Magic, Witchcraft, and Religion

Cover photograph by Terry Heffernan

The artifacts shown (from the Lowie Museum of Anthropology, University of California, Berkeley) were made by the Tlingit Indians of the Pacific Northwest. At top is a dance mask of carved and painted alder. At middle left is a carved and painted wooden rattle. At middle right is a shaman's piece, a "soul catcher," of carved ivory, probably representing a man killed by whales. At lower left is a wooden rattle with puffin beaks. At lower right is a dance baton of carved and painted red cedar.

Magic, Witchcraft, and Religion
An Anthropological Study of the Supernatural
Second Edition

Arthur C. Lehmann and James E. Myers

California State University, Chico

Mayfield Publishing Company
Mountain View, California

*This book is dedicated to the memory of
Alan P. Merriam and Allan Holmberg.*

Library of Congress Cataloging-in-Publication Data

Magic, witchcraft, and religion : an anthropological study of the
  supernatural / [compiled by] Arthur C. Lehmann and James E. Myers.
  –2nd ed.
      p.   cm.
   Bibliography: p.
   Includes index.
   ISBN 0-87484-898-9
   1. Religion. 2. Occultism. I. Lehmann, Arthur C. II. Myers,
James E. (James Edward), 1931–
   BL50.M26   1989
   291—dc19   88-29762
                                                            CIP

Manufactured in the United States of America
10 9 8 7 6 5 4 3

Mayfield Publishing Company
1240 Villa Street
Mountain View, California 94041

The verse quotation on p. 403 is from "The Seven Spiritual Ages of Mrs. Marmaduke Moore," in *Verses from
1919 On* by Ogden Nash. Copyright 1933 by Ogden
Nash. Used by permission of Little, Brown and Company.

Sponsoring editor, Janet M. Beatty; production editor,
Sondra Glider; manuscript editor, Joy Dickinson; cover
designer, Jeanne M. Schreiber; text designer, Marilyn
Langfeld; mask drawings, Betty Armstrong; cover pho-
tograph, Terry Heffernan. The text was set in 9/11
Palatino by Interactive Composition Corporation and
printed on 50# Finch Opaque by Malloy Lithographing,
Inc.

Contents

Foreword

It has often been remarked that the challenge to anthropologists, as well as their opportunity, is to show the familiar in the strange and the strange in the familiar. Nowhere in anthropology are that challenge and opportunity more present than in the comparative study of religion. It is our task as anthropologists to encounter, study, record, understand, and interpret the social practices and cultural patterns of human groups, wherever and whenever they have gathered—from the Arctic to the tropics; from Neanderthal times to the present. We have thus brought together in our literature a vast collection of religious beliefs and practices, many of which may seem strange indeed to twentieth-century North Americans. Yet if we bring these beliefs and practices wisely under anthropological focus, as Professors Lehmann and Myers have done in this reader, they will be seen to be strangely familiar. They are beliefs, we discover, that under other circumstances we might have believed ourselves. They are ritual practices, we see, that we might have engaged in, as, often enough, did our own ancestors. In these beliefs and practices we come to recognize needs, desires, appetites, and satisfactions ultimately characteristic of all human experience.

It is not enough, then, to study strange practices unless that study somehow enables us to gain perspective on our own way of life—to understand better because we see as from a distance. That is what is meant by seeing the strange in the familiar. Anthropology, by taking us out to dwell, if only momentarily, among unfamiliar practices elsewhere, should by that act alone give us perspective on our own lifeways when we return. It is the particular virtue of this collection of readings, however, to give a convincing additional twist to the distancing we obtain from contemplating strange religious practices elsewhere in the world: The editors have included in each section studies of practices taking place in modern Western societies today, mostly in North America. They show us the "strange" not only in exotic circumstances but also in a society with which we are extremely familiar. Although we may not always be familiar with the specific behavior described—the health food movement or contemporary Satanism, for example—the fact that such beliefs and practices are active among us today underscores the continuing relevance and vitality of the anthropological study of religion, wherever it is conducted. The religious impulse, with all its variegated manifestations, remains at work even in the so-called secular societies of present-day North America.

Why, especially, should we want to make the strange familiar and the familiar strange? What can we gain from the added perspective achieved by seeing ourselves as from a distance? At least three answers may be given to this question: tolerance, diversity, and adaptability. We now live in an increasingly interdependent world in which we are constantly being brought into contact with the strange and with strangers. Order in such a world demands an increased tolerance for lifeways that are strange to us. Moreover, familiarity with the exotic not only creates respect for, but may also help preserve, an enlivening diversity in the world, rather than the homogenized, consumption-oriented, worldwide popular culture toward which we seem to be irrevocably moving. A homogenized world culture gives us a much less interesting world in which to live. Finally, an increased perspective on our own beliefs and practices (which is not incompatible with continuing satisfaction in them) helps us avoid inert or fanatical overcommitment to them. (This is particularly the case with religious practices, which have so often been attended by intolerance, if not fanaticism.) The hallmark of the human career as compared with other creatures has been our adaptability: our ability to change our lifeways to fit into many diverse environments and to respond quickly and effectively to the challenge of changing circumstances. The maintenance of a balanced perspective on our own beliefs and practices—the avoidance of overcommitment to them because we have come to see them as strange in their own way—is part and parcel of our adaptability, our readiness to meet and master changing circumstances.

Beyond these values of tolerance, diversity, and adaptability that can emerge from the study of comparative religion lies the fact of religion itself.

Religion is a human universal: It is found in every culture known to anthropologists, in a great diversity and variety of forms of expression. No reader who embarks on an attentive reading of this rewarding selection of articles can fail to recognize the human creativity that lies in this diversity. Nor can he or she fail to recognize the particular power through which religion enables men and women to speak to and cope with the ultimate circumstances of human life: injustice, unpredictability, suffering, death. An attentive reading, then, will offer insight both into what makes us human and into some of the more effective ways we have of battling that frail humanity. Such insight and understanding are a main object of anthropological study of any aspect of culture, but the study of religion has been particularly rewarding in this respect. The anthropological study of comparative religion stretches out to embrace diversity, as does this collection of readings. It stretches out to diversity to try to show us not only what being human is but what it might be.

James W. Fernandez
University of Chicago

Preface

We designed this reader to reach a broad spectrum of students and to demonstrate a comparative approach to the major elements and categories of religion. The volume provides teachers and students with contemporary, provocative readings on both non-Western and Western subjects. These readings allow students not only to investigate their own religious belief systems but also to compare those systems with others outside their culture. We believe this text thus illustrates the importance of understanding religion in our own culture as well as in those of the non-Western world. Primarily designed to reach undergraduate students, it is appropriate as a supplemental reader for graduate students as well.

In preparing this volume, we carefully searched through the literature of comparative religion, sociology, psychology, and anthropology, intensively screening hundreds of articles on the basis of their readability, academic quality and level, topical interest, and subject matter (including geographical and cultural area). Our overall goal was to achieve a final collection that would introduce students to the main topics in the study of magic, witchcraft, and religion, while at the same time introducing them to the major ethnographic areas of the world. Although the book does center on the non-Western world, we placed in each chapter at least one article from contemporary Western culture, both to increase students' interest and to heighten their cross-cultural perspective.

Using the recommendations of students and the evaluations and suggestions of faculty from various universities who have taught a similar course over the years, we narrowed the field to the existing selections, which are organized topically into ten chapters: (1) the anthropological study of religion; (2) myth, ritual, symbolism, and taboo; (3) shamans, priests, and prophets; (4) the religious use of drugs; (5) ethnomedicine (religion and healing); (6) witchcraft, sorcery, and other forces of evil; (7) demons, exorcism, divination, and magic; (8) ghosts, souls, and ancestors (power of the dead); (9) old and new religions (the search for salvation); and (10) the occult (paths to the unknown).

New to this Edition

Based on suggestions from users of the text, we have made several substantive changes in the second edition:

• We've deleted several articles and replaced them with works that offer readers a better grasp of the breadth of comparative religion. With the wealth of good classic and contemporary articles to choose from, we've added 16 new selections and have brought the total number of readings up to 50.

• We've rearranged the chapters into a sequence that users and reviewers find more suitable for their courses: the chapter on ethnomedicine now precedes the chapter on witchcraft, sorcery, and other forces of evil.

• To help readers get their geographical bearings, we've added a frontispiece map of the principal societies and locations cited in the articles.

Features from the First Edition

We believe this volume is unique and especially valuable because of the following features:

- The content not only covers every major traditional topic in comparative religion, but also features separate chapters on the religious use of drugs, old and new religions, ethnomedicine, and the occult.
- Each chapter includes both a core of non-Western articles and at least one reading from contemporary Western culture.
- Although the majority of the articles are the most recent available, classic readings are also included.
- The selections were chosen specifically for students on the basis of compelling subject matter and readability.
- The readings represent a broad sample of the world's geographic areas and economic levels.
- Each selection is preceded by a headnote that draws out the main theoretical and substantive points in the work.

- An introduction to each chapter presents a historical and theoretical overview of the major topics that follow, thus providing students with a framework for understanding the contemporary importance of the subject.

Acknowledgments

A number of people contributed significantly to the preparation and development of this volume. We acknowledge with thanks the comments and suggestions made by the following reviewers of the second edition: Amy Burce, University of Texas at Austin; James F. Garber, Southwest Texas State University; Paul G. Hiebert, Fuller Seminary; Phillips Stevens, Jr., State University of New York at Buffalo; Melford S. Weiss, California State University at Sacramento.

In addition, we thank Frank Graham for encouraging us to write the first edition, Jan Beatty for expertly guiding us through the second edition, Pam Trainer for dauntless efforts to acquire reprint permissions, Sondra Glider for bringing this edition smoothly through production, and Joy Dickinson for a rigorous and thoughtful editing of the final draft.

A.C.L.
J.E.M.

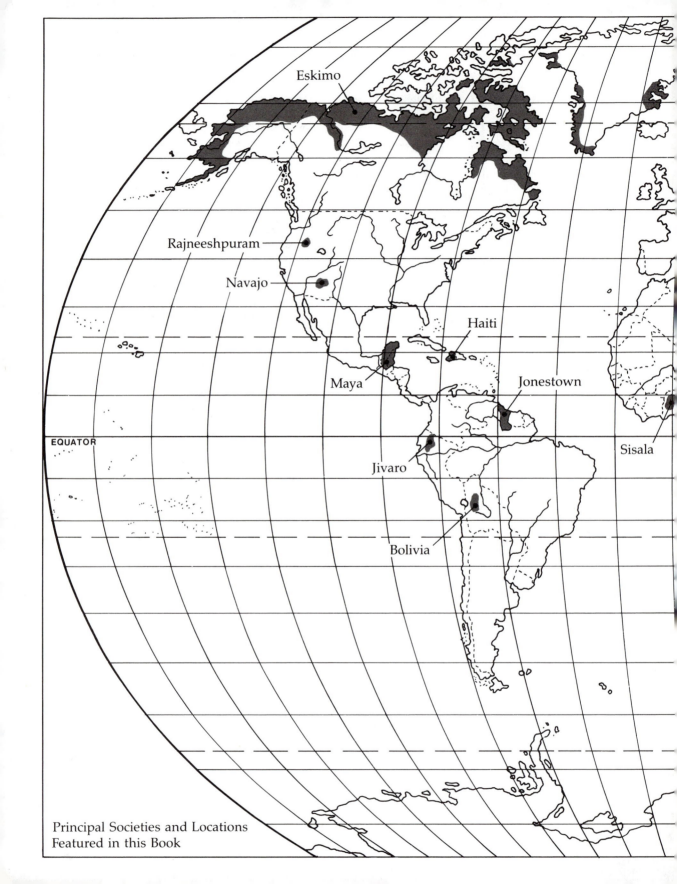

Eskimo

Rajneeshpuram

Navajo

Haiti

Maya

Jonestown

Jivaro

Sisala

EQUATOR

Bolivia

Principal Societies and Locations
Featured in this Book

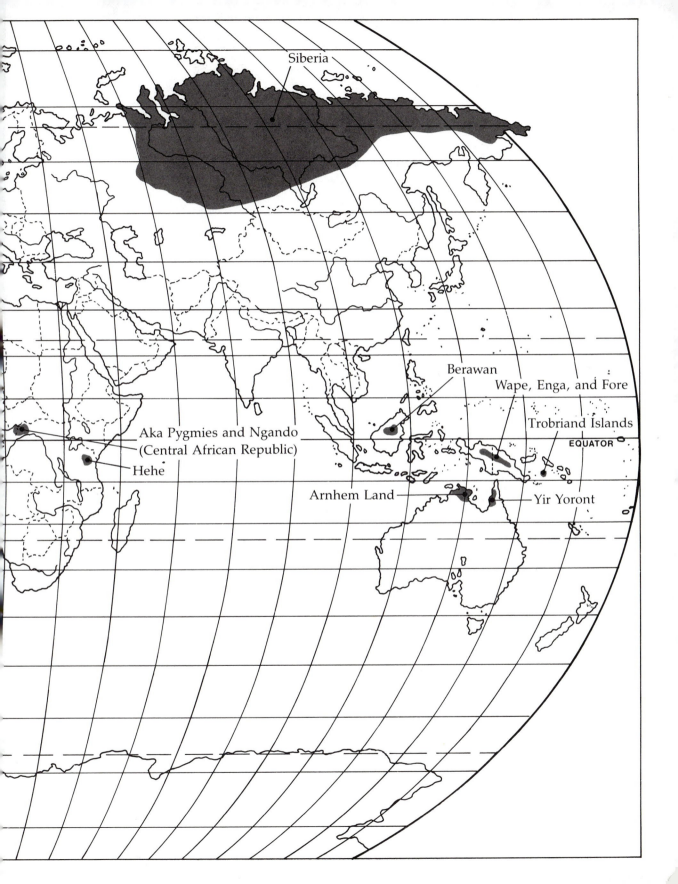

Siberia

Berawan

Wape, Enga, and Fore

Trobriand Islands

EQUATOR

Aka Pygmies and Ngando
(Central African Republic)

Hehe

Arnhem Land

Yir Yoront

1
The Anthropological Study of Religion

Anthropologists have always been interested in the origins of religion, although the lack of both written records and archaeological evidence has made the subject speculative. It is reasonable to assume, however, that religion, like material culture, has a prehistory. Surely, uncertainty and change have always existed, exposing people in all ages to real and imagined threats and anxieties. The human animal alone senses a pattern behind the facts of existence and worries about life here and in the hereafter. We are born, we live, and we die. And although this is true of other animals, only humans are aware of the precariousness of life and the inevitability of death. As William Howells has observed, "Man's life is hard, very hard. And he knows it, poor soul; that is the vital thing. He knows that he is forever confronted with the Four Horsemen—death, famine, disease, and the malice of other men" (1962: 16).

The earliest surviving anthropological evidence of humans possibly expressing these concerns through religious practices dates from

Buffalo mask of the Bobo, Upper Volta.

1

the era of *Homo sapiens neanderthalensis*, approximately a hundred thousand years ago. Because the Neanderthals buried their dead with tools, weapons, and other funerary objects, many anthropologists have held that they were the first humans to believe in an afterlife of some sort. The era of *Homo sapiens sapiens* (modern man in the biological sense), approximately thirty thousand years ago, has yielded increasing evidence of religious beliefs—more elaborate burials, carved figurines ("Venuses"), and magnificent cave art. And during the Neolithic period, which began about ten thousand years ago, burials indicate a deep respect for the power of the dead. It is likely that during this period, which is marked by the cultivation of crops and the domestication of animals, cycles of nature became an important feature of magic and religious beliefs. Drought, storms, and other natural perils of the farmer could have created a growing dependence on supernatural powers.

The antiquity of religion indirectly testifies to its utility; however, the usefulness of supernaturalism to contemporary societies is a clearer, more provable demonstration of its functions. The many forms of adversity facing individuals and groups require explanation and action; we are unwilling to let challenges to health, safety, and salvation go unchecked. Just as adversity is universal, so too is the use of religion as an explanation for and solution to adversity. Although the form religion takes is as diverse as its practitioners, all religions seek to answer questions that cannot be explained in terms of objective knowledge—to permit people reasonable explanations for often unreasonable events and phenomena by demonstrating a cause-and-effect relationship between the supernatural and the human condition. This may be its most important function.

In his article "Religion: Problems of Definition and Explanation" (1966: 109–17), Melford E. Spiro has distinguished three sets of basic desires (cognitive, substantive, and expressive), each of which is satisfied by a corresponding function of religion (adjustive, adaptive, and integrative). Spiro's first and second functions are basically those of explanation and solution: the adjustive function of religion, as he defines it, is to satisfy the cognitive desires we experience as we attempt to understand what goes on around us (illness, natural phenomena); the adaptive function seeks to satisfy substantive desires (the desire for rain, or for victory in war). In his third category, however, Spiro moves to different territory: the often unconscious, expressive desires made up of what Spiro calls painful drives and painful motives.

According to Spiro, painful drives are anxieties concerning infantile and primitive fears (fears of destruction, or of one's own destructiveness). Painful motives are culturally forbidden—for example, types of aggressive or sexual behavior that result in feelings of shame, inadequacy, and moral anxiety. Because of the pain they create in an individual, these drives and motives are usually relegated to the unconscious, where, "in the absence of other, or of more efficient means," religion becomes the vehicle "by which, symbolically, they can be handled and expressed." Thus, in what Spiro calls the integrative function of supernaturalism, "religious belief and ritual provide the content for culturally constituted projective mechanisms by which unconscious fears and anxieties may be reduced and repressed motives may be satisfied" (1966: 115).

Over the years, scholars have taken several approaches in their attempts to understand the reasons for the existence of religious behavior. The most prominent of these approaches are psychological, sociological, and anthropological. Melford Spiro's belief that religious behavior serves to reduce unconscious fears typifies the psychological approach, which, briefly stated, sees religion as functioning to reduce anxiety. For example, the famous British social anthropologist Bronislaw Malinowski held that the proper use of religious rites reduced anxieties brought on by crisis. (Like all theorists who apply the psychological approach, Freud also believed that religion and ritual functioned to reduce anxieties, but, unlike others, he saw religion as a neurotic need that humans would eventually outgrow.) In contrast, the sociological viewpoint stresses the societal origins of religion. The French sociologist Emile Durkheim, for example, viewed religion as a manifestation of social solidarity and collective beliefs. According to Durkheim, members of society create religious objects, rituals, beliefs, and symbols in order to integrate their cultures. A. R. Radcliffe-Brown, a British social anthropologist, agreed with Durkheim that participation in annual religious rites functioned to increase social solidarity.

Although their functional analyses of religious behavior and phenomena do explain, in part, the universality of religion, neither the psychological nor the sociological theorists adequately provide answers to the origin of religion. Both approaches are too limited in focus, centered as they are on human emotions and social structure respectively; neither explores the wide variety of cultural expressions of religion. Because religious experience, wherever it is observed, displays such great variation of cognitive and phenomenal expression, anything less than a wide-ranging holistic approach would not allow true comparisons; as a result, generalizations about the nature of religious systems would be incomplete as well as inaccurate.

The third, the anthropological approach to the study of religion, is by its very nature holistic, combining not only sociological and psychological, but historical, semantic, and evolutionary perspectives as well. As Clifford Geertz demonstrates in the lead article of this book, anthropologists attempt to go beyond the observable to the analysis of symbolic forms. In order to make generalizations on pan-human religious behavior, symbology, and ideology, however, anthropologists must work from the common basis of a definition of religion. Without an acceptable and accurate definition, anthropologists would be unable to establish a common basis for comparison of religion cross-culturally.

Many definitions of religion have been generated by anthropologists. Tylor, the father of modern anthropology, described religion as the belief in spiritual beings, what he called "animism," the most primitive form of religion. At the opposite extreme from Tylor's open-ended definition, which set no limits as to what the study of spiritual beings would embrace, are a majority of contemporary anthropologists who, like Spiro, define religion more narrowly as "an institution consisting of culturally postulated superhuman beings" (1966: 96). At first glance, Tylor's and Spiro's definitions appear similar, but Spiro's use of the term "superhuman," unlike Tylor's "spiritual beings," emphasizes an aura of omnipotence unknown to the living. Further, Spiro's position

that religion is an "institution" places it in the realm of phenomena that can be empirically studied, as any other cultural institution can be. Still, similarities in Tylor's and Spiro's definitions are apparent: both show, for example, that religion is the study of the nature of the unnatural. Spirits are not of this world, nor are superhumans; indeed, both are "supernatural," which has been defined by the anthropologist Edward Norbeck "to include all that is not natural, that which is regarded as extraordinary, not of the ordinary world, mysterious or unexplainable in ordinary terms" (1961: 11).

Expanding the definition of religion beyond spiritual and superhuman beings to include the extraordinary, the mysterious, and unexplainable allows a more comprehensive view of religious behaviors among the peoples of the world and permits the anthropological investigation of phenomena such as magic, sorcery, curses, and other practices that hold meaning for both pre-literate and literate societies. For this reason, this book focuses on the concept of the "supernatural" and incorporates a wide variety of contemporary examples of religious beliefs and practices that demonstrate the breadth of human ideology.

Through their comparative research anthropologists have shown that religious practices and beliefs vary in part as a result of the level of social structure in a given society. In *The Birth of the Gods* (1960), Guy Swanson applied a statistical approach to support the argument that religious forms are related to social development, and in *Religion: An Anthropological View* (1966: 84–101), Anthony F. C. Wallace presented a provocative typology of religious behavior based on the concept of the cult institution—"a set of rituals all having the same general goal, all explicitly rationalized by a set of similar or related beliefs, and all supported by the same social group" (p. 75). Ranging from the simplest to the most complex, Wallace describes individualistic, shamanic, communal, and ecclesiastical cult institutions. Each succeeding or more complex level contains all components of those preceding it. The ecclesiastical, for example, contains all of the elements of the less complex individualistic, shamanistic, and communal cult institutions.

According to Wallace, in the simplist, *individualistic* cult institution, each person functions as

4 • 1 • THE ANTHROPOLOGICAL STUDY OF RELIGION

his or her own specialist without need for such intermediaries as shamans or priests. Examples occur in both modern and primitive societies (the dream cult among the Iroquois, sealing magic among the Trobriand Islanders, and various cults among the Americans). The next level, the *shamanic*, also found in cultures around the world, marks the beginning of a religious division of labor. Individual part-time practitioners are designated by experience, birth, or training to help lay clients enlist the aid of the supernatural. The *communal* cult institution is even more complex, with laypeople handling important religious rituals for people in such special categories as secret societies, kinship groups, and age groups. (Examples include the ancestor ceremonies of the Chinese and some African tribal groups, Iroquois agricultural rituals, and Australian puberty rituals.) Although specialists such as shamans, skilled speakers, and dancers may participate, the lay group assumes the primary responsibility for conducting the sacred performance; an extensive religious hierarchy is still not in evidence. It is in the fourth, *ecclesiastical* cult institution that a professional religious clergy is formally elected or appointed and the division of labor is sharply drawn, with the laymen usually passive participants instead of active performers. Ecclesiastical cult institutions have characteristically worshipped either an Olympian pantheon of gods (as among the ancient Greeks and Romans) or a monotheistic deity (as among the Judeo-Christian and Moslem religions).

The differences between religious behavior and belief in so-called primitive and modern cultures has been of great interest to anthropologists over the years. William Howells (1962: 5) observed several characteristics that he believed distinguished the major world religions from the belief systems of more primitive cultures. First, the "great faiths" are messianic, their origins stemming from such charismatic figures as Jesus, Buddha, and Muhammed. Second, they have a rigid ethical form. Third, each has a missionary, imperialistic aspect, seeing itself as the one and only religion. Finally, each displays an exclusiveness in its belief system to the degree of being intolerant of other faiths. Howells is quick to point out that he has been generalizing, reminding the reader that the varied nature and heter-

ogeneity of native cults may make an understanding of their nature arduous, especially for anyone aware only of the differences among Christian sects (1962: 6). His concluding remark is important to an understanding of all the articles in this book; referring to the "perfect legitimacy" of native cults, he states that the "primitive devotees are not people of another planet, but are essentially exactly like us, and are engaged with precisely the same kind of religious appetite as the civilized. And that appetite is fed and stilled by their own religions. This is very important; it is why we are taking those religions seriously. They are not toys. They are what we might be doing ourselves; and they are what most of our ancestors were indeed doing, two thousand years ago today" (1962: 7).

The four articles in this chapter have been selected to provide a basic understanding of the anthropological approach to the study of the supernatural. Each stresses the use of the comparative method, the very anchor for anthropological thought.

In the first selection Clifford Geertz offers us a taste of the comparative approach, not so much by comparing the religious behaviors of several different cultures—as occurs throughout the book—as by comparing various academic approaches to the study of the supernatural. What is the historical approach? How does it differ from the psychological approach? What are the sociological and semantic approaches, and how does the anthropological approach differ from all the above?

Next, Dorothy Lee's article on religious perspectives in anthropology shows how religion is part and parcel of a pre-literate people's total way of life. Lee tells us about pre-literate societies in which ceremonies and their preparation occupy most of a year.

In the third selection, I. M. Lewis provides several examples of the reaction of anthropologists when they themselves encounter the supernatural in non-Western societies. In the last selection, Lauriston Sharp provides the reader with a classic example of the cultural disruption that can occur when an outside group intervenes in the life of another group without careful consideration of the consequences.

References

Howells, William
    1962 *The Heathens: Primitive Man and His Religions.* Garden City, N.Y.: Doubleday.

Norbeck, Edward
    1961 *Religion in Primitive Society.* New York: Harper and Brothers.

Spiro, Melford E.
    1966 "Religion: Problems of Definition and Explanation." In Michael Banton, ed., *Anthropological Approaches to the Study of Religion,* pp. 85–126. London: Tavistock Publications Limited for the Association of Social Anthropologists of the Commonwealth.

Swanson, Guy
    1960 *The Birth of the Gods: The Origin of Primitive Beliefs.* Ann Arbor: University of Michigan Press.

Wallace, A. F. C.
    1966 *Religion: An Anthropological View.* New York: Random House.

Religion

Clifford Geertz

In Clifford Geertz's classic work, "Religion as a Cultural System" (1966), the author argued for a broadened analysis of religion. This argument, aimed primarily at the narrowness of the British sociological approach to the study of comparative religion, was accepted by American ethnologists and reflected in their contemporary research. In the following 1972 article Geertz pursues his goal, demonstrating the importance of his historical, psychological, sociological, and semantic approaches to the study of religion, and concluding that a mature theory of religion will consist of an integration of them all into a conceptual system whose exact form remains to be discovered. In addition to extensive field work in Java, Professor Geertz has also conducted research in Bali and Morocco.

Reprinted by permission of the publisher from *International Encyclopedia of the Social Sciences*, David L. Sills, Editor. Vol. 13, pp. 398–406. Copyright © 1972 by Crowell Collier and Macmillan, Inc.

THE ANTHROPOLOGICAL STUDY OF RELIGION HAS been highly sensitive to changes in the general intellectual and moral climate of the day; at the same time, it has been a powerful factor in the creation of that climate. Since the early discussion by Edward Tylor, interest in the beliefs and rituals of distant, ancient, or simpler peoples has been shaped by an awareness of contemporary issues. The questions that anthropologists have pursued among exotic religions have arisen from the workings—or the misworkings—of modern Western society, and particularly from its restless quest for self-discovery. In turn, their findings have profoundly affected the course that quest has taken and the perspective at which it has arrived.

Perhaps the chief reason for the rather special role of comparative religious studies is that issues which, when raised within the context of Western culture, led to extreme social resistance and personal turmoil could be freely and even comfortably handled in terms of bizarre, presumably primitive, and thus—also presumably—fanciful materials from long ago or far away. The study of "primitive religions" could pass as the study of superstition, supposedly unrelated to the serious religious and moral concerns of advanced civilization, at best either a sort of vague foreshadowing of them or a grotesque parody upon them. This made it possible to approach all sorts of touchy subjects, such as polytheism, value relativism, possession, and faith healing, from a frank and detached point of view. One could ask searching questions about the historicity of myth among Polynesians; when asked in relation to Christianity, these same questions were, until quite recently, deeply threatening. One could discuss the projection of erotic wishes found in the "totemic" rites of Australian aborigines, the social roots and functions of African "ancestor worship," or the protoscientific quality of Melanesian "magical thought," without involving oneself in polemical debate and emotional distress. The application of the comparative method—the essence of anthropological thought—to religion permitted the growth of a resolutely scientific approach to the spiritual dimensions of human life.

Through the thin disguise of comparative method the revolutionary implications of the work of such men as Tylor, Durkheim, Robertson Smith, Freud, Malinowski, and Radcliffe-Brown soon became apparent—at first mainly to philosophers, theologians, and literary figures, but eventually to the educated public in general. The meticulous descriptions of tribal curiosities such as soul loss, shamanism, circumcision, blood sacrifice, sorcery, tree burial, garden magic, symbolic cannibalism, and animal worship have been caught up in some of the grander intellectual battles of the last hundred years—from those over evolutionism and historicism in the late nineteenth century to those over positivism and existentialism today. Psychoanalysts and phenomenologists, Marxists and Kantians, racists and egalitarians, absolutists and relativists, empiricists and rationalists, believers and skeptics have all had recourse to the record—partial, inconsistent, and shot through with simple error as it is—of the spiritual life of tribal peoples to support their positions and belabor those of their opponents. If interest in "primitive religion" among savants of all sorts has been remarkably high, consensus concerning its nature and significance has not.

At least three major intellectual developments have exercised a critical influence on the anthropological study of religion: (1) the emergence, in the latter half of the nineteenth century, of history as the sovereign science of man; (2) the positivist reaction against this sovereignty in the first decades of the twentieth century and the radical split of the social sciences into resolutely psychological approaches, on the one hand, and resolutely sociological ones, on the other; and (3) the growth, in the interwar period, of a concern with the role of ideational factors in the regulation of social life. With the first of these came an emphasis on the nature of primitive reasoning and the stages of its evolution into civilized thought. With the second came an investigation of the emotional basis of religious ritual and belief and the separate examination of the role of ritual and belief in social integration. The concern with value systems and other features of the ideational realm led to an exploration of the philosophical dimensions of religious ideas, particularly the symbolic vehicles in terms of which those ideas are expressed.

Evolutionism and Its Enemies

Like so much else in anthropology, the study of the religious notions of primitive peoples arose within the context of evolutionary theory. In the nineteenth century, to think systematically about human affairs was to think historically—to seek out survivals of the most elementary forms and to trace the steps by which these forms subsequently developed. And though, in fact, Tylor, Morgan, Frazer, and the rest drew more on the synthetic social-stage theories of such men as Comte and Hegel than on the analytic random-variation and natural-selection ideas of Darwin, the grand concept of evolution was shared by both streams of thought: namely, that the complex, heterogeneous present has arisen, more or less gradually, out of a simpler, more uniform past. The relics of this past are still to be found scattered, like Galápagos turtles, in out-of-the-way places around us. Tylor, an armchair scholar, made no "voyage of the *Beagle*." But in combing and organizing the reports of missionaries, soldiers, and explorers, he proceeded from the same general premise as did Darwin, and indeed most of the leading minds of the day. For them a comprehensive, historically oriented comparison of all forms of a phenomenon, from the most primitive to the most advanced, was the royal road to understanding the nature of the phenomenon itself.

In Tylor's view, the elementary form out of which all else developed was spirit worship—*animism*. The minimal definition of religion was "a belief in spiritual beings." The understanding of religion thus came down to an understanding of the basis upon which such a belief arose at its most primitive level. Tylor's theory was intellectualistic. Belief in spirits began as an uncritical but nonetheless rational effort to explain such puzzling empirical phenomena as death, dreams, and possession. The notion of a separable soul rendered these phenomena intelligible in terms of soul departure, soul wandering, and soul invasion. Tylor believed that the idea of a soul was used to explain more and more remote and hitherto inexplicable natural occurrences, until virtually every tree and rock was haunted by some sort of gossamer presence. The higher, more developed forms of "belief in spiritual beings," first polytheism, ultimately monotheism, were founded upon this animistic basis, the urphilosophy of all mankind, and were refined through a process of critical questioning by more advanced thinkers. For this earnest Quaker the religious history of the world was a history of progressive, even inevitable, enlightenment.

This intellectualistic, "up from darkness" strain has run through most evolutionist thought about religion. For Frazer, a nineteenth-century figure who lived for forty years into the twentieth century without finding it necessary to alter either his views or his methods, the mental progress involved was from magic to religion to science. Magic was the primordial form of human thought; it consisted in mistaking either spatiotemporal connection ("sympathetic magic," as when drinking the blood of an ox transfers its strength to the drinker) or phenomenal similarity ("imitative magic," as when the sound of drumming induces thunderheads to form) for true scientific causality. For Durkheim, evolutionary advance consisted in the emergence of specific, analytic, *profane* ideas about "cause" or "category" or "relationship" from diffuse, global, *sacred* images. These "collective representations," as he called them, of the social order and its moral force included such sacra as "mana," "totem," and "god." For Max Weber, the process was one of "rationalization": the progressive organization of religious concern into certain more precisely defined, more specifically focused, and more systematically conceived cultural forms. The level of sophistication of such theories (and, hence, their present relevance) varies very widely. But, like Tylor's, they all conceive of the evolution of religion as a process of cultural differentiation: the diffuse, all-embracing, but rather unsystematic and uncritical religious practices of primitive peoples are transformed into the more specifically focused, more regularized, less comprehensively authoritative practices of the more advanced civilizations. Weber, in whom both intellectualism and optimism were rather severely tempered by a chronic apprehensiveness, called this transformation the "disenchantment (*Entzauberung*) of the world."

On the heels of evolutionism came, of course, anti-evolutionism. This took two quite different forms. On one side there was a defense, mainly by Roman Catholic scholars, of the so-called degradation theory. According to this theory, the original revelation of a high god to primitive peoples was later corrupted by human frailty into the idol worship of present-day tribal peoples. On the other side there was an attack, mainly by American scholars of the Boas school, upon the "armchair speculation" of evolutionary thinkers and a call for its replacement by more phenomenological approaches to the study of tribal custom.

The first of these reactions led, logically enough, to a search among the most primitive of existing peoples for traces of belief in a supreme being. The resulting dispute, protracted, often bitter, and stubbornly inconclusive as to the existence of such "primitive monotheism," turned out to be unproductive—aside from some interesting discussions by Lang (1898) concerning culture heroes and by Eliade (1949) concerning sky gods—and both the issue and the theory that gave rise to it have now receded from the center of scholarly attention. The second reaction has had a longer life and great impact on ethnographic methodology, but it too is now in partial eclipse. Its main contributions—aside from some devastating empirical demolitions of evolutionist generalization—came in the field of cultural diffusion. Leslie Spier's study of the spread of the Sun Dance through the Great Plains (1921) and A. L. Kroeber's application of the age-area approach to aboriginal religion in California are good examples of productive diffusion studies. However, apart from their importance for culture history, the contribution of such distributional studies to our understanding of religious ideas, attitudes, and practices as such has not been great, and few students now pursue these studies. The call of the Boas school for thorough field research and disciplined inductive analysis has been heeded; but its fruits, insofar as religious studies are concerned, have been reaped by others less inhibited theoretically.

Psychological Approaches

The major reaction against the intellectual tradition of the cultural evolutionists took place not within anthropology, however, but in the general context of the positivist revolt against the domination of historicist modes of thought in the social sciences. In the years before World War I the rise of the systematic psychologism of psychoanalysis and of the equally systematic sociologism of the *Année sociologique* forced evolutionist theorizing into the background, even though the leaders of both movements—Freud and Durkheim—were themselves still very strongly influenced by it. Perhaps even more relevant, it introduced a sharp split into anthropological studies of religion which has resolved into the militantly psychodynamic and the militantly social-structural approaches.

Freud's major work in this field is, of course, *Totem and Taboo*, a book anthropologists in general have had great difficulty in evaluating—as Kroeber's two reviews of it, the first facilely negative, the second, two decades later, ambivalently positive, demonstrate. The source of the difficulty has been an inability or an unwillingness to disentangle Freud's basic thesis—that religious rituals and beliefs are homologous with neurotic symptoms—from the chimerical ethnology and obsolete biology within which he insisted upon setting it. Thus, the easy demolition of what Kroeber called Freud's "just so story" concerning primal incest, parricide, and guilt within some protohuman horde ("in the beginning was the deed") was all too often mistaken for total rejection of the rather more penetrating proposition that the obsessions, dreams, and fantasies of collective life spring from the same intrapsychic sources as do those of the isolated individual.

For those who read further in Freud's writings, however—especially in "Mourning and Melancholia" and "Obsessive Acts and Religious Practices"—it became apparent that what was at issue was the applicability of theories concerning the forms and causes of individual psychopathology to the explanation of the forms and causes of public myth and group ritual. Róheim (1950) analyzed Australian circumcision rites against the background of orthodox Freudian theories of psychosexual development, especially those clustered around the Oedipal predicament. However, he explicitly avoided recourse to speculations about buried memories of primordial occurrences. Bettelheim (1954) adopted a similar, though more systematic and less orthodox, approach to initiation practices generally, seeing them as socially instituted symbolic mechanisms for the definition and stabilization of sexual identity. Kardiner (1945), taking a neo-Freudian position,

sought to demonstrate that th⌐ ⌐tions of tribal peoples were pr⌐, personality structure," formed not by ⌐ an unconsciously remembered historical ⌐ but by the more observable traumas produced by child-training practices, an approach later extended and cast into quantitative form by Whiting (Whiting and Child 1953). Erikson (1950), drawing upon developments in ego psychology which conceived the emergence of the adult personality to be a joint product of psychobiological maturation, cultural context, and historical experience, interpreted the religious notions of the Yurok and the Sioux in terms of certain basic modes of relating to the world. These relationships gradually developed during the whole course of childhood and adolescence. Others—notably Devereux (1951)—have attempted to use the autobiographical, case-history approach to determine the relations between personality dynamics and religious orientation in particular individuals; still others—notably Hallowell (1937–1954)—have employed projective tests, questionnaires, reports of dreams, or systematic interviews toward similar ends.

In all such studies, even when individual authors have dissented from many of Freud's specific views, the basic premise has been Freudian: that religious practices can be usefully interpreted as expressions of unconscious psychological forces— and this has become, amid much polemic, an established tradition of inquiry. In recent years, however, responsible work of this type has come to question the degree to which one is justified in subjecting historically created and socially institutionalized cultural forms to a system of analysis founded on the treatment of the mental illnesses of individuals. For this reason, the future of this approach depends perhaps more upon developments within psychoanalysis, now in a somewhat uncertain state, than within anthropology. So far, perhaps only Kluckhohn's pioneering *Navaho Witchcraft* (1944) has attempted to systematically relate psychological factors to social and cultural aspects of primitive religion. The great majority of psychoanalytic studies of tribal beliefs and rites remain willfully parochial.

In any case, not all psychological approaches to religion have been Freudian. Jungian influences have had a certain impact, especially on studies of myth. Campbell (1949), for example, has stressed he continuity of certain themes both cross-culturally and temporally. These themes have been interpreted as expressions of transpersonal constancies in unconscious mental functioning which are at the same time expressions of fundamental cosmic realities.

Simple emotionalist theories have also been extremely popular. There have been two main varieties of these: awe theories and confidence theories. Awe theories have been based on some usually rather vague notion of "religious thrill" experienced by human beings when brought face to face with cosmic forces. A wide range of ethnologists, from Max Müller through Lang and Marett to Lowie and Goldenweiser, have accepted such theories in one form or another. However, awe theories remain mere notations of the obvious—that religious experience is, in the nature of the case, touched with intense feelings of the grandeur of the universe in relation to the self and of the vulnerability of the self in relation to the universe. This is not explanation, but circular reasoning.

Confidence theories also begin with a notion of man's inward sense of weakness, and especially of his fears—of disease, of death, of ill fortune of all kinds—and they see religious practices as designed to quiet such fears, either by explaining them away, as in doctrines of the afterlife, or by claiming to link the individual to external sources of strength, as in prayer. The best-known confidence theory was that set forth by Malinowski. He regarded magic as enabling man to pursue uncertain but essential endeavors by assuring him of their ultimate success. Confidence, or anxiety-reduction, theories, like awe theories, clearly have empirical foundation but do not adequately explore the complex relationship between fear and religious activity. They are not rooted in any systematic conceptualization of mental functioning and so merely point to matters desperately in need of clarification, without in fact clarifying them.

Sociological Approaches

The sociological approach to the analysis of the religions of nonliterate peoples proceeded independent of, and even at variance with, the psychoanalytic approach, but it shared a concern with the same phenomenon: the peculiar "otherness," the extraordinary, momentous, "set apart" quality of

sacred (or "taboo") acts and objects, as contrasted with the profane. The intense aura of high seriousness was traced by Freud to the projection of unacceptable wishes repressed from consciousness onto external objects. The dramatic ambivalence of the sacred—its paradoxical unification of the commanded and the forbidden, the pure and the polluted, the salutary and the dangerous—was a symbolic expression of the underlying ambivalence of human desires. For Durkheim, too, the extraordinary atmosphere surrounding sacred acts and objects was symbolic of a hidden reality, but a social, not a psychological one: the moral force of the human community.

Durkheim believed that the integrity of the social order was the primary requisite for human survival, and the means by which that integrity superseded individual egocentricity was the primary problem of sociological analysis. He saw Australian totemism (which he, like Freud, made the empirical focus of his work) as a mechanism to this end. For example, the collective rituals involving the emblems of the totemic beings—the so-called bull roarers—aroused the heightened emotions of mass behavior and evoked a deep sense of moral identification among the participants. The creation of social solidarity was the result of the common public veneration, by specific groups of persons, of certain carefully designated symbolic objects. These objects had no intrinsic value except as perceptible representations of the social identity of the individuals. Collective worship of consecrated bits of painted wood or stone created a moral community, a "church," upon which rested the viability of the major social units. These sanctified objects thus represented the system of rights and obligations implicit in the social order and the individual's unformulated sense of its overriding significance in his life. All sacred objects, beliefs, and acts, and the extraordinary emotions attending them, were outward expressions of inward social necessities, and, in a famous phrase, God was the "symbol of society." Few anthropologists have been able to swallow Durkheim's thesis whole, when put this baldly. But the more moderate proposition that religious rituals and beliefs both reflect and act to support the moral framework underlying social arrangements (and are in turn animated by it) has given rise to what has become perhaps the most popular form of analysis in the anthropological study of religion. Usually called "functionalism" —or sometimes, to distinguish it from certain variants deemed objectionable, "structuralism"—this approach found its champion in Radcliffe-Brown and its major development in Great Britain, though its influence has now spread very much more widely.

Radcliffe-Brown (1952) agreed with Durkheim's postulate that the main role (or "function") of religion was to celebrate and sustain the norms upon which the integration of society depends. But unlike Durkheim (and like Freud), Radcliffe-Brown was concerned with the content of sacred symbols, and particularly with the reasons why one object rather than another was absorbed into rite or woven into myth. Why here stones, there water holes, here camp circles, there personified winds?

Durkheim had held this to be an arbitrary matter, contingent upon historical accident or psychological proclivity, beyond the reach of and irrelevant to sociological analysis. Radcliffe-Brown considered, however, that man's need for a concrete expression of social solidarity was not sufficient explanation of the structure of a people's religious system. Something was needed to tie the particular objects awarded sacred status (or, in his terminology, "ritual value") to the particular social interests they presumably served and reflected. Radcliffe-Brown, resolute empiricist that he was, chose a solution Durkheim had already magisterially demolished: the utilitarian. The objects selected for religious veneration by a given people were either directly or indirectly connected to factors critical to their collective well-being. Things that had real, that is, practical, "social value" were elevated to having spiritual, or symbolic, "ritual value," thus fusing the social and the natural into one overarching order. For primitives at least (and Radcliffe-Brown attempted to establish his theory with regard to the sanctified turtles and palm leaves of the pre-agricultural Andaman Islanders and, later on, with regard to Australian totemism), there is no discontinuity, no difference even, between moral and physical, spiritual and practical relationships and processes. These people regard both men and things as parts of a single normative system. Within that system those elements which are critical to its effective functioning (or, sometimes, phenomena empirically associated with such elements, such as the Andaman cicada cycle and

the shifting monsoons) are made the objects of that special sort of respect and attention which we call religious but which the people themselves regard as merely prudential.

Radcliffe-Brown focused upon the content of sacred symbols and emphasized the relation between conceptions of the moral order of existence and conceptions of its natural order. However, the claim that the sanctity of religious objects derives from their practical social importance is one of those theories which works when it works and doesn't when it doesn't. Not only has it proved impossible to find even an indirect practical significance in most of the enormous variety of things tribal peoples have regarded as sacred (certain Australian tribes worship vomit), but the view that religious concerns are mere ritualizations of real-life concerns leaves the phenomenon of sacredness itself—its aura of mystery, power, fascination—totally unexplained.

More recent structuralist studies have tended to evade both these questions and to concentrate on the role played by religion in maintaining social equilibrium. They attempt to show how given sets of religious practices (ancestor worship, animal sacrifice, witchcraft and sorcery, regeneration rites) do in fact express and reinforce the moral values underlying crucial processes (lineage segmentation, marriage, conflict adjudication, political succession) in the particular society under investigation. Arnold van Gennep's study of crisis rites was perhaps the most important forerunner of the many analyses of this type. Although valuable in their own right as ethnography and as sociology, these structural formulations have been severely limited by their rigid avoidance on the one side, of the kind of psychological considerations that could account for the peculiar emotions which permeate religious belief and practice, and, on the other, of the philosophical considerations that could render their equally peculiar content intelligible.

The Analysis of Symbolic Forms

In contrast to other approaches—evolutionary psychological sociological—the field of what we may loosely call "semantic studies" of religion is extremely jumbled. There is, as yet, no well-established central trend to analysis, no central figure around whom to order debate, and no readily apparent system of interconnections relating the various competing trends to one another.

Perhaps the most straightforward strategy—certainly the most disarming—is merely to *accept* the myriad expressions of the sacred in primitive societies, to consider them as actual ingressions of the divine into the world, and to trace the forms these expressions have taken across the earth and through time. The result would be a sort of natural history of revelation, whose aim would be to isolate the major classes of religious phenomena considered as authentic manifestations of the sacred—what Eliade, the chief proponent of this approach, calls hierophanies—and to trace the rise, dominance, decline, and disappearance of these classes within the changing contexts of human life. The meaning of religious activity, the burden of its content, is discovered through a meticulous, wholly inductive investigation of the natural modalities of such behavior (sun worship, water symbolism, fertility cults, renewal myths, etc.) and of the vicissitudes these modalities undergo when projected, like the Son of God himself, into the flux of history.

Metaphysical questions (here uncommonly obtrusive) aside, the weaknesses of this approach derive from the same source as its strengths: a drastic limiting of the interpretations of religion to the sort that a resolutely Baconian methodology can produce. On the one hand, this approach has led, especially in the case of a scholar as erudite and indefatigable as Eliade, to the uncovering of some highly suggestive clusterings of certain religious patterns with particular historical conditions—for example, the frequent association of sun worship, activist conceptions of divine power, cultic veneration of deified heroes, elitist doctrines of political sovereignty, and imperialist ideologies of national expansion. But, on the other hand, it has placed beyond the range of scientific analysis everything but the history and morphology of the phenomenal forms of religious expression. The study of tribal beliefs and practices is reduced to a kind of cultural paleontology whose sole aim is the reconstruction, from scattered and corrupted fragments, of the "mental universe of archaic man."

Primitive Thought

Other scholars who are interested in the meaningful content of primitive religion but who are incapable of so thoroughgoing a suspension of disbelief as Eliade, or are repelled by the cultic overtones of this somewhat mystagogic line of thought, have directed their attention instead toward logical and epistemological considerations. This has produced a long series of studies that view "primitive thought" as a distinctive mode of reasoning and/or a special body of knowledge. From Lévy-Bruhl through Lévi-Strauss, and with important contributions from members of the evolutionary, psychoanalytic, and sociological schools as well, this line of exploration has persisted as a minor theme in anthropological studies of religion. With the recent advances in linguistics, information theory, the analysis of cognition, semantic philosophy, modern logic, and certain sorts of literary investigation, the systematic study of symbolic activity bids fair to become, in a rather thoroughly revised form, the major theme for investigation. The "new key" Susanne K. Langer heard being struck in philosophy in the early 1940s—"the concern with the concept of meaning in all its forms"—has, like the historicist and positivist "keys" before it, begun to have its echo in the anthropological study of religion. Anthropologists are increasingly interested in ideational expression, increasingly concerned with the vehicles, processes, and practical applications of human conceptualization.

The development of this approach has come in two fairly distinct phases, one before and one after World War II. In the first phase there was a concern with "the mind of primitive man" and in particular with its capacity for rational thought. In a sense, this concern represented the evolutionists' interest in primitive reasoning processes detached from the historicist context. In the second phase, which is still in process, there has been a move away from, and in part a reaction against, the subjectivist emphasis of the earlier work. Ideational expression is thought of as a public activity, rather like speech, and the structure of the symbolic materials, the "language," in whose terms the activity is conducted becomes the subject of investigation.

The first, subjectivist, phase was animated by a protracted wrangle between those who used the religious beliefs and practices of tribal peoples as evidence to prove that there was a qualitative difference between the thought processes of primitives and those of civilized men and the anthropologists who considered such religious activity as evidence for the lack of any such differences. The great protagonist of the first school was the French philosopher Lévy-Bruhl whose theories of "prelogical mentality" were as controversial within anthropology as they were popular outside it. According to Lévy-Bruhl, the thought of primitives, as reflected in their religious ideas, is not governed by the immanent laws of Aristotelian logical reasoning, but by affectivity—by the vagrant flow of emotion and the dialectical principles of "mystical participation" and "mystical exclusion."

The two most effective antagonists of Lévy-Bruhl's theories concerning primitive religion were Radin and Malinowski. Radin, influenced by Boas' more general attacks on theories of "primitive mentality," sought to demonstrate that primitive religious thought reaches, on occasion, very high levels of logical articulation and philosophical sophistication and that tribal society contains, alongside the common run of unreflective doers ("men of action"), contemplative intellectuals ("men of thought") of boldness, subtlety, and originality. Malinowski attacked the problem on an even broader front. Using his ethnographic knowledge of the Trobriand Islanders, Malinowski argued that alongside their religious and magical notions (which he, too, regarded as mainly emotionally determined) the "savages" also had a rather well-developed and, as far as it went, accurate empirical knowledge of gardening, navigation, housebuilding, canoe construction, and other useful arts. He further claimed that they were absolutely clear as to the distinction between these two sorts of reasoning, between mystical-magical and empirical-pragmatic thinking, and never confused them in actual practice. Of these two arguments, the former seems to be today nearly universally accepted and was perhaps never in fact really questioned. But with respect to the latter, serious doubts have arisen concerning whether the lines between "science," "magic," and "religion" are as simple and clear-cut in the minds of tribal peoples (or any peoples) as Malinowski, never one for shaded judgments, portrayed them. Nevertheless, between them, Radin and Malinowski rather definitively demolished the notion of a radical qualitative gap between the thought processes of primitive and civilized men. Indeed, toward the end of his life even Lévy-Bruhl admitted that his arguments

had been badly cast and might better have been phrased in terms of different modes of thinking common to all men. (In fact, Freud, with his contrast between primary and secondary thinking processes, had already made this distinction.)

Thus, the debate about what does or does not go on in the heads of savages exhausted itself in generalities, and recent writers have turned to a concern with the symbolic forms, the conceptual resources, in terms of which primitives (and non-primitives) think. The major figure in this work has been Claude Lévi-Strauss, although this line of attack dates back to Durkheim and Mauss's influential 1903 essay in sociological Kantianism, *Primitive Classification*. The writings of E. E. Evans-Pritchard on Zande witchcraft, Benjamin Whorf on Hopi semantics, and Gregory Bateson on Iatmul ritual and, among non-anthropologists, works by Granet, Cassirer, and Piaget have directed attention to the study of symbolic formulation.

Symbolic Systems

Lévi-Strauss, whose rather highly wrought work is still very much in progress, is concerned with the systems of classification, the "homemade" taxonomies, employed by tribal peoples to order the objects and events of their world (see Lévi-Strauss 1958; 1962). In this, he follows in the footsteps of Durkheim and Mauss. But rather than looking, as they did, to social forms for the origins and explanations of such categorical systems, he looks to the symbolic structures in terms of which they are formulated, expressed, and applied. Myth and, in a slightly different way, rite are systems of signs that fix and organize abstract conceptual relationships in terms of concrete images and thus make speculative thought possible. They permit the construction of a "science of the concrete"—the intellectual comprehension of the sensible world in terms of sensible phenomena—which is no less rational, no less logical, no more affect-driven than the abstract science of the modern world. The objects rendered sacred are selected not because of their utilitarian qualities, nor because they are projections of repressed emotions, nor yet because they reflect the moral force of social organization ritualistically impressed upon the mind. Rather, they are selected because they permit the embodiment of general ideas in terms of the immediately perceptible realities—the turtles, trees, springs, and caves—of everyday experience; not, as Lévi-Strauss says, apropos of Radcliffe-Brown's view of totems, because they are "good to eat," but because they are "good to think."

This "goodness" exists inherently in sacred objects because they provide the raw materials for analogical reasoning. The relationships perceived among certain classes of natural objects or events can be analogized, taken as models of relationships—physical, social, psychological, or moral—obtaining between persons, groups, or other natural objects and events. Thus, for example, the natural distinctions perceived among totemic beings, their species differentiation, can serve as a conceptual framework for the comprehension, expression, and communication of social distinctions among exogamous clans—their structural differentiation. Thus, the sharp contrast between the wet and dry seasons (and the radical zoological and botanical changes associated with it) in certain regions of Australia is employed in the mythology of the native peoples. They have woven an elaborate origin myth around this natural phenomenon, one that involves a rain-making python who drowned some incestuous sisters and their children because the women polluted his water hole with menstrual blood. This model expresses and economizes the contrasts between moral purity and impurity, maleness and femaleness, social superiority and inferiority, fertilizing agent (rain) and that which is fertilized (land), and even the distinction between "high" (initiate) and "low" (noninitiate) levels of cultural achievement.

Lévi-Strauss contends that primitive religious systems are, like all symbolic systems, fundamentally communications systems. They are carriers of information in the technical Shannon-Weaver sense, and as such, the theory of information can be applied to them with the same validity as when applied to any physical systems, mechanical or biological, in which the transfer of information plays a central regulative role. Primitives, as all men, are quintessentially multichanneled emitters and receivers of messages. It is merely in the nature of the code they employ—one resting on analogies between "natural" and "cultural" distinctions and relationships—that they differ from ourselves. Where there is a distinguishing difference, it lies in the technically specialized codes of modern abstract thought, in which semantic properties are radically and deliberately severed from physical ones. Religion, primitive or modern, can be understood only as an integrated system of thought, logically sound, epistemologically valid, and as flourishing in France as in Tahiti.

It is far too early to evaluate Lévi-Strauss's work with any assurance. It is frankly incomplete and explorative, and some parts of it (the celebration of information theory, for example) are wholly programmatic. But in focusing on symbol systems as conceptual models of social or other sorts of reality, he has clearly introduced into the anthropology of religion a line of inquiry which, having already become common in modern thought generally, can hardly fail to be productive when applied to tribal myth and ritual.

Whether his own particular formulation of this approach will prove to be the most enduring remains, however, rather more of a question. His rejection of emotional considerations and his neglect of normative or social factors in favor of an extreme intellectualism which cerebralizes religion and tends to reduce it yet again to a kind of undeveloped (or, as he puts it, "undomesticated") science are questionable. His nearly exclusive stress on those intellectual processes involved in classification, i.e., on taxonomic modes of thought (a reflex of his equally great reliance on totemic ideas as type cases of primitive beliefs), at the expense of other, perhaps more common, and certainly more powerful styles of reasoning, is also doubtful. His conception of the critical process of symbolic formulation itself remains almost entirely undeveloped—hardly more than a sort of associationism dressed up with some concepts from modern linguistics. Partly as a result of this weakness and partly as a result of a tendency to consider symbol systems as entities functioning independently of the contextual factor, many of his specific interpretations of particular myths and rites seem as strained, arbitrary, and oversystematized as those of the most undisciplined psychoanalyst.

But, for all this, Lévi-Strauss has without doubt opened a vast territory for research and begun to explore it with theoretical brilliance and profound scholarship. And he is not alone. As the recent work of such diverse students as Evans-Pritchard, R. G. Lienhardt, W. E. H. Stanner, Victor W. Turner, Germaine Dieterlen, Meyer Fortes, Edmund R.

Leach, Charles O. Frake, Rodney Needham, and Susanne K. Langer demonstrates, the analysis of symbolic forms is becoming a major tradition in the study of primitive religion—in fact, of religion in general. Each of these writers has a somewhat different approach. But all seem to share the conviction that an attempt must be made to approach primitive religions for what they are: systems of ideas about the ultimate shape and substance of reality.

Whatever else religion does, it relates a view of the ultimate nature of reality to a set of ideas of how man is well advised, even obligated, to live. Religion tunes human actions to a view of the cosmic order and projects images of cosmic order onto the plane of human existence. In religious belief and practice a people's style of life, what Clyde Kluckhohn called their *design for living*, is rendered intellectually reasonable; it is shown to represent a way of life ideally adapted to the world "as it 'really' ('fundamentally,' 'ultimately') is." At the same time, the supposed basic structure of reality is rendered emotionally convincing because it is presented as an actual state of affairs uniquely accommodated to such a way of life and permitting it to flourish. Thus do received beliefs, essentially metaphysical, and established norms, essentially moral, confirm and support one another.

It is this mutual confirmation that religious symbols express and celebrate and that any scientific analysis of religion must somehow contrive to explain and clarify. In the development of such an analysis historical, psychological, sociological, and what has been called here semantic considerations are all necessary, but none is sufficient. A mature theory of religion will consist of an integration of them all into a conceptual system whose exact form remains to be discovered.

Religious Perspectives in Anthropology

Dorothy Lee

At first glance the study of the religion of non-Western cultures may appear somewhat esoteric, albeit interesting. In reality, however, religion is very much a part of everyday, practical activities in these cultures, and knowledge of a society's religion is essential for the successful introduction of social changes. In the following article Dorothy Lee dramatically shows how religion is part and parcel of pre-literate people's world view, or
Weltanschauung: *the corpus of beliefs about the life and environment in which members of a society find themselves. Among pre-literate societies, economic, political, and artistic behavior is permeated by religion. Lee points out that anthropologists make every attempt to understand the insiders' "emic" view of their universe, which they share with other members of their group, and demonstrates that an outsider's "etic" view is too limited a base of cultural knowledge on which to introduce innovations that do not violate the religious tenets of the society and meet with acceptance.*

Reprinted from Lowell D. Holmes, ed., *Readings in General Anthropology* (New York: Ronald Press, 1971), pp. 416–27.

IN PRIMITIVE SOCIETIES, WE DO NOT ALWAYS find the worship of God or a god, nor the idea of the supernatural. Yet religion is always present in man's view of his place in the universe, in his relatedness to man and nonhuman nature, to reality and circumstance. His universe may include the divine or may itself be divine. And his patterned behavior often has a religious dimension, so that we find religion permeating daily life—agriculture and hunting, health measures, arts and crafts.

We do find societies where a Supreme Being is recognized; but this Being is frequently so far removed from mundane affairs, that it is not present in the consciousness of the people except on the specific occasions of ceremonial or prayer. But in these same societies, we find communion with the unperceivable and unknowable in nature, with an ultimate reality, whether spirit, or power, or intensified being, or personal worth, which evokes humility, respect, courtesy or sometimes fear, on man's part. This relationship to the ultimate reality is so pervasive, that it may determine, for example, which hand a man will use in adjusting his loin cloth, or how much water he will drink at a time, or which way his head will point when he sleeps, or how he will butcher and utilize the carcass of a caribou. What anthropologists label "material culture," therefore, is never purely material. Often we would be at least as justified to call the operation involved religious.

All economic activities, such as hunting, gathering fuel, cultivating the land, storing food, assume a relatedness to the encompassing universe, and with many cultures, this is a religious relationship. In such cultures, men recognize a certain spiritual worth and dignity in the universe. They do not set out to control, or master, or exploit. Their ceremonials are often periods of intensified communion, even social affairs, in a broad sense, if the term may be extended to include the forces of the universe. They are not placating or bribing or even thanking; they are rather a formal period of concentrated, enjoyable association. In their relationships with nature, the people may see themselves as the offspring of a cherishing mother, or the guests of a generous hostess, or as members of a democratic society which proceeds on the principle of consent. So, when the Baiga in India were urged to change over to the use of an iron plow, they replied with horror that they could not tear the flesh of their mother with knives. And American Indians have hunted many animals with the consent of the generic essence of these—of which the particular animal was the carnal manifestation—only after establishing a relationship or reciprocity; with man furnishing the ceremonial, and Buffalo or Salmon or Caribou making a gift of the countless manifestations of his flesh.

The great care with which so many of the Indian groups utilized every portion of the carcass of a hunted animal, was an expression, not of economic thrift, but of courtesy and respect; in fact, an aspect of the religious relationship to the slain. The Wintu Indians of California, who lived on land so wooded that it was difficult to find clear land for putting up a group of houses, nevertheless used only dead wood for fuel, out of respect for nature. An old Wintu woman, speaking in prophetic vein, expressed this: "The White people never cared for land or deer or bear. When we Indians kill meat, we eat it all up. When we dig roots we make little holes. When we build houses, we make little holes. When we burn grass for grasshoppers, we don't ruin things. We shake down acorns and pinenuts. We don't chop down the trees. We only use dead wood. But the White people plow up the ground, pull up the trees, kill everything. The tree says, 'Don't. I am sore. Don't hurt me.' But they chop it down and cut it up. The spirit of the land hates them. They blast out trees and stir it up to its depths. They saw up the trees. That hurts them. The Indians never hurt anything, but the white people destroy all. They blast rocks and scatter them on the ground. The rock says, 'Don't! You are hurting me.' But the White People pay no attention. When the Indians use rocks, they take little round ones for their cooking. . . . How can the spirit of the earth like the white man? . . . Everywhere the White man has touched it, it is sore.'"

Here we find people who do not so much *seek* communion with environing nature as *find themselves* in communion with it. In many of these societies, not even mysticism is to be found, in our sense of the word. For us, mysticism presupposes a prior separation of man from nature; and communion is achieved through loss of self and subsequent merging with that which is beyond; but for many cultures, there is no such distinct separation between self and other, which must be overcome. Here, man is *in* nature already, and we cannot speak properly of man *and* nature.

Take the Kaingang, for example, who chops out a wild beehive. He explains his act to the bees, as he would to a person whom he considered his coordinate. "Bee, produce! I chopped you out to make beer of you! Yukui's wife died, and I am making beer of you so that I can cut his hair." Or he may go up to a hive and say simply, "Bee, it is I." And the Arapesh of New Guinea, going to his yam garden, will first introduce to the spirit of the land, the brother-in-law whom he has brought along to help him with the gardening. This is not achieved communication, brought about for definite ends. It implies an already present relatedness with the ultimate reality, with that which is accepted in faith, and which exists irrespective of man's cognition or perception or logic. If we were to abstract, out of this situation, merely the food getting or the operational techniques, we would be misrepresenting the reality.

The same present relatedness is to be found in some societies where the deity is more specifically defined. The Tikopia, in the Solomon Islands Protectorate, sit and eat their meals with their dead under the floor, and hand food and drink to them; the dead are all somewhat divine, progressively so as they come nearer to the original, fully divine ancestor of the clan. Whatever their degree of divinity, the Tikopia is at home with them; he is aware of their vague presence, though he requires the services of a medium whenever he wants to make this presence definite.

Firth describes an occasion when a chief, having instructed a medium to invite his dead nephew to come and chew betel with him, found himself occupied with something else when the dead arrived, and so asked the medium to tell the spirit—a minor deity—to chew betel by himself. At another time, during an important ceremonial, when this chief was receiving on his forehead the vertical stripe which was the symbol that he was now the incarnation of the highest god, he jokingly jerked his head aside, so that the stripe, the insignium of the presence of the god, went crooked. These are the acts of a man who feels accepted by his gods, and is at one with them. And, in fact, the Tikopia appear to live in a continuum which includes nature and the divine without defining bounds; where communion is present, not achieved; where merging is a matter of being, not of becoming.

In these societies, where religion is an everpresent dimension of experience, it is doubtful that religion as such is given a name; Kluckhohn reports that the Navaho have no such word, but most ethnographers never thought to inquire. Many of these cultures, however, recognized and named the spiritual ingredient or attribute, the special quality of the wonderful, the very, the beyondness, in nature. This was sometimes considered personal, sometimes not. We have from the American Indians terms such as *manitou*, or *wakan*, or *yapaitu*, often translated as power; and we have the well-known Melanesian term *mana*. But this is what they reach through faith, the other end of the relationship; the relationship itself is unnamed. Apparently, to behave and think religiously, is to behave and think. To describe a way of life in its totality is to describe a religious way of life.

When we speak of agricultural taboos and rites, therefore, we often introduce an analytical factor which violates the fact. For example, when preparing seed for planting, one of the several things a Navaho traditionally does is to mix ground "mirage stone" with the seed. And in the process of storing corn, a double-eared stalk is laid at the bottom of the storage pit. In actual life, these acts are a continuous part of a total activity.

The distinction between the religious and the secular elements may even separate an act from the manner of performance, a verb from its adverb. The direction in which a man is facing when performing a secular act, or the number of times he shakes his hand when spattering water, often have their religious implications. When the Navaho planted his corn sunwise, his act reflected a total world view, and it would be nonsense for us to separate the planting itself from the direction of the planting.

Those of us who present religion as separate from "everyday" living, reflect moreover the distinctions of a culture which will identify six days with the secular in life and only the seventh with religion. In many primitive societies, religion is rarely absent from the details of everyday living, and the ceremonials represent a formalization and intensification of an everpresent attitude. We have societies such as that of the Hopi of Arizona, where ceremonials, and the preparation for them, cover most of the year. Some years ago, Crowwing, a Hopi, kept a journal for the period of a year, putting down all events of ceremonial import. Day after day, there are entries containing some casual reference to a religious activity, or describing a ritual, or the preparation for a ceremonial. After a few weeks of such entries, we come to a sequence of four days' entries which are devoted to a description of a ball game played by two opposing groups of children and enjoyed by a large number of spectators. But, in the end, this also turns out to have been ceremonial in nature, helping the corn to grow.

Among many groups, agriculture is an expression of man's religious relatedness to the universe. As Robert Redfield and W. Lloyd Warner have written: "The agriculture of the Maya Indians of southeastern Yucatan is not simply a way of securing food. It is also a way of worshipping the gods. Before a man plants, he builds an altar in the field and prays there. He must not speak boisterously in the cornfield; it is a sort of temple. The cornfield is planted as an incident in a perpetual sacred contract between supernatural beings and men. By this agreement, the supernaturals yield part of what is theirs—the riches of the natural environment—to men. In exchange, men are pious and perform the traditional ceremonies in which offerings are made to the supernaturals. . . . The world is seen as inhabited by the supernaturals; each has his appropriate place in the woods, the sky, or the wells from which the water is drawn. The village is seen as a reflection of the quadrilateral pattern of the cosmos; the cornfield too is oriented, laid out east, west, north, and south, with reference to the supernaturals that watch over the cardinal points; and the table altars erected for the ceremonies again remind the individual of this pattern. The stories that are told at the time when men wait to perform the ceremony before the planting of the corn or that children hear as they grow up are largely stories which explain and further sanction the traditional way of life."

Art also is often so permeated with religion that sometimes, as among the Navaho, what we classify as art is actually religion. To understand the rhythm of their chants, the "plot" of their tales, the making of their sand paintings, we have to understand Navaho religion: the concept of harmony between man and the universe as basic to health and well being; the concept of continuity, the religious significance of the groups of four, the door of contact opened through the fifth repetition, the need to have no completely enclosing frame around any of their works so that continuity can be maintained and the evil inside can have an opening through which to leave.

The sand paintings are no more art than they are ritual, myth, medical practice or religious belief. They are created as an integral aspect of a ceremonial which brings into harmony with the universal order one who finds himself in discord with it; or which intensifies and ensures the continuation of a harmony which is already present. Every line and shape and color, every interrelationship of form, is the visible manifestation of myth, ritual and religious belief. The making of the painting is accompanied with a series of sacred songs sung over a sick person, or over someone who, though healed of sickness by emergency measures has yet to be brought back into the universal harmony; or in enhancing and giving emphasis to the present harmony. What we would call purely medical practices may or may not be part of all this. When the ceremonial is over, the painting is over too; it is destroyed; it has fulfilled its function.

This is true also of the art of the neighboring Hopi, where the outstanding form of art is the drama. In this we find wonderfully humorous clowning, involving careful planning and preparation, creation of magnificent masks and costumes, rehearsals, organization. Everyone comes to see and responds with uproarious hilarity. But this is not mere art. It is an important way of helping nature in her work of growing the corn. Even the laughter of the audience helps in this.

More than dramatic rehearsal and creation of costumes has gone into the preparation. The actors have prepared themselves as whole persons. They have refrained from sexual activity, and from anything involving conflict. They have had good

thoughts only. They have refrained from anger, worry and grief. Their preparations as well as their performance have had a religious dimension. Their drama is one act in the great process of the cyclical growing of corn, a divinity indispensable to man's well being, and to whose well being man is indispensable. Corn wants to grow, but cannot do so without the cooperation of the rest of nature and of man's acts and thoughts and will. And, to be happy, corn must be danced by man and participate in his ceremonials. To leave the religious dimension out of all this, and to speak of Hopi drama as merely a form of art, would be to present a fallacious picture. Art and agriculture and religion are part of the same totality for the Hopi.

In our own culture, an activity is considered to be economic when it deals with effective utilization or exploitation of resources. But this definition cannot be used when speaking of Hopi economics. To begin with, it assumes an aggressive attitude toward the environment. It describes the situation of the homesteader in Alaska, for example, who works against tremendous odds clearing land for a dairy farm, against the inexorable pressure of time, against hostile elements. By his sweat, and through ingenuity and know-how and the use of brutally effective tools, he tames nature; he subjugates the land and exploits its resources to the utmost.

The Hopi Talayesua, however, describing his work on the land, does not see himself in opposition to it. He works *with* the elements, not *against* them. He helps the corn to grow; he cooperates with the thunderstorm and the pollen and the sun. He is in harmony with the elements, not in conflict; and he does not set out to conquer an opponent. He depends on the corn, but this is part of a mutual interdependence; it is not exploitation. The corn depends on him too. It cannot grow without his help; it finds life dull and lonely without his company and his ceremonials. So it gives its body for his food gladly, and enjoys living with him in his granary. The Hopi has a personal relationship with it. He treats it with respect, and houses it with the care and courtesy accorded to an honored guest. Is this economics?

In a work on Hopi economics we are given an account of the Hopi Salt Journey, under the heading, "Secondary Economic Activities." This expedition is also described in a Hopi autobiography, and here we discover that only those men who have achieved a certain degree of experience in the Hopi way, can go on this journey, and then, only if their minds are pure and they are in a state of harmony with the universe. There is a period of religious preparation, followed by the long and perilous journey which is attended by a number of rituals along the way. Old men, lowering themselves from the overhanging ledge onto the salt deposits, tremble with fear, knowing that they may be unable to make the ascent. The occasion is solemnly religious. This is no utilization of resources, in the eyes of the Hopi who makes the journey. He goes to help the growing corn; the Salt Journey brings needed rain. Twelve adult men will spend days and court dangers to procure salt which they can buy for two dollars from the itinerant peddler. By our own economic standards, this is not an efficient use of human resources. But Hopi ends transcend our economic categories and our standards of efficiency are irrelevant to them.

In many societies, land tenure, or the transference of land, operations involved in hunting and agriculture, are often a part of a religious way of life. In our own culture, man conceives of his relationship to his physical environment, and even sometimes his human environment, as mechanistic and manipulative; in other cultures, we often find what Ruth Benedict has called the animistic attitude toward nature and man, underlying practices which are often classified miscellaneously together in ethnographics, under the heading of superstitions or taboos. The courteous speech to the bear about to be killed, the offering to the deer world before the hunter sets out, the introduction of the brother-in-law to the garden spirit, or the sacrifice to the rice field about to be sold, the refraining from intercourse, or from the eating of meat or from touching food with the hand, are expressive of such an attitude. They are the practices we find in a democratic society where there is consideration for the rights of everyone as opposed to the brutal efficiency of the dictator who feels free to exploit, considering the rights of none. They reflect the attitude of people who believe in conference and consent, not in coercion; of people who generally find personality or mana in nature and man, sometimes more, sometimes less. In this framework, taboo and superstitious act mean that man acts and refrains from acting in the name of a wider democracy which includes nature and the divine.

With such a conception of man's place in nature, what is for us land tenure, or ownership, or rights of use and disposal, is for other societies an intimate belongingness. So the Arapesh conceive of themselves as belonging to the land, in the way that flora and fauna belong to it. They cultivate the land by the grace of the immanent spirits, but they cannot dispose of it and cannot conceive of doing so.

This feeling of affinity between society and land is widespread and appears in various forms and varying degrees of intensity, and it is not found only among sedentary peoples. We have Australian tribes where the very spirit of the men is believed to reside in the land, where a bush or a rock or a peculiar formation is the present incarnation of myth, and contains security and religious value; where a social class, a structured group of relatives, will contain in addition to human beings, an animal and a feature of the landscape. Here, when a man moves away from the land of his group, he leaves the vital part of himself behind. When a magistrate put people from such societies in jail in a distant city, he had no idea of the terrifying severity of the punishment he was meting; he was cutting the tribesman off from the very source of his life and of his self, from the past, and the future which were incorporated and present in his land.

In the technology of such societies we are again dealing with material where the religious and secular are not distinct from each other. We have, for example, the description which Raymond Firth gives of the replacing of a wornout wash strake on a canoe, among the Tikopia. This operation is expertly and coherently carried out, with secular and religious acts performed without distinction in continuous succession or concurrently. A tree is cut down for the new wash strake, a libation is poured out to the deities of the canoe to announce this new timber, and a kava rite is performed to persuade the deities to step out of the canoe and on to a piece of bark cloth, where they can live undisturbed, while the canoe is being tampered with. Then comes the unlashing of the old wash strake, the expert examination of the body of the canoe in search of lurking defects, the discovery of signs indicating the work of a borer, the cutting of the body of the canoe with a swift stroke to discover whether the borer is there, accompanied by an appeal to the deities of the canoe by the expert, to witness what he is doing, and the necessity for doing it.

Now a kinsman of the original builder of the canoe, now dead and a tutelary deity, spontaneously drops his head on to the side of the canoe and wails over the wounding of the body of the canoe. The borer is discovered, in the meantime, to be still there; but only a specially consecrated adze can deal with him successfully. The adze is sent for, dedicated anew to the deity, invoked, and finally wielded with success by the expert.

All this is performed with remarkable expedition and economy of motion yet the Tikopia workers are not interested in saving time; they are concerned neither with time limits nor with speed in itself. Their concern is with the dispossessed deities whose home must be made ready against their return; and the speed of their work is incidental to this religious concern. The end result is efficiency; but unlike our own efficiency, this is not rooted in the effort to utilize and exploit material and time resources to the utmost; it is rooted in that profound religious feeling which also gives rise to the time-consuming rites and the wailing procedures which, from the purely economic point of view, are wasteful and interfering.

The world view of a particular society includes that society's conception of man's own relation to the universe, human and non-human, organic and inorganic, secular and divine, to use our own dualisms. It expresses man's view of his own role in the maintenance of life, and of the forces of nature. His attitude toward responsibility and initiative is inextricable from his conception of nature as deity-controlled, man-controlled, regulated through a balanced cooperation between god and man, or perhaps maintained through some eternal homeostasis, independent of man and perhaps of any deity. The way a man acts, his feeling of guilt and achievement, and his very personality, are affected by the way he envisions his place within the universe.

For example, there are the Tiv of Southern Nigeria who as described by one of them in the thirties, people the universe with potentially hostile and harmful powers, the *akombo*. Man's function in the maintenance of his own life and the moderate well-being of the land and of his social unit, is to prevent the manifestation of *akombo* evil, through performing rites and observing taboos. So his rites render safe through preventing, through expulsion and purging. His role is negative, defending the normal course against the interference. Vis-à-vis the universe, his acts arise out of negative motives. Thus what corresponds to a gift of first fruits to a deity in other cultures is phrased as a rite for preventing the deities from making a man's food go bad or diminish too quickly; fertility rites for a field are actually rites preventing the evil-intentioned from robbing the fields of their normal fertility.

In the writings of R. F. Barton, who studied the Ifugao of Luzon in the early part of this century, these people also appear to see deities as ready to interfere and bring evil; but their conception of man's role within the structure of the universe is a different one from that of the Tiv. In Barton's descriptive accounts, the Ifugao either accept what comes as deity-given, or act without being themselves the agents; they believe that no act can come to a conclusive end without the agency of a specific deity. They have a specific deity often for every step within an operation and for every part of the implement to be used. R. F. Barton recorded the names of 1,240 deities and believed that even so he had not exhausted the list.

The Ifugao associate a deity with every structured performance and at least a large number of their deliberate acts. They cannot go hunting, for example, without enlisting the aid of the deity of each step of the chase, to render each effective, or to nullify any lurking dangers. There is a deity for the level spot where "the hunter stands watching and listening to the dogs"; one for when the dogs "are sicced on the game"; one for when "the hunter leans on his spear transfixing the quarry"; twelve are listed as the deities of specific ways of rendering harmless to the hunter's feet the snags and fangs of snakes which he encounters. If he is to be successful in the hunt, a man does not ask the blessing of a deity. He pays all the particular deities of every specific spot and act, getting them to transitivize each act individually.

Even so, in most cases an Ifugao remains non-agentive, since the function of many of the deities is to save man from encounter, rather than to give him success in his dealing with it. For example, in the area of interpersonal relations, we have Tupya who is invoked so that, "the creditor comes for dun for what is owed, but on the way he forgets and goes about other business"; and Dulaiya, who is invoked so that, "the enemies just don't think about us, so they don't attack." His tools, also, are ineffective of themselves; so that, when setting a deadfall, he invokes and bribes such deities as that for the Flat Stone of the Deadfall, the Main Posts of the Deadfall, the Fall of the Deadfall, the Trigger of the Deadfall. Most of the Ifugao economy is involved in providing sacrifices to the deities, big or little according to the magnitude of the operation and the importance of the deities. There is no warmth in the sacrifices; no expression of gratitude or appeal or belongingness. As the Ifugaos see it, the sacrifice is a bribe. With such bribes, they buy the miraculous intervention and transitivization which are essential for achievement, health, and good personal relations.

The Ifugao show no humility in the face of this ineffective role in the universe; they merely accept it as the state of things. They accept their own failures, the frequent deaths, the sudden and disastrous flaring up of tempers, as things that are bound to happen irrespective of their own desires and efforts. But they are neither passive nor helpless. They carry on great undertakings, and, even now they go on forbidden head hunts. They know when and how and whom to bribe so as to perfect their defective acts. When however, a deity states a decision, they accept it as immutable. A Catholic priest tells a story about the neighboring Iloko which illustrates this acceptance. A Christian Iloko was on his deathbed, and the priest, trying to persuade him to repent of his sin, painted to him vividly the horrors of hell; but the dying man merely answered, "If God wants me to go to hell, I am perfectly willing."

Among the Wintu Indians of California we find that man sees himself as effective but in a clearly limited way. An examination of the myths of the Wintu shows that the individual was conceived as having a limited agentive role, shaping, using, intervening, actualizing and temporalizing the given, but never creating; that man was viewed as needing skill for his operations, but that specific skill was useless without "luck" which a man received through communion and pleading with some universal power.

It is to this limited role of man, geared to the working of the universe, that I referred when I spoke earlier of Hopi drama and agriculture. With-

out an understanding of this role, no Hopi activity or attitude or relationship can be understood. The Hopi have developed the idea of man's limited effectiveness in their own fashion, and have elaborated it systematically in what they call the "Hopi Way." Laura Thompson says of the Hopi, "All phenomena relevant to the life of the tribe—including man, the animals, and plants, the earth, sun, moon, clouds, the ancestors, and the spirits—are believed to be interdependent. . . . In this system each individual—human and non-human—is believed to have . . . a definite role in the universal order." Traditionally, fulfillment of the law of nature—the growth of the corn, the movements of the sun—can come only with man's participation, only with man's performance of the established ceremonials. Here man was effective, but only in cooperation with the rest of the phenomena of nature.

The Indians of the Plains, such as the Crow and the Sioux, have given a somewhat different form to this conception of man's circumscribed agency. The aggressive behavior for which they have been known, their great personal autonomy, their self-assurance and assertiveness and in recent years, their great dependence and apathy, have been explained as an expression of this conception. These societies envisioned the universe as pervaded by an undifferentiated religious force on which they were dependent for success in their undertakings and in life generally. The specific formulation different in the different tribes, but, essentially, in all it was believed that each individual and particularly each man, must tap this universal force if his undertakings were to be successful. Without this "power" a man could not achieve success in any of the valued activities, whether warfare or the hunt; and no leadership was possible without this power. This was a force enhancing and intensifying the being of the man who acted; it was not, as with the Ifugao, an effectiveness applied to specific details of activities. The individual himself prepared himself in the hardihood, self-control, skills and areas of knowledge necessary. Little boys of five or seven took pride in their ability to withstand pain, physical hardship, and the terrors of running errands alone in the night. The Sioux did not appeal for divine intervention; he did not want the enemy to forget to come. Yet neither was he fearless. He appealed for divine strength to overcome his own fears as well as the external enemy.

The relationship with the divine, in this case, is personal and intense. The Plains Indian Sioux did not, like the Hopi, inherit a specific relatedness when he was born in a specific clan. Each man, each pre-adolescent boy, had to achieve the relationship for himself. He had to go out into the wilderness and spend days and nights without food or drink, in the cold, among wild beasts, afraid and hungry and anxious, humbling himself and supplicating, sometimes inflicting excruciating pain upon himself, until some particular manifestation of the universal force took pity upon him and came to him to become his life-long guardian and power. The appeals to the universal force were made sometimes in a group, through the institution of the Sun Dance. But here also they were individual in nature. The relationship with the divine was an inner experience; and when the Dakota Black Elk recounted his autobiography, he spoke mainly of these intense, personal religious experiences. Within this range of variation in form and concept and world view, we find expressed by all the same immediate relatedness to the divine.

The Anthropologist's Encounter with the Supernatural

I. M. Lewis

In this article I. M. Lewis takes the reader through a series of examples of anthropologists' encounters with the supernatural in non-Western societies. Reactions range from the skepticism of E. E. Evans-Pritchard, on the one hand, to the outright belief in mystic experiences of Carlos Castaneda, on the other. These encounters are ambiguous, and Lewis sets out to test supernatural experiences through what he terms "the most impressive psychic evidence of the divine—that dramatic invasion of the human body we call 'spirit possession.'" Using the Umbanda cult of Brazil and the Cuban Santeria cult, Lewis demonstrates that women are especially prominent in cult activities, and that cults, almost without exception, employ sexual imagery. Lewis's focus on possession does not, in the final summary, prove supernatural activity of spirits or gods, but it tells us a great deal about the nature of man, in particular in terms of stress and conflict situations. However, Lewis is unable to show that spiritual forces do not exist.

Reprinted from Allan Angoff and Diana Barth, eds., *Parapsychology and Anthropology*, pp. 22–31, by permission of The Parapsychology Foundation, Inc.

THERE MUST BE FEW ANTHROPOLOGISTS WHO HAVE not had a brush with the supernatural in the course of their field work in the "high-spirited," exotic communities which they customarily study. Such encounters have, moreover, often been as unexpected as they were unsolicited. Let me give a few random illustrations. Recalling his field work in Ireland many years ago, the very serious American anthropologist S. T. Kimball has recently described how he encountered a ghost at his hotel (Kimball and Watson 1972: 189). This meeting, he tells us, turned out to be very fortunate, for it finally convinced his Irish informants that their anthropologist was, after all, a normal human being (and that, of course, is one of the most difficult things for the anthropologist to achieve). Other anthropologists have heard the wail of the banshee, seen mysterious lights in the night, and witnessed amazing cures. Even very skeptical anthropologists have had daunting experiences. Illnesses or misadventures after slighting or quarreling with a local witch doctor or medicine man are frequently reported. Certainly there are few of us who could cross our hearts and honestly say that we had not felt discomfort, qualms about what might happen, when threatened with cursing—or the evil eye. A very distinguished psychologist told me recently how, when he was working in West Africa, a fetish priest once threatened to kill one of his children (who was incidentally thousands of miles away). My friend, who is a very firm skeptic, confesses that he felt acutely uncomfortable, resisting the blackmail but guiltily thinking: "What if there is something in it." On a happier note, I can recount a personal experience involving more benevolent powers. In the course of carrying out research amongst the Muslim Somali of northeast Africa I spent a lot of time visiting the shrines of the most famous local saints. These, of course, are a potent source of *baraka*, that miracle-working energy which brings life and blessing. The fact that I now have four children has, as I have heard on a number of occasions, been ascribed by Somalis to my prudent piety in communing so closely with their saints. So, whether they like it or not, anthropologists are drawn into the web of the mystical beliefs they study. How they respond is another matter.

"The anthropologist," Edmund Leach primly asserts, "rejects the idea of supernatural forces" (1969: 9). He should know. He is President of the Royal Anthropological Institute and of the British Humanist Association. However, the matter is far from being as simple or straightforward as this. The truth is rather that the anthropologist's credulity (or incredulity) is often highly selective. It is very noticeable, for instance, that anthropologists (even those who are avowed agnostics or atheists) have been much more "objective" and analytical in their treatment of topics like witchcraft or sorcery than in that of other, less immediately implausible, mystical experiences. So, for instance, precisely because it does *not* take their faith at face value, Evans-Pritchard's classic study of witchcraft among the Zande people of the southern Sudan is, paradoxically, able to show how such a closed system of ostensibly untenable beliefs makes sense (1937). The author, a highly sophisticated Catholic, does not seem to find it necessary to spend quite as much time justifying the *theistic* religion of the Nuer (1956).

These two famous books—*Nuer Religion* and *Witchcraft, Oracles and Magic among the Azande*—make, indeed, a most interesting contrast. Whereas the Zande study is filled with references to "skepticism," this word hardly occurs at all (so far as I can discover) in *Nuer Religion*. Interestingly enough, the skepticism referred to is actually mostly that of the Zande themselves. Indeed, it is quite clear that the Zande, at a certain level of experience, see their witchcraft with precisely the same analytical clarity as Evans-Pritchard. They know as well as he does that it is a philosophy of misfortune and a strategy for the release of social tension. They too fully appreciate that withcraft is a pseudonym for malice, envy, and spite. Evans-Pritchard's approach, it will be understood, is very different from the recent sorcerer's apprenticeship so evocatively described by Carlos Castaneda in *The Teachings of Don Juan* (1968).

Up to a point then, I am suggesting that Evans-Pritchard's skepticism about witchcraft and that of the Zande happen to coincide. In other cases, we find credulous anthropologists shocked by the irreverence and skepticism of their informants: shamans, for instance, like the skeptic encountered by Lévi-Strauss in South America, who do not really believe in their own powers. But they do believe in the authentic shamanistic powers of *other* shamans. Somebody, somewhere, is a true, genuine exponent of an art which others can only sham. This selective skepticism is familiar to us all. More recently, as in the case of Carlos Castaneda, the boot is on the other foot. The disinterested, "objective," scientist returns to his own world a convert to the exotic beliefs he has studied. Actually, as I have argued in *The Anthropologist's Muse* (1973), anthropologists are always more influenced by the people they study than they think. And certain younger anthropologists, at least, thus find themselves more in tune with contemporary trends than that stern guardian of the old rational order, Edmund Leach, whom I quoted earlier. Today western cultures export Marxism and import oriental mysticism. Our traditional God having withered away, the stage is cleared for the appearance of novel, exotic supernatural forces. The baneful influence of this in the field of parapsychology has been brilliantly delineated by Dr. Eric J. Dingwall (1972). The God you don't know is very much more attractive than the one you do.

What has been said will I hope establish that the anthropologist's encounter with the supernatural is decidedly ambiguous, even problematical. The same is true, I believe, of all the evidence the anthropologist can adduce relating to the supernatural. It is, of course, true, as Dr. Van de Castle argues, that "non-Western societies will display more frequent examples of psychic phenomena because of their strong belief in such phenomena and because greater cultural sanction exists for participation in altered states of consciousness" (1973). But what of it? This scarcely produces confirmatory evidence in any scientific sense. A much more impressive test would be a high level of psychic phenomena among skeptics! It would require a voluminous study to demonstrate this bold claim across the whole field of supernatural phenomena. So I shall have to restrict myself to a particular topic, and thus choose what I think many people would agree is the most impressive psychic evidence of the divine—that dramatic invasion of the human body we call "spirit possession." Since this is a particularly confusing and controversial topic, we must begin with a few definitions.

First, possession is a state of mind and being, or rather it is an interpretation of a person's condition, which may or may not be shared by other members of the "possessed" subject's community. It may or may not coincide with trance. As a culturally conditioned phenomenon, possession may be diagnosed in someone who is far from being in a state of trance, or altered consciousness. Contrariwise, trance may not be interpreted as possession. Nevertheless, in most cultures in which possession by God, spirits, or devils is a common event, possessed people are likely to experience trance.

Second, for all its gloriously subjective exaltation, possession bears the stamp of the culture where it is experienced and the social circumstances in which it occurs. It is both a cultural and social fact, as amenable to sociological and anthropological study and interpretation as any other cultural and social phenomenon. Its incidence is thus just as open to scrutiny—without prejudice to the quality of the subjective experience—as is that of, let us say, suicide.

Third, the ecstatic states which a variety of cultures choose to interpret as possession can be achieved or induced in many different ways. We are currently very conscious of the use (and abuse) of powerful hallucinogenic drugs such as LSD. Indeed, there is a strong temptation, vigorously pursued by that well-known "mushroom-man" R. Gordon Wasson (and others), to look everywhere in man's past as well as present existence for a common set of chemical stimulants. But we should not forget that while mankind, in many places at any rate, has always had ready access to drug-induced mysticism, the same effects can be produced in other ways. There are many well-tried routes to ecstatic agony—including those we now lump together as sensory deprivation. We must not get bogged down in biochemistry or physiology.

These assertions help to clarify a number of persistent confusions and false problems in the literature. Even the most antireligious of anthropologists betray a touching anxiety to discover whether what they witness in the field is or is not "true possession." Are the magnificently abandoned figures, with their wildly thrashing limbs and their glazed eyes *really* "possessed"? Or is it all a sham, like the old tricks of the "charlatan" shaman? Perhaps these anthropologists feel they are entitled to their money's worth and fear they may not get it! But the source of their confusion is their inability to distinguish between "trance" and "possession," and their quaint supposition that there is some universal touchstone by which to identify and assess the authenticity of mystical experience. In fact, this can only be determined by the individual subjects and the other members of their culture. Whether people are or are not in trance can, with some difficulty, be established cross-culturally. But only God and the members of the religions concerned are competent to judge whether those who claim to be possessed really are!

This obsession with authenticity continues to bedevil the most recent anthropological discussions of spirit possession and shamanism, thus continuing a tradition that gets back at least to the misconceptions of Mircea Eliade (1951). In their most recent writings both Mary Douglas (1970) and Erika Bourguignon (1973) stress what they take to be a critical distinction between "voluntary" and "involuntary" ecstatic states. This is simply a reformulation of the allegedly critical dichotomy between "authentic" and "inauthentic" or "positive" and "negative" possession. One might be forgiven for thinking that electricity was under discussion. The trademark of "authentic" or "positive" or "voluntary" ecstasy is that it is represented as a desired, approved state of exaltation. It is a beatific experience and therefore divine. The opposite is feared and is therefore a manifestation of hostile, evil powers. Each of these contrary experiences entails a contrary cult, even must exist in a different society. This, frankly, is arrant nonsense. Have these writers never heard of "bad trips"? Are they unfamiliar with that basic psychological principle—ambivalence? Have they forgotten the old cliché of the "agony and ecstasy"? The answer of course is, apparently, yes, and they have thus allowed themselves to be misled by incomplete ethnographic data.

The truth, as I have tried to explain elsewhere, is that typically these are simply different phases, or episodes, in an ongoing spectrum of religious experience. What begins as an "unsolicited" intrusion, even as an illness, or psychic trauma, usually ends as a glorious communion with the divine. The wild spirit which to the patient's consternation seizes hold of him, becomes gradually domesticated. In more familiar parlance, perhaps, the patient learns to live with his problems. And affliction endured and overcome becomes a source of strength. For only those who have themselves suffered the violent pangs of first possession and mastered them can diagnose and treat the same symptoms in others. The parallel with induction into the psychoanalytic fraternity through a training analysis is obvious. I want to emphasize, however, that possession is not simply a primitive psychoanalysis. Rather, psychoanalysis is a primitive form of shamanism.

Finally, before we proceed to our findings and conclusions, a few more remarks on the question of the "authenticity" of mystical experience. Faced with the many competing claims of mystics in rival religious traditions, anthropologists have suggested various tests. One of the ostensibly most culture-free and reliable of these puts the onus of proof on the subject. The more the latter struggles to resist the call, the more we should be impressed when, at last, he does succumb. For that, we are told (among others by Professor O'Brien, 1965), is the true sign of true possession. Those who accept this view fall into the trap cunningly prepared for us by ecstasy.

I am prepared to assert that in all settings where ecstatic experiences flourish, this is the standard convention signifying the onset of the ecstatic career. And being a convention, those concerned know how to produce the appropriate manifestations. It follows that what appears in the guise of extreme reluctance may in fact be extreme eagerness. This consideration creates serious (and I think insuperable) obstacles for those who would seek to establish a reliable register of "authentic" mystics on a global basis.

We are now in a position, at last, to confront the facts. Any thorough, unprejudiced cross-cultural investigation will reveal two outstanding features. The first is that, with certain exceptions, men uncharacteristically here cede pride of place to women who dominate the ecstatic scene in most religions. The second is the universal currency of sexual imagery to describe ecstatic experience.

There is a great deal of evidence which shows that women are especially prominent in subsidiary "mystery" cults. These often have a highly rebellious content, and express difficulties which women experience in their relationship with men, particularly in accepting the subordinate position traditionally assigned to them. Deprived of power and of words which carry weight in the councils of men, "inarticulate" women are seized by spirits which unmistakenly give tongue to their complaints. To this extent they are the authentic, if seldom recognized, founders of Women's Lib. Such cults frequently expand their membership to include men of low status (e.g., slaves or ex-slaves) or those with individual personality problems. The membership of these movements thus provides a regular commentary on the prevailing social conditions. Changes in the one are reflected in the other.

Let me give two examples which I have not employed in my book *Ecstatic Religion*. The first concerns the thriving Umbanda cult of contemporary Brazil, as described recently by Esther Pressel (1973), working in São Paulo. Dr. Pressel reports that here (as elsewhere) possession states in a novice are usually provoked by difficulties experienced in trying to fulfill expected roles. One of her main informants was a 52-year-old mulatto woman of rural origins, who after a stormy childhood moved to São Paulo when she was seventeen and married when she was twenty. At first things went well and the couple had three children. Later her luck changed. Her husband became quarrelsome after losing the bar he had been running; the eldest daughter died when her mother was twenty-eight, and her twin brother was killed in a motor accident the following year. Friends advised her to seek spiritual aid at an Umbanda center. There she was urged by a spirit to seriously consider becoming a medium, which, after further spiritual encounters, is precisely what she did. One of the spirits who descended on her during her novitiate was, significantly, a Japanese spirit. He was a prisoner in solitary confinement and desperately concerned to save children from being killed. Clearly his characteristics related quite specifically to this poor woman's personal tragedies. Dr. Pressel records that this Umbanda medium felt that she had been liberated by becoming a medium. And indeed she did. Her spirits had imperiously forced her into a position in which she was often obliged to leave her husband and home several nights a week because of the call of duty.

Now the question of the way in which Umbanda relates to the wider sociocultural setting. Umbanda is a dynamic movement changing as Brazil changes. The older Candomblé cult was frankly African in its orientation and involved direct possession by the West African *orishas* imported with the original slave colonies. In Umbanda, which is Brazilian rather than Afro-Brazilian in the identity it projects, the *orishas* have, as Pressel puts it, been "kicked upstairs" to a more remote, if loftier, position from which they send spirit emissaries. Since the late 1920s, as Brazilian ethnicity has developed, four major classes of spirits have emerged in Umbanda. One represents the African element; another, the Amerindian; a third, European influence; and a fourth, very appropriately characterized as that of an innocent child, seems to symbolize the nascent new Brazilian identity.

My other example, which again is not restricted in its membership only to women, is the fascinating Cuban Santeria cult to which my attention was first drawn by Mrs. Joan Halifax-Grof. In its original Cuban form, this cult was patronized by the descendants of Yoruba slaves. However, since Fidel Castro's assumption of power, the cult has become immensely popular among the frustrated Cuban refugee community in Miami. Its adherents there are no longer all of servile origin. On the contrary, its clientele has widened very remarkably to include what is by Cuban standards a strongly middle-class element. For them, however, Santeria has become an alternative expression of Cuban identity in a setting where they feel themselves to be an alien minority, as indeed they are. Deprivation, here as elsewhere, is always relative.

Let me now turn to the second feature which I mentioned as being so striking in these cults: the sexual imagery which they almost without exception employ. The spirits are regularly described as "horses" riding their human "mounts," and women devotees are regularly possessed—in all the most frankly sexual connotations of the word—by their spiritual lovers. This divine intimacy is, too, frequently regularized in formal marriages. A woman cult member or medium thus may, like the Virgin Mary, enjoy two husbands—one mortal, the other entirely spiritual. She may be required to sleep on appointed nights with her celestial spouse, spurning her mundane partner. These unions may even be blessed with issue, again as in the case of the Blessed Virgin, or as with so many of the Greek gods. Those who love the gods clearly feel they are entitled to make love to them.

Now all this is a familiar theme in mystical poetry in the Old Testament, in Islam, and in Hinduism. I wish to assert that, if people (and women in particular) all over the world are using the same vocabulary, namely the language of love, to express their feelings and relationships towards the gods they love, we are entitled to assume that they are all talking about the same thing. I do not mean by this that all their internal emotions are identical, but only that there is a significant area of shared common ground. When St. Teresa describes the exultant raptures of her Spiritual Marriage she may be more articulate than millions of possessed tribeswomen down the ages. But, how do we know that her feelings are in any significant manner radically different from theirs? Who are we to say that the quality of her devotion is on another plane entirely? Indeed, we might reverse the usual ethnocentric judgment and ask: What can all these dreary Christian spinsters know about love that is not known to their humbler tribal sisters, most of whom have actually known men! Surely there must be an advantage in first loving men—before loving God?

Some will interpret me as saying: Ecstasy is simply repressed sex. I do not deny that the evidence clearly shows that religious enthusiasm has its attractions for sexually repressed women. But I contend that it would be a gross oversimplification to see ecstasy in these terms. The ranks of the enthusiasts include many sexually liberated women—to say nothing of the men involved. Nor, I think, can the men's interest here always by any means be seen as it is among the Tukano Indians of Colombia described by Reichel-Dolmatoff (1972). Tukano shamans employ hallucinogens to achieve ecstatic visions which they explicitly compare to incestuous intercourse. Indeed, the supreme aim of their visionary quest is to be "suffocated," as they put it, in a mystic uterine union. There seems little evidence, however, that the male members of other ecstatic cults always seek to fulfill the same oedipal fantasies.

Where, in conclusion, does all this lead? Not, I think, in the direction currently being pursued in the Department of Sexology at the University of Quebec where, apparently, researchers claim to have found neurophysiological differences between orgasm and ecstasy. (It would be interesting to see how the Tukano referred to above would make out here.) The much wider and more significant issue is: What does our evidence on possession tell us about the supernatural?

Following the slogan "Spiritualism proves survival," some Christians have claimed that we see here conclusive proof of the existence of God. Weston La Barre (1972) makes a similar claim, though from a radically different point of view. He asserts that the visions of hallucinating shamans are literally the origins of religion. As we have seen, however, though a ready supply of hallucinogenic drugs certainly helps, ecstasy can be achieved without them. So we can dismiss the first part of Weston La Barre's claim. The second part also requires amendment. All the evidence shows that shamanism is not the origin of religion, but of religions. To explain the origins of religion *in any complete sense* it is necessary to explore man's need for religion to which possession and shamanism are responses rather than causes. Of course the ready procurement of rapturous visions helps, as we see so

clearly in the drug-cultures of Western industrial society. For is not seeing believing?

But does all this add conclusive weight to other evidence of supernatural activity? Does it prove that there really are spirits, gods, powers—call them what you like—out there? I think not. It certainly tells us a great deal about the nature of man and his needs, particularly in situations of stress and conflict. It tells us, I would argue, that normal people everywhere are readily capable of ecstatic experiences. And we all know that man, when pressed to his utmost, does need to believe in a "separate reality." But the wish is after all very often father to the idea as well as to the deed. The stock psychoanalytical explanations (reproduced with great eloquence and persuasiveness by La Barre) which reduce all these powers to projections of man's unconscious wishes, certainly offer an attractively parsimonious explanation of much, if not all, possession ideology and behavior. However, this can only represent a hypothesis. It does not entitle us to affirm categorically that there are *no* spiritual forces save those that well up from man's subconscious. It is for that reason that I said at the beginning of this paper that the anthropologist's encounter with the supernatural seems to me destined to remain ambiguous and inconclusive.

Steel Axes for Stone-Age Australians

Lauriston Sharp

In this article Lauriston Sharp discusses the introduction of the steel axe into the Yir Yoront culture and the startling impact this seemingly minor innovation had on their religion and social structure. He outlines a classic example of the cultural disruption that can occur when an outside group intervenes in the life of another group without careful consideration of the various consequences that may occur. Sharp's article is a good selection for Chapter 1 because it gives us an excellent account of the anthropological fieldworker's traditional stance of non-involvement in a group's religious life versus the missionary's tendency to plunge wholeheartedly into the everyday life and decision-making of a people.

Reproduced by permission of the Society for Applied Anthropology from *Human Organization*, Vol. 11, no. 2 (1952) pp. 457–64.

LIKE OTHER AUSTRALIAN ABORIGINALS, THE YIR YOR-ont group which lives at the mouth of the Coleman River on the west coast of Cape York Peninsula originally had no knowledge of metals. Technologically their culture was of the old stone age or paleolithic type. They supported themselves by hunting and fishing, and obtained vegetables and other materials from the bush by simple gathering techniques. Their only domesticated animal was the dog; they had no cultivated plants of any kind. Unlike some other aboriginal groups, however, the Yir Yoront did have polished stone axes hafted in short handles, which were most important in their economy.

Towards the end of the nineteenth century, metal tools and other European artifacts began to filter into the Yir Yoront territory. The flow increased with the gradual expansion of the white frontier outward from southern and eastern Queensland. Of all the items of western technology thus made available, the hatchet, or short-handled steel axe, was the most acceptable to and the most highly valued by all aboriginals.

In the mid 1930s an American anthropologist lived alone in the bush among the Yir Yoront for thirteen months without seeing another white man. The Yir Yoront were thus still relatively isolated and continued to live an essentially independent economic existence, supporting themselves entirely by means of their old stone age techniques. Yet their polished stone axes were disappearing fast and being replaced by steel axes, which came to them in considerable numbers, directly or indirectly, from various European sources to the south.

What changes in the life of the Yir Yoront still living under aboriginal conditions in the Australian bush could be expected as a result of their increasing possession and use of the steel axe?

Relevant Factors

If we concentrate our attention on Yir Yoront behavior centering about the original stone axe (rather than on the axe—the object—itself) as a cultural trait or item of cultural equipment, we should get some conception of the role this implement played in aboriginal culture. This, in turn, should enable us to foresee with considerable accuracy some of the results stemming from the displacement of the stone axe by the steel axe.

The production of a stone axe required a number of simple technological skills. With the various details of the axe well in mind, adult men could set about producing it (a task not considered appropriate for women or children). First of all a man had to know the location and properties of several natural resources found in his immediate environment: pliable wood for a handle, which could be doubled or bent over the axe head and bound tightly; bark, which could be rolled into cord for the binding; and gum, to fix the stone head in the haft. These materials had to be correctly gathered, stored, prepared, cut to size, and applied or manipulated. They were in plentiful supply, and could be taken from anyone's property without special permission. Postponing consideration of the stone head, the axe could be made by any normal man who had a simple knowledge of nature and of the technological skills involved, together with fire (for heating the gum), and a few simple cutting tools—perhaps the sharp shells of plentiful bivalves.

The use of the stone axe as a piece of capital equipment used in producing other goods indicates its very great importance to the subsistence economy of the aboriginal. Anyone—man, woman, or child—could use the axe; indeed, it was used primarily by women, for theirs was the task of obtaining sufficient wood to keep the family campfire burning all day, for cooking or other purposes, and all night against mosquitoes and cold (for in July, winter temperature might drop below 40 degrees). In a normal lifetime a woman would use the axe to cut or knock down literally tons of firewood. The axe was also used to make other tools or weapons, and a variety of material equipment required by the aboriginal in his daily life. The stone axe was essential in the construction of the wet-season domed huts which keep out some rain and some insects; of platforms which provide dry storage; of shelters which give shade in the dry summer when days are bright and hot. In hunting and fishing and in gathering vegetable or animal food the axe was also a necessary tool, and in this tropical culture, where preservatives or other means of storage are lacking, the natives spend more time obtaining food than in any other occupation—except sleeping. In only two instances was the use of the stone axe strictly limited to adult men: for gathering wild honey, the most prized food known to the Yir Yoront; and for making the secret paraphernalia for ceremonies. From this brief listing of some of the activities involving the use of the axe, it is easy to understand why there was at least one stone axe in every camp, in every hunting or fighting party, and in every group out on a "walk-about" in the bush.

The stone axe was also prominent in interpersonal relations. Yir Yoront men were dependent upon interpersonal relations for their stone axe heads, since the flat, geologically recent, alluvial country over which they range provides no suitable stone for this purpose. The stone they used came from quarries four hundred miles to the south, reaching the Yir Yoront through long lines of male trading partners. Some of these chains terminated with the Yir Yoront men; others extended on farther north to other groups, using Yir Yoront men as links. Almost every older adult man had one or more regular trading partners, some to the north and some to the south. He provided his partner or partners in the south with surplus spears, particularly fighting spears tipped with the barbed spines of sting ray, which snap into vicious fragments when they penetrate human flesh. For a dozen such spears, some of which he may have obtained from a partner to the north, he would receive one stone axe head. Studies have shown that the sting-ray barb spears increased in value as they moved south and farther from the sea. One hundred and fifty miles south of Yir Yoront one such spear may be exchanged for one stone axe head. Although actual investigations could not be made, it was presumed that farther south, nearer the quarries, one sting-ray barb spear would bring several stone axe heads. Apparently people who acted as links in the middle of the chain and who made neither spears nor axe heads would receive a certain number of each as a middle man's profit.

Thus trading relations, which may extend the individual's personal relationships beyond that of his own group, were associated with spears and axes, two of the most important items in a man's equipment. Finally, most of the exchanges took place during the dry season, at the time of the great aboriginal celebrations centering about initiation rites or other totemic ceremonials which attracted hundreds and were the occasion for much exciting activity in addition to trading.

Returning to the Yir Yoront, we find that adult men kept their axes in camp with their other equipment, or carried them when traveling. Thus a woman or child who wanted to use an axe—as might frequently happen during the day—had to get one from a man, use it promptly, and return it in good condition. While a man might speak of "my axe," a woman or child could not.

This necessary and constant borrowing of axes from older men by women and children was in accordance with regular patterns of kinship behavior. A woman would expect to use her husband's axe unless he himself was using it; if unmarried, or if her husband was absent, a woman woud go first to her older brother or to her father. Only in extraordinary circumstances would she seek a stone axe from other male kin. A girl, boy, or a young man would look to a father or an older brother to provide an axe for their use. Older men, too, would follow similar rules if they had to borrow an axe.

It will be noted that all of these social relationships in which the stone axe had a place are pair relationships and that the use of the axe helped to define and maintain their character and the roles of the two individual participants. Every active relationship among the Yir Yoront involved a definite and accepted status of superordination or subordination. A person could have no dealings with another on exactly equal terms. The nearest approach to equality was between brothers, although the older was always superordinate to the younger. Since the exchange of goods in a trading relationship involved a mutual reciprocity, trading partners usually stood in a brotherly type of relationship, although one was always classified as older than the other and would have some advantage in case of dispute. It can be seen that repeated and widespread conduct centering around the use of the axe helped to generalize and standardize these sex, age, and kinship roles both in their normal benevolent and exceptional malevolent aspects.

The status of any individual Yir Yoront was determined not only by sex, age, and extended kin relationships, but also by membership in one of two dozen patrilineal totemic clans into which the entire community was divided. Each clan had literally hundreds of totems from one or two of which the clan derived its name, and the clan members their personal names. These totems included natural species or phenomena such as the sun, stars, and daybreak, as well as cultural "species": imagined ghosts, rainbow serpents, heroic ancestors; such eternal cultural verities as fires, spears, huts; and such human activities, conditions, or attributes as eating, vomiting, swimming, fighting, babies and corpses, milk and blood, lips and loins. While individual members of such totemic classes or species might disappear or be destroyed, the class itself was obviously ever-present and indestructible. The totems, therefore, lent permanence and stability to the clans, to the groupings of human individuals who generation after generation were each associated with a set of totems which distinguished one clan from another.

The stone axe was one of the most important of the many totems of the Sunlit Cloud Iguana clan. The names of many members of this clan referred to the axe itself, to activities in which the axe played a vital part, or to the clan's mythical ancestors with whom the axe was prominently associated. When it was necessary to represent the stone axe in totemic ceremonies, only men of this clan exhibited it or pantomimed its use. In secular life, the axe could be made by any man and used by all; but in the sacred realm of the totems it belonged exclusively to the Sunlit Cloud Iguana people.

Supporting those aspects of cultural behavior which we have called technology and conduct is a third area of culture which includes ideas, sentiments, and values. These are most difficult to deal with, for they are latent and covert, and even unconscious, and must be deduced from overt actions and language or other communicating behavior. In this aspect of the culture lies the significance of the stone axe to the Yir Yoront and to their cultural way of life.

The stone axe was an important symbol of masculinity among the Yir Yoront (just as pants or pipes are to us). By a complicated set of ideas the axe was defined as "belonging" to males, and everyone in the society (except untrained infants) accepted these ideas. Similarly spears, spear throwers, and fire-making sticks were owned only by men and were also symbols of masculinity. But the masculine values represented by the stone axe were constantly being impressed on all members of society by the fact that females borrowed axes but not other masculine artifacts. Thus the axe stood for an important theme of Yir Yoront culture: the superiority and rightful dominance of the male, and the greater value of his concerns and of all things associated with him. As the axe also had to be borrowed by the younger people it represented the prestige of age, another important theme running through Yir Yoront behavior.

To understand the Yir Yoront culture it is necessary to be aware of a system of ideas which may be called their totemic ideology. A fundamental belief of the aboriginal divided time into two great epochs: (1) a distant and sacred period at the beginning of the world when the earth was peopled by mildly marvelous ancestral beings or culture heroes who are in a special sense the forebears of the clans; and (2) a period when the old was succeeded by a new order which includes the present. Originally there was no anticipation of another era supplanting the present. The future would simply be an eternal continuation and reproduction of the present which itself had remained unchanged since the epochal revolution of ancestral times.

The important thing to note is that the aboriginal believed that the present world, as a natural and cultural environment, was and should be simply a detailed reproduction of the world of the ancestors. He believed that the entire universe "is now as it was in the beginning" when it was established and left by the ancestors. The ordinary cultural life of the ancestors became the daily life of the Yir Yoront camps, and the extraordinary life of the ancestors remained extant in the recurring symbolic pantomimes and paraphernalia found only in the most sacred atmosphere of the totemic rites.

Such beliefs, accordingly, open the way for ideas of what *should be* (because it supposedly *was*) to influence or help determine what actually *is*. A man called Dog-chases-iguana-up-a-tree-and-barks-at-him-all-night had that and other names because he believed his ancestral alter ego had also had them; he was a member of the Sunlit Cloud Iguana clan because his ancestor was; he was associated with particular countries and totems of this same ancestor; during an initiation he played the role of a dog

and symbolically attacked and killed certain members of other clans because his ancestor (conveniently either anthropomorphic or kynomorphic) really did the same to the ancestral alter egos of these men; and he would avoid his mother-in-law, joke with a mother's distant brother, and make spears in a certain way because his and other people's ancestors did these things. His behavior in these specific ways was outlined, and to that extent determined for him, by a set of ideas concerning the past and the relation of the present to the past.

But when we are informed that Dog-chases-etc. had two wives from the Spear Black Duck clan and one from the Native Companion clan, one of them being blind, that he had four children with such and such names, that he had a broken wrist and was left handed, all because his ancestor had exactly these same attributes, then we know (though he apparently didn't) that the present has influenced the past, that the mythical world has been somewhat adjusted to meet the exigencies and accidents of the inescapably real present.

There was thus in Yir Yoront ideology a nice balance in which the mythical was adjusted in part to the real world, the real world in part to the ideal preexisting mythical world, the adjustments occurring to maintain a fundamental tenet of native faith that the present must be a mirror of the past. Thus the stone axe in all its aspects, uses, and associations was integrated into the context of Yir Yoront technology and conduct because a myth, a set of ideas, had put it there.

The Outcome

The introduction of the steel axe indiscriminately and in large numbers into the Yir Yoront technology occurred simultaneously with many other changes. It is therefore impossible to separate all the results of this single innovation. Nevertheless, a number of specific effects of the change from stone to steel axes may be noted, and the steel axe may be used as an epitome of the increasing quantity of European goods and implements received by the aboriginals and of their general influence on the native culture. The use of the steel axe to illustrate such influences would seem to be justified. It was one of the first European artifacts to be adopted for regular use by the Yir Yoront, and whether made of stone or steel, the axe was clearly one of the most important items of cultural equipment they possessed.

The shift from stone to steel axes provided no major technological difficulties. While the aboriginals themselves could not manufacture steel axe heads, a steady supply from outside continued; broken wooden handles could easily be replaced from bush timbers with aboriginal tools. Among the Yir Yoront the new axe was never used to the extent it was on mission or cattle stations (for carpentry work, pounding tent pegs, as a hammer, and so on); indeed, it had so few more uses than the stone axe that its practical effect on the native standard of living was negligible. It did some jobs better, and could be used longer without breakage. These factors were sufficient to make it of value to the native. The white man believed that a shift from steel to stone axe on his part would be a definite regression. He was convinced that his axe was much more efficient, that its use would save time, and that it therefore represented technical "progress" towards goals which he had set up for the native. But this assumption was hardly borne out in aboriginal practice. Any leisure time the Yir Yoront might gain by using steel axes or other western tools was not invested in "improving the conditions of life," nor certainly, in developing aesthetic activities, but in sleep—an art they had mastered thoroughly.

Previously, a man in need of an axe would acquire a stone axe head through regular trading partners from whom he knew what to expect, and was then dependent solely upon a known and adequate natural environment, and his own skills or easily acquired techniques. A man wanting a steel axe, however, was in no such self-reliant position. If he attended a mission festival when steel axes were handed out as gifts, he might receive one either by chance or by happening to impress upon the mission staff that he was one of the "better" bush aboriginals (the missionaries definition of "better" being quite different from that of his bush fellows). Or, again almost by pure chance, he might get some brief job in connection with the mission which would enable him to earn a steel axe. In either case, for older men a preference for the steel axe helped change the situation from one of self-reliance to one of dependence, and a shift in behavior from well-structured or defined situations in technology or conduct to ill-defined situations in conduct alone. Among the men, the older ones whose earlier experience or knowledge of the white man's harshness made them suspicious were particularly careful to avoid having relations with the mission, and thus excluded themselves from acquiring steel axes from that source.

In other aspects of conduct or social relations, the steel axe was even more significantly at the root of psychological stress among the Yir Yoront. This was the result of new factors which the missionary considered beneficial: the simple numerical increase in axes per capita as a result of mission distribution, and distribution directly to younger men, women, and even children. By winning the favor of the mission staff, a woman might be given a steel axe which was clearly intended to be hers, thus creating a situation quite different from the previous custom which necessitated her borrowing an axe from a male relative. As a result a woman would refer to the axe as "mine," a possessive form she was never able to use of the stone axe. In the same fashion, young men or even boys also obtained steel axes directly from the mission, with the result that older men no longer had a complete monopoly of all the axes in the bush community. All this led to a revolutionary confusion of sex, age, and kinship roles, with a major gain in independence and loss of subordination on the part of those who now owned steel axes when they had previously been unable to possess stone axes.

The trading partner relationship was also affected by the new situation. A Yir Yoront might have a trading partner in a tribe to the south whom he defined as a younger brother and over whom he would therefore have some authority. But if the partner were in contact with the mission or had other access to steel axes, his subordination obviously decreased. Among other things, this took some of the excitement away from the dry season fiesta-like tribal gatherings centering around initiations. These had traditionally been the climactic annual occasions for exchanges between trading partners, when a man might seek to acquire a whole year's supply of stone axe heads. Now he might find himself prostituting his wife to almost total strangers in return for steel axes or other white man's goods. With trading partnerships weakened there was less reason to attend the ceremonies, and less fun for those who did.

Not only did an increase in steel axes and their distribution to women change the character of the relations between individuals (the paired relationships that have been noted), but a previously rare type of relationship was created in the Yir Yoront's conduct towards whites. In the aboriginal society there were few occasions outside of the immediate family when an individual would initiate action to several other people at once. In any average group, in accordance with the kinship system, while a person might be superordinate to several people to whom he could suggest or command action, he was also subordinate to several others with whom such behavior would be tabu. There was thus no overall chieftainship or authoritarian leadership of any kind. Such complicated operations as grass-burning animal drives or totemic ceremonies could be carried out smoothly because each person was aware of his role.

On both mission and cattle stations, however, the whites imposed their conception of leadership roles upon the aboriginals, consisting of one person in a controlling relationship with a subordinate group. Aboriginals called together to receive gifts, including axes, at a mission Christmas party found themselves facing one or two whites who sought to control their behavior for the occasion, who disregarded the age, sex, and kinship variables of which the aboriginals were so conscious, and who considered them all at one subordinate level. The white also sought to impose similar patterns on work parties. (However, if he placed an aboriginal in charge of a mixed group of post-hole diggers, for example, half of the group, those subordinate to the "boss," would work while the other half, who were superordinate to him, would sleep.) For the aboriginal, the steel axe and other European goods came to symbolize this new and uncomfortable form of social organization, the leader-group relationship.

The most disturbing effects of the steel axe, operating in conjunction with other elements also being introduced from the white man's several subcultures, developed in the realm of traditional ideas, sentiments, and values. These were undermined at a rapidly mounting rate, with no new conceptions being defined to replace them. The result was the erection of a mental and moral void which foreshadowed the collapse and destruction of all Yir Yoront culture, if not, indeed, the extinction of the biological group itself.

From what has been said it should be clear how changes in overt behavior, in technology and conduct, weakened the values inherent in a reliance on nature, in the prestige of masculinity and of age, and in the various kinship relations. A scene was set in which a wife, or a young son whose initiation may not yet have been completed, need no longer defer to the husband or father who, in turn, became confused and insecure as he was forced to borrow a steel axe from them. For the woman and boy the steel axe helped establish a new degree of freedom which they accepted readily as an escape from the unconscious stress of the old patterns—but they, too, were left confused and insecure. Ownership became less well defined with the result that stealing and trespassing were introduced into technology and conduct. Some of the excitement surrounding the great ceremonies evaporated and they lost their previous gaiety and interest. Indeed, life itself became less interesting, although this did not lead the Yir Yoront to discover suicide, a concept foreign to them.

The whole process may be most specifically illustrated in terms of totemic system, which also illustrates the significant role played by a system of ideas, in this case a totemic ideology, in the breakdown of a culture.

In the first place, under pre-European aboriginal conditions where the native culture has become adjusted to a relatively stable environment, few, if any, unheard of or catastrophic crises can occur. It is clear, therefore, that the totemic system serves very effectively in inhibiting radical cultural changes. The closed system of totemic ideas, explaining and categorizing a well-known universe as it was fixed at the beginning of time, presents a considerable obstacle to the adoption of new or the dropping of old culture traits. The obstacle is not insurmountable and the system allows for the minor variations which occur in the norms of daily life. But the inception of major changes cannot easily take place.

Among the bush Yir Yoront the only means of water transport is a light wood log to which they cling in their constant swimming of rivers, salt creeks, and tidal inlets. These natives know that tribes forty-five miles further north have a bark canoe. They know these northern tribes can thus fish from midstream or out at sea, instead of clinging to the river banks and beaches, that they can cross coastal waters infested with crocodiles, sharks, sting rays, and Portuguese men-of-war without danger. They know the materials of which the canoe is made exist in their own environment. But they also know, as they say, that they do not have canoes because their own mythical ancestors did not have them. They assume that the canoe was part of the ancestral universe of the northern tribes. For them, then, the adoption of the canoe would not be simply a matter of learning a number of new behavioral skills for its manufacture and use. The adoption would require a much more difficult procedure; the acceptance by the entire society of a myth, either locally developed or borrowed, to explain the presence of the canoe, to associate it with some one or more of the several hundred mythical ancestors (and how decide which?), and thus establish it as an accepted totem of one of the clans ready to be used by the whole community. The Yir Yoront have not made this adjustment, and in this case we can only say that for the time being at least, ideas have won out over very real pressures for technological change. In the elaborateness and explicitness of the totemic ideologies we seem to have one explanation for the notorious stability of Australian cultures under aboriginal conditions, an explanation which gives due weight to the importance of ideas in determining human behavior.

At a later stage of the contact situation, as has been indicated, phenomena unaccounted for by the totemic ideological system begin to appear with regularity and frequency and remain within the range of native experience. Accordingly, they cannot be ignored (as the "Battle of the Mitchell" was apparently ignored), and there is an attempt to assimilate them and account for them along the lines of principles inherent in the ideology. The bush Yir Yoront of the mid-thirties represent this stage of the acculturation process. Still trying to maintain their aboriginal definition of the situation they accept European artifacts and behavior patterns, but fit them into their totemic system, assigning them to various clans on a par with original totems. There is an attempt to have the myth-making process keep up with these cultural changes so that the idea system can continue to support the rest of the culture. But analysis of overt behavior, of dreams, and of some of the new myths

indicates that this arrangement is not entirely satisfactory, that the native clings to his totemic system with intellectual loyalty (lacking any substitute ideology), but that associated sentiments and values are weakened. His attitudes towards his own and towards European culture are found to be highly ambivalent.

All ghosts are totems of the Head-to-the-East Corpse clan, are thought of as white, and are of course closely associated with death. The white man, too, is closely associated with death, and he and all things pertaining to him are naturally assigned to the Corpse clan as totems. The steel axe, as a totem, was thus associated with the Corpse clan. But as an "axe," clearly linked with the stone axe, it is a totem of the Sunlit Cloud Iguana clan. Moreover, the steel axe, like most European goods, has no distinctive origin myth, nor are mythical ancestors associated with it. Can anyone, sitting in the shade of a *ti* tree one afternoon, create a myth to resolve this confusion? No one has, and the horrid suspicion arises as to the authenticity of the origin myths, which failed to take into account this vast new universe of the white man. The steel axe, shifting hopelessly between one clan and the other, is not only replacing the stone axe physically, but is hacking at the supports of the entire culture system.

The aboriginals to the south of the Yir Yoront have clearly passed beyond this stage. They are engulfed by European culture, either by the mission or cattle station subcultures or, for some natives, by a baffling, paradoxical combination of both incongruent varieties. The totemic ideology can no longer support the inrushing mass of foreign culture traits, and the myth-making process in its native form breaks down completely. Both intellectually and emotionally a saturation point is reached so that the myriad new traits which can neither be ignored nor any longer assimilated simply force the aboriginal to abandon his totemic system. With the collapse of this system of ideas, which is so closely related to so many other aspects of the native culture, there follows an appallingly sudden and complete cultural disintegration, and a demoralization of the individual such as has seldom been recorded elsewhere. Without the support of a system of ideas well devised to provide cultural stability in a stable environment, but admittedly too rigid for the new realities pressing in

from outside, native behavior and native sentiments and values are simply dead. Apathy reigns.
The aboriginal has passed beyond the realm of any
outsider who might wish to do him well or ill.

Returning from the broken natives huddled on
cattle stations or on the fringes of frontier towns to
the ambivalent but still lively aboriginals settled on
the Mitchell River mission, we note one further
devious result of the introduction of European artifacts. During a wet season stay at the mission, the
anthropologist discovered that his supply of tooth
paste was being depleted at an alarming rate. Investigation showed that it was being taken by old
men for use in a new tooth paste cult. Old materials
of magic having failed, new materials were being
tried out in a malevolent magic directed towards
the mission staff and some of the younger aboriginal men. Old males, largely ignored by the missionaries, were seeking to regain some of their lost
power and prestige. This mild aggression proved

hardly effective, but perhaps only because confidence in any kind of magic on the mission was by
this time at a low ebb.

For the Yir Yoront still in the bush, a time could
be predicted when personal deprivation and
frustration in a confused culture would produce an
overload of anxiety. The mythical past of the
totemic ancestors would disappear as a guarantee
of a present of which the future was supposed to be
a stable continuation. Without the past, the present
could be meaningless and the future unstructured
and uncertain. Insecurities would be inevitable.
Reaction to this stress might be some form of symbolic aggression, or withdrawal and apathy, or
some more realistic approach. In such a situation
the missionary with understanding of the processes going on about him would find his opportunity to introduce his forms of religion and to help
create a new cultural universe.

2

Myth, Ritual, Symbolism, and Taboo

Tales, legends, proverbs, riddles, adages, and myths make up what anthropologists call *folklore*, an important subject for the study of culture. Because of its sacred nature, myth is especially significant in the analysis of comparative religion. Myth functions in a society as a ''charter,'' as Malinowski puts it—a model for behavior that also explains the origins of the world, life on earth, death, and all other experiences of human existence: ''[Myth] is a statement of primeval reality which lives in the institutions and pursuits of a community. It justifies by precedent the existing order and it supplies a retrospective pattern of moral values, of sociological discriminations and burdens and of magical belief. . . . The function of myth is to strengthen tradition and to endow it with a greater value and prestige by tracing it back to a higher, better, more supernatural, and more effective reality of initial events'' (1931: 640–41).

Some anthropologists apply a psychological approach to myth analysis and see myths as symbolic expressions of sibling rivalry, male-

Indian mask of painted wood, Northwest Coast, North America.

female tensions, and other themes. Others—structural anthropologists such as Claude Lévi-Strauss—view myths as cultural means of resolving critical binary oppositions (life-death, matrilineal-patrilineal, nature-culture) that serve as models for members of a society (1976: 280–81). Whether in Judeo-Christian and Moslem cultures, where myths have been transcribed to form the Tora, Bible, and Koran, or in other, less familiar cultures, these sacred narratives still serve their time-honored function for the bulk of humanity as the basis of religious belief. What is important to remember is that myths in traditional societies are considered to be truthful accounts of the past, just as the writings of the so-called great religions.

Like myth, ritual and ceremony are of crucial significance to all human societies, and are important for the understanding of religion in culture. According to Victor Turner, in a definition widely quoted from his article that appears later in this chapter, "A ritual is a stereotyped sequence of activities involving gestures, words, and objects, performed in a sequestered place and designed to influence preternatural [magical] entities or forces on behalf of the actors' goals and interests." As described by Anthony Wallace, ritual is "the primary phenomenon of religion": "Ritual is religion in action; it is the cutting edge of the tool. Belief, although its recitation may be part of the ritual, or a ritual in its own right, serves to explain, to rationalize, to interpret and direct the energy of the ritual performance. . . . It is ritual which accomplishes what religion sets out to do" (1966: 102).

It is through ritual that religion is able to impress on people a commitment to their system of religious beliefs. Participants in a religious ritual are able to express group solidarity and loyalty. Indeed, Emile Durkheim argued that the true nature of religion was ritual participation. Of course, history abounds with examples of the importance of the individual experience in religion; yet there is no denying the overwhelming effect of group participation. As William Howells has pointed out, ritual helps individuals but does so by treating them as a whole group: "they are like a tangled head of hair, and ritual is the comb" (1962: 243).

Although in this chapter Max Gluckman urges

the rejection of any simple explanation of ritual as a response to anxiety, most anthropologists believe, along with Malinowski and other early functionalists, that ritual at least allays anxiety. Through the shared performance of group dances and ceremonies, humans are able to reduce the fears that often come when life's events threaten their security and sense of well-being. Other scholars, such as A. R. Radcliffe-Brown, have taken the opposite tack, claiming that ritual may actually create rather than allay anxiety and fears.

Most introductory textbooks in anthropology divide religious ritual into rites of passage and rites of intensification. Rites of passage mark transition points in the lives of individuals—for example, birth, puberty, marriage, and death. Rites of intensification occur during a crisis for a group and are thus more important in maintaining group equilibrium and solidarity. They are typically associated with natural phenomena, such as seasonal changes or a lack of rain, but other events, such as impending warfare, could also trigger a rite of intensification. Whatever precipitates the crisis, there is need of a ritual to lessen the anxiety that is felt by the group.

Although the division of rituals into this twofold scheme is useful, it does not adequately represent the variety of ritual occurring in the world's cultures. Anthony Wallace, for example, has outlined five major categories of ritual (1966: 107–66).

1. *Technological rituals*, designed to control nature for the purpose of human exploitation, comprise three subdivisions:

   a. Divination rites, which help predict the future and gain hidden information.

   b. Rites of intensification, designed to help obtain food and alcohol.

   c. Protective rites, aimed at coping with the uncertainty of nature (for example, stormy seas, floods, crop disease, and bad luck).

2. *Therapy and anti-therapy rituals* are designed to control human health. Curative rites exemplify therapy rituals; witchcraft and sorcery, anti-therapy.

3. *Ideological rituals*, according to Wallace, are "intended to control, in a conservative way, the behavior, the mood, the sentiments and values of

groups for the sake of the community as a whole." They consist of four subcategories:

a. Rites of passage, which deal with role change and geographic movement (for example, marriages).

b. Rites of intensification, to ensure people adhere to values and customs (for example, Sunday church service).

c. Taboos (ritual avoidances), courtesies (positive actions), and other arbitrary ceremonial obligations, which serve to regulate human behavior.

d. Rites of rebellion, which provide a form of "ritualized catharsis" that contributes to order and stability by allowing people to vent their frustrations.

4. *Salvation rituals* aim at repairing damaged self-esteem and other forms of impaired identity. Wallace sees three common subdivisions in this category:

a. Possession, in which an individual's identity is altered by the presence of an alien spirit that occupies the body (exorcism is the usual treatment).

b. Ritual encouragement of an individual to accept an alternate identity, a process similar to the ritual procedure shamans undergo upon assuming a shamanic role.

c. The mystic experience—loss of personal identity by abandoning the old self and achieving salvation by identifying with a sacred being.

5. *Revitalization rituals* are aimed at what can be described as an identity crisis of an entire community. The revitalization movement may be seen as a religious movement (a ritual) that, through the help of a prophet, strives to create a better culture.

Just as myth and ritual are expressions of ideology, the study of symbolism too is vital to the study of religion. Anthropology has been less than clear in its attempt to define the meaning of this important concept. Minimally, a symbol may be thought of as something that represents something else. The development of culture, for example, was dependent on human beings having the ability to assign symbolic meanings of words—to

create and use a language. Religion is also a prime example of man's proclivity to attach symbolic meanings to a variety of behavior and objects. "The object of symbolism," according to Alfred North Whitehead, "is the enhancement of the importance of what is symbolized" (1927: 63).

That anthropological interest in the topic of symbolism had its start with the study of religious behavior is not surprising, especially in light of the plethora of symbols present in religious objects and ceremonies. Reflect for a moment on any religious service. Immediately on entering the building, be it a church, synogogue, or mosque, one is overwhelmed by symbolic objects—the Christian cross, the Star of David, paintings, statues, tapestries, and assorted ceremonial paraphernalia—each representing a religious principle. Fittingly, Geertz has noted that a religious system may be viewed as a "cluster of sacred symbols" (1957: 424). Unlike the well-defined symbols in mathematics and the physical sciences, these religious symbols assume many different forms and meanings: witness Victor Turner's concept of the multivocalic nature of symbols (their capacity to have many meanings), outlined in his article in this chapter.

More than a simple reminder of some remote aspect of a religion's history, religious symbols are often considered to possess a power or force (*mana*) emanating from the spiritual world itself. The symbols provide people with an emotional and intellectual commitment to their particular belief system, telling them what is important to their society, collectively and individually, and helping them conform to the group's value system. Durkheim accounted for the universality of symbols by arguing that a society kept its value system through their use; that is, the symbols stood for the revered values. Without the symbols, the values and, by extension, the society's existence would be threatened.

Whereas symbols, like myths and rituals, prescribe thoughts and behaviors of people, taboos restrict actions. Because the term *taboo* (also known as *tabu* and *kapu*) originated in the Pacific Islands, beginning anthropology students often associate it with images of "savage" Polynesians observing mystical prohibitions. It is true that Pacific Islanders did cautiously regard these restrictions, being careful to avoid the supernatural retribution that was certain to follow violations. Taboos are not limited to the Pacific, however: every society has restrictions that limit behavior in one respect or another, usually in association with sex, food, rites of passage, sacred objects, and sacred people. The incest taboo is unique in that it is found in all societies. Although anthropologists have yet to adequately explain why the incest taboo exists everywhere, they have demonstrated that most taboos are reinforced by the threat of punishments meted out by supernatural forces.

As anthropologists have pointed out, taboos are adaptive human mechanisms: they function to counter dangers of both the phenomenal and ideational world. It is possible to theorize that the existence of fewer real or imagined dangers would result in fewer taboos, but it is equally safe to argue that all societies will continue to establish new taboos as new threats to existence or social stability arise. Certainly taboos function at an ecological level, for example, to preserve plants, animals, and resources of the sea. Taboos also function to distinguish between and control social groups, threatening violators with supernatural punishments as severe as the denial of salvation. Depending on the culture, sacred authority is often as compelling as the civil codes to which people are required to comply. Simply stated, the breaking of a sacred taboo, as opposed to a civil sanction, is a sin. The impersonal power of *mana* made certain objects and people in Pacific cultures taboo. Although the concept of *mana* does not exist in contemporary Western cultures, certain symbols and objects are similarly imbued with such an aura of power or sacredness that they too are considered taboo.

Using both a case study and an encyclopedic approach to myth, ritual, symbolism, and taboo, the six articles selected for this chapter clearly show the importance of these topics to the study of comparative religion. Leach, Gluckman, Turner, and Douglas bring to the reader the results of their field work in the non-Western world; Dubisch, on the other hand, discusses the religious aspects evidenced in the American health food movement—a phenomenon that displays common elements of all this chapter's major topics. In the final article Miner examines the body rituals of the Nacirema, a North American group who devote a considerable portion of the day to ritual activity.

References

Geertz, Clifford
  1957 "Ethos, World-View and the Analysis of Sacred Symbols," *Antioch Review* 17: 421–37.
Howells, William
  1962 *The Heathens*. Garden City, N.Y.: Doubleday.
Hunter, David E., and Phillip Whitten
  1976 *Encyclopedia of Anthropology*. New York: Harper and Row.
Malinowski, Bronislaw
  1931 "Culture." In David L. Sills, ed., *Encyclopedia of the Social Sciences*, Vol. 4, pp. 621–46. New York: Macmillan Free Press.
Wallace, A. F. C.
  1966 *Religion: An Anthropological View*. New York: Random House.
Whitehead, Alfred N.
  1927 *Symbolism*. New York: G. P. Putnam's Sons.

Genesis as Myth

Edmund R. Leach

Rather than analyze myths that have originated in non-Western societies, Edmund R. Leach here dissects a familiar story: the Old Testament recounting of the beginning of the world. Leach argues that although myths such as the Book of Genesis are repetitive, intricate, and contradictory, their construction is logical. He also shows how modern information theory throws new light on myths as a form of communication. Because to the true believer these mythic messages are the word of God, their very redundancy is reassuring. Each version confirms and reinforces the meaning of all the others and thereby reifies man's faith in the unknowable, making it the known. Leach explains the role of opposites as a basic construct of human minds, and maintains that the structure of binary opposites in myth reflects our natural cognitive map as we separate, for example, God from man. Myth not only creates the oppositions, but sets as a common mythic element how these separations are eliminated through supernatural intermediaries and rituals, which bring the opposites together.

Reprinted from *Discovery* (May 1982), pp. 30–35, by permission of the author.

A DISTINGUISHED GERMAN THEOLOGIAN HAS DEfined myth as "the expression of unobservable realities in terms of observable phenomena" (Bartsch 1953). All stories which occur in the Bible are myths for the devout Christian, whether they correspond to historical fact or not. All human societies have myths in this sense, and normally the myths to which the greatest importance is attached are those which are the least probable. The non-rationality of myth is its very essence, for religion requires a demonstration of faith by the suspension of critical doubt.

But if myths do not mean what they appear to mean, how do they come to mean anything at all? What is the nature of the esoteric mode of communication by which myth is felt to give "expression to unobservable realities"?

This is an old problem which has lately taken on a new shape because, if myth be a mode of communication, then a part of the theory which is embodied in digital computer systems ought to be relevant. The merit of this approach is that it draws special attention to precisely those features of myth which have formerly been regarded as accidental defects. It is common to all mythological systems that all important stories recur in several different versions. Man is created in Genesis (chapter I, verse 27) and then he is created all over again (II, 7). And, as if the two first men were not enough, we also have Noah in chapter VIII. Likewise in the New Testament, why must there be four gospels each telling "the same" story yet sometimes flatly contradictory on details of fact? Another noticeable characteristic of mythical stories is their markedly binary aspect; myth is constantly setting up opposing categories: "In the beginning God created the heaven and the earth," "they crucified Him and two others with him, on either side one, and Jesus in the midst," "I am the Alpha and the Omega, the beginning and the end, saith the Lord." So always it is in myth— God against the world and the world itself forever dividing into opposites on either side—male and female, living and dead, good and evil, first and last . . .

Now, in the language of communication engineers, the first of these common characteristics of myth is called *redundancy*, while the second is strongly reminiscent of the unit of information—the *bit*. "Information" in this technical sense is a measure of the freedom of choice in selecting a message. If there are only two messages and it is arbitrary which you choose then "information is unity," that is = 1 bit (*bit* stands for "binary digit") (Shannon and Weaver 1949).

Communication engineers employ these concepts for the analysis of problems which arise when a particular individual (the sender) wishes to transmit a coded message correctly to another individual (the receiver) against a background of interference (noise). "Information" refers on the one hand to the degrees of choice open to the sender in encoding his transmission and on the other to the degrees of choice open to the receiver in interpreting what he receives (which will include noise in addition to the original transmitted signal). In this situation a high level of redundancy makes it easy to correct errors introduced by noise.

Now in the mind of the believer, myth does indeed convey messages which are the Word of God. To such a man the redundancy of myth is a very reassuring fact. Any particular myth in isolation is like a coded message badly snarled up with noisy interference. Even the most confident devotee might feel a little uncertain as to what precisely is being said. But, as a result of redundancy, the believer can feel that, even when the details vary, each alternative version of a myth confirms his understanding and reinforces the essential meaning of all the others.

Binary Structure of Myth

The anthropologist's viewpoint is different. He rejects the idea of a supernatural sender. He observes only a variety of possible receivers. Redundancy increases information—that is the uncertainty of the possible means of decoding the message. This explains what is surely the most striking of all religious phenomena—the passionate adherence to sectarian belief. The whole of Christendom shares a single corpus of mythology so it is surely very

remarkable that the members of each particular Christian sect are able to convince themselves that they alone possess the secret of revealed truth. The abstract propositions of communication theory help us to understand this paradox.

But if the true believer can interpret his own mythology in almost any way he chooses, what principle governs the formation of the original myth? Is it random chance that a myth assumes one pattern rather than another? The binary structure of myth suggests otherwise.

Binary oppositions are intrinsic to the process of human thought. Any description of the world must discriminate categories in the form "*p* is what not-*p* is not." An object is alive or not alive and one could not formulate the concept "alive" except as the converse of its partner "dead." So also human beings are male or not male, and persons of the opposite sex are either available as sexual partners or not available. Universally these are the most fundamentally important oppositions in all human experience.

Religion everywhere is preoccupied with the first, the antinomy of life and death. Religion seeks to deny the binary link between the two words; it does this by creating the mystical idea of "another world," a land of the dead where life is perpetual. The attributes of this other world are necessarily those which are not of this world; imperfection here is balanced by perfection there. But this logical ordering of ideas has a disconcerting consequence—God comes to belong to the other world. The central "problem" of religion is then to reestablish some kind of bridge between Man and God.

This pattern is built into the structure of every mythical system; the myth first discriminates between gods and men and then becomes preoccupied with the relations and intermediaries which link men and gods together. This much is already implicit in our initial definition.

So too with sex relations. Every human society has rules of incest and exogamy. Though the rules vary they always have the implication that for any particular male individual all women are divided by at least one binary distinction, there are women of *our kind* with whom sex relations would be incestuous and there are women of the *other kind* with whom sex relations are allowed. But here again we are immediately led into paradox. How was it in the beginning? If our first parents were persons of two kinds, what was that other kind? But if they were both of our kind, then their relations must have been incestuous and we are all born in sin. The myths of the world offer many different solutions to this childish intellectual puzzle, but the prominence which it receives shows that it entails the most profound moral issues. The crux is as before. If the logic of our thought leads us to distinguish *we* from *they*, how can we bridge the gap and establish social and sexual relations with "the others" without throwing our categories into confusion?

So, despite all variations of theology, this aspect of myth is a constant. In every myth system we will find a persistent sequence of binary discriminations as between human/superhuman, mortal/immortal, male/female, legitimate/illegitimate, good/bad . . . followed by a "mediation" of the paired categories thus distinguished.

"Mediation" (in this sense) is always achieved by introducing a third category which is "abnormal" or "anomalous" in terms of ordinary "rational" categories. Thus myths are full of fabulous monsters, incarnate gods, virgin mothers. This middle ground is abnormal, non-natural, holy. It is typically the focus of all taboo and ritual observance.

This approach to myth analysis derives originally from the techniques of structural linguistics associated with the name of Roman Jakobson (Jakobson and Halle 1956) but is more immediately due to C. Lévi-Strauss, one of whose examples may serve to illustrate the general principle.

Certain Pueblo Indian myths focus on the opposition between life and death. In these myths we find a threefold category distinction: agriculture (means to life), war (means to death), and hunting (a mediating category since it is means to life for men but means to death for animals). Other myths of the same cluster deploy a different triad: grass-eating animals (which live without killing), predators (which live by killing), and carrion-eating creatures (mediators, since they eat meat but do not kill in order to eat). In accumulation this total set of associated symbols serves to imply that life and death are *not* just the back and the front of the same penny, that death is *not* the necessary consequence of life (Lévi-Strauss 1955).

My Figure 1 has been designed to display an analogous structure for the case of the first four chapters of Genesis. The three horizontal bands

of the diagram correspond to (i) the story of the seven-day creation, (ii) the story of the Garden of Eden, and (iii) the story of Cain and Abel. The diagram can also be read vertically: column 1 in band (ii) corresponds to column 1 in band (i) and so on. The detailed analysis is as follows:

Upper Band

First Day (I, 1–5; not on diagram). Heaven distinguished from Earth; Light from Darkness; Day from Night; Evening from Morning.

Second Day (I, 6–8; col. 1 of diagram). (Fertile) water (rain) above; (infertile) water (sea) below. Mediated by firmament (sky).

Third Day (I, 9–10; col. 2 and I, 11–12; col. 3). Sea opposed to dry land. Mediated by "grass, herb yielding seed (cereals), fruit trees." These grow on dry land but need water. They are classed as things "whose seed is in itself" and thereby contrasted with bisexual animals, birds, etc.

The creation of the world as a static (that is, dead) entity is now complete and this whole phase of the creation is opposed to the creation of moving (that is, living) things.

Fourth Day (I, 13–18; col. 4). Mobile sun and moon are placed in the fixed firmament of col. 1. Light and darkness become alternations (life and death become alternates).

Fifth Day (I, 20–23; col. 5). Fish and birds are living things corresponding to the sea/land opposition of col. 2 but they also mediate the col. 1 oppositions between sky and earth and between salt water and fresh water.

Sixth Day (I, 24–25; col. 6). Cattle (domestic animals), beasts (wild animals), creeping things. These correspond to the static triad of col. 3. But only the grass is allocated to the animals. Everything else, including the meat of the animals, is for Man's use (I, 29–30). Later at Leviticus XI creatures which do not fit this exact ordering of the world—for instance, water creatures with no fins, animals and birds which eat meat or fish, etc.—are classed as "abominations." Creeping Things are anomalous with respect to the major categories, Fowl, Fish, Cattle, Beast and are thus abominations *ab initio* (Leviticus XI, 41–42). This classification in turn leads to an anomalous con-

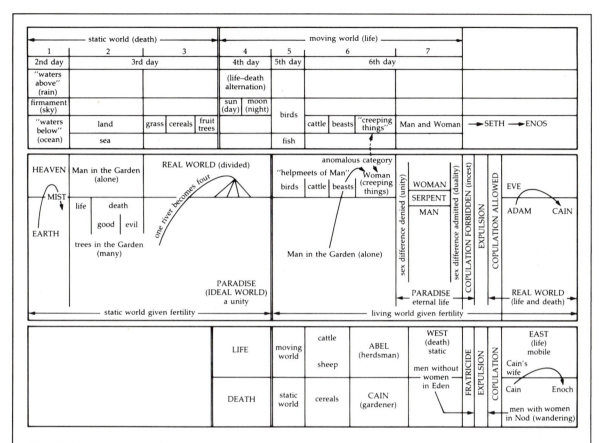

FIGURE 1

The first four chapters of Genesis contain three separate creation stories. Horizontal bands correspond to (a) 7-day creation; (b) Garden of Eden; (c) Cain and Abel. Each story sets up opposition of Death versus Life, God versus Man. World is "made alive" by using categories of "woman" and "creeping things" to mediate this opposition.

tradition. In order to allow the Israelites to eat locusts the author of Leviticus XI had to introduce a special qualification to the prohibition against eating creeping things: "Yet these ye *may* eat: of every flying creeping thing that goeth on all four which have legs above their feet, to leap withal upon the earth" (v. 21). The procedures of binary discrimination could scarcely be carried further!

(I, 26–27; col. 7), Man and Woman are created simultaneously. The whole system of living creatures is instructed to "be fruitful and multiply"

but the problems of Life versus Death, and Incest versus Procreation are not faced at all.

Center Band

The Garden of Eden story which now follows tackles from the start these very problems which have been evaded in the first version. We start again with the opposition Heaven versus Earth, but this is mediated by a fertilizing mist drawn from the dry infertile earth (II, 4–6). This theme, which blurs the distinction life/death, is repeated. Living Adam is formed from the dead dust of the ground (II, 7);

so are the animals (II, 19); the garden is fertilized by a river which "went out of Eden" (II, 10); finally fertile Eve is formed from a rib of infertile Adam (II, 22–23).

The opposition Heaven/Earth is followed by further oppositions—Man/Garden (II, 15); Tree of Life/Tree of Death (II, 9, 17); the latter is called the tree of the "knowledge of good and evil" which means the knowledge of sexual difference.

Recurrent also is the theme that unity in the other world (Eden, Paradise) becomes duality in this world. Outside Eden the river splits into four and divides the world into separate lands (II, 10–14). In Eden, Adam can exist by himself, Life can exist by itself; in this world, there are men and women, life and death. This repeats the contrast between monosexual plants and bisexual animals which is stressed in the first story.

The other living creatures are now created specifically because of the loneliness of Man in Eden (II, 18). The categories are Cattle, Birds, Beasts. None of these is adequate as a helpmeet for Man. So finally Eve is drawn from Adam's rib . . . "they are of one flesh" (II, 18–24).

Comparison of Band 1 and Band 2 at this stage shows that Eve in the second story replaces the "Creeping Things" of the first story. Just as Creeping Things were anomalous with respect to Fish, Fowl, Cattle and Beast so Eve is anomalous to the opposition Man versus Animal. And, as a final mediation (chapter III), the Serpent, a creeping thing, is anomalous to the opposition Man versus Woman. Christian artists have always been sensitive to this fact; they manage to give the monster a somewhat hermaphrodite appearance while still indicating some kind of identification between the Serpent and Eve herself.

Hugo Van der Goes puts Eve and the Serpent in the same posture; Michelangelo makes Adam and Eve both gaze with loving adoration on the Serpent, but the Serpent has Eve's face.

Adam and Eve eat the forbidden fruit and become aware of sexual difference, death becomes inevitable (III, 3–8). But now for the first time pregnancy and reproduction become possible. Eve does not become pregnant until after she has been expelled from Paradise (IV, 1).

Lower Band

Cain the Gardener and Abel the Herdsman repeat the antithesis between the first three days of the creation and the last three days in the first story. Abel's living world is more pleasing to God (IV, 4–5). Cain's fratricide compares with Adam's incest and so God's questioning and cursing of Cain (IV, 9–12) has the same form and sequence as God's questioning and cursing of Adam, Eve and the Serpent (III, 9–19). The latter part of III, 16, is later repeated exactly (IV, 7) so Cain's sin was not only fratricide but also incestuous homosexuality. In order that immortal monosexual existence in Paradise may be exchanged for fertile heterosexual existence in reality, Cain, like Adam, must acquire a wife (IV, 17). To this end Adam must eliminate a sister; Cain a brother. The symmetry is complete.

Cross-Cultural Comparison

The issue here is the logical basis of incest categories and closely analogous patterns must occur in all mythologies regardless of their superficial content. Cross-cultural comparison becomes easier if we represent the analysis as a systematic pattern of binary discriminations as in Figure 2.

Adam/Eve and Cain/Abel are then seen to be variants of a theme which can also occur in other forms as in the well-known myth of Oedipus. The actual symbolism in these two cases is nearly identical. Oedipus, like Adam and Cain, is initially earthbound and immobile. The conclusion of the Athenian version of the Oedipus story is that he is an exiled wanderer, protected by the gods. So also is Cain (IV, 14–15). The Bible also includes the converse of this pattern. In Genesis XXVIII Jacob is a lonely exile and wanderer under God's protection but (XXXII, 24–32) he is renamed Israel and thus given the status of a first ancestor with a territorial autochthonous base, and he is lamed by God. Although Jacob dies abroad in Egypt he is buried on his own ancestral soil in Israel (XL, 29–32; L, 5–7).

In the Oedipus story, in place of Eve's Serpent we have Jocasta's Sphinx. Like Jocasta the Sphinx is female, like Jocasta the Sphinx commits suicide, like the Serpent the Sphinx leads men to their doom by verbal cunning, like the Serpent the Sphinx is an anomalous monster. Eve listens to the Serpent's words and betrays Adam into incest; Oedipus solves the Sphinx riddle and is led into incest. Again, Oedipus's patricide replaces Cain's fratricide—Oedipus, incidentally, meets Laius "at a cross roads."

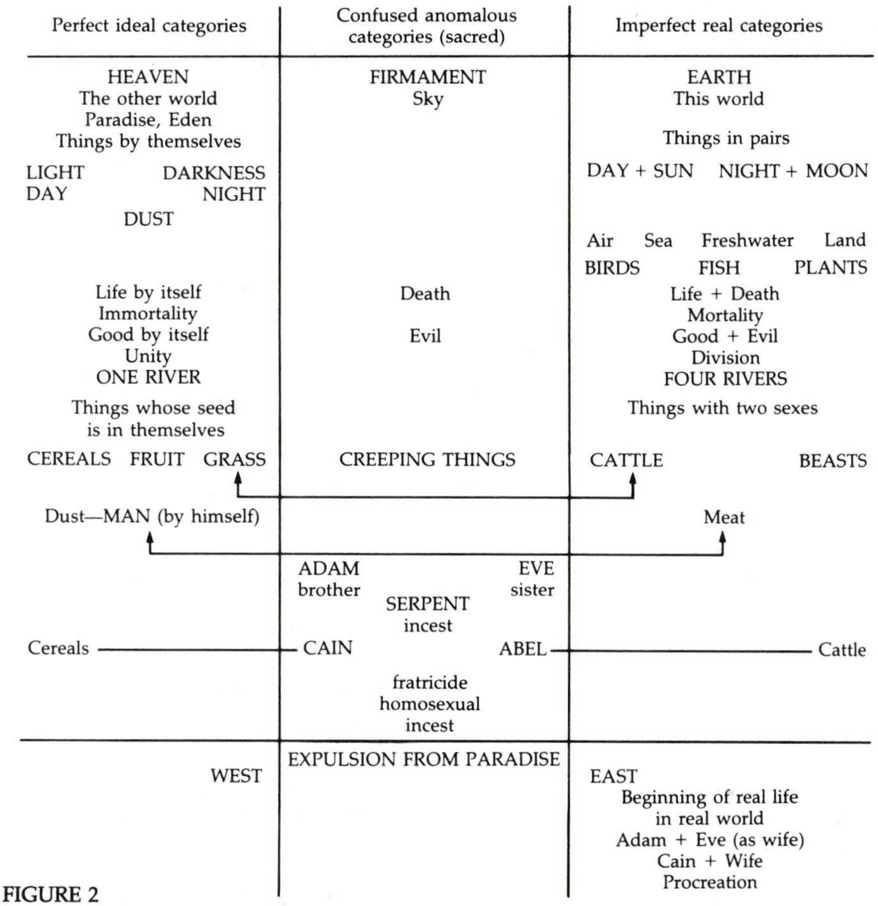

Perfect ideal categories	Confused anomalous categories (sacred)	Imperfect real categories
HEAVEN The other world Paradise, Eden Things by themselves	FIRMAMENT Sky	EARTH This world Things in pairs
LIGHT　　　　DARKNESS DAY　　　　　　NIGHT 　　　DUST		DAY + SUN　NIGHT + MOON
		Air　Sea　Freshwater　Land BIRDS　　FISH　　PLANTS
Life by itself Immortality Good by itself Unity ONE RIVER	Death Evil	Life + Death Mortality Good + Evil Division FOUR RIVERS
Things whose seed is in themselves		Things with two sexes
CEREALS　FRUIT　GRASS	CREEPING THINGS	CATTLE　　　　　　BEASTS
Dust—MAN (by himself)		Meat
	ADAM　　　　　　EVE brother　　　　　sister 　　SERPENT 　　incest	
Cereals —————————— CAIN　　　　ABEL ——————————— Cattle		
	fratricide homosexual incest	
	EXPULSION FROM PARADISE	
WEST		EAST Beginning of real life in real world Adam + Eve (as wife) Cain + Wife Procreation

FIGURE 2

Incest categories have a logical basis in all myths. Similarity between myths is seen most clearly if they are analysed in a binary form as shown in this table.

Parallels of this kind seem too close to be accidental but this kind of algebra is unfamiliar and more evidence will be needed to convince the skeptical. Genesis contains several further examples of first ancestors.

Firstly, Noah survived the destruction of the world by flood together with three sons and their wives. Prior to this the population of the world had included three kinds of being—"sons of God," "daughters of men" and "giants" who were the offspring of the union of the other two (VI, 1–4). Since the forbears of Noah's daughters-in-law have all been destroyed in the Flood, Noah becomes a unique ancestor of all mankind without the implication of incest. Chapter IX, 1–7, addressed to Noah is almost the duplicate of I, 27–30, addressed to Adam.

Though heterosexual incest is evaded, the theme of homosexual incest in the Cain and Abel story recurs in the Noah saga when drunken Noah is seduced by his own son Ham (IX, 21–25). The Canaanites, descendants of Ham, are for this reason accursed. (That a homosexual act is intended is evident from the language "Ham saw the nakedness of his father." Compare Leviticus XVIII, 6–19, where "to uncover the nakedness of" consistently means to have sexual relations with.)

In the second place Lot survives the destruction of the world by fire together with two nubile daughters. Drunken Lot is seduced by his own daughters (XIX, 30–38). The Moabites and the Ammonites, descendants of these daughters, are for this reason accursed. In chapter XIX the men of Sodom endeavour to have homosexual relations with two angels who are visiting Lot. Lot offers his nubile daughters instead but they escape unscathed. The implication is that Lot's incest is less grave than heterosexual relations with a foreigner, and still less grave than homosexual relations.

Thirdly, the affair of the Sodomites and the Angels contains echoes of "the sons of God" and "the daughters of men" but links specifically with chapter XVIII where Abraham receives a visit from God and two Angels who promise that his ageing and barren wife Sarah shall bear a son. Sarah is Abraham's half-sister by the same father (XX, 12) and his relations with her are unambiguously incestuous (Leviticus XVIII, 9). Abraham loans Sarah to Pharaoh saying that she is his sister (XII, 19). He does the same with King Abimelech (XX, 2). Isaac repeats the game with Abimelech (XXVI, 9–11) but with a difference. Isaac's wife Rebekah is his father's brother's son's daughter (second cousin) and the relation is *not* in fact incestuous. The barrenness of Sarah is an aspect of her incest. The supernatural intervention which ultimately ensures that she shall bear a child is evidence that the incest is condoned. Pharaoh and Abimelech both suffer supernatural penalties for the lesser offence of adultery, but Abraham, the incestuous husband, survives unscathed.

There are other stories in the same set. Hagar, Sarah's Egyptian slave, bears a son Ishmael to Abraham, whose descendants are wanderers of low status. Sarah's son Isaac is marked out as of higher status than the sons of Abraham's concubines, who are sent away to "the east country" (c.f. wandering Cain who made his home in Nod "eastward of Eden"). Isaac marries a kinswoman in preference to a Canaanite woman. Esau's marriage to a Hittite woman is marked as a sin. In contrast his younger and favored twin brother Jacob marries two daughters of his mother's brother, who is in turn Jacob's father's father's brother's son's son.

All in all, this long series of repetitive and inverted tales asserts:

1. the overriding virtue of close kin endogamy;

2. that the sacred hero ancestor Abraham can carry this so far that he marries his paternal half-sister (an incestuous relationship). Abraham is thus likened to Pharaoh, for the Pharaohs of Egypt regularly married their paternal half-sisters; and

3. that a rank order is established which places the tribal neighbors of the Israelites in varying degrees of inferior status depending upon the nature of the defect in their original ancestry as compared with the pure descent of Jacob (Israel).

The myth requires that the Israelites be descended unambiguously from Terah, the father of Abraham. This is achieved only at the cost of a breach of the incest rule; but by reciting a large number of similar stories which entail even greater breaches of sexual morality the relations of Abraham and Sarah finally stand out as uniquely virtuous. Just as Adam and Eve are virtuous as compared to Cain and Abel, so Abraham's incest can pass unnoticed in the context of such outrageous characters as Ham, Lot's daughters, and the men of Sodom.

I have concentrated here upon the issue of sexual rules and transgressions so as to show how a multiplicity of repetitions, inversions, and variations can add up to a consistent "message." I do not wish to imply that this is the only structural pattern which these myths contain.

The novelty of the analysis which I have presented does not lie in the facts but in the procedure. Instead of taking each myth as a thing in itself with a "meaning" peculiar to itself it is assumed, from the start, that every myth is one of a complex and that any pattern which occurs in one myth will recur, in the same or other variations, in other parts of the complex. The structure that is common to all variations becomes apparent when different versions are "superimposed" one upon the other.

Whenever a corpus of mythology is recited in its religious setting such structural patterns are "felt" to be present, and convey meaning much as poetry conveys meaning. Even though the ordinary listener is not fully conscious of what has been communicated, the "message" is there in a quite objective sense. If the labor of programming could be performed the actual analysis could be done by a computer far better than by any human. Furthermore, it seems evident that much the same patterns exist in the most diverse kinds of mythology. This seems to me to be a fact of great psychological, sociological, and scientific significance. Here truly are observable phenomena which are the expression of unobservable realities.

Ritual

Max Gluckman

Religious ritual is of crucial importance in all human societies. Ritual is the heart of religious behavior, or, as William Howells describes it, "the meat which goes on the bones of a cult's beliefs" (1986: 224). As a perusal of the literature makes clear, however, there is an endless variety not only in types of religious rituals, but also in modes of interpreting them. In this article, Max Gluckman briefly discusses various psychoanalytical, sociological, and anthropological explanations regarding the purpose and function of religious ritual. Using Swazi first-fruits rites and a Ndembu nubility ritual as ethnographic examples, Gluckman rejects any simple explanation of ritual as a response to anxiety, the transference of aggression into scapegoats, or the reinforcement of social sentiments. Rather, he prefers Victor W. Turner's more complicated analysis of the significance of ritual ceremonies. Briefly, Turner would collect from participants information on the meaning of ritual ceremonies and their symbols. Although the explanations given by the participants varied, Turner felt that in general they would stress the "socially valuable attributes of the symbol."

Reprinted from Richard Cavendish, ed., *Man, Myth, and Magic* (London, 1970), Vol. 17, pp. 2392–98, by permission of the author and BPCC/Phoebus Publishing.

MANY DIFFERENT KINDS OF PHENOMENA HAVE BEEN described as ritual. The term has been applied, for example, to the mating habits of birds and animals, such as the dance on the water of the crested grebe; by psychoanalysts to the obsessive behavior of neurotics, as when a man persistently checks whether he has turned off a tap, only to check anew after each check; and by anthropologists and sociologists to the established forms of behavior of devotees of cults and religions. But while it is important to try to establish common explanations for the phenomena thus categorized, it is essential to grasp that there are fundamental differences between them and also between modes of interpreting them.

Freud himself argued that there were marked similarities between the obsessive "rituals" of neurotics and psychotics, and the "rituals" of what he called primitive society. Indeed, he postulated in *Totem and Tabu* (1913) from his theory of the development of the Oedipus complex (a theory derived from depth analyses of his patients), that the origin of sacrifice and religion in general was to be derived from a primordial killing and devouring of a patriarchal male, who dominated a group of females and their offspring, by the young males of the group. Overcome with guilt, they instituted a symbolic rekilling of the father-figure, now transformed into a god, and partaking of his being in a ritual of sacrifice and communion. If this be taken as what the anthropologist A. Kroeber called a "Just-so Story" (that is, a story which explains the origin of some well-known phenomenon), then there is no evidence for it, and more recent studies of the social life of the apes make it highly improbable. On the other hand, Kroeber allowed that it might represent a psychological process which most human males undergo, in symbolical form, in the course of their development. Then it might well be one of the springs of emotion which feed into social rituals. Even so, sociologists and anthropologists would argue that Freud's theory cannot be used to explain the development, and the complexity, of the social and cultural relationship involved in rituals.

Variations in Response

Similarly, anthropologists would reject any claim by psychoanalysts that, for example, cirumcision ceremonies of boys near puberty can be "explained" by saying that they create castration anxiety and fix the incest taboo firmly in the boys' minds. While the above is the standard psychoanalytical explanation of circumcision, one psychoanalyst, B. Bettelheim, has argued from a study of four schizoid children who developed their own initiation ceremonies, that the practice of circumcision arises among males through envy of the productive wombs of females.

Anthropologists would concede that particular persons, passing through circumcision ceremonies, may feel castration anxiety or womb envy; but that this would have to be demonstrated by appropriate methods of research, and that the structure of the personalities of the persons enforcing, or undergoing, such ceremonial operations should be taken into account. It may well be that in all men and women, at very deep levels of the psyche, similar syndromes of feeling are to be found; but psychoanalysis itself shows that people vary in their degree of adjustment to those syndromes, in their more conscious feelings and their actions. Thus there is a considerable degree of variation in both the type and the intensity of individuals' reaction to participation in the same ritual.

Examples of this were noted by the present writer at circumcision ceremonies held among certain African tribes. At the ritual circumcision each candidate (aged from seven to 15), while being operated on, should be supported by his father, who is supposed to hold his son's penis and help the circumciser, a ritual adept, turn back the foreskin. On one occasion, the hands of the first father shook so much that it was impossible for the circumciser to act; and the father was replaced by his brother-in-law, the boy's mother's brother, who strictly was not appropriate. The hands of the second father were very steady, and he watched the operation steadily. The hands of the third father were steady, but he could not watch the operation and turned his head away to look over his shoul-

der. One must draw the conclusion that the circumcision of each boy meant something quite different to each father, in terms of present relationships, of what each had felt and suffered when he himself as a boy underwent the operation, of the psychological syndromes established in each during infancy, and so on. Hence it seems that psychological analysis can only be effective if it is applied to bring out the significance of a particular ritual, or part of a ritual, for particular individuals, each with his own history of psychological development and his own established personality. Thereafter psychological analysis may feed into sociological-anthropological analysis; and of course the reverse is also true.

Swazi Songs of Hate

The Swazi of southern Africa, at the ripening of the first fruits, stage elaborate national ceremonies, at certain phases of which they are required to hurl insults at their king, who is the central figure of the rituals, and to sing sacred national songs stating how much the king is hated by his subjects. In social-anthropological analysis these rites have been successfully related to the low density of population as a result of the simple system of husbandry; the low variation in standards of living; and the delegation of authority from the king to subordinates ruling numbers of men who, because of the simplicity of weapons, are all warriors, constituting a private army which can help its leader in attempts to gain power. These leaders are of royal blood and may organize rebellions aimed at the kingship. There is therefore present in the national ceremony a symbolic representation of political processes built into the nation, which is riven by periodic armed civil wars.

The rites emphasize that while the kingship itself is sacred and is "strengthened" in the rites, the king is beset by internal enemies on whose loyalty he cannot rely. But this does not mean that each warrior who insults the king or who sings the songs of hatred against him, must necessarily have sentiments of disloyalty awakened, or go through a severe crisis of loyalty. For one warrior, though he may feel the sacredness of the occasion, it may be in some ways like a fete, a kind of carnival when license is allowed. At the other extreme, other warriors may go through an emotional turmoil in which strong resentments against authority are awakened, and perhaps a reliving of childhood difficulties in their relationships with their fathers. Again, analysis of individual, possibly variable, reactions to ritual is required.

One must similarly reject any simple direct explanation of ritual as the expression of tension, of despair, of anxiety or aggression, or as the transference of stifled feelings of aggression onto scapegoats, or as simply and directly strengthening social sentiments. In the Swazi ceremony summarily analyzed above, it is justified to say that the rites are calculated to arouse the sentiments that support national solidarity. Since we know that acting an emotion is likely to produce feelings of that emotion, it is probable that occasions of group celebration will arouse the sentiments which are appropriate to group solidarity and which support adherence to certain group values and morals, in most participants at least.

But we know equally well that the most complex and intensive reaction to a religious ceremony may come from the sinners in the congregation: they may be most deeply moved by emotions evoked by ritual, particularly ritual in which they have participated as children and as adolescents, and they may then feel determined during the ritual to sin no more. Their intensive emotional reaction may well be provoked by strong feelings of guilt and unworthiness. On the other hand, the man who conforms in his daily life with the precepts of religion and morality is likely to worship with a much more restrained and consistent devotion, while those who are betwixt and between will respond in moderate degree. So in the Swazi ritual cited above, loyal men may have their sentiments of patriotism evoked less strongly than the potential traitors.

Milk Tree Society

A much more complicated theory to relate rituals to emotional predispositions is therefore required, and the best as yet advanced is that of Victor W. Turner, in a series of analyses of the significance of ritual symbols. His highly complex argument can be summarized as follows. Information on the meaning of ritual symbols can be collected from participants, who will give interpretations of various degrees of complexity, depending on whether they are ritual adepts or not. In general, explanations of this kind stress the harmonious, socially valuable

attributes of the symbol. Thus, when the Ndembu of Zambia, whom Turner studied, are initiating a nubile girl into womanhood, the key symbol is a tree which exudes a white substance, like milk. The Ndembu specifically compare the white sap of the "milk tree" with mother's milk, and state that it represents the tie between mother and child: it thus represents the tie between the girl being initiated and her own mother, and her future, nurturing tie with the children whom it is hoped she will produce.

Further, since the Ndembu are a matrilineal society (reckoning descent and succession and inheritance from brother to sister's son), they are organized in groups of kinsfolk related to one another by descent through females. The milk tree therefore represents these groups, technically called matrilineages. As the matrilineages are the persisting groups of Ndembu society, and villages are to some extent combinations of matrilineages, the matrilineal principle in the abstract is vertebral to Ndembu society, and the milk tree symbolizes this, and symbolizes both the continuity of the society and its whole culture, its customs and its laws. In a graphic comparison, one of the Ndembu compared it with the Union Jack flying over the administrative headquarters of the district, then under British rule. He described the milk tree as "our flag."

But Turner showed that if one examined actions around the milk tree, in the ritual itself, these were not altogether harmonious, and did not reflect a continual state of harmony in accordance with the values stressed in the Ndembu's own account of the ritual. In practice, there was considerable competition and "strife" among the people assembled around the milk tree. Women were separated from the men, and had to behave "hostilely" towards them. Married women and unmarried girls, women of different matrilineages, and women of different villages, formed also competing pairs of contraposed groups. These alignments reflected the fact that while succession and inheritance passed through women, the women themselves dispersed, during their childbearing lives, to live at their husbands' villages—one example of the contradictory principles on which Ndembu society is built. These contradictory principles appear in the rituals and thus deny the very abstract harmony which is stated in the Ndembus' interpretation of them.

Duty Made Desirable

Turner shows that all the dominant ritual symbols of Ndembu society can be similarly analyzed. His thesis is that two sharply different poles of reference for the symbols—the sensory and the ideological—must be distinguished. At the sensory pole are clustered meanings which refer to physiological facts and processes, such as mother's milk, blood, blood of menstruation and birth, semen, genitalia, copulation, excreta, death, and so on. While at the ideological pole are clustered social values and allegiances: conformity with the law, morality and custom; motherhood as a nurturing relationship; the established relationships between women and men, married women and girls, membership of matrilineages and villages, and so on. Symbols cover these diverse meanings because they can condense many meanings, can unify disparate meanings and can polarize meanings.

Turner argues that in the course of ritual, marked by feasting, drinking, dancing and music—all physiologically stimulating—as well as by fellowship, strong and varied emotions are evoked in response both to the feasting, drinking and so on, and to the sensory associations of the rites and symbols. The energy thus aroused is then transferred to, and fixed upon, the values evoked at the ideological pole. Thus there occurs a process in which the obligatory is felt also to be desirable.

Clearly this theory involves a much more complex approach to the relation between emotions evoked and forms of ritual, than the notions briefly criticized above. We can appreciate why it is that singing songs of hate and hurling insults at the king may act to strengthen, at least temporarily, sentiments of loyalty to him. Moreover, it is a theory which is in accord with the psychoanalytic theory of the sublimation of instinctual drives and demands towards socially approved ends.

If the step from psychological interpretation of ritual to understanding of its sociological functioning is so complicated, it is even more mistaken to relate ritual directly to the behavior of animals, in mating dances, display, and the like.

Ritual from Relationships

Turner's theory was worked out on tribal rituals, but it seems that it could equally be applied to the ritual symbols of the great religions. These types of rituals, however, differ markedly from each other. Sociologists who have written on the general evolution of human society have all stressed that this development, associated with more complex technology and a greater division of labor, is marked by an increasing obsolescence of ritual and its replacement by what have been called universal religions, such as Christianity, Islam, and Buddhism, which any person can join as a convert, and in which any adherent can join any congregation assembled to worship. The examples above, of the Swazi first-fruits rites and the Ndembu nubility ritual, show that in tribal society rituals are constituted to specific social relationships according to the domestic, kinship, sexual, local, or political affiliations of the members of the cult. Only persons occupying specific positions in those relationships can participate, and they do so in terms of the specific ways in which they are related to one another. Moreover, in the ritual, apart from using special symbols (in the form of things, words, or actions), they act their specific roles in secular life, either directly, or sometimes invertedly (as in transvestism, by women dressing as men and men as women), or in some particular symbolic form. Hence an analysis of tribal rituals leads one into a detailed analysis of secular relationships because these are of the fabric of the ritual, and because it is believed that the symbolic representation of those relationships in some hidden, occult way creates and directs occult power so as to bless, purify, protect, strengthen, make fruitful, and otherwise successful, the persons involved in those relationships.

This type of analysis has shown that in some of the rituals the enactment of secular relationships involves a statement, in an exaggerated form, not only of the harmonious and unifying aspects of the relationships, but also of the conflicts which reside in them. This is one of the main means by which emotion is aroused, which is then fixed on socially approved values: out of the very conflicts which exist in normal life, on special occasions the value of an ideal of life without conflict is emotionally and intellectually established.

It has therefore been argued that ritual, occult beliefs, and practices will tend to occur in crisis situations in which the discrepant principles out of which social organization is formed, principles which are in conflict, produce actual or potential disputes which cannot be settled by judicial and other purely intellectual procedures. Ritual then may operate where there are fundamental disharmonies within the theoretical harmony of a social system.

This theory is based on the perception that in human, as against animal, society, there is a consistent tendency to exaggerate the differences between categories of persons. Thus belief in the occult contaminating effect of menstrual blood and its threat to things virile exaggerates the biological difference between women and men. There are other beliefs, and associated practices, of this kind, based on distinctions of age, the facts of locality, different kinds of relationship through birth and kinship, the relationship of ruler and subject, and so forth. This tendency is more marked in tribal society than in complex industrial societies where people's roles, the material things which they handle, the places they work and worship and play in, are more differentiated. This may explain why in tribal society we find a "ritualization" of secular roles, while as society develops a more complex technology on which is based a more complex division of labor, there is a movement towards universal religions.

E. R. Leach and other anthropologists have argued from studies of tribal rituals that ritual is only a symbolic statement of status. This is undoubtedly one of the aspects of ritual, as has been shown. Others assert that rituals mainly manifest competition for power. This too is present in tribal rituals, and is also to be found within the congregations of universal religions. But there is clearly much more to ritual than these two aspects.

Complex problems are involved in the question of when actions referring to beliefs in occult power occur, and how they operate. It therefore seems advisable to use a more complicated vocabulary in discussing these problems. The term *ceremonial* may be used to describe all actions which involve symbolic statements of social status (for instance, All Saints' Day and the October Revolution parade). As a further distinction, *ceremoniousness* could be used to describe ceremonial where the practitioners have no idea of occult powers being involved (such as standing when "God Save the Queen" is played). Ritual describes ceremonial where ideas of occult power are present. Within the field of ritual in this sense, there is in tribal society a *ritualization* of secular social roles, of domestic places, and so forth. As this ritualization decreases with advancing civilization, some religions will be austere, while others will be marked by a high *ritualism*, symbolic itself, drawing on the same complex of emotions maybe, but not involving the enacting of everyday roles.

Symbols in African Ritual

Victor W. Turner

In the preceding article by Max Gluckman, reference is made to Victor Turner's analysis of the significance of ritual symbols. It is not unusual for even a scholar of Gluckman's stature to refer to Turner for assistance in an analysis of symbols, for Victor Turner has over the years established an excellent reputation in the field of symbolic analysis. In the present article, Professor Turner discusses three significant dimensions of symbols: the exegetic, the operational, and the positional. The exegetic involves any explanations given the field worker by the participants in a given ritual. The operational dimension is determined by the researcher seeking the relationship between a symbol's meaning and its use. In the last dimension, the positional, the anthropologist attempts to find the meaning of a symbol by studying the relationship between that symbol and other symbols in a given ritual.

Turner also applies Morris Opler's concept of cultural themes ("dynamic affirmations that can be identified in every culture") to an analysis of ritual, noting that ritual constitutes a base for the playing out of themes, while the themes themselves are passed along by the ritual symbols.

Interestingly, just as Edmund Leach used the technique of binary oppositions in the lead article of this chapter to help him analyze myths, so too does Turner apply this aspect of modern information theory to help him understand symbolism within ritual.

Reprinted from *Science*, Vol. 179 (1973), pp. 1100–1105, by permission of the author and the American Association for the Advancement of Science. Copyright © 1973 by the AAAS.

NO ONE WHO HAS LIVED FOR LONG IN RURAL sub-Saharan Africa can fail to be struck by the importance of ritual in the lives of villagers and homesteaders and by the fact that rituals are composed of symbols.

A ritual is a stereotyped sequence of activities involving gestures, words, and objects, performed in a sequestered place, and designed to influence preternatural entities or forces on behalf of the actors' goals and interests. Rituals may be seasonal, hallowing a culturally defined moment of change in the climatic cycle or the inauguration of an activity such as planting, harvesting, or moving from winter to summer pasture; or they may be contingent, held in response to an individual or collective crisis. Contingent rituals may be further subdivided into life-crisis ceremonies, which are performed at birth, puberty, marriage, death, and so on to demarcate the passage from one phase to another in the individual's life cycle, and rituals of affliction, which are performed to placate or exorcise preternatural beings or forces believed to have afflicted villagers with illness, bad luck, gynecological troubles, severe physical injuries, and the like. Other classes of rituals include divinatory rituals; ceremonies performed by political authorities to ensure the health and fertility of human beings, animals, and crops in their territories; initiation into priesthoods devoted to certain deities, into religious associations, or into secret societies; and those accompanying the daily offering of food and libations to deities or ancestral spirits or both. Africa is rich indeed in ritual genres, and each involves many specific performances.

Each rural African society (which is often, though not always, coterminous with a linguistic community) possesses a finite number of distinguishable rituals that may include all or some of the types listed above. At varying intervals, from a year to several decades, all of a society's rituals will be performed, the most important (for example, the symbolic transference of political authority from one generation to another, as among the Nyakyusa of Tanzania) being performed perhaps the least often. Since societies are processes responsive to change, not fixed structures, new rituals are devised or borrowed, and old ones decline and disappear. Nevertheless, forms survive through flux, and new ritual items, even new ritual configurations, tend more often to be variants of old themes than radical novelties. Thus it is possible for anthropologists to describe the main features of a ritual system, or rather ritual round (successive ritual performances), in those parts of rural Africa where change is occurring slowly.

The Semantic Structure of the Symbol

The ritual symbol is "the smallest unit of ritual which still retains the specific properties of ritual behavior . . . the ultimate unit of specific structure in a ritual context." This structure is a semantic one (that is, it deals with relationships between signs and symbols and the things to which they refer) and has the following attributes: (i) multiple meanings (significata)—actions or objects perceived by the senses in ritual contexts (that is, symbol vehicles) have many meanings; (ii) unification of apparently disparate significata—the essentially distinct significata are interconnected by analogy or by association in fact or thought; (iii) condensation—many ideas, relations between things, actions, interactions, and transactions are represented simultaneously by the symbol vehicle (the ritual use of such a vehicle abridges what would verbally be a lengthy statement or argument); (iv) polarization of significata—the referents assigned by custom to a major ritual symbol tend frequently to be grouped at opposed semantic poles. At one pole of meaning, empirical research has shown that the significata tend to refer to components of the moral and social orders—this might be termed the ideological (or normative) pole of symbolic meaning; at the other, the sensory (or orectic) pole, are concentrated references to phenomena and processes that may be expected to stimulate desires and feelings. Thus, I have shown that the mudyi tree, or milk tree (*Diplorrhyncus mossambicensis*), which is the focal symbol of the girls' puberty ritual of the Ndembu

people of northwestern Zambia, at its normative pole represents womanhood, motherhood, the mother-child bond, a novice undergoing initiation into mature womanhood, a specific matrilineage, the principle of matriliny, the process of learning "women's wisdom," the unity and perdurance of Ndembu society, and all of the values and virtues inherent in the various relationships—domestic, legal, and political—controlled by matrilineal descent. Each of these aspects of its normative meaning becomes paramount in a specific episode of the puberty ritual; together, they form a condensed statement of the structural and communal importance of femaleness in Ndembu culture. At its sensory pole, the same symbol stands for breast milk (the tree exudes milky latex—indeed, the significata associated with the sensory pole often have a more or less direct connection with some sensorily perceptible attribute of the symbol), mother's breasts, and the bodily slenderness and mental pliancy of the novice (a young slender sapling of mudyi is used). The tree, situated a short distance from the novice's village, becomes the center of a sequence of ritual episodes rich in symbols (words, objects, and actions) that express important cultural themes.

Ritual Symbols and Cultural Themes

Opler has defined a theme as a part of a limited set of "dynamic affirmations" that "can be identified in every culture." In the "nature, expression, and relationship" of themes is to be found the "key to the character, structure, and direction of the specific culture." The term "theme" denotes "a postulate or position, declared or implied, and usually controlling behavior or stimulating activity, which is tacitly approved or openly promoted in a society." Every culture has multiple themes, and most themes have multiple expressions, some of which may be in one or more parts of the institutional culture. Ritual forms an important setting for the expression of themes, and ritual symbols transmit themes. Themes have multiple expressions, and ritual symbols, such as the mudyi tree (and thousands of others in the ethnographic literature of African ritual), have multiple significata. The major difference between themes and symbols is that themes are postulates or ideas inferred by an observer from the data of a given culture, while ritual symbols are one class of such data. Ritual symbols are multivocal—that is, each symbol expresses not one theme but many themes simultaneously by the same perceptible object or activity (symbol vehicle). Symbols *have* significata, themes may *be* significata.

Themes, in their capacity as significata (including both conceptions and images), may be disparate or grouped, as we have seen, at opposed semantic poles. Thus the mudyi signifies aspects of female bodily imagery (milk, suckling, breasts, girlish slenderness) and conceptions about standards of womanhood and motherhood, as well as the normative ordering of these in relation to group membership, the inheritance of property, and succession to such political offices as chieftainship and village headmanship through matrilineal descent. These are rules of exclusion connected with the mudyi in this ritual context—all that is not concerned with the nurtural, procreative, and esthetic aspects of human femaleness and with their cultural control and structuring, is excluded from the semantic field of mudyi symbolism. This is a field of themes with varying degrees of concreteness, abstraction, and cognitive and orectic quality. The impulse that leads advanced cultures to the economical use of signs in mathematics finds its equivalent here in the use of a single symbol vehicle to represent simultaneously a variety of themes, most of which can be shown to be related, logically or pragmatically, but some of which depend for their association on a sensed likeness between variables rather than on cognitive criteria. One is dealing with a "mathematics" of sociocultural experience rather than with a mathematics of logical relationships.

Ritual symbols differ from other modes of thematic expression, particularly from those unformalized modes that arise in spontaneous behavior and allow for individual choice in expression. Indeed, it might be argued that the more ritualized the expression, the wider the range of themes that may be signified by it. On the other hand, since a ritual symbol may represent disparate, even contradictory themes, the gain in economy may be offset by a loss in clarity of communication. This would be inevitable if such symbols existed in a vacuum, but they exist in cultural and operational contexts that to some extent overcome the loss in intelligibility and to some extent capitalize on it.

Dominant Symbols in Ritual Cycles

Rituals tend to be organized in a cycle of performances (annual, biennial, quinquennial, and so on); even in the case of contingent rituals, each is performed eventually. In each total assemblage, or system, there is a nucleus of dominant symbols, which are characterized by extreme multivocality (having many senses) and a central position in each ritual performance. Associated with this nucleus is a much larger number of enclitic (dependent) symbols. Some of these are univocal, while others, like prepositions in language, become mere relations or function signs that keep the ritual action going (for example, bowings, lustrations, sweepings, and objects indicative of joining or separation). Dominant symbols provide the fixed points of the total system and recur in many of its component rituals. For example, if 15 separate kinds of ritual can be empirically distinguished in a given ritual system, dominant symbol A may be found in 10 of them, B in 7, C in 5, and D in 12. The mudyi tree, for example, is found in boys' and girls' initiation ceremonies, in five rituals concerned with female reproductive disorders, in at least three rituals of the hunters' cults, and in various herbalistic practices of a magical cast. Other dominant symbols of Ndembu rituals . . . recur almost as frequently in the ritual round. Each of these symbols, then, has multiple referents, but on each occasion that it is used—usually an episode within a ritual performance—only one or a related few of its referents are drawn to public attention. The process of "selectivity" consists in constructing around the dominant symbol a context of symbolic objects, activities, gestures, social relationships between actors of ritual roles, and verbal behavior (prayers, formulas, chants, songs, recitation of sacred narratives, and so on) that both bracket and underline those of its referents deemed pertinent in the given situation. Thus, only a portion of a dominant symbol's full semantic wealth is deployed in a single kind of ritual or in one of its episodes. The semantic structure of a dominant symbol may be compared with a ratchet wheel, each of whose teeth represents a conception or theme. The ritual context is like a pawl, which engages the notches. The point of engagement represents a meaning that is important in the particular situation. The wheel is the symbol's total meaning, and the complete range is only exposed when the whole cycle of rituals has been performed. Dominant symbols represent sets of fundamental themes. The symbol appears in many rituals, and its meanings are emphasized separately in many episodes. Since the settings in which the themes are ritually presented vary, and since themes are linked in different combinations in each setting, members of the culture who have been exposed to the entire ritual cycle gradually learn, through repetition, variation, and contrast of symbols and themes, what the values, rules, behavioral styles, and cognitive postulates of their culture are. Even more important, they learn in what cultural domains and with what intensity in each domain the themes should apply.

Positional Role of Binary Opposition

The selection of a given theme from a symbol's theme assemblage is a function of positioning—that is, of the manner in which the object or activity assigned symbolic value is placed or arranged vis-à-vis similar objects or activities. One common mode of positioning is binary opposition, the relating of two symbol vehicles whose opposed perceptible qualities or quantities suggest, in terms of the associative rules of the culture, semantic opposition. Thus when a grass hut is made at the Ndembu girls' puberty ceremony for the seclusion of the novice for several months, the two principal laths of the wooden frame are made respectively from mudyi and mukula (blood tree) wood. Both species are dominant symbols. To the Ndembu, mukula represents the husband whom the girl will marry immediately after the puberty rites, and the mudyi stands for the bride, the novice herself. Yet when mukula is considered as a dominant symbol of the total ritual system, it is found to have a wide range (what has aptly been called a "fan") of significata. Its primary and sensory meaning is blood—the Ndembu point to the dusky red gum secreted by the tree from cracks in its bark to justify their interpretation. But some bloods, they say, are masculine and some feminine. The former include blood shed by warriors, hunters, and circumcisers in the call of duty; the latter represents blood shown at menstruation and parturition. Another binary opposition within the semantic field of blood is between running blood and coagulating blood. The

latter is good, the former is dangerous. Thus, prolonged menstruation means that a woman's blood is ebbing away uselessly; it should coagulate to form fetus and placenta. But since men are the dangerous sex, the blood they cause to flow in hunting and war may be good—that is, beneficial for their own group.

Mukula symbolism is adroitly manipulated in different rituals to express various aspects of the human condition as the Ndembu experience it. For example, in the *Nkula* ritual, performed to placate the spirit of a dead kinswoman afflicting the female patient with menstrual troubles causing barrenness, mukula and other red symbols are contextually connected with symbols characteristic of the male hunting cults to convey the message: the patient is behaving like a male shedder of blood, not like a female conserver of blood, as she should be. It is her "masculine protest" that the ritual is mainly directed at overcoming and domesticating into the service of her female role. Mukula means many other things in other contexts, when used in religious ritual or in magical therapy. But the binary opposition of mudyi to mukula restricts the meaning of mudyi to young mature femininity and that of mukula to young mature masculinity, both of which are foundations of a hut, the prototypical domestic unit. The binding together of the laths taken from these trees is said to represent the sexual and the procreative union of the young couple. If these meanings form the sensory pole of the binary opposition as symbol, then the legitimated union by marriage represents the normative pole. In other words, even the binary opposition does not stand alone; it must be examined in the context of building the novice's seclusion hut and of the symbolic objects comprising the hut and its total meaning. There are, of course, many types of binary opposition. The members of pairs of symbols may be asymmetrical ($A>B$, $A<B$); they may be like or unlike but equal in value; they may be antithetical; one may be thought of as the product or offspring of the other; one may be active, the other passive; and so on. In this way, the Ndembu are induced to consider the nature and function of relationships as well as of the variables being related, for nonverbal symbol systems have the equivalents of grammar, syntax, accidence, and parts of speech.

Sometimes binary opposition may appear between complexes of symbol vehicles, each carrying a system of dominant and secondary symbols. Thus, in the circumcision rites of the Wiko, in Zambia, one group of masked dancers may mime opposition to another group; each mask and head-piece is already a combination of multivocal symbols. Yet one team may represent protectiveness and the other, aggressiveness. It is, in fact, not uncommon to find complex symbol vehicles, such as statues or shrines, with simple meanings, while simple vehicles, such as marks drawn in white or red clay, may be highly multivocal in almost every ritual situation in which they are used. A simple vehicle, exhibiting some color, shape, texture, or contrast commonly found in one's experience (such as the whiteness of the mudyi or the redness of the mukula), can literally or metaphorically connect a great range of phenomena and ideas. By contrast, a complex vehicle is already committed, at the level of sensory perception, to a host of contrasts that narrow and specify its message. This is probably why the great religious symbol vehicles such as the cross, the lotus, the crescent moon, the ark, and so on are relatively simple, although their significata constitute whole theological systems and control liturgical and architectural structures of immense complexity. One might almost hypothesize that the more complex the ritual (many symbols, complex vehicles), the more particularistic, localized, and socially structured its message; the simpler the ritual (few symbols, simple vehicles), the more universalistic its message. Thus, ecumenical liturgiologists today are recommending that Christian ritual be essentially reduced to the blessing, distribution, and partaking of bread and wine, in order to provide most denominations with a common ground.

Actors Experience Symbols as Powers and as Meanings

The second characteristic of ritual condensation, which compensates in some measure for semantic obscurity, is its efficacy. Ritual is not just a concentration of referents, of messages about values and norms; nor is it simply a set of practical guidelines and a set of symbolic paradigms for everyday action, indicating how spouses should treat each other, how pastoralists should classify and regard cattle, how hunters should behave in different wild habitats, and so on. It is also a fusion of the powers believed to be inherent in the persons, objects, relationships, events, and histories represented by ritual symbols. It is a mobilization of energies as well as messages. In this respect, the objects and activities in point are not merely things that stand for other things or something abstract, they participate in the powers and virtues they represent. I use "virtue" advisedly, for many objects termed symbols are also termed medicines. Thus, scrapings and leaves from such trees as the mudyi and the mukula are pounded together in meal mortars, mixed with water, and given to the afflicted to drink or to wash with. Here there is direct communication of the life-giving powers thought to inhere in certain objects under ritual conditions (a consecrated site, invocations of preternatural entities, and so on). When an object is used analogously, it functions unambiguously as a symbol. Thus, when the mudyi tree is used in puberty rites it clearly *represents* mother's milk; here the association is through sight, not taste. But when the mudyi is used as medicine in ritual, it is felt that certain qualities of motherhood and nurturing are being communicated physically. In the first case, the mudyi is used because it is "good to think" rather than "good to eat"; in the second, it is used because it has maternal power. The same objects are used both as powers and symbols, metonymically and metaphorically—it is the context that distinguishes them. The power aspect of a symbol derives from its being a part of a physical whole, the ideational aspect from an analogy between a symbol vehicle and its principal significata.

Each symbol expresses many themes, and each theme is expressed by many symbols. The cultural weave is made up of symbolic warp and thematic weft. This weaving of symbols and themes serves as a rich store of information, not only about the natural environment as perceived and evaluated by the ritual actors, but also about their ethical, esthetic, political, legal, and ludic (the domain of play, sport, and so forth in a culture) ideas, ideals, and rules. Each symbol is a store of information, both for actors and investigators, but in order to specify just which set of themes any particular ritual or ritual episode contains, one must determine the relations between the ritual's symbols and their vehicles, including verbal symbolic behavior. The advantages of communication by means of rituals in non-literate societies are clearly great, for the individual symbols and the patterned relations between them have a mnemonic function. The symbolic vocabulary and grammar to some extent make up for the lack of written records.

The Semantic Dimensions

Symbols have three especially significant dimensions: the exegetic, the operational, and the positional. The exegetic dimension consists of the explanations given the investigator by actors in the ritual system. Actors of different age, sex, ritual role, status, grade of esoteric knowledge, and so forth provide data of varying richness, explicitness, and internal coherence. The investigator should infer from this information how members of a given society think about ritual. Not all African societies contain persons who are ready to make verbal statements about ritual, and the percentage of those prepared to offer interpretations varies from group to group and within groups. But, as much ethnographic work attests, many African societies are well endowed with exegetes.

In the operational dimension, the investigator equates a symbol's meaning with its use—he observes what actors do with it and how they relate to one another in this process. He also records their gestures, expressions, and other nonverbal aspects of behavior and discovers what values they represent—grief, joy, anger, triumph, modesty, and so on. Anthropologists are now studying several genres of non-verbal language, from iconography (the study of symbols whose vehicles picture the conceptions they signify, rather than being arbitrary, conventional signs for them) to kinetics (the study of bodily movements, facial expressions, and so forth as ways of communication or adjuncts and intensifiers of speech). Several of these fall under the rubric of a symbol's operational meaning. Non-exegetical, ritualized speech, such as formalized prayers or invocations, would also fall into this category. Here verbal symbols approximate non-verbal symbols. The investigator is interested not only in the social organization and structure of those individuals who operate with symbols on this level, but also in what persons, categories, and groups are absent from the situation, for formal exclusion would reveal social values and attitudes.

In the positional dimension, the observer finds in the relations between one symbol and other symbols an important source of its meaning. I have shown how binary opposition may, in context, highlight one (or more) of a symbol's many referents by contrasting it with one (or more) of another symbol's referents. When used in a ritual context with three or more other symbols, a particular symbol reveals further facets of its total "meaning." Groups of symbols may be so arrayed as to state a message, in which some symbols function analogously to parts of speech and in which there may be conventional rules of connection. The message is not about specifications and circumstances, but about the given culture's basic structures of thought, ethics, esthetics, law, and modes of speculation about new experience.

In several African cultures, particularly in West Africa, a complex system of rituals is associated with myths. These tell of the origins of the gods, the cosmos, human types and groups, and the key institutions of culture and society. Some ritual episodes reenact primordial events, drawing on their inherent power to achieve the contemporary goals of the members of the culture (for example, adjustment to puberty and the healing of the sick). Ritual systems are sometimes based on myths. There may coexist with myths and rituals standardized schemata of interpretation that may amount to theological doctrine. But in wide areas of East and Central Africa, there may be few myths connected with rituals and no religious system interrelating myths, rituals, and doctrine. In compensation, there may be much piecemeal exegesis of particular symbols.

Foundations of Meaning

Most African languages have terms for ritual symbol. The Nyakyusa, for example, speak of *ififwani* (likenesses); the Ndembu use *chijikijilu* (a landmark, or blaze), which is derived from *kujikijila* (to blaze a trail or set up a landmark). The first connotes an association, a feeling of likeness between sign and signified, vehicle and concept; the second is a means of connecting known with unknown territory. (The Ndembu compare the ritual symbol to the trail a hunter blazes in order to find his way back from unexplored bush to his village.) Other languages possess similar terms. In societies that do not have myths, the meaning of a symbol is built up by analogy and association of three foundations—

nominal, substantial, and artifactual—though in any given instance only one of these might be utilized. The nominal basis is the name of the symbol, an element in an acoustic system; the substantial basis is a symbol's sensorily perceptible physical or chemical properties as recognized by the culture; and its artifactual basis is the technical changing of an object used in ritual by human purposive activity.

For example: At the start of a girl's puberty ritual among the Nyakyusa of Tanzania, she is treated with a "medicine" called *undumila*. This medicine is also an elaborate symbol. Its nominal basis is the derivation of the term from *ukulumila*, meaning "to bite, to be painful." The substantial basis is a natural property of the root after which the medicine is named—it is pungent-tasting. As an artifact, the medicine is a composite of several symbolic substances. The total symbol involves action as well as a set of objects. Wilson writes that the root "is pushed through the tip of a funnel or cup made of a leaf of the bark-cloth tree, and salt is poured into the cup. The girl takes the tip of the root in her mouth and pulls it inward with her teeth, thus causing the salt to trickle into her mouth." The root and leaf funnel, together with their ritual use, constitute an artifact. These three bases of significance are substantiated by the Nyakyusa Wilson talked to. One woman told her: "The pungent root is the penis of the husband, the cup is her vagina, the salt, also pungent, is the semen of her husband. Biting the root and eating the salt is copulation." Another woman confirmed this: "The *undumila* is put through the leaf of a bark-cloth tree, shaped into a cup, and it is a sign of man and woman, the penis in the vagina. It is similar to the plantains which we give her when we wash her. The plantains are a symbol of the husband. If we do not give her . . . the *undumila*, she constantly has periods and is barren." A third informant said: "It is the pain of periods that we symbolize in the sharpness of the *undumila* and salt." Thus *undumila* is at once a symbol of sexual intercourse, a prophylactic against pain in intercourse and against frequent or painful periods, and (according to other accounts) a ritual defense against those who are "heavy"—that is, those actively engaged in sexual intercourse, especially women who have just conceived. If a heavy person steps over the novice's footprints, the novice will not bear a child, but will menstruate con-

tinually. These explanations also demonstrate the multivocality and economy of reference of a single dominant symbol. The same symbol vehicles can represent different, even disparate, processes—marital intercourse and menstrual difficulty—although it may be argued that the Nyakyusa, at an unconscious level, regard a woman's "distaste" for intercourse as a cause of her barrenness or menorrhagia.

Symbols and Cosmologies

Similar examples abound in the ethnography of subsaharan Africa, but in the great West African cultures of the Fon, Ashanti, Yoruba, Dahomeyans, and Dogon, piecemeal exegesis gives way to explicit, complex cosmologies. Among the Dogon, for example, a symbol becomes a fixed point of linkage between animal, vegetable, and mineral kingdoms, which are themselves regarded as parts of "ungigantesque organisme humaine." The doctrine of correspondences reigns—everything is a symbol of everything else, whether in ritual context or not. Thus the Dogon establish a correspondence between the different categories of minerals and the organs of the body. The various soils in the area are conceived of as the organs of "the interior of the stomach," rocks are regarded as the bones of the skeleton, and various hues of red clay are likened to the blood. Sometimes these correspondences are remarkably precise: one rock resting on another represents the chest; little white river pebbles stand for the toes of the feet. The same *parole du monde* principles hold true for the relationship between man and the vegetable kingdom. Man is not only the grain of the universe, but each distinct part of a single grain represents part of the human body. In fact, it is only science that has emancipated man from the complex weave of correspondences, based on analogy, metaphor, and mystical participation, and that enables him to regard all relations as problematical, not preordained, until they have been experimentally tested or systematically compared.

The Dogon further conceive of a subtle and finely wrought interplay between speech and the components of personality. The body constitutes a magnet or focus for man's spiritual principles, which nevertheless are capable of sustaining an independent existence. The Dogon contrast visible and invisible ("spiritual") components of the human personality. The body is made up of four elements: water (the blood and bodily fluids), earth (the skeleton), air (breath), and fire (animal warmth). There is a continuous interchange between these internal expressions of the elements and their external aspects. The body has 22 parts: feet, shins, thighs, lumbar region, stomach, chest, arms, neck, and head make up nine parts (it would seem that Dogon reckon double parts, as they do twins, as a unit); the fingers (each counting as a unit), make up ten parts; and the male genitals make up three parts. Further numerical symbolism is involved: there are believed to be eight symbolic grains—representing the principal cereal crops of the region—lodged in the collarbones of each Dogon. These grains represent the mystical bond between man and his crops. The *body* of speech itself is, like the human body, composed of four elements: water is saliva, without which speech is dry; air gives rise to sound vibrations; earth gives speech its weight and significance; and fire gives speech its warmth. There is not only homology between personality and speech, but also a sort of functional interdependence, for words are selected by the brain, stir up the liver, and rise as steam from the lungs to the clavicles, which decide ultimately whether the speech is to emerge from the mouth.

To the 22 parts of the personality must be added the 48 types of speech, which are divided into two sets of 24. Each set is under the sign of a supernatural being, one of the androgynous twins Nommo and Yourougou. Here I must draw on Griaule and Dieterlen's extensive work on the Dogons' cosmogonic mythology. The twins are the creations of Amma. Yourougou rebelled against Amma and had sexual relations with his mother—he was punished by being changed into a pale fox. Nommo saved the world by an act of self-sacrifice, brought humans, animals, and plants to the earth, and became the lord of speech. Nommo's speech is human and can be heard; the Fox's is silent, a sign language made by his paw marks, and only diviners can interpret it. These myths provide a classification and taxonomy of cosmos and society; explain many details of ritual, including the forms and color symbolism of elaborate masks; and, indeed, determine where and how houses are constructed. Other West African cultures have equally elaborate

cosmologies, which are manifested in ritual and divinatory symbolism. Their internal consistency and symmetry may be related to traditions of continuous residence and farming in a single habitat, combined with exposure to trans-Saharan cultural elements, including religious beliefs, for thousands of years—ancient Egyptian, Roman, Christian, Neo-Platonic, Gnostic, Islamic. The history of West Africa contrasts with that of Central Africa, where most societies descend from groups that migrated in a relatively short period of time across several distinct ecological habitats and that were then exposed to several centuries of slave raiding and slave trading. Groups were fragmented and then combined with the social detritus of other societies into new, temporary polities. There were conquests, assimilations, reconquests, the rise and fall of "kingdoms of the savannah," and temporary centralization followed by decentralization into localized clans. Swidden (slash-and-burn) agriculture kept people constantly on the move; hunting and pastoralism compounded the mobility. Because of these circumstances, there was less likelihood of complex, integrated religious and cosmological systems arising in Central Africa than in West Africa. Yet the needs and dangers of social and personal survival provided suitable conditions for the development of rituals as pragmatic instruments (from the standpoint of the actors) for coping with biological change, disease, and natural hazards of all kinds. Social action in response to material pressures was the systematic and systematizing factor. Order, cosmos, came from purpose, not from an elaborate and articulated cosmology. It is an order that accords well with human experience at preindustrial technological levels; even its discrepancies accurately reflect the "facts of life"—in contrast to consistent and harmonious cosmologies whose symbols and myths mask and cloak the basic contradictions between wishes and facts.

The Continuing Efficacy of African Ritual Symbols

Nevertheless, from the comparative viewpoint, there are remarkable similarities among symbols used in ritual throughout sub-Saharan Africa, in spite of differences in cosmological sophistication. The same ideas, analogies, and modes of association underlie symbol formation and manipulation from the Senegal River to the Cape of Good Hope. The same assumptions about powers prevail in kingdoms and nomadic bands. Whether these assemblages of similar symbols represent units of complex orders or the debris of formerly prevalent ones, the symbols remain extraordinarily viable and the themes they represent and embody tenaciously rooted. This may be because they arose in ecological and social experiences of a kind that still prevails in large areas of the continent. Since they are thus sustained and since there is a continuous flux and reflux of people between country and city, it is not surprising that much of the imagery found in the writings of modern African novelists and in the rhetoric of politicians is drawn from ritual symbolism—from which it derives its power to move and channel emotion.

Taboo

Mary Douglas

One of the most difficult tasks anthropologists face in their study of non-Western cultures is isolating the bases for rules of right conduct. In the following article, Mary Douglas succinctly demonstrates that unlike modern industrialized nations, which have shared common experiences for centuries, primitive cultures have remained separated by distance and language and have developed unique world views. Pointing out, for example, that Westerners' separation of the natural and the supernatural is peculiar to us, Douglas explains how our reality and, therefore, our taboos are so different from those of the non-Western world.

Douglas's functional analysis of taboos shows that they underpin social structure everywhere. Anthropologists, studying taboos over extensive periods of time, have learned that taboo systems are not static and forever inviolate; on the contrary, they are dynamic elements of learned behavior that each generation absorbs. Taboos, as rules of behavior, are always part of a whole system and cannot be understood outside their social context. Douglas's explanation of taboos holds as much meaning for us in the understanding of ourselves as it does for our understanding of rules of conduct in the non-Western world. Whether considering the taboos surrounding a Polynesian chief's mana *or the changing sexual taboos in the Western world, it is apparent that taboo systems function to maintain cultural systems.*

Reprinted from Richard Cavendish, ed., *Man, Myth, and Magic* (London, 1979), Vol. 20, pp. 2767–71, by permission of the author and BPCC/Phoebus Publishing.

A TABOO (SOMETIMES SPELLED TABU) IS A BAN OR prohibition; the word comes from the Polynesian languages where it means a religious restriction, to break which would entail some automatic punishment. As it is used in English, taboo has little to do with religion. In essence it generally implies a rule which has no meaning, or one which cannot be explained. Captain Cook noted in his log-book that in Tahiti the women were never allowed to eat with the men, and as the men nevertheless enjoyed female company he asked the reason for this taboo. They always replied that they observed it because it was right. To the outsider the taboo is irrational, to the believer its rightness needs no explaining. Though supernatural punishments may not be expected to follow, the rules of any religion rate as taboos to outsiders. For example, the strict Jewish observance forbids the faithful to make and refuel the fire, or light lamps or put them out during the Sabbath, and it also forbids them to ask a Gentile to perform any of these acts. In his book *A Soho Address*, Chaim Lewis, the son of poor Russian Jewish immigrants in London's Soho at the beginning of this century, describes his father's quandary every winter Sabbath: he did not want to let the fire go out and he could not ask any favor outright. Somehow he had to call in a passerby and drop oblique hints until the stranger understood what service was required. Taboos always tend to land their observers in just such a ridiculous situation, whether it is a Catholic peasant of the Landes who abstains from meat on Friday, but eats teal (a bird whose fishy diet entitles it in their custom to be counted as fish), or a Maori hairdresser who after he had cut the chief's hair was not allowed to use his own hands even for feeding himself and had to be fed for a time like a baby.

In the last century, when the word gained currency in European languages, taboo was understood to arise from an inferior mentality. It was argued that primitive tribes observed countless taboos as part of their general ignorance about the physical world. These rules, which seemed so peculiar to Europeans, were the result of false science, leading to mistaken hygiene, and faulty medicine. Essentially the taboo is a ban on touching or eating or speaking or seeing. Its breach will unleash dangers, while keeping the rules would amount to avoiding dangers and sickness. Since the native theory of taboo was concerned to keep certain classes of people and things apart lest misfortune befall, it was a theory about contagion. Our scholars of the last century contrasted this false, primitive fear of contagion with our modern knowledge of disease. Our hygiene protects from a real danger of contagion, their taboos from imaginary danger. This was a comfortably complacent distinction to draw, but hygiene does not correspond to all the rules which are called taboo. Some are as obviously part of primitive religion in the same sense as Friday abstinence and Sabbath rest. European scholars therefore took care to distinguish on the one hand between primitive taboo with a mainly secular reference, and on the other hand rules of magic which infused the practice of primitive religion. They made it even more difficult to understand the meaning of foreign taboos by importing a classification between true religion and primitive magic, and modern medicine and primitive hygiene; and a very complicated web of definitions was based on this misconception.

In the Eye of the Beholder

The difficulty in understanding primitive taboo arose from the difficulty of understanding our own taboos of hygiene and religion. The first mistake was to suppose that our idea of dirt connotes an objectively real class from which real dangers to health may issue, and whose control depends on valid rules of hygiene. It is better to start by realizing that dirt, like beauty, resides in the eye of the beholder. We must be prepared to put our own behavior under the same microscope we apply to primitive tribes. If we find that they are busy hedging off this area from that, stopping X from touching Y, preventing women from eating with men, and creating elaborate scales of edibility and inedibility among the vegetable and animal worlds, we should realize that we too are given to this ordering and classifying activity. No taboo can ever make

sense by itself. A taboo is always part of a whole system of rules. It makes sense as part of a classification whose meaning is so basic to those who live by it that no piecemeal explanation can be given. A native cannot explain the meaning of a taboo because it forms part of his own machinery of learning. The separate compartments which a taboo system constructs are the framework or instrument of understanding. To turn round and inspect that instrument may seem to be an advanced philosophic exercise, but it is necessary if we are to understand the subject.

The nineteenth-century scholars could not understand taboo because they worked within the separate compartments of their own taboo system. For them religion, magic, hygiene, and medicine were as distinct as civilized and primitive; the problem of taboo for them was only a problem about native thought. But put in that form it was insoluble. We approach it nowadays as a problem in human learning.

First, discard the idea that we have anything like a true, complete view of the world. Between what the scientists know and what we make of their knowledge there is a synthesis which is our own rough-and-ready approximation of rules about how we need to behave in the physical world. Second, discard the idea that there can ever be a final and correct world view. A gain in knowledge in one direction does not guarantee there will be no loss or distortion in another; the fullness of reality will always evade our comprehension. The reasons for this will become clear. Learning is a filtering and organizing process. Faced with the same events, two people will not necessarily register two identical patterns, and faced with a similar environment, two cultures will construe two different sets of natural constraints and regular sequences. Understanding is largely a classifying job in which the classifying human mind is much freer than it supposes itself to be. The events to be understood are unconsciously trimmed and filtered to fit the classification being used. In this sense every culture constructs its own universe. It attributes to its own world a set of powers to be harnessed and dangers to be avoided. Each primitive culture, because of its isolation, has a unique world view. Modern industrial nations, because and insofar as they share a common experience, share the same rules about the powers and dangers aroused. This is a valid difference between "Us" and "Them," their primitive taboos and ours.

For all humans, primitive or not, the universe is a system of imputed rules. Using our own distinctions, we can distinguish firstly, physical Nature, inorganic (including rocks, stars, rivers) and organic (vegetable and animal bodies, with rules governing their growth, lifespan and death); secondly, human behavior; thirdly, the interaction between these two groups; fourthly, other intelligent beings whether incorporeal like gods, devils and ghosts or mixtures of human and divine or human and animal; and lastly, the interaction between this fourth group and the rest.

The use of the word supernatural has been avoided. Even a small amount of reading in anthropology shows how very local and peculiar to our own civilization is the distinction between natural and supernatural. The same applies even to such a classification as the one just given. The fact that it is our own local classification is not important for this argument as the present object is to make clear how taboos should be understood. Taboos are rules about our behavior which restrict the human uses of things and people. Some of the taboos are said to avoid punishment or vengeance from gods, ghosts and other spirits. Some of them are supposed to produce automatically their dreaded effects. Crop failures, sickness, hunting accidents, famine, drought, epidemic (events in the physical realm), they may all result from breach of taboos.

The Seat of Mana

Taboos can have the effect of expressing political ideas. For example, the idea of the state as a hierarchy of which the chief is the undisputed head and his officials higher than the ordinary populace easily lends itself to taboo behavior. Gradings of power in the political body tend to be expressed as gradings of freedom to approach the physical body of the person at the top of the system. As Franz Steiner says, in *Taboo* (1956):

> In Polynesian belief the parts of the body formed a fixed hierarchy which had some analogy with the rank system of society. . . . Now the backbone was the most important part of the body, and the limbs that could be regarded as continuations of the backbone derived importance from it. Above the body was, of course, the

head, and it was the seat of mana. When we say this, we must realize that by "mana" are meant both the soul aspect, the life force, and a man's ritual status. This grading of the limbs concerned people of all ranks and both sexes. It could, for example, be so important to avoid stepping over people's heads that the very architecture was involved: the arrangements of the sleeping rooms show such an adaptation in the Marquesas. The commoner's back or head is thus not without its importance in certain contexts. But the real significance of this grading seems to have been in the possibilities it provided for cumulative effects in association with the rank system. The head of a chief was the most concentrated mana object of Polynesian society, and was hedged around with the most terrifying taboos which operated when things were to enter the head or when the head was being diminished; in other words when the chief ate or had his hair cut. . . . The hands of some great chiefs were so dangerous that they could not be put close to the head.

Since the Polynesian political system was very competitive and chiefs had their ups and downs, great triumphs or total failures, the system of taboo was a kind of public vote of confidence and register of current distributions of power. This is important to correct our tendency to think of taboo as a rigidly fixed system of respect.

We will never understand a taboo system unless we understand the kind of interaction between the different spheres of existence which is assumed in it. Any child growing up learns the different spheres and interactions between them simultaneously. When the anthropologist arrives on the scene, he finds the system of knowledge a going concern. It is difficult for him to observe the changes being made, so he gets the wrong impression that a given set of taboos is something hard-and-fast handed down the generations.

In fact, the classifying process is always active and changing. New classifications are being pushed by some and rejected by others. No political innovation takes place without some basic reclassification. To take a currently live issue, in a stratified society, if it is taboo for lower classes or Negroes to sit down at table or to join sporting events with upper classes or whites, those who assert the rule can make it stronger if they find a basis in Nature to support the behavior they regard as right. If women in Tahiti are forbidden to eat with men, or in Europe to enter certain male occupations, some ultimate justification for the rule needs to be found. Usually it is traced back to their physical nature. Women are said to be constitutionally feeble, nervous or flighty; Negroes to smell; lower classes to be hereditarily less intelligent.

Rules of the Game

Perhaps the easiest approach is to try to imagine what social life would be like without any classification. It would be like playing a game without any rules; no one would know which way to run, who is on his side or against him. There would be no game. It is no exaggeration to describe social life as the process of building classification systems. Everyone is trying to make sense of what is happening. He is trying to make sense of his own behavior, past and present, so as to capture and hold some sense of identity. He is trying to hold other people to their promises and ensure some kind of regular future. He is explaining continually, to himself and to everyone else. In the process of explaining, classifications are developed and more and more meanings successfully added to them, as other people are persuaded to interpret events in the same way. Gradually even the points of the compass get loaded with social meanings. For example, the west room in an Irish farmer's house used to be the room where the old couple retired to, when the eldest son married and brought his wife to the farm. West meant retirement as well as sundown. In the Buddhist religion, east is the high status point; Buddha's statue is on a shelf on the east wall of the east room; the husband always sleeps to the east of his wife. So east means male and social superior. Up and down, right and left, sun and moon, hot and cold, all the physical antitheses are able to carry meanings from social life, and in a rich and steady culture there is a steady core of such agreed classifications. Anyone who is prepared to support the social system finds himself impelled to uphold the classification system which gets meaning from it. Anyone who wants to challenge the social system finds himself up against a set of manifold classifications which will have to be rethought. This is why breach of taboo arouses such strong feeling. It is not because the minor classification is threatened, but because the whole social system (in which a great investment has been made) looks like tottering, if someone can get away with challenging a taboo.

Classification involves definition; definition involves reducing ambiguity; ambiguity arises in several ways and it is wrong to think that it can ever be excluded. To take the classification of animal species, they can be classified according to their obvious features, and according to the habitat they live in, and according to how they behave. This gives three ways of classifying animals which could each place the same beasts in different classes. Classed by behavior, using walking, swimming or flying as basic types, penguins would be nearer to fish; classed by bone structure and egg laying, penguins would count more clearly as birds than would flying fish, which would be birds in the other classification. Animal life is much more untidy and difficult to fit into a regular system of classification than at first appears. Human social life is even more untidy. Girls behave like boys, there are adults who refuse to grow up, every year a few are born whose physical make-up is not clearly male or female. The rules of marriage and inheritance require clear-cut categories but always there will be some cases which do not fit the regularities of the system. For human classifications are always too crude for reality. A system of taboos covers up this weakness of the classification system. It points in advance to defects and insists that no one shall give recognition to the inconvenient facts or behave in such a way as to undermine the acceptability and clarity of the system as a whole. It stops awkward questions and prevents awkward developments.

Sometimes the taboo ban appears in ways that seem a long way from their point of origin. For example, among the Lele tribe, in the Kasai district of the Congo, it was taboo to bring fishing equipment direct into the village from the streams or lakes where it had been in use. All round the village fishing traps and baskets would be hung in trees overnight. Ask the Lele why they did this and they replied that coughs and disease would enter the village if the fishing things were not left out one night. No other answer could be got from them except elaboration of the danger and how sorcerers could enter the village if this barrier were not kept up. But another kind of answer lay in the mass of other rules and regulations which separated the village and its human social life from the forest and streams and animal life. This was the basic classification at stake; one which never needed to be explained because it was too fundamental to mention.

Injecting Order into Life

The novelist William Burroughs describes the final experiences of disgust and depression of some forms of drug addiction. What he calls the "Naked Lunch" is the point where all illusions are stripped away and every thing is seen as it really is. When everyone can see what is on everyone's fork, nothing is classed as edible. Meat can be animal or human flesh, caterpillars, worms, or bugs; soup is equally urine, lentils, scotch broth, or excreta; other people are neither friends nor enemies, nor is oneself different from other people since neither has any very clear definition. Identities and classifications are merged into a seething, shapeless experience. This is the potential disorder of the mind which taboo breaks up into classes and rules and so judges some activities as right and proper and others as horrifying.

This kind of rationality is the justification for the taboos which we ourselves observe when we separate the lavatory from the living room and the bed from the kitchen, injecting order into the house. But the order is not arbitrary; it derives from social categories. When a set of social distinctions weakens, the taboos that expressed it weaken too. For this reason sex taboos used to be sacred in England but are no longer so strong. It seems ridiculous that women should not be allowed in some clubs or professions, whereas not so long ago it seemed obviously right. The same for the sense of privacy, the same for hierarchy. The less we ourselves are forced to adopt unthinking taboo attitudes to breaches of these boundaries, the easier it becomes to look dispassionately at the taboos of other societies and find plenty of meaning in them.

In some tribal societies it is thought that the shedding of blood will cause droughts and other environmental disasters. Elsewhere any contact with death is dangerously polluting, and burials are followed by elaborate washing and fumigation. In other places they fear neither homicide nor death pollution but menstrual blood is thought to be very dangerous to touch. And in other places again, adultery is liable to cause illness. Some people are thickly beset with taboos so that everything they do is charged with social symbolism. Others observe only one or two rules. Those who are most taboo-minded have the most complex set of social boundaries to preserve. Hence their investment of so much energy into the control of behavior.

A taboo system upholds a cultural system and a culture is a pattern of values and norms; social life is impossible without such a pattern. This is the dilemma of individual freedom. Ideally we would like to feel free to make every choice from scratch and judge each case on its merits. Such a freedom would slow us down, for every choice would have to be consciously deliberated. On the one hand, education tries to equip a person with means for exercising private judgment, and on the other hand, the techniques of education provide a kind of mechanical decision-making, along well-oiled grooves. They teach strong reactions of anxiety about anything which threatens to go off the track. As education transmits culture, taboos and all, it is a kind of brainwashing. It only allows a certain way of seeing reality and so limits the scope for private judgment. Without the taboos, which turn basic classifications into automatic psychological reflexes, no thinking could be effective, because if every system of classification was up for revision at every moment, there would be no stability of thought. Hence there would be no scope for experience to accumulate into knowledge. Taboos bar the way for the mind to visualize reality differently. But the barriers they set up are not arbitrary, for taboos flow from social boundaries and support the social structure. This accounts for their seeming irrational to the outsider and beyond challenge to the person living in the society.

You Are What You Eat: Religious Aspects of the Health Food Movement

Jill Dubisch

In this article Jill Dubisch shows that the health food movement in this country may be seen as more than a way of eating and more than an alternative healing system. Using Clifford Geertz's definition of religion as a "system of symbols," Dubisch maintains that the health food movement has many of the characteristics of a religion. For example, the anthropological concepts of mana *and* taboo *are used in a discussion of the merits of "health foods" (mana) versus the detrimental nature of "junk foods" (taboo). The health food movement, like religion, offers its adherents salvation of the body, psyche, and even society itself. Followers strive to gain new values and a new world view. Comparing health food devotees to people undergoing a religious revitalization, Dubisch describes how converts learn to criticize prevailing social values and institutions. She notes the process of conversion that individuals entering the movement undergo, their concern for the maintenance of purity, the "temples" (health food stores), the "rabbis" (health food experts), and the sacred writings that establish the movement's principles. Provocative and entertaining, Dubisch's analysis of the religious aspects of the health food movement is sound anthropology and is certain to remind each of us of our own, or an acquaintance's, "religious" involvement with health food.*

Reprinted from Susan P. Montague and W. Arens, eds., *The American Dimension: Culture Myths and Social Realities*, 2nd ed. (Palo Alto, Calif., 1981), pp. 115–27, by permission of the author and Mayfield Publishing Company.

Dr. Robbins was thinking how it might be interesting to make a film from Adelle Davis' perennial best seller, *Let's Eat Right to Keep Fit*. Representing a classic confrontation between good and evil—in this case nutrition versus unhealthy diet—the story had definite box office appeal. The role of the hero, Protein, probably should be filled by Jim Brown, although Burt Reynolds undoubtedly would pull strings to get the part. Sunny Doris Day would be a clear choice to play the heroine, Vitamin C, and Orson Welles, oozing saturated fatty acids from the pits of his flesh, could win an Oscar for his interpretation of the villainous Cholesterol. The film might begin on a stormy night in the central nervous system. . . .

—Tom Robbins, *Even Cowgirls Get the Blues*

I INTEND TO EXAMINE A CERTAIN WAY OF EATING; that which is characteristic of the health food movement, and try to determine what people are communicating when they choose to eat in ways which run counter to the dominant patterns of food consumption in our society. This requires looking at health foods as a system of symbols and the adherence to a health food way of life as being, in part, the expression of belief in a particular world view. Analysis of these symbols and the underlying world view reveals that, as a system of beliefs and practices, the health food movement has some of the characteristics of a religion.

Such an interpretation might at first seem strange since we usually think of religion in terms of a belief in a deity or other supernatural beings. These notions, for the most part, are lacking in the health food movement. However, anthropologists do not always consider such beliefs to be a necessary part of a religion. Clifford Geertz, for example, suggests the following broad definition:

> A *religion* is (1) a system of symbols which acts to (2) establish powerful, pervasive, and long-lasting moods and motivations in men by (3) formulating conceptions of a general-order of existence and (4) clothing these conceptions with such an aura of factuality that (5) the moods and motivations seem uniquely realistic. (Geertz 1965: 4)

Let us examine the health food movement in the light of Geertz's definition.

History of the Health Food Movement

The concept of "health foods" can be traced back to the 1830s and the Popular Health movement, which combined a reaction against professional medicine and an emphasis on lay knowledge and health care with broader social concerns such as feminism and the class struggle (see Ehrenreich and English 1979). The Popular Health movement emphasized self-healing and the dissemination of knowledge about the body and health to laymen. One of the early founders of the movement, Sylvester Graham (who gave us the graham cracker), preached that good health was to be found in temperate living. This included abstinence from alcohol, a vegetarian diet, consumption of whole wheat products, and regular exercise. The writings and preachings of these early "hygienists" (as they called themselves) often had moral overtones, depicting physiological and spiritual reform as going hand in hand (Shryock 1966).

The idea that proper diet can contribute to good health has continued into the twentieth century. The discovery of vitamins provided for many health food people a further "natural" means of healing which could be utilized instead of drugs. Vitamins were promoted as health-giving substances by various writers, including nutritionist Adelle Davis, who has been perhaps the most important "guru" of health foods in this century. Davis preached good diet as well as the use of vitamins to restore and maintain health, and her books have become the best sellers of the move-

ment. (The titles of her books, *Let's Cook It Right*, *Let's Get Well*, *Let's Have Healthy Children*, give some sense of her approach.) The health food movement took on its present form, however, during the late 1960s, when it became part of the "counterculture."

Health foods were "in," and their consumption became part of the general protest against the "establishment" and the "straight" life-style. They were associated with other movements centering around social concerns, such as ecology and consumerism (Kandel and Pelto 1980: 328). In contrast to the Popular Health movement, health food advocates of the sixties saw the establishment as not only the medical profession but also the food industry and the society it represented. Food had become highly processed and laden with colorings, preservatives, and other additives so that purity of food became a new issue. Chemicals had also become part of the food-growing process, and in reaction terms such as "organic" and "natural" became watchwords of the movement. Health food consumption received a further impetus from revelations about the high sugar content of many popular breakfast cereals which Americans had been taught since childhood to think of as a nutritious way to start the day. (Kellogg, an early advocate of the Popular Health movement, would have been mortified, since his cereals were originally designed to be part of a hygienic regimen.)

Although some health food users are members of formal groups (such as the Natural Hygiene Society, which claims direct descent from Sylvester Graham), the movement exists primarily as a set of principles and practices rather than as an organization. For those not part of organized groups, these principles and practices are disseminated, and contact is made with other members of the movement, through several means. The most important of these are health food stores, restaurants, and publications. The two most prominent journals in the movement are *Prevention* and *Let's Live*, begun in 1920 and 1932 respectively (Hongladarom 1976).

These journals tell people what foods to eat and how to prepare them. They offer advice about the use of vitamins, the importance of exercise, and the danger of pollutants. They also present testimonials from faithful practitioners. Such testimonials take the form of articles that recount how the author overcame a physical problem through a health food approach, or letters from readers who tell how they have cured their ailments by following methods advocated by the journal or suggested by friends in the movement. In this manner, such magazines not only educate, they also articulate a world view and provide evidence and support for it. They have become the "sacred writings" of the movement. They are a way of "reciting the code"—the cosmology and moral injunctions—which anthropologist Anthony F. C. Wallace describes as one of the important categories of religious behavior (1966: 57).

Ideological Content of the Health Food Movement

What exactly is the health food system? First, and most obviously, it centers around certain beliefs regarding the relationship of diet to health. Health foods are seen as an "alternative" healing system, one which people turn to out of their dissatisfaction with conventional medicine (see, for example, Hongladarom 1976). The emphasis is on "wellness" and prevention rather than on illness and curing. Judging from letters and articles found in health food publications, many individuals' initial adherence to the movement is a type of conversion. A specific medical problem, or a general dissatisfaction with the state of their health, leads these converts to an eventual realization of the "truth" as represented by the health food approach, and to a subsequent change in life-style to reflect the principles of that approach. "Why This Psychiatrist 'Switched'," published in *Prevention* (September 1976), carries the following heading: "Dr. H. L. Newbold is a great advocate of better nutrition and a livelier life style. But it took a personal illness to make him see the light." For those who have experienced such conversion, and for others who become convinced by reading about such experiences, health food publications serve an important function by reinforcing the conversion and encouraging a change of life-style. For example, an article entitled "How to Convert Your Kitchen for the New Age of Nutrition" (*Prevention*, February 1975) tells the housewife how to make her kitchen a source of health for her family. The article suggests ways of reorganizing kitchen supplies and reforming cooking by substituting health foods for substances detrimental to health, and also offers ideas

on the preparation of nutritious and delicious meals which will convert the family to this new way of eating without "alienating" them. The pamphlet *The Junk Food Withdrawal Manual* (Kline 1978), details how an individual can, step by step, quit eating junk foods and adopt more healthful eating habits. Publications also urge the readers to convert others by letting them know how much better health foods are than junk foods. Proselytizing may take the form of giving a "natural" birthday party for one's children and their friends, encouraging schools to substitute fruit and nuts for junk food snacks, and even selling one's own baking.

Undergoing the conversion process means learning and accepting the general features of the health food world view. To begin with, there is great concern, as there is in many religions, with purity, in this case, the purity of food, of water, of air. In fact, there are some striking similarities between keeping a "health food kitchen" and the Jewish practice of keeping kosher. Both make distinctions between proper and improper foods, and both involve excluding certain impure foods (whether unhealthful or non-kosher) from the kitchen and table. In addition, a person concerned with maintaining a high degree of purity in food may engage in similar behavior in either case—reading labels carefully to check for impermissible ingredients and even purchasing food from special establishments to guarantee ritual purity.

In the health food movement, the basis of purity is healthfulness and "naturalness." Some foods are considered to be natural and therefore healthier; this concept applies not only to foods but to other aspects of life as well. It is part of the large idea that people should work in harmony with nature and not against it. In this respect, the health food cosmology sets up an opposition of nature (beneficial) versus culture (destructive), or, in particular, the health food movement against our highly technological society. As products of our industrialized way of life, certain foods are unnatural; they produce illness by working against the body. Consistent with this view is the idea that healing, like eating, should proceed in harmony with nature. The assumption is that the body, if allowed to function naturally, will tend to heal itself. Orthodox medicine, on the other hand, with its drugs and surgery and its non-holistic approach to health, works against the body. Physicians are frequently criticized in the literature of the movement for their narrow approach to medical problems, reliance on drugs and surgery, lack of knowledge of nutrition, and unwillingness to accept the validity of the patient's own experience in healing himself. It is believed that doctors may actually cause further health problems rather than effecting a cure. A short item in *Prevention*, "The Delivery Is Normal—But the Baby Isn't," recounts an incident in which drug-induced labor in childbirth resulted in a mentally retarded baby. The conclusion is "nature does a good job—and we should not, without compelling reasons, try to take over" (*Prevention*, May 1979: 38).

The healing process is hastened by natural substances, such as healthful food, and by other "natural" therapeutic measures such as exercise. Vitamins are also very important to many health food people, both for maintaining health and for healing. They are seen as components of food which work with the body and are believed to offer a more natural mode of healing than drugs. Vitamins, often one of the most prominent products offered in many health food stores, provide the greatest source of profit (Hongladarom 1976).

A basic assumption of the movement is that certain foods are good for you while others are not. The practitioner of a health food way of life must learn to distinguish between two kinds of food: those which promote well-being ("health foods") and those which are believed to be detrimental to health ("junk foods"). The former are the only kind of food a person should consume, while the latter are the antithesis of all that food should be and must be avoided. The qualities of these foods may be described by two anthropological concepts, *mana* and *taboo*. Mana is a type of beneficial or valuable power which can pass to individuals from sacred objects through touch (or, in the case of health foods, by ingestion). Taboo, on the other hand, refers to power that is dangerous; objects which are taboo can injure those who touch them (Wallace 1966: 60–61). Not all foods fall clearly into one category or the other. However, those foods which are seen as having health-giving qualities, which contain *mana*, symbolize life, while *taboo* foods symbolize death. ("Junk food is . . . dead. . . . Dead food produces death," proclaims one health food manual [Kline 1978: 2–4].) Much of the space in health food publications is devoted to

telling the reader why to consume certain foods and avoid others ("Frozen, Creamed Spinach: Nutritional Disaster," *Prevention*, May 1979; "Let's Sprout Some Seeds," *Better Nutrition*, September 1979).

Those foods in the health food category which are deemed to possess an especially high level of *mana* have come to symbolize the movement as a whole. Foods such as honey, wheat germ, yogurt, and sprouts are seen as representative of the general way of life which health food adherents advocate, and Kandel and Pelto found that certain health food followers attribute mystical powers to the foods they consume. Raw food eaters speak of the "life energy" in uncooked foods. Sprout eaters speak of their food's "growth force" (1980: 336).

Qualities such as color and texture are also important in determining health foods and may acquire symbolic value. "Wholeness" and "whole grain" have come to stand for healthfulness and have entered the jargon of the advertising industry. Raw, coarse, dark, crunchy, and cloudy foods are preferred over those which are cooked, refined, white, soft, and clear. (See chart.)

Thus dark bread is preferred over white, raw milk over pasteurized, brown rice over white. The convert must learn to eat foods which at first seem strange and even exotic and to reject many foods which are components of the Standard American diet. A McDonald's hamburger, for example, which is an important symbol of America itself (Kottack 1978), falls into the category of "junk food" and must be rejected.

Just as the magazines and books which articulate the principles of the health food movement and serve as a guide to the convert can be said to comprise the sacred writings of the movement, so the health food store or health food restaurant is the temple where the purity of the movement is guarded and maintained. There individuals find for sale the types of food and other substances advocated by the movement. One does not expect to find items of questionable purity, that is, substances which are not natural or which may be detrimental to health. Within the precincts of the temple adherents can feel safe from the contaminating forces of the larger society, can meet fellow devotees, and can be instructed by the guardians of the sacred area (see, for example, Hongladarom 1976). Health food stores may vary in their degree

HEALTH FOOD WORLD VIEW

	Health Foods	Junk Foods	
cosmic oppositions basic values and desirable attributes	LIFE NATURE holistic, organic harmony with body and nature natural and real harmony, self- sufficiency, independence homemade, small scale layman competence and understanding	DEATH CULTURE fragmented, mechanistic working against body and nature manufactured and artificial disharmony, dependence mass-produced professional esoteric knowledge and jargon	undesirable attributes
beneficial qualities of food	whole coarse dark crunchy raw cloudy	processed refined white soft cooked clear	harmful qualities
specific foods with mana	yogurt* honey* carob soybeans* sprouts* fruit juices herb teas foods from other cultures: humus, falafel, kefir, tofu, stir-fried vegetables, pita bread	ice cream, candy sugar* chocolate beef overcooked vegetables soft drinks* coffee,* tea "all-American" foods: hot dogs, McDonald's hamburgers,* potato chips, Coke	specific taboo foods
	return to early American values, "real" American way of life	corruption of this original and better way of life and values	

* Denotes foods with especially potent mana or taboo.

of purity. Some sell items such as coffee, raw sugar, or "natural" ice cream which are considered questionable by others of the faith. (One health food store I visited had a sign explaining that it did not sell vitamin supplements, which it considered to be "unnatural," i.e., impure.)

People in other places are often viewed as living more "naturally" and healthfully than contemporary Americans. Observation of such peoples may be used to confirm practices of the movement and to acquire ideas about food. Healthy and long-lived people like the Hunza of the Himalayas are studied to determine the secrets of their strength and longevity. Cultures as yet untainted by the food systems of industrialized nations are seen as examples of what better diet can do. In addition, certain foods from other cultures—foods such as humus, falafel, and tofu—have been adopted into the health food repertoire because of their presumed healthful qualities.

Peoples of other times can also serve as models for a more healthful way of life. There is in the health food movement a concept of a "golden age," a past which provides an authority for a better way of living. This past may be scrutinized for clues about how to improve contemporary American society. An archaeologist, writing for *Prevention* magazine, recounts how "I Put Myself on a Cave-man Diet—Permanently" (*Prevention*, September 1979). His article explains how he improved his health by utilizing the regular exercise and simpler foods which he had concluded from his research were probably characteristic of our prehistoric ancestors. A general nostalgia about the past seems to exist in the health food movement, along with the feeling that we have departed from a more natural pattern of eating practiced by earlier generations of Americans (see, for example, Hongladarom 1976). (Sylvester Graham, however, presumably did not find the eating habits of his contemporaries to be very admirable.)

The health food movement is concerned with more than the achievement of bodily health. Nutritional problems are often seen as being at the root of emotional, spiritual, and even social problems. An article entitled "Sugar Neurosis" states "Hypoglycemia (low blood sugar) is a medical reality that can trigger wife-beating, divorce, even suicide" (*Prevention*, April 1979: 110). Articles and books claim to show the reader how to overcome depression through vitamins and nutrition and the movement promises happiness and psychological well-being as well as physical health. Social problems, too, may respond to the health food approach. For example, a probation officer recounts how she tried changing offenders' diets in order to change their behavior. Testimonials from two of the individuals helped tell "what it was like to find that good nutrition was their bridge from the wrong side of the law and a frustrated, unhappy life to a vibrant and useful one" (*Prevention*, May 1978: 56). Thus, through more healthful eating and a more natural life-style, the health food movement offers its followers what many religions offer: salvation—in this case salvation for the body, for the psyche, and for society.

Individual effort is the keystone of the health food movement. An individual can take responsibility for his or her own health and does not need to rely on professional medical practitioners. The cor-

ollary of this is that it is a person's own behavior which may be the cause of ill health. By sinning, by not listening to our bodies, and by not following a natural way of life, we bring our ailments upon ourselves.

The health food movement also affirms the validity of each individual's experience. No two individuals are alike: needs for different vitamins vary widely; some people are more sensitive to food additives than others; each person has his or her best method of achieving happiness. Therefore, the generalized expertise of professionals and the scientifically verifiable findings of the experts may not be adequate guides for you, the individual, in the search of health. Each person's experience has meaning; if something works for you, then it works. If it works for others also, so much the better, but if it does not, that does not invalidate your own experience. While the movement does not by any means disdain all scientific findings (and indeed they are used extensively when they bolster health food positions), such findings are not seen as the only source of confirmation for the way of life which the health food movement advocates, and the scientific establishment itself tends to be suspect.

In line with its emphasis on individual responsibility for health, the movement seeks to deprofessionalize knowledge and place in every individual's hands the information and means to heal. Drugs used by doctors are usually available only through prescription, but foods and vitamins can be obtained by anyone. Books, magazines, and health food store personnel seek to educate their clientele in ways of healing themselves and maintaining their own health. Articles explain bodily processes, the effects of various substances on health, and the properties of foods and vitamins.

The focus on individual responsibility is frequently tied to a wider concern for self-sufficiency and self-reliance. Growing your own organic garden, grinding your own flour, or even, as one pamphlet suggests, raising your own cow are not simply ways that one can be assured of obtaining healthful food; they are also expressions of independence and self-reliance. Furthermore, such practices are seen as characteristic of an earlier "golden age" when people lived natural lives. For example, an advertisement for vitamins appearing in a digest distributed in health food stores shows a mother and daughter kneading bread together. The heading reads "America's discovering basics." The copy goes on, "Baking bread at home has been a basic family practice throughout history. The past several decades, however, have seen a shift in the American diet to factory-produced breads. . . . Fortunately, today there are signs that more and more Americans are discovering the advantage of baking bread themselves." Homemade bread, home-canned produce, sprouts growing on the window sill symbolize what are felt to be basic American values, values supposedly predominant in earlier times when people not only lived on self-sufficient farms and produced their own fresh and more natural food, but also stood firmly on their own two feet and took charge of their own lives. A reader writing to *Prevention* praises an article about a man who found "new life at ninety without lawyers or doctors," saying "If that isn't the optimum in the American way of living, I can't imagine what is!" (*Prevention*, May 1978: 16). Thus although it criticizes the contemporary American way of life (and although some vegetarians turn to Eastern religions for guidance—see Kandel and Pelto 1980), the health food movement in general claims to be the true faith, the proponent of basic American-ness, a faith from which the society as a whole has strayed.

Social Significance of the Health Food Movement for American Actors

Being a "health food person" involves more than simply changing one's diet or utilizing an alternative medical system. Kandel and Pelto suggest that the health food movement derives much of its popularity from the fact that "food may be used simultaneously to cure or prevent illness, as a religious symbol and to forge social bonds. Frequently health food users are trying to improve their health, their lives, and sometimes the world as well" (1980: 332). Use of health foods becomes an affirmation of certain values and a commitment to a certain world view. A person who becomes involved in the health food movement might be said to experience what anthropologist Anthony F. C. Wallace has called "mazeway resynthesis." The "mazeway" is the mental "map" or image of the world which each individual holds. It includes val-

ues, the environment and the objects in it, the image of the self and of others, the techniques one uses to manipulate the environment to achieve desired end states (Wallace 1966: 237). Resynthesis of this mazeway—that is, the creation of new "maps," values, and techniques—commonly occurs in times of religious revitalization, when new religious movements are begun and converts to them are made. As individuals, these converts learn to view the world in a new manner and to act accordingly. In the case of the health food movement, those involved learn to see their health problems and other dissatisfactions with their lives as stemming from improper diet and living in disharmony with nature. They are provided with new values, new ways of viewing their environment, and new techniques for achieving their goals. For such individuals, health food use can come to imply "a major redefinition of self-image, role, and one's relationship to others" (Kandel and Pelto 1980: 359). The world comes to "make sense" in the light of this new world view. Achievement of the desired end states of better health and an improved outlook on life through following the precepts of the movement gives further validation.

It is this process which gives the health food movement some of the overtones of a religion. As does any new faith, the movement criticizes the prevailing social values and institutions, in this case the health-threatening features of modern industrial society. While an individual's initial dissatisfaction with prevailing beliefs and practices may stem from experiences with the conventional medical system (for example, failure to find a solution to a health problem through visits to a physician), this dissatisfaction often comes to encompass other facets of the American way of life. This further differentiates the "health food person" from mainstream American society (even when the difference is justified as a return to "real" American values).

In everyday life the consumption of such substances as honey, yogurt, and wheat germ, which have come to symbolize the health food movement, does more than contribute to health. It also serves to represent commitment to the health food world view. Likewise, avoiding those substances, such as sugar and white bread, which are considered "evil" is also a mark of a health food person. Ridding the kitchen of such items—a move often advocated by articles advising readers on how to "convert" successfully to health foods—is an act of ritual as well as practical significance. The symbolic nature of such foods is confirmed by the reactions of outsiders to those who are perceived as being inside the movement. An individual who is perceived as being a health food person is often automatically assumed to use honey instead of sugar, for example. Conversely, if one is noticed using or not using certain foods (e.g., adding wheat germ to food, not eating white sugar), this can lead to questions from the observer as to whether or not that individual is a health food person (or a health food "nut," depending upon the questioner's own orientation).

The symbolic nature of such foods is especially important for the health food neophyte. The adoption of a certain way of eating and the renunciation of mainstream cultural food habits can constitute "bridge-burning acts of commitment" (Kendel and Pelto 1980: 395), which function to cut the individual off from previous patterns of behavior. However, the symbolic activity which indicates this cutting off need not be as radical as a total change of eating habits. In an interview in *Prevention*, a man who runs a health-oriented television program recounted an incident in which a viewer called up after a show and announced excitedly that he had changed his whole life-style—he had started using honey in his coffee! (*Prevention*, February 1979: 89). While recognizing the absurdity of the action on a practical level, the program's host acknowledged the symbolic importance of this action to the person involved. He also saw it as a step in the right direction since one change can lead to another. Those who sprinkle wheat germ on cereal, toss alfalfa sprouts with a salad, or pass up an ice cream cone for yogurt are not only demonstrating a concern for health but also affirming their commitment to a particular life-style and symbolizing adherence to a set of values and a world view.

Conclusion

As this analysis has shown, health foods are more than simply a way of eating and more than an alternative healing system. If we return to Clifford Geertz's definition of religion as a "system of symbols" which produces "powerful, pervasive, and long-lasting moods and motivations" by "formulating conceptions of a general order of existence" and making them appear "uniquely realistic," we see that the health food movement definitely has a religious dimension. There is, first, a system of symbols, in this case based on certain kinds and qualities of food. While the foods are believed to have health-giving properties in themselves, they also symbolize a world view which is concerned with the right way to live one's life and the right way to construct a society. This "right way" is based on an approach to life which stresses harmony with nature and the holistic nature of the body. Consumption of those substances designated as "health foods," as well as participation in other activities associated with the movement which also symbolize its world view (such as exercising or growing an organic garden) can serve to establish the "moods and motivations" of which Geertz speaks. The committed health food follower may come to experience a sense of spiritual as well as physical well-being when he or she adheres to the health food way of life. Followers are thus motivated to persist in this way of life, and they come to see the world view of this movement as correct and "realistic."

In addition to its possession of sacred symbols and its "convincing" world view, the health food movement also has other elements which we usually associate with a religion. Concepts of mana and taboo guide the choice of foods. There is a distinction between the pure and impure and a concern for the maintenance of purity. There are "temples" (health food stores and other such establishments) which are expected to maintain purity within their confines. There are "rabbis," or experts in the "theology" of the movement and its application to everyday life. There are sacred and instructional writings which set out the principles of the movement and teach followers how to utilize them. In addition, like many religious movements, the health food movement harkens back to a "golden age" which it seeks to recreate and assumes that many of the ills of the contemporary world are caused by society's departure from this ideal state.

Individuals entering the movement, like individuals entering any religious movement, may undergo a process of conversion. This can be dramatic, resulting from the cure of an illness or the reversal of a previous state of poor health, or it can be gradual, a step-by-step changing of eating and other habits through exposure to health food doctrine. Individuals who have undergone conversion and mazeway resynthesis, as well as those who have tested and confirmed various aspects of the movement's prescriptions for better health and a better life, may give testimonials to the faith. For those who have adopted, in full or in part, the health food world view, it provides, as do all religions, explanations for existing conditions, answers to specific problems, and a means of gaining control over one's existence. Followers of the movement are also promised "salvation," not in the form of afterlife, but in terms of enhanced physical well-being, greater energy, longer life-span, freedom from illness, and increased peace of mind. However, although the focus is this-worldly, there is a spiritual dimension to the health food movement. And although it does not center its world view around belief in supernatural beings, it does posit a higher authority—the wisdom of nature—as the source of ultimate legitimacy for its views.

Health food people are often dismissed as "nuts" or "food faddists" by those outside the movement. Such a designation fails to recognize the systematic nature of the health food world view, the symbolic significance of health foods, and the important functions which the movement performs for its followers. Health foods offer an alternative or supplement to conventional medical treatment, and a meaningful and effective way for individuals to bring about changes in lives which are perceived as unsatisfactory because of poor physical and emotional health. It can also provide for its followers a framework of meaning which transcends individual problems. In opposing itself to the predominant American life-style, the health food movement sets up a symbolic system which opposes harmony to disharmony, purity to pollution, nature to culture, and ultimately, as in many religions, life to death. Thus while foods are the beginning point and the most important symbols of the health food movement, food is not the ultimate focus but rather a means to an end: the organization of a meaningful world view and the construction of a satisfying life.

Body Ritual Among the Nacirema

Horace Miner

This article is a classic of anthropological literature. In it Horace Miner gives readers a thorough and exciting ethnographic account of the myriad of taboos and ceremonial behaviors that permeate the everyday activities of the members of a magic-ridden society. Focusing on secret rituals that are believed to prevent disease while simultaneously beautifying the body, Miner demonstrates the importance of ceremonial specialists such as the "holy-mouth-men" and the "listeners" in directing even the most routine aspects of daily life among the Nacirema.

Reproduced by permission of the American Anthropological Association from *American Anthropologist*, Vol. 58 (1956), pp. 503–507. Not for further reproduction.

THE ANTHROPOLOGIST HAS BECOME SO FAMILIAR with the diversity of ways in which different peoples behave in similar situations that he is not apt to be surprised by even the most exotic customs. In fact, if all of the logically possible combinations of behavior have not been found somewhere in the world, he is apt to suspect that they must be present in some yet undescribed tribe. This point has, in fact, been expressed with respect to clan organization by Murdock (1949: 71). In this light, the magical beliefs and practices of the Nacirema present such unusual aspects that it seems desirable to describe them as an example of the extremes to which human behavior can go.

Professor Linton first brought the ritual of the Nacirema to the attention of anthropologists twenty years ago (1936: 326), but the culture of this people is still very poorly understood. They are a North American group living in the territory between the Canadian Cree, the Yaqui and Tarahumare of Mexico, and the Carib and Arawak of the Antilles. Little is known of their origin, though tradition states that they came from the east. According to Nacirema mythology, their nation was originated by a culture hero, Notgnishaw, who is otherwise known for two great feats of strength—the throwing of a piece of wampum across the river Pa-To-Mac and the chopping down of a cherry tree in which the Spirit of Truth resided.

Nacirema culture is characterized by a highly developed market economy which has evolved in a rich natural habitat. While much of the people's time is devoted to economic pursuits, a large part of the fruits of these labors and a considerable portion of the day are spent in ritual activity. The focus of this activity is the human body, the appearance and health of which loom as a dominant concern in the ethos of the people. While such a concern is certainly not unusual, its ceremonial aspects and associated philosophy are unique.

The fundamental belief underlying the whole system appears to be that the human body is ugly and that its natural tendency is to debility and disease. Incarcerated in such a body, man's only hope is to avert these characteristics through the use of the powerful influences of ritual and ceremony. Every household has one or more shrines devoted to this purpose. The more powerful individuals in the society have several shrines in their houses and, in fact, the opulence of a house is often referred to in terms of the number of such ritual centers it possesses. Most houses are of wattle and daub construction, but the shrine rooms of the more wealthy are walled with stone. Poorer families imitate the rich by applying pottery plaques to their shrine walls.

While each family has at least one such shrine, the rituals associated with it are not family ceremonies but are private and secret. The rites are normally only discussed with children, and then only during the period when they are being initiated into these mysteries. I was able, however, to establish sufficient rapport with the natives to examine these shrines and to have the rituals described to me.

The focal point of the shrine is a box or chest which is built into the wall. In this chest are kept the many charms and magical potions without which no native believes he could live. These preparations are secured from a variety of specialized practitioners. The most powerful of these are the medicine men, whose assistance must be rewarded with substantial gifts. However, the medicine men do not provide the curative potions for their clients, but decide what the ingredients should be and then write them down in an ancient and secret language. This writing is understood only by the medicine men and by the herbalists who, for another gift, provide the required charm.

The charm is not disposed of after it has served its purpose, but is placed in the charm-box of the household shrine. As these magical materials are specific for certain ills, and the real or imagined maladies of the people are many, the charm-box is usually full to overflowing. The magical packets are so numerous that people forget what their purposes were and fear to use them again. While the natives are very vague on this point, we can only

assume that the idea in retaining all the old magical materials is that their presence in the charm-box, before which the body rituals are conducted, will in some way protect the worshipper.

Beneath the charm-box is a small font. Each day every member of the family, in succession, enters the shrine room, bows his head before the charm-box, mingles different sorts of holy water in the font, and proceeds with a brief rite of ablution. The holy waters are secured from the Water Temple of the community, where the priests conduct elaborate ceremonies to make the liquid ritually pure.

In the hierarchy of magical practitioners, and below the medicine men in prestige, are specialists whose designation is best translated ''holy-mouth-men.'' The Nacirema have an almost pathological horror and fascination with the mouth, the condition of which is believed to have a supernatural influence on all social relationships. Were it not for the rituals of the mouth, they believe that their teeth would fall out, their gums bleed, their jaws shrink, their friends desert them, and their lovers reject them. (They also believe that a strong relationship exists between oral and moral characteristics. For example, there is a ritual ablution of the mouth for children which is supposed to improve their moral fiber.)

The daily body ritual performed by everyone includes a mouth-rite. Despite the fact that these people are so punctilious about care of the mouth, this rite involves a practice which strikes the uninitiated stranger as revolting. It was reported to me that the ritual consists of inserting a small bundle of hog hairs into the mouth, along with certain magical powders, and then moving the bundle in a highly formalized series of gestures.

In addition to the private mouth-rite, the people seek out a holy-mouth-man once or twice a year. These practitioners have an impressive set of paraphernalia, consisting of a variety of augers, awls, probes, and prods. The use of these objects in the exorcism of the evils of the mouth involves almost unbelievable ritual torture of the client. The holy-mouth-man opens the client's mouth and, using the above-mentioned tools, enlarges any holes which decay may have created in the teeth. Magical materials are put into these holes. If there are no naturally occurring holes in the teeth, large sections of one or more teeth are gouged out so that the supernatural substance can be applied. In the client's view, the purpose of these ministrations is to arrest decay and to draw friends. The extremely sacred and traditional character of the rite is evident in the fact that the natives return to the holy-mouth-men year after year, despite the fact that their teeth continue to decay.

It is to be hoped that, when a thorough study of the Nacirema is made, there will be a careful inquiry into the personality structure of these people. One has but to watch the gleam in the eye of a holy-mouth-man, as he jabs an awl into an exposed nerve, to suspect that a certain amount of sadism is involved. If this can be established, a very interesting pattern emerges, for most of the population shows definite masochistic tendencies. It was to these that Professor Linton referred in discussing a distinctive part of the daily body ritual which is performed only by men. This part of the rite involves scraping and lacerating the surface of the face with a sharp instrument. Special women's rites are performed only four times during each lunar month, but what they lack in frequency is made up in barbarity. As part of this ceremony, women bake their heads in small ovens for about an hour. The theoretically interesting point is that what seems to be a preponderantly masochistic people have developed sadistic specialists.

The medicine men have an imposing temple, or latipso, in every community of any size. The more elaborate ceremonies required to treat very sick patients can only be performed at this temple. These ceremonies involve not only the thaumaturge but a permanent group of vestal maidens who move sedately about the temple chambers in distinctive costume and headdress.

The latipso ceremonies are so harsh that it is phenomenal that a fair proportion of the really sick natives who enter the temple ever recover. Small children whose indoctrination is still incomplete have been known to resist attempts to take them to the temple because "that is where you go to die." Despite this fact, sick adults are not only willing but eager to undergo the protracted ritual purification, if they can afford to do so. No matter how ill the supplicant or how grave the emergency, the guardians of many temples will not admit a client if he cannot give a rich gift to the custodian. Even after one has gained admission and survived the ceremonies, the guardians will not permit the neophyte to leave until he makes still another gift.

The supplicant entering the temple is first stripped of all his or her clothes. In every-day life the Nacirema avoids exposure of his body and its natural functions. Bathing and excretory acts are performed only in the secrecy of the household shrine, where they are ritualized as part of the body-rites. Psychological shock results from the fact that body secrecy is suddenly lost upon entry into the latipso. A man, whose own wife has never seen him in an excretory act, suddenly finds himself naked and assisted by a vestal maiden while he performs his natural functions into a sacred vessel. This sort of ceremonial treatment is necessitated by the fact that the excreta are used by a diviner to ascertain the course and nature of the client's sickness. Female clients, on the other hand, find their naked bodies are subjected to the scrutiny, manipulation, and prodding of the medicine men.

Few supplicants in the temple are well enough to do anything but lie on their hard beds. The daily ceremonies, like the rites of the holy-mouth-men, involve discomfort and torture. With ritual precision, the vestals awaken their miserable charges each dawn and roll them about on their beds of pain while performing ablutions, in the formal movements of which the maidens are highly trained. At other times they insert magic wands in the supplicant's mouth or force him to eat substances which are supposed to be healing. From time to time the medicine men come to their clients and jab magically treated needles into their flesh. The fact that these temple ceremonies may not cure, and may even kill the neophyte, in no way decreases the people's faith in the medicine men.

There remains one other kind of practitioner, known as a "listener." This witch-doctor has the power to exorcise the devils that lodge in the heads of people who have been bewitched. The Nacirema believe that parents bewitch their own children. Mothers are particularly suspected of putting a curse on children while teaching them the secret body rituals. The counter-magic of the witch-doctor is unusual in its lack of ritual. The patient simply tells the "listener" all his troubles and fears, beginning with the earliest difficulties he can remember. The memory displayed by the Nacirema in these exorcism sessions is truly remarkable. It is not uncommon for the patient to bemoan the rejection he felt upon being weaned as a babe, and a few individuals even see their troubles going back to the traumatic effects of their own birth.

In conclusion, mention must be made of certain practices which have their base in native esthetics but which depend upon the pervasive aversion to the natural body and its functions. There are ritual fasts to make fat people thin and ceremonial feasts to make thin people fat. Still other rites are used to make women's breasts large if they are small, and smaller if they are large. General dissatisfaction with breast shape is symbolized in the fact that the ideal form is virtually outside the range of human variation. A few women afflicted with almost inhuman hyper-mammary development are so idolized that they make a handsome living by simply going from village to village and permitting the natives to stare at them for a fee.

Reference has already been made to the fact that excretory functions are ritualized, routinized, and relegated to secrecy. Natural reproductive functions are similarly distorted. Intercourse is taboo as a topic and scheduled as an act. Efforts are made to avoid pregnancy by the use of magical materials or by limiting intercourse to certain phases of the moon. Conception is actually very infrequent. When pregnant, women dress so as to hide their condition. Parturition takes place in secret, without friends or relatives to assist, and the majority of women do not nurse their infants.

Our review of the ritual life of the Nacirema has certainly shown them to be a magic-ridden people. It is hard to understand how they have managed to exist so long under the burdens which they have imposed upon themselves. But even such exotic customs as these take on real meaning when they are viewed with the insight provided by Malinowski when he wrote (1948: 70):

> Looking from far and above, from our high places of safety in the developed civilization, it is easy to see all the crudity and irrelevance of magic. But without its power and guidance early man could not have mastered his practical difficulties as he has done, nor could man have advanced to the higher stages of civilization.

3

Shamans, Priests, and Prophets

In Chapters 1 and 2 the reader was introduced to the anthropological approach to the study of religion and to the complex variety of symbols, rites, ceremonies, and belief structures that constitute the heart of supernatural belief systems everywhere. We now turn to the role and place of the supernatural leader. Where and how do religious leaders get their power? What is the distinction between a shaman and a priest, or a prophet and a priest? How do sorcerers, diviners, and magicians differ? In short, this chapter introduces the topic of religious specialists.

Any member of society may approach the supernatural on an individual basis; for example, a person may kneel to the ground, all alone, and recite a prayer for help from the spiritual world. But the religions of the world, whether small animistic cults or the "great faiths," also have intermediaries: religious people who, acting as part-time or full-time specialists, intervene on behalf of an individual client or an entire community. Paul Radin (1937: 107) argued that the development of religion can be traced to the social roles undertaken by each of these "priest-thinkers"—at once, a philosopher of religion, a theologian of

Eskimo mask, Ingalik, Alaska.

beliefs, a person who is the recognized master of worship.

If all religions appear to have specialists, anthropologists have also found that some societies place more emphasis on these religious experts than others do. Robert Textor has noted, for example, that the societies that are more likely to have religious specialists tend to produce food rather than collect it, use money as a medium of exchange, and display different social classes and a complex political system (1967). In other words, the more complex the society, the greater is the likelihood of having religious intermediaries.

Early anthropologists were drawn to the view of unilineal evolution: how institutions progressed from savagery to barbarism, finally achieving a civilized state. As societies advance, all institutions become more complex and specialized. In his classic work *Primitive Culture* (1871), E. B. Tylor posited an early definition of religion that prompted his colleagues to concern themselves with religious specialization. Describing religion as the belief in spiritual beings, what he called "animism," Tylor implied that a society's degree of religious specialization was directly related to its position on the evolutionary scale. Unilineal evolutionary theory was pockmarked with faulty premises, of course: although cultures do evolve, they do not necessarily follow a prescribed series of stages. What is important to note here, however, is that Tylor and his contemporaries began to look carefully at religious specialization and categories of religious phenomena. J. G. Frazer, in the *Golden Bough* (1890), distinguished between magic and religion and described the role of specialists. And Herbert Spencer's approach, in the *Principles of Sociology* (1896), that religious stages could only be comprehended if the functions of religion and the interrelationships of religion with other institutions were known, demanded that religious specialization be studied in terms of its functions in society—an approach that anthropologists still adhere to today. Anthropological data have shown the importance of shamans, priests, prophets, and other specialists to the maintenance of economic, political, social, and educational institutions of their societies.

The anthropological literature devoted to religious specialists is extensive; much work remains, however, to adequately define and distinguish between the actual functions they perform for members of their societies. Shamans, for example, have duties and religious obligations that differ from society to society, although their basic duty of curing through the use of the supernatural is accepted by anthropologists. The same kinds of differences exist in the tasks performed by prophets, priests, sorcerers, and others designated as "intermediaries" with the supernatural. Without a clear understanding of these distinctions, systematic cross-cultural comparisons would be impossible. Differentiation of specialists through an analysis of their functions tells anthropologists a great deal about the structure of society.

In addition to the definitional problem associated with specialists, anthropologists must also determine whether or not to place the tasks performed by these experts under the rubric of "the religious" or to create other categories for such activities. Is the performance of magic, witchcraft, and sorcery "religious" behavior, or are these examples of non-religious, indeed anti-religious acts? If those who practice these acts are outside the religious realm, then what, if any, connection do they have with the sacred? The real question becomes, What is religion? In Western culture witchcraft, magic, and sorcery are assigned to the occult and are considered outside of and, ordinarily, counter to religion. In the non-Western world, however, specialists who take part in these kinds of activities are often considered to be important parts of the total religious belief system. It is a common view in Africa south of the Sahara that people are often designated witches by God, and that sorcerers and magicians receive their power from the spirit world, that is, from supernatural agencies controlled by God. In these terms, is drawing upon supernatural aid from shamans, priests, or prophets more "religious" than turning to magicians, sorcerers, and other specialists who also call upon supernatural agents but for different ends? In light of these questions, anthropologists have found it necessary to consider all specialists whose power emanates from supernatural agents and power to be in the realm of the religious, although some specialists serve while others harm society through their actions.

Because not all societies contain identical

religious specialists, determining why certain specialists exist and others do not is important to our understanding both of the structure of a society and its supernatural world, and of the causal forces behind good and bad fortune. In societies where witches do not exist, for example, it is frequently malicious ghosts or ancestors who are believed to bring misfortune and illness. In such cases elders may play an important role as diviners, in contrast to the diviner specialists that exist in other groups. Such data not only aid our understanding of supernatural causation and specialization but also demonstrate the connection between the social structure of the living—the position of the elder in society—and that of the ancestor or ghost in the afterworld. The example of the elder as religious specialist is problematic in some societies. Eugene Mendonsa, in speaking of the Sisala of Ghana, for example, makes clear that not all elders have the ability to divine and those who can are only specialists in a part-time sense (1976).

The difficulty inherent in making distinctions among non-Western specialists may be further realized by considering the position of the religious lay person in this country. Although not a specialist in the traditional sense, this individual is nevertheless more involved and usually more knowledgeable than the typical church member. Is the lay person significantly different from one of the more traditional part-time specialists? Immediately, the problem of the degree of participation comes to mind—part-time versus full-time—accompanied by the complicating factor of training—formal versus "on-the-job" learning. Making distinctions such as these is an important part of analytic accounts of religious functionaries.

The four excellent articles that follow tell us much about the religious specialist. Victor Turner's lead-off essay provides a broad-spectrum account of the various specialists who appear in ethnographic descriptions of religions around the world. Next, C. Von Furer-Haimendorf delineates the role of priests, and William Howells discusses the positive functions offered by Siberian shamans to the societies they serve. Shamanistic leadership, the result of psychological and physiological aid given their followers, is also based on their control of malevolent powers that can be dangerous to the people. But these powers, for good or evil, contribute to the awe in which the shaman is held. How does trickery assist the shaman? Do shamans really believe they have the power to cure? Or is shamanism a charlatan's game?

References

Frazer, J. G.
   1890 *The Golden Bough*. London: MacMillan.

Mendonsa, Eugene L.
   1976 "Characteristics of Sisala Diviners." In *The Realm of the Extra-Human: Agents and Audiences*, pp. 179–95. World Anthropology Series, ed. Agehananda Bharati. The Hague: Mouton Publishers.

Radin, Paul
   1937 *Primitive Religion: Its Nature and Origin*. New York: Dover Publications.

Spencer, H.
   1896 *Principles of Sociology*. New York: D. Appleton.

Textor, Robert
   1967 *A Cross-Cultural Summary*. New Haven: HRAF Press.

Tylor, E. B.
   1871 *Primitive Culture: Researches into the Development of Mythology, Philosophy, Religion, Language, Art and Custom*.

Religious Specialists
Victor W. Turner

Noted for his specialization in the study of symbolism and symbolic behavior, Victor Turner here presents an outstanding general discussion of religious specialists and lays the groundwork for the more specialized articles to follow, which deal specifically with shamans, priests, and prophets. Turner not only deals with these avocations but includes other, less prominent but often equally important religious specialists—diviners, seers, mediums, witches, sorcerers, and magicians. Unlike many theorists of the past, Turner stresses that all should be included under the umbrella of the term "religion," for all, in special ways, manipulate the supernatural to their own or society's ends.

Turner's is no small theoretical accomplishment, for controversy over the definition of the term "religion" has long occupied anthropologists. His discussion illuminates the subtle but important differences among specialists, without which religions of the non-Western world would remain unintelligible.

Reprinted by permission of the publisher from the *International Encyclopedia of the Social Sciences*, David L. Sills, Editor. Vol. 13, pp. 437–44. Copyright © 1972 by Crowell Collier and Macmillan.

A RELIGIOUS SPECIALIST IS ONE WHO DEVOTES himself to a particular branch of religion or, viewed organizationally, of a religious system. "Religion" is a multivocal term whose range of meanings varies in different social and historical contexts. Nevertheless, most definitions of religion refer to the recognition of a transhuman controlling power that may be either personal or impersonal. A religious specialist has a culturally defined status relevant to this recognition. In societies or contexts where such power is regarded as impersonal, anthropologists customarily describe it as *magic*, and those who manipulate the power are magicians. Wherever power is personalized, as deity, gods, spirits, daemons, genii, ancestral shades, ghosts, or the like, anthropologists speak of *religion*. In reality, religious systems contain both magical and religious beliefs and procedures: in many of them the impersonal transhuman (or mystical, or non-empirical, or supernatural) power is considered to be a devolution of personal power, as in the case of the mystical efficacy of rites established *in illo tempore* by a deity or divinized ancestor.

Priest and Prophet

Scholars have tended to distinguish between two polarities of religious specialization. Max Weber, for example, although well aware of numerous historical instances of their overlap and interpenetration, contrasts the roles of priest and prophet. He begins by making a preliminary distinction between priest and magician. A priest, he writes, is always associated with "the functioning of a regularly organized and permanent enterprise concerned with influencing the gods—in contrast with the individual and occasional efforts of magicians." Accordingly, the crucial feature of priesthood is that it represents the "specialization of a particular group of persons in the continuous operation of a cultic enterprise, permanently associated with particular norms, places and times, and related to specific social groups." In Weber's view, the prophet is distinguished from the priest by "personal call." The priest's claim to religious authority derives from his service in a sacred tradition; the authority of the prophet is founded on revelation and personal "charisma." This latter term has been variously defined by Weber (in some contexts it seems almost to represent the *Führerprinzip*), but it may broadly be held to designate extraordinary powers. These include, according to Weber, "the capacity to achieve the ecstatic states which are viewed, in accordance with primitive experience, as the preconditions for producing certain effects in meteorology, healing, divination and telepathy." But charisma may be either ascribed or achieved. It may be an inherent faculty ("primary charisma") or it may be "produced artificially in an object or person through some extraordinary means." Charisma may thus be "merited" by fastings, austerities, or other ordeals. Even in such cases, Weber asserts, there must be some dormant capacity in the persons or objects, some "germ" of extraordinary power, already vested in them. The prophet, then, is a "purely individual bearer of charisma," rather than the representative of a sacred tradition. He produces discontinuity in that cultic enterprise which it is the priest's major role to keep "in continuous operation." Weber's prophet feels that he has a "mission" by virtue of which he "proclaims religious doctrine or divine commandment." Weber refuses to distinguish sharply between a "renewer of religion" who preaches "an older revelation, actual or suppositious" and a "founder of religion" who claims to bring completely new "deliverances," for, he says, "the two types merge into one another." In Weber's view, the charisma of a prophet appears to contain, in addition to ecstatic and visionary components, a rational component, for he proclaims "a systematic and distinctively religious ethic based upon a consistent and stable doctrine which purports to be a revelation" [(1922)].

Weber's distinction between priest and prophet has its main relevance in an analytical frame of reference constructed to consider the relationship between religion as "a force for dynamic social change" and religion as "a reinforcement of the stability of societies" (Parsons 1963). It has been found effective by such anthropologists as Evans-Pritchard ([1956] 1962) and Worsley (1957a; 1957b)

who are dealing directly with social transitions and "the prophetic break," or what Parsons calls "the primary decision point [between] a direction which makes for a source of evolutionary change in the . . . established or traditional order, and a direction which tends either to reinforce the established order or at least not to change it drastically" (1963; p. xxix in 1964 edition).

Priest and Shaman

Anthropologists who are less concerned than Weber with the genesis of religions and with internal developments in complex societies or their impact on the "primitive" world are inclined to contrast priest not with prophet but with shaman or spirit medium and to examine the relationship between these statuses as part of the normal working of the religious system in the simpler societies. In their excellently representative *Reader in Comparative Religion* (1958), the editors W. A. Lessa and E. Z. Vogt devote a whole section to this distinction.

Often, where there is a priest the shaman is absent, and vice versa, although both these roles may be found in the same religion, as among the Plains Indians. According to Lowie (1954), a Plains Indian shaman is a ritual practitioner whose status is acquired through a personal communication from a supernatural being, whereas a priest does not necessarily have a face-to-face relationship with the spirit world but must have competence in conducting ritual. Lessa and Vogt ([1958] 1965, p. 410) expand these differences: a shaman's powers come by "divine stroke," a priest's power is inherited or is derived from the body of codified and standardized ritual knowledge that he learns from older priests and later transmits to successors. They find that shamanism tends to predominate in food-gathering cultures, where the shaman most frequently performs a curing rite for the benefit of one or more patients and within the context of an extended family group. Shamanistic rites are "noncalendrical," or contingent upon occasions of mishap and illness. The priest and priestly cult organization are characteristically found in the more structurally elaborated food-producing—usually agricultural—societies, where the more common ceremonial is a public rite performed for the benefit of a whole village or community. Such rites are often calendrical, or performed at critical points in the ecological cycle.

Shaman and Medium

Raymond Firth (1964*a*, p. 638) regards shamanism as itself "that particular form of spirit mediumship in which a specialist (the *shaman*) normally himself a medium, is deemed to exercise developed techniques of control over spirits, sometimes including mastery of spirits believed to be possessing another medium." This definition, like that of Howells (1948), stresses the *control* exercised over spirits. Howells describes the shaman as "bullyragging" gods or spirits and emphasizes his intellectual qualities as a leader. This element of mastery makes the shaman a distinctive type of spirit medium, one who is believed to be "possessed by a spirit (or closely controlled by a spirit) [and who] can serve as a means of communication between other human beings and the spirit world" (Firth 1964*b*, p. 689). The spirit medium per se need not exert mastery; he is rather the vessel or vehicle of the transhuman entity.

Thus, although we sometimes find the two functions of priest and shaman combined in the same individual (Piddington 1950), mediums, shamans, and prophets clearly constitute subtypes of a single type of religious functionary. The priest communicates with transhuman entities through ritual that involves cultural objects and activities. The medium, shaman, and prophet communicate in a person-to-person manner: they are in what Buber (1936) would describe as an I-thou relationship with the deities or spirits. The priest, on the other hand, is in what may be called an I-it relationship with the transhuman. Between the priest and the deity intervenes the institution. Priests may therefore be classified as institutional functionaries in the religious domain, while medium, shaman, and prophet may be regarded as subtypes of inspirational functionaries. This distinction is reflected in characteristically different modes of operation. The priest presides over a rite; the shaman or medium conducts a seance. Symbolic forms associated with these occasions differ correlatively: the symbols of a rite are sensorily perceptible to a congregation and have permanence in that they are culturally transmissible, while those of a seance are mostly in the mind of the entranced functionary as elements of his visions or fantasies and are often generated by and limited to the unique occasion. The inspirational functionary may describe what he has clair-voyantly perceived (or "been shown" as he might put it), but the institutional functionary manipulates symbolic objects with prescribed gestures in full view of this congregation.

Sociocultural Correlates

Since the priest is an actor in a culturally "scripted" drama, it is but rarely that priests become innovators, or "dramatists." If they do assume this role it is mainly as legislative reformers—by altering the details of liturgical procedure—that they do so. If a priest becomes a radical innovator in religion, he is likely to become a prophet to his followers and a heretic to his former superiors. From the priestly viewpoint it is the office, role, and script that are sacred and "charismatic" and not the incumbent of priestly office. The priest is concerned with the conservation and maintenance of a deposit of beliefs and practices handed down as a sacred trust from the founders of the social or religious system. Since its symbols at the semantic level tend to condense the critical values, norms, and principles of the total cultural system into a few sensorily perceptible representations, the sanctification of these symbols is tantamount to a preservative of the entire culture. What the priest is and does keeps cultural change and individual deviation within narrow limits. But the energy and time of the inspirational functionary is less bound up with the maintenance of the total cultural system. His practice has more of an ad hoc flavor; he is more sensitive and responsive than the priest to the private and personal, to the mutable and idiosyncratic. This type of functionary thrives in loosely structured food-gathering cultures, where he deals individually with specific occasions of trouble, or during periods of social turbulence and change, when societal consensus about values is sharply declining and numerically significant classes of persons and social groups are becoming alienated from the orthodox social order. The shaman subtype is completely a part of the cultural system of the food-gatherers; the prophet may well stand outside the cultural system during such a period of decomposition and propose new doctrines, ethics, and even economic values.

The shaman is not a radical or a reformer, since the society he services is traditionally flexible and mobile; the prophet is an innovator and reformer, for he confronts a tightly structured order that is moribund and points the way to religious forms that will either provide an intensified cognitive dynamic for sociocultural change or codify the new moral, ideational, and social structures that have been inarticulately developing.

There are of course significant differences in the scale of the societies in which shaman and prophet operate. The shaman enacts his roles in small-scale, multifunctional communities whose religious life incorporates beliefs in a multitude of deities, daemons, nature spirits, or ancestral shades—societies that Durkheim might have described as possessing mechanical solidarity, low moral density, and segmental organization. The prophet tends to come into his own when the division of labor is critically replacing "mechanical" by "organic" solidarity, when class antagonisms are sharpened, or when small-scale societies are decisively invaded by the powerful personnel, ideas, techniques, and cultural apparatus (including military skills and armaments) of large-scale societies. The shaman deals in a personal and specific way with spirits and lesser deities; the prophet enters into dialogue, on behalf of his whole community, with the Supreme Being or with the major deities of a traditional pantheon, whose tutelary scope embraces large numbers of persons and groups, transcending and transecting their traditional divisions and animosities. Alternatively he communicates with the generalized ancestors or *genii loci*, conceived to be a single anonymous and homogeneous collectivity rather than a structure of known and named shades, each representing a specific segment of society. Whereas the shaman's function is associated with looseness of structure in small-scale societies, the prophet's is linked with loosening of structure in large-scale societies or with incompatibilities of scale in culture-contact situations.

Divination and Religious Specialists

In its strict etymological sense the term "divination" denotes inquiry about future events or matters, hidden or obscure, directed to a deity who, it is believed, will reply through significant tokens. It usually refers to the process of obtaining knowledge of secret or future things by mechanical means or manipulative techniques—a process which may or may not include invoking the aid of non-empirical (transhuman) persons or powers but

does not include the empirical methods of science.

In the analysis of pre-literate societies divination often is concerned with the immediate problems and interests of individuals and subgroups and but seldom with the destinies of tribes and nations. It is this specificity and narrowness of reference that primarily distinguishes divination from prophecy. Nadel (1954, p. 64) has called the kind of guidance it offers "mechanical and of a case-to-case kind." The diviner "can discover and disentangle some of the hidden influences which are at work always and everywhere. . . . He cannot uncover any more embracing design. . . . Yet within the limits set to it divination has a part to play, providing some of the certainty and guidance required for provident action." Thus, although its range and scope are more circumscribed than those of prophecy, divination is believed to reveal what is hidden and in many cases to forecast events, auspicious and inauspicious.

Divination further refers to the analysis of past events, especially untoward events; this analysis often includes the detection and ascription of guilt with regard to their perpetrators, real or alleged. Where such untoward events are attributed to sorcerers and witches the diviner has great freedom of judgment in detecting and determining guilt. Diviners are frequently consulted by victims' relatives and show intuitive and deductive virtuosity in discovering quarrels and grudges in their clients' kin groups and local communities. Social anthropologists find important clues to areas and sources of social strain and to the character and strength of supportive social norms and values in the diviners' diagnoses.

There is evidence that mediums, shamans, and priests in various cultures have practiced divination. The medium and shaman often divine without mechanical means but with the assistance of a tutelary spirit. In the work of Lessa and Vogt there is a translation of a vivid first-person account by a Zulu informant of a diviner's seance. This mediumistic female diviner

> dramatically utilizes some standard procedures of her art—ventriloquism, prior knowledge of the clients, the overhearing of the client's unguarded conversation, and shrewd common sense—to enable her spirits to provide the clients with advice. In this example, . . . a boy is suffering from a convulsive ailment. The spirits discover

that an ancestral spirit is spitefully causing the boy's illness: the spirits decree that the location of the family's village must be moved; a goat must be sacrificed to the ancestor and the goat's bile poured over the boy; the boy must drink *Itongo* medicine. The treatment thus ranges from physical to social actions—from propitiation of wrathful ancestors to prescription of a medicinal potion (Lessa & Vogt [1958] 1965, p. 340).

Similar accounts of shamanistic divinatory seances have been recorded by anthropologists working among North and South American Indians, Eskimos, and Siberian tribes, in many parts of Africa, and among Afro-Americans.

Divination was a function of members of the priesthood in many of the complex religious systems of Polynesia, west Africa, and ancient Mexico; in the religions of Israel, Greece, Etruria, and Rome; in Babylonia, India, China, Japan, and among the Celts. According to Wach,

> The Etruscans made these practices so much a part of their culture that the discipline has been named after them (*disciplina Etrusca* or *auguralis*). Different phenomena and objects were used as media to ascertain the desires of the gods (regular and irregular celestial events, lightning, fire, and earthquakes, the shape or utterances of animals, flights of birds, movements of serpents, barking of dogs, forms of liver or entrails). Both in Etruria and Rome a numerous and well-organized hierarchy of functionaries existed for the practice of the sacred arts (1958, p. 111 in 1961 edition).

Indeed, diffused through the Roman world, many of these techniques passed into medieval and modern culture.

Diviner and Doctor

Callaway's account (1868–1870) of the combined divinatory and curative seance in Zululand emphasizes the close relationship believed to hold in many preliterate societies between the functions of divination and therapy. Sometimes, as in the case cited, the diviner and "doctor" are the same person, but more often the roles are specialized and performed by different individuals. Modern therapy is taking increasingly into account the psychosomatic character of many maladies and the importance of sociological factors in their etiology. In most pre-literate societies bodily symptoms are

regarded as signs that the soul or life principle of the patient is under attack or has been abstracted by spiritual forces or beings. Furthermore, it is widely held that these attacks are motivated by animosities provoked by breaches of cultural, mainly religious, prescriptions and/or breaches of social norms regarded as binding on members of kin groups or local communities. Thus, to acquire a comprehensive understanding of why and how a patient was afflicted with certain symptoms by a spirit or witch, primitives seek out a diviner who will disclose the secret antagonisms in social relations or the perhaps unconscious neglect of ritual rules (always a threat to the cultural order) that incited mystical retribution or malice. The diviner is a "diagnostician" who refers his clients to his colleague, the doctor or "therapist." The doctor in question has both shamanistic and priestly attributes. The division of labor which in more complex societies segregates and institutionalizes the functions of priest and medical man has hardly begun to make its influence felt. The diviner-doctor dichotomy does not depend, as does the priest-shaman dichotomy, upon contrasting roles in regard to the transhuman realm but upon different phases in a social process which involves *total* human phenomena—integral personalities, many psychosomatic complexes, multiple social relationships, and multiform communities.

Modes of Religious Specialization

As the scale and complexity of society increase and the division of labor develops, so too does the degree of religious specialization. This process accompanies a contraction in the domain of religion in social life. As Durkheim stated with typical creative exaggeration in his *Division of Labor in Society* ([1893] 1960, p. 169): "Originally [religion] pervades everything; everything social is religious; the two words are synonymous. Then, little by little, political, economic, scientific functions free themselves from the religious function, constitute themselves a part and take on a more and more acknowledged temporal character."

Simple Societies

In the simplest societies every adult has some religious functions and the elders have most; as their capacity to hunt or garden wanes, their priestlike role comes into ever greater prominence. Women tend to receive more recognition and scope as religious functionaries than in more developed societies. There is some tendency toward religious specialization in such societies, based on a variety of attributes, such as knowledge of herbalistic lore, skill in leechcraft, the capacity to enter a state of trance or dissociation, and sometimes physical handicap that compels a man or woman to find an alternative means of support to subsistence activities. (I have met several diviners in central Africa with maimed hands or amputated limbs.) But such specialization can hardly be defined, in the majority of cases, as more than part-time or even spare-time specialization. Michael Gelfand's description of the Shona *nganga*, variously translated in the ethnographic literature as "medicine man," "doctor," or "witch doctor," exemplifies the socio-cultural situation of similar practitioners in very many pre-literate societies (1964). The Shona *nganga* is at once a herbalist, a medium, and also a diviner who, possessed by a spirit of a dead relative, diagnoses both the cause of illness and of death. Yet, reports Gelfand,

> when he is not engaged in his medical practice he leads exactly the same life as the other men of his village. He cultivates his land, looks after his cattle, repairs his huts, makes blankets or other equipment needed by his family. And the same applies to a woman *nganga*, who busies herself with the tasks expected of every Shona woman. . . . The amount the *nganga* does in his village depends, of course, on the demands of his patients, but on the average he has a fair amount of spare time. . . . A fair guess would be [that there is a *nganga*] to every 800 to 1,000 persons. . . . The *nganga* is given no special status in his village, his chances of being appointed headman are the same as anyone else's (1964, pp. 22–23).

Complex Societies

To bring out best the effects of increase in scale and the division of labor it is necessary to examine religious systems at the opposite end of the gradient of complexity. Religion no longer pervades all social domains; it is limited to its own domain. Furthermore, it has acquired a contractual and associational character; people may choose both the form and extent of their religious participation or may opt out of any affiliation. On the other hand,

within each religious group a considerable amount of specialization has taken place. Much of this has been on the organizational level. Processes of bureaucratization, involving rationality in decision making, relative impersonality in social relations, routinization of tasks, and a hierarchy of authority and function, have produced a large number of types, grades, and ranks of religious specialists in all the major religious systems.

For example, the Catholic clerical hierarchy may be considered as (1) the hierarchy of order, whose powers are exercised in worship and in the administration of the sacraments, and (2) as the hierarchy of jurisdiction, whose power is over the members of the church. Within the hierarchy of jurisdiction alone we find such manifold statuses as pope and bishop (which are held to be of divine institution); cardinal, patriarch, exarch, and primate (whose powers are derived by delegation expressed or implied from the holy see); metropolitan and archbishop (who derive their powers from their patriarch, exarch, or primate); archdeacon, vicar general, vicar forane, rural dean, pastor, and rector (who derive their powers from their diocesan bishop).

In addition to the clerical hierarchy there are in the Catholic church numerous institutes of the religious, that is, societies of men and women approved by ecclesiastical superiors, in which the members in conformity with the special laws of their association take vows, perpetual or temporary, and by this means aspire to religious perfection. This is defined as "the heroic exercise of the virtue of supernatural charity" and is pursued by voluntary maintenance of the vows of poverty, chastity, and obedience, by ascetical practices, through charitable works, such as care of the poor, sick, aged, and mentally handicapped, and by contemplative techniques, such as prayer. Within each religious institution or congregation there is a marked division of function and gradation of office.

Thus there are many differences of religious status, rank, and function in a developed religious system such as the Catholic church. Differences in charismata are also recognized in such terms as "contemplative," "ascetic," "mystic," "preacher," "teacher," "administrator." These gifts may appear in any of the major divisions of the church: among clergy or laity, among hermits, monks, or friars, among female as well as male religious. Certain of these charismata are institutionalized and constitute the devotional pattern particular to certain religious institutions: thus there are "contemplative orders," "friars preachers," and the like.

Medium-Scale Societies

Other developed religions, churches, sects, cults, and religious movements exhibit degrees of bureaucratic organization and specialization of role and function. Between the situational specialization of religious activities found in small-scale societies and the full-time and manifold specialization in large-scale societies falls a wide variety of intermediate types. A characteristic religious dichotomy is found in many of the larger, politically centralized societies of west and east Africa, Asia, Polynesia, and pre-Columbian Central and South America. National and tribal gods are worshiped in the larger towns, and minor deities, daemons, and ancestral shades are venerated in the villages. At the village level we find once more the multifunctional religious practitioner. But where there are national gods there are usually national priests, their official servants, and worship tends to take place in temples or at fixed and elaborate shrines. Parrinder writes:

> In the cults of the West African gods [for example, in Dahomey, Yoruba, and Ashanti] there are priests who are highly trained to do their work. These priests are often set aside from birth, or they may be called to the service of the god by being possessed by his spirit. They will then retire from there families and public life, and submit to the training of an older priest. The training normally lasts several years, during which time the novice has to apply himself to learn all the secrets of consulting and serving the god. The training of a priest is an arduous matter. . . . [He] has to observe chastity and strict taboos of food and actions. He frequently has to sleep on a hard floor, have insufficient food, and learn to bear hardship. He is regarded as married to the god, though later he may take a wife. Like an Indian devotee, he seeks by self-discipline to train himself to hear the voice of his god. He learns the ritual and dances appropriate to the cult, receives instruction in the laws and taboos of the god, and gains some knowledge of magical medicines (1954, pp. 100–101).

In these west African cults of deities there is a formal division of function between priests and mediums. In general, priests control mediums and carefully regulate their experience of possession. This situation is one solution to the perennial problem posed for priesthoods by what Ronald Knox (1950) has termed "enthusiasm," that is, the notion that one can become possessed by or identified with a god or God and that one's consequent acts and words are divinely inspired, even if they transgress religious or secular laws. In Dahomey, for example (Herskovits 1938), there are communal training centers, called cult houses or "convents," for mediums and assistants to priests. Here the novices are secluded for considerable periods of time. Part of their training involves the attempt to induce the return of the initial spirit possession that marked their calling. They learn later to produce coherent messages in a state of trance. During this period they are under the surveillance of priests. The Catholic church has similarly brought under its control as members of contemplative orders mystics and visionaries who claim "experiential knowledge of God's presence."

Religious and Political Specialization

In many primitive societies an intimate connection exists between religion and politics. If by politics we denote those behavioral processes of resolution of conflict between the common good and the interests of groups by the use of or struggle for power, then religion in such societies is pragmatically connected with the maintenance of those values and norms expressing the common good and preventing the undue exercise of power. In centralized political systems that have kings and chiefs, these dignitaries themselves have priestly functions; in many parts of Africa, for example, they take charge of observances which safeguard many of the basic needs of existence, such as rainmaking, sowing, and harvest rites, ritual to promote the fertility of men, domestic and wild animals, and so on. On the other hand, even where this is the case, there are frequently other specialized religious functionaries whose duties are bound up with the office of kingship. An illustration of this occurs among the Bemba of Zambia, where the *Bakabilo*

> are in charge of ceremonies at the sacred relic shrines and take possession of the *babenye* when the chief dies. They alone can purify the chief

from the defilement of sex intercourse so that he is able to enter his relic shrine and perform the necessary rites there. They are in complete charge of the accession ceremonies of the paramount and the bigger territorial chiefs, and some of their number are described as *bafingo*, or hereditary buriers of the chief. Besides this, each individual *mukabilo* has his own small ritual duty or privilege, such as lighting the sacred fire, or forging the blade of the hoe that is to dig the foundations of the new capital (Richards 1940, p. 109 in 1955 edition).

The *Bakabilo* constitute a council that exerts a check on the paramount's power, since the members are hereditary officials and cannot be removed at will. They are immune to the paramount's anger and can block the implementation of decisions that they consider to be detrimental to the interests of the Bemba people by refusing to perform the ritual functions that are necessary to the exercise of his office. A priesthood of this type thus forms a constituent part of the interior structure of the government of a primitive state.

In stateless societies in Africa and elsewhere, incumbents of certain ritual positions have similar functions in the maintenance of order and the resolution of conflict. The " leopard-skin chief" or "priest of the earth" (as this specialist has been variously called) among the Nuer of the Nilotic Sudan is a person whose ritual relationship with the earth gives him power to bless or curse, to cleanse a killer from the pollution of bloodshed, and, most important, to perform the rites of reconciliation between persons who are ready to terminate a blood feud. A similar role is performed by the "masters of the fishing spear" among the Dinka and the *tendaanas*, or earth priests, among the Tallensi and their congeners in the northern territories of Ghana. Similar religious functionaries are found in many other regions of Africa. They serve to reduce, if not to resolve, conflict within the society. As against sectional and factional interests they posit the commonweal. In these contexts, moreover, the commonweal is regarded as part of the cosmic order; breach, therefore, is mystically punished. The religious specialists are accorded the function of restoring the right relation that should obtain between society, the cosmos, and the deities or ancestral shades.

Priests

C. Von Furer-Haimendorf

In the following article Von Furer-Haimendorf, a specialist in the ethnology of Asian societies, calls on his own field data to demonstrate the important roles of priests in society. Utilizing case studies of the aboriginal Hill Reddis and the Saora tribe of India, the Ifugao of the Philippines, and West African societies, he focuses on the functions of priests as experts on ritual, preservers of myths and religious belief systems, and conduits for communication with the supernatural.

Distinguishing between priests, shamans, magicians, and prophets, Professor Von Furer-Haimendorf also demonstrates that the functions of these religious specialists often overlap. Unlike other specialists, the position of priest is more precarious and constantly threatened with loss of power from a variety of sources, both human and superhuman. As a result, taboos evolved into important protective mechanisms for priests, functioning to guard them against innumerable forms of pollution that could drain away the priestly powers necessary to properly serve society. The respect given priests and the awe surrounding their station can be, in part, correlated with their quality of charisma, the subject of Douglas Barnes's article, which follows this one.

Reprinted from Richard Cavendish, ed., *Man, Myth, and Magic* (London, 1970), Vol. 16, pp. 2248–55, by permission of the author and BPCC/Phoebus Publishing.

The priests, medicine men, or shamans of primitive societies are "specialists in the supernatural" who provide a channel of communication between human beings and the divine: more sophisticated societies also have specialist priesthoods.

AT MOST LEVELS OF CIVILIZATION PRIESTS ACT AS THE socially recognized mediators between men and supernatural beings. They are the experts in the performances of rituals, and in preliterate societies it is they who preserve, by oral tradition, the myths and the body of religious concepts and ideas which constitute a people's intellectual heritage. The functions, selection, training, and social position of priests differ widely even within simpler societies, and the designation "priest" has been applied to a large variety of religious practitioners, who may have little in common except for their alleged ability to establish contact with gods and spirits, or to manipulate supernatural forces.

In some societies there is a distinction between priests, who are the official religious leaders and representatives of the community, and magicians, shamans, and prophets, whose power derives from individual supernatural experiences or what is presumed to be direct inspiration by deities or spirits. In practice, the functions of these two types of religious practitioners often overlap, and the distinction is not universal.

At the lowest level of economic development, there is little scope for the emergence of ritual experts or any other form of occupational specialization. Most societies of nomadic food gatherers and hunters lack religious specialists comparable to the priests of more advanced peoples. All adults are considered capable of invoking gods or spirits and of soliciting their favor by way of prayers and offerings. Cult acts involving all the members of a group may be conducted by old men experienced in the performance of ritual, but no training or hereditary qualification is required for such activity, nor do those engaging in the organization of religious rites enjoy any special privileges.

Priest and Magician

Where larger and more stable social groups have developed, increased economic efficiency enables man to divert some energies to the elaboration of religious practices. In most societies of some complexity the task of establishing contact with transcendental powers tends to be vested in individuals who act as the representatives of their clan or village. Such individuals need not possess outstanding intellectual gifts, but the ability and the right to perform priestly functions may be hereditary in certain families, lineages or clans. Another claim to priesthood is derived from psychological states interpreted as possession or selection by a divinity or spirit, who is supposed to invest the priest with powers and knowledge not accessible to other men. Priests who base their position on hereditary rights and priests called to their vocation by the gods may coexist in the same society.

The Hill Reddis, an aboriginal tribe of southern India, for instance, depend on two classes of intermediaries in their relations with the supernatural world; the hereditary priest of the local group or village and the magician who derives his powers from an intimate connection with a specific god or spirit. The hereditary priest is normally a descendant of the village-founder, and membership of the lineage of the man who first settled in the locality is sufficient qualification for his office. He is regarded as the head of the village, and as the appropriate mediator between man and the deities and spirits who dwell in the area.

As representative of the village he performs those rites and ceremonies that are believed to secure the prosperity of the community as a whole. And since this prosperity is intimately linked with the thriving of the crops, it is above all the agricultural rites that call for the intercession of the priest. He must inaugurate the sowing of the grain, propitiate the earth deity with sacrifices, and perform the rites at the great seasonal feasts. No special intuition or skill is required for these tasks.

Less simple are those that fall to the magician. While the hereditary spiritual head of the community follows the broad and well-trodden path of long-established ritual, the magician must battle through the wilderness of the supernatural world to discover the cause of disease and threatening disaster, and must devise the means of placating the wrath of malignant spirits. The priest acts, so to speak, while all is well; his offerings are tendered to gods while their mood is benevolent, and his prayers are designed to solicit their favor for the welfare of the community, and their protection against dangers not yet arisen. It is only when misfortune is rife that the magician is called in to restore the disturbed relations with supernatural powers, to draw the sick from the jaws of death or to counteract the black magic of an enemy. This power, which he could not wield unless he himself possessed a thorough knowledge of magical practices, justifies his being called a "magician."

Every Reddi village must have a priest, but there may or may not be a magician in the community. Being a magician is an art, acquired by learning or bestowed by supernatural beings on an eager apprentice. It is an art and a power within reach only of those men and women who are predisposed towards it by particular mental qualities. Naturally these may occur in a priest as well as in any other man, and his frequent performance of ritual acts is bound to favor their development. Nothing debars a priest from learning the practices of a magician, and the combination of both functions is fairly common.

No Reddi is born a magician and aptitude for the work does not manifest itself in childhood. A magician frequently owes his knowledge to the instruction of his father or an older kinsman, but not every son of a famous magician has the talent or the desire to assimilate his parent's teaching. The cooperation of a deity is indispensable to the process of becoming a magician, and it is not only men who seek the gods; on occasion the gods themselves take the initiative. Reddi magicians agree that they receive their inspiration and knowledge from the gods, either while in a state of trance or through the medium of dreams. When a magician is called on to treat a sick person, it is usually his guardian deity who tells him what medicines to apply and what animals to sacrifice.

Married to a Spirit

While the roles of priest and magician are clearly distinguished in some of the simpler societies, they overlap in others and a distinction between the functions of priests and magicians is hardly perceptible. Both deal with the control of supernatural forces and priests are generally expected to influence the gods through prayer and ritual performances, while magicians exert their power through spells and the manipulation of certain material objects possessed of mysterious efficacy. But as the principal duty of priests is to mediate between mankind and the higher powers, the faculty of communicating with gods and spirits is a primary qualification for the priesthood in many societies. This ability may be proved in different ways. When a person falls into a state of trance or ecstasy, people think that he or she is under the influence of a supernatural power, and therefore suitable for the role of mediator between men and gods. Or the supposed connection between priests and the spirit world may be that they have one or more tutelary deities of their own who assist them when required.

A striking example of this type of link between priests and supernatural beings occurs among the Saora tribe of Orissa in India. Among these primitive hill farmers, placating the vast otherworld of invisible and often hostile beings occupies the energy of a small band of dedicated men and women. Armed with a few fragile implements, and devoting themselves to supplication of spirits and the sacrifice of animals, these people strive bravely to protect mankind.

There are two types of religious practitioner among the Saoras, the village priest and the shaman or magician. The priest's special function is to maintain the cult of the local shrines and to guard the village lands from the interference of hostile spirits and sorcerers. When a new priest is to be appointed a shaman is called and, falling into a trance, he asks the gods and ancestors whether the proposed candidate is acceptable to them. If they agree that he is, the shaman summons the ghost of the last priest to hold office in the village. If he too approves, the shaman—possessed by, and representing, the dead man—puts his hands on the head of the new priest and tells him to do his work well. This selection and installation of a Saora village priest demonstrates the coexistence and friendly cooperation of two quite different types of ritual expert.

For practical purposes, however, the shaman, who may be male or female, is the most important religious figure in a Saora village. He has the power not only to diagnose the source of trouble or disease, but to cure it. He is doctor as well as priest, psychologist as well as magician, the repository of tradition, the source of sacred knowledge. His primary duty is that of divination; in case of sickness he seeks the cause in trance or dream. Every male shaman has a spirit-wife in the underworld and every female shaman has a spirit-husband, whom she visits in her dreams. These tutelary spouses are the strength and inspiration of Saora shamans. The marriages are absolutely real in their own minds, and they believe themselves to be chosen by the direct intervention of the guardian spirit, through whom they subsequently have immediate access to the world of spirits and deities. A female shaman may have to be wooed by a spirit for a long time before she consents to accept him as husband. Usually such calls from the spirit world come as hallucinations or dream experiences, and a girl may appear to be deranged and ill until the "marriage" to her suitor from the underworld has been performed.

After the marriage, the shaman's spirit-husband visits her regularly and lies with her till dawn. He may even take her away into the jungle for days at a time. In due course a spirit-child is born, and the ghostly father brings it every night to be nursed by the human wife. This imaginary marriage is no bar to marrying a human husband, but the dream-spouse seems as real to a Saora shaman as her husband of flesh and blood, and it is believed that she will become a spirit herself after death.

The Master of Ecstasy

The term "shaman," now widely current in anthropological literature, was first applied to the religious practitioners of central and northern Asia, where the magico-religious life of most of the indigenous population traditionally centers on the shaman. He is the dominating figure, though in many tribes there are also priests concerned with the performance of animal sacrifices, and every head of a family is also the head of the domestic cult. The ecstatic state is considered to be the supreme religious experience, and the shaman is the great master of ecstasy. Unlike persons possessed by spirits and temporarily in their power, the shaman controls spirits. He is able to communicate with the dead, or with demons and Nature spirits, without becoming their instrument.

Shamans are separated from the rest of society by the intensity of their religious experience, and in this sense they resemble the mystics of historic religions. The mental disposition which qualifies a person for the functions of a shaman points to an important feature of early priesthood. Among many peoples, priests must display a certain excitability of temperament, which in modern Western society might be considered as bordering on a psychopathic condition. The ability to fall into trance may be an essential prerequisite for the performance of certain rites, in which case only those capable of such psychological states are suitable as priests.

The importance attached to ecstasy as a visible means of divine inspiration is shown in the numerous instances of priests obtaining their initiation by inducing a state of delirium or trance through the use of narcotics or fasting. The convulsive movements and seemingly irrational utterances of the inspired person suggest that his own controlling will is in abeyance, and that an external force or being has taken possession of his body. In many cases a god or spirit is supposed to speak through his mouth and determine his actions.

Not all priests need to undergo a formal course of training, or be initiated into the mystery of relations with supernatural powers by a specific ritual. Those who succeed to the priesthood through inheritance, for example, are usually believed to have powers acquired by birth into a family or clan. On the other hand, there are many pre-literate societies which require potential religious practitioners to be subjected to a rigorous training in self-control and in the sacred lore of the tribe. Among the Eskimo, for instance, the priests are trained in their profession from childhood.

Where priests receive formal instruction, their education often consists of two different phases. During the first period the novice is under the care of an experienced practitioner, who initiates him into the body of religious beliefs and teaches him how to perform various rites. A later phase is devoted mainly to self-training, in the course of which the novice seeks mystic experiences, and through them a direct relationship with supernatural powers. During this preparation for the priesthood he may have to live in seclusion or submit himself to austerities such as prolonged fasting or exposure to the elements.

In some primitive societies the period of instruction and training culminates in an elaborate initiation ceremony which confirms upon the candidate the full status of an ordained priest.

In many societies, however, priests are trained in a much more casual way. Among the Ifugao tribe of the Philippines, for instance, there is no institutionalized method of initiating priests into the labyrinth of an immensely rich and complicated mythology. There is no organized priesthood recruited from a special social class. Any Ifugao possessing intellectual ability and a good memory may attach himself to an experienced priest of his kin-group or locality as an apprentice; but in many cases sons follow in the footsteps of fathers enjoying a reputation as knowledgeable and successful priests. Ifugao priests also act as chroniclers and genealogists, for the frequently repeated incantations of ancestors give them an unrivalled knowledge of genealogies. The ministrations of priests form an essential part of all the innumerable rituals by which Ifugaos mark social as well as religious occasions.

Some of these rituals may extend over a whole day or even over several days, and the demands they make on the memory can be prodigious. The priests are of supreme importance to the Ifugao, for only they are thought to be capable of manipulating the gods and coaxing them to aid human endeavor. The relation between man and deities is looked upon as one of bargaining and of give and take, and the priests must exert all their skill to get favorable terms for their clients. Ifugao gods are regarded as morally neutral and unconcerned with the ethical conduct of men, and the priests do not take any stand on moral questions. They do not feel any need to behave in an exemplary way in their private lives, nor do they attempt to influence the moral conduct of their clients and fellow villagers.

Unlike Christian priests or other holy men who regard themselves as representatives of a moral order that derives its sanction from a supreme deity, most priests in primitive societies act simply as the agents of their fellow men, and are intent only on obtaining material benefits for them. They have no interest in giving them any guidance in moral matters. Priests of this kind do not preach to men, but address themselves solely to the deities they seek to influence.

In addition, whatever the circumstances in which a priest acts as an intermediary between men and gods, the quality which makes his mediation effective often resides in his office rather than in himself as an individual. Consequently it may not greatly matter what sort of person he is, socially, psychologically, or morally.

A Sense of Awe

Because of his usefulness and power a priest may enjoy considerable prestige and authority, but his position is so precarious and easily damaged that he tends to be surrounded with taboos to protect him against harmful contacts with forces that might render him ineffective. The social position of priests varies greatly from one society to another. The ability to experience states of trance and spirit-possession is usually not combined with great economic efficiency or political acumen, and priests who on ritual occasions will act as the mouthpiece of gods may be withdrawn and comparatively ineffective personalities in ordinary life. On the other hand, someone who holds the position of clan priest by hereditary right, and functions as the sole mediator between a powerful clan and its protective deities, may derive considerable prestige and material advantages from his office.

In some societies, as among certain West African tribes for instance, priests tend to increase the respect in which they are held by enveloping their proceedings in mystery. They often create a sense of awe and fear among the laity, in order to enhance their power. The special and sometimes fantastic attire donned by some priests is intended partly to distinguish them from the rest of the population, and partly to impress deities and spirits or avert malignant forces. Masks worn by priests have similar purposes, and occasionally signify a mystical connection between the priest and an ancestor spirit or deity whom he embodies.

In primitive societies priesthood is not exclusively a male occupation, and there are many instances of women functioning as priestesses and magicians. It is rare for them to be debarred from marriage, just as male priests are usually expected to marry and lead a life not basically different from that of other members of their society. Though their priestly status may provide them with certain privileges and material benefits, occupational specialization among primitive populations normally does not go far enough to free religious practitioners from the need to till the soil or herd cattle. At that level of material development priesthood is seldom an exclusive profession, and a priest does not diminish his spiritual status or prestige by engaging in normal secular occupations.

Restrictions on the sexual life of priests and priestesses are usually found in the more advanced civilizations. Primitive peoples rarely place any value on celibacy and chastity, and priests are expected to have normal family lives. They may be obliged to abstain from sexual activities during periods of training or at the time of major rituals, in the same way as fasting is regarded as a preparation for spiritual experiences; but in general primitive priests are not expected to lead a life basically different from that of laymen.

The Shaman: A Siberian Spiritualist

William Howells

In this classic work, William Howells demonstrates the many positive functions of Siberian and Eskimo shamans in their roles as mediums and diviners, clearly differentiating their character from the evil nature of witches. Like witches, however, shamans have "familiars"—animal souls that give them their powers. Through their familiars, for example, shamans might travel into all three realms of nature (upper, middle, and lower) to recapture the lost souls of villagers enticed into the lower realm of darkness and evil by a demon. At the same time, the power of animal souls allows the shamans to do witch-like harm, and this, along with their ability to cure and keep the balance between the spirits of the upper and lower realms of nature, inspires awe in the villagers' minds. The shamans foster this awe through their artful use of prestidigitation and ventriloquism, justifying their trickery because it enables them to help their followers in the cause of good and to perpetuate their religion.

Although shamanism is both dangerous and burdensome, in Siberia as many women as men become shamans, and each sex often takes on the behavior of its opposite. Members of society may disapprove of this behavior, but don't voice their disapproval due to fear of shamanic retribution. It is the shaman's power, expressed in dramatic performance, that provides the psychological benefits for the society by reducing tensions in both individuals and groups and thereby returning emotional balance.

Howells's view of the functions of shamanism anticipated the current view of medical anthropologists who have positively reappraised the role of the traditional healer.

WITCHES ARE ALL EVIL, AND HIDE THEMSELVES FROM common men; they are "secret, black and midnight hags"; fell creatures, they hypocritically put on the mien of ordinary folk, the better to stalk and strike their prey unknown. But there are other men and women with extraordinary powers of their own, who have no need to skulk, because their purposes are good, and who are given public recognition and respect. The type specimen of such people is known under the Tungus word *shaman*, and the shaman is a figure of importance among the aboriginal people of Siberia and the Eskimos, among most of the American Indians, and to a lesser extent among various other primitive tribes elsewhere in the world. He has been sometimes called a witch doctor, especially with reference to Africa.

A shaman is a medium and a diviner, but his powers do not stop there. He differs from men in general, and resembles a witch, because he can shift gears and move in the plane of the supernatural. He can go at will to the other world, and he can see and treat with souls or spirits, meeting them on their own ground. And that is his business. He differs from a witch, who exists solely in the heads of the victimized, in that he is an actual person, who not only conducts his profession publicly, making the people think that he goes on brave errands among ghosts and goblins, but in many if not most cases really believes he has the powers he claims. This, of course, would be something difficult to get the truth of. Nonetheless he acts as though he can and does do the things which are traditionally his to do, and the public believes and acclaims him. That is the important thing.

His duties are to ride herd on the souls of the departed and to discover the general disposition of other important spirits, according as it is swayed by the behavior of human beings. He may do only a little of this; among some people there is a shaman in every family, who simply makes contact with the spirits from time to time to flatter them and assure himself of their serene humor, as we look at a barometer. Elsewhere he may do it as his trade: general divining, diagnosis of sickness, and ghost chasing. And he may be the most important person of the village, as well as the center of religion; this position he has in easternmost Siberia and among the Eskimos. With such people communities are small and religion is otherwise crude, and the people look to the shaman to take care of their relations with the supernatural both public and private. While he thus acts for them much as does a medicine man or a diviner, he is no magician. He does not endeavor to find the formula to the supernatural, working it as though it were made up of wires and joints, while remaining on the outside; instead, he boldly enters it himself and meets its inhabitants man to man. Nor is he a priest, who leads the people in supplication and represents them before their gods. He may work in their behalf, but he does not represent them; he is acting on his own hook, and through skill and power, not through supplication.

The stronghold of the shaman is among the reindeer herders and fishers of northeast Asia: the Yakuts and the Tungus, two widespread groups of tribes, and others living around the western shore of the Bering Sea: the Chuckchis, the Koryaks, the Gilyaks, and the Kamchadals of Kamchatka. Some of these live nomadically in felt tents and others in wooden villages, and in the long arctic nights of their bleak environment the comfort and entertainment that the shaman gives them is very well received. Typically it is believed that there are three realms of nature: an upper one, of light and of good spirits; a middle one, which is the world of men and of the spirits of the earth; and a lower one, for darkness and evil spirits. Men of the usual sort can move about the middle realm, and have some dealings with its spirits, but only a shaman can go above or below. A shaman also has the power of summoning spirits to come to him. Thus he can speak directly to spirits and ask what they want, which is his form of divining. Not only this, but a shaman deals with sickness in various ways through these same powers. If you have a disease spirit inside you, he can detect it and he knows how to send it off, perhaps by having a personal contest with it. Or you may have lost your soul—

this explanation of illness turns up almost everywhere in the world—and the shaman gets it back. It has probably been enticed against its will by a stronger demon, and taken to the lower regions, and only the shaman can go after it, see it, identify it, and return it.

Both in Asia and America shamans, like witches, are generally believed to have familiar spirits, or animal souls, which are the things that give them their peculiar qualities and powers. A Yakut shaman has two or three (Casanowicz 1924; Czaplicka 1914). One, called *emekhet*, is the shaman's own guardian angel, which is not only a sort of impersonal power like mana but also a definite spirit, usually that of a shaman already dead. This spirit hovers around its protégé, guiding and protecting him all the time, and comes at once when he calls for it, and gives him the advice he needs. Another spirit, the *yekyua*, has more character but is less accommodating. This one is an external soul, which belongs both to the shaman and to a living wild animal, which may be a stallion, a wolf, a dog, an eagle, a hairy bull, or some mythical creature, like a dragon. The yekyua is unruly and malevolent; it is dangerous and enables the shaman to do harm, rather like a witch, so that the people are in awe of him, but at the same time it has no consideration for the shaman himself and gives him continual trouble and anxiety, because his own fortunes are bound up with it. It is independent and lives far away, rather than upon the immediate tribal scene, and only another shaman can see it anyway.

"Once a year, when the snow melts and the earth is black, the yekyua arise from their hiding places and begin to wander" (Czaplicka 1914). When two of them meet, and fight, the human shamans to whom they are linked undergo the evil effects and feel badly. If such an animal dies or is killed, its shaman dies as well, so that a shaman whose yekyua is a bear or a bull can congratulate himself that his life expectancy is good. Of this phantasmal zoo the least desirable soul partners to have are carnivorous animals, especially dogs, because the shaman must keep them appeased, and if they go hungry they are not above taking advantage of their connection with the poor shaman to gnaw at his vitals to stay their appetites. When a person takes to shamanizing, the other shamans round about can tell whether a new yekyua has made its appearance far away, which will cause them to recognize the new shaman and accept him into the profession.

Siberian shamans all dress the part, as do so many shamans and medicine men of North America. The north-eastern Asiatics wear clothing which is made of skin and tailored. A shaman has a cap and a mask, but it is his coat which distinguishes him like a collar turned around. It is a tunic made of hide—goat, elk, etc.—and usually comes down to his knees in front and to the ground behind, and is decorated to the point of being a textbook of shamanistic lore. On the front may be sewed metal plates which protect him from the blows of hostile spirits which he is always encountering. One of these plates represents his emekhet, and usually two others suggest a feminine appearance, since shamans have a hermaphroditic character, as we shall see. All over the tunic are embroidered or appliquéd the figures of real and mythical animals, to represent those he must face on his travels in spirit realms, and from the back there hang numerous strips of skin falling clear to the ground, with small stuffed animals attached to some of them, all this alleged to be for attracting to the shaman any spiritual waifs of the vicinity, who might like to join his retinue. The whole getup would remind you of the unusual headdresses and paraphernalia in which medicine men are turned out among Indians of the Plains and Canada.

Siberian shamans have a tambourine drum whenever they are working, and this is true of Eskimo shamans as well. It is a round or oval drum, covered like a tambourine on one side only, and decorated with the same kind of symbolism as the coat. It is held by a crosspiece or strips of hide in the frame, and is beaten to accompany all the invocations of spirits.

When a shaman goes into action the result is not a rite but a séance, which is full of drama and which the people enjoy immensely. A typical performance is a summoning of spirits, and is carried out in the dark (for the same reasons as among ourselves—i.e., to hide the shenanigans), in a house, a tent, or an Eskimo igloo. The people all gather, and the shaman says what he is going to do, after which he puts out the lamps and the fire, being sure that there is little or no light. Then he begins to sing. There may be a wait, and he beats his tambourine drum first of all, an immediate

dramatic effect. The song starts softly. The sense of the song is of no consequence as far as the listeners are concerned; it is often incomprehensible, and may have no words at all. Jochelson knew a Tungus shaman who sang his songs in Koryak (1908). He explained that his spirits were Koryak and said that he could not understand Koryak himself. Jochelson found this last suspicious statement to be quite true; the shaman had memorized the songs subconsciously when he had first heard them.

As the singing goes on, other sounds begin to make themselves heard, supposedly made by animal spirits and said to be remarkably good imitations. The shaman may announce to the audience that the spirits are approaching, but he is apt to be too absorbed or entranced himself to bother. Soon voices of all kinds are heard in the house, in the corners and up near the roof. The house now seems to have a number of independent spirits in it, all moving around, speaking in different voices, and all the time the drum is sounding, changing its tempo and its volume; the people are excited, and some of them who are old hands help the shaman out by making responses and shouting encouragement, and the shaman himself is usually possessed by a spirit or spirits, who are singing and beating the drum for him. The confusion of noises goes on increasing in intensity, with animal sounds and foreign tongues as well as understandable communications (among the Chuckchis, the wolf, the fox, and the raven can speak human language), until it finally dies down; the spirits give some message of farewell, the drumming ceases, and the lights are lit. Often the shaman will be seen lying exhausted or in a faint, and on coming to he will assert that he cannot say what has been happening.

This is all a combination of expert showmanship and management and of autohypnosis, so that while the shaman knows perfectly well he is faking much of the performance he may at the same time work himself into a trance in which he does things he believes are beyond his merely human powers. He warns his audience strictly to keep their places and not try to touch the spirits, who would be angered and assault the offender, and perhaps even kill the shaman. When the show starts, the shaman produces his voices by moving around in the dark and by expert ventriloquism, getting the audience on his side and rapidly changing the nature and the force of the spirit sounds he is making. He may allow the impression that some of the visiting spirits are possessing him and speaking through his mouth and beating on his drum, but he may hide the fact that he is using his own mouth at all.

A shaman need not perform only in the dark. He carries out some of his business in full view, especially when it is a matter of his going to the spirit world himself, rather than summoning the spirits to this world. The idea seems to be that he is in two places at once; i.e., his soul is traveling in spiritdom while he himself is going through the same actions before his watchers. He does a furious dramatic dance, rushing about, advancing and retreating, approaching the spirits, fighting them or wheedling them, all in a seeming trance. He may foam at the mouth and be so wild that he must be held for safety in leather thongs by some of the onlookers. After vivid adventures in the other realms, portrayed in his dance, he will accomplish his purpose, which may be to capture a wandering soul or to get some needed information from his spectral hosts. Then he becomes his normal self again and gives an account of what he has done.

After a death it is a regular thing for a Mongolian shaman to be called in to "purify" the *yurt* (felt hut) of the deceased's family, by getting rid of the soul of the dead, which of course cannot be allowed to hang around indefinitely. The mourners assemble late in the day, and at dusk the shaman himself comes, already drumming in the distance. He enters the yurt, still drumming, lowering the sound until it is only a murmur. Then he begins to converse with the soul of the newly departed, which pitifully implores to be allowed to stay in the yurt, because it cannot bear to leave the children or the scenes of its mortal days. The shaman, faithful to his trust, steels himself and pays no attention to this heartrending appeal. He goes for the soul and corners it by means of the power in his drum, until he can catch it between the drum itself and the drum stick. Then he starts off with it to the underworld, all in play acting. Here at the entrance he meets the souls of other dead members of the same family, to whom he announces the arrival of the new soul. They answer that they do not want it and refuse it admission. To multiply the difficulties, the homesick soul, which is slippery, generally makes its escape from the shaman as the two of them are on the way down, and comes rushing back to the yurt, with the shaman after it; he catches it all over again. It is lucky the people have a shaman! Back at the gate of the lower world he makes himself affable to the older souls and gives them vodka to drink, and in one way or another he manages to smuggle the new one in.

Europeans who have seen Siberian shamans perform say that it is tremendous and exciting melodrama for them, and it must therefore have still more of an impact on the natives, whose belief and interest are greater. Aside from ventriloquism and histrionics, shamans use other tricks to heighten their effects, and even give small magic shows to maintain the awe of the populace. They are masters of prestidigitation, especially considering that they must work with little apparatus—no trap doors or piano wire. In their séances they can make it appear that there are spirits in several parts of the yurt at once, mischievously throwing things around. Many stick knives into themselves and draw them out again, making the wound heal immediately (all faked, of course). Or they will have themselves trussed up, like Houdini, and call on their spirits, who will set them free. Bogoras saw a Chuckchi woman shaman take a rock between her hands and, without changing it in any way, produce a pile of smaller stones from it, and to defy the skeptics she wore nothing above her waist (Bogoras 1904–09). She repeated the trick at Bogoras's request, but he could not find out what she did.

The shamans know, of course, that their tricks are impositions, but at the same time everyone who has studied them agrees that they really believe in their power to deal with spirits. Here is a point, about the end justifying the means, which is germane to this and to all conscious augmenting of religious illusion.* The shaman's main purpose is an honest one and he believes in it, and does not consider it incongruous if his powers give him the right to hoodwink his followers in minor technical

---

*Shaw has the following to say about it, through two characters in *Saint Joan*:

THE ARCHBISHOP: A miracle, my friend, is an event which creates faith. That is the purpose and nature of miracles. They may seem very wonderful to the people who witness them, and very simple to those who

matters. If shamanism were a conspiracy or a purposeful fraud, it would attract only the clever and the unscrupulous, interested in their own aggrandizement, and the public would shortly see the snare, being no bigger fools than we are. But shamanism is an institution, and the things that keep the public from rejecting it are religious characteristics: shamanism does something to help them, and the shamans themselves are inside the system and believe in it too. A sick shaman will call in a superior shaman to cure him. Actually, shamans are among the most intelligent and earnest people of the community, and their position is one of leadership.

Evans-Pritchard has the same thing to say about Zande witch doctors, who do shamanizing of a less distinct type. They divine for the people, usually dancing in a group. A question will be asked one of them, and he will "dance" to it, very vigorously, working himself into a transport or half frenzy, throwing himself on the ground and perhaps gashing himself. In this state he begins to make an answer to the question, at first tentatively and in a faraway voice, but then more certainly and finally in loud and arrogant tones, although the terms of the answer remain a little obscure, with no names mentioned, and probably phrased in such a way that only the questioner can gather up the meaning. They do not claim to be guided by spirits, and they could be accused of making any answer they

___

perform them. That does not matter; if they confirm or create faith they are true miracles.

LA TRÉMOUILLE: Even when they are frauds, do you mean?

THE ARCHBISHOP: Frauds deceive. An event which creates faith does not deceive; therefore it is not a fraud, but a miracle.

Elsewhere the archbishop says: "Miracles are not frauds because they are often—I do not say always—very simple and innocent contrivances by which the priest fortifies the faith of his flock. When this girl picks out the Dauphin from among his courtiers, it will not be a miracle for me, because I shall know how it has been done, and my faith will not be increased. But as for the others, if they feel the thrill of the supernatural, and forget their sinful clay in a sudden sense of the glory of God, it will be a miracle and a blessed one. And you will find that the girl herself will be more affected than anyone else. She will forget how she really picked him out. . . ."

chose. It is unlikely, however, that they do such a thing consciously; actually they possess a knowledge of the village and its people, and of the background of any question asked them, so that they have a good basis for judgment, and they juggle all these elements loosely in their heads until, under the stimulation of their abandoned physical activity, they feel struck by an inspiration, an effect which they would not experience without the dancing. These witch doctors also cure by sucking intrusive magical objects out of their patients, if that is the cause of illness, and at their shindigs the doctors who are not busy dancing to a question will stage contests of shooting the same kind of thing—bones or beetles—into one another, or into the spectators, if they are unruly, and then removing them again. This is generally known by the Azande to be nothing but sleight of hand, good as it is, and the doctors will admit it, saying that their success is really due to their medicines; the people are also often skeptical of them to the point of laughing outright at them, because a doctor may fail completely when tested by so simple a question as what is hidden in a pot. Nonetheless Evans-Pritchard feels that these doctors, who do not occupy as responsible a position as the Asiatic shamans, are basically honest; and also that they are usually above the average mentally. In spite of their higher intelligence, and their awareness of their own trickery, they believe in their magic and their powers as much as anyone else, and the people, laugh as they may, always go to them when taken sick.

In Asia and North America some tribes think that shaman spirits run in the family, and that a boy or young man will sooner or later be seized by such a legacy. This is the usual thing on the Northwest Coast of America, so that normally only the descendants of shamans became shamans. However, a man with none of them in the family tree may nevertheless become one by going to the bier of a newly dead shaman, which in the northern region was set out in a hut on a point of land, and there he will sit and bite the dead man's little finger all night long. This will offend the departed soul, who will react by sending a small spirit to torment the offender, and the latter, if he is courageous and has his wits about him, may capture the spirit for his own ends, and so become a shaman.

The most general belief as to recruitment is

simply that a spirit appears, to anyone at all, and insists on the person's becoming a shaman, which is tantamount to accepting the spirit as an internal boarder, whether it is wanted or not. Being a shaman is considered dangerous and burdensome, because you are committed to it and have to observe certain tabus, and so people generally try to avoid it. If you play on a drum, or show yourself in any way receptive, you are laying yourself open, and anyone not wishing to become a shaman will be careful to do no such thing. Usually the spirits pick out young men. In Siberia there are as many woman shamans as men, and they are by no means subservient to their male colleagues. In this area also, there is something of an assimilation of male and female shamans; the former, as I said, wear some marks suggestive of femininity, and may braid their hair, and vice versa, female shamans acting somewhat like men. They may go so far as to marry someone of their own sex, a woman getting a wife to keep house for her. This is considered strange, as you might think, and it is not approved of by right-thinking people, but right-thinking people do not like to antagonize shamans and so they keep their mouths shut. Actually, shamans are not thought of as bisexual so much as sexless.

This is one significant thing about the temperamental nature of individuals who become shamans. Another is the reason often given as to why they do so deliberately. A Siberian will say that he became ill, and that in desperation over being melancholy, or on the verge of dying, he began to solicit a spirit and prepare for a shaman's career, whereupon he got well; he now has a bull by the tail, however, and must continue to shamanize or fall ill again. He has to undergo a long training, under the tutelage of an older shaman, and during this period he is subject to mental suffering and sickness; but once he is a practicing shaman he regains his balance, and no shamans suffer from insanity. Europeans report that they can distinguish a shaman by his expression, which is nervous and bright compared to that of ordinary people. Furthermore, the Buriats allege that a future shaman can be told while he is still a child, by certain signs: he is meditative and likes to be alone, and he has mysterious dreams, and sometimes fits, in which he faints.

It is clear from these clues that shamanism is a calling for a certain psychological type: those who are less stable and more excitable than the average, but who have at the same time intelligence, ability, and what is vulgarly called "drive." They are familiar to us, perhaps most so in what we think of as the artistic temperament; they fail of the balance and solidity and self-confidence, not to say aggressiveness, that are necessary in a business executive, or a politician, but their mental powers and their quickness demand expression, goaded by their dissatisfaction at being somewhat maladjusted socially. We are given to calling them introverted, and think them somewhat difficult. They find the expression they need mainly in the arts. Now of course I do not mean that every artist must have bats in his belfry, but only that there is some relation between one variety of human temperament and the insistence of artistic expression. There are plenty of placid and well-adjusted artists; nevertheless, we often say that artists are temperamental people, actually meaning that it is temperamental people who become artists. So it is with shamans, who have in their profession a socially useful exhibitionist release, and a device by which they can discipline their own nervous tendencies by orienting them according to a defined pattern. We have a somewhat stereotyped parallel in people who soothe their nerves by playing the piano; and Conan Doyle made Sherlock Holmes (who was such a bad case that he was addicted to the needle) play the violin.

Some of the native diviners of South Africa, of either sex, are much the same as shamans, being recognized as people of a special type (Hoernle 1937). They enter into this life because of an illness, or hallucinations, or spirit possession; and since the novitiate involves months of solitude, training, and medical treatment by an older diviner, few go into it voluntarily, and most will try to resist it as long as possible. When they come out of this phase they are believed to have second sight and spirit connections, and have developed a peculiar faraway look. As elsewhere, the profession automatically picks out people of a high-strung temperament and appears to give them social satisfaction and psychiatric help.

Shamanism is the more adapted to Siberian and North American native cultures because hysterical tendencies seem to be common among the peoples of the Arctic, giving rise to the term "Arctic hysteria" (Czaplicka 1914; Jochelson 1926). Hysterical seizures, cramps, and trances are the simpler expressions of it. Eskimos will suddenly run wild, tearing off their clothes and rushing out, plunging into a snowbank and sometimes freezing before they can be caught. In Siberia, victims fall into a state, generally on being startled, in which they lose command of themselves and cannot help repeating the words and actions of others. Jokers used to tease known sufferers by tricking them in this way into throwing their belongings into the water, and a Russian colonel was once faced with a troop of natives who had gone hysterical in a body, and were helplessly roaring his orders back at him, and his curses too. A native boy, who knew two older men were both subject to this failing, managed to get them each repeating the other, which they kept up until they both collapsed. I do not know what the basis for this is—i.e., whether it is culturally suggested, like running amok among the Malays—but it is not as merry for the people concerned as it sounds, and is a disturber of the normal social welfare of a group. The contribution of shamanism is not only that it exhausts the special tensions of the shaman himself, and makes him a figure of consequence rather than a slightly psychopathic social liability, but also that it drains off the potential hysteria of the whole community, through the excitement and the drama of the shaman's performances.

Shamans seem to flourish, as might be expected, mainly among people whose religion is not highly organized and whose social structure is also simple and loosely knit. Something that can be called shamanizing often exists in other cultures and cults, but when it does, it is apt to be subservient to some higher political or religious authority. A true shaman is a lone wolf, following his own dictates, and so a well-developed cult, with important gods in it, cannot tolerate any such freebooting approach to the supernatural, and is bound to restrict this kind of activity, and to deprecate the importance of shamans, mediums, and their like. Two generally similar examples will show this. I have already described the *kaula* of the Polynesians, the prophet who was temporarily occupied by a god, and who then spoke with the voice of the god, often going into violent frenzies while possessed. These prophets also held séances of an entirely shamanistic kind, conducted in a dark house, with ventriloquism, sleight of hand, and all the other appurte-

nances of shamans as I have described them. Handy (1927) refers to a well-known story about a Maori priest whom a missionary was assiduously trying to convert: he stopped the missionary in his tracks by holding up a sprig of dry brown leaves and causing it to turn green before the good man's eyes. The report does not say whether the missionary saw the light and became a Maori. At any rate, the public business of the Polynesian prophets was limited to divining—the primary overt, if not actual, office of all shamans—and in their public appearances at Tahitian feasts they were kept under the thumb of the priests proper, who received the word of the gods in the indistinct mutterings and shouts of the kaula, and then interpreted it themselves and divulged it to the people.

A good parallel to this exists in female functionaries, called *woyei* (singular *woyo*) by the Gã of West Africa, and common to many tribes of the same region (Field 1937). It is an area of polytheistic cults, in which worshipers are free to choose their favorite god, with each god having his own temple, manned by a priest. Such a god enters and possesses certain women, who will therefore be officially appointed to his temple; and their duty is to dance and become possessed at any ceremony, and while possessed to speak for the god. They show various typical signs of possession, and dance in a semi-abandoned manner. If a practicing woyo becomes possessed while no ceremony is going on, a dance is organized at once in order to maintain the possession and get the message which the god is transmitting. Such a woman generally has her first seizure at a dance, having an apparently genuine fit, and acting bewildered and abstracted, talking incoherently. This is a sign that the god has chosen her, and she must leave home and go into training. Eventually she becomes able to deliver the words of her god with more coherence. Sometimes one has been found to talk in languages of other tribes, which she once knew but can no longer speak in her ordinary conscious state. On completing her training she resumes her normal life, and may be appointed to a temple, serving under the priest at ceremonies, and becoming possessed; or else she may practice free lance, as she sees fit.

I have not seen any comments of the same sort on Polynesian kaulas, but Miss Field states that Gã women who become woyei are, like shamans, individuals of a more nervous and less stable temperament than the average, and that the satisfactions of office, together with the license to throw a periodic fit of prophylactic hysterics, actually result in their living more serene, well-balanced, and happier everyday lives than perfectly "normal" women.

If you follow native philosophy, shamanism can be made to look something like witchcraft, as I said earlier. And it also resembles witchcraft, as we have seen, in the psychological benefits it bestows. Both of them relieve certain kinds of tensions in individuals, such as can be harmful to the social climate, and both of them do it dramatically, which means artistically, which in turn means in a manner calculated to give emotional satisfaction. Shamanism should be the more successful, because witchcraft is more of a fantasy and brings its own difficulties, while shamanism is a real emotional exercise, with practically no drawbacks. It allows some of the people to let off steam by indulging in uninhibited antics, while it allows the others to enjoy these antics and at the same time to make use of some of the shaman's real gifts.

Apocalypse at Jonestown

John R. Hall

The tragic end of the People's Temple utopian experiment in Guyana is unparalleled in the history of humankind. Hall's article is more than an exploration of a religion gone mad, however: by viewing the Reverend Jim Jones and his followers through an anthropological lens, Hall has been able to compare charismatic leadership and prophetism in the West with non-Western examples (discussed both in this chapter and in Chapter 9, on "Old and New Religions"). Hall challenges the labeling of the People's Temple as a "cult," and demonstrates that the apostolic character of the Reverend Jones fits the profile of charismatic leaders the world over. Using a social psychological, structural approach, Hall discusses the membership of the sect, why they were attracted to it, and how Jones's leadership was vital to the subordination of individual rights that ended with the death of the nine hundred adherents at Jonestown. The rapid erosion of traditional values is but one of the many prerequisites necessary to precipitate a revitalization movement, that rapid and intentional process of socio-cultural change that has occurred so frequently in the non-Western world and for which Jones offered a Western alternative.

Reprinted by permission of Transaction, Inc., from *Society*, Vol. 16, no. 6 (September/October 1979), pp. 52–61. Copyright © 1979.

THE EVENTS OF NOVEMBER 1978 AT JONESTOWN, Guyana, have been well documented, indeed probably better documented than most incidents in the realm of the bizarre. Beyond the wealth of "facts" which have been drawn from interviews with survivors of all stripes, there remain piles of as yet unsifted documents and tapes; if they can ever be examined, these will perhaps add something in the way of detail. But it is unlikely they will change very much the broad lines of our understanding of Jonestown. The major dimensions of the events and the outlines of various intrigues are already before us. But so far we have been caught in a flood of instant analysis; some of this has been insightful, but much of the accompanying moral outrage has clouded our ability to comprehend the events themselves. We need a more considered look at what sort of social phenomenon Jonestown was, and why (and how) Reverend Jim Jones and his staff led the 900 people of Jonestown to die in mass murder and suicide. On the face of it, the action is unparalleled and incredible.

"Crazy Like a Fox"

The news media have sought to account for Jonestown largely by looking for parallels "in history"; yet we have not been terribly enlightened by the ones they have found, usually because they have searched for cases which bear the outer trappings of the event, but which have fundamentally different causes. Thus, at Masada, in 73 A.D., the Jews who committed suicide under siege by Roman soldiers knew their fate was death, and chose to die by their own hands rather than at those of the Romans. In World War II, Japanese kamikaze pilots acted with the knowledge that direct, tangible, strategic results would stem from their altruistic suicides, if they were properly executed. And in Hitler's concentration camps, though there was occasional cooperation by Jews in their own executions, the Nazi executioners had no intentions of dying themselves.

Besides pointing to parallels which don't quite fit, the news media have targeted Jim Jones as irrational, a madman who had perverse tendencies from early in his youth. They have labelled the Peoples Temple as a "cult," perhaps in the hope that a label will suffice when an explanation is unavailable. And they have quite correctly plumbed the key issue of how Jones and his staff were able to bring the mass murder/suicide to completion, drawing largely on the explanations of psychiatrists who have prompted the concept of "brainwashing" as the answer.

But Jones was crazy like a fox. Though he may have been "possessed" or "crazed," both the organizational effectiveness of the Peoples Temple for more than 15 years, and the actual carrying out of the mass murder/suicide show that Jones and his immediate staff knew what they were doing.

Moreover, the Peoples Temple only became a "cult" when the media discovered the mass suicide. As an Indiana woman whose teenager died at Jonestown commented, "I can't understand why they call the Peoples Temple a cult. To the people, it was their church. . . ." It is questionable whether the term "cult" has any sociological utility. As Harold Fallding has observed, it is a value-laden term most often used by members of one religion to describe a heretical or competing religion, of which they disapprove. Of course, even if the use of the term "cult" in the press has been sloppy and inappropriate, some comparisons, for example to the Unification Church, the Krishna Society, and the Children of God, have been quite apt. But these comparisons have triggered a sort of guilt by association; in this view, Jonestown is a not-so-aberrant case among numerous exotic and weird religious "cults." The only thing stopping some people from "cleaning up" the "cult" situation is the constitutional guarantee of freedom of religion.

Finally, "brainwashing" is an important but incomplete basis for understanding the mass murder/suicide. There can be no way to determine how many people at Jonestown freely chose to drink the cyanide-laced Flav-r-ade distributed after Jonestown received word of the murders of U.S. Congressman Leo Ryan and four other visitors at the airstrip. Clearly over 200 children and an undetermined number of adults were murdered. Thought control and blind obedience to authority ("brainwashing") surely account for some additional number of suicides. But the obvious cannot be ignored: a substantial number of people—"brainwashed" or not—committed suicide. Insofar as "brainwashing" occurs in other social organizations besides the Peoples Temple, it can only be a necessary and not a sufficient cause of the mass murder/suicide. The coercive persuasion involved in a totalistic construction of reality may explain in part *how* large numbers of people came to accept the course proposed by their leader, but it leaves unanswered the question of *why* the true believers among the inhabitants of Jonestown came to consider "revolutionary suicide" a plausible course of action.

In all the instant analysis of Jones' perversity, the threats posed by "cults" and the victimization of people by "brainwashing," there has been little attempt to account for Jonestown sociologically, and as a religious phenomenon. The various facets of Jonestown remain as incongruous pieces of seemingly separate puzzles; we need a close examination of the case itself to try to comprehend it. In the following discussion based on ideal type analysis and *verstehende* sociology, I will suggest that the Peoples Temple Agricultural Project at Jonestown was an apocalyptic sect. Most apocalyptic sects gravitate toward one of three ideal typical possibilities: (1) preapocalyptic Adventism, (2) preapocalyptic war, or (3) postapocalyptic otherworldly grace. Insofar as the Adventist group takes on a communal form, it comes to approximate the postapocalyptic tableau of other-worldly grace. Jonestown was caught on the saddle of the apocalypse: it had its origins in the vaguely apocalyptic revivalist evangelism of the Peoples Temple in the United States, but the Guyanese communal settlement itself was an attempt to transcend the apocalypse by establishing a "heaven-on-earth." For various reasons, this attempt was frustrated. The Peoples Temple at Jonestown was drawn back into a preapocalyptic war with the forces of the established order. "Revolutionary suicide" then came to be seen as a way of surmounting the frustration, of moving beyond the apocalypse, to "heaven," albeit not "on earth."

In order to explore this account, let us first

consider the origins of Jonestown and the ways in which it subsequently came to approximate the ideal typical other-worldly sect. Then we can consider certain tensions of the Jonestown group with respect to its other-worldly existence, so as to understand why similar groups did not (and are not likely to) encounter the same fate as Jonestown.

"A Prophet Calls the Shots"

An other-worldly sect, as I have described it in *The Ways Out*, is a utopian communal group which subscribes to a set of beliefs based on an apocalyptic interpretation of current history. The world of society-at-large is seen as totally evil, and in its last days; at the end of history as we know it, it is to be replaced by a community of the elect—those who live according to the revelation of God's will. The convert who embraces such a sect must, perforce, abandon any previous understanding of life's meaning and embrace the new worldview, which itself is capable of subsuming and explaining the individual's previous life, the actions of opponents to the sect, and the demands which are placed on the convert by the leadership of the sect. The other-worldly sect typically establishes its existence on the "other" side of the apocalypse by withdrawing from "this" world into a timeless heaven-on-earth. In this millennial kingdom, those closest to God come to rule. Though democratic consensuality or the collegiality of elders may come into play, more typically, a preeminent prophet or messiah, legitimated by charisma or tradition, calls the shots in a theocratic organization of God's chosen people.

The Peoples Temple had its roots in amorphous revivalistic evangelical religion, but in the transition to the Jonestown Agricultural Mission, it came to resemble an other-worldly sect. The Temple grew out of the interracial congregation Jim Jones had founded in Indiana in 1953. By 1964, the Peoples Temple Full Gospel Church was federated with the Disciples of Christ. Later, in 1966, Jones moved with 100 of his most devout followers to Redwood Valley, California. From there they expanded in the 1970s to San Francisco and Los Angeles—more promising places for liberal, interracial evangelism than rural Redwood Valley. In these years before the move to Guyana, Jones engaged himself largely in the manifold craft of revivalism. Jones learned from others he observed—Father Divine in Philadelphia and David Martinus de Miranda in Brazil, and Jones himself became a purveyor of faked miracles and faith healings. By the California years, the Peoples Temple was prospering financially from its somewhat shady "tent meeting" style activities, and from a variety of other petty and grand money-making schemes; it was also gaining political clout through the deployment of its members for the benefit of various politicians and causes.

These early developments give cause to wonder why Jones did not establish a successful but relatively benign sect like Jehovah's Witnesses, or, alternatively, why he did not move from a religious base directly into the realm of politics, as did the Reverend Adam Clayton Powell, from his Harlem congregation to the U.S. House of Representatives. The answer seems twofold. In the first place, Jim Jones seems to have had limitations both as an evangelist and as a politician. He simply did not succeed in fooling key California observers with his faked miracles. And for all the political support he peddled in California politics, Jones was not always able to draw on his good political "credit" when he needed it. A certain mark of political effectiveness concerns the ability to sustain power in the face of scandal. By this standard, Jones was not totally successful in either Indiana or California: there always seemed to be investigators and reporters on the trails of various questionable financial and evangelical dealings.

Quite aside from the limits of Jones' effectiveness, the very nature of his prophecy directed his religious movement along a different path from either "worldly" politics or sectarian Adventism. Keyed to the New Testament Book of Revelation, Adventist groups receive prophecy about the apocalyptic downfall of the present evil order of the world and the second coming of Christ to preside over a millennial period of divine grace on earth. For all such groups, the Advent itself makes social action to reform "this" world's institutions irrelevant. Adventist groups differ from one another in their exact eschatology of the last days, but the groups that have survived, like the Seventh Day Adventists and Jehovah's Witnesses, have juggled their doctrines which fix an exact date for Christ's appearance. Thus they have moved away from any intense chiliastic expectation of an imminent appearance, to engage in more mundane conversionist activities which are intended to pave the way for the Millennium.

"Apocalypse Now"

Reverend Jones himself seems to have shared the pessimism of the Adventist sects about reforming social institutions in this world (for him, the capitalist world of the United States). True, he supported various progressive causes, but he did not put much stake in their success. Jones' prophecy was far more radical than those of contemporary Adventist groups; he focused on imminent apocalyptic disaster rather than on Christ's millennial salvation, and his eschatology therefore had to resolve a choice between preapocalyptic struggle with "the beast" or collective flight to establish a postapocalyptic kingdom of the elect. Up until the end, the Peoples Temple was directed toward the latter possibility. Even in the Indiana years, Jones had embraced an apocalyptic view. The move from Indiana to California was in part justified by Jones' claim that Redwood Valley would survive nuclear holocaust. In the California years, the apocalyptic vision shifted to Central Intelligence Agency persecution and Nazi-like extermination of blacks. In California too, the Peoples Temple gradually became communalistic in certain respects; it established a community of goods, pooled resources of elderly followers to provide communal housing for them, and drew on state funds to act as foster parents by establishing group homes for displaced youth. In its apocalyptic and communal aspects, the Peoples Temple more and more came to exist as an ark of survival. Jonestown, the Agricultural Project in Guyana, was built beginning in 1974 by an advance crew that by early 1977 still amounted to less than 60 people, most of them under 30 years old. The mass exodus of the Peoples Temple to Jonestown really began in 1977, when the Peoples Temple was coming under increasing scrutiny in California.

In the move to Guyana, the Peoples Temple began to concertedly exhibit many dynamics of other-worldly sects, though it differed in ways which were central to its fate. Until the end, Jonestown was similar in striking ways to contemporary sects like the Children of God and the Krishna Society (ISKCON, Inc.). Indeed, the Temple bears a more than casual (and somewhat uncomfortable) resemblance to the various Protestant sects which emigrated to the wilderness of North America beginning in the seventeenth century. The Puritans, Moravians, Rappites, Shakers, Lutherans, and many others like them sought to escape religious persecution in Europe in order to set up theocracies where they could live out their own visions of the earthly millennial community. So it was with Jonestown. In this light, neither disciplinary practices, the daily round of life, nor the community of goods at Jonestown seem so unusual.

"The Jungle Is Only a Few Yards Away"

The disciplinary practices of the Peoples Temple—as bizarre and grotesque as they may sound, are not uncommon aspects of other-worldly sects: these practices have been played up in the press in an attempt to demonstrate the perverse nature of the group, so as to "explain" the terrible climax to their life. But as Erving Goffman has shown in *Asylums*, sexual intimidation and general psychological terror occur in all kinds of total institutions, including mental hospitals, prisons, armies, and even nunneries. Indeed, Congressman Leo Ryan, just prior to his fateful visit to Jonestown, accepted the need for social control: ". . . you can't put 1,200 people in the middle of a jungle without some damn tight discipline." Practices at Jonestown may well seem restrained in comparison to practices of, say, seventeenth-century American Puritans who, among other things, were willing to execute "witches" on the testimony of respected churchgoers or even children. Meg Greenfield observed in *Newsweek* in reflecting on Jonestown, "the jungle is only a few yards away." It seems important to recall that some revered origins of the United States lie in a remarkably similar "jungle."

Communal groups of all types, not just otherworldly sects, face problems of social control and commitment. Rosabeth Kanter has convincingly shown that successful communal groups in the nineteenth-century United States often drew on mechanisms of mutual criticism, mortification, modification of conventional dyadic sexual mores, and other devices in order to decrease the individual's ties to the outside or personal relationships within the group, and increase the individual's commitment to the collectivity as a whole.

Such commitment mechanisms are employed most often in religious communal groups, especially those with charismatic leaders. Other-worldly communal groups, where a special attempt is being made to forge a wholly new interpretation of reality, where the demand for commitment is especially pronounced (in a word, where it is sectarian)—these groups have tremendously high stakes in maintaining commitment. These groups are likely to seek out the procedures most effective at guaranteeing commitment. After all, defection from "the way" inevitably casts doubt on the sanctity of the way, no matter how it is rationalized among the faithful. Thus, it is against such groups that the charges of "brainwashing," chicanery, and mistreatment of members are most often leveled. Whatever their basis in fact, these are the likely charges of families and friends who see their loved ones abandon them in favor of committing material resources and persona to the religious hope of a new life. Much like other-worldly sects, families suffer a loss of legitimacy in the "defection" of one of their own.

The abyss that comes to exist between other-worldly sects and the world of society-at-large left behind simply cannot be bridged. There is no encompassing rational connection between the two realities, and, therefore, the interchange between the other-worldly sect and people beyond its boundaries becomes a struggle either between "infidels" and the "faithful" from the point of view of the sect, or between rationality and fanaticism from the point of view of outsiders. Every sectarian action has its benevolent interpretation and legitimation within the sect and a converse interpretation from the outside. Thus, from inside the sect, various practices of "confession," "mutual criticism," or "catharsis" sessions seem necessary to prevent deviant worldviews from taking hold within the group. In the Peoples Temple, such practices included occasional enforced isolation and drug regimens for "rehabilitation" akin to contemporary psychiatric treatment. From the outside, all this tends to be regarded as "brainwashing," but insiders will turn the accusation outward, claiming that it is those in the society-at-large who are "brainwashed." Though there can really be no resolution to this conflict of interpretations, the widespread incidence of similar "coercive persuasion" outside Jonestown suggests that the fact it

was practiced at Jonestown is not so unusual, at least within the context of other-worldly sects, or total institutions in general, for that matter.

What is unusual is the direction which coercive persuasion or "brainwashing" took. Jones worked to instill devotion in unusual ways—ways which fostered the acceptability of "revolutionary suicide" among his followers. During "white nights" of emergency mobilization, he conducted rituals of proclaimed mass suicide, giving "poison" to all members, saying they would die within the hour. According to one defector, Deborah Blakey, Jones "explained that the poison was not real and we had just been through a loyalty test. He warned us that the time was not far off when it would be necessary for us to die by our own hands." This event initially left Blakey "indifferent" to whether she "lived or died." A true believer in the Peoples Temple was more emphatic: disappointed by the string of false collective suicides, in a note to Jones he hoped for "the real thing" so that they could all pass beyond the suffering of this world. Some people yielded to Jim Jones only because their will to resist was beaten down; others, including many "seniors"— the elderly members of the Peoples Temple—felt they owed everthing to Jim Jones, and provided him with a strong core of unequivocal support. Jones allowed open dissension at "town meetings" apparently because, with the support of the "seniors," he knew he could prevail. Thus, no matter what they wanted personally, people learned to leave their fates in the hands of Jim Jones, and accept what he demanded. The specific uses of coercive persuasion at Jonestown help explain how (but not why) the mass murder/suicide was implemented. But it is the special use, not the general nature of "brainwashing" which distinguishes Jonestown from most other-worldly sects.

Meat Eaters and Bean Eaters

Aside from "brainwashing," a second major kind of accusation about Jonestown, put forward most forcefully by Deborah Blakey, concerns the work discipline and diet there. Blakey swore in an affidavit that the work load was excessive and the food served to the average residents of Jonestown inadequate. She abhorred the contradiction between the conditions she reported and the privileged diet of Reverend Jones and his inner circle.

Moreover, because she had dealt with the group's finances, she knew that money could have been directed to providing a more adequate diet.

Blakey's moral sensibilities notwithstanding, the disparity between the diet of the elite and of the average Jonestowner should come as no surprise: it parallels Erving Goffman's description of widespread hierarchies of privilege in total institutions. Her concern about the average diet is more the point. But here, other accounts differ from Blakey's report. Maria Katsaris, a consort of Reverend Jones, wrote her father a letter extolling the virtues of the Agricultural Project's "cutlass" beans used as a meat substitute. And Paula Adams, who survived the Jonestown holocaust because she resided at the Peoples Temple house in Georgetown, expressed ambivalence about the Jonestown community in an interview after the mass murder/suicide. But she also remarked, "My daughter ate very well. She got eggs and milk every day. How many black children in the ghetto eat that well?" The accounts of surviving members of Reverend Jones' personal staff and inner circle, like Katsaris and Adams, are suspect, of course, in exactly the opposite way as those of people like the "Concerned Relatives." But the inside accounts are corroborated by at least one outsider, *Washington Post* reporter Charles Krause. On his arrival at Jonestown in the company of U.S. Congressman Leo Ryan, Krause noted, "contrary to what the Concerned Relatives had told us, nobody seemed to be starving. Indeed, everyone seemed quite healthy."

It is difficult to assess these conflicting views. Beginning early in the summer of 1977, Jones set in motion the mass exodus of some 800 Peoples Temple members from California to Jonestown. Though Jonestown could adequately house only about 500 people by then, the population quickly climbed well beyond that mark, at the same time ballooning way past the agricultural base of the settlement. The exodus also caused Jonestown to become "top heavy" with less-productive seniors and children. Anything close to agricultural self-sufficiency then became a more elusive and long-range goal. As time wore on during the group's last year of existence, Jones himself became ever more fixated on the prospect of a mass emigration from Guyana, and in this light, any sort of long-range agricultural development strategy seemed increasingly irrational. According to *The New York Times*, the former

Jonestown farm manager, Jim Bogue, suggested that the agricultural program at Jonestown would have succeeded in the long run, if it had been adhered to. But with the emerging plans for emigration, it was not followed, and thus became merely a charade for the benefit of the Guyanese government. This analysis would seem to have implications for *internal* conflicts about goals within Jonestown: for example, Jim Jones' only natural son, Stephan Jones, as well as several other young men in the Peoples Temple, came to believe in Jonestown as a socialist agrarian community, not as an other-worldly sect headed up by Jim Jones. Reflecting about his father after the mass murder/suicide, Stephan Jones commented, "I don't mind discrediting him, but I'm still a socialist, and Jim Jones will be used to discredit socialism. People will use him to discredit what was built. Jonestown was not Jim Jones, although he believed it was."

The "seniors" who provided social security checks, gardened, and produced handicraft articles for sale in Georgetown in lieu of heavy physical labor, as well as the fate of agricultural productivity—these both reinforce the assessment that Jim Jones' vision of the Peoples Temple approximates the "other-worldly sect" as an ideal type. In such sects, as a rule, proponents seek to survive *not* on the basis of productive labor (as in more "worldly utopian" communal groups), but on the basis of patronage, petty financial schemes, and the building of a "community of goods" through prosely-tism. This was just the case with Jonestown: the community of goods which Jones built up is valued at more than $12 million. As a basis for satisfying collective wants, any agricultural production at Jonestown would have paled in comparison to this amassed wealth.

But even if the agricultural project itself became a charade, it is no easy task to create a plausible charade in the midst of relatively infertile soil reclaimed from dense jungle; this would have required the long hours of work which Peoples Temple defectors described. Such a charade could serve as yet another effective means of social control. In the first place, it gave a purposeful role to those who envisioned Jonestown as an experimental socialist agrarian community. Beyond this, it monopolized the waking hours of most of the populace in exhausting work, and gave them only a minimal (though probably adequate) diet on which to do it. It is easy to imagine that many city people, or those with bourgeois sensibilities in general, would not find this their cup of tea in any case. But the demanding daily regimen, however abhorrent to the uninitiated, is widespread in other-worldly sects. Various programs of fasting and work asceticism have long been regarded as signs of piety and routes to religious enlightenment or ecstasy. In the contemporary American Krishna groups, an alternation of nonsugar and high-sugar phases of the diet seems to create an almost addictive attachment to the food which is communally dispersed. And we need look no later in history than to Saint Benedict's order to find a situation in which the personal time of participants is eliminated for all practical purposes, with procedures of mortification for offenders laid out by Saint Benedict in his *Rule*. The concerns of Blakey and others about diet, work, and discipline may have some basis, but they have probably been exaggerated, and in any case, they do not distinguish Jonestown from other-worldly sects in general.

Community of Goods

One final public concern with the Peoples Temple deserves mention because it so closely parallels previous sectarian practice: the Reverend Jim Jones is accused of swindling people out of their livelihoods and life circumstances by tricking them into signing over their money and possessions to the Peoples Temple or its inner circle of members. Of course, Jones considered this a "community of goods" and correctly pointed to a long tradition of such want satisfaction among other-worldly sects; in an interview just prior to the mass murder/suicide, Jones cited Jesus' call to hold all things in common. There are good grounds to think that Reverend Jones carried this philosophy into the realm of a con game. Still, it should be noted that in the suicidal end, Jones did not benefit from all the wealth the way a good number of other self-declared prophets and messiahs have done.

As with its disciplinary practices and its round of daily life, the community of goods in the Peoples Temple at Jonestown emphasizes its similarities to other-worldly sects—both the contemporary ones labelled "cults" by their detractors, and historical examples which are often revered in retrospect by contemporary religious culture. The elaboration of these affinities is in no way intended to suggest

that we can or should vindicate the duplicity, the bizarre sexual and psychological intimidation, and the hardships of daily life at Jonestown. But it must be recognized that the Jonestown settlement was a good deal less unusual than some of us might like to think: the things which detractors find abhorrent in the life of the Peoples Temple at Jonestown prior to the final "white night" of murder and suicide are the core nature of other-worldly sects. It should come as no surprise that practices like those in Jonestown are widespread, both in historical and contemporary other-worldly sects. Granted that the character of such sects—the theocratic basis of authority, the devices of mortification and social control, and the demanding regimen of everyday life—predispose people in such groups to respond to the whims of their leaders, whatever fanatic and zealous directions they may take. But given the widespread occurrence of other-worldly sects, the other-worldly features of Jonestown are in themselves insufficient to explain the bizarre fate of its participants. If we are to understand the unique turn of events at Jonestown, we must look to certain distinctive features of the Peoples Temple—things which make it unusual among other-worldly sects, and we must try to comprehend the subjective meanings of these features for various of Jonestown's participants.

Race and Ideology

If the Peoples Temple was distinctive among other-worldly sects, it is for two reasons: first, the group was far and away more thoroughly racially integrated than any other such group today. Second, the Peoples Temple was distinctively proto-communist in ideology. Both of these conditions, together with certain personal fears of Jim Jones (mixed perhaps with organic disorders and assorted drugs), converged in the active mind of the reverend to give a special twist to the apocalyptic quest of his flock. Let us consider these matters in turn.

In the Peoples Temple, Jim Jones had consistently sought to transcend racism in peace rather than in struggle. The origins of this approach, like most of Jones' early life, are by now shrouded in myth. But it is clear that Jones was committed to racial harmony in his Indiana ministry. In the 1950s, his formation of an interracial congregation met with much resistance in Indianapolis, and this persecution was one impetus for the exodus to California. There is room for debate on how far Jones' operation actually went toward racial equality, or to what degree it simply perpetuated racism, albeit in a racially harmonious microcosm. But the Peoples Temple fostered greater racial equality and harmony than that of the society-at-large, and in this respect, it has few parallels in present-day communal groups, much less mainstream religious congregations. The significance of this cannot easily be assayed, but one view of it is captured in a letter from a 20-year-old Jonestown girl. She wrote to her mother in Evansville, Indiana, that she could "walk down the street now without the fear of having little old white ladies call me nigger."

Coupled with the commitment to racial integration, and again in contrast with most other-worldly sects, the Peoples Temple moved strongly toward ideological communism. Most other-worldly sects practice religiously inspired communism—the "clerical" or "Christian" socialism which Marx and Engels railed against. But few, if any, to date have flirted with the likes of Marx, Lenin, and Stalin. By contrast, it has become clear that, whatever the contradictions other socialists point to between Jones' messianism and socialism, the Reverend Jim Jones and his staff considered themselves socialists. In his column "Perspectives from Guyana," Jim Jones maintained, "neither my colleagues nor I are any longer caught up in the opiate of religion. . . ." Though the practice of the group prior to the mass murder/suicide was not based on any doctrinaire Marxism, at least some of the recruits to the group were young radical intellectuals, and one of the group's members, Richard Tropp, gave evening classes on radical political theory. In short, radical socialist currents were unmistakably present in the group.

Preaching Atheism

It is perhaps more questionable whether the Peoples Temple was religious in any conventional sense of the term. Of course, all utopian communal groups are religious in that they draw together true believers who seek to live out a heretical or heterodox interpretation of the meaningfulness of social existence. In this sense, the Peoples Temple was a religious group, just as Frederick Engels once observed that socialist sects of the nineteenth century paralleled the character of primitive Christian and Reformation sects. Clearly, Jim Jones was more self-consciously religious than the socialist sects were. Though he "preached atheism," and did not believe in a God that answers prayer, he did embrace reincarnation, and a surviving resident of Jonestown remembers him saying, "Our religion is this: your highest service to God is service to your fellow man." On the other hand, it seems that the outward manifestations of conventional religious activity—revivals, sermons, faith healings—were, at least in Jim Jones' view, calculated devices to draw people into an organization which was something quite different. It is a telling point in this regard that Jones ceased the practice of faith healings and cut off other religious activities once he moved to Jonestown. Jones' wife Marceline once noted that Jim Jones considered himself a Marxist who "used religion to try to get some people out of the opiate of religion." In a remarkable off-the-cuff interview with Richard and Harriet Tropp—the two Jonestown residents who were writing a book about the Peoples Temple—Jones reflected on the early years of his ministry, claiming, "what a hell of a battle that [integration] was—I thought 'I'll never make a revolution. I can't even get those fuckers to integrate, much less get them to any communist philosophy.'" In the same interview, Jones intimated that he had been a member of the U.S. Communist party in the early 1950s. Of course, with Jones' Nixonesque concern for his place in history, it is possible that his hind-sight, even in talking with sympathetic biographers, was not the same as his original motives. In the interview with the Tropps, Jones hinted that the entire development of the Peoples Temple down to the Jonestown Agricultural Project derived from his communist beliefs. This interview and Marceline Jones' comment give strong evidence of an early communist orientation in Jones. Whenever this orientation originated, the move to Jonestown was in part predicated on it. The socialist government of Guyana was generally committed to supporting socialists seeking refuge from capitalist societies, and they apparently thought Jones' flexible brand of Marxism fit well within the country's political matrix. By 1973, when negotiations with Guyana about an agricultural project were initiated, Jones and his aides were professing identification with the world-historical communist movement.

The Persecution Complex

The convergence of racial integration and crude communism gave a distinctly political character to what in many other respects was an other-worldly religious sect. The injection of radical politics gave a heightened sense of persecution to the Jonestown Agricultural Project. Jim Jones seems to have both fed this heightened sense of persecution to his followers, and to have been devoured by it himself. Jones manipulated fears among his followers by controlling information and spreading false rumors about news events in the United States. With actual knowledge of certain adversaries, and fed by his own premonitions, Jones spread premonitions among his followers, thereby heightening their dedication. In the process, Jones disenchanted a few, who became Judas Iscariots, in time bringing the forces of legitimated external authority to "persecute" Jones and his true believers in their jungle theocracy.

The persecution complex is a stock-in-trade of other-worldly sects. It is naturally engendered by a radical separation from the world of society-at-large. An apocalyptic mission develops in such a way that "persecution" from the world left behind is taken as a sign of the sanctity of the group's chosen path of salvation. Though racial and political persecution are not usually among the themes of other-worldly persecution, they do not totally break the other-worldly way of interpreting experience. But the heightened sense of persecution at Jonestown did reduce the disconnection from society-at-large which is the signature of other-worldly sects.

Most blacks in the United States have already experienced "persecution": if Jim Jones gave his black followers some relief from a ghetto existence (which many seem to have felt he did), he also made a point of reminding the blacks in his group that persecution still awaited them back in the ghettos and rural areas of the United States. In the California years, for example, the Peoples Temple would stage mock lynchings of blacks by the Ku Klux Klan as a form of political theater. And according to Deborah Blakey, Jones "convinced black Temple members that if they did not follow him to Guyana, they would be put into concentration camps and killed."

Similarly, white socialist intellectuals could easily develop paranoia about their activities: as any participant in the New Left movement of the 1960s and early 1970s knows, paranoia was a sort of badge of honor to some people. Jones fed this sort of paranoia by telling whites that the CIA listed them as enemies of the state.

Jones probably impressed persecution upon his followers to increase their allegiance to him. But Jones himself was caught up in a web of persecution and betrayal. The falling out between Jones and Grace and Tim Stoen seems central here. In conjunction with the imminent appearance of negative news articles, the fight over custody of John Victor Stoen—Grace's son whom both Jones and Tim Stoen claimed to have fathered—triggered Jones' 1977 decision to remove himself from the San Francisco Temple to Guyana.

We may never know what happened between the Stoens and Jones. According to Terri Buford, a former Jonestown insider, Tim Stoen left the Peoples Temple shortly after it became known that in the 1960s he had gone on a Rotary-sponsored speaking tour denouncing communism. Both sides have accused the other of being the progenitors of violence in the Peoples Temple. To reporters who accompanied Congressman Ryan, Jones charged that the Stoen couple had been government agents and provocateurs who had advocated bombing, burning, and terrorism. This possibility could have been regarded as quite plausible by Jones and his staff, for they possessed documents about alleged similar Federal Bureau of Investigation moves against the Weather Underground and the Church of Scientology. The struggle between Jones and the Stoens thus could easily have personified to Jones the quintessence of a conspiracy against him and his work. It certainly intensified negative media attention on the Temple.

For all his attempts to garner favor from the press, Jones failed in the crucial instance. The San Francisco investigative reporters gave horror stories about the Peoples Temple and Jones' custody battle a good deal of play. Jones may well have been correct in his suspicion that he was not being treated fairly in the press. After the mass murder/suicide, the managing editor of the *San Francisco Examiner* proudly asserted in a January 15, 1979, letter to the *Wall Street Journal* that his paper had not been "morally neutral" in its coverage of the Peoples Temple.

The published horror stories were based on the allegations by defectors, the Stoens and Deborah Blakey foremost among them. How true, widespread, exaggerated, or isolated the incidents reported were, we do not know. Certainly they were generalized in the press to the point of creating an image of Jones as a total ogre. The defectors also initiated legal proceedings against the Temple. And the news articles began to stir the interest of government authorities in the operation. These developments were not lost on Jim Jones. The custody battle with the Stoens seems to have precipitated Jones' mass suicide threat to the Guyanese government. Not coincidentally, according to Jim Jones' only natural son, Stephan Jones, at this point the first "white night" drills for mass suicide were held (Stephan Jones connects these events with the appearance of several negative news articles).

With these sorts of events in mind, it is not hard to see how it came to be that Jim Jones felt betrayed by the Stoens and the other defectors, and persecuted by those who appeared to side with the defectors—the press and the government foremost among them. In September 1978, Jones went so far as to retain well-known conspiracy theorist and lawyer Mark Lane to investigate the possibility of a plot against the Peoples Temple. In the days immediately after he was retained by Jones, Mark Lane (perhaps self-servingly) reported in a memorandum to Jones that "even a cursory examination" of the available evidence "reveals that there has been a coordinated campaign to destroy the Peoples Temple and to impugn the reputation of its leader." Those involved were said to include the U.S. Customs Bureau, the Federal Communications Commission, the Central Intelligence Agency, the Federal Bureau of Investigation, and the Internal Revenue Service. Lane's assertions probably had little basis in fact: though several of the named agencies independently had looked into certain Temple activities, none of them had taken any direct action against the Temple, even though they may have had some cause for doing so. The actual state of affairs notwithstanding, with Lane's assertions, Jones had substantiation of his sense of persecution from a widely touted theorist of conspiracies.

The sense of persecution which gradually developed in the Peoples Temple from its beginning and increased markedly at Jonestown must have come to a head with the visit there of U.S. Congressman Leo Ryan. The U.S. State Department has revealed that Jones had agreed to a visit by Ryan, but withdrew permission when it became known that a contingent of "Concerned Relatives" as well as certain members of the press would accompany Ryan to Guyana. Among the Concerned Relatives who came with Ryan was the Stoen couple; in fact, Tim Stoen was known as a "leader" of the Concerned Relatives. Reporters with Ryan included two from the *San Francisco Chronicle*, a paper which had already pursued investigative reporting on the Peoples Temple, as well as Gordon Lindsay, an independent newsman who had written a negative story on the Peoples Temple intended to be (but never actually) published in the *National Enquirer*. This entourage could hardly have been regarded as objective or unbiased by Jim Jones and his closer supporters. Instead, it identified Ryan with the forces of persecution, personified by the Stoens and the investigative press, and it set the stage for the mass murder/suicide which had already been threatened in conjunction with the custody fight.

The ways in which the Peoples Temple came to differ from more typical other-worldly sects are more a matter of degree than of kind, but the differences together profoundly altered the character of the scene of Jonestown. Though the avowed radicalism, the interracial living, and the defector-media-government "conspiracy" are structurally distinct from one another, Jim Jones drew them together into a tableau of conspiracy which was intended to increase his followers' attachment to him, but ironically brought his legitimacy as a messiah into question, undermined the other-worldly possibilities of the Peoples Temple Agricultural Project, and placed the group on the stage of history in a distinctive relationship to the apocalypse.

Virtuosi of the Collective Life

Other-worldly sects by their very nature are permeated with apocalyptic ideas. The sense of a decaying social order is personally experienced by the religious seeker in a life held to be untenable, meaningless, or both. This interpretation of life is collectively affirmed and transcended in other-worldly sects, which purport to offer "heaven-on-earth," beyond the effects of the apocalypse. Such sects promise the grace of a theocracy in which followers can sometimes really escape the "living hell" of society-at-large. Many of Reverend Jones' followers seem to have joined the Peoples Temple with this in mind. But the predominance of blacks and the radical ideology of the Temple, together with the persistent struggle against the defectors and the "conspiracy" which formed around them in the minds of the faithful each gave the true believers' sense of persecution a more immediate and pressing, rather than "other-worldly" cast. Jones used these elements to heighten his followers' sense of persecution from the outside, but this device itself may have drawn into question the ability of the supposed charismatic leader to provide an other-worldly sanctuary. By the middle of October, a month before Congressman Ryan's trip in November 1978, Jones' position of preeminent leadership was beginning to be questioned not only by disappointed religious followers, but also by previously devoted "seniors" who were growing tired of the ceaseless meetings and the increasingly untenable character of everyday life, and by key virtuosi of collective life who felt Jones was responsible for their growing inability to deal successfully with Jonestown's material operations. Once those who were dissatisfied circumvented Jones' intelligence network of informers and began to establish solidarity with one another, the "conspiracy" can truly be said to have taken hold within Jonestown itself. If the times were apocalyptic, Reverend Jones was like the revolutionary millenarians described by Norman Cohn and Gunther Levy. Rather than successfully proclaiming the postapocalyptic sanctuary, Jones was reduced to declaiming the web to web of "evil" powers in which he was ensnared, and searching with chiliastic expectation for the imminent cataclysm which would announce the beginning of the kingdom of righteousness.

Usually, other-worldly sects have a sense of the eternal about them: having escaped "this" world, they adopt the temporal trappings of "heaven," which amounts to a timeless bliss of immortality. But Jim Jones had not really established a postapocalyptic heavenly plateau. Even if he had promised this to his followers, it was only just being built in the form of the Agricultural Project. And it was not even clear that Jonestown itself was the promised land. Jones did not entirely trust the Guyanese government, and he was considering seeking final asylum in Cuba or the Soviet Union. Whereas

other-worldly sects typically assert that heaven is at hand, Jones could only hold it out as a future goal, and one which became more and more elusive as the forces of "persecution" tracked him to Guyana. Thus, Jones and his followers were still within the throes of the apocalypse, still, as they conceived it, the forces of good battling against the evil and conspiratorial world which could not tolerate a living example of a racially integrated American socialist utopia.

In the struggle against evil, Jones and his true believers took on the character of what I have termed a "warring sect"—fighting a decisive Manichean struggle with the forces of evil. Such a struggle seems almost inevitable when political rather than religious themes of apocalypse are stressed, and it is clear that Jones and his staff at times acted within this militant frame of reference. For example, they maintained armed guards around the settlement, held "white night" emergency drills, and even staged mock CIA attacks on Jonestown. By doing so, they undermined the plausibility of an other-worldly existence. The struggle of a warring sect takes place in historical time, where one action builds on another, where decisive outcomes of previous events shape future possibilities. The contradiction between this earthly struggle and the heaven-on-earth Jones would have liked to proclaim (for example, in "Perspectives from Guyana") gave Jonestown many of its strange juxtapositions—of heaven and hell, of suffering and bliss, of love and coercion. Perhaps even Jones himself, for all his megalomaniacal ability to transcend the contradictions which others saw in him (and labelled him an "opportunist" for), could not endure the struggle for his own immortality. If he were indeed a messianic incarnation of God, as he sometimes claimed, presumably Jones could have either won the struggle of the warring sect against its evil persecutors or delivered his people to the bliss of another world.

In effect, Jones had brought his flock to the point of straddling the two sides of the apocalypse. Had he established his colony beyond the unsympathetic purview of defectors, Concerned Relatives, investigative reporters, and governmental agencies, the other-worldly tableau perhaps could have been sustained with less-repressive methods of social control. As it was, Jones and the colony experienced the three interconnected limitations of group totalism which Robert Jay Lifton described with respect to the Chinese Communist revolution: (1) diminishing conversions, (2) inner antagonism (that is, of disillusioned participants) to the suffocation of individuality, and (3) increasing penetration of the "idea-tight milieu control" by outside forces. As Lifton noted, revolutionaries are engaged in a quest for immortality. Other-worldly sectarians in a way short-circuit this quest by the fiat of *asserting* their immortality—positing the timeless heavenly plateau which exists *beyond* history as the basis of their everyday life. But under the persistent eyes of external critics, and because Jones himself exploited such "persecution" to increase his social control, he could not sustain the illusion of other-worldly immortality.

On the other hand, the Peoples Temple could not achieve the sort of political victory which would have been the goal of a warring sect. Since revolutionary war involves a struggle with an established political order in unfolding historical time, revolutionaries can only attain immortality in the wide-scale victory of the revolution over the "forces of reaction." Ironically, as Lifton pointed out, even the initial political and military victory of the revolutionary forces does not end the search for immortality: even in victory, revolution can only be sustained through diffusion of its principles and goals. But as Max Weber observed, in the long run, it seems impossible to maintain the charismatic enthusiasm of revolution; more pragmatic concerns come to the fore, and as the ultimate ends of revolution are faced off against everyday life and its demands, the quest for immortality fades, and the immortality of the revolutionary moment is replaced by the myth of a grand revolutionary past.

The Peoples Temple could not begin to achieve revolutionary immortality in historical time, for it could not even pretend to achieve any victory against its enemies. If it had come to a pitched battle, the Jonestown defenders—like the Symbionese Liberation Army against the Los Angeles Police Department S.W.A.T. (strategic weapons and tactics) Team—would have been wiped out.

But the Peoples Temple could create a kind of "immortality" which is really not a possibility for political revolutionaries. They could abandon apocalyptic hell by the act of mass suicide. This would shut out the opponents of the Temple: they could not be the undoing of what was already undone, and there could be no recriminations against the dead. It could also achieve the other-worldly salvation Jones had promised his more religious followers. Mass suicide united the divergent public threads of meaningful existence at Jonestown—those of political revolution and religious salvation. It was an awesome vehicle for a powerful statement of collective solidarity by the true believers among the people of Jonestown—that they would rather die together than have the life that was created together subjected to gradual decimation and dishonor at the hands of authorities regarded as illegitimate.

Most warring sects reach a grisly end: occasionally, they achieve martyrdom, but if they lack a constituency, their extermination is used by the state as proof of its monopoly on the legitimate use of force. "Revolutionary" suicide is a victory by comparison. The event can be drawn upon for moral didactics, but this cannot erase the stigma that Jonestown implicitly places on the world that its members left behind. Nor can the state punish the dead who are guilty, among other things, of murdering a U.S. Congressman, three newsmen, a Concerned Relative, and however many Jonestown residents that did not willingly commit suicide. Though they paid the total price of death for their ultimate commitment, and though they achieved little except perhaps sustenance of their own collective sense of honor, still those who won this hollow victory cannot have it taken away from them. In the absence of retribution, the state search for living guilty, as well as the widespread outcry against "cults," takes on the character of scapegoating. Those most responsible are beyond the reach of the law: unable to escape the hell of their own lives by creating an other-worldly existence on earth, they instead sought their "immortality" in death, and left it to others to ponder the apocalypse which they have unveiled.

4

The Religious Use of Drugs

Because the peoples of the world have such a myriad of uses for and attitudes toward what we call "drugs," it is impossible to define the term to the satisfaction of all. In the West, for example, chemical substances are prescribed to alleviate disease, but they are also used, often illegally, to provide "kicks" for the user; in many non-Western societies religious specialists utilize these materials as a vehicle for entry into the realm of the supernatural. Perhaps Marston Bates has most correctly defined the term, as "almost all materials taken for other than nutritional reasons" (1971: 113). Using this definition, one can count an extraordinary number of substances as falling into the category of "drugs."

Every culture, whatever the level of technological accomplishment, has an inventory of drugs and a medical system. The use of drugs is so ancient that Weston La Barre has posited the theory that shamanism itself developed from the use of hallucinogens (1972). The aim of this chapter is to describe the religious functions of drugs. This purpose almost totally eliminates the role of drugs in the West, where they are either medicinal or used for pleasure. At varying periods in Western history, most recently in the social ferment

Zapotec mask representing life and death, from Oaxaca, Mexico.

of the 1960s, drug usage was proclaimed by some people to have religious overtones, but few fool themselves today by believing that drugs provide the taker with a religious experience. Hedonism and escapism leading to addiction are the most prominent characteristics of Western drug use, and pose immense problems for governments that recognize the changing values that have encouraged the availability of illicit drugs. Certainly anthropologists have found the pleasure and escape motivation for drug use in non-Western societies as well, but the interrelationship of drugs and religion is dominant in traditional societies, where specialists such as shamans utilize plant and animal substances to contact the spirit world. Cross-cultural comparison demonstrates not only that drugs are perceived differently but also that they may actually have different effects on the users from one society to the next (despite having identical chemical makeup). Indeed, physiological and psychological reactions to drugs vary among individuals in the same society, a phenomenon that is often explained in terms of supernatural intervention.

Because most of us know little of the scientific properties of drugs, it is worthwhile to categorize them as to their effects on users. Lewis Lewin, the famous German toxicologist, whose drug classification is still basically sound and continues to be used by pharmacologists, offered the following categories (after Lewin as quoted by Bates [1971]: 115–16):

I. *Euphoria*: sedatives which reduce mental activity and induce mental and physical comfort, such as morphine, cocaine and the like.

II. *Phantastica*: hallucinogens, bringing on visions and illusions which vary greatly in chemical composition, but may be followed by unconsciousness or other symptoms of altered brain states. This group includes: mescal buttons, hashish and its source, marijuana.

III. *Inebriantia*: drugs which produce an initial phase of cerebral excitation followed by a state of depression which sometimes leads to unconsciousness. Chloroform, alcohol, ether, and others are members of this group.

IV. *Hypnotica*: sedatives or sleep producers such as chloral, sulphonol and some recent synthetic barbiturates.

V. *Excitania*: mental stimulants today referred to as analeptics. Coffee, tea, betel, and tobacco;

that is, all plants containing caffeine, nicotine and the like.

Today we would add a sixth category to the above—the tranquilizers, sometimes termed "ataraxics." In reality none are new drugs; rather, they are relatively newly discovered.

Interestingly, none of the first five categories, indeed, even the sixth (ataraxics), was unknown to so-called primitive people. Although the history of the use of these drugs is so ancient as to make attempts at tracing their origins academic exercises, it wasn't until the development of synthetics, prompted by the shortages of natural products during World War II, that hunting and gathering societies knew of and used the same basic chemical substances of medicines as modern technological cultures. For their knowledge of the chemical properties of the plants and animals in their environments, modern man's debt to "primitive man" is great.

The focus of drug use in traditionally based non-Western cultures is on the religious specialist, particularly the shaman, whose duty it is to control the spirit world for the benefit of the members of his society. Of all the categories of drugs, it is the hallucinogens, Lewin's "phantastica," that command our attention, for it is these psychotropic plant and animal substances that provide the shamans with their visions of the supernatural realm. Importantly, what one society considers to be real or unreal is not always shared by another society. Michael Harner's article in this chapter demonstrates, for example, that the Jívaro of the Ecuadorian Amazon consider reality to be what is found in the hallucinogenic state that results from drinking a tea made from the Banisteriopsis vine; the non-hallucinogenic, ordinary state is considered to be an illusion. Indeed, some drugs not considered hallucinogens in Western pharmacology do cause a visionary state; such is the case of the Warao shamans' use of tobacco. The point is that whether we agree or not with the folk categories of drugs in other societies, the mainspring of shamanistic power is centered on drugs that produce visual hallucinations as well as hallucinations of the other senses.

The shamanistic use of a variety of hallucinogenic drugs for trance inducement has not in itself guaranteed that a shaman's patient would recover, or that an enemy would suffer. To this end many other, non-hallucinogenic drugs and practices have also been used, some of which involved effective chemical properties or constituted successful non-drug techniques, such as the sucking-out of evil forces. Even substances having only inert chemicals were often effective in the hands of the shaman. Surely, other reasons must be offered for those successes. The illnesses of non-Western traditional societies have sometimes been described as being due to imbalances or disruptions of the patients' social environment. Physical and mental illnesses are difficult to separate, particularly in groups where belief systems are shared by a high percentage of the population. The treatment offered by shamans is relatively standard and almost always considered correct by patients, as well as by their families and friends, who are often present for the curing process and ceremony. The anxiety of the patient, on the one hand, and the confidence of the shaman, on the other, work to develop a level of suggestibility that literally sets the stage for effective treatment. Shamans, with their secret formulas, chants, and personal contact and control over spirit helpers—knowledge and power the patient does not possess—appear omnipotent and inordinately powerful. The encouragement and support of family and friends in a familiar environment all count toward the eventual cure. Westerners have learned much from shamanistic treatment, for it treats the physical and the psychological, both of which are irrevocably intertwined with the supernatural causes of illness.

The first three articles in this chapter were chosen because each one focuses on a different aspect of drug use in traditional societies. Francis Huxley takes a broad approach to the subject, discussing the general use of drugs in primitive societies. Furst and Coe's work on "Ritual Enemas" is an ethnohistorical reconstruction of Maya drug usage through an analysis of their pottery. In "The Sound of Rushing Water," Michael Harner offers an insight to Jívaro reality, a state that can be achieved only through consumption of the hallucinogenic tea, natema. Finally, in the fourth article, Raziel Abelson, Allen Ginsberg, and Michael Wyschogrod, as members of a symposium on drugs, demonstrate that the functions of hallucinogenic drugs in the West are highly disputed and draw attention to the changes in Western attitudes toward drugs in the 1960s and today.

References

Bates, Marston
  1971 *Gluttons and Libertines: Human Problems of Being Natural.* New York: Vintage Books.

La Barre, Weston
  1972 "Hallucinogens and the Shamanistic Origins of Religion." In Peter T. Furst, ed., *Flesh of the Gods: The Ritual Use of Hallucinogens,* pp. 261–78. New York: F. Praeger.

Wilbert, Johannes
  1972 "Tobacco and Shamanistic Ecstasy Among the Warao Indians of Venezuela." In Peter T. Furst, ed., *Flesh of the Gods: The Ritual Use of Hallucinogens,* pp. 55–83. New York: Praeger.

Drugs

Francis Huxley

Field workers' interest in religious specialists inevitably drew anthropologists' attention to the religious use of drugs. The important role of drugs in human life, particularly in aboriginal South America where they are used in the most traditional manner, has prompted Marston Bates to refer to us as Homo medicans, *man the drug taker. His definition of drugs as almost all materials taken for other than nutritional reasons may be vague, but it does demonstrate the extraordinary variety of substances that are eaten, drunk, smoked, chewed, or rubbed on the skin but lack food value as their primary function (1971: 112–13). Francis Huxley's article discusses uses of drugs the world over, but focuses on such religious purposes as curing illnesses of the soul and body, divining, gaining supernatural knowledge, and contacting spirits. Huxley argues that drugs used in many religious rites tend to be hallucinogenic rather than those that suppress mental and physical activity. Unlike users of hallucinogens in contemporary society, however, primitive groups have long recognized the need for a ritual setting to channel the dangerous forces contained in drugs.*

Reprinted from Richard Cavendish, ed., *Man, Myth, and Magic* (London, 1970), Vol. 5, pp. 711–16, by permission of the author and BPCC/Phoebus Publishing.

THE POET BAUDELAIRE DESCRIBED DRUGS WHICH affect the mind as "artificial paradises." The phrase is apt and Lewis Lewin, the German biochemist, repeated it in his pioneering study of these drugs (*Phantastica*, 1924), where he divided paradise into categories: five of them in all, the paradises of narcosis, stimulation, euphoria, intoxication and hallucination. More simply we might say: of dreaming sleep, energetic wakefulness, well-being, drunkenness and the inspired imagination.

In palmistry, a certain small line near the bottom edge of the palm is called the paradise line. Some people, however, call it the poison line, because it indicates the capacity to enjoy a private and rarefied pleasure which in large doses cuts a man off from reality and infects him with an unattainable hope. A substance known as a drug in the pejorative sense of that word also has the characteristic of being paradisiacal and poisonous, as though it were one product of the serpent coiled about the Tree of Life.

One cannot read widely about drugs these days without coming across persistent references to the "drug problem." Drugs are indeed a problem in that they are addictive and encourage strange forms of narcissism which, though they may end fatally, are still attempts to regain paradise. The desire to do so is one of the fundamental ambitions of human nature which nearly every religion encourages, and this illuminates the drug problem from another aspect. If drugs can be used to enter paradise, what are the uses of paradise itself?

Drugs are used the world over, sometimes for entertainment, often for therapy or as a religious observation. Thus the soma plant celebrated in the early Vedic hymns of the East gave such bliss to those who took its juices that it was regarded as a divinity, and the visionary worlds of splendor praised by its devotees are certainly descriptions of the images which it induced. Opinions are divided as to what plant soma was originally;

at one time it was thought to be a species of either *Asclepias* or of *Sarcostemma*, though it has recently been identified as *Amanita muscaria*, the fly agaric.

The use of this toadstool and of other hallucinogenic (hallucination-producing) mushrooms may have been much more widespread in the past than we realize, and its effects quite possibly helped to give form to a number of traditional descriptions of heaven. Indeed, the most famous mysteries of antiquity, those of Eleusis, may have used the fly agaric in order to initiate the worshippers into a realization of the divine, which could well account for the veneration in which the mysteries were held. In Mexico before and after the Spanish Conquest several plants were held sacred because of their illuminating properties, ranging from the peyote cactus from which mescalin is derived to a species of *ipomea* containing a relative of lysergic acid (LSD); the *psilocybe* mushroom which was called *teonanactl* or "god's flesh," whose active principle is psilocybine, and *Datura stramonium* or thornapple with its scopolamine and atropine.

Such plants were used to cure illnesses of the soul and of the body, to divine the future and to gain a sense of supernatural knowledge. In South America other plants are used for similar purposes: one Brazilian curer has tracked down some 80 such plants in his own country, including a hallucinatory tree-toadstool. These plants include lianas like *Banisteria caapi*, peppers like *Piptadenia*, cocaine in the Andes, and at least one hallucinogenic animal, a caterpillar found inside bamboo stems.

In Africa, Asia, Siberia and Australia the list of plants which produce psychotropic (mind-changing) effects is long, and where no such plant is available alcohol may be used instead. Modern pharmacology has added to the number of psychotropic substances with highly potent and dangerous derivatives of opium, with anaesthetics, synthetic narcotics, tranquillizers—the original one being a synthetic based on the active principle of *Rauwolfia*, a plant used for centuries in India to calm the mind—pep pills, hallucinogens, and others. However, no modern doctor considers such substances to be sacred, as they would be amongst traditional cultures and as they are, up to a point, among those who use these products for their own enjoyment. This fact in itself has much to do with the existence of a drug problem.

The Religious Use of Drugs

The widespread use of drugs around the world, and especially in our society, makes it plain that man is a discontented animal beset by psychological and physical troubles, by boredom and spiritual ambitions. He uses drugs to relieve pain and illness, and also to change his entire way of looking at things. In religious language, human nature is always wishing to transcend its usual limitations. For waking consciousness is by no means the only kind which it is possible or desirable to experience, and other states can be reached by the use of psychophysical techniques and also by drugs.

Because they change the degree of alertness of the mind in one way or another, it seems probable that drugs interfere with the sleep cycle, either by allowing one to dream while still awake or by using the force of dreams to power action. It seems hardly credible, however, that maté tea, made from the leaf of a South American shrub and containing caffeine, could ever be used to induce trance. Tea, which contains tannin as well as caffeine in quite large quantities, certainly does not have this effect normally, and it was originally celebrated in India and China for its refreshing qualities that allowed the mind to stay awake during meditation. By itself maté could not bring about an oracular state of trance—as it does amongst Indians still living in the Mato Grosso—unless its actions reinforce a process already set in motion by the seer and, by this working together of a psychological technique with a physiological agent, bring about a state of dissociation in which the mind finds a new faculty of expression.

The religious use of drugs, in fact, usually accompanies the practice of shamanism, though shamanism often does without drugs. Shamanism is a technique by which a man, and sometimes a woman, prepares himself by singing, dancing, training and long periods of seclusion during which he meditates, for an influx of untoward inspiration that can carry him into the world of spirits where events on earth are ordained and carried out. It is often a hereditary calling, but may equally well be embraced by those who have either a surplus of mental energy or who have suffered from what we would call a nervous complaint of some severity. Such unsatisfied or unbalanced states of mind are continually looking for a resolution of their frustrations and ambitions, and they do so by using traditional methods which articulate their powers coherently.

Drugs can help to do this because their effects are so similar to those produced by other methods of shamanistic training. An instructive case concerns tobacco, which like maté was used for getting into trance. Throughout the Americas this plant was used much as we use it today, for pleasure and to aid concentration, though it was sometimes accounted a fault in an ordinary man if he smoked it in private. But its most significant use was by shamans who smoked large amounts at one sitting to achieve their ecstatic experiences. The combination of tobacco smoke and overbreathing (causing oxygen intoxication) produces that kind of giddiness and nausea which most people experience with their first cigarette. Giddiness is one of the universal symptoms of ecstasy—the word giddy comes from the Old English *gidig*, meaning possessed by a god—and it is by entering into this giddiness and following down the physiological pathways which it opens up that a shaman is able to dissociate himself from his normal waking self and arrive at a place in his mind where all is certain and a quite different conscious process begins.

What such people have done is to use the forces within the paradisiacal experience for definite ends. The lack of such ends in modern society, as has already been implied, is one reason why we have a drug problem: without a ritual support the mind is often not strong enough to resist the effects of a drug, and so loses its sense of direction. When we consider the power of some drugs, this is not surprising. The incredibly small quantity of 100 microgrammes of lysergic acid is enough to bring about a psychedelic experience in which the mind is profoundly altered in its normal functioning and of which it previously had but the barest suspicion. Indeed many investigators have been so taken aback by these changes that they prefer to call the drug a psychosomimetic, one which produces a condition resembling madness.

The purpose of a ritual setting for the taking of a drug is to prevent madness, by directing the energies which the drug releases into a number of specific channels, and to put paradise into relation with objects in the outside world by establishing a dogmatic plan within the imagination, through which social events can be seen as psychological

ones, psychological as physical ones, and physical ones as spiritual.

By such a method even opium, the grandmother of all narcotics, has occasionally been used not merely to enjoy its sumptuous and pearly visions but to carry out a conscious intention. Such is the habit of shamans in parts of Southeast Asia, who take opium to increase the ecstatic effects of dancing and through them to send their spirits upon a supernatural adventure for the curing of illness or the foretelling of the future. The soporific effect of opium is such, however, that its devotees are much more liable to become physically passive, which must be why it is so seldom used in an active and practical manner. It is true that opium is used in the East for conviviality, but its solitary use is difficult to control. Coleridge, who first took laudanum, a derivative of opium, to dull a particularly ferocious toothache and eventually became addicted to it, did manage to write at least one great poem under its influence: or perhaps we should say that *Kubla Khan* composed itself when his mind, still active in its poetic function, directed the opium into a creative activity. But such feats are rare, for the mind's ability to hold its own against the sweetly insidious effects of opium in large quantities is limited, and the drug soon brings about that passive state in which, as Henri Michaux, the modern French poet, has said, "One no longer dreams, one is dreamed."

"O just, subtle and all-conquering opium!" cried de Quincey, author of *Confessions of an English Opium Eater* (1822), who took laudanum as an elixir for his neurasthenia and declared it to be the center of the true religion of which he was the high priest. But religions have hells as well as heavens, and the last stages of his addiction were marked, as they always are, by psychic and physical horrors from which he at last managed to free himself. What is this paradise, as Baudelaire said of hashish, which one buys at the price of one's eternal damnation? But this progression from paradise to the inferno allows one to draw a most interesting parallel between the possessive effects of a drug and those of a spirit, as in Voodoo.

In Voodoo ceremonies we might say that a pact has been entered into with any one of the many gods or spirits of the Haitian pantheon, which are called *loa*. The worshipper is possessed by the loa in such a way that he no longer has conscious control of his actions, and has no memory of what passed when he was possessed. The loa who rides him, as the phrase goes, always has a definite way of behaving—a stereotype, we might say, or schema—and this ability to act out the character of a loa is only achieved after training and initiation. Those who feel the influx of divine energy before they are initiated into Voodoo suffer not only from unfortunate accidents but often from manic outbursts ending in madness. It is the business of Voodoo to avoid this outcome and to see that its initiates can become possessed by this energy and still remain sane.

A Pact with the Devil

We might thus call an addict one who has been possessed by a drug after a private initiation which has no aim other than the desire continually to be possessed, unlike a Voodoo ceremony with its definite beginning and end. The addict cannot but wish his experience will continue for ever, even if he realizes that his body will disintegrate under the impact of the drug and that he then can no longer call his soul his own. The narcotic drugs, which slow down physical activity, and the excitants like amphetamine which speed it up, are particularly apt to bring about this state of living on borrowed time; this is presumably not only because they bring out long-term metabolic changes but also because the will cannot detach itself from the pleasures it seeks.

The question of whether it is ethical to take drugs is a difficult one to answer. They have been and still are being used as an aid to meditation, but the masters of this art are unanimous in condemning them, since they tend to inflame the imagination and give it a wrong idea of its powers. From his own experience, Jean Cocteau has said that no one becomes an opium addict unless he has made a pact with it: a pact in which he dedicates his will to the power of the drug. There is no doubt that the mythology surrounding drug-taking reflects certain basic notions about black magic for this reason. Black magic is rightly regarded as a dangerous pastime because it provides immediate gains without immediate payment: it is a pact with the Devil, who comes later when it suits him and presents a bill on which are written the ominous words, One Soul.

What does it mean, to enter into a pact with the Devil? Freud was much interested in the subject and wrote a study of it at the time when he was still taking cocaine, which he did for ten years. The traditional reasons for such a pact include the obtaining of wealth, of power over men and Nature, and over the hearts of women. But Freud concluded from the case he studied that the central reason was to overcome depression and to find a father-substitute. About cocaine he wrote: "One senses an increase of self-control and feels more vigorous and more capable of work," and he suggested that its effects were due, not to direct stimulation but to the removal of anxiety symptoms, which produced a return to a state of normal euphoria. Anxiety has to do with the superego in his system, and we can enlarge this description by remarking that by removing the "censor" cocaine also removes anxiety. Because of this cocaine may have been an indispensable tool for Freud during his self-analysis: it allowed him to follow the lines of his reasoning into the subconscious without his mental censor putting up a resistance. That Freud escaped from addiction while one of his friends, to whom he had recommended it, died from its effects, suggests that he only did so because he had found a method by which the effects of the drug became subservient to the force of his intellectual drive. He had created a special form of ritual.

Separating Mind from Body

Without this drive cocaine is undoubtedly a danger, as we may see from the religious taking of coca amongst the Kogi of Colombia. This tribe uses it ceremonially to learn the lengthy genealogies and liturgies of their worship, and to fill their minds with the proper religious awe and sense of significance. Coca however has the unfortunate effect of making its takers impotent after a while, and the Kogi are suspicious of their womenfolk (who are not allowed to chew it) and so inefficient as farmers that their children are undernourished. Ironically, the atheists of the tribe who have dropped out of the religion altogether are much healthier and happier, though their neighbors scorn them for losing their chance of immortality. This petrifying effect of coca, even with a religious system to direct it, is certainly partly caused by the fact that the Kogi way of life is beset on all sides by the creole population and has withdrawn into a state of apathy.

Coca is used elsewhere in the Andes to ward off hunger and fatigue, and it does so by numbing these sensations and dissociating the mind from anxieties arising in the body. But anxiety may persist even if its symptoms disappear with the use of a drug. These symptoms emerge again after a long time in an even more disagreeable form, as the nightmare effects of addiction show. When at such a time the use of the drug is stopped, this anxiety must be at least one of the constituents of the most unpleasant withdrawal symptoms.

Attacking the Self

The drugs used in other religious rites tend to be hallucinogenic rather than narcotic or stupefying, and these have a quite different effect upon anxiety. Common to plants with such different active principles as *Banisteria*, *Amanita* and *Datura* is the production of a sudden and violent surge of energy with visions in which terror and splendor may be equally present. The Viking berserkers seem to have used *Amanita* to endow themselves with a blind and warlike frenzy no opponent could withstand, a frenzy that might last more than a day and after which they sank into a long torpor of exhaustion.

In South America the Indians who take *Banisteria* and other plants fall victim to a similar frenzy (though they do not use it when on war parties), and European travellers who have tried the drug in their company report experiencing the traditional visions, amongst which are those of beasts of prey about to tear them into pieces. Such drugs seem to work by putting psychological anxieties into touch with the musculature, and what is dissociated is the ego from the imagination rather than, as in narcotics, the imagination from anxiety. There may be a connection between the fact that hallucinogens are not physically addictive and that they do not inhibit anxiety.

All these drugs, however, can be used for delicate purposes as well as frenzied ones. One must remember that all shamanistic traditions speak of an initiatory experience in which the body is felt to be torn apart, after which a crystalline body is given by the spirits. Both the dismemberment and the illumination of the body are commonly felt under hallucinogens, even if in a mild fashion, and one can understand dismemberment as the outcome of a drug-induced dissociation in which the normal persona or expression of the personality, is forced to give up its defensive reactions. What is known as a "bad trip" is caused by the anxiety which the approach of such a psychological dismemberment evokes, and which generates an increasing feeling of loss and horror when it cannot be properly discharged. From all accounts a really bad trip has certain similarities to a schizophrenic attack, and hospitals report many instances of bad trips which last for days or even months. The taking of tranquillizers is certainly one way of bringing such an episode to an end, but the traditional method is to accept the attack which the drug makes on the self without fear, an acceptance which transforms anxiety into knowledge and makes it give up its energy to a higher faculty.

But no two drugs attack the self in quite the same way, and they activate different parts of the same underlying process and give rise to different types of anxiety. The drug found in *Amanita* seems to be particularly effective in putting the motor system into spasm, and the shamans who use it must go through a long education in this experience and have grappled with the startling visions it produces before they can master its immediate effects and use them according to their will. *Datura* also activates a sense of physical power together with a psychic ambition that may lead a man so far out of his normal range that a spasm of timidity at the wrong moment may leave him stranded upon an ungovernable activity. Different is the effect of the *psilocybe* mushroom which clinically is said to be that of depersonalization. But there are two sides of every coin, and what is depersonalization to one man may be dematerialization to another: tribal practitioners in fact call upon this effect when they wish to penetrate material obstacles, to free consciousness from its bodily entanglements and allow it to inhabit bodies other than its own.

Drug of the Aztecs

Peyote traditionally used has yet other consequences. It was one of the first hallucinogens to be experimented with in Europe, and is famous for its visions of fantastic and grotesque architecture, of prodigious landscapes and giant figures striding about or petrified into ancient statuary, and of jewels shining with abundant color. All these visions occur without apparent reason, and the Indians phrase this by saying that peyote is a power in itself that works from the outside, a teacher who can show a man the right way to live and answer his questions by giving him an experience to live through.

This quality of the peyote experience allows one to qualify the remark of Michaux that under such drugs one does not dream, one is dreamed. If used correctly peyote has the power of personifying a dream in such a way that it allows the dreamer to keep some part of his self-awareness intact and still questioning. The consequence of searching for a meaning within the visions which inhabit one is that they become increasingly full of meaning themselves.

Peyote is of particular interest because it is the sacrament of the Native American Church, a religion based upon Indian practices and having Christianity for its justification. It was used by the Aztecs for divinatory purposes, and by the Tarahumara and Huichot of northern Mexico as the body of divinity on which all their beliefs centered. This religion was picked up by the Plains Indians at the time of their defeat by the whites and used to rally the wisdom of the Indian past to cope with the degrading changes that overcame them. It was in fact a type of cult such as we often find springing into existence when old ways of life are being destroyed by a powerful and technically more advanced culture, and it is also the only surviving one of several such cults which arose in the Plains.

The Search for Power

The drug problem in the West should probably be seen in the same light: the popularity of drugs is at least partly due to the very rapid changes now occurring in our society. Drugs have always been used to search for power, a power which can be used to enlarge the capacity of the imagination and to bring about change in society. When society itself changes, drugs give a certain kind of life to the imagination which is being stripped of its ancient forms, and a confidence in its ability to live in a strange world. Cannabis has certainly been used in this way from time to time: in Jamaica, for instance, the Rastafari smoke it both for religious and political reasons in the hope that they may soon return to their promised land—Abyssinia, where the Lion of Judah still reigns. Half a century ago or

more, cannabis was also the motive cause for a new religion being set up by the Baluba of the Congo: they destroyed their fetish houses, and proclaimed the drug to be a power under which they could live in perpetual friendship and protected from calamity. The drinking of alcohol was forbidden, and those who had committed misdeeds were condemned to smoke a number of pipes of cannabis in order to reform their misconceptions.

Wherever a drug is used by a religion to gain a view and foretaste of divinity, it is treated as though it were a god itself. ''We have drunk Soma, we have become immortals, we have arrived at the light, we have reached the gods: what power has malevolence over us now, what can the perfidy of mortals do to us, O Immortal?'' So runs one of the hymns of the *Rig Veda*, one of the sacred texts of the East. Opium has been called the hand of God and anchor of salvation, though Cocteau has remarked that it resembles religion as an illusionist resembles Jesus. Tobacco has been called the blessed plant, honor of the earth and gift from Olympus, and both wine and beer have been similarly praised down the centuries. "Our glass was the full moon, the wine is the sun. If the grave is moistened with such a wine, the dead man will rediscover his soul and the corpse will revive," said Ibn al Farid, the medieval Arabian poet. But the wine he talks of here is that of the Spirit, which also descended upon the Apostles at Pentecost so that they spoke with tongues and were accused of being drunk.

A drug is nothing unless it kindles the spirit in a man, though this spirit may be thought of as divine or demoniacal according to predilection. Whichever it may be, the spirit is not man's possession but a gift made to him, and as a gift it has a nature and a morality of its own which must be both wrestled with and obeyed if it is not to bring harm to its host. Every religion has its own way of experiencing and ordering this power, and their often stringent ritual requirements are the product of a long experience in bringing the spirit in touch with the world of men. The religious taking of drugs is one particular example of this: it says plainly enough that amateurism in these matters does little but create a problem, and that if the mind is to reach beyond itself by the use of a drug it must be placed in the service of an idea and a method that makes for wisdom and communion rather than folly and isolation.

Ritual Enemas

Peter T. Furst
Michael D. Coe

As we have seen in earlier articles, many of the world's cultures contain religious specialists and lay people who routinely undergo, for ritual purposes, an altering of their normal state of consciousness. Although this state can be obtained by non-drug related methods, it is not uncommon to find ethnographic accounts of drugs being used to enhance and quicken an altered state of consciousness. This article is about the religious use of various psychoactive substances among the Mayan Indians of Central Mexico. The authors note that although hallucinogenic mushrooms, morning glories, and other psychedelic plants were known and used by the Maya, yet another substance seems to have been employed—intoxicating enemas. This phenomenon quite clearly appears in Maya art as early as the first millennium A.D.; it is curious that it has not been described in the literature over the years. Ritual enemas were well known in South America, where rubber-tree sap was used for bulbed syringes. Furst and Coe reason that a rectal infusion of intoxicants could result in a more quickly and more radically changed state of consciousness, with fewer negative side effects.

Reprinted with permission from *Natural History*, Vol. 86, no. 3 (1977), pp. 88–91. Copyright the American Museum of Natural History, 1977.

WHEN THE SPANIARDS CONQUERED MEXICO IN the sixteenth century, they were at once fascinated and repelled by the Indians' widespread use not only of alcoholic beverages but also of numerous hallucinogenic plants.

From the Spaniards' point of view, however, both served the same purpose—to conjure up visions of demons and devils and to take imbibers from their daily life to supernatural realms.

Distillation was unknown in the New World before the conquest, but Mesoamerican Indians were making, as they still do, a variety of intoxicating ritual drinks, principally by fermenting cactus fruit; agave, or century plant, sap; or maize kernels. Among the Maya, the ritual beverage was balche, made from fermented honey mixed with a bark extract from the balche tree, *Lonchocarpus longistylus*. These concoctions were all taken orally.

But according to a Spanish writer known only as the Anonymous Conqueror, the Huastec people of northern Veracruz and southern Tamaulipas had pulque (fermented agave sap) "squirted into their breech," meaning that they used intoxicating enemas. There are indications that the Aztecs, as well as several other Mesoamerican groups, also followed this practice.

Mesoamerican Indians generally used liquor only on sacred occasions, when, according to such sixteenth-century observers as Bishop Diego de Landa of Yucatán, the Indians often drank themselves into states approaching oblivion. Similarly, the use of many botanical hallucinogens, first described by Fray Bernardino de Sahagún and his contemporaries, was strictly limited to occasions when direct communication with the otherworld was required. Today, the best known of these is peyote, *Lophophora williamsii*, a small, spineless cactus native to the north-central desert of Mexico and southern Texas. The plant now serves as sacrament for 225,000 adherents of the Native American Church and also plays an important role in the religious life of the Huichol Indians of western Mexico. Before the conquest, peyote was widely traded throughout Mexico, where the Aztec priests numbered it among their important magical and medicinal plants.

At the time of the conquest the seeds of the white-flowered morning glory *Turbina corymbosa* were a widely used hallucinogen. In 1960, Albert Hofmann, the Swiss discoverer of LSD (a synthetic hallucinogenic drug), isolated the active alkaloids in this morning glory species and a related species, the purple- or blue-flowered *Ipomoea violacea*, and found them to be lysergic acid derivatives closely resembling LSD-25. The latter species is often referred to as "heavenly blue"   the United States.

Mushrooms also played an important role in preconquest Mesoamerican Indian life. Certain species, most of them now known to belong to the genus *Psilocybe*, were perhaps the most extraordinary natural hallucinogens in use in Mexico. The Aztecs called them *teonanácatl*, or "God's flesh." Psychedelic fungi were widely employed in Mexico when the Spaniards came, and their use in divination and supernatural curing survives to this day in central Mexico, as well as in the state of Oaxaca (*see* "Drugs, Chants, and Magic Mushrooms," *Natural History*, December 1975). The Indians even used tobacco to induce ecstatic trance states, which the Spanish only saw as diabolic communication.

While Spanish writers of the sixteenth and seventeenth centuries left us relatively detailed accounts of the use of hallucinogens in central Mexico, there is little mention of this intriguing aspect of native religion among the Maya, who lived farther to the south. The silence is the more puzzling because we have circumstantial evidence of a very early cult of sacred mushrooms in the Maya highlands of Guatemala and the adjacent lowlands, in the form of more than 250 mushroom effigies made of carved stone, many dating to the first millennium B.C.

The Maya were an integral part of Mesoamerican civilization and shared many of its basic assumptions about the nature of the universe and the relationship of humans to the natural and supernatural environment. Like the central Mexicans, they divided the cosmos into upperworlds and underworlds with their respective gods, believed in the cyclical destruction and regeneration of the earth and its inhabitants, and followed the 260-day ritual calendar.

In view of these many similarities, as the Maya scholar J. Eric Thompson has written, it was hard to believe that the Maya did not use intoxicating plants. Thompson searched the pages of sacred traditional books of the Yucatec Maya, set down in the European alphabet in the colonial period, for hints of ecstatic visionary trances through which the priests made their prophecies. In the *Books of Chilam Balam* (jaguar-priest) of Tizimín and Maní, he found mention of trancelike states but no hint whatever of any hallucinogenic plants. He also discovered scattered scenes in Maya relief sculpture that suggested visionary experiences characteristic of hallucinogenic ritual.

This is slim evidence, however, compared with the data from central Mexico, and some Maya scholars are not convinced that the Maya practiced the kinds of ecstatic shamanistic rituals or vision quests with botanical hallucinogens that played so pervasive a role in central Mexico, or among the Zapotecs, Mixtecs, Mazatecs, and other peoples of Oaxaca.

The silence of Spanish colonial writers on the subject of hallucinogenic plants or rituals among the Maya accords well with the view, once widely held among scholars, that the Maya were quite unlike their Mexican contemporaries in temperament, being less preoccupied with warfare and the Dionysian excesses than with the contemplative interpretation of the heavens and the passage of time. But the discovery at Bonampak, Chiapas, of mural paintings that depict, among other events, a fierce battle among Maya warriors, indicate that this traditional view is very wide of the mark.

As specialists have more closely examined Maya art and iconography in recent years, they have accumulated increasing evidence that among the classic Maya, ecstatic ritual was important. One suggestion for this is that some of the major Mexican hallucinogens—among them the morning glories and the hallucinogenic mushroom *Stropharia cubensis*—occur in the Maya country. These and other psychedelic plants were undoubtedly known to the Maya.

Had Maya specialists looked more closely at the earliest dictionaries of the Quiché and Cakchiquel languages, compiled in the first centuries after the conquest of highland Guatemala, they would have discovered mention of several varieties of mushrooms with hallucinogenic properties. One is called *xibalbaj okox* (*xibalba* means "underworld," or "land of the dead," and *okox*, "mushroom"), said by the sixteenth-century compiler to give those who eat it visions of hell. If the association of this species with the Maya underworld left any doubt of its psychedelic nature, it is dispelled by a later reference to the same species in Fray Tomas Coto's dictionary of the Cakchiquel language. According to him, *xibalbaj okox* was also called *k'aizalah okox*, which translates as the "mushroom that makes one lose one's judgment." Still another fungus, *k'ek-c'un*, had inebriating characteristics, and another, *muxan okox*, apparently brought on insanity or caused one to "fall into a swoon."

We have recently come across a wholly unexpected use of psychoactive substances among the Maya—the ritual use of intoxicating enemas, unmistakably depicted in classic Maya art of the first millennium A.D., but not mentioned either in the colonial or the modern literature. This practice is well documented among the inhabitants of South American tropical forests as well as among the Inca and their contemporaries in the Andes, where archeologists have discovered enema syringes.

Sixteenth-century sources describe the Incas as regularly intoxicating themselves with infusions of *willka*, now known to be the potent hallucinogenic seeds of the acacialike *Anadenanthera colubrina* tree. Lowland Indians also used tobacco enemas.

South American Indians were the first people known to use native rubber tree sap for bulbed enema syringes. While medical enemas had a long history in the Old World, having been used by ancient Sumerians and Egyptians, as well as by Hindus, Arabs, Chinese, Greeks, and Romans, the rubber bulb syringe was unknown in Europe until two centuries after the discovery of the New World.

The native Amerindian enema was distinguished from its Old World counterpart in that its primary purpose was to introduce medicines and intoxicants into the body, while the Old World enema was employed principally to clear the bowels. During the seventeenth and eighteenth centuries, the enema as a relief for constipation, real or imagined, became a craze in Europe—so much so, that Louis XIV had more than 2,000 enemas administered to him during his reign, sometimes even

receiving court functionaries and foreign dignitaries during the procedure.

The wide dissemination of the intoxicating enema in South America suggests the discovery by Indians that the rectal administration of intoxicants could radically alter one's state of consciousness more rapidly, and with fewer undesirable side effects, such as nausea, than oral administration. The physiological reason is simple: Substances injected into the rectum enter the colon, the last segment of the large intestine; the principal function of the large intestine is the reabsorption of liquids into the system and the storage of wastes until they can be evacuated. The absorbed liquid immediately enters the bloodstream, which carries it to the brain. An intoxicant or hallucinogen injected rectally closely resembles an intravenous injection in the rapidity of its effects.

The first evidence that not only the Huastecs, whose language is related to the Maya languages, but also the classic Maya knew of and employed the intoxicating enema came to light this past year through the examination of a painted vase in a private collection in New York. This polychrome jar, with a high, vertical neck and flaring rim, was probably painted in the heavily forested Petén district of northern Guatemala during the classic Maya phase, which dated from the third century A.D. to the first decades of the seventh century. Seven male-female pairs, the women easily distinguished by their robes and long hair, are depicted in two horizontal rows. That one woman is fondling a child suggests a familial setting. The activity being portrayed would have brought blushes to the cheeks of the traditional Maya specialist, for while one man is inserting a syringe into his rectum, this delicate task is being carried out for another male by his consort. One male also has a bulbed enema syringe tucked into his belt.

Nine vases, identical in shape to the actual vessel, are painted between the couples, and painted dots at the mouth of each represents a foaming, fermented liquid that is probably balche, the common alcoholic drink among the Maya at the time of the conquest. We must conclude that the people on the vase are taking intoxicating enemas, a practice previously unrecorded for this culture.

An understanding of the scenes depicted on the Maya vase was only the first link in a chain of iconographic discovery of the Mesoamerican enema phenomenon. Suddenly, several previously enigmatic scenes and objects in classic Maya art had new meaning. A small clay figurine from a burial excavated in 1964 by Mexican archeologists on the island of Jaina, in the Gulf of Campeche, depicts a male in squatting position, his hand reaching back to his rectum. For a long time Maya experts were puzzled because the figure's position seemed to represent defecation. But would the Maya have interred such a scene as an offering to their dead?

A small hole in the anus suggested that a piece was missing—that some small object previously inserted there had either become lost during excavation or had been made of some perishable material, long since decayed. The discovery of the enema vase from the Petén district seems to have solved the riddle. The little Maya was probably not defecating but was in the act of giving himself an enema.

The gods themselves were also depicted as indulging in the enema ritual. One Maya vase has the figures of thirty-one underworld deities painted on it. A naturalistically designed enema syringe dangles from the paw of one of the principal figures. Maya experts did not recognize the significance of the object until they had examined the enema vase in New York. As another example, a polychrome bowl from Yucatán, now in the National Museum of Anthropology in Mexico City, shows a naked being with a pointed head injecting himself with liquid.

The ritual importance of the intoxicating enema is highlighted by the involvement in the rite of one of the greatest underworld deities, an old lord associated with earth, water, and agricultural fertility. The Maya may have believed that this god—now identified by Mayanists only by the letter N, but very likely the same deity as the ancient Yucatecan god Pauhatun—consisted of four parts, each part livng in the underworld and supporting the four corners of the earth.

The quadripartite god is depicted on a fine vase in a private collection in Chicago. Each of the four parts has a characteristically chapfallen face. Four young and fetching consorts are apparently preparing each of the god's representations for the enema rite. Enema pots with syringes on top are in front of two of the consorts. The female consorts may well represent the important Mother Goddess

of the Maya, known as Ixchel, as several figurine examples of the god N embracing this goddess have been found.

The same association of the god N, females and enemas is depicted on another pottery vase, with a consort shown standing behind each god representation and untying his loincloth. Again, the same enema pots are in front of the consorts. So often are the pottery forms and syringes encountered together that we must conclude that they were commonly used in the enema rite.

The explicit depiction of enema rituals on Maya vases has led us to take a new look at a hitherto puzzling type of clay figurine from central Veracruz, which also dates from the classic Maya period. Some archeologists have interpreted these curious sculptures as representing human sacrifice. They are usually of males whose facial expressions suggest pleasure or ecstatic trance, not death. Their legs are raised, either draped over a high pillow or some other type of support or else slightly spread, with the feet up in the air. The posture—and the enraptured look—suggest the intoxicating enema. The reclining position also conforms to the Anonymous Conqueror's description of the method of enema intoxication among the Huastecs.

The hallucinogenic, or intoxicating, enema has apparently not disappeared altogether from Middle America. While conducting linguistic research in the Sierra Madre Occidental in western Mexico some years ago, ethnographer Tim Knab was shown a peyote apparatus reportedly used by an elderly woman curer. The bulb was made from a deer's bladder and the tube from the hollow femur of a small deer. The curer prepared peyote by grinding it to a fine pulp and diluting it with water. Instead of taking the peyote by mouth, as for example, the Huichols normally do, either whole or ground (see "An Indian Journey to Life's Source," *Natural History*, April 1973), she injected it rectally, experiencing its effects almost at once while avoiding its bitter and acrid taste and the nausea that even some experienced Indian *peyoteros* continue to feel as they chew the sacred plant.

We do not know what materials the ancient Maya used for their syringes. The deer was sacred to the Maya, as it still is to Indians in western Mexico. Still, to make the transition from contemporary western Mexico to the Maya requires an enormous jump in time and space. Fish bladders and the bones of birds, which are prominent in Maya art, might have served for the syringe, as might rubber from the latex tree, which is native to the Maya region. More important than the precise technology, however, is the discovery that, no less than the simpler folk of the South American tropical rain forests, the creators of the most flamboyant and intellectually advanced native civilization in the New World hit upon the enema as a technique of intoxication or ecstasy—a practical means of ritually altering or transforming the ordinary state of consciousness.

The Sound of Rushing Water

Michael Harner

Amazonian Indians, as in the case of forest dwellers everywhere, have a tremendous depth of understanding of the chemical properties of plants indigenous to their habitats. Extracts of plants are prepared as medicines that are used both in the Western pharmacological sense and in the supernatural sense. Preparations take a variety of forms and range from ebene, *the snuff used by the Yanomamo of Brazil and Venezuela, to the tea-like drink* natema, *used by the Jívaro of Ecuador. Both contain hallucinogenic properties, provide the taker entry into the spirit world, and offer powers otherwise unattainable without ingestion of potent alkaloid compounds. Yet, elsewhere, as among the Warao of South America, non-hallucinogenic drugs such as tobacco are consumed by shamans to achieve a similar ecstatic state, which, as in the case of* ebene *and* natema, *provides visions of spirit helpers and other agents of the supernatural world (Wilbert 1972). Comparisons such as these give anthropologists insight into the importance of shared belief systems and suggestibility. Describing the use of the Banisteriopsis vine by Jívaro shamans, Michael Harner draws on his field data to illustrate the use of the hallucinogenic drink* natema. *Called by a variety of names in other Amazonian societies, this drug gives extraordinary powers to cure or bewitch, and shamans specialize in either one or the other.*

Reprinted with permission from *Natural History*, Vol. 77, no. 6 (June/July 1968), pp. 28–33. Copyright the American Museum of Natural History, 1968.

HE HAD DRUNK, AND NOW HE SOFTLY SANG. Gradually, faint lines and forms began to appear in the darkness, and the shrill music of the *tsentsak*, the spirit helpers, arose around him. The power of the drink fed them. He called, and they came. First, *pangi*, the anaconda, coiled about his head, transmuted into a crown of gold. Then *wampang*, the giant butterfly, hovered above his shoulder and sang to him with its wings. Snakes, spiders, birds, and bats danced in the air above him. On his arms appeared a thousand eyes as his demon helpers emerged to search the night for enemies.

The sound of rushing water filled his ears, and listening to its roar, he knew he possessed the power of *tsungi*, the first shaman. Now he could see. Now he could find the truth. He stared at the stomach of the sick man. Slowly, it became transparent like a shallow mountain stream, and he saw within it, coiling and uncoiling, *makanchi*, the poisonous serpent, who had been sent by the enemy shaman. The real cause of the illness had been found.

The Jívaro Indians of the Ecuadorian Amazon believe that witchcraft is the cause of the vast majority of illnesses and non-violent deaths. The normal waking life, for the Jívaro, is simply "a lie," or illusion, while the true forces that determine daily events are supernatural and can only be seen and manipulated with the aid of hallucinogenic drugs. A reality view of this kind creates a particularly strong demand for specialists who can cross over into the supernatural world at will to deal with the forces that influence and even determine the events of the waking life.

These specialists, called "shamans" by anthropologists, are recognized by the Jívaro as being of two types: bewitching shamans or curing shamans. Both kinds take a hallucinogenic drink, whose Jívaro name is *natema*, in order to enter the supernatural world. This brew, commonly called *yagé*, or *yajé*, in Colombia, *ayahuasca*

(Inca "vine of the dead") in Ecuador and Peru, and *caapi* in Brazil, is prepared from segments of a species of the vine *Banisteriopsis*, a genus belonging to the Malpighiaceae. The Jívaro boil it with the leaves of a similar vine, which probably is also a species of *Banisteriopsis*, to produce a tea that contains the powerful hallucinogenic alkaloids harmaline, harmine, d-tetrahydroharmine, and quite possibly dimethyltryptamine (DMT). These compounds have chemical structures and effects similar, but not identical, to LSD, mescaline of the peyote cactus, and psilocybin of the psychotropic Mexican mushroom.

When I first undertook research among the Jívaro in 1956–57, I did not fully appreciate the psychological impact of the *Banisteriopsis* drink upon the native view of reality, but in 1961 I had occasion to drink the hallucinogen in the course of field work with another Upper Amazon Basin tribe. For several hours after drinking the brew, I found myself, although awake, in a world literally beyond my wildest dreams. I met bird-headed people, as well as dragon-like creatures who explained that they were the true gods of this world. I enlisted the services of other spirit helpers in attempting to fly through the far reaches of the Galaxy. Transported into a trance where the supernatural seemed natural, I realized that anthropologists, including myself, had profoundly underestimated the importance of the drug in affecting native ideology. Therefore, in 1964 I returned to the Jívaro to give particular attention to the drug's use by the Jívaro shaman.

The use of the hallucinogenic *natema* drink among the Jívaro makes it possible for almost anyone to achieve the trance state essential for the practice of shamanism. Given the presence of the drug and the felt need to contact the "real," or supernatural, world, it is not surprising that approximately one out of every four Jívaro men is a shaman. Any adult, male or female, who desires to become such a practitioner, simply presents a gift to an already practicing shaman, who administers the *Banisteriopsis* drink and gives some of his own supernatural power—in the form of spirit helpers, or *tsentsak*—to the apprentice. These spirit helpers, or "darts," are the main supernatural forces believed to cause illness and death in daily life. To the non-shaman they are normally invisible, and even shamans can perceive them only under the influence of *natema*.

Shamans send these spirit helpers into the victims' bodies to make them ill or to kill them. At other times, they may suck spirits sent by enemy shamans from the bodies of tribesmen suffering from witchcraft-induced illness. The spirit helpers also form shields that protect their shaman masters from attacks. The following account presents the ideology of Jívaro witchcraft from the point of view of the Indians themselves.

To give the novice some *tsentsak*, the practicing shaman regurgitates what appears to be—to those who have taken *natema*—a brilliant substance in which the spirit helpers are contained. He cuts part of it off with a machete and gives it to the novice to swallow. The recipient experiences pain upon taking it into his stomach and stays on his bed for ten days, repeatedly drinking *natema*. The Jívaro believe they can keep magical darts in their stomachs indefinitely and regurgitate them at will. The shaman donating the *tsentsak* periodically blows and rubs all over the body of the novice, apparently to increase the power of the transfer.

The novice must remain inactive and not engage in sexual intercourse for at least three months. If he fails in self-discipline, as some do, he will not become a successful shaman. At the end of the first month, a *tsentsak* emerges from his mouth. With this magical dart at his disposal, the new shaman experiences a tremendous desire to bewitch. If he casts his *tsentsak* to fulfill this desire, he will become a bewitching shaman. If, on the other hand, the novice can control his impulse and reswallow the first *tsentsak*, he will become a curing shaman.

If the shaman who gave the *tsentsak* to the new man was primarily a bewitcher, rather than a curer, the novice likewise will tend to become a bewitcher. This is because a bewitcher's magical darts have such a desire to kill that their new owner will be strongly inclined to adopt their attitude. One informant said that the urge to kill felt by bewitching shamans came to them with a strength and frequency similar to that of hunger.

Only if the novice shaman is able to abstain from sexual intercourse for five months, will he have the power to kill a man (if he is a bewitcher) or cure a victim (if he is a curer). A full year's abstinence is considered necessary to become a really effective bewitcher or curer.

During the period of sexual abstinence, the new shaman collects all kinds of insects, plants, and other objects, which he now has the power to convert into *tsentsak*. Almost any object, including living insects and worms, can become a *tsentsak* if it is small enough to be swallowed by a shaman. Different types of *tsentsak* are used to cause different kinds and degrees of illness. The greater the variety of these objects that a shaman has in his body, the greater is his ability.

According to Jívaro concepts, each *tsentsak* has a natural and supernatural aspect. The magical dart's natural aspect is that of an ordinary material object as seen without drinking the drug *natema*. But the supernatural and "true" aspect of the *tsentsak* is revealed to the shaman by taking *natema*. When he does this, the magical darts appear in new forms as demons and with new names. In their supernatural aspects, the *tsentsak* are not simply objects but spirit helpers in various forms, such as giant butterflies, jaguars, or monkeys, who actively assist the shaman in his tasks.

Bewitching is carried out against a specific, known individual and thus is almost always done to neighbors or, at the most, fellow tribesmen. Normally, as is the case with intratribal assassination, bewitching is done to avenge a particular offense committed against one's family or friends. Both bewitching and individual assassination contrast with the large-scale headhunting raids for which the Jívaro have become famous, and which were conducted against entire neighborhoods of enemy tribes.

To bewitch, the shaman takes *natema* and secretly approaches the house of his victim. Just out of sight in the forest, he drinks green tobacco juice, enabling him to regurgitate a *tsentsak*, which he throws at his victim as he comes out of his house. If the *tsentsak* is strong enough and is thrown with sufficient force, it will pass all the way through the victim's body causing death within a period of a few days to several weeks. More often, however, the magical dart simply lodges in the victim's body. If the shaman, in his hiding place, fails to see the intended victim, he may instead bewitch any member of the intended victim's family who appears, usually a wife or child. When the shaman's mission is accomplished, he returns secretly to his own home.

One of the distinguishing characteristics of the bewitching process among the Jívaro is that, as far as I could learn, the victim is given no specific indication that someone is bewitching him. The bewitcher does not want his victim to be aware that he is being supernaturally attacked, lest he take protective measures by immediately procuring the services of a curing shaman. Nonetheless, shamans and laymen alike with whom I talked noted that illness invariably follows the bewitchment although the degree of the illness can vary considerably.

A special kind of spirit helper, called a *pasuk*, can aid the bewitching shaman by remaining near the victim in the guise of an insect or animal of the forest after the bewitcher has left. This spirit helper has his own objects to shoot into the victim should a curing shaman succeed in sucking out the *tsentsak* sent earlier by the bewitcher who is the owner of the *pasuk*.

In addition, the bewitcher can enlist the aid of a *wakani* ("soul," or "spirit") bird. Shamans have the power to call these birds and use them as spirit helpers in bewitching victims. The shaman blows on the *wakani* birds and then sends them to the house of the victim to fly around and around the man, frightening him. This is believed to cause fever and insanity, with death resulting shortly thereafter.

After he returns home from bewitching, the shaman may send a *wakani* bird to perch near the house of the victim. Then if a curing shaman sucks out the intruding object, the bewitching shaman sends the *wakani* bird more *tsentsak* to throw from its beak into the victim. By continually resupplying the *wakani* bird with new *tsentsak*, the sorcerer makes it impossible for the curer to rid his patient permanently of the magical darts.

While the *wakani* birds are supernatural servants available to anyone who wishes to use them, the *pasuk*, chief among the spirit helpers, serves only a single shaman. Likewise a shaman possesses only one *pasuk*. The *pasuk*, being specialized for the service of bewitching, has a protective shield to guard it from counterattack by the curing shaman. The curing shaman, under the influence of *natema*, sees the *pasuk* of the bewitcher in human form and size, but "covered with iron except for its eyes." The curing shaman can kill this *pasuk* only by shooting a *tsentsak* into its eyes, the sole vulnerable area in the *pasuk's* armor. To the person who has not taken the hallucinogenic drink, the *pasuk* usually appears to be simply a tarantula.

Shamans also may kill or injure a person by using magical darts, *anamuk*, to create supernatural animals that attack a victim. If a shaman has a small, pointed armadillo bone *tsentsak*, he can shoot this into a river while the victim is crossing it on a balsa raft or in a canoe. Under the water, this bone manifests itself in its supernatural aspect as an anaconda, which rises up and overturns the craft, causing the victim to drown. The shaman can similarly use a tooth from a killed snake as a *tsentsak*, creating a poisonous serpent to bite his victim. In more or less the same manner, shamans can create jaguars and pumas to kill their victims.

About five years after receiving his *tsentsak*, a bewitching shaman undergoes a test to see if he still retains enough *tsentsak* power to continue to kill successfully. This test involves bewitching a tree. The shaman, under the influence of *natema*, attempts to throw a *tsentsak* through the tree at the point where its two main branches join. If his strength and aim are adequate, the tree appears to split the moment the *tsentsak* is sent into it. The splitting, however, is invisible to an observer who is not under the influence of the hallucinogen. If the shaman fails, he knows that he is incapable of killing a human victim. This means that, as soon as possible, he must go to a strong shaman and purchase a new supply of *tsentsak*. Until he has the goods with which to pay for this new supply, he is in constant danger, in his proved weakened condition, of being seriously bewitched by other shamans. Therefore, each day, he drinks large quantities of *natema*, tobacco juice, and the extract of yet another drug, *pirípirí*. He also rests on his bed at home to conserve his strength, but tries to conceal his weakened condition from his enemies. When he purchases a new supply of *tsentsak*, he can safely cut down on his consumption of these other substances.

The degree of illness produced in a witchcraft victim is a function of both the force with which the *tsentsak* is shot into the body, and also of the character of the magical dart itself. If a *tsentsak* is shot all the way through the body of a victim, then "there is nothing for a curing shaman to suck out," and the patient dies. If the magical dart lodges within the body, however, it is theoretically possible to cure the victim by sucking. But in actual practice, the sucking is not always considered successful.

The work of the curing shaman is complementary to that of a bewitcher. When a curing shaman is called in to treat a patient, his first task is to see if the illness is due to witchcraft. The usual diagnosis and treatment begin with the curing shaman drinking *natema*, tobacco juice, and pirípirí in the late afternoon and early evening. These drugs permit him to see into the body of the patient as though it were glass. If the illness is due to sorcery, the curing shaman will see the intruding object within the patient's body clearly enough to determine whether or not he can cure the sickness.

A shaman sucks magical darts from a patient's body only at night, and in a dark area of the house, for it is only in the dark that he can perceive the drug-induced visions that are the supernatural reality. With the setting of the sun, he alerts his *tsentsak* by whistling the tune of the curing song; after about a quarter of an hour, he starts singing. When he is ready to suck, the shaman regurgitates two *tsentsak* into the sides of his throat and mouth. These must be identical to the one he has seen in the patient's body. He holds one of these in the front of the mouth and the other in the rear. They are expected to catch the supernatural aspect of the magical dart that the shaman sucks out of the patient's body. The *tsentsak* nearest the shaman's lips is supposed to incorporate the sucked-out *tsentsak* essence within itself. If, however, this supernatural essence should get past it, the second magical dart in the mouth blocks the throat so that the intruder cannot enter the interior of the shaman's body. If the curer's two *tsentsak* were to fail to catch the supernatural essence of the *tsentsak*, it would pass down into the shaman's stomach and kill him. Trapped thus within the mouth, this essence is shortly caught by, and incorporated into, the material substance of one of the curing shaman's *tsentsak*. He then "vomits" out this object and displays it to the patient and his family saying, "Now I have sucked it out. Here it is."

The non-shamans think that the material object itself is what has been sucked out, and the shaman does not disillusion them. At the same time, he is not lying, because he knows that the only important thing about a *tsentsak* is its supernatural aspect, or essence, which he sincerely believes he has removed from the patient's body. To explain to the layman that he already had these objects in his mouth would serve no fruitful purpose and would prevent him from displaying such an object as proof that he had effected the cure. Without incontrovertible evidence, he would not be able to convince the patient and his family that he had effected the cure and must be paid.

The ability of the shaman to suck depends largely upon the quantity and strength of his own *tsentsak*, of which he may have hundreds. His magical darts assume their supernatural aspect of spirit helpers when he is under the influence of *natema*, and he sees them as a variety of zoomorphic forms hovering over him, perching on his shoulders, and sticking out of his skin. He sees them helping to suck the patient's body. He must drink tobacco juice every few hours to "keep them fed" so that they will not leave him.

The curing shaman must also deal with any *pasuk* that may be in the patient's vicinity for the purpose of casting more darts. He drinks additional amounts of *natema* in order to see them and engages in *tsentsak* duels with them if they are present. While the *pasuk* is enclosed in iron armor, the shaman himself has his own armor composed of his many *tsentsak*. As long as he is under the influence of *natema*, these magical darts cover his body as a protective shield, and are on the lookout for any enemy *tsentsak* headed toward their master. When these *tsentsak* see such a missile coming, they immediately close up together at the point where the enemy dart is attempting to penetrate, and thereby repel it.

If the curer finds *tsentsak* entering the body of his patient after he has killed *pasuk*, he suspects the presence of a *wakani* bird. The shaman drinks *maikua* (*Datura* sp.), an hallucinogen even more powerful than *natema*, as well as tobacco juice, and silently sneaks into the forest to hunt and kill the bird with *tsentsak*. When he succeeds, the curer returns to the patient's home, blows all over the house to get rid of the "atmosphere" created by the numerous *tsentsak* sent by the bird, and completes his sucking of the patient. Even after all the *tsentsak* are extracted, the shaman may remain another night at the house to suck out any "dirtiness" (*pahuri*) still inside. In the cures which I have witnessed, this sucking is a most noisy process, accompanied by deep, but dry, vomiting.

After sucking out a *tsentsak*, the shaman puts it into a little container. He does not swallow it because it is not his own magical dart and would therefore kill him. Later, he throws the *tsentsak* into

the air, and it flies back to the shaman who sent it originally into the patient. *Tsentsak* also fly back to a shaman at the death of a former apprentice who had originally received them from him. Besides receiving "old" magical darts unexpectedly in this manner, the shaman may have *tsentsak* thrown at him by a bewitcher. Accordingly, shamans constantly drink tobacco juice at all hours of the day and night. Although the tobacco juice is not truly hallucinogenic, it produces a narcotized state, which is believed necessary to keep one's *tsentsak* ready to repel any other magical darts. A shaman does not even dare go for a walk without taking along the green tobacco leaves with which he prepares the juice that keeps his spirit helpers alert. Less frequently, but regularly, he must drink *natema* for the same purpose and to keep in touch with the supernatural reality.

While curing under the influence of *natema*, the curing shaman "sees" the shaman who bewitched his patient. Generally, he can recognize the person, unless it is a shaman who lives far away or in another tribe. The patient's family knows this, and demands to be told the identity of the bewitcher, particularly if the sick person dies. At one curing session I attended, the shaman could not identify the person he had seen in his vision. The brother of the dead man then accused the shaman himself of being responsible. Under such pressure, there is a strong tendency for the curing shaman to attribute each case to a particular bewitcher.

Shamans gradually become weak and must purchase *tsentsak* again and again. Curers tend to become weak in power, especially after curing a patient bewitched by a shaman who has recently received a new supply of magical darts. Thus, the most powerful shamans are those who can repeatedly purchase new supplies of *tsentsak* from other shamans.

Shamans can take back *tsentsak* from others to whom they have previously given them. To accomplish this, the shaman drinks *natema*, and, using his *tsentsak*, creates a "bridge" in the form of a rainbow between himself and the other shaman. Then he shoots a *tsentsak* along this rainbow. This strikes the ground beside the other shaman with an explosion and flash likened to a lightning bolt. The purpose of this is to surprise the other shaman so that he temporarily forgets to maintain his guard over his magical darts, thus permitting the other shaman to suck them back along the rainbow. A shaman who has had his *tsentsak* taken away in this manner will discover that "nothing happens" when he drinks *natema*. The sudden loss of his *tsentsak* will tend to make him ill, but ordinarily the illness is not fatal unless a bewitcher shoots a magical dart into him while he is in this weakened condition. If he has not become disillusioned by his experience, he can again purchase *tsentsak* from some other shaman and resume his calling. Fortunately for anthropology some of these men have chosen to give up shamanism and therefore can be persuaded to reveal their knowledge, no longer having a vested interest in the profession. This divulgence, however, does not serve as a significant threat to practitioners, for words alone can never adequately convey the realities of shamanism. These can only be approached with the aid of *natema*, the chemical door to the invisible world of the Jívaro shaman.

Psychedelics and Religion: A Symposium

Raziel Abelson
Allen Ginsberg
Michael Wyschogrod

The primary purpose of this article is to discuss the religious and philosophical aspects of the so-called consciousness-expanding drugs. Allen Ginsberg assumes the position that there is a positive value in using such drugs as marijuana and LSD to attain a more intensive religious experience, while Professor Wyschogrod emphasizes the "artificiality" of any religious experience based on drugs. Wyschogrod is not basing his argument on the question of the legality or morality of drugs, but rather on his belief that a drug-induced religious experience results only in a synthetic or "illusory" religious experience.

As we have seen in the preceding articles of this chapter, psychotropic (mind-changing) drugs are used throughout the world to bring about or enhance religious experiences. In the United States today, however, as well as in other countries, drug usage is considered a major social problem. The amount of popular media coverage devoted to the topic of drugs in this country is staggering, reflecting the deep social, philosophical, and moral conflict over their use. This article stemmed from a 1967 drug symposium held at New York University. It is not difficult to understand why the symposium was convened. In the 1960s, millions of young Americans turned to drugs as one aspect of their rejection of what they felt was an unsuccessful system of American values. Difficult as it was for an older generation to cope with the sudden popularity of such drugs as marijuana and LSD in the profane world of the streets and the college campus, to many the thought of their use in the sacred world was frightening, even terrifying.

This article first appeared in the *Humanist* issue of Fall 1967 (September/December), pp. 153–56 and 190–91, and is reprinted by permission.

Introduction: Raziel Abelson

THE PURPOSE OF THIS SYMPOSIUM IS TO DISCUSS THE religious and philosophical aspects of the so-called "consciousness expanding" drugs, particularly LSD and marijuana. It occurs to me that the title of this symposium is much too pretentious and stuffy; I would prefer to call it something simpler and more cozy. I suggest we call this a "Trip-in," for a reason not quite what you would naturally think. My reason is a personal one: it has to do with various trips I have made recently and a new one I am reluctant to take until I can see a good reason for it.

I am particularly interested in the subject of our discussion because of my feeling of closeness to the generation that has made it an issue, the generation that came of age or will come of age in the 1960s. I consider it an extraordinarily interesting generation, the most exciting that I have had contact with. My own generation of the 40s was, I think, not a bad one; it was interested in its fellowmen, it was dynamic and hard working, it fought a world war against barbarism, but it was not as free as the present one because it was enslaved to ideologies. For the conservative prejudices of our parents we substituted the radical and neo-Puritanical prejudices of Marxism and Freudianism. I began to teach in the 1950s, and the generation of students who attended my lectures in that decade was, I think, the dullest, most boring of my time. It was enslaved to things far worse than ideologies: to chrome-plated Cadillacs, large houses, good jobs and social status. Its heroes were McCarthy on the "right" and Eisenhower on the "left." I first began to enjoy teaching in the 60s, because only then did I feel a rapport with students, whom I found so remarkably free that I felt myself liberated by them—free of pretentious ideology, free of mechanical rules of grammar, spelling, etiquette and sexual behavior, free of parental authoritarianism, of superstitions and phobias, willing to explore and appreciate any kind of human experience, able to say, like Marsiglio of Padua: "Nothing human is alien to me." Unfortunately, my age disqualifies me from full, card-carrying membership in this new generation, but, unlike Lewis Feuer and Ronald Reagan, I recognize its superiority to my own and I would like to be at least an honorary or associate member. For this reason I have tried to share its experience by taking various "trips" with it. In 1963 I took a trip on a rickety old school bus at four in the morning, to the Washington March for civil rights legislation. The following summer I took a trip to Mississippi to observe the Freedom Schools and voter registration drive; although I wasn't there long, I did get a taste of the "agony and the ecstasy" of the students who fought nonviolently and valiantly for reason and decency. I believe that summer of 1964 was the most glorious moment in the history of American youth; it was the moment at which the older generations began to look to the youth for the leadership they did not have the courage to assume. Two summers later I took another trip on a rickety old school bus, full of students, to march on Washington to end the war in Viet Nam, and this year I marched with them in New York, surrounded by Viet Cong banners and hippies with bananas, flowers, and electric guitars. Up to that point, the generation of the 60s had always turned me on. Their skeptical rebelliousness and their intense social involvement seemed to me to promise a far better world when they would take control. But something very disturbing has been happening in the last two years. This generation, that created in me and many others so much hope for the future, has itself lost hope and nerve, and has turned from social concern inward toward its own private experience: it has turned from iconoclasm to quietism, from humanistic liberalism to passivity and drugs. The revolutionary generation is "copping out."

The "trips" I had taken with it were all outward, other-centered, and to get things done that needed doing. Now, if I listen to the proselytes of Liberation Through Drugs, I am to take a trip in the exact opposite direction—inward, toward passivity, hal-

lucination, inconsequence. Maybe I can understand the motives for this shift into reverse gear—disappointment at the snail's pace of social reforms, moral revulsion and despair about the abominable, uncontrollable and endless war in Viet Nam—but motives are not reasons, and I would like to know the *reason* why, before I take this trip backward into darkness. I am in search of enlightenment: why are drug induced fantasies better than the light of cool reason; why is sensual overstimulation more worthwhile than the pursuit of rational social ideals? I look to two extremely well-qualified experts to enlighten me on these questions. From Mr. Ginsberg I hope for a clear answer to the question, "Why?" and from Professor Wyschogrod, an equally clear explanation of "Why not?"

Turning On with LSD and Pot: Allen Ginsberg

I would like to begin by introducing some data from comparative religion. Those who have done any dilettanting around in Tantric Hinduism or its esoteric erotic sexual practices will no doubt know of the book, *The Serpent Power*, by Arthur Avalon. It is a translation of an ancient Hindu text, the *Mahanirvana tantra*, one of the older, more conservative texts of the Shaivite school of Hinduism. This text deals with ritual, prayer, and the formal religious use of marijuana. If one reads just a few sentences from the text, he can get an appreciation of the importance of the use of marijuana in the religious rituals. One who engages in mantra prayer and chanting will use this narcotic hemp in his ceremonies.

I should point out that I am a formally initiated member of the Shiva sect, and I assume that my presentation of its rituals is protected by the First Amendment of the U.S. Constitution. Since I have a central preoccupation within my heart with religious matters, I wish to stay off legal problems and to focus upon the actual subject matter on a more realistic level, without worrying about whether it's going to be against the law, whether it's moral or immoral to break the law, whether you'll go mad or you won't go mad. I want to deal with the phenomenology of LSD and pot and their philosophical implications. Professor Elia Rubichek of Prague, who has done a lot of work on LSD, defines it in

Pavlovian and Marxian terminology, the terminology the "Iron Curtain" would use in dealing with the effects of LSD. The phraseology is really interesting. What he said was, "It inhibits conditioned reflexes." Now that's a big deal out there in Russia where there's a Pavlovian conception of consciousness, because it means that there is a way of reversing or wiping out the conditioning that would make a member of the former upper class no longer eligible to be condemned by the bureaucrat. Anybody could take LSD and say that he had his conditioned reflexes wiped out and was now just as good as the proletariat.

What it means in terms of our country is something you have been digging lately—Marshall McLuhan's generalizations about the effects of the conditioning of our technology on our consciousness. He's saying that the media or environment we have created around us is a giant conditioning mechanism, a giant teaching machine. We are hardly aware of it as a teaching machine. We are hardly aware of its effect. We are hardly aware that consciousness is not necessarily a conceptual or verbal matter, that there are other levels of consciousness, depths of consciousness, that there is feeling consciousness, that there is touch consciousness, that there is smelling, seeing, hearing, and levels of memory consciousness that we are not generally aware of. But McLuhan has been saying recently that the verbal and language consciousness that we have been conditioned to over the last centuries has atrophied our other senses. That is, the universe into which we have projected ourselves and developed has atrophied our other sense—smell, touch, taste—in a way that he could even quantify. McLuhan told me that he wanted to work out a way to quantify in scientific terminology the difference caused by our preoccupation with visual consciousness; that is, the difference caused to the other senses. There is a quantitative mode of measurement that he could apply. What has this to do with LSD? McLuhan didn't know the connection because he hasn't taken LSD or read much about it. Yet given a chemical which can reverse conditioning, we have a kind of open consciousness which receives almost all of the data present to us and takes account of it all, as if that which we usually are not aware of or is unconscious within us is presented to our awareness during the time that we are high on LSD. This goes on without any

screening structure—something that Leary has been saying over and over—to the point where something is either understood and is boring or is not understood and is still a koan for people to solve.

What good is that kind of consciousness? I don't know if I have presented it clearly enough to have any value for you. It involves a consciousness that is not socially conditioned (though conditioned by our bodies surely), a consciousness where the social conditioning is reversed, and where we had eight hours to look around us as newborn babes to see our bodies, to see our relationships, to see our architecture around us, to see our relationships to other forms of life. It involves eight hours of experience of ourselves as mammalian sentient beings. Is that a socially useful experience?

I think it always has been considered a socially useful experience. I think that the LSD experience approximates the mystical experience, as it is called, the religious experience, or the peak experience, as Maslow calls it. It approximates the kind of experience that one reads about in William James's *The Varieties of Religious Experience*. I'm not sure it's identical with what people would call the classical religious experience, but then in William James one also finds that very few of those experiences are identical experiences. Their common quality is that there is a break in the normal mode of consciousness, an opening up of another universe of awareness, so that from one description to another in any of the books describing mystical experiences the forms are not the same. One thing that everybody cries out in delight at is that the universe they had taken for granted had suddenly opened and revealed itself as something much deeper and fuller, much more exquisite, something more connected with a divine sense of things—a Self perhaps. So I would say that the LSD experience does approximate what we humans have been recording over millennia as a flight of higher imagination or a flight of higher awareness. Now that experience has always been accorded a very honored status in society. A few people have been burned at the stake or crucified for attempting to manifest the insights that they've experienced. But at least in the academies, in religion, in the church, and even among truck drivers, there is a respect for the non-conditioned, non-verbal, non-conceptual opening up of the mind to all of the data of experience flooding in at once, newly perceived, or perceived as a newborn babe or early child.

Its usefulness in our society is extra. That's why I began talking about McLuhan, inasmuch as we have arrived at sort of a Buck Rogers space age, science-fiction society in which everybody is electronically intercommunicated, in which visual images and verbal images are multiplied, stereotyped and implanted in everybody's brain so that it is very difficult to escape the automatic, mechanistic forms that are constantly being played on our bodies by radio, television, newspapers, by our own university, or by our own parents.

In a world now facing apocalypse, in the sense that America, the largest world power, is perhaps preparing for a war on the Asiatic life form, it becomes important not only to see what we have in common with the Asiatic life form and what we actually have distinct and separate from it but also to find those points, to control the angers built up in us, to measure the actual universe around, to lose the conditioning that brought us to this path of anger, fear and paranoia, to experience what is original in our nature as distinct from what has been educated into our nature since our birth. The problem, however, that still arises, particularly when people have had religious experience and have not had LSD experience, is this question: "Is this experience like an evil specter or is it something that can be reconciled with the older religious experience? Does it have any relationship to the norms of human experience, or at least the high norms of human experience, that are described in the religious books?"

Of these we have neither enough experiments nor enough data. My own experience is as follows: When I was younger (when I was about 28) I had a series of visionary or religious or illuminative experiences which are best categorized as the aesthetic experience, since they became catalyzed by reading poems of Blake. I had an auditory hallucination of Blake's voice and also experienced a number of moments of guilelessness about the world around me and feeling that the father of the universe had existed all along but I had not realized it, that the father of the universe loved me and that I was identical with the father. So this was an experience of bliss. I realized that I had my place in the universe. I tried to describe this a few times in poetry or in prose but it's very difficult to describe.

At the time that I had it (it was about in 1948) this kind of experience was, at least in the circles where I ran (Columbia University), an experience which was practically unknown and was considered madness. I remember that when this happened I went to Lionel Trilling and said, "I've seen light." And he looked at me and seemed to be wondering, "What am I going to do with this?" He looked as if he wondered where I was going to wind up. There were two people at Columbia at the time who had enough inner experience to be able to understand, to talk to me, to reassure me. One was Raymond Weaver who had been the first biographer for Herman Melville and who had lived in Japan and was for those at Columbia in the forties *the* great light, a secret light because he was a cranky cat. He used to know Hart Crane and Wanda Landowska. He was the most eminent professor at Columbia. He shared an office with Mark Van Doren. Weaver could deal with this kind of experience without slipping out and becoming anxious. Mark Van Doren also could deal with it. When I went to him in an overexcited and totally disoriented state and said, "I have seen some light, I heard Blake's voice!" he said, "What kind of light was it?" Then he began questioning me about the quality of the experience, asking for data. Everybody else thought I was nuts. However I am what I am. So I'll stand in my own body and believe my own senses and experiences.

Later I found that LSD catalyzed a variety of consciousness that was very similar to the natural experience. I've used a variety of other hallucinogenics—maybe about thirty times over a fifteen-year period. This is very small actually compared to the usage now being made by the younger people. I found that there has not been any contradiction between the kind of consciousness I had under LSD and my height of rapture of consciousness in natural moments. I also found that I faced the same difficulties with LSD as I had faced with my original visionary experience. Those difficulties were that, having gotten into a state of high perception, how to maintain my normal life, my awareness on a higher level, incorporating in my daily experience some of the concrete perceptions that I had in a moment of ecstasy. Specifically I had had a non-drug vision in the Columbia book store. I'd gone in there for years, and I went in there this day and suddenly I saw that everybody looked like tortured animals. I was reading Blake's poem about—

> I wander through London's chartered streets
> Near where the chartered Thames doth flow
> On every face I meet I see
> Marks of weakness
> Marks of woe

Well, in those moments I saw marks of suffering on the faces of the bookstore clerks, the enormous-like mammalism sexual deliciousness of their being and the contrary stultified, rigid, unsexualized, non-feeling, day-to-day commerce over the books with a few camp jokes mixed in to refer to the unknown. I asked, How, in coming down to a day-to-day dealing with the bookstore people or anyone on the campus, how to deal with such persons, such deep persons as exist in everybody? And that took very slow practice and continuous awareness of the fact that everyone was a deep person and a divine mammal rather than a bookstore clerk. The same problem exists in relation to LSD. Having had a vision on LSD of either your parents' or your own role, how do you manifest that in your school life or whatever life you are pursuing? Henri Michaud, a great French poet who did a lot of early experiments, finally told me that he had concluded that what was important was not the visions, but what people did with the visions afterward, and how they manifested them in their daily life. I think that the really basic practical problem to be faced is the problem common to all mysticism. How is one in day-to-day life to keep continuous high consciousness of the eternal which he had experienced in separated moments of a larger consciousness? What good is it if they are separated moments; if they are not totally, distinctly integrated into everyday life? Having experienced only separated moments of divine consciousness without drugs, I find that the drugs do make possible a return to more native awareness which is useful when I have to take stock of my activities. For instance, a year and a half ago I was involved in the Viet-Nam Day Committee in Berkeley. There was a great deal of anger and outrage about the war. I found myself being swept along into that outrage and vowing vengeance on the murderers of innocent children; and my wits were astray because of all of that senseless tumult; and I all but cried for vengeance on the murderers. I took some LSD the day the President went for his gall bladder operation and I realized that he was another suffering deep person, perhaps one almost ignorant of his own state of consciousness and so suffering a great deal more because of that ignorance, one however entering the valley of the shadow. My hatred simply disappeared. What was left was a funny kind of compassion for him in his ignorance, a prayer for him for his return from the valley of the shadow. In a state of awareness, less hostile, less fearful, less paranoid than his entrance, I found myself praying for him, praying for his own understanding. The thing that I did realize was that my piling up my own hatred on top of the general hatred of the Pentagon and the *New York Daily News* and the military and industrial complex only added to the anti-Vietnam War reaction. Piling up my hatred and my curses and my magic on top of that was going to make the situation worse. I wanted to move to liquidate the anger hallucination that was controlling everybody.

Finally, we have a few other details that might interest you. A poet friend of mine has worked for ten years in Zen monasteries, has done formal meditation, and is an accomplished Zen student. He was here in America a few months ago, and we had several conversations about the rising LSD culture and the Haight-Ashburys. He felt that the LSD experience was not contradictory to the experience of Satori as described by Zen. The younger, qualified, completely trained Zen masters in Japan who had tried LSD were interested in it and considered it a useful tool for education in relation to their own discipline. They were not against its use and were themselves beginning to employ it. The Roshi Suzuki—Roshi means master—who is the head of the meditation sect in San Francisco, said he felt the LSD experience is not the same as Zazen sitting meditation. However he finds that most of the meditators in his group are people who are originally turned on by LSD. As far as he can see, it does open people up to a widening area of consciousness, which can then be worked in with other disciplines. I find the same report coming in now from the schools of Tibetan Buddhism. There is a Geshe who has a monastery in New Jersey. He has some American disciples who have been equally experienced in Tibetan meditation and psychedelics. Wanga and his disciple, Tenjin, who is an ex-Harvard student, have prepared translations of old Tibetan meditation texts and are preparing them for publication with the foreword note that the Tibetan prayers, methods and procedures may be found useful in collaboration with psychedelic experiments. Thus it seems clear to me that there is a close relationship between psychedelic drugs and mystical experience.

Instant Mysticism: Michael Wyschogrod

I think the point of view expressed by Allen Ginsberg is a very good one—an attitude of reason, of peace, of affection, of understanding, and therefore, I am not in a polemical spirit. I do not wish to disagree, to forbid, to outlaw, or to consider LSD and marijuana evil or immoral. They exist like many other things in the world, and it's very superficial to take a simple "no" attitude to what one finds in the world.

Nevertheless there are a number of issues that deserve deeper analysis. I think the two issues we do not want to discuss are these: first, I think it a mistake to approach this problem from the point of view of the dangers involved. The dangers, of course, are not irrelevant. I think anyone who contemplates taking psychedelic drugs deserves to have all of the knowledge necessary so that he can make an intelligent choice as to just what risk is involved; but that is not a final word because many things in life involve risk and yet we don't shun them. In this country the automobile kills forty thousand people a year, and yet I have not heard anyone advocate the abolition of the automobile. For some reason we feel that the advantages of the automobile outweigh the disadvantages. In any case if the psychedelic substances have substantial spiritual and religious advantages, then I would be prepared to say that this outweighs a great many perils and disadvantages. So the element of peril, though relevant, in my opinion is not crucial and is not the final consideration. Secondly, I think that this problem ought not to be approached essentially from the legal point of view, because whether we ought or ought not to outlaw something is again a secondary question.

The first consideration is, is this a good thing or a bad thing? Outlawing is only secondary. Even if we decide that this is a bad thing, it does not necessarily follow that it ought to be outlawed. The heart of the matter is the question: what good are

these drugs? And the moment we ask this question we are in the religious realm. My thesis can be stated very simply: it's a thesis of wonder and surprise. I find that the younger generation to which Professor Abelson referred senses that there is something wrong with the technological mode of existence into which we have been projected in the middle of the twentieth century. There is something wrong with the artificiality of our existence. We no longer experience reality. We live through artificial media such as the television and radio, which have a life of their own and stand as a screen between man and reality. Life in our times is in essence artificial. And because it is artificial there are those people who want to break through this artificiality on all levels, who want to live as a man ought to live and was intended to live, in serenity and peace, with direct contact with reality, not in a life of instant coffee, instant pudding, instant bake mixes, and instant this and that and the other thing—but a wholesale life of cooking vegetables as they grow and taking flour and using it for baking, of brewing coffee, instead of getting it out of an instant mix. Our lives are nightmares of instant experiences. And this, of course, is a profound truth. But then something amazing has happened and I am genuinely amazed—suddenly there is instant mysticism, there is technological mysticism, instead of patience, serenity, humility and waiting for enlightenment and praying for it and loving our fellow man. Instead we look to chemistry: "better living through better things through chemistry."

It seems to me that the genuinely religious person cannot want to buy his relationship to God in a sugar cube, a bottle, or a chemical. It is true that these substances are not yet mass-produced by the pharmaceutical companies. But perhaps that won't take long, if this thing catches on and if people go for it. I assure you that in a few years *Life* and *Time* will be full of ads and every drug company will be selling the stuff and holding out the hope of a quick road to God. And there will be competition, there will be the jingles. I don't want that. I think that would be a travesty on genuine religion, genuine mysticism, and genuine religious experience.

The real thing is always harder and more difficult to achieve than the imitation. And with the real thing you run the risk of never quite making it. There is one element and thought that is universally agreed on among scholars of religion, and that is this: there is a profound distinction between magic and religion. The distinction is simple: Magic is power; religion is prayer. The magician is of the opinion that there is some secret formula which, when discovered, gives him power over the spirit. Once he has that, the spirit cannot refuse his demands. The spirit of magic and the spirit of modern technology are very close indeed because both see man in the driver's seat. Both see man as the power that controls the world around him, and human destiny as a destiny with ever greater control over human existence. Just as through technology we control our environment, the heat and the cold, and the world around us, so by means of magic was the same attempted. The only difference was that we think that science works better than magic. But the spirit is the same; and against science and against magic stands genuine religion. Genuine religion is prayer. Prayer is asking God, and he can say "no."

There is the story of the little kid who prayed; and his cynical uncle said, "Well God didn't answer you, did he?" And the little kid answered, "Yes, he did. He said, 'No.'"

This is the spirit of true religion. In genuine religion we hand ourselves over to the greater spirit, whether one calls it "God," "the Father," or "the spirit of the universe." Fundamentally it doesn't matter. But you see yourself as worshipping that being, that spirit, loving Him. He loves you in return. And you live in peace and union with Him.

Drug mysticism is the conversion of mysticism into magic. It is the illusion that one can have power over the spirit; and this never has happened and never will happen. What comes in a bottle or in a chemical is not the spirit of God. What comes in a bottle or a chemical is an illusion. It is the epitome of just that technological threat against which well-meaning people are fighting and succumbing to through drugs and narcotics. It is the victory of the slogan of the chemical industry, and I don't want to see that happen.

Ginsberg Replies to Wyschogrod

For all I know perhaps Professor Wyschogrod is right! I have no idea about the victory of the chemical industry, or victory of artificial madness, or black magic technology. Burroughs, a former teacher of mine and someone I respect a great deal, has had considerable experience with hallucinogens and has stopped using them. Occasionally he turns on; but lately he has taken to saying, "No, I'd better watch out. The Pentagon is going to poison us all. Things have gotten too Orwellian."

As to religious reality, I don't agree with Professor Wyschogrod as to what constitutes a valid religious experience. The spirit of religion is investigation and practice, of which prayer is only an element. But there isn't a pre-supposition, or what I call a hang-up on a Jehovah, that you've got up there that you've got to be humble to, that you've got to pray to, or to be said "no" by. Jehovah is within in Buddhism and Hinduism and in some aspects of Christianity and actually in some Hebraic traditions also. The external Jehovah is just high camp. In some schools that sense of an external authority is not relied on, certainly not in Buddhism where one of the major koans is that Buddha is not a divine being to be worshipped. The saying is that, "If you meet the Buddha on the way to enlightenment and he bars your way, cut him down!"

As to LSD coming in a bottle and whether or not it is the spirit of God, it all depends on the way we are using the term "god." If there were a Jehovah I wouldn't put it past him to come through a bottle any way. Certainly it would be within his power. Certainly a God would see it as equally charming to come through a bottle as through prayer. So I don't think there is anything to be feared in that sense. What might be feared is dependence on the drug and lack of ritual or lack of prayer or lack of humility or lack of earnestness in the yoga of the drug. I tried to provide the suggestions for ritual, the suggestions for prayer, the suggestions for the application of the drug vision to daily life. But I think that purely verbal terminologies are a bit over-dramatized in speaking of LSD as merely "magic" as opposed to religion. I think those are verbal distinctions. I think they are basically stereotypes of thought. I don't think they fit the enormity and eloquence of the experience which many of us have felt.

Wyschogrod Replies to Ginsberg

I agree with Mr. Ginsberg that these are very serious matters and it's presumptuous for anyone to say what is the case and what is not the case. Yet each of us talks from his own experience. I do not speak out of LSD experience but I talk out of religious experience and I think that I am reporting what I see. I don't think that I have the last word. I don't think that I am right, but do feel deeply that there is profound danger here.

I would add just one word. I don't know much about eastern religion. I deeply respect it. I have an intuitive sense that there is something very real and very deep there, but I'm not a Japanese, Chinese or a Far Easterner. I'm a Westerner. What goes on in the Far East in the setting of that civilization over the thousands of years of art, poetry, and history, and what has gone into the development of those religions I cannot enter into. Therefore I think it is spiritually dangerous for men of New York, for example, to take one aspect of foreign or eastern civilization and transport it here and to think that we have the same thing here that they have. We are Jews or Christians and there is very much to Judaism and Christianity, and we must be what we are. I think there is something very sad about a person trying to be something that he is not and never can be.

Mr. Ginsberg advises people to take pot and LSD. Now I grant an individual the full freedom to act as he wishes and to be what he wishes and I'd be the last person to take that away. But at the same time I must express my convictions. Life poses a peculiar problem: to become what you are. Now this sounds paradoxical, because if you are what you are, why do you need to become what you are? Here there is always tension between becoming what you are, and becoming what you are meant to be. And that's the job for each of us to find. All I can do for you is to say, Look once more before you embark on this strange new path of psychedelic religion. Look once more at your heritage. Just give it a second look and after that you're on your own.

Post Mortem: Raziel Abelson

I must confess that I do not feel I have received the enlightenment I had hoped for—I am not exactly in a state of Satori. The trouble with this discussion is that both participants have assumed something to be the case which, it seems to me, is even more doubtful than the qualities of the drugs they have argued about. Both Ginsberg and Wyschogrod

have assumed that religious experience is necessarily good, and I do not see any reason for accepting that assumption. Ginsberg has argued that, because religious experience is always good, and (he claims) LSD and marijuana help produce religious experience, these drugs are very good and useful things. Wyschogrod has argued, to the contrary, that drugs cannot *possibly* (later he modified his claim to the effect that they do not, so far as he can see) produce genuine religious experience, but only spurious, synthetic, "instant," "bottled," in a word, *illusory* religious experience. Thus he takes it for granted that there is a clear distinction between illusion and reality in religious experience. On this point, it seems to me, Ginsberg has much the better of the argument. To Wyschogrod's claim "You can't get God out of a bottle" Ginsberg replied, very sensibly, "Why not?"

Why not, indeed? I am reminded of Philip Roth's story, *The Conversion of the Jews*, in which the Rabbi pontificates to his Hebrew school class that Christianity is more irrational than Judaism, because it (Christianity) claims that Jesus was born without sexual intercourse; and little Ozzie then demands to know why an omnipotent God, who can divide the Red Sea and send plagues over Egypt, cannot make a woman become pregnant without any sexual intercourse. Once we begin talking about the transcendental (a fancy word for supernatural) anything goes—each one makes up his own rules. One says you can't find God in a bottle, but you can in a burning bush; another says God can't make a woman pregnant without intercourse but that the Holy Ghost in the form of a dove can. How adjudicate such theological claims, and why bother? How one can find God depends very much on just what one means by "God," and it is not at all clear what either Ginsberg or Wyschogrod means, and still less clear whether whatever they mean exists. And if He doesn't exist, you can no more find Him through prayer than through drugs or in a bottle.

Now it seems to me that the distinction between real and unreal, whether it is applied to religious experience, to God, or to the beauty and goodness allegedly revealed by psychedelic drugs, is crucial to this discussion. And my own objection to the claims made for such drugs is on the philosophical ground that this distinction is being applied to a type of experience to which it cannot properly be applied, because there are no established criteria for making the distinction. Indeed, the experience, being hallucinatory, is that there cannot possibly be criteria for distinguishing the real from the apparent. Mr. Ginsberg made this clear in describing how, under LSD, he felt compassion for everyone and anything, for President Johnson (he said to me later) for Adolph Hitler. Now what sense is there in compassion that does not distinguish the executioner from his victims? How can one have real compassion for the sufferer without hating the agent who makes him suffer? What good is such compassion; indeed, is it really compassion, or is this feeling of compassion not as hallucinatory as everything else in the state of being drugged? To be more exact, the trouble here is that there is no objective way of distinguishing what is real from what is imaginary, hallucinatory, apparent, spurious, or in any sense unreal. The psychedelic experience is one that, by its very nature, leads one beyond (or below) all criteria of reality. One can, of course, easily say that it leads one to a "higher reality," but this verbalism is empty because "real" makes no sense where it cannot be distinguished from unreal. And this breakdown of the distinction is, of course, typical of all modes of irrationality, including religious mysticism. Consequently, it is impossible to judge whether psychedelic experience and religious experience are the same or different. All we can say is that they are equally hallucinatory. Why the speakers should assume that that is a very good thing is still a mystery to me.

In effect, Mr. Ginsberg has made two claims: first that psychedelic drugs are good in an instrumental sense because they have beneficial effects on one's personality and abilities, and second, that the experience they induce is intrinsically good. The first claim, it seems to me, cannot be authoritatively established by Mr. Ginsberg or anyone else who testifies only from personal experience, any more than the therapeutic value of psychoanalysis can be established by brainwashed patients who have been persuaded by their analyst that they are much improved (when no one else can see any difference in their behavior). Such a claim can only be proved by carefully controlled scientific studies, and no conclusive studies have yet been made. So I would discount this claim completely, just as anyone with sense would discount the claims made by Krebiozen enthusiasts, and just as Freud came close

to discrediting himself as a doctor when he made premature claims for the therapeutic value of cocaine.

The second claim, that the psychedelic experience is intrinsically good, is more difficult to assess, for the reason that its value has to be judged within the experience (I am frequently rebuked by students when I question the value of taking drugs. I am told I haven't tried them, so I can't possibly know whether they are good or bad). Yet the experience is such that within it, all established criteria of good or bad are dissolved, just as, in a dream, the criteria for distinguishing real from apparent cease to apply. One dreams that something is real and something else is not, but this distinction is itself dreamt, and therefore ineffectual. Consequently, it makes no more sense to say that what one experiences is bad than to say that it is good. We simply have no standards for evaluating the hallucinatory objects of a psychedelic experience, for we have no standards for evaluating any hallucinatory objects. So far, the human race is a reality-oriented species. If enough people take drugs, this may change, and then the philosophical premises of a discussion such as this will be different, but it is as useless to speculate on such a state of affairs as to try to imagine what the world would be like if the laws of physics ceased to hold.

I do not mean to question the right of anyone, including Mr. Ginsberg, to express a preference for any type of experience he chooses to enjoy. If someone likes to smoke pot or take acid, and injures no one else in doing so, that so far as I am concerned, is his affair; and I no more support legislation against such activities than I support legislation against suicide. But to say that one likes something is not the same as to say that that something is good. I do very strongly object to the proselytizing of drugs, because, as I have tried to explain, there are no objective grounds for making a claim either to intrinsic value or to instrumental value with respect to such drugs. I still see one rather compelling reason not to take them, a reason that I tried to indicate in my opening remarks. To steep oneself in illusion is to escape from the irksome necessity to distinguish illusion from reality—in a word, to cop out. My conclusion from this discussion is: there's a lot of work to be done in the real world, and a lot of real beauty to enjoy— let's get on with it.

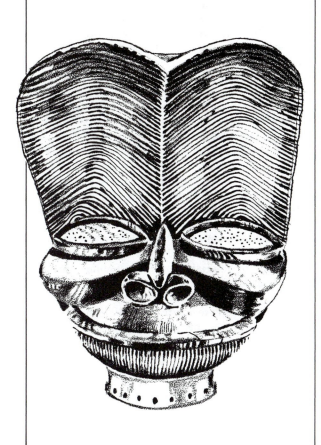

5

Ethnomedicine: Religion and Healing

If a single pervasive thought were to be singled out in this chapter, it would be the importance of culture in determining the etiology and treatment of disease and mental disorders. Just as humans have always suffered from disease, so too have we always responded to it, seeking ways to reduce its debilitating nature or, we hope, to banish it completely. All human societies have belief systems and practices that people turn to in order to identify disease and effect a cure. The integration of the study of these systems of beliefs and practices into the study of non-Western societies has created medical anthropology, the most recent addition to the discipline of anthropology.

Explanations and cures of illnesses may be either natural or supernatural (a naturalistic response would not involve supernatural aid). As P. Stanley Yoder has clearly pointed out, one of the medical anthropologist's most important tasks is to distinguish between different types of causation and to understand the relationship between them, especially because "different types of casual explanations may be involved at different points during the process of diagnosis

Bacham dance mask from Cameroun.

and treatment, or may characteristically demand differing treatments" (1982: 15). Moreover, because the range and variability of medical beliefs and practices among the nonliterate peoples of the world is immense, there will be no easy explanation or simple generalization regarding causation and treatment of diseases. But always it will be possible to see the close relationship between medicine and religion, a cultural bonding that occurs in non-literate, non-industrialized cultures as well as in modern, technological cultures.

The importance of our understanding of ethnomedical systems is made clear by the fact that a great percentage of the non-Western world's population reside in areas that are not exposed to Western medical treatment. Primary among the concerns of such international groups as the World Health Organization is the role that improved health care can play in the socioeconomic development of Third World countries. The lack of implementation of modern medical care in these areas of the world is caused by a lack both of available funds and of information. Partly in response to the dearth of funding, some health planners have proposed that the most effective way to expand modern primary care would be for Western-trained practitioners to collaborate with traditional practitioners (Bichmann 1979: 175); however, lack of information is the greatest barrier to assessing the feasibility of such proposals in relation to national health goals and planning (Good 1977: 705). Because little substantive information concerning indigenous health care systems is available for non-Western countries, the identification and use of agents of change such as local curers to improve the quality of life in rural areas is extremely difficult.

It is noteworthy to point out also that intercultural contact seems to have caused an increase in both physical and psychological Western-based diseases among non-Western populations; the frustrations of not being able to cure these modern illnesses are liable to increase the use of traditional methods of healing. Other problems of contact also exist. Western-trained medical practitioners find little in traditional systems of health care they consider effective in either the physical or mental realms. On the other hand, modern medical treatment is also often rejected by those

in the culture. For example, in rural contemporary Kenya modern medical technology is not interfering with the pervasive "ancestor spirit-sorcery theory" of disease causation that has traditionally been used to account for all major misfortunes (Kramer and Thomas 1982: 169): as late as 1969 there was still no indication among the rural Kamba of Kenya that modern medicine had made prominent inroads at the level of prevention, either in effecting behavioral change or in modifying etiological beliefs, despite their long exposure to Western techniques.

Determining why the ill choose to accept or reject a system of treatment not only would define who the people in the culture perceive as the proper healer but also would delineate their etiology of disease and their perception of appropriate treatment. What applied anthropologists are attempting to determine are the advantages and disadvantages of each of the health care systems—traditional and modern—in the eyes of the patients, as well as the nature of the knowledge healers and their clients draw upon in the process of selecting treatment. Unfortunately, previous research in traditional medical systems has essentially ignored the studied people's own explanations of these criteria, criteria that ordinarily include both natural and supernatural explanations.

Knowledge of the naturalistic treatments and ethnopharmacological systems of non-Western societies is also important, for much of the pharmacopoeia administered by traditional healers does work. (Societies everywhere, including preliterate peoples, possess naturalistic explanations and treatments. Cures derived from hundreds of wild plants were used by the North American Indians, for example, and techniques for treating headaches and stomachaches, setting broken bones, bloodletting, lancing, cauterization, and other naturalistic skills are well known to the nonliterate world.) However, since the effectiveness of the traditional healer is dependent upon more than the use of proper chemical treatment, diagnosis is made not only at the empirical level but also at the psychological and social levels as well. In speaking of Africa, for example, Wolfgang Bichmann notes that illness does not mean so much an individual event but a disturbance of social relations (1979: 177), and M. F. Lofchie points out that "African medical research has much to contribute to Western medicine: its wholism, emphasis on treatment of the entire family as well as the 'ill' person, and its encyclopedic lore of information about the curative properties of items available in nature—all of these principles are now working their way into Western medical vocabulary" (1982: vii).

For years it was widely believed that only "civilized" peoples were subject to mental illness, while the pre-literates of the world led a blissful life free of neuroses and psychoses. It did not take anthropology long to prove that Rousseau's Noble Savage was just as susceptible to the major disorders of the mind as was the individual coping with life in the so-called civilized societies of the world. Anthropologists have sought answers to such important questions as whether mental illness rates differ in pre-literate and modern societies; whether styles and types of illnesses vary; and whether it is more difficult to adjust to life in modern cultures than in pre-literate cultures. Anthropologists and others have shown, moreover, that traditional healers are particularly effective in the treatment of mental illness, and that their approaches to curing are beneficial to physical diseases as well. Not only are traditional healers' services readily available to the ill, for example, but their system of care is also non-disruptive to those in the culture, and the patient has the support of family members who are nearby or in actual attendance during the treatment. Beyond these advantages, and in contrast with the Western world, Third World countries frequently are much more accepting of those having mental illnesses. Sufferers of these disorders are often stigmatized in the West, and often attempt to hide their medical history.

In a seven-year multi-cultural pilot study of severe mental illness by the World Health Organization reported in the magazine *Science '80* it was shown that relatively fast and complete recoveries from major psychoses are achieved in developing countries like Nigeria and India. In the United States and other Western countries, however, almost one-half of those who suffer psychotic breakdowns never recover. For example, whereas 58 percent of the Nigerians and 51 percent of the Indians studied had a single psychotic episode and were judged cured after treatment, the cure

rate in the industrialized countries ranged from only 6 percent in Denmark to a high of 27 percent in China (1980: 7). Certainly non-Western healing techniques are effective in the treatment of the mentally ill; however, the treatment of physiological diseases cannot match that of the West. The fact that many non-Western pharmaceuticals may be effective in one society and not in another demonstrates the important relationship of beliefs and cures, in particular the interaction of the healer and the supernatural.

Throughout the world it is possible to place supernaturally caused illnesses into five categories: (1) sorcery, (2) breach of taboo, (3) intrusion of a disease object, (4) intrusion of a disease-causing spirit, and (5) loss of soul (Clements, 1932: 252). It is important to note that these categories may not be recognized by certain societies. Indeed, it is a difficult task to determine the frequency and incidence of illnesses, especially mental illnesses, in non-Western, non-industrialized countries. Native peoples may avoid seeking medical help from a modern health facility, for example; or, if they do seek treatment, there may be a question of accurate recordkeeping.

Anthropologists have correctly noted that the types of cures sought are based not only on the cause but also on the severity of the illness in terms of level of pain and difficulty of curing. Treatment based on cause and severity varies greatly; some non-Western groups maintain that most diseases are of natural origin, whereas others blame the supernatural realm for the misfortunes.

It is apparent that anthropologists must understand the integration of ethnomedical systems with the other areas of culture if they are successfully to conduct comparative studies. Ethnomedical systems are deeply ingrained in the structure of societies, functioning in ways that create a positive atmosphere for health care . No longer can we view pre-literate medical methods as inferior; indeed, Western society owes much to traditional medicine, not the least of which is the support given to the patient by the family and the community.

The selection of readings in this chapter for the most part deals with supernaturally caused diseases and mental illnesses and their etiology and treatment.

Arthur Lehmann opens the chapter with an analysis of ethnomedicine among the Aka hunters and Ngando farmers. He stresses disease categories, disease etiology, treatment, and the role the traditional healers (*ngangas*) play in interethnic contacts. In the second article, Ari Kiev investigates psychotherapy in non-Western societies that have different patterns of food production. He demonstrates a relationship between technology and the complexity of ethnopsychological approaches by traditional healers. Robert Bergman's article, "A School for Medicine Men," helps us see the similarities and dissimilarities between Navajo medicine men and Western-trained psychiatrists. Bergman also discusses the establishment of a school for Navajo medicine men. Robert Edgerton describes the training and psychiatric approach used by one particular Hehe traditional psychiatrist from Tanzania. Although this traditional psychiatrist normally emphasizes witchcraft and magic, invoking the aid of the supernatural when necessary, he remains primarily a pragmatic psycho-pharmacologist, always ready to use botany and pharmacology to cure his patients. Claude Lévi-Strauss reminds us of the power of belief and faith in understanding certain psycho-physiological mechanisms underlying death and illness caused by magic. In the final article, Wayland D. Hand demonstrates that the use of folk medical magic and symbolism is not restricted to non-Western cultures. On the contrary, Hand's folkloric research illustrates that in the contemporary western United States, magical beliefs and the symbols that attend them are still popular and practiced in healing.

References

Bichmann, Wolfgang
    1979 "Primary Health Care and Traditional Medicine—Considering the Background of Changing Health Care Concepts in Africa." *Social Science and Medicine* 13B: 175–82.

Clements, Forrest E.
    1932 "Primitive Concepts of Disease." University of California *Publications in American Archaeology and Ethnology* 32, No. 2: 252.

Good, Charles M.
    1977 "Traditional Medicine: An Agenda for Medical Geography." *Social Science and Medicine* 11: 705–13.

Lofchie, M. F.
    1982 "Foreword." In P. Stanley Yoder, ed., *African Health and Healing Systems: Proceedings of a Symposium*, pp. vii–ix. Los Angeles: Crossroads Press, University of California.

"World Psychosis." *Science '80*, Vol. 1, no. 6, p. 7.

Yoder, P. Stanley
    1982 "Issues in the Study of Ethnomedical Systems in Africa." In P. Stanley Yoder, ed., *African Health and Healing Systems: Proceedings of a Symposium*, pp. 1–20. Los Angeles: Crossroads Press, University of California.

Eyes of the Ngangas: Ethnomedicine and Power in Central African Republic

Arthur C. Lehmann

Peoples of the Third World have a variety of therapies available for combating diseases, but because of cost, availability, and cultural bias most rely on ethnomedical, or traditional, treatment rather than "biomedical" or Western therapies. Dr. Lehmann's field research focuses on the importance of ngangas (traditional healers) as a source of primary health care for both the Aka Pygmy hunters and their horticultural neighbors, the Ngando of Central African Republic. Tracing the basis and locus of the ngangas' mystical diagnostic and healing powers, he shows that they are particularly effective with treatments for mental illness and, to an unknown extent, with herbal treatment of physical illnesses as well. The powers of the Aka ngangas, however, are also used to reduce the tensions between themselves and their patrons and to punish those Ngando who have caused the hunters harm. Lehmann points out the necessity of recognizing and treating the social as well as the biological aspects of illness and appeals to health-care planners to establish counterpart systems that mobilize popular and biomedical specialists to improve primary health care in the Third World.

This selection was written for this volume and appears here in print for the first time.

"ETHNOMEDICINE" (ALSO REFERRED TO AS FOLK, traditional, or popular medicine) is the term used to describe the primary health care system of indigenous people whose medical expertise lies outside "biomedicine," the "modern" medicine of Western societies. Biomedicine does exist in the Third World, but it is unavailable to the masses of inhabitants, for a number of reasons. Conversely, although popular medicine has largely been supplanted by biomedicine in the Western world, it still exists, and is revived from time to time by waves of dissatisfaction with modern medicine and with the high cost of health care, by the health food movement, and by a variety of other reasons. The point is, all countries have pluralistic systems of health care, but for many members of society the combat against the diseases that have plagued mankind is restricted to the arena of popular medicine.

This is particularly true in the developing nations, such as those of the sub-Saharan regions of Africa, where over 80 percent of the population live in rural areas with a dearth of modern medical help (Bichmann 1979, Green 1980). During 1984, 1985, and 1986, I made three fieldtrips to one such rural area, to study the primary health care practices of Aka Pygmy hunter-gatherers and their horticultural neighbors, the Ngando of Central African Republic (C.A.R.).

The Aka and the Ngando

Several groups of the Pygmies live in a broad strip of forested territory stretching east and west across the center of Equatorial Africa. The two largest societies are the Mbuti of the Ituri Forest of Zaire and the Aka, who live in the Southern Rainforest that extends from the Lobaye River in Central African Republic into the People's Republic of the Congo and into Cameroun (Cavalli-Sforza 1971). Like the Mbuti, the Aka are long-time residents of their region. It is on the edge of the Southern Rainforest in and near the village of Bagandu that the Aka Pygmies and the Ngando come into most frequent contact. The close proximity, particularly during the dry season from December to April, allows for comparisons of health care systems that would be difficult otherwise, for the Aka move deep into the forest and are relatively inaccessible for a good portion of the year.

Since Turnbull described the symbiotic relationship between Mbuti Pygmies and villagers in Zaire (1965), questions remain as to why Pygmy hunters continue their association with their sedentary neighbors. Bahuchet's work shows that the relationship between the Aka and the Ngando of C.A.R. is one of voluntary mutual dependence in which both groups benefit; indeed, the Aka consider the villagers responsible for their well-being (1985: 549). Aka provide the Ngando with labor, meat, and forest materials, while the Ngando pay the Aka with plantation foods, clothes, salt, cigarettes, axes and knives, alcohol, and infrequently, money.

This mutual dependence extends to the health care practices of both societies. Ngando patrons take seriously ill Aka to the dispensary for treatment; Aka consider this service a form of payment that may be withheld by the villagers as a type of punishment. On the other hand, Aka *ngangas* (traditional healers) are called upon to diagnose and treat Ngando illnesses. The powers believed to be held by the ngangas are impressive, and few, particularly rural residents, question these powers or the roles they play in everyday life in Central African Republic.

Eyes of the Ngangas

The people believe that the ngangas both intervene on their behalf with the supernatural world to combat malevolent forces, and also use herbal ex-

pertise to protect them from the myriad of tropical diseases. Elizabeth Motte [1980] has recorded an extensive list of medicines extracted by the ngangas from the environment to counter both natural and supernatural illnesses; 80 percent are derived from plants and the remaining 20 percent from animals and minerals.

Both Aka and Ngando ngangas acquire their power to diagnose and cure through an extensive apprenticeship ordinarily served under the direction of their fathers, who are practicing healers themselves. This system of inheritance is based on primogeniture, although other than first sons may be chosen to become ngangas. Although Ngando ngangas may be either male or female, the vast majority are males; all Aka ngangas are males. In the absence of the father or if a younger son has the calling to become a healer, he may study under an nganga outside the immediate family.

During my three trips to the field, ngangas permitted me to question them on their training and initiation into the craft; it became apparent that important consistencies existed. First, almost all male ngangas are first sons. Second, fathers expect first sons to become ngangas; as they said, "It is natural." Third, the apprenticeship continues from boyhood until the son is himself a nganga, at which time he trains his own son. Fourth, every nganga expresses firm belief in the powers of his teacher to cure and, it follows, in his own as well. As is the case with healers around the world, despite the trickery sometimes deemed necessary to convince clients of the effectiveness of the cure, the ngangas are convinced that their healing techniques will work unless interrupted by stronger powers. Fifth, every nganga interviewed maintained strongly that other ngangas who are either envious or have a destructive spirit can destroy or weaken the power of a healer, causing him to fail. Sixth, and last, the origin and locus of the ngangas' power is believed to be in their eyes.

Over and over I was told that during the final stages of initiation, the master nganga had vaccinated the initiate's eyes and placed "medicine" in the wound, thus giving the new nganga power to divine and effectively treat illnesses. At first I interpreted the term *vaccination* to simply mean the placement of "medicine" in the eyes, but I was wrong. The master actually cuts the lower eyelids with a razor blade or both blade and a needle, inserts the "medicine," and concludes the ceremony of initiation. I have no information that shows that the eye itself is vaccinated, but it is clear that the multiple powers of the ngangas are believed to reside in the eyes.

It follows that the actual divinatory act involves a variety of techniques, particular to each nganga, that allow him to use his powers to "see" the cause of the illness and determine its treatment. Some burn a clear amber resin called *paka*, staring into the flames to learn the mystery of illness and the appropriate therapy. Some stare into the rays of the sun during diagnosis, and others gaze into mirrors to unlock the secret powers of the ancestors through their vaccinated eyes. Western methods of divining—of knowing the unknown—were not, and to some degree are not now, significantly different from the techniques of the ngangas. Our ways of "seeing," involving gazing at and "reading" tea leaves, crystal balls, cards, palms, and stars, are still considered appropriate techniques by many.

Therapy Choices and Therapy Managers

A wide variety of therapies coexist in contemporary Africa, and the situation in the village of Bagandu is no exception. The major sources of treatment are Aka ngangas, Ngando ngangas, kinship therapy (family councils called to resolve illness-causing conflicts between kin), home remedies, Islamic healers (marabouts), and the local nurse at the government dispensary, who is called "doctor" by villagers and hunters alike. In addition, faith healers, herbalists, and local specialists (referred to as "fetishers") all attempt, in varying degrees, to treat mental or physical illness in Bagundu. Intermittently Westerners, such as missionaries, personnel from the U.S. Agency for International Development, and anthropologists, also treat physical ailments. Bagandu is a large village of approximately 3,000 inhabitants, however; most communities are much smaller and have little access to modern treatment. And, as Cavalli-Sforza has noted,

> If the chances of receiving Western medical help for Africans living in remote villages are very limited, those of Pygmies are practically nonexistent. They are even further removed from hospitals. African health agents usually do not treat Pygmies. Medical help comes exceptionally and almost always from rare visiting foreigners (Cavalli-Sforza 1986: 421).

Residents of Bagandu are fortunate in having both a government dispensary and a pharmacy run by the Catholic church, but prescriptions are extremely costly relative to income, and ready cash is scarce. A more pressing problem is the availability of drugs. Frequently the "doctor" has only enough to treat the simplest ailments such as headaches and small cuts; he must refer thirty to forty patients daily to the Catholic pharmacy, which has more drugs than the dispensary but still is often unable to fill prescriptions for the most frequently prescribed drugs such as penicillin, medicine to counteract parasites, and antibiotic salves. While the doctor does the best he can under these conditions, patients must often resort only to popular medical treatment—in spite of the fact that family members, the therapy managers, have assessed the illness as one best treated by biomedicine. In spite, too, of the regular unavailability of medicine, the doctor's diagnosis and advice is still sought out—although many people will consent to go to the dispensary only "after having exhausted the resources of traditional medicine" [Motte 1980: 311].

Popular, ethnomedical treatment is administered by kin, ngangas (among both the Aka and Ngando villagers), other specialists noted for treatment of specific maladies, and Islamic marabouts, who are recent immigrants from Chad. (According to both Aka and Ngando informants, the heaviest burden for health care falls to these ethnomedical systems.) Ngando commonly utilize home, kin remedies for minor illnesses, but almost 100 percent indicated that for more serious illnesses they consulted either the doctor or ngangas (Aka, Ngando, or both); to a lesser extent they visited specialists. The choice of treatment, made by the family therapy managers, rests not only on the cause and severity of the illness, but also on the availability of therapists expert in the disease or problem, their cost, and their proximity to the patient. Rarely do the residents of Bagandu seek the aid of the marabouts, for example, in part because of the relatively high cost of consultation. Clearly, both popular and biomedical explanations for illness play important roles in the maintenance of health among Bagandu villagers, although popular medicine is the most important therapy resource available. Popular medicine is especially vital for the Aka hunters, whose relative isolation and inferior status (in the eyes of the Ngando) have resulted in less opportunity for biomedical treatment. Yet even they seek out modern medicine for serious illnesses.

Whatever the system of treatment chosen, it is important to understand that "the management of illness and therapy by a set of close kin is a central aspect of the medical scene in central Africa. . . . The therapy managing group . . . exercises a brokerage function between the sufferer and the specialist . . ." (Janzen 1978: 4). It is the kingroup that determines which therapy is to be used.

Explanations of Illness

The choice of therapy in Bagandu is determined by etiology and severity, as in the West. Unlike Western medicine, however, African ethnomedicine is not restricted to an etiology of only natural causation. Both the Aka and the Ngando spend a great deal of time, energy, and money (or other forms of payments) treating illnesses perceived as being the result of social disorders and cultural imbalances, often described in supernatural terms. Aka and Ngando nosology has accommodated biomedicine without difficulty, but traditional etiology has not become less important to the members of these societies. Frequent supernatural explanations of illness by Aka and Ngando informants inevitably led me to the investigation of witchcraft, curses, spells, or the intervention of ancestors and nameless spirits, all of which were viewed as being responsible for poor health and misfortune. The Aka maintain, for example, that the fourth leading cause of death in Bagandu is witchcraft (diarrhea is the principal cause; measles, second, and convulsions, third [Hewlett 1986: 56]). During my research it became apparent that a dual model of disease explanation exists among the Aka and Ngando: first, a naturalistic model that fits its Western biomedical counterpart well and, second, a supernaturalistic explanation.

Interviews with village and Pygmy ngangas indicated that their medical systems are not significantly different. Indeed, both groups agree that their respective categories of illness etiology are identical. Further, the categories are not mutually exclusive: an illness may be viewed as being natural, but it may be exacerbated by supernatural forces such as witchcraft and spells. Likewise, this phenomenon can be reversed: an illness episode may be caused by supernatural agents but progress into a form that is treatable through biomedical

techniques. For example, my relatively educated and ambitious young field assistant, a villager, was cut on the lower leg by a piece of stone while working on a new addition to his house. The wound, eventually becoming infected, caused swelling throughout the leg and groin. As was the case in some of his children's illnesses, the explanation for the wound was witchcraft. It was clear to him that the witch was a neighbor who envied his possessions and his employment by a foreigner. Although the original cut was caused by a supernatural agent, the resulting infection fitted the biomedical model. Treatment by a single injection of penicillin quickly brought the infection under control, although my assistant believed that had the witch been stronger the medicine would not have worked. Here is a case in which, "in addition to the patient's physical signs and social relationships," the passage of time is also crucial to "the unfolding of therapeutic action" (Feierman 1985: 77). As the character of an illness changes with time as the illness runs its course, the therapy manager's decisions may change, because the perceived etiology can shift as a result of a variety of signs, such as a slow-healing wound or open conflict in the patient's social group (Janzen 1978: 9)

Studies on disease etiologies among select African societies (Bibeau 1979, Janzen 1978, and Warren 1974) reported that most illnesses had natural causes, and this finding holds for the Ngando villagers as well. At first glance these data would seem to reduce the importance of ngangas and of popular medicine generally, but it is necessary to recognize that ngangas treat both natural and supernatural illnesses utilizing both medical and mystical techniques. The question posed by Feierman, "Is popular medicine effective?" (1985: 5), is vital to the evaluation of ngangas as healers. Surely some traditional medicines used by these cures must in many cases work, and work regularly enough to earn the sustained support of the general public.

Illness of God and Illnesses of Man

Both the Ngando and Aka explanations for natural illnesses lack clarity. Some ngangas refer to them as "illnesses of God"; others simply identify them as "natural"; and still others frequently use both classifications, regularly assigning each label to specific ailments. Hewlett maintains that the Aka sometimes labeled unknown maladies as illnesses of God (1986: personal communication). On the other hand, the Bakongo of neighboring Zaire defined illnesses of God as those "generally, mild conditions which respond readily to therapy when no particular disturbance exists in the immediate social relationships of the sufferer. . . . The notion of 'god' does not imply divine intervention or retribution but simply that the cause is an affliction in the order of things unrelated to human intentions" (Janzen 1978: 9).

Both Janzen's and Hewlett's data are accurate, by my field data show as well that the explanations of natural illnesses among the Ngando and Aka not only refer to normal mild diseases and sometimes unknown ones, but also to specific illnesses named by the ngangas and the residents of Bagandu. The confusion surrounding these mixed explanations of disease causation is an important topic for future ethnosemantic or other techniques of emic inquiry by ethnographers.

Residents of Bagandu and both Aka and Ngando ngangas categorized sickness caused by witchcraft, magic, curses, spells, and spirits as "illnesses of man." This is the second major disease category. Witchcraft, for example, while not the main cause of death, is the most frequently named cause of illness in Bagandu. Informants in Bagandu cite the frequency of witchcraft accusations as proof of their viewpoint. Antisocial or troublesome neighbors are frequently accused of being witches and are jailed if the charge is proven. Maladies of all sorts, such as sterility among females, are also commonly attributed to the innate and malevolent power of witches. These types of explanations are not unusual in rural Africa. What is surprising are reports of new illnesses in the village caused by witches.

All Ngando informants claimed, furthermore, that the problem of witchcraft has not diminished over time; on the contrary, it has increased. The thinking is logical: because witchcraft is believed to be inherited, any increase in population is seen also as an inevitable increase in the number of witches in the village. Population figures in the region of the Southern Rainforest have increased somewhat in the past few decades, despite epidemics such as measles; accordingly, the incidence of maladies attributed to witches has increased. One informant from Bagandu strongly insisted that witches are not

only more numerous but also much more powerful today than before. Offiong (1983) reported a marked increase of witchcraft in Nigeria and adjacent states in West Africa, caused not by inflation of population but by the social strain precipitated by the frustration accompanying lack of achievement after the departure of colonial powers.

Insanity is not a major problem among the Ngando. When it does occur, it is believed to be caused by witchcraft, clan or social problems, evil spirits, and breaking taboos. Faith healers, marabouts, and ngangas are seen as effective in the treatment of mental illness due to witchcraft or other causes. The role of faith healers is particularly important in the lives of members of Prophetical Christian Church in Bagandu. They have strong faith in the healing sessions and maintain that the therapy successfully treats the victims of spirits' attacks. Informants also claim the therapy lasts a long time.

The curse is a common method of venting anger in Bagandu, used by both male and female witches. Informants stated that women use curses more than men and that the subjects of their attacks are often males. The curses of witches are counted as being extremely dangerous in the intended victim. One villager accused the elderly of using the curse as a weapon most frequently. Spell-casting is also common in the area, and males often use spells as a method of seduction.

Most, if not all, residents of Bagandu use charms, portable "fetishes," and various types of magical objects placed in and around their houses for protection. Some of these objects are counter-magical: they simultaneously protect the intended victim and turn the danger away from the victim to the attackers. Counter-magic is not always immediate; results may take years to appear. Charms, fetishes, and other forms of protection are purchased from ngangas, marabouts, and other specialists such as herbalists. For example, the Aka and Ngando alike believe that wearing a mole's tooth on a bracelet is the most powerful protection from attacks by witches.

To a lesser extent, spirits are also believed to cause illness. It is problematic whether or not this source of illness deserves a separate category of disease causation. Bahuchet thinks not; rather, he holds that spirit-caused illnesses should be labeled illnesses of God (1986: personal communication). It is interesting to note that in addition to charms and other items put to use in Bagandu, residents supplicate ancestors for aid in times of difficulty. If the ancestors do not respond, and if the victim of the misfortune practices Christianity, he or she will seek the aid of God. Non-Christians and Christians alike commonly ask diviners the cause of their problem, after which they seek the aid of the proper specialist. Revenge for real or imagined attacks on oneself or on loved ones is common. One method is to point a claw of a mole at the wrongdoer. Ngando informants maintain the victim dies soon after. Simple possession of a claw, if discovered, means jail for the owner.

My initial survey of Aka and Ngando ngangas in 1984 brought out other origins of illness. Two ngangas in Bagandu specifically cited the devil, rather than unnamed evil spirits, as a cause for disease. The higher exposure of villagers to Christianity may account for this attribution: seven denominations are currently represented in the churches of Bagandu. Urban ngangas questioned in Bangui, the capital, stressed the use of poison as a cause of illness and death. Although poisonings do not figure prominently as a cause of death among the Aka and Ngando, it is common belief that ngangas and others do use poison.

Finally, while not a cause for illness, informants maintained that envious ngangas have the power to retard or halt the progress of a cure administered by another. Every nganga interviewed in 1984 and 1985 confirmed not only that they have the power to interrupt the healing process of a patient, but also that they frequently invoke it. Interestingly, ngangas share this awesome power with witches, who are also believed by members of both societies to be able to spoil the "medicine" of healers. This kind of perception of the ngangas' power accounts, in part, for their dual character: primarily beneficial to the public, they can also be dangerous.

While the numerical differences in the frequency of physiologically and psychologically rooted illnesses in Bagandu are unknown, Ngando respondents in a small sample were able to list a number of supernaturally caused illnesses that are treatable by ngangas, but only a few naturally caused ones. Among the naturalistic illnesses were illnesses of the spleen; *katungba*, deformation of the back; and *Kongo*, "illness of the rainbow." According to Hewlett (1986: 53), *Kongo* causes paralysis of the legs (and sometimes of the arms) and death after the victim steps on a dangerous mushroom growing on a damp spot in the forest where a rainbow-colored snake has rested. Had the Ngando sample been more exhaustive, it is probable that the list of natural diseases would have been greater, although perhaps not as high as the twenty natural illnesses the ngangas said they could treat successfully. That impressive list includes malaria, hernia, diarrhea, stomach illness, pregnancy problems, dysentery, influenza, abscesses, general fatigue, traumas (snake bite, miscellaneous wounds, and poisoning), and general and specific bodily pain (spleen, liver, ribs, head, and uterus).

Powers of the Ngangas

The powers of the ngangas are not limited to controlling and defeating supernatural or natural diseases alone. In the village of Bagandu and in the adjacent Southern Rainforest where the Ngando and Aka hunters come into frequent contact, tensions exist due to the patron-client relationship, which by its very economic nature is negative. These tensions are magnified by ethnic animosity. Without the Akas' mystical power, their economic and social inferiority would result in an even more difficult relationship with the Ngando. Here the powers of the Pygmy ngangas play an important part in leveling, to bearable limits, the overshadowing dominance of the Ngando, and it is here that the ngangas demonstrate their leadership outside the realm of health care. Each Aka has some form of supernatural protection provided by the nganga of his camp to use while in the village. Still, the need exists for the extraordinary powers of the nganga himself for those moments of high tension when Aka are confronted by what they consider the most menacing segments of the village population: the police, the mayor, and adolescent males, all of whom, as perceived by the Aka, are dangerous to their personal safety while in the village.

In the summer of 1986 I began to study the attitudes of village patrons toward their Aka clients and, conversely, the attitudes of the so-called "wayward servants" (Turnbull's term for the Mbuti Pygmy of Zaire, 1965) toward the villagers. Participant observation and selective interviews of patrons, on the one hand, and of hunters, on the other, disclosed other important tangents of power of the Aka in general and of their ngangas in particular. First, the Aka often have visible sources of power such as scarification, cords worn on the wrist and neck, and bracelets strung with powerful charms for protection against village witches. These protective devices are provided the Aka by their ngangas. Second, and more powerful still, are the hidden powers of the Aka in general, bolstered by the specific powers of the ngangas. Although the villagers believe the hunters' power is strongest in the forest, and therefore weaker in the village setting, Aka power commands the respect of the farmers. Third, the villagers acknowledge the Aka expertise in the art of producing a variety of deadly poisons, such as *sepi*, which may be used to punish farmers capable of the most serious crimes against the Pygmies. The obvious functions of these means of protection and retribution, taken from the standpoint of the Aka, are positive. Clearly these powers reduce the tension of the Aka while in the village, but they also control behavior of villagers toward the hunters to some undefinable degree.

Villagers interpret the variety of punishments which the Aka are capable of meting out to wrongdoers as originating in their control of mystical or magical powers. Interestingly, even poisonings are viewed in this way by villagers, because of the difficulty of proving that poison rather than mystical power caused illness or death. Although the use of poison is rare, it is used and the threat remains. Georges Guille-Escuret, a French ethnohistorian working in Bagandu in 1985, reported to me that prior to my arrival in the field that year three members of the same household had died on the same day. The head of the family had been accused of repeated thefts of game from the traps and from the camp of an Aka hunter. When confronted with the evidence—a shirt the villager had left at the scene of the thefts—the family rejected the demands of the hunter for compensation for the stolen meat. Soon thereafter, the thief, his wife, and his mother died on the same day. Villagers, who knew of the accusations of theft, interpreted the deaths as the result of poisoning or the mystical powers of the hunter.

Stories of Aka revenge are not uncommon, nor are the Akas' accusations of wrongdoing leveled against the villagers. To the Ngando farmers, the powers of the Aka ngangas include the ability to

cause death through the use of fetishes, to cause illness to the culprit's eyes, and to direct lightning to strike the perpetrator. These and other impressive powers to punish are seen as real threats to the villagers—but the power of the ngangas to cure is even more impressive.

Attempts in my research to delineate the strengths and weaknesses of the ngangas and other health care specialists discovered a number of widely held qualities/characteristics associated with each. First, each specialist is known for specific medical abilities; that is, Aka and Ngando ngangas recognize the therapeutic expertise of others in a variety of cures. A nganga from Bangui maintained that Aka ngangas were generally superior to the village healers in curing. This view is shared by a number of villagers interviewed, who maintained that the power of Aka ngangas is greater than that of their own specialists.

The Aka strongly agree with this view, and in a sense the Aka are more propertied in the realm of curing than are the villagers. There is no question that the Aka are better hunters. Despite the Ngandos' greater political and economic power in the area and the social superiority inherent in their patron status, the Ngando need the Aka. All of these elements help balance the relationship between these two societies, although the supernatural and curative powers of Aka ngangas have not previously been considered to be ingredients in the so-called symbiotic relationship between Pygmy hunters and their horticultural neighbors.

Second, ngangas noted for their ability to cure particular illnesses are often called upon for treatment by other ngangas who have contracted the disease. Third, with one exception, all of the ngangas interviewed agree that European drugs, particularly those contained in hypodermic syringes and in pills, are effective in the treatment of natural diseases. One dissenting informant from the capital disdained biomedicine altogether because, as he said, "White men don't believe in us." Fourth, of the fourteen Aka and Ngando ngangas interviewed in 1985, only five felt that it was possible for a nganga to work successfully with the local doctor (male nurse) who directed the dispensary in Bagandu. All five of these ngangas said that if such cooperation did come about, their special contribution would be the treatment of patients having illnesses of man, including mental illness resulting from witchcraft, from magical and spiritual attacks, and from breaking taboos. None of the ngangas interviewed had been summoned to work in concert with the doctor. Fifth, as a group the ngangas held that biomedical practitioners are unable to successfully treat mental illnesses and other illnesses resulting from attacks of supernatural agents. In this the general population of the village agree. This is a vitally important reason for the sustained confidence in popular therapy in the region—a confidence that is further strengthened by the belief that the ngangas can treat natural illnesses as well. Sixth, the village doctor recognized that the ngangas and marabouts do have more success in the treatment of mental illnesses than he does. Although the doctor confided that he has called in a village nganga for consultation in a case of witchcraft, he also disclosed that upon frequent occasions he had to remedy the treatment administered by popular specialists for natural diseases. It is important to recognize, that unlike biomedical specialists in the capital, the local doctor does appreciate the talents of traditional therapists who successfully practice ethnopsychiatry.

All respondents to this survey recognized the value of biomedicine in the community, and little variation in the types of cures the doctor could effect was brought out. No doubts were raised regarding the necessity of both biomedicine and popular therapy to the proper maintenance of public health. The spheres of influence and expertise of both types of practitioners, while generally agreed upon by participants of the Ngando survey, did show some variation, but these were no more serious than our own estimates of the abilities of our physicians in the West. In short, all informants utilized both systems of therapy when necessary and if possible.

The continuation of supernatural explanations of illness by both the Ngando and the Aka results in part from tradition, in combination with their lack of knowledge of scientific disease etiology, and in part because of the hidden positive functions of such explanations. Accusations of witchcraft and the use of curses and malevolent magic function to express the anxiety, frustrations, and social disruptions in these societies. These are traditional explanations of disease, with more than a single focus, for they focus on both the physical illness and its sociological cause. "Witchcraft (and by extension other supernatural explanations for illness and disaster) provides an indispensable component in many philosophies of misfortune. It is the friend rather than the foe of mortality . . ." (Lewis 1986: 16). Beyond this rationale, reliance upon practitioners of popular medicine assures the patient that medicine is available for treatment in the absence of Western drugs.

The Role of Ethnomedicine

Among the Aka and Ngando and elsewhere, systems of popular medicine have sustained African societies for centuries. The evolution of popular medicine has guaranteed its good fit to the cultures that have produced it; even as disruptive an element of the system as witchcraft can claim manifest and latent functions that contribute to social control and the promotion of proper behavior.

Unlike Western drug therapies, no quantifiable measure exists for the effectiveness of popular medicine. Good evidence from World Health Organization studies can be brought forth, however, to illustrate the relatively high percentage of success of psychotherapeutic treatment through ethnomedicine in the Third World compared to that achieved in the West. The results of my research in Bagandu also demonstrate the strong preference of villagers for popular medicine in cases involving mental illness and supernaturally caused mental problems. At the same time, the doctor is the preferred source of therapy for the many types of natural disease, while ngangas and other specialists still have the confidence of the public in treating other maladies, referred to as illnesses of man and some illnesses of God. Whatever the perceived etiology by kingroup therapy managers, both popular and biomedical therapists treat natural illnesses. It is in this realm of treatment that it is most important to ask, "What parts of popular medicine work?" rather than, "Does popular medicine work?" Since evidence has shown that psychotherapy is more successful in the hands of traditional curers, it is therefore most important to question the effectiveness of popular therapy in handling natural illnesses. Currently, the effectiveness of traditional drugs used for natural diseases is unknown; however, the continued support of popular therapists by both rural and urban Africans indicates a strength in the system. The effectiveness of the ngangas may be both psychological and pharmaceutical, and if the ecological niche does provide drugs that do cure natural illnesses, it is vital that these be determined and manufactured commercially in their countries of origin. If we can assume that some traditional drugs are effective, governments must utilize the expertise of healers in identifying these.

It is unrealistic to attempt to train popular therapists in all aspects of biomedicine, just as it is unrealistic to train biomedical specialists in the supernatural treatments applied by popular practitioners. However, neither type of therapist, nor the public, will benefit from the expertise of the other if they remain apart. The task is to make both more effective by incorporating the best of each into a counterpart system that focuses on a basic training of healers in biomedicine. This combination must certainly be a more logical and economic choice than attempting to supply biomedical specialists to every community in Central African Republic, a task too formidable for any country north or south of the Sahara. The significance of this proposal is magnified by the massive numbers for whom biomedicine is unavailable, those who must rely only upon ethnomedicine.

Even if available to all, biomedicine alone is not the final answer to disease control in the Third World. Hepburn succinctly presents strong arguments against total reliance upon the biomedical approach:

Biomedicine is widely believed to be effective in the cure of sickness. A corollary of this is the belief that if inadequate facilities could be provided in the Third World and "native" irrationalities and cultural obstacles could be overcome, the health problems of the people would largely be eliminated. However, this belief is not true, because the effectiveness of biomedicine is limited in three ways. First, many conditions within the accepted defining properties of biomedicine (i.e., physical diseases) cannot be treated effectively. Second, by concentrating on the purely physical, biomedicine simply cannot treat the social aspects of sickness (i.e., illness). Third, cures can only be achieved under favorable environmental and political conditions: if these are not present, biomedicine will be ineffective (1988: 68).

The problems facing societies in Africa are not new. These same issues faced Westerners in the past, and our partial solutions, under unbelievably better conditions, took immense time and effort to achieve. If primary health care in the non-Western world is to improve, the evolutionary process must be quickened by the utilization of existing popular medical systems as a counterpart of biomedicine, by the expansion of biomedical systems, and by the cooperation of international funding agencies with African policymakers who themselves must erase their antagonism toward ethnomedicine.

The Psychotherapeutic Aspects of Primitive Medicine

Ari Kiev

The purpose of Ari Kiev's article is to explore various aspects of primitive medicine (i.e., traditional healing) in order to achieve insight into the nature of psychotherapy. Kiev is primarily interested in discovering what particular behavior of the medicine man bestows upon him the "power to cure" in the eyes of patients. Recognizing the great significance of subsistence patterns and technological development in the complexity of medical activities, Kiev examines three types of societies according to their primary method of food production. At the lowest level, where food gathering is the basic means of existence, there is little medical leadership. In the more complex fishing-hunting societies, healers have more prestige, and social influence is maintained by medical influence. But it is in agricultural societies, the highest level, where one finds all the features characteristic of modern psychotherapy. Kiev also concludes that the nature of the medical role seems related to the nature of the social organization, and that as societies become more complex, the healer increasingly shares the responsibility for success with the patient.

Reproduced by permission of the Society for Applied Anthropology from *Human Organization*, Vol. 21 (1), pp. 25–29.

MEDICAL THINKERS IN WESTERN SOCIETY HAVE ONLY recently come to recognize the importance of psychological and sociological factors in disease and treatment. In primitive societies, however, where the germ theory, antibiotics, and steroids have not as yet been introduced, the emotional, attitudinal, and interpersonal components of disease receive the chief emphasis. Primitive peoples have integrated their medical arts into the conceptual framework of their societies, and all members share the same theories of disease and treatment.

The purpose of this article is to examine certain aspects of primitive medicine in the hope of gaining some insight into the nature of psychotherapy. Following the suggestions of Ackerknecht (1942a) that much of the success of primitive medicine is attributable to the psychotherapeutic aspects of the witch doctor's role, the inquiry focuses on that aspect of the role which affords the witch doctor the "power to cure" in the eyes of his patients. As Frank (1959) has written:

> From the moment the prospective patient approaches psychotherapy until his treatment terminates he is confronted with cues and procedures which tend to impress him both with the importance of the procedure and its promise of relief. These heighten the therapist's potential influence over the patient and . . . probably have some therapeutic effects in themselves by mobilizing his favorable expectancies.

The expectation of cure seems as important in methods of primitive healing as in modern psychotherapy.

We have selected three types of society to examine, classifying each society according to the dominant means of food production: food gathering, fishing-hunting, or agricultural. The significance of food supply is great. With an abundance of it populations can flourish, specialized classes can develop, and societies can prosper and progress. The degree of technological development in dealing with problems relating to food seems to correlate well with the degree of societal development in other spheres. The aspect of the medical role which affords its possessor the "power to cure" seems also to be related to the degree of advancement and complexity of the society to which he belongs. Thus where there is little development of economic techniques and little specialization or division of labor, there should be similar evidences of minimal organization, technical development, and specialization in medical activities. Where surplus supplies are made possible through advanced technology, there should be some interrelationship between medical performance and the economic rewards of the social system.

Food-Gathering Societies

In food-gathering societies, medicine is dominated by magic. There is little systematic organization of theories and practices. Individuals gain power to deal with disease through special personal experiences with supernatural forces. Among the Australian Murngin the healer gains his power to cure through extraordinary experiences with two or three "soul children" (spirits of the dead) (Warner 1958). His magical rituals are exclusively owned and can only be exercised by him. For the Cheyenne a unique dream experience was necessary before a man could learn the special medical lore and language from an elder (Ackerknecht 1942b). Among the Shoshoni the shamans obtained their powers through dreams or by experiencing visions in special situations (Harris 1940). Likewise among the Southern Colorado Ute the unique endowments of the medicine men were attained through dream encounters with the supernatural (Opler 1940).

In these most-primitive societies the therapeutic prowess of the medicine men was due to the conviction of tribesmen that they had special power to cure. As the medicine men shared the same world view, they were able to exert influence partly because of their own belief in their magical powers. They also subscribed to prevalent notions of dis-

ease causation and in treatment utilized expected maneuvers. Among the Dobuans the diviner consistently selects disease-causing witches or sorcerers from those who have justified economic grievances against the sick person. Economic reparations suffice to pacify the injured and to repair the sick (Ackerknecht 1942b). The Dobuan diviner acts in accordance with the expectancies of his society and by virtue of his special powers exerts a therapeutic effect.

The close relationship between shaman and sick in terms of beliefs, expectancies, and shared values is demonstrated by Warner's observations on the Murngin (Warner 1958). Here the medicine men rely heavily on the power inherent in group pressure during ceremonials. Among the Murngin it is not only the supernatural power of the healer which is the effective vehicle of cure but also the impact of group attitudes reinforcing the therapist's position during cures. The medicine man in these simpler cultures does not develop his own theories and formulations about disease and cure. He relies on the beliefs of the group and his supernatural capacities in his work but functions as an ordinary citizen at all other times. Elaborate formulations seem to be unnecessary for the continuation of his practices, and since such work usually yields no extra prestige or remuneration in these barely subsisting societies and since there is little leisure time to pursue such intellectual pursuits, we find little evidence of any specifically medical theories among these groups.

Fishing-Hunting

In fishing-hunting societies the nature of the medical role changes. Increased control of environmental forces (particularly food sources) makes possible division of labor, specialization, and increased leisure time. There is greater emphasis on the qualifications for the medical role and a clearly outlined pattern for attaining this role. There is much elaboration of religious and medical beliefs by the medicine men, which ensures their security and strengthens their authority. Demonstrating clearly the manipulative and utilitarian aspects of this role in Eskimo society, Radin (1957) has written:

> In a society where murder is a common phenomenon they are rarely murdered. Similarly in a society where women are scarce they have

established and maintained the right to cohabit with all women. This unusual priority has come about through organization which has been associated with a complex religious theory and a spectacular shamanistic technique. Their system is designed to keep the contact with the supernatural exlusively in the hands of the angakok (shaman), and to manipulate and exploit the sense of fear of the ordinary man. Fear seems to be the all embracing focus of this religion—fear for the food supply or uncertainty of broken taboos and fear of dead and of malevolent ghosts. The shamans have combined the fear of economic insecurity with the magical formulas and taboos and with the fear of deceased human beings.

The Eskimo shaman attain this influence through special experiences involving genuine suffering from neurotic or epileptoid disorders, trance experiences, ordeals of physical and spiritual isolation away from the group, and adherence to special rituals and taboos while preparing for the assumption of the role. Such experiences are oftentimes sought after by non-neurotic individuals desirous of becoming medicine men. As Radin (1957) has pointed out:

> What was originally due to psychic necessity became the prescribed and mechanical formulae to be employed by anyone who desired to enter the priestly profession or for any successful approach to the supernatural.

The special experiences, status, and abilities of the medicine men in fishing-hunting economies is demonstrated by the Andaman Islanders (Radcliffe-Brown 1948). Here the oko-jumu, or medicine men, acquire power to communicate with the spirits, causing illness through "jungle meetings" with the spirits, dream exeriences, fainting episodes, or epileptic fits. This supernatural endowment gives the oko-jumu the power to cure illness. Often medicine men circulate legends and lore about their derived power and therapeutic prowess, further bolstering their reputations. As a result they receive a good share of the game caught by tribesmen seeking their good will.

Where surplus economy allows for privileged roles the medicine men seem to have self-consciously recognized the value of maintaining power. Writing about Apache shamanistic technique, Opler (1936) has pointed out that the seasoned shaman is often

reluctant to accept responsibility for the cure of serious organic disturbances:

> The seasoned shaman who eschews the incurables is usually quick to treat the less serious indispositions and solidify his reputation by rendering prompt relief . . . The shaman will insist on the impossibility of curing one who is skeptical of the efficacy of the ceremony to be performed or unconvinced of the integrity of the practitioner.

In fishing-hunting societies special experiences were not always the sole criterion for assumption of the medical role. Thus among the Alkatchko Carriers of British Columbia the medicine men obtained only part of their power through visions (Goldman 1940). It was also necessary for the selected individual to be cured by another medicine man and complete a potlatch first. Here therapeutic power derived from actual achievement as well as special experience.

The enhanced social status acquired by the shamans contributed to their personal power and the efficacy of their technique. Privileged status reflected on the power of the individual who attained such status. The shaman among the Puyallup of Puget Sound lived in a bigger house than the other tribesmen and was treated deferentially by all (Smith 1940). Similarly among the Arapaho of Northern Wyoming the medicine men had vested interests in traditional religious forms and derived much material gain from the treatment of disease (Elkin 1940).

Agricultural

Agricultural techniques led to the development of larger and firmer social units. As the security and independence of the average man increased, the medicine man altered the methods used to maintain influence. Thus the prominent features of the medical role in agricultural societies are increased social organization, increased training, and systematization of techniques. There is increased competition, specialization, an emphasis on knowledge and heredity as qualifications for the role, and changes in the notions of disease causation.

Magic becomes increasingly less important. Less emphasis is placed on spirit causation, and illness more often is viewed as the outcome of the sick individual's own activities. Patient responsibility for success of treatment, which is intimately tied in with the medicine man's efforts to maintain status and control, is clearly illustrated by the Nandi of Kenya (Huntingford 1953). There the medicine man does not tolerate any suggestions that his predictions or medicines have failed. Failure of cure is attributed to the neglect of the patient to follow the specific instructions as to their use.

Specialization of medical roles is also prominent. Among the Chiga of Western Uganda homemade treatments such as poultices, blood-letting, or ingestion of herbs are tried first. If these fail the neighborhood specialist not infrequently tries the same cures. Lastly, the expensive diviner with greater diagnostic and therapeutic ability to cure with complicated techniques of purification and sacrifice is consulted (Edel 1957).

Agricultural societies, in contrast to more primitive societies, make a clear-cut distinction between medicine and religion. Among the Mano of Liberia the first specialist to be consulted is usually an old woman or the local midwife, who is expected to know all the common remedies (Harley 1941). During the first stage of illness a priestess or head of a girl's initiation school might also be consulted. The next specialist would be a man of the medical guild. He might also be a priest of the boy's school. He would have access to the ancestral spirits but would not appeal to them directly except in a general way once a month for personal success. He would know remedies and procedures of a more magical nature calculated to reach evil influences causing the disease. Next would be a diviner to find out what person among the sick man's acquaintances might have cast a spell upon him. The guilty one might be able to do something about it by confessing and removing the spell. With increasing fear and uncertainty and lack of success there is an increased reliance on less empirical and more magical techniques. If death follows, a diviner would try to catch the guilty one by using a poison ordeal.

In many agricultural societies cure is attributed to the medicines rather than to the supernatural powers of the practitioners. Thus among the Fox of Iowa the power to cure was obtained through learning of medical techniques and through vision quests (Joffe 1940). Only intelligent children were taught the correct usage of herbs, and prestige was maintained by a broad knowledge of techniques.

Ackerknecht (1942a), writing about the Thonga of South Africa, has commented:

> Medicine men are hereditary. . . . Sometimes the heritage of knowledge is small but a good medicine man tries to combine the activities not only of the diviner and therapist but also of the witchdoctor of the rain and the warm-magician-priest and thus gains a high social standing.

In Tahiti only the able-bodied and sure-footed who were free from personal defects were chosen as candidates for medical training. After a training period novitiates were required to pass examinations in order to graduate (Radin 1957). The Ashanti of West Africa required a three-year novitiate under a recognized master for those who received a call to be medicine men. In the first year, the novitiate must observe such strict taboos as not tapping palm wine, not setting fish traps, and refraining from sexual intercourse. If married he must leave his wife for the training period. During the second year elaborate fetishes are worn and ceremonial ablutions undertaken. In the final year, the candidate is taught water-gazing, divining, how to impregnate charms with various spirits, and other information and techniques for proper performance of the medical arts (Radin 1957).

Discussion

Examination of therapeutic factors in primitive medical roles reveals that it is only in the most advanced primitive societies (agricultural) that all the features characteristic of modern psychotherapy are found. In all societies examined, only some of the features delineated by Frank (1959) as characterizing the dynamics of the patient-doctor relationship are found. In all, the patient relies on the doctor to relieve distress, and favorable expectancies are reinforced by the setting of treatment and the technique of cure. In all, the medicine man has faith in the treatment method, faith in the patient's capacity to respond to the treatment, and adheres to a definite procedure, much as Western psychiatrists do.

All the features characteristic of the Western patient-psychiatrist relationship are found only in the primitive agricultural societies. Thus, among the Navaho, ambiguity is introduced and skillfully manipulated by the medicine man (Kluckholn and

Leighton 1947). The Navaho singer "conveys to patients that they know what is wrong with them but that they [the patients] must find out themselves," a situation which, according to Frank (1959) would heighten ambiguity, which heightens suggestibility and anxiety and increases the desire to please the therapist. This attitude compels patient participation, which, too, increases the likelihood of favorable therapeutic results.

Primitive therapies differ from modern psychiatry in the short-term nature of treatment. Therapeutic ceremonials are familiar to all. Faith in, and expectancy of relief from, the healer is established long before the patient seeks help. The tie-in of treatment with dominant values further increases therapeutic potential. In all societies examined, the medicine man, irrespective of his technical armamentarium, retained and utilized certain prestigious and influential notions about his person. In the most primitive societies, this quality is assigned by the group. In more advanced societies, the shaman cultivates this special quality himself. Coupled with the utilization of a special technique, it permits the medicine man to avoid entering into the intense emotional involvements characteristic of families and friends of the ill. He can remain "objective" and neutral and receive institutional support for this behavior. The support the medicine man receives from the community not only reinforces the patient's belief in the efficacy of the treatment but also minimizes the patient's fears about the medicine man's motives, which might be greater if the medical role was not community sanctioned. This orientation permits the patient to place greater trust in the medicine man as he does in the doctor in Western communities. By adhering to a socially acceptable standardized role, the medicine man gains the power of the role irrespective of personal qualities or abilities. Dissociation from the usual emotional reciprocities between human beings creates a psychological and perhaps therapeutic advantage for the person filling this medical role.

Conclusions

1. A survey of medical roles in a number of primitive societies suggests certain generalizations of interest to psychiatry. In contrast to the notion that all primitive medicines are fundamentally the same, examination reveals certain differences in medical systems which seem related to economic and technological development. In the most primitive societies, where food gathering is the basic means of food supply, there is little medical leadership, few privileges accorded to the medicine men, and little evidence of a systematized set of medical ideas. The medicine men assume their roles by virtue of extraordinary experiences with the supernatural forces believed to be responsible for illness.

In the fishing-hunting societies where medicine men obtain greater prestige and economic reward there is a deliberate attempt to maintain social influence by maintaining medical influence. More specific qualifications are devised for assumption of medical roles and there is a more elaborate systematization of medical theory. Where changes in economic structure have been introduced, as for example when the Fox of Iowa were moved on to reservations, the influence of the shaman declines and his therapeutic powers abate as well.

Agricultural societies place a greater emphasis on knowledge and acquire skills as qualifications for the medical roles. Medicine men are more often organized into medical societies, and one often finds specialization of functions and elaborate training programs.

2. The nature of the medical role seems related to the nature of the social organization. As economic differentiation becomes possible the shamans exert influences to provide themselves with surplus, special privileges, etc. Where the shamans have obtained valued wealth and prestige they utilize the social power inherent in such attainments in their medical work. The special power of the shaman is tied in with the dominant belief and value systems of his society. Where supernatural forces are deemed responsible for illness the shaman is the one who can contact the supernatural. Where successful cures are attributed to drugs his power is his "knowledge" of the drugs or herbs. The relationship between therapeutic effectiveness and social values has been demonstrated by Redlich and Hollingshead (1958) to exist in our society, where, for example, lower-class patients come to psychiatrists expecting pills and injections, not anticipating that psychotherapy entails talking.

3. With increasing complexity of society the medicine man increasingly shares the responsibility for treatment success with the patient. In food-gathering societies the shaman's success in treatment seems to be due to their belief and the patient's belief in their supernatural powers. In fishing-hunting societies the shaman increases his influence over the society and his patients through induction or perpetuation of fear among patients, through careful selection of curable patients and through much secrecy and exclusiveness about his techniques and medicines. In agricultural societies the shaman is less compelled to resort to sleight of hand. His power derives more from knowledge and skill and he derives security from medical organizations. He deliberately utilizes the guilt feelings of the sick and manipulates the extent of patient participation in treatment. He seems more aware of the relationship between taboo violation and the development of illness than in the more primitive societies. This is akin to modern Western notions ascribing psychiatric illness primarily to the interpersonal and intrapsychic conflicts of the patient.

A School for Medicine Men

Robert Bergman

The anthropological study of mental illness demonstrates that the types and frequency of mental disorders vary from one culture to another, as do the diagnosis and treatment of the illness. In this article Robert Bergman discusses a training school for Navajo medicine men founded by the Navajo themselves at Rough Rock, Arizona, a community on the Navajo reservation. As a non-Indian psychiatrist working for the Indian Health Service, the author volunteered his professional services to the fledgling school. Working side-by-side with the Navajo medicine men, or "singers," as they are called, Bergman analyzed the nature of Navajo curative ceremonies and their effects on patients. The clash of folk medicine and modern scientific medicine has received considerable attention by anthropologists, and reports of fear and grief felt by non-Western patients undergoing modern medical treatment are common. If pre-literate patients and their curers are ignorant of the procedures and philosophies underlying modern medicine, so too are those trained in modern medicine ignorant of folk medicine and its accomplishments.

Reprinted from the *American Journal of Psychiatry*, Vol. 130, no. 6 (1973), pp. 663–66, by permission of the author and the American Psychiatric Association. Copyright 1973 the American Psychiatric Association.

THIS PAPER IS AN ACCOUNT OF HOW A NAVAJO community set up its own medical school and how a non-Indian psychiatrist became involved in it. In order to understand what happened one must have some acquaintance with the nature of Navajo medicine. This subject has received an enormous amount of attention from anthropologists and other behavioral scientists. I will make no attempt here to review the extensive anthropologic literature except to recommend the great works of Haile (1950), Reichard (1938), and Kluckhohn and associates (1940, 1956, 1967 [See "References" in the Bibliography]). The psychiatric literature is less extensive. It includes the early article of Pfister (1932), which seems to me to be remarkably insightful and sound in spite of having been based on very little and quite secondhand evidence. The Leightons in 1941 described Navajo ceremonials beautifully and explained many of their beneficial elements. Sandner (1970) reported his work with Navajo medicine men to the APA three years ago. Almost everyone agrees that the ceremonies work.

Background

Navajo practitioners generally fall into three categories. The herbalists know a variety of medicinal plants, which are used primarily for symptomatic relief. The diagnosticians are shamans who work by inspiration. By one of several techniques, such as hand trembling, crystal gazing, or star gazing, they divine the nature and cause of an illness and make an appropriate referral to a member of the third and highest status group, the singers. The singers (I will use the terms "ceremonialist," "medicine man," and "singer" synonymously) do the only truly curative work, and it is a school to train them that I will be discussing.

Navajo nosology classes diseases by etiology; identical illnesses often have similar symptoms, but they need not. Note that psychiatric nosology is similar, e.g., depression is often characterized by insomnia, but sometimes the reverse can be true. A seriously oversimplified statement of Navajo etiology is that disease is caused by a disharmony with the universe, including the universe of other men. A singer restores this harmony by performing a ceremony proper to the case. Little or no reliance is placed on herbs or other medicines and, as is the case with psychiatry (at least from the psychoanalytic viewpoint), this absence of organic measures confers high status.

No one seems to know precisely how many ceremonies there are, but there are many. Important ones last five or nine nights and are difficult and elaborate to a degree approached among us physicians, I think, only by open heart surgery. The proper performance of a major sing requires the presence of the entire extended family and many other connections of the patient. The immediate family must feed all of these people for days. Many of the people present have important roles in the performance, such as chanting, public speaking, dancing in costume, leading group discussions, and many other prescribed activities of a more or less ritualized nature. For the singer himself the performance requires the letter-perfect performance of 50 to 100 hours of ritual chant (something approaching the recitation of the New Testament from memory), the production of several beautiful and ornate sand paintings, the recitation of the myth connected with the ceremony, and the management of a very large and difficult group process.

Non-Navajo explanations of why all this effort helps anyone tend to be rather offensive to the medicine men themselves, and *their* explanations, if they should feel like giving any, tend to be unsatisfying to us since they are based on the supernatural. The difference may not be as great as it appears, however. Traditional Navajos talk frequently in symbols: "We are glad you came from Washington to talk with us. There are many mountains between here and Washington," which translates as, "Communication with the federal government is difficult. We are glad you are making an effort to improve it." They also reject the notion that they are using figures of speech. They do not attach as much significance to the distinctions among different levels of reality as we do, and

like some poets, they reject as stupid and destructive any attempt to translate their words into ordinary language. Though it seems to me that their myths and chants are symbols of human social-psychological forces and events, they would regard such a statement as silly and missing the point. Nevertheless, I will make a slight attempt in that direction.

The Rituals

For the past six years, I have been practicing psychiatry among the Navajo people. I have often referred patients to medicine men (who in turn occasionally refer patients to me). I have also often consulted medicine men, and patients have often told me about the medicine men's traditional cures and their feelings about these cures. It seems to me, although my knowledge of the sings is very limited, that the ceremony performed is almost always symbolically appropriate to the case. Pathologically prolonged grief reactions, for example, are almost always treated with a ceremony that removes the influence of the dead from the living and turns the patient's attention back toward life. "Treatment of a dream by a dream," Pfister called it.

It seems to me that the singers and we psychiatrists are the converse of one another with regard to our attitude toward ritual. To them ritual is the main focus: What is unvaryingly their practice from one case to another is at the center of their thought. Informal interaction with the patient and his family is considered important in an informal sort of way. This kind of interaction is not what is taught explicitly but only what is taught by the by. Our ritual, which I would argue is fairly elaborate, is not taught as the central part of psychiatry; rather, the more varying interaction is taught explicitly to psychiatry residents—ritual being taught by the by. In any event the singers do manage an intricate family interaction that, I think, has several important effects: (1) the patient is assured that his family cares for him by the tremendous effort being made; (2) the prolonged and intense contact makes it inevitable that conflicts are revealed and, if things are handled skillfully, resolved; and (3) a time of moratorium and turning point are established.

At the time I first heard of the medicine-man school in 1967, I was already quite convinced of the value of Navajo medicine. Aside from the cases I had seen, I was greatly influenced by my contact with a singer named Thomas Largewhiskers. Mr. Largewhiskers, who is now 100 years old, agreed to be my consultant and to teach me a little of what he knew. I first looked him up after seeing a formerly psychotic patient who attributed her remarkable and well-documented improvement to him. At the time of our first meeting I tried to explain what I do and said that I wanted to learn from him. He replied, "I don't know what you learned from books, but the most important thing I learned from my grandfathers was that there is a part of the mind that we don't really know about and that it is that part that is most important in whether we become sick or remain well." When he told me some of his life story it impressed me that he had become interested in being a singer when, as a young man, he had had an accident and the singer who took care of him explained that it had been unconsciously determined.

Mr. Largewhiskers and many other extremely old men are still practicing very actively. There is a growing demand for their services—growing because the population is increasing and their belief in traditional medicine is continuing. The trouble is that younger people are not becoming singers. The reasons behind the lack of students are largely economic. To learn to perform even one short ceremony takes at least a year of full-time effort. To learn a major ceremony takes much longer, and many medicine men know several. Since the end of the old herding economy, almost no one can afford to give up earning a living for such a long time. At the time of starting the school for medicine men Yazzie Begay, one of its founders, said "I have been acquainted with several medicine men who have recently died. They were not able to teach the ceremonies which they knew to their grandchildren or to anyone else. Today their sacred instruments and paraphernalia are sitting unused."

The School

The school is at Rough Rock, Ariz., a community near the center of the Navajo Reservation. It is part of the Rough Rock Demonstration School, the first community-controlled Indian school. The Demonstration School was started in 1965, when the Bureau of Indian Affairs (BIA) gave the buildings and equipment to a nonprofit corporation of Navajo leaders called Dine, Inc. Dine helped the Rough

Rock chapter of the tribe set up and elect its own board of education (no one on the original board could speak English and all were ceremonialists) and then contracted with the board to operate an elementary boarding school. BIA contributed funds that would have been equal to the budget of such a school if they had been operating it; funds also came from the Office of Economic Opportunity (OEO) and other sources. Soon after the school began operations in 1966, the people became convinced that their ideas really were taken seriously in its daily workings, and several local people suggested setting up the medicine-man school to the board. It was pointed out at a board meeting that white people have medical schools and give students scholarships to attend them and that what was needed most on the reservation were new medicine men. Therefore they felt Rough Rock should set up a school for singers and provide scholarships.

The idea was taken up enthusiastically by the board, and the details, were worked out over the course of the next year. It was decided to alter the traditional method of teaching and learning sings as little as possible. (The old way is by apprenticeship and takes place in the teacher's home.) It was also decided that each medicine man would teach two apprentices of his own selection; that is, application for admission to the school would be made by trios consisting of a medicine man and two trainees. The school board would select among them on the basis of the medicine man's reputation, the trainees' apparent ability, and the importance of and threat of extinction to the ceremony that was proposed to be taught. The medicine men were to be paid a very modest salary and the trainees considerably less for their subsistence.

Obtaining Funds

Ever since the Demonstration School started, I had been going there once a month or more to consult with the guidance counselor and teachers. At one time the school administration, at the direction of the board, was preparing a project proposal in an attempt to obtain funds; I was asked to attend a meeting about the project, and here my support for the proposal was enlisted. This was the first of several project discussions in which I took part, and ultimately the board kindly included me in the proposal. It was decided that I should meet regularly with the trainees to discuss non-Navajo medicine, particularly psychiatry. I strongly suspect that my inclusion was a move to make the project look more reasonable to funding agencies.

I flatter myself that from time to time my colleagues in the school and the trainees have been glad to have me around, but I am sure that I have gained much more from this than they have. Before the project could materialize, however, we had to obtain funds.

The first proposal was made to OEO, which turned it down. The second proposal went to the Training and Special Projects Branch of the National Institute of Mental Health (NIMH). This one was accepted, although not, I suspect, without some trepidation. At the time of the site visit by NIMH it became apparent how many mountains there really were between Rough Rock and Bethesda, Md. First of all, the weather became very bad and the site visitors felt they were stranded in Albuquerque, which is 250 miles away from Rough Rock. Luckily the school board was able to go to Albuquerque, so we had a meeting. Two incidents seemed to me to epitomize the meeting. The first was a question from the visitors: "How can a project that supports the continuance of superstition promote mental health?" The reaction of the ceremonialist school board members was more restrained than I had expected. They answered at length, and I added my endorsement. The visitors seemed satisfied. Later one of them, in leafing through the documents, said, "The project director is to be full-time, and the salary listed here is $5000. Can that possibly be right?" When that question had been translated, Mr. John Dick, the director in question, who was a medicine man and a former school board member, asked anxiously, "Is it too much?" I am very grateful that the project was funded, and I know that the board is also appreciative.

The Training Program

The work began in September 1969 and is still continuing. There are six medicine men and 12 trainees. Most of the original trainees are still in the program. One of the faculty members died during the first year and was replaced. The ceremonies being taught so far have been one and two nights in length, and almost all of the trainees have completed learning them. Soon they will be performing

them for the first time. They will then go on to major ceremonies. Although the lessons (excluding the ones I teach) are conducted at various homes scattered over considerable territory in which there are no paved roads, Mr. Dick as director maintains close supervision. He travels to each home and watches over the teaching and its results. As the trainees have progressed, he and other medicine men have tested them. My only criticism has been that Mr. Dick's supervision seems rather harsh at times. He has demanded continuous effort and has been very hard on some people whom he surprised when he thought they should be working and they weren't. Still, apart from minor professional jealousy, the group's morale seems high. The program has been well accepted, and there clearly will be a demand for the services of the graduates. Other communities are trying to start similar schools. Recently one of the medicine men had one of his students perform a sing over him.

My sessions are a full day every two weeks. Before I started holding them I met with the medicine men to describe what I intended to do and to ask their permission. To my great pleasure they not only agreed to my plans but said they would like to attend along with the trainees. Attendance has varied from time to time, but usually most of the trainees are present as well as three to five of the medicine men. During the first year I talked about somatic medicine, attempting to cover elements of anatomy, physiology, pathology, diagnosis, and treatment. I discovered that the entire group, including the trainees, had considerable knowledge of anatomy and some of physiology. The sessions were lively. The medicine men and the trainees enjoyed trying out stethoscopes, otoscopes, ophthalmoscopes, and blood-pressure cuffs. Microscope slides of blood smears and pathology specimens were also very popular. In return I was learning more about ceremonial practice, although not as much as I was to learn the next year when we began discussing psychology.

One of the high points of the first year was a visit that the group made to the Gallup Indian Medical Center. It was characteristic, I thought, that the two things the medicine men most enjoyed seeing at the hospital were an operation and a particularly good view of a sacred mountain peak from the windows of the psychiatric ward. They also had criticisms and suggestions. They were horrified by the pediatric ward because the children were so lonely. They kept asking, "Where are the parents?" They urged that better provisions be made for parents to stay with their children. They also suggested that we build two hogans at the hospital for ceremonial purposes. They remarked that they all had performed brief ceremonies in the hospital but that they could do more in a real hogan. They said that the medical staff could see the patients during the sing and could go back and forth if necessary. Their suggestion still has not been followed, but I hope that it will be soon.

During the second year I began discussing psychiatry, and in this area there has been more of a two-sided interchange. We have spent much time on European and Navajo notions of the unconscious, a subject in which difficulties in translation have been great. Navajo metapsychology still largely eludes me, but it is clear that the medicine men know about the dynamic interpretation of errors and dreams and were pleased to discover that all of us followed the same custom with regard to them. We all, it turned out, spend our first waking moments in the morning contemplating and interpreting our dreams. One of the medicine men gave an example. He had dreamt about an automobile accident and said that that kind of a dream meant something serious was going on within him and that in order to prevent some disaster from happening to him, it was important to perform a chant about it.

There has been a good deal of case presentation on both sides, particularly, for some reason not clear to me, regarding returned Viet Nam veterans. My feeling of trust and closeness to this group ultimately became such that I presented my own case, describing some things that had led me to enter my analysis and something of the analysis itself. When I finished this rather long account, one of the singers asked me the name of my analyst and where he is now. When I told him, he said, "You were very lucky to find a man who could do so much for you. He must be a very intelligent person."

Another high point for me was demonstrating hypnosis. The group ordinarily looks half asleep—as seems to be the custom with medicine men in meetings. This was unnerving at first, until I found out from their questions and comments that they had been paying very close attention. When hypnosis was demonstrated, however, they were obviously wide awake, although at times I wondered if they were breathing. Working with a carefully prepared subject (I was unwilling to face failure before this audience), I demonstrated a number of depth tests, somnambulism, age regression, positive and negative hallucinations, and some posthypnotic suggestions. When I was done, one of the faculty members said, "I'm 82 years old, and I've seen white people all my life, but this is the first time that one of them has ever surprised me. I'm not surprised to see something like this happen because we do things like this, but I am surprised that a white man should know anything so worthwhile." They also pointed out the resemblance of hypnosis to hand trembling, a diagnostic procedure in which the shaman goes into a trance and his hand moves automatically and indicates the answers to important questions. After we had discussed the similarity, they asked that my subject, a young Navajo woman, diagnose something. I objected, saying that neither she nor I knew how to do this and that it was too serious a matter to play with. They insisted that we try, however, and finally we decided that a weather prediction was not too dangerous to attempt. They were particularly interested in the weather at that time because we were in the midst of an especially severe drought, and someone in the community had predicted that it would continue for another year. When my subject was in a deep trance, I instructed her to visualize the weather for the next six months. She predicted light rain within the week, followed by a dry spell of several months and finally by a good rainy season in late summer. I make no claim other than the truthful reporting of facts: She was precisely correct.

My involvement in this project has, of course, been extremely interesting to me. It is hard, however, to assess the effects of the project on the medicine men and on me. The medicine men say that they know better when and how to refer patients to the white doctors, and I think they feel more kindly toward us. In turn, I feel better able to understand my Navajo patients and know better when to refer them to medicine men. I have adopted some Navajo styles of thought, I think. I use hypnosis more than I used to. And one of my Navajo colleagues in the Indian Health Service Mental Health Program claims that I try to act like a medicine man all the time.

A Traditional African Psychiatrist

Robert B. Edgerton

Tracing the education of an African traditional doctor from his early training to his mature status as an effective man of medicine, Robert Edgerton in the following article characterizes Hehe shamans as rational, logical empiricists and keen observers and diagnosticians. Edgerton demonstrates that the Hehe make no clear distinction between shamanism and Western science and that Hehe shamans recognize a host of physical and mental illnesses. The shaman Abedi, for example, recognizes five psychotic conditions that, depending on their origin, are treated either magically or with pharmaceuticals, physical therapy, or actual removal of the patient from the situation causing the psychological distress. Illustrating the interaction of healers and their clients, Edgerton well shows the importance of traditional doctors in Africa, where a permanent lack of funds has prevented the implementation of Western-type medical systems.

Reprinted from the *Southwestern Journal of Anthropology*, Vol. 27, no. 3 (1971), pp. 259–78, by permission of the author and the *Journal of Anthropological Research*.

INTEREST IN NON-WESTERN PSYCHIATRY IN THE past decade has produced a substantial literature, much of it relating to Africa. Nevertheless, the coverage of African societies has only begun, and the preliminary findings that we now possess may be one-sided. Thus, despite the sometimes positive evaluations of such men as Prince (1964), Collis (1966) and Lambo (1964) in Nigeria, and Gelfand (1964) and Loudon (1960) in Southeast Africa, many writers continue to feel that traditional African psychiatric practices have little instructive value for Western psychiatry. Others have been even more critical, believing that the magical practices of African healers are inimical to science. For example, Margetts (1965: 115) writes that native healers "can do little good in a mental health programme and may do harm. They have no rational place in the modern technological world . . ."; however, he adds that analyses should be made of their folk medicines.

Before any considered opinion on the nature of traditional African medicine or "psychiatry" can be reached, we not only need more research from additional areas of Africa, but research which adopts additional perspectives. The following report is offered because its practitioner, a Hehe of Tanzania, is a specialist in psychiatry, and his beliefs and practices, particularly as they emphasize botanical and pharmacological empiricism, complement our knowledge of African ethnopsychiatry as it is practiced in other parts of Africa.

The Hehe

The Hehe are a Bantu-speaking people located in the Southern Highlands Region of Tanzania, formerly Tanganyika. Their territory stretches from the Great Ruaha River on the north and west to the escarpment of the Kilombero Valley on the south and east. Most of this area is high rolling woodland or grassland, but some Hehe occupy arid lowland savanna areas and others live at higher elevations in the mountain rain forest. The Hehe were a congeries of small chieftancies until they were united by the agressive military and diplomatic actions of Muyugumba and his son, Mkwawa. By extending Hehe hegemony over much of south-central Tanganyika, these men established the Hehe as a kingdom of considerable military and political power. After early victories over the Germans, Mkwawa was defeated and killed in 1894. The Germans restored the independence of territories conquered by the Hehe and confined the Hehe state to its present boundaries.

The Hehe, who now number over 200,000, live in dispersed homesteads which are organized into neighborhoods. A homestead is typically occupied by a man, his wife or wives, and their children. It is surrounded by its fields of maize, millet, beans, cassava, and squash and by small numbers of cattle, sheep, and goats. Each Hehe neighborhood is bound together by ties of kinship and friendship, by ceremonial activities, and by cooperative work parties. In addition to the strong ties of kinship, the Hehe recognize a hierarchy of lesser and greater chiefs who possess considerable traditional authority and have obligations to the British administration.

When the Hehe fall ill, as they often do, they may attribute their misfortune to any of several sources: to natural phenomena such as worry, impure water, or faulty inheritance, to witchcraft, or to legitimate retribution for the violation of Hehe norms. If the source of illness is seen as natural, a Hehe may seek help from a European-trained physician or medical helper in a nearby town. But even for "natural" illnesses, the patient is likely also to seek out a traditional doctor—an *mbombwe*—and where the source of illness is other than natural, he is certain to do so. There are many such doctors (the Swahili term is *mganga*) throughout Hehe territory, and their advice is continually sought. Some, of course, are more highly regarded than others. The best known native doctor in the Iringa area was a man whom I shall name Abedi. Unlike most traditional Hehe doctors who attempt to treat any disorder, Abedi is a specialist in mental disorders—he is a Hehe psychiatrist.

Abedi's Training

Abedi was the headman (*jumbe*) of an area near Iringa until early in the 1950's when he encountered some sort of difficulty with the British administration. Accused of malfeasance, he left the post in 1955 and turned to full-time practice as an *mbombwe*. Abedi was born around 1910 to a man who had been a renowned *mbombwe*, a doctor to the king, Mkwawa, himself. Thus Abedi's father had access to the traditional medicine not only of the royal clan and court of the Hehe, but also from those neighboring tribes whom the Hehe conquered. Abedi's mother was also an *mbombwe*, who, like Abedi, was known as a specialist (her specialty was female disorders).

Abedi's formal training as an *mbombwe* did not begin until he was an adult, by which time his father was quite elderly. Abedi learned primarily from his father, but also studied with his mother who gave him intensive instruction in botany. Much of his training was highly practical, giving attention to the method of diagnosis and treatment, observation of symptoms, collection of plants and roots, knowledge of inherited disorders, etc. But an equal emphasis was placed upon the supernatural. Abedi inherited his father's *lyang'ombe*, a small metal object that appeared to be an old European belt buckle. Through prayer, the *lyang'ombe* could be imbued with God's power to cure. Abedi learned to pray to God (*Nguluvi*), to practice divination, to discover the cause of witchcraft, to defend against witchcraft, and to employ magic. His father also gave him protection against the malevolence of witches, who might be angered because he cured those whom they had sickened, by rubbing a secret medicine (*gondola*) into a series of cuts (*nyagi*). These cuts are located on the thumb of the right hand, the third joint of the small finger of the left hand, the wrist, elbow, both temples, forehead, hairline, sternum, chest, neck, nipples, ribs, spine, ankles, knees, and toes. Abedi must reinforce this protection from time to time by reopening the cuts and adding fresh *gondola*. Abedi has also purchased magical knowledge and herbal medications from other traditional doctors over a large area of southern Tanzania.

Abedi's specialization in mental illnesses began during his apprenticeship when he first hallucinated ("hearing voices of people I could not see") and ran in terror to hide in the bush. He was discovered and returned to his father's care, but lay ("completely out of my senses") for two weeks before being cured. The cause was diagnosed as witchcraft and since the cure, Abedi has never been sick again. This experience initiated Abedi's interest in mental illness, and the subsequent mental disorders of his sister and his wife reinforced it. At different times, both women became violently psychotic, but Abedi quickly cured them both. These two cures not only heightened Abedi's interest in psychiatric phenomena, but they led to his reputation as a skillful psychiatrist.

Diagnosis, Etiology, and Prognosis

Although, as we shall see later, Abedi sometimes makes home visits, almost all of his patients came to him in what we might call his "office." The office is a small house, 10 by 20 feet, flimsy and poorly thatched, unlike ordinary Hehe houses, which are massive and solid structures. It has the look of a temporary building, but Abedi has been practicing medicine in it for eight years. The inside of his "office" is remarkably cluttered, with large pots, baskets, and gourds in every corner and hanging from the walls. These containers are filled with the roots and leaves from which Abedi mixes his medicines on a small table in one corner of the office. In his small office he stores, sorts, grinds, and boils his medications before packaging them in a variety of bottles, leaves, horns, small gourds, and leather pouches.

Seeking treatment from Abedi in his office often requires interrupting him in the course of preparing his medications, but he always greets a patient warmly as he asks him (and the usual family members or kinsmen who attend him) to be seated by the fireplace before he begins his diagnostic routine.

In proceeding with his diagnosis, Abedi must keep in mind his nosology of disorders (the catalogue of illness categories that he knows), the signs and symptoms, and the patient's biography—including past illnesses and, especially, antagonists who might want to bewitch him. In short, Abedi is concerned with the entire social context of the patient and his illness—a context which Abedi enters and typically alters—for while successful treatment pleases some, it may displease others (Winans and Edgerton 1964).

In a general way, Abedi recognizes a great variety of illnesses such as impotence, venereal infections, infertility, stomach and bowel ailments, respiratory disorders (including pneumonia and asthma), orthopedic malfunctions, and fevers. He also recognizes more specific diseases such as trachoma, tetanus, malaria, and smallpox. While he may choose to treat all such disorders with specific medications he has developed for that purpose, it is only when the disorders are "mental" (when the locus of disorder, in his perspective, is in the mind) that his diagnosis categories achieve any prognostic differentiation. Indeed, his categories of mental illness are defined by criteria that are based far less upon symptoms than they are upon etiology and prognosis.

Hehe men and women who live in the area near Abedi typically described mental illness in behavioral terms, perceiving its onset as sudden, with aggressive behavior that can result in human injury, but rapidly "cooling" to a fearful and stuporous retreat from human interaction (Edgerton 1966). They made no distinctions among psychotics. Abedi's views of mental illness were more complex. He recognized two symptoms as being indicators of excessive worry: headache and stomach pain. He felt that both responded well to removal of the source of worry and to his herbal medications. For extreme cases, he recommended that the patient move away from his neighborhood for a prolonged vacation with kinsmen. He denied, however, that worry was a common cause of psychotic conditions. He also recognized epilepsy by its *grand mal* seizures, and mental retardation by the fact that intellectual ability was deficient from birth. Mental retardation he deemed untreatable, but he felt that epilepsy, which he said was an inherited condition, was curable by medication if treatment were begun in the first few days after the initial seizure.

Among psychotic conditions, he recognized five: *litego, mbepo, lisaliko, kuhavila* and *erishitani*. *Litego* is marked by depression and guilt, by fever and headache, and sometimes by unusual or bizarre behavior. It never produces thought disturbances. Because it is caused by moral retributive magic brought on by wrong-doing, it cannot be treated medically (or the *mbombwe*, too, would be sickened by the moral magic). Instead it requires confession, apology, and the payment of compensation. Without such restitution, *litego* can be fatal (Winans and Edgerton 1964).

Mbepo is marked by disturbances of behavior (running wildly, destroying property, and assaulting people) as well as by thought disturbances (inability to concentrate, hallucinations, visions, and a loss of touch with reality). It is a product of evil—in this case, witchcraft—and hence it can be cured without wrongdoing by a skilled and protected *mbombwe* (the protection is essential lest the thwarted witch turn his evil upon the doctor).

Lisaliko is indistinguishable from *mbepo* in its symptoms but its causes are natural, not supernatural. These causes include faulty inheritance, febrile illness, poisoning, and, very rarely, excessive worry. It is curable if treated early.

Kuhavila is a particularly violent sort of psychosis, even more so than *mbepo*. Persons afflicted with *kuhavila* actually kill others, and abuse them violently if unable to kill them. They also have prolonged fevers, go naked, eat feces, and run about without apparent purpose except to attack others. The disorder is caused by a specific sort of magic, which can only be acquired by a woman who has intercourse with her father. Such women must continue the incestuous relationship to maintain their power, but their male offspring may inherit the power without continuing the incestuous relationship. This form of psychosis is easily cured by a native doctor who possesses the appropriate magic to "see" the witch and establish protective magic, as well as the requisite medications.

Erishitani is produced only by Muslims who direct "devils" (*erishitani*) to enter the body of their victim, and "like the wind, squeeze out a person's blood, leaving him mad." The symptoms are an affectlessness and mental vacuity—literally, an emptiness. It can only be cured successfully by other Muslims; Abedi attempted two such cures and failed both times.

In his diagnostic search for symptoms, Abedi never touches the patient. He observes carefully, although usually unobtrusively and he carefully questions the patient and any available kinsmen or friends. The questioning is often lengthy, involving what appears to the patient (or kinsmen) to be nothing more than an exchange of pleasantries and a concern for mutual acquaintances. In reality, it appeared that Abedi was probing carefully for an understanding of the social context of the illness. Who might be an enemy? What is the patient fearful about? Has he had a similar problem before? Do such illnesses run in his family?

Following the period of informal conversation, Abedi initiates his formal divinatory procedures. He begins by praying to *Nguluvi* to give him the power to see the cause of the sickness and to understand what ought to be done. He then takes out his *lyang'ombe*, kisses it to imbue it with God's power, and begins to divine by means of his *bao*. The *bao* is a paddle-shaped board about 8 inches long and 3 inches wide, with a groove in which a small wooden cylinder is rubbed running diagonally along its upper surface. Abedi places the board on the ground, puts the *lyang'ombe* on its narrow end, and holds both objects down with his foot. He then sprinkles water on the groove and begins rubbing the wooden cylinder in it. As he manipulates the *bao*, he chants in a low liturgical voice interrupted from time to time by a question he addresses to the *bao*. As the water in the groove dries up, the counter moves less easily and at some point it will stick. This is taken as an affirmative answer to the last question addressed to the *bao*. As long as the counter moves freely, the answers to questions addressed to it are usually taken to be negative. In any case of illness, Abedi asks five preliminary questions: Did the patient commit adultery? Did he steal? Did he borrow money and refuse to repay it? Did he quarrel with someone? Did he actually have a fight with someone? In some instances, the answer to all the questions is negative. This indicates that the patient has become ill for no good reason and hence the cause is natural. Or, it means that effective counter magic must be made against the evil person who has performed magic or witchcraft against the patient without cause. This Abedi determines by further questions. He then asks specific questions about his ability to cure the patient, alternating "yes" and "no" questions until the *bao* answers. Finally he asks about the effectiveness of various medicines until the *bao* selects for him the medicine favored by God.

Throughout the investigations and supplications Abedi takes great care, for both he and his patient realize that the treatment of illness is dangerous, involving as it does not merely natural phenomena but such critical matters as moral magic, witchcraft, spirits, and the like. All realize that a faulty diagnosis endangers the doctor as well as the patient.

Treatment

Although Abedi's treatment routine varies somewhat depending upon the diagnosis he reaches, for almost all of the "mental illnesses" that he recognizes (*mbepo, lisaliko,* etc.), his treatment follows a prescribed course. First, the patient must be made tractable. Only a few patients are quiet enough that Abedi will begin their treatment without subjecting them to some degree of restraint. Most patients are agitated and difficult to manage, and they are either tied sitting to the center post of Abedi's office or, if treated at home, they are shackled to a bed. Next, all patients are purged. For this purpose Abedi maintains a ready supply of purgatives and emetics. The emetic is administered first; if the patient will not cooperate by swallowing the medication, a liquid preparation, his nose is held until he is compelled to swallow. If vomiting should not quickly ensue, Abedi assists by tickling the patient's throat with a feather. As soon as vomiting has taken place, a purgative is given with almost universal success within a few hours. Once purged, the patient is allowed to rest but is usually permitted only water until Abedi's specific medications have been prepared and administered.

As we have seen, Abedi's *bao* has already identified the appropriate medications, but it may take Abedi several hours, or even overnight, to prepare the prescriptions. In some cases, the necessary ingredients have already been collected, ground into powder, and stored, but in other instances Abedi must sort out the correct mixture of leaves, roots, patent medicines, and other substances before mixing them. Occasionally, he must actually go out to collect the ingredients. Some medications cannot even be selected until Abedi has gone to a crossroad (a place where village footpaths intersect or, ideally, trisect), stood naked at midnight, and used his magical powers to "see" the correct medicine (the *bao* is not involved in this form of divination). Sometimes the medication must be mixed at the crossroad as well, and in rare circumstances, the patient must ingest the medicine at the same crossing. Where selection of a medication has

proven particularly difficult, and where the cause of the psychosis has been diagnosed as witchcraft, the patient himself may be made to act as an oracle in the selection of his own medication. This is done by burning a mass of *Cannabis sativa*, covering the patient with a blanket, and forcing him to inhale the smoke for a period of an hour or more. The patient identifies the person who has bewitched him, and by answering Abedi's questions with "yes" or "no," selects an effective medicine.

Once assured that the medication of choice is known and available Abedi "cooks" it by boiling the powdered ingredients over a fire in full view of the patient and his kinsmen. Most of the resulting medications are taken as liquids, usually drunk in a glass of tea. A few medications are rubbed on the skin as ointment, others are rubbed into shallow linear incisions, and a few are inhaled. Before the medicine is actually given, Abedi offers a brief *sotto voce* prayer for the success of the medicine and spits once or three times upon the patient's head as a blessing for good luck. Doses of medicine are repeated at varying intervals until a cure is effected. Abedi accepts no payment for his treatment (except a small retainer for house calls) until such time as the patient has recovered.

An Illustrative Case

The following case is one which I was able to follow closely from its inception to its remission. A 17-year-old boy, related to a Hehe man whom I knew, was stricken with a high fever. When his fever continued for six days his parents took him to a nearby hospital for European medical care. Once in the hospital, he lay in a coma for the better part of six days, occasionally returning to consciousness with violent efforts to escape his bed and flee. He became so violent in his delirium that he was tied to his bed, but it was not until his struggles tipped the bed over that he would lie quietly. No sedatives calmed him and no diagnosis was made, although malaria was suspected. At no time was he able to speak coherently, although he did mutter to himself.

His parents complained that he was receiving inadequate care (the European medical officer was on leave) and that his condition had not improved. They took him home where he continued to be delirious. When he showed no improvement and refused food by the seventh day of treatment, his parents and his uncle asked me if I would take them to see Abedi, who was some 45 minutes away by automobile. This we did immediately. Abedi could have had no warning that we were coming, and it is difficult to believe that he knew anything about so distant a family and their sick child. After customary greetings, the sick boy's uncle said, "I want to ask you about a sick person." Abedi sat down with his *bao* and after a few minutes he announced that the person was male, about 18 years old. The uncle was suitably impressed and asked Abedi to undertake treatment. Abedi asked to see the patient, but was told that the boy could not be moved. Abedi accepted this necessity and began at once his prayer to *Nguluvi* to give him the power to see and to cure. After praying in his monotonous manner for four minutes, he began to divine, sliding the piece of wood along his *bao* while asking the routine questions.

After five minutes of divination, Abedi found an answer: the boy had been bewitched by someone in a mountainous area several miles from his home. The witch's identity could not be seen, but it was known that the boy's illness was *mbepo*, caused by eating a "medicine" which was lodged in his chest making breathing difficult, disorienting his mind, and threatening his life. When he heard this, the uncle asked that Abedi go and treat the boy without delay. Abedi said that he had made plans to be elsewhere and such a trip would be most inconvenient. The uncle then threw one shilling (14 cents) at Abedi's feet. He picked it up, committing himself to walk over 25 miles round trip.

Once this matter was settled, Abedi again consulted his *bao*, asking which of his medicines would cure the boy. The *bao* chose first the usual emetic and purgative, next, a "tranquilizer" called *ngambe* ("to cool his heart and stop his wildness"), and then another to counteract the evil "medicine." Each medication was already available in Abedi's containers so he poured out the correct amounts, perfunctorily tasting each with his tongue ("to prove that it is not a poison") before wrapping each separately in a corn husk and tying it with bark. Before leaving, Abedi again consulted his *bao*, this time to determine the order in which the medications should be given. The answers were given quickly and the order was the standard one used with most patients.

I then offered to take everyone to see the sick boy. Abedi probably knew that I would do so on this occasion, but he must also have known that I could not be counted upon to do so on subsequent days. When we arrived, the boy lay bound to a bed. Seven days without food had left him emaciated. He stared at me, the only non-African, but did not speak. He had a massive facial tic and there was a marked tremor of his extremities. Abedi approached him without any ceremony and attempted to force the emetic past his lips. The boy struggled and moaned and it was only with assistance and by holding the boy's nose that Abedi compelled him to swallow. The purgative followed without delay. Abedi then unwrapped his second medication—the "tranquilizer"—and mixed it with water, creating a cup full of a foul-smelling, rather slimy, green liquid. Filling his mouth with this preparation, Abedi spat three times on the boy's head. Briefly reciting his prayer for healing, Abedi rubbed the remainder of the medication on the boy's head, pulling three hairs as he did so. To these three hairs he added the green paste that he next scraped off the boy's head, tying them together in a rag that was tied to the patient's wrist. Later, the same medication would be given internally, but first the patient must vomit.

While waiting for the emetic to take effect, Abedi unwrapped his third medicine, a powder to provide protection against witchcraft. It was rubbed into the boy's nostrils; it too he would later take by mouth. Although Abedi said that the emetic usually takes effect in ten minutes, this time nothing happened. Abedi and the assembled kin agreed that the boy's seven day fast was the reason for the delay. Abedi instructed everyone to wait, deciding not to tickle his throat with a feather or to administer more of the emetic. Everyone waited quietly, sometimes leaving the room to talk in the courtyard. After two hours, the boy vomited, and all gathered around to examine the two long yellow strands of vomitus carefully. All agreed that the vomitus was unique—not mucous, not worms, nor any normal contents of the stomach. They agreed that it must be as Abedi said: the boy had vomited the "medicine" that was the source of his illness.

Abedi next gave the second and third medication by mouth, saying that the patient would sleep and that he need not be tied any longer—"his heart has been cooled." At this point, Abedi left to walk back to his office where he would see other patients. The boy slept all afternoon, awakening at about six o'clock to ask for food. He ate, to the joy of everyone, then slept quietly all night. Abedi returned each morning to see his patient and to repeat applications of the second and third medications. For two more days the boy slept and ate without speaking. On the fourth day of treatment he spoke rationally. By the eighth day he was able to leave the bed for short periods. After 15 days Abedi pronounced him cured, and the boy did indeed appear to be normal.

Abedi said, following the cure, that the original diagnosis had been incorrect (Edgerton 1969). The boy suffered from *kuhavila*, not *mbepo*, because there is no fever with *mbepo*. When asked how the *bao* could be wrong he said, "It happens sometimes." He explained further that he could have cured the boy in one day had he seen him on the initial day of illness, but that once the "medicine" had time to take effect the recovery was always protracted. The parents were said to have paid Abedi 100 shillings for his services, but I do not know how the fee was settled upon or whether it was paid in several installments.

Discussion

The foregoing case is intended to illustrate some of the typical features of Abedi's therapeutic routine, but it is also directed to the point that his therapy for "mental" illness is often, perhaps even usually, rewarded by the remission of symptoms. There are obvious reasons why this pattern of apparent remission should not be construed as a "cure." For one thing, the symptoms presented by Abedi's patients are so diverse as to challenge the therapeutic arsenal of any doctor, African or Western. What is more, while my four week study of his practice revealed striking success in the remission of symptoms, it would be naive to suppose that failures could not have been hidden from me had Abedi chosen to do so. Finally we have no way of knowing how often the symptoms would have vanished under differing treatment or with no treatment at all. We do know, however, that rapid and seemingly complete recovery from apparently psychotic conditions has been reported from several parts of Africa. Any discussion of the efficacy of Abedi's treatment must await properly designed research

of the sort begun in West Africa by Collis (1966). The purpose of this discussion is to compare Abedi's treatment routine with principles of treatment reported from other parts of Africa and to ask why his therapeutic practices have taken their particular form.

Analysts of "primitive medicine" from Ackerknecht (1943) to Frank (1961) have emphasized the role of suggestion in treatment. Recently, Kiev (1964) concluded that two universals of non-Western psychiatry were suggestion and confession. Others have expanded this list to include faith, catharsis, group support, and suggestion (Kennedy, MS). Let us examine the role of each of these in Abedi's psychiatric practice.

Faith

By faith I mean the generalized expectation on the part of the patient that treatment of the sort offered by the traditional doctor *can* be effective. These expectations are difficult to determine and research reports regarding them are generally superficial. The Hehe data are also superficial, although here at least some quantification and comparison is possible. For example, 36 of 123 Hehe respondents in a neighborhood near Abedi's office said that psychotic patients could be cured, 12 said that they could not, and 75 were unsure. This degree of expressed faith was much greater than that shown by the Pokot of Kenya or the Sebei of Uganda, but less than that indicated by the Kamba of Kenya (Edgerton 1966: 416). We can probably conclude that while the Hehe have some faith in psychiatric treatment they also maintain ample skepticism. Turning now to Abedi, who is certainly the most highly regarded doctor in this area, we see that even where his ability is concerned, a degree of what might be considered skepticism remains. For example, in the case presented earlier of serious and prolonged illness, the boy's parents were in no hurry to see a native doctor and while they had heard of Abedi's reputation, they had no blind faith in his ability. They, as did others, began their contact with Abedi by testing him— could he identify the sick boy and his illness? And all patients withhold payment until a cure has taken place (a practice which is as unusual in Africa as in the West). Thus while Hehe patients approach Abedi with some faith in his reputation as a doctor, most enter treatment with an attitude that combines hope and doubt. For his part, Abedi does nothing to foster or require a testimonial of faith before treatment begins. Instead he is content to rely upon his treatment itself.

Catharsis

For the Hehe, as for other African peoples, catharsis through confession is a commonplace. In childbirth, as in many forms of illness, both Hehe patient and spouse or other kinsmen must confess and apologize for wrongful thoughts or acts before birth or recovery can take place (Winans and Edgerton 1964). Nevertheless, Abedi makes virtually no use of catharsis in his practice. He never asks a patient or kinsman to act out any hidden desire and only very infrequently do his questions to the *bao* elicit any sort of confession from a patient. Asked about this anomaly, Abedi said, "Talking cures nothing. Medicines cure."

Group Support

There are reports from several African societies that point to the importance of group support in the treatment of mental illness. In West Africa, for example, group support may be supplied by religious cults (Prince 1964), secret societies (Dawson 1964), or by elaborate "discharge" ceremonies that ritualize the patient's cleansing of illness, death, and rebirth into a new life (Prince 1964). Elsewhere, the patient may receive support by moving from one area and social network to another. Among the Ndembu of Northern Rhodesia, the patient's kinsmen may join with hostile persons in what amounts to group therapy, complete with catharsis and social reintegration (Turner 1964).

While Abedi permits kinsmen of his patients to be present throughout his diagnosis and treatment he does nothing to solicit group support. As with his disavowal of confession, this neglect of group concern is remarkable, for just such group support is a regular feature of childbirth and the recovery from many illnesses. As with catharsis, other Hehe doctors I knew did require that their patients undergo treatment within a larger social nexus.

Suggestion

Research on African psychiatric practice has emphasized the role that suggestion plays in treatment. For example, Prince (1964: 110), writing about the Yoruba, refers to a "continuous barrage of suggestions at all levels from the most intellectual to the most concrete and primitive." Others have attributed whatever success the African therapies may have had entirely to suggestion, noting that Africans are highly suggestible. There can be no doubt that suggestion plays an important part in Abedi's practice, and yet Abedi makes little or no use of a variety of practices widely employed in Africa to heighten suggestibility or to implant specific ideas. For example, Abedi never alters his own personality to indicate special powers nor does he claim direct communication with supernatural powers through dissociation or possession. Neither does he employ special effects through legerdemain or ventriloquism. He makes no attempt at indirect communication by means of allegory, simile, traditional, or sacramental stories. He never gives commands, nor does he attempt to change his patient's consciousness through hypnosis, drumming, or dancing to exhaustion (cf. Whisson 1964). What is more, he utilizes none of the many versions of body contact common in Africa such as rubbing, sucking, bathing, or such stressful ones as whipping, burning, or steaming.

Kennedy (MS) and others have noted the significance of dramatic rituals and powerful symbolism in psychiatric practice in Africa and throughout the non-Western world. For example, Gelfand (1964) notes the flamboyant regalia of Shona "medicine men"; the Yoruba, Luo, and Ndembu all enact potent rituals in the service of therapy. However, Abedi's use of ritual is minimal, being confined almost entirely to a few ritual acts on the first day of treatment. Others have noted that non-Western psychiatrists rely upon settings so suffused by religious or magical symbolism that they are set apart from the ordinary world (Kennedy MS). Again, nothing could be more prosaic than the settings in which Abedi works.

Abedi's principal uses of suggestion lie in his appeals for supernatural guidance or power and in his utilization of potent medications. Although Abedi's frequent prayers for divine assistance are understated and humble, they nonetheless must serve to impress patients, as must also the divine and magical power that resides in his *lyang'ombe*. And, of course, the *bao* is an impressive divinatory device, especially when it reveals information about the patient that would seem to be inaccessible to Abedi by normal means. It is possible that

Abedi maintains an "intelligence system" in the form of boys who inform him of matters relevant to actual or prospective patients, but I saw no evidence that he did so. Abedi's knowledge of magic and his occasional visits to crossroads and the like must also contribute to the supernatural aura that he is able to establish.

Probably of equal importance, however, is the placebo effect of Abedi's medications. Several of his preparations contain copper sulphate which has the impressive property of turning from blue-green to white when heated. The patients whom I watched during their first exposure to this transformation were visibly startled. Similarly, his infrequent but copious use of *Cannabis sativa* may produce impressive psychological changes, and the reliable effects of his standard emetics and purgatives must alike create in a patient a sense of the dramatic power of Abedi's medications. The resulting alteration of psychological and bodily states should produce a heightening of suggestibility. Such effects from the use of herbal remedies by African doctors have been widely noted. However, in recognizing the prominent place of suggestion in Abedi's use of drugs, we should not overlook the possibility that some of his medications possess specific psychopharmacological action that may have value in the treatment of mental illness (Gelfand 1964).

Abedi as Pharmacologist

Abedi's pharmacopoeia is extensive. In addition to emetics, purgatives, and his specific preparations for mental illness or epilepsy, he keeps on hand many drugs for gastro-intestinal disorders, as well as a variety of aphrodisiacs for men, and, for women, various drugs specific for infertility, miscarriage, menorrhagia, and the like. Most of the botanical knowledge that underlies his drugs was inherited from his father and mother, but some knowledge was purchased and some preparations were purchased ready-made (e.g., copper sulphate). I collected seven preparations said to be specific for mental illness or epilepsy. Of these, several were described by Abedi as (and were seen by me to have the apparent effect of) soporifics or tranquilizers. Of these, the most potent was called *mwini*.

Following this lead, the botanist, Mildred Mathias,

and the pharmacologist, Dermot Taylor, visited Abedi. Concentrating their collection upon plants that might affect the central nervous system, they went with Abedi while he collected the plants essential to his medications for mental illness and epilepsy. They traveled throughout the Southern Highlands Province, finding medicinal plants in all of the micro-habitats in that diverse area. In all, 37 species of plants were collected, representing 35 genera in 25 plant families. Some individual medications contained as many as 11 species of plants (Mathias 1965: 87–88).

Abedi's empirical knowledge of the botany of Hehe territory was considerable, and so was his pharmacological skill in preparing and administering these medications. For example, several of these plants contain violent emetics and purgatives which can produce death in overdose (Mathias 1965: 87). Yet, of over 120 Hehe questioned, none had heard of so much as an accusation that Abedi's medications had ever killed a patient. Recall, too, that Abedi refused to increase the standard dosage of his emetics and purgatives when they did not have an immediate effect upon the boy in the previous case. In the mixing of each medication, Abedi takes care to prepare and measure each ingredient, and he does so with the secular manner of a pharmacist, not that of a magician. Yet his preparations are not confined to the leaves and roots of plants with at least potential psychopharmacological effect. He often adds to his medicine such magical substances as the aforementioned copper sulphate, powdered rock from the sea coast, corn flour, the blood of a black cock, and the urine or powdered bones of a sheep. Abedi insists that these latter substances are as essential to certain of his medications as the plant components. In this sense, he is not without full commitment to the Hehe world of supernatural belief. But other medications contain only leaves and roots. For these, no magic in preparation, content, or administration is employed. Abedi's pharmacopoeia has its supernatural elements, but they are relatively few, and may be relatively unimportant.

Neither is there evidence that he regularly employs his medications in the manner of a charlatan. To be sure, we can point to the fact that he feels the need for copper sulphate, which he says that he regards as just another vital ingredient, and that he sometimes uses *Cannabis sativa* to evoke witchcraft accusations from his patients. But unlike doctors among the Yoruba, he does not use hallucinogenics to worsen a patient's condition simply in order to achieve a spectacular treatment success by withdrawing the toxin (Prince 1964: 118). Nor does he employ *Datura* to evoke confessions of witchcraft or to induce psychosis, although he knows of its properties, is aware that it grows in many accessible places, and knows that other "medicine men" in Tanzania, including those among the nearby Mtumbi, use it for those purposes (Lienhardt 1968: 75–76). He said, "*Datura* can cause madness but it cannot cure it." I agree with Lienhardt (1968: 74) that the medications used or sold by many a *mganga* in Tanzania are known to be useless by the so-called doctor himself. Abedi stands apart from fraud. He believes in the efficacy of his medications.

Demonstrating that Abedi is a serious empiricist about his medications is one thing; demonstrating that the medicines have any specific effect upon the central nervous system is quite another. The final word here must await complete pharmacological analysis, of course, but we might note that Abedi's treatment regimen follows that of the Yoruba of Nigeria—emetics and purgatives followed by a drug that seems to induce sleep and tranquility. For the Yoruba, this drug is *Rauwolfia*, the source of reserpine (Prince 1964: Hordern 1968). Abedi's "tranquilizing" drugs, especially the one he calls *mwini*, were observed to induce both sleep and, following sleep, tranquility. These effects may be a product of verbal suggestion, but if this is so, then the suggestion must be very subtle, for I have witnessed the use of this drug on ten occasions, and on none of these occasions could I detect any verbal suggestion that would lead to sleep or tranquility. My Hehe-speaking interpreter also failed to discover any such cues. On the other hand, this drug (and others he employs) *could* have soporific or tranquilizing effects since Abedi's pharmacopoeia included 19 alkaloid-producing plant families.

Although the pharmacological analysis of *mwini* has proven difficult in research with laboratory animals, psychopharmacological activity (some of it soporific) has been noted. The drug had a quietening effect upon mice, reducing their activity noticeably. It also doubled the barbiturate sleeping time (modern tranquilizers will increase it six or seven times). Because of difficulties in acquiring

sufficient quantities of the plant and in developing techniques for the assay of this plant material, a more active fraction from the plant could not be obtained. The plant involved was *Limosella major* Diels, a member of the Scrophulariaceae. The family has not been noted for its medicinal properties.

Conclusion

In his practice as a traditional African psychiatrist, Abedi not only must, but does, live within the belief systems of his culture, and these beliefs center around the etiological and prognostic significance of magic and witchcraft. Abedi diagnoses and treats mental disorders within the constraints posed by this supernatural system, constraints that emphasize his vulnerability to danger in equal measure to that of his patients. He believes in supernatural causes of illness, and he excels in discovering and in thwarting such causes. At the same time, however, he recognizes natural causes of illness and he seeks medication that will cure, not merely impress. He has stated this conviction, and his actions have given his convictions legitimacy. Only extensive botanical and pharmacological research can determine to what extent he has succeeded in locating medications whose successes are due to specific action and not to the placebo effect. If future analyses should show that the medications have specific actions upon the central nervous system, it would be an error to conclude that such action is a fortuitous product of the more or less random collection of leaves and roots. Abedi, and other Hehe doctors before him, have believed not only in supernatural causation and treatment of illness, but also in herbal remedies.

For example, Mkwawa, the King, and members of his court, were highly pragmatic men who displayed a keen interest in innovation. Their empiricism was especially notable in regard to botany. Mkwawa imported several plants to his kingdom from other parts of East Africa, seeking not only better medicinal plants but better food sources and even superior shade trees. He also experimented with cross-breeding cattle. At the same time, Mkwawa and his court retained their traditional beliefs in witchcraft, divination, and the like. Abedi's father, as physician to Mkwawa, was a member of this elite, among whom traditional belief in supernatural causation coexisted with an intense pragmatic interest in natural cause and effect. Years of empirical effort have yielded Abedi's pharmacopoeia and his knowledge of it. It would be surprising indeed if his medications did not possess some specific pharmacological effectiveness.

In comparison to traditional doctors in other parts of Africa, as well as among the Hehe, Abedi is notable for his secular approach to medicine. He does not reject the supernatural beliefs or practices of his culture. On the contrary, he excels in their use. But he does attempt to go beyond them by formulating principles of natural causation and by empirically discovering chemical cures. In this sense, he has transcended his culture, and such transcendance is an achievement for any man. Yet, whether Abedi's success in treating mental illness has anything to do with the pharmacological action of his drugs or not, he possesses the essential attitude of a scientist—a belief in natural causes and effects, and an empirical method of seeking out causal relationships. His story is worth recording simply because he has made the effort to find useful drugs, to continue the beginnings of science within a pre-scientific system of medicine.

There is nothing necessarily contradictory about Abedi's continuing commitment to a world of supernatural cause and effect. As Koestler (1963) has pointed out, such beliefs were very much a part of the lives of Kepler, Galileo, Newton, and others who nevertheless brought about scientific revolution. Abedi is no Newton either in intent or accomplishment, but neither is he simply a magician-herbalist. He believes that supernatural practices are necessary but not sufficient for a cure. Only medicines are sufficient, and he is devoted to the discovery of more effective chemical agents. Abedi's own words best reflect this quest: "I became a doctor to cure people. Medicines cure, nothing else works. I have some very strong medicines, but always hope to find better ones. I would like to be able to travel to a place where roots stronger than those around here grow. My medicines cure some things. If I had stronger roots I could cure more." Abedi undoubtedly undervalues the importance of suggestion in his practice of psychiatry, just as he no doubt overvalues the efficacy of his medications. His commitment to empiricism is botanical, not psychological.

Abedi is not the first of his kind in pre-scientific societies: curare, quinine, digitalis, atropine, reserpine, and many other valuable drugs attest to that. The dominant presence of a scientific ethos does not exclude magical practices in modern Western psychiatry. This we realize all too well. We should remind ourselves that the dominance of a supernatural ethos in non-Western psychiatry does not exclude the presence of beliefs and practices that are of significance for science.

The Sorcerer and His Magic

Claude Lévi-Strauss

Lévi-Strauss, the leading exponent of the French structural school of anthropology, here analyzes the elements of the "shamanistic complex" and demonstrates by example their reliance on one another. The overall effectiveness of the sorcerer's treatment relies on the integration of his own belief in the effectiveness of his powers, the patient's belief in therapy, and the support of and faith in the shaman and his herbal and supernatural powers by members of society. An important component of the success or failure of shamans is directly related to the powerful elements of suggestion that pervade the interaction of shamans with patients and society. The marked difference between the confidence, indeed omnipotence, of the shaman, on the one hand, and the anxiety of the patient and his family, on the other, is important to the cure. So too is the sorcerer's secret knowledge of formulas, incantations, and other methods of control over supernatural agents who work at his command to help effect the cure. The final element in suggestion is the homogeneous belief system of the members of the patient's society, who reify and validate the power of the sorcerer. All these elements aid the sorcerer and demonstrate a marked difference between Western and non-Western treatment of psychophysical ailments.

SINCE THE PIONEERING WORK OF CANNON, WE understand more clearly the psycho-physiological mechanisms underlying the instances reported from many parts of the world of death by exorcism and the casting of spells. An individual who is aware that he is the object of sorcery is thoroughly convinced that he is doomed according to the most solemn traditions of his group. His friends and relatives share this certainty. From then on the community withdraws. Standing aloof from the accursed, it treats him not only as though he were already dead but as though he were a source of danger to the entire group. On every occasion and by every action, the social body suggests death to the unfortunate victim, who no longer hopes to escape what he considers to be his ineluctable fate. Shortly thereafter, sacred rites are held to dispatch him to the realm of shadows. First brutally torn from all of his family and social ties and excluded from all functions and activities through which he experienced self-awareness, then banished by the same forces from the world of the living, the victim yields to the combined effect of intense terror, the sudden total withdrawal of the multiple reference systems provided by the support of the group, and, finally, to the group's decisive reversal in proclaiming him—once a living man, with rights and obligations—dead and an object of fear, ritual, and taboo. Physical integrity cannot withstand the dissolution of the social personality.

How are these complex phenomena expressed on the physiological level? Cannon showed that fear, like rage, is associated with a particularly intense activity of the sympathetic nervous system. This activity is ordinarily useful, involving organic modifications which enable the individual to adapt himself to a new situation. But if the individual cannot avail himself of any instinctive or acquired response to an extraordinary situation (or to one which he conceives of as such), the activity of the sympathetic nervous system becomes intensified and disorganized; it may, sometimes within a few hours, lead to a decrease in the volume of blood and a concomitant drop in blood pressure, which result in irreparable damage to the circulatory organs. The rejection of food and drink, frequent among patients in the throes of intense anxiety, precipitates this process; dehydration acts as a stimulus to the sympathetic nervous system, and the decrease in blood volume is accentuated by the growing permeability of the capillary vessels. These hypotheses were confirmed by the study of several cases of trauma resulting from bombings, battle shock, and even surgical operations; death results, yet the autopsy reveals no lesions.

There is, therefore, no reason to doubt the efficacy of certain magical practices. But at the same time we see that the efficacy of magic implies a belief in magic. The latter has three complementary aspects: first, the sorcerer's belief in the effectiveness of his techniques; second, the patient's or victim's belief in the sorcerer's power; and, finally, the faith and expectations of the group, which constantly act as a sort of gravitational field within which the relationship between sorcerer and bewitched is located and defined. Obviously, none of the three parties is capable of forming a clear picture of the sympathetic nervous system's activity or of the disturbances which Cannon called homeostatic. When the sorcerer claims to suck out of the patient's body a foreign object whose presence would explain the illness and produces a stone which he had previously hidden in his mouth, how does he justify this procedure in his own eyes? How can an innocent person accused of sorcery prove his innocence if the accusation is unanimous—since the magical situation is a consensual phenomenon? And, finally, how much credulity and how much skepticism are involved in the attitude of the group toward those in whom it recognizes extraordinary powers, to whom it accords corresponding privileges, but from whom it also requires adequate satisfaction? Let us begin by examining this last point.

It was in September, 1938. For several weeks we had been camping with a small band of Nambicuara Indians near the headwaters of the Tapajoz, in those desolate savannas of central Brazil where the natives wander during the greater part of the year, collecting seeds and wild fruits, hunting small mammals, insects, and reptiles, and whatever else might prevent them from dying of starvation. Thirty of them were camped together there, quite by chance. They were grouped in families under frail lean-tos of branches, which give scant protection from the scorching sun, nocturnal chill, rain, and wind. Like most bands, this one had both a secular chief and a sorcerer; the latter's daily activities—hunting, fishing, and handicrafts—were in no way different from those of the other men of the group. He was a robust man, about forty-five years old, and a *bon vivant*.

One evening, however, he did not return to camp at the usual time. Night fell and fires were lit; the natives were visibly worried. Countless perils lurk in the bush: torrential rivers, the somewhat improbable danger of encountering a large wild beast—jaguar or anteater—or, more readily pictured by the Nambicuara, an apparently harmless animal which is the incarnation of an evil spirit of the waters or forest. And above all, each night for the past week we had seen mysterious campfires, which sometimes approached and sometimes receded from our own. Any unknown band is always potentially hostile. After a two-hour wait, the natives were convinced that their companion had been killed in ambush and, while his two young wives and his son wept noisily in mourning for their dead husband and father, the other natives discussed the tragic consequences, foreshadowed by the disappearance of their sorcerer.

Toward ten that evening, the anguished anticipation of imminent disaster, the lamentations in which the other women began to join, and the agitation of the men had created an intolerable atmosphere, and we decided to reconnoiter with several natives who had remained relatively calm. We had not gone two hundred yards when we stumbled upon a motionless figure. It was our man, crouching silently, shivering in the chilly night air, disheveled and without his belt, necklaces, and arm-bands (the Nambicuara wear nothing else). He allowed us to lead him back to the camp site without resistance, but only after long exhortations by his group and pleading by his family was he persuaded to talk. Finally, bit by bit, we extracted the details of his story. A thunderstorm, the first of the season, had burst during the afternoon, and the thunder had carried him off to a site several miles distant, which he named, and then, after stripping him completely, had brought him back to the spot where we found him. Everyone went off to sleep commenting on the event. The next day the thunder victim had recovered his joviality and, what is more, all his ornaments. This last detail did not appear to surprise anyone, and life resumed its normal course.

A few days later, however, another version of these prodigious events began to be circulated by certain natives. We must note that this band was actually composed of individuals of different origins and had been fused into a new social entity as a result of unknown circumstances. One of the groups had been decimated by an epidemic several years before and was no longer sufficiently large to lead an independent life; the other had seceded from its original tribe and found itself in the same straits. When and under what circumstances the two groups met and decided to unite their efforts, we could not discover. The secular leader of the new band came from one group and the sorcerer, or religious leader, from the other. The fusion was obviously recent, for no marriage had yet taken place between the two groups when we met them, although the children of one were usually betrothed to the children of the other; each group had retained its own dialect, and their members could communicate only through two or three bilingual natives.

This is the rumor that was spread. There was good reason to suppose that the unknown bands crossing the savanna belonged to the tribe of the seceded group of which the sorcerer was a member. The sorcerer, impinging on the functions of his colleague the political chief, had doubtless wanted to contact his former tribesmen, perhaps to ask to return to the fold, or to provoke an attack upon his new companions, or perhaps even to reassure them of the friendly intentions of the latter. In any case, the sorcerer had needed a pretext for his absence, and his kidnapping by thunder and its subsequent staging were invented toward this end. It was, of course, the natives of the other group who spread this interpretation, which they secretly believed and which filled them with apprehension. But the official version was never publicly disputed, and until we left, shortly after the incident, it remained ostensibly accepted by all.

Although the skeptics had analyzed the sorcerer's motives with great psychological finesse and political acumen, they would have been greatly astonished had someone suggested (quite plausibly) that the incident was a hoax which cast doubt upon the sorcerer's good faith and competence. He had probably not flown on the wings of thunder to the Rio Ananaz and had only staged an act. But these things might have happened, they had certainly happened in other circumstances, and they belonged to the realm of real experience. Certainly the sorcerer maintains an intimate relationship with the forces of the supernatural. The idea that in a particular case he had used his power to conceal a secular activity belongs to the realm of conjecture and provides an opportunity for critical judgment. The important point is that these two possibilities were not mutually exclusive; no more than are, for us, the alternate interpretations of war as the dying gasp of national independence or as the result of the schemes of munitions manufacturers. The two explanations are logically incompatible, but we admit that one or the other may be true; since they are equally plausible, we easily make the transition from one to the other, depending on the occasion and the moment. Many people have both explanations in the back of their minds.

Whatever their true origin, these divergent interpretations come from individual consciousness not as the result of objective analysis but rather as complementary ideas resulting from hazy and unelaborated attitudes which have an experiential character for each of us. These experiences, however, remain intellectually diffuse and emotionally intolerable unless they incorporate one or another of the patterns present in the group's culture. The assimilation of such patterns is the only means of objectivizing subjective states, of formulating inexpressible feelings, and of integrating inarticulated experiences into a system.

These mechanisms become clearer in the light of some observations made many years ago among the Zuni of New Mexico by an admirable fieldworker, M. C. Stevenson. A twelve-year-old girl was stricken with a nervous seizure directly after an adolescent boy had seized her hands. The youth was accused of sorcery and dragged before the court of the Bow priesthood. For an hour he denied having any knowledge of occult power, but this defense proved futile. Because the crime of sorcery was at that time still punished by death among the Zuni, the accused changed his tactics. He improvised a tale explaining the circumstances by which he had been initiated into sorcery. He said he had received two substances from his teachers, one which drove girls insane and another which cured them. This point constituted an ingenious precaution against later developments. Having been ordered to produce his medicines, he went home under guard and came back with two roots, which he proceeded to use in a complicated ritual. He simulated a trance after taking one of the drugs, and after taking the other he pretended to return to his normal state. Then he administered the remedy to the sick girl and declared her cured. The session was adjourned until the following day, but during the night the alleged sorcerer escaped. He was soon captured, and the girl's family set itself up as a court and continued the trial. Faced with the reluctance of his new judges to accept his first story, the boy then invented a new one. He told them that all his relatives and ancestors had been witches and that he had received marvelous powers from them. He claimed that he could assume the form of a cat, fill his mouth with cactus needles, and kill his victims—two infants, three girls, and two boys—by shooting the needles into them. These feats, he claimed, were due to the magical powers of certain plumes which were used to change him and his family into shapes other than human. This last detail was a tactical error, for the judges called upon him to produce the plumes as proof of his new story. He gave various excuses which were rejected one after another, and he was forced to take his judges to his house. He began by declaring that the plumes were secreted in a wall that he could not destroy. He was commanded to go to work. After breaking down a section of the wall and carefully examining the plaster, he tried to excuse himself by declaring that the plumes had been hidden two years before and that he could not remember their exact location. Forced to search again, he tried another wall, and after another hour's work, an old plume appeared in the plaster. He grabbed it eagerly and presented it to his prosecutors as the magic device of which he had spoken. He was then made to explain the details of its use. Finally, dragged into the public plaza, he had to repeat his entire story (to which he added a wealth

of new detail). He finished it with a pathetic speech in which he lamented the loss of his supernatural power. Thus reassured, his listeners agreed to free him.

This narrative, which we unfortunately had to abridge and strip of all its psychological nuances, is still instructive in many respects. First of all, we see that the boy tried for witchcraft, for which he risks the death penalty, wins his acquittal not by denying but by admitting his alleged crime. Moreover, he furthers his cause by presenting successive versions, each richer in detail (and thus, in theory, more persuasive of guilt) than the preceding one. The debate does not proceed, as do debates among us, by accusations and denials, but rather by allegations and specifications. The judges do not expect the accused to challenge their theory, much less to refute the facts. Rather, they require him to validate a system of which they possess only a fragment; he must reconstruct it as a whole in an appropriate way. As the field-worker noted in relation to a phase of the trial, "The warriors had become so absorbed by their interest in the narrative of the boy that they seemed entirely to have forgotten the cause of his appearance before them." And when the magic plume was finally uncovered, the author remarks with great insight, "There was consternation among the warriors, who exclaimed in one voice: 'What does this mean?' Now they felt assured that the youth had spoken the truth." Consternation, and not triumph at finding a tangible proof of the crime—for the judges had sought to bear witness to the reality of the system which had made the crime possible (by validating its objective basis through an appropriate emotional expression), rather than simply to punish a crime. By his confession, the defendant is transformed into a witness for the prosecution, with the participation (and even the complicity) of his judges. Through the defendant, witchcraft and the ideas associated with it cease to exist as a diffuse complex of poorly formulated sentiments and representations and become embodied in real experience. The defendant, who serves as a witness, gives the group the satisfaction of truth, which is infinitely greater and richer than the satisfaction of justice that would have been achieved by his execution. And finally, by his ingenious defense which makes his hearers progressively aware of the vitality offered by his corroboration of their system (especially since the choice is not between this system and another, but between the magical system and no system at all—that is, chaos), the youth, who at first was a threat to the physical security of his group, became the guardian of its spiritual coherence.

But is his defense merely ingenious? Everything leads us to believe that after groping for a subterfuge, the defendant participates with sincerity and—the word is not too strong—fervor in the drama enacted between him and his judges. He is proclaimed a sorcerer; since sorcerers do exist, he might well be one. And how would he know beforehand the signs which might reveal his calling to him? Perhaps the signs are there, present in this ordeal and in the convulsions of the little girl brought before the court. For the boy, too, the coherence of the system and the role assigned to him in preserving it are values no less essential than the personal security which he risks in the venture. Thus we see him, with a mixture of cunning and good faith, progressively construct the impersonation which is thrust upon him—chiefly by drawing on his knowledge and his memories, improvising somewhat, but above all living his role and seeking through his manipulations and the ritual he builds from bits and pieces, the experience of a calling which is, at least theoretically, open to all. At the end of the adventure, what remains of his earlier hoaxes? To what extent has the hero become the dupe of his own impersonation? What is more, has he not truly become a sorcerer? We are told that in his final confession, "The longer the boy talked the more absorbed he became in his subject. . . . At times his face became radiant with satisfaction at his power over his listeners." The girl recovers after he performs his curing ritual. The boy's experiences during the extraordinary ordeal become elaborated and structured. Little more is needed than for the innocent boy finally to confess to the possession of supernatural powers that are already recognized by the group.

We must consider at greater length another especially valuable document, which until now seems to have been valued solely for its linguistic interest. I refer to a fragment of the autobiography of a Kwakiutl Indian from the Vancouver region of Canada, obtained by Franz Boas.

Quesalid (for this was the name he received when he became a sorcerer) did not believe in the power of the sorcerers—or, more accurately, shamans, since this is a better term for their specific type of activity in certain regions of the world. Driven by curiosity about their tricks and by the desire to expose them, he began to associate with the shamans until one of them offered to make him a member of their group. Quesalid did not wait to be asked twice, and his narrative recounts the details of his first lessons, a curious mixture of pantomime, prestidigitation, and empirical knowledge, including the art of simulating fainting and nervous fits, the learning of sacred songs, the technique for inducing vomiting, rather precise notions of auscultation and obstetrics, and the use of "dreamers," that is, spies who listen to private conversations and secretly convey to the shaman bits of information concerning the origins and symptoms of the ills suffered by different people. Above all, he learned the *ars magna* of one of the shamanistic schools of the Northwest Coast: The shaman hides a little tuft of down in the corner of his mouth, and he throws it up, covered with blood, at the proper moment—after having bitten his tongue or made his gums bleed—and solemnly presents it to his patient and the onlookers as the pathological foreign body extracted as a result of his sucking and manipulations.

His worst suspicions confirmed, Quesalid wanted to continue his inquiry. But he was no longer free. His apprenticeship among the shamans began to be noised about, and one day he was summoned by the family of a sick person who had dreamed of Quesalid as his healer. This first treatment (for which he received no payment, any more than he did for those which followed, since he had not completed the required four years of apprenticeship) was an outstanding success. Although Quesalid came to be known from that moment on as a "great shaman," he did not lose his critical faculties. He interpreted his success in psychological terms—it was successful "because he [the sick person] believed strongly in his dream about me." A more complex adventure made him, in his own words, "hesitant and thinking about many things." Here he encountered several varieties of a "false supernatural," and was led to conclude that some forms were less false than others—those, of course, in which he had a personal stake and whose system he was, at the same time, surreptitiously building up in his mind. A summary of the adventure follows.

While visiting the neighboring Koskimo Indians, Quesalid attends a curing ceremony of his illustrious colleagues of the other tribe. To his great astonishment he observes a difference in their technique. Instead of spitting out the illness in the form of a "bloody worm" (the concealed down), the Koskimo shamans merely spit a little saliva into their hands, and they dare to claim that this is "the sickness." What is the value of this method? What is the theory behind it? In order to find out "the strength of the shamans, whether it was real or whether they only pretended to be shamans" like this fellow tribesmen, Quesalid requests and obtains permission to try his method in an instance where the Koskimo method has failed. The sick woman then declares herself cured.

And here our hero vacillates for the first time. Though he had few illusions about his own technique, he has now found one which is more false, more mystifying, and more dishonest than his own. For he at least gives his clients something. He presents them with their sickness in a visible and tangible form, while his foreign colleagues show nothing at all and only claim to have captured the sickness. Moreover, Quesalid's method gets results, while the other is futile. Thus our hero grapples with a problem which perhaps has its parallel in the development of modern science. Two systems which we know to be inadequate present (with respect to each other) a differential validity, from both a logical and an empirical perspective. From which frame of reference shall we judge them? On the level of fact, where they merge, or on their own level, where they take on different values, both theoretically and empirically?

Meanwhile, the Koskimo shamans, "ashamed" and discredited before their tribesmen, are also plunged into doubt. Their colleague has produced, in the form of a material object, the illness which they had always considered as spiritual in nature and had thus never dreamed of rendering visible. They send Quesalid an emissary to invite him to a secret meeting in a cave. Quesalid goes and his foreign colleagues expound their system to him: "Every sickness is a man: boils and swellings, and itch and scabs, and pimples and coughs and consumption and scrofula; and also this, stricture of the bladder and stomach aches. . . . As soon as we get the soul of the sickness which is a man, then dies the sickness which is a man. Its body just dis-

appears in our insides." If this theory is correct, what is there to show? And why, when Quesalid operates, does "the sickness stick to his hand"? But Quesalid takes refuge behind professional rules which forbid him to teach before completing four years of apprenticeship, and refuses to speak. He maintains his silence even when the Koskimo shamans send him their allegedly virgin daughters to try to seduce him and discover his secret.

Thereupon Quesalid returns to his village at Fort Rupert. He learns that the most reputed shaman of a neighboring clan, worried about Quesalid's growing renown, has challenged all his colleagues, inviting them to compete with him in curing several patients. Quesalid comes to the contest and observes the cures of his elder. Like the Koskimo, this shaman does not show the illness. He simply incorporates an invisible object, "what he called the sickness" into his head-ring, made of bark, or into his bird-shaped ritual rattle. These objects can hang suspended in mid-air, owing to the power of the illness which "bites" the house-posts or the shaman's hand. The usual drama unfolds. Quesalid is asked to intervene in cases judged hopeless by his predecessor, and he triumphs with his technique of the bloody worm.

Here we come to the truly pathetic part of the story. The old shaman, ashamed and despairing because of the ill-repute into which he has fallen and by the collapse of his therapeutic technique, sends his daughter to Quesalid to beg him for an interview. The latter finds his colleague sitting under a tree and the old shaman begins thus: "It won't be bad what we say to each other, friend, but only I wish you to try and save my life for me, so that I may not die of shame, for I am a plaything of our people on account of what you did last night. I pray you to have mercy and tell me what stuck on the palm of your hand last night. Was it the true sickness or was it only made up? For I beg you have mercy and tell me about the way you did it so that I can imitate you. Pity me, friend."

Silent at first, Quesalid begins by calling for explanations about the feats of the head-ring and the rattle. His colleague shows him the nail hidden in the head-ring which he can press at right angles into the post, and the way in which he tucks the head of his rattle between his finger joints to make it look as if the bird were hanging by its beak from his hand. He himself probably does nothing but lie and fake, simulating shamanism for material gain, for he admits to being "covetous for the property of the sick men." He knows that shamans cannot catch souls, "for . . . we all own a soul"; so he resorts to using tallow and pretends that "it is a soul . . . that white thing . . . sitting on my hand." The daughter then adds her entreaties to those of her father: "Do have mercy that he may live." But Quesalid remains silent. That very night, following this tragic conversation, the shaman disappears with his entire family, heartsick and feared by the community, who think that he may be tempted to take revenge. Needless fears: He returned a year later, but both he and his daughter had gone mad. Three years later, he died.

And Quesalid, rich in secrets, pursued his career, exposing the impostors and full of contempt for the profession. "Only one shaman was seen by me, who sucked at a sick man and I never found out whether he was a real shaman or only made up. Only for this reason I believe that he is a shaman; he does not allow those who are made well to pay him. I truly never once saw him laugh." Thus his original attitude has changed considerably. The radical negativism of the free thinker has given way to more moderate feelings. Real shamans do exist. And what about him? At the end of the narrative we cannot tell, but it is evident that he carries on his craft conscientiously, takes pride in his achievements, and warmly defends the technique of the bloody down against all rival schools. He seems to have completely lost sight of the fallaciousness of the technique which he had so disparaged at the beginning.

We see that the psychology of the sorcerer is not simple. In order to analyze it, we shall first examine the case of the old shaman who begs his young rival to tell him the truth—whether the illness glued in the palm of his hand like a sticky red worm is real or made up—and who goes mad when he receives no answer. Before the tragedy, he was fully convinced of two things—first, that pathological conditions have a cause which may be discovered and second, that a system of interpretation in which personal inventiveness is important structures the phases of the illness, from the diagnosis to the cure. This fabulation of a reality unknown in itself—a fabulation consisting of procedures and representations—is founded on a threefold experience: first, that of the shaman himself, who, if his

calling is a true one (and even if it is not, simply by virtue of his practicing it), undergoes specific states of a psychosomatic nature; second, that of the sick person, who may or may not experience an improvement of his condition; and, finally, that of the public, who also participate in the cure, experiencing an enthusiasm and an intellectual and emotional satisfaction which produce collective support, which in turn inaugurates a new cycle.

These three elements of what we might call the "shamanistic complex" cannot be separated. But they are clustered around two poles, one formed by the intimate experience of the shaman and the other by group consensus. There is no reason to doubt that sorcerers, or at least the more sincere among them, believe in their calling and that this belief is founded on the experiencing of specific states. The hardships and privations which they undergo would often be sufficient in themselves to provoke these states, even if we refuse to admit them as proof of a serious and fervent calling. But there is also linguistic evidence which, because it is indirect, is more convincing. In the Wintu dialect of California, there are five verbal classes which correspond to knowledge by sight, by bodily experience, by inference, by reasoning, and by hearsay. All five make up the category of knowledge as opposed to conjecture, which is differently expressed. Curiously enough, relationships with the supernatural world are expressed by means of the modes of knowledge—by bodily impression (that is, the most intuitive kind of experience), by inference, and by reasoning. Thus the native who becomes a shaman after a spiritual crisis conceives of his state grammatically, as a consequence to be inferred from the fact—formulated as real experience—that he has received divine guidance. From the latter he concludes deductively that he must have been on a journey to the beyond, at the end of which he found himself—again, an immediate experience—once more among his people.

The experiences of the sick person represent the least important aspect of the system, except for the fact that a patient successfully treated by a shaman is in an especially good position to become a shaman in his own right, as we see today in the case of psychoanalysis. In any event, we must remember that the shaman does not completely lack empirical knowledge and experimental techniques, which may in part explain his success. Furthermore, disorders of the type currently termed psychosomatic, which constitute a large part of the illnesses prevalent in societies with a low degree of security, probably often yield to psychotherapy. At any rate, it seems probable that medicine men, like their civilized colleagues, cure at least some of the cases they treat and that without this relative success magical practices could not have been so widely diffused in time and space. But this point is not fundamental; it is subordinate to the other two. Quesalid did not become a great shaman because he cured his patients; he cured his patients because he had become a great shaman. Thus we have reached the other—that is, the collective—pole of our system.

The true reason for the defeat of Quesalid's rivals must then be sought in the attitude of the group rather than in the pattern of the rivals' successes and failures. The rivals themselves emphasize this when they confess their shame at having become the laughingstock of the group; this is a social sentiment *par excellence*. Failure is secondary, and we see in all their statements that they consider it a function of another phenomenon, which is the disappearance of the *social consensus*, recreated at their expense around another practitioner and another system of curing. Consequently, the fundamental problem revolves around the relationship between the individual and the group, or, more accurately, the relationship between a specific category of individuals and specific expectations of the group.

In treating his patient the shaman also offers his audience a performance. What is this performance? Risking a rash generalization on the basis of a few observations, we shall say that it always involves the shaman's enactment of the "call," or the initial crisis which brought him the revelation of his condition. But we must not be deceived by the word *performance*. The shaman does not limit himself to reproducing or miming certain events. He actually relives them in all their vividness, originality, and violence. And since he returns to his normal state at the end of the séance, we may say, borrowing a key term from psychoanalysis, that he *abreacts*. In psychoanalysis, abreaction refers to the decisive moment in the treatment when the patient intensively relives the initial situation from which his disturbance stems, before he ultimately overcomes it. In this sense, the shaman is a professional abreactor.

We have set forth elsewhere the theoretical hypotheses that might be formulated in order for us to accept the idea that the type of abreaction specific to each shaman—or, at any rate, to each shamanistic school—might symbolically induce an abreaction of his own disturbance in each patient. In any case, if the relationship is that between the shaman and the group, we must also state the question from another point of view—that of the relationship between normal and pathological thinking. From any non-scientific perspective (and here we can exclude no society), pathological and normal thought processes are complementary rather than opposed. In a universe which it strives to understand but whose dynamics it cannot fully control, normal thought continually seeks the meaning of things which refuse to reveal their significance. So-called pathological thought, on the other hand, overflows with emotional interpretations and overtones, in order to supplement an otherwise deficient reality. For normal thinking there exists something which cannot be empirically verified and is, therefore, "claimable." For pathological thinking there exist experiences without object, or something "available." We might borrow from linguistics and say that so-called normal thought always suffers from a deficit of meaning, whereas so-called pathological thought (in at least some of its manifestations) disposes of a plethora of meaning. Through collective participation in shamanistic curing, a balance is established between these two complementary situations. Normal thought cannot fathom the problem of illness, and so the group calls upon the neurotic to furnish a wealth of emotion heretofore lacking a focus.

An equilibrium is reached between what might be called supply and demand on the psychic level—but only on two conditions. First, a structure must be elaborated and continually modified through the interaction of group tradition and individual invention. This structure is a system of oppositions and correlations, integrating all the elements of a total situation, in which sorcerer, patient, and audience, as well as representations and procedures, all play their parts. Furthermore, the public must participate in the abreaction, to a certain extent at least, along with the patient and the sorcerer. It is this vital experience of a universe of symbolic effusions which the patient, because he is ill, and the sorcerer, because he is neurotic—in other words, both having types of experience which cannot otherwise be integrated—allow the public to glimpse as "fireworks" from a safe distance. In the absence of any experimental control, which is indeed unnecessary, it is this experience alone, and its relative richness in each case, which makes possible a choice between several systems and elicits adherence to a particular school or practitioner.

In contrast with scientific explanation, the problem here is not to attribute confused and disorganized states, emotions, or representations to an objective cause, but rather to articulate them into a whole or system. The system is valid precisely to the extent that it allows the coalescence or precipitation of these diffuse states, whose discontinuity also makes them painful. To the conscious mind, this last phenomenon constitutes an original experience which cannot be grasped from without. Because of their complementary disorders, the sorcerer-patient dyad incarnates for the group, in vivid and concrete fashion, an antagonism that is inherent in all thought but that normally remains vague and imprecise. The patient is all passivity and self-alienation, just as inexpressibility is the disease of the mind. The sorcerer is activity and self-projection, just as affectivity is the source of symbolism. The cure interrelates these opposite poles, facilitating the transition from one to the other, and demonstrates, within a total experience, the coherence of the psychic universe, itself a projection of the social universe.

Thus it is necessary to extend the notion of abreaction by examining the meanings it acquires in psychotherapies other than psychoanalysis, although the latter deserves the credit for rediscovering and insisting upon its fundamental validity. It may be objected that in psychoanalysis there is only one abreaction, the patient's, rather than three. We are not so sure of this. It is true that in the shamanistic cure the sorcerer speaks and abreacts *for* the silent patient, while in psychoanalysis it is the patient who talks and abreacts *against* the listening therapist. But the therapist's abreaction, while not concomitant with the patient's, is nonetheless required, since he must be analyzed before he himself can become an analyst. It is more difficult to define the role ascribed to the group by each technique. Magic readapts the group

predefined problems through the patient, while psychoanalysis readapts the patient to the group by means of the solutions reached. But the distressing trend which, for several years, has tended to transform the psychoanalytic system from a body of scientific hypotheses that are experimentally verifiable in certain specific and limited cases into a kind of diffuse mythology interpenetrating the consciousness of the group, could rapidly bring about a parallelism. (This group consciousness is an objective phenomenon, which the psychologist expresses through a subjective tendency to extend to normal thought a system of interpretations conceived for pathological thought and to apply to facts of collective psychology a method adapted solely to the study of individual psychology.) When this happens—and perhaps it already has in certain countries—the value of the system will no longer be based upon real cures from which certain individuals can benefit, but on the sense of security that the group receives from the myth underlying the cure and from the popular system upon which the group's universe is reconstructed.

Even at the present time, the comparison between psychoanalysis and older and more widespread psychological therapies can encourage the former to re-examine its principles and methods. By continuously expanding the recruitment of its patients, who began as clearly characterized abnormal individuals and gradually become representative of the group, psychoanalysis, transforms its treatments into conversions. For only a patient can emerge cured; an unstable or maladjusted individual can only be persuaded. A considerable danger thus arises: The treatment (unbeknown to the therapist, naturally), far from leading to the resolution of a specific disturbance within its own context, is reduced to the reorganization of the patient's universe in terms of psychoanalytic interpretations. This means that we would finally arrive at precisely that situation which furnishes the point of departure as well as the theoretical validity of the magico-social system that we have analyzed.

If this analysis is correct, we must see magical behavior as the response to a situation which is revealed to the mind through emotional manifestations, but those essence is intellectual. For only the history of the symbolic function can allow us to understand the intellectual condition of man, in which the universe is never charged with sufficient meaning and in which the mind always has more meanings available than there are objects to which to relate them. Torn between these two systems of reference—the signifying and the signified—man asks magical thinking to provide him with a new system of reference, within which the thus-far contradictory elements can be integrated. But we know that this system is built at the expense of the progress of knowledge, which would have required us to retain only one of the two previous systems and to refine it to the point where it absorbed the other. This point is still far off. We must not permit the individual, whether normal or neurotic, to repeat this collective misadventure. The study of the mentally sick individual has shown us that all persons are more or less oriented toward contradictory systems and suffer from the resulting conflict; but the fact that a certain form of integration is possible and effective practically is not enough to make it true, or to make us certain that the adaptation thus achieved does not constitute an absolute regression in relation to the previous conflict situation.

The reabsorption of a deviant specific synthesis, through its integration with the normal syntheses, into a general but arbitrary synthesis (aside from critical cases where action is required) would represent a loss on all fronts. A body of elementary hypotheses can have a certain instrumental value for the practitioner without necessarily being recognized, in theoretical analysis, as the final image of reality and without necessarily linking the patient and the therapist in a kind of mystical communion which does not have the same meaning for both parties and which only ends by reducing the treatment to a fabulation.

In the final analysis we could only expect this fabulation to be a language, whose function is to provide a socially authorized translation of phenomena whose deeper nature would become once again equally impenetrable to the group, the patient, and the healer.

Folk Medical Magic and Symbolism in the West

Wayland D. Hand

In this selection folklorist Wayland Hand turns to the United States to give us several fascinating examples of magical medicine and folk medical symbolism. In Utah there are those who believe walnuts are good for diseases of the brain (because the meat of the nut looks like the brain), while in other western states some people wear a red string around the neck to stop a nosebleed. In California, Arkansas, and Oklahoma children with chickenpox may be taken to a chicken coup in order to let chickens fly over them and thus effect a cure. These and dozens of other magical beliefs from the western United States are discussed in this article, which will help the reader to realize that folk medical magic and symbolism are not just part of a system of quaint beliefs and practices from Africa, New Guinea, or aboriginal Australia, but continue to be well known and practiced in the contemporary United States.

Reprinted from Austin and Alfa Fife and Henry H. Glassie, eds., *Forms Upon the Frontier*. Utah State University, Monograph Series, XVI, no. 2 (April 1969), pp. 103–18. By permission of the publisher. The article's citations, originally numbered footnotes, have been interpolated into the text in this volume for consistency of presentation.

THE COLLECTING OF FOLK MEDICINE IN THE WEST has not been under way long enough to permit anything approaching a full survey of the causes and cures of disease and matters having to do with the medical aspects of the life cycle, particularly with birth and death. Even so, there is at hand a sufficiently representative body of medical folklore to constitute at least an adumbration of the kinds of material that still await the hand of the collector in the sprawling country beyond the Mississippi (Anderson 1968; Fife 1957; Hand 1971; Lathrop 1961). It is my purpose here to concentrate on the more neglected areas of folk medical study in the West, namely magical medicine and folk medical symbolism as it derives from elementary forms of magic.

In putting this paper together, I have drawn on archival material for California and other western states that has been accumulating from student collectanea for the past fifteen or twenty years in the Archive of California and Western Folklore at the University of California at Los Angeles. Systematic collecting in Utah, also through students, has been undertaken by my colleague at the University of Utah, Professor Anthon S. Cannon, who is collaborating with me in the preparation of the Utah volume tributary of the Dictionary of American Popular Beliefs and Superstitions. The extensive Austin and Alta Fife collections, made in Moab, Utah, in 1953, have also been at my disposal. To the heavy unpublished material from California and Utah have been added much lighter samplings from other western states, but the footnotes to this paper contain a backup of published material from older parts of the country, particularly from the eastern seaboard and the South. (In the main, these references are found in the notes to the entries from the Brown Collection.) For the purposes of defining the West, I am including all states west of the Mississippi, including Minnesota, when it has served my purposes to do so. In taking only unpublished material to illustrate magical folk medicine I have sought to show field collectors that it is still possible to collect magical medical lore in the West in addition to turning up accounts of the use of plant and animal samples, the preparation and administration of various kinds of medicines, teas, and tonics, the application of different sorts of dressings and poultices, and resort to manipulative therapy of one kind and another.

Homeopathic principles of medicine are well known, and are based on analogic magic, wherein it is assumed that external similarity rests on what would seem to be an apparent internal connection and a basic inner unity and dependence (Bakker 1960; *Dictionnaire encyclopedique des sciences medicales* 1881; *Handwortenbuch* 1927–1942; Jungbauer 1934; Wuttke 1900). Under this premise, cures are undertaken on the theory that similar things are cured by similar means, as set forth in the celebrated Latin phrase, *similia similibus curantur* (Bonser 1963; Mogk 1906).

Though these notions were known in antiquity, it remained for later medical practitioners such as the Italian physician Jean Baptiste Porta to state these principles of unity in more specific terms. Porta, among other things, enunciated the "doctrine of signatures," whereby the efficacy of a plant for the cure of a certain malady could be assessed in terms of its shape, its color, its appendages, and the essences secreted as they related to the diseased part or the impeded function (*Dictionnaire encyclopedique 1881*). These simple preliminary observations on magic and symbolism, then, will prepare us for assorted folk medical notions that involve homeopathy which are still to be found in the West.

Similarity of shape is seen in a Utah belief, supported by seven texts from different parts of Salt Lake County, that walnuts are good for diseases of the brain, one informant declaring that the efficacy rested in the fact that "the meat of the nut looks like the brain, and the shell resembles the skull" Also from Salt Lake County comes a variation on the doctrine of signatures affecting shape and relative position, namely, the belief that the tops of plants should be used to cure diseases of the head, while the roots of plants should be utilized

for maladies of the legs. Kissing a pain better is an age-old custom of the nursery employed by mothers to assure children that the pain will go away. The kissing of a person's thumb when he stubs his toe, rests on an extension of the principles of analogy stated above, and is made necessary by the fact that a person is actually unable to kiss his own toe. Examples of this whimsical notion come from California, one entry being possibly of ultimate Polish provenience. The other allusion comes from Helena, Montana.

The use of appropriate colors to combat disease is seen in the following examples from western states: in Missouri, South Dakota, Washington, and Utah, a nosebleed is stanched by wearing either a red string, red yarn, a red handkerchief, or a red necklace about the neck (Brown 1952–64; Fife 1957; Hand 1961–64; Neal 1955). Two additional items from Utah prescribe carrying the red yarn or red string in one's pocket.

A Salt Lake doctor reports having heard many times in his practice that yellow jaundice should be treated with yellow drugs, on the theory that "yellow rids yellow" (*Journal of American Folklore* 1944). A variation on this general prescription, also from Salt Lake, is the hanging of a carrot in the basement, which is supposed to absorb the jaundice as the carrot dries up (Neal 1955). Scarlet fever was treated in Utah by wrapping the patients up in scarlet blankets, and doctoring them with medicine scarlet or red in color.

The curing of frostbite and other conditions brought on by cold are treated in their own terms in Minnesota, where frozen members are treated with snow; in Kansas, where frostbitten ears are likewise rubbed with snow; and in Utah, where chilblains are combatted by the same agent that caused them, namely, snow (Brown 1952–64; Lathrop 1961). In Los Angeles, for example, it is recommended that one swim in the ocean to combat a cold. In heat therapy, on the contrary, an old lady in Moab, Utah, reported to be a witch, cured burns by holding the wound over heat until it supposedly drew the heat out of the burn (Brown 1952–64; Fife 1957). In Ogden, Utah, in an entry dating back to 1885, it was recommended that a hot stone be placed on the head of a person suffering from fever. This application supposedly caused the fever to leave.

The almost classical cure of a disease by the

agent causing it, is seen in the well-known example of curing the bite of a mad dog by "the hair of the dog that bit you" (Brown 1952–64; Hendricks 1966). Three recent California examples and one from Oregon dating from 1915, attest to this old folk medical belief and practice, as do a spate of examples from Utah, including a prescription from Park City (1930) to the effect that the mad dog be killed immediately so that the person bitten would not go insane. Two other Utah items employ this same primitive logic, one recommending the eating of a snake that has inflicted a bite, and the other, from Provo about 1900, merely dictating that the snake's head should be bitten off (Brown 1952–64).

The taking of children to chicken coops to let the chickens fly over them is reported from Arkansas and Oklahoma and is found also in two entries from California, one of which indicates that "when the chickens fly over the kids, they take the pox away" (Brown 1952–64; Hendricks 1966). In parts of California as widely separated as San Luis Obispo, Ojai, and Los Angeles, the eating of poison oak is supposed to convey a lasting immunity against skin poisoning by this plant.

Space precludes a treatment of the sympathetic principles related to the marking of unborn children, a situation, or course, in which contagious magic as well as homeopathic principles come into play (Brown 1952–64). I shall cite but a single example from the unpublished Fife collection: "during the pregnancy the father or some close relative had an accident . . . and the child was born with a mark resembling the injury the father had." Here, you see, the child's most immediate connection, namely, the mother, is not mentioned at all. One might think of this as a secondary situation on which the analogy rests. Even so, a purely external event is magically communicated to the child by its mother.

The following four items—none related to each other—have in common only the sympathetic enlistment of a similar response, or the avoidance of an act that will induce a similar reaction. In Moab, Utah, for example, in order to get a child to fall asleep, it was prescribed that the person holding the child must herself yawn. In a California belief that probably came from Russia before 1900 it was feared that if a person swallowed string he would tie up his intestines. Another Utah example, and one involving contagious magic also, indicates that

if a person carries the crutches of someone with a broken arm or leg, he or she too will be the next to break a limb. A New Mexico belief that if one has boils, and a menstruating woman comes into the room, the boils will get worse, rests on the notion that one ailing person can influence another adversely. It does not matter that the respective maladies have nothing whatsoever in common.

The ancient notion of treating the weapon that has inflicted a wound (*Handwortenbuch* 1927–42), raised to a doctrine and widely advertised by Sir Kenelm Digby in 17th-century England, is seen in the West by the fact that lard or turpentine is put on a rusty nail after it has inflicted a puncture wound. Treatments of this kind are reported from Missouri and Oklahoma, and from three different parts of Utah. The Salt Lake version is summed up in a neat prescription: "Treat the weapon that made the wound" (Brown 1952–64).

Contrary measures, or a sort of reverse magic, are seen in the notion, for example, that playing with fire or matches will induce bed-wetting. Reports of this folk belief come from Utah, North Dakota, and New Mexico, the last-named instance stemming from the Latin-American tradition (Brown 1952–64). It must be noted that the principle of reversal, or *contraria contrariis* (*Handwortenbuch* 1927–42; Jungbauer 1934) as seen here, represents the cause of this noisome frailty in young children. Cures are seen in the combatting of a cold with hot drinks of various kinds, sweating, etc., etc. These are so common that I have not listed them. An unusual cure for sore throat—perhaps a bit of whimsy—involves reverse magic so extraordinary that one is tempted hardly to take it seriously. This cure from New Mexico prescribes rubbing Vicks Vaporub into the rectum to cure a sore throat.

Contagious magic opens up an even wider range of unusual folk medical beliefs and practices than those we have considered under homeopathic magic. All of these rest on the fundamental assumption that things once conjoined remain magically connected, even though dissevered (Frazer 1911–15). In folk medicine the law of contact, and of contagion, almost invariably has to do with the magical divestment of disease, whereby the malady is passed off wholly, or in a part which still represents the whole. This is a corollary of contagious magic known under the Latin formulation *pars pro toto* (Jungbauer 1934). In the ensuing discussions we shall see various manifestations of contagious magic. Intermingled will also be some symbolic cures not resting on actual contact. In handling material of this kind, one must bear in mind that contagious magic, as well as homeopathic magic, are part of the broader category of sympathetic magic.

Let us begin with the transference of disease (see Hand 1965). The cure of venereal diseases by transmitting the malady to a virgin, as found elsewhere in the United States, but not widely, is reported from Oakland and Hanford, California, for gonorrhea. A less sensational kind of transference is recommended from Montana for the cure of a cold, simply by passing it on to another person, and making a scapegoat of him. The transference of warts either to a willing or an unwary host is one of the commonplaces of magical transference of disease (Brown 1952–64; Fife 1957; Stout 1936). This is usually done outright by "sale." In various examples from Iowa, Nebraska, New Mexico, Utah, and California, the buyer usually pays a small sum of money, for instance, a penny, for each wart, or a dime. Contagious principles are not at work here (Brown 1952–64; Mckinney 1952; Stout 1936), except where the owner of the wart himself makes the sale, and pays out his own money to be freed of the wart. Under these circumstances the buyer, as in a California example, must bury the money to avoid getting the wart himself. Equally common with an outright sale is the use of a penny as a so-called *Zwischenträger*, or an intermediate agent (Hand 1965). Once rubbed on the wart, and hence impregnated with part of it, the coin may be thrown away, buried, or sold, as is seen in various practices from Iowa, North Dakota, Washington, Idaho, Utah, and California (Brown 1952–1964). A common way of wishing the wart onto others is to cast it off in such a way that it will be picked up by another person, who is thus sure to contract the wart (Brown 1952–64). This traffic is seen in a riddance cure from Salt Lake (Hand 1965). A unique cure from Iowa, dating from 1902, and involving a reversal, is seen in the following prescription: "Pick out a special dime and rub it over the wart, and give it to the person with the wart. As soon as the dime is spent the wart will disappear. The dime is kept with the patient's other money so it cannot be distinguished." Warts may be transferred to another person merely by his counting them, or by

placing as many pebbles in a candy bag, or other kind of container, as there are warts. The bag is then left in some likely place to be picked up by an inquisitive person (Brown 1952–64). Utah, Idaho, and California examples do not involve rubbing the wart to impregnate the pebbles, but an instance from Vernal, Utah, runs true to the more traditional form, wherein stones, peas, and beans are rubbed on the warts and then disposed of in a roadway. Even so, the picking up of the new host objects is not recorded in this last-named instance. The use of a transient in the ritual of divestment is seen in a California prescription from Hollywood, wherein the itinerant person counts the warts, writes them (the number?) on the inside of his hatband, and then magically takes the warts with him when he leaves town.

Aid of the dead in disposing of warts and other excrescences, and maladies of all kinds, is known in the United States, but this practice is no longer as common as it once was. From the western area of the country under survey, however, I have only two or three good examples, and two of these are from California. A friend of mine in Canoga Park, California, who had a goiter was once waiting for a green light at an intersection, when an unknown woman walked up and said: "Lady, if you place your hand on a dead person's throat, your goiter will go away" (Hand, n.d.). The other item is a less striking variant of this well-known cure for goiter. As late as 1960 there is a report from Salt Lake City that a dead hand touched to a cancer will cure it (Black 1935). In another Utah cure involving the dead, or objects connected with the dead, it was believed in Helper years ago that the cutting of a wart with a razor used to shave a dead person would cause the wart to disappear. Two other wart cures, both reported from California, involve traffic with the corpse. "When a corpse (in a funeral procession) goes by," the entry reads, "flick your wart, and say, 'Corpse take my wart with you.' Then forget about it, and the wart will soon be gone." The other instance reveals the common practice of rubbing the wart with a rag, but instead of burying the rag in the usual way, it is placed in the coffin with the dead person. When the rag rots, the wart will be gone.

Communicating disease to animals and thus ridding oneself of the malady is a prominent form of magical divestment of sickness (Hand 1965). This transfer is accomplished by contact with the animal, usually a dog or a cat, in sleeping or in other kinds of contact. In the classical sense of magical transference, however, as I have discussed it elsewhere (Hand 1965), the animal manifestly contracts the disease, and often dies as a result. Three Utah examples, the earliest from Grantsville, about 1880, display this cardinal feature. The Grantsville item reads: "Three hairs taken from the cross of an ass will cure whooping cough, but the ass will die." A cure for this same disease is reported from Salt Lake in 1928: "Tie a hairy caterpillar in a bag around a child's neck. As the insect dies, the whooping cough will vanish" (Black 1883; *Folklore* 1913; *Notes and Queries* 1903). The sacrificial role of the caterpillar, of course, is envisioned as part of the cure, and actually is thought to insure its success. The final Utah example, which was recorded in Salt Lake in 1953, is equally illuminating, and bears out the traditional pattern of eventual death to the creature to whom the disease has been communicated. "To cure warts, impale a frog on a stick and rub the warts on the frog. They will disappear as the frog dies" (Brown 1952–64). In less drastic kinds of transference to animals, rheumatic diseases are cured by contact with the animal, usually a dog or a cat, in sleeping or in other kinds of contact. (Brown 1952–64). Sleeping with a cat at the foot of the bed is recommended in Nebraska, and a dog is thought to accomplish the same purpose in California. It is claimed in this same California entry that a cat sleeping with you will result in your contracting arthritis from the cat. The wearing of a cat's fur on one's skin is recommended in Utah for the cure of pneumonia and consumption, and in California and Nebraska the fur of both cats and dogs is recommended for rheumatism (Brown 1952–64; Hendricks 1966). Merely keeping a Mexican Chihuahua dog in the house will ward off asthma, it is claimed in two entries from the Los Angeles area (Hendricks 1966). In an item from Murray, Utah, it is believed that sleeping on a bear rug will cure backache. In a very rare item from California, but possibly referable to Michigan, the cure of tuberculosis by sleeping in the hay with horses is recommended. Riddance of stone bruises by contact with a frog according to Oklahoma belief, and the loss of a wart in California by touching a frog are reported, while in Utah it is recommended to let a horny toad crawl on the victim's

bare skin so he can carry off the rheumatism (Brown 1952–64). In the same way, a snake wrapped around the neck will take the goiter with it when it disengages itself and crawls away, according to a Colorado belief (Black 1935).

Chickens are used to consume grains of barley after the barley has been rubbed on the wart. In this way, both by symbolic and contagious principles, the fowl takes the wart as it ingests the kernel of barley. This belief and practice is reported from Oklahoma, but the observance is widely reported wherever standard collections of folk medicine have been made (Brown 1952–64). Another item from Oklahoma, far more inscrutable than the first, recommends a cure for night blindness wherein a chicken is made to jump over the sleeping victim. No explanation is given, nor can I offer one.

In folk medicine swallows figure importantly in maladies of the eye, and there is an interesting Utah belief in the ability of this bird to help in restoring sight. The first time you hear the swallow in the spring, it is said, if you go to a stream or fountain and wash your eyes, at the same time making a silent prayer, the swallows will carry away all your eye troubles. A brutal ritual in contagious magic is reported from California, wherein a congenitally blind person must secure a frog, gouge its eyes out, return the frog to the water alive, and then place the animal's eyeballs on his own neck, in order to regain his eyesight.

Oral contact with animals, or breathing their expired breath, is a category of folk medical therapy found in the area under survey, even though the tradition is not well known (Hand 1968). Kissing a donkey for the relief of toothache is reported from California and Utah, and having a full-bred stallion blow its breath in the face of the victim of whooping cough, is also reported from California (Brown 1952–64; Hand 1968), although this cure ultimately comes from West Virginia. Spitting into the mouth of a frog is supposed to cure one of asthma, as reported in an instance from California. From the same state a recommended cure of whooping cough is to have the child cough into the mouth of a live fish (Brown 1952–64; Hand 1968). In Utah, as three Salt Lake entries attest, toads are credited with being able to suck the poison of cancer from the system. One other magical cure involving the passage of air into the respiratory tract of the patient is the well-known cure of thrush by having a posthumous child breathe into the mouth of a baby with thrush, as is reported in a case from Bakersfield, California (Brown 1952–64; Hand 1968).

A curious connection between headache and discarded hair combings that eventually are used in birds' nests is found in some California items, two of which stem from Louisiana and Georgia before the turn of the century (Brown 1952–64). Loss of hair is also reported from the misappropriation of a person's hair for nest building, as is seen in two Los Angeles county entries. Here, of course, harm to the hair, even though it is no longer connected with the person, results in harm to the person himself.

Transference of diseases to trees, generally rare in America, is found in only two reports. In Utah, around 1918, warts were transferred to an aspen tree by means of a piece of bacon. According to the classical requirements of such a transfer, the warts were thought to "grow on the tree and vanish from you," as the report states. Transference of diseases to trees by "plugging," "nailing," "wedging," and kindred means is more common in my sampling than communication to trees by means of strings, rubbing against the tree, and the like (Hand 1966; *Handwortenbuch* 1927–42), but, once more, it must be remembered that records of the practice in the western part of the country are scanty. In Missouri before the turn of the century, the victim probed a wart with a pin until it bled, and then stuck the pin into the tree (Brown 1952–64). Instead of the tree's getting the wart, as in normal procedures of this kind, it was supposed to be passed on to the first person who touched the pin. A more typical example of this general kind of transference, and one which I have called "wedging," is seen in a Utah example collected in Salt Lake as late as 1959: "Rub your warts with a piece of bacon, and then put the bacon in the slit of a tree. The warts will grow on the tree as knobs." To cure chills and fever in California, an "X" mark was cut in a persimmon tree, but details are lacking as to how the magical transfer took place. The incisions were made on different sides of the tree according to the seasons, as follows: summer: south; fall: west; winter: north; spring: east. In a wart cure reported from Los Angeles, a lock of the victim's hair is placed in the natural cleft of a tree, and he is supposed never to return to it. At best this is a secondary contagion, since the hair apparently was not brought into contact with the wart. Another California account

of plugging runs truer to form: "To cure asthma cut a square from the door facing where the person gasped for breath. Take out a chunk of wood, cut a lock of hair off the person, and place it back in the hole; then cover it up with a chunk of wood (Hand 1966).

Magical "plugging" of diseases is frequently confused with magically outgrowing a disease by a procedure of "measuring." A good example of this confusion is contained in a curative ritual reported as a memorat from Tarzana, California. "To cure a child of asthma, stand he or she (sic) against a door-jamb and drill a hole just above the head. Put a hank of hair in the hole and plug. After the child has grown above the hole he or she will never have asthma again." In another cure for asthma, a prescription recorded in North Hollywood, a lock of the child's hair is cut and placed in the window sill. When the child grows as high as where the hair was placed, he will have outgrown the disease. Measuring a wart with a pine needle in Spanish Fork, Utah, and then burying it, seems to emphasize the magic of burial and decay more than that of measurement (Brown 1952–64). This would be true, too, of course, for all counting rituals having to do with warts, in which the string or thread is ultimately buried, there to await rotting and the magical disappearance of the warts.

The accounts at my disposal of "notching" as a magical folk medical practice are inadequate to convey this complicated ritual, which involves, in its various manifestations, not only notching as a measurement (Brown 1952–64), but also as a means of counting warts, and the like, and in some cases it also involves elements of plugging. A South Dakota entry, dating from World War I, simply involved notching a piece of wood and throwing it away to get rid of a wart. A more detailed procedure is indicated in a practice reported from Moab, Utah, in 1953, but referable to a much earlier date, wherein a notch was cut in a stick for every wart, and then some other person made to bury the stick. When the stick decayed, it was thought that the warts would be gone.

"Passing through," or "pulling through," as this symbolic curing ritual is known, is little reported from the western part of the United States, and it is also rapidly becoming a thing of the past elsewhere in America. A good example that fits the usual description of this healing ritual is an item from San Diego, California. If a child gets a rupture, to heal it one has to find a young living willow, or any other young suitable tree, cut it lengthwise at the time of the full moon, and then pass the child through the willow. Tie the two parts together, and as the tree grows together, so will the rupture heal together (Hand 1968b). The Utah examples fill out the picture a bit. In Southern Utah about 1920, for example, a person suffering from blackheads was made to creep on hands and knees under a bramble bush three times with the sun (clockwise) in order to be cured. In Logan, it was claimed as recently as 1938 that a child's cough could be cured by passing him three times underneath the belly of a horse. In enquiring for old medical practices of this sort, including such additional practices as pulling people through water-worn holes in stones, through rungs of ladders, and the like, one should not fail to mention the ailments for which these passing-through rituals are most often employed, namely, rupture, fits, whooping cough, rheumatism, rickets, epilepsy, and even boils. Blackheads, mentioned above, I should regard as being exceptional.

The circumscribing of an area within which the disease must remain, or an area within which the cure will be carried out, is one of the rarities of magical medicine. For this purpose rings or other ring-shaped objects are used, or string and thread are also pressed into service. In Moab, Utah, for example, some people wear lead around their necks, tied with buckskin, to keep mumps from "going down." For this same purpose a sock was tied around the neck in Centerville, Utah, in 1920, and a plain string as late as 1955 in Morgan County of the same state (Brown 1952–64). A Utah physician had encountered in his practice the custom of tying string around an infected area to confine the malady to that spot. It was stated that this was to "keep the spirit from going deeper into the body." Los Angeles public health nurses, for example, frequently find ribbons or strings around the abdomens of pregnant Mexican women who wear them to protect the unborn child from harm and fairy influences of all kinds. Ringworm is circumscribed in New Mexico by placing a gold ring on it, drawing a circle around the ring, and then wearing the ring until the rash disappears (Brown 1952–64). In Los Angeles, for the same malady, one should spit on a golden thimble, place it on the affected spot, and turn it three times. This should be done by the light of the moon (Brown 1952–64).

Spitting as a means of divestment is seen in California and Utah cures for sideache, wherein the sufferer spits on a rock and either throws it away, or he spits under a stone, which he then replaces (Brown 1952–64). This is an aspect of burial of disease, it would seem. A more magical cure involves going to a crossroads at night and spitting to rid oneself of a sty (Thomas 1920), as reported in a Utah item a few years ago. According to the belief, the sty will be gone by morning.

I am sorry that lack of space precludes my doing more with such relatively common magical practices as getting rid of warts by burial, measurement, notching, floating away, and the like. Likewise, curing rheumatism by various kinds of absorptive measures has had short shrift, and I have said nothing at all about the supposed magnetic and galvanic cures of this dread disease. These are subjects for independent treatment (Brown 1952–64), as is also the widespread use of various kinds of amulets in folk medical practice, including the still popular buckeye and the whole nutmeg pierced and suspended on a string around the throat. Verbal magic, finally, is also widely used in folk medicine, but this subject, too, must await a later discussion.

6

Witchcraft, Sorcery, and Other Forces of Evil

All societies recognize the frailness of the human condition; wherever pain, illness, injury, and unjustness exist, so too do culturally prescribed explanations. In many parts of the world, where opportunities for formal education are limited to an elite whose numbers are small, although their economic and political power may be considerable, explanations of events and phenomena are still rooted deeply in traditional interpretations passed from generation to generation by word of mouth. In rural Africa, for example, where between 70 and 90 percent of the population is not covered by public health services (Shehu 1975: 29), mental and physical illness are often accounted for in terms of a formidable array of supernatural sources, including witchcraft, sorcery, magic, curses, spirits, or a combination of these. The point is that, whether explanations for illness are "scientific" or "mystical," all societies must have explanations for crises. Mental and physical illness cannot be permitted to go unchecked.

Devil mask from the Tyrol.

In pre-literate societies a vast number of daily crises are attributed to witchcraft, particularly in sub-Saharan Africa, where the highest level of belief in witchcraft exists today. Here witchcraft explanations are logical, indeed, some say indispensable. In short, witchcraft is an integral part of traditional African belief systems, as are sorcery and magic, and it is considered by many anthropologists to be essential to African religions.

Lucy Mair, a British social anthropologist and a leading authority on African witchcraft, points out that the belief in witchcraft is universal. Around the world, greed and sexual motifs are commonly associated with witches, as is the "nightmare" witch that prowls at night and is distinguished from the everyday witch by nocturnal habits (1969: 36–37). Women are more often labeled witches than men, and societies frequently associate particular types of personalities with individuals who they feel have the highest probability of becoming witches. According to Mair (1969: 43), many of the qualities associated with being a poor neighbor, such as unsociability, isolation, stinginess, unfriendliness, and moroseness, are the same qualities ascribed to the everyday witch. Nothing compares in terms of sheer evil, however, to the nightmare witch, whose hatred of the most basic tenets of human decency earns it a special place of infamy.

Witches, wherever they exist, are the antithesis of proper behavior. Their antisocial acts, moreover, are uncontrollable. A final commonality of witch beliefs is that their powers are innate, unlike those of the sorcerer, whose powers are learned; the witch inherits the power for evil or is given the power by God.

To the beginning student in anthropology, witchcraft surely must appear to affect a society negatively; a careful analysis of belief systems demonstrates more positive than negative functions, however. In his analysis of the functions of witchcraft among the Navaho, Clyde Kluckhohn evaluated the belief more positively than negatively in terms of economic and social control and the psychological states of a group (1967; Kluckhohn and Leighton, 1962). Beliefs in witchcraft act to level economic differences, for example. Among the Navaho, the rich are believed to have gained their wealth by secret supernatural techniques. In such cases, the only way to quell this

kind of rumor is through a variety of forms of generosity that may take the form of redistribution of wealth among relatives and friends (Kluckhohn and Leighton 1962: 247). In his later work, Kluckhohn demonstrated that witchcraft beliefs help reinforce social values. For example, the belief that uncared-for elderly will turn into witches demands that the Navaho treat the aged with proper care. The worry that the death of a close relative may cast suspicion of witchcraft on survivors, particularly siblings, also reinforces their social values regarding obligations to kin. Ironically, because leaders are thought to be witches, people were hesitant to be disobedient for fear of supernatural retribution (1967: 113).

Kluckhohn maintained that at the psychological level witchcraft was an outlet for hostility because frustrated individuals used witches, rather than relatives or neighbors, as scapegoats. Anxiety and neglect could also be accommodated through commonly held witchcraft beliefs, for people showing symptoms of witchcraft-caused illnesses, usually those neglected or of low status, would have their importance to kinsmen and the group reaffirmed at the public curing ceremonies (1967: 83–84).

The terms *witchcraft* and *sorcery* are often used interchangeably to mean any kind of evil magic; however, E. E. Evans-Pritchard's (1937) analysis of Azande witchcraft and sorcery resulted in a distinction between the two terms that is accepted by most anthropologists today. Generally speaking, a sorcerer intentionally seeks to bring about harm. Sorcerers have learned how to cast spells and use certain formulas and objects to inflict evil. The sorcerer's methods are real, not psychic like those of the witch. Sorcery is conscious and an acquired skill, whereas witchcraft is unconscious and innate. Contrary to witchcraft, sorcery is not always antisocial or illegitimate, and occurs with a higher frequency than does witchcraft.

Interestingly, some scholars believe that witchcraft does not, in truth, exist despite the strong beliefs of those in the culture. Witchcraft, they argue, exists only in the minds of the people, whereas sorcery is proven by the presence of paraphernalia, medicines, and the identification of sorcerer specialists in the community. The point is, however, that witchcraft serves so many functions it is hard to believe its importance can be whittled away by the difficulties involved in trying to prove its existence or in distinguishing it from sorcery. Everywhere there is social conflict: people become angry, get insulted, or perhaps become jealous of someone's success; it is during such uncomfortable times that witches may be found at fault and sorcerers may be called upon for help.

When someone in North American culture thinks of witches and witchcraft, the usual association is with early modern European witchcraft and the Salem trials in New England in 1692. Yet, these European-based witch beliefs, including the Salem case, were quite different from those of the pre-literate societies in which witchcraft occurs, where it functions as an everyday, socially acceptable way of managing tension, explaining the otherwise unexplainable, leveling disparities in wealth and status, and resolving social conflict. In contrast, early modern European witchcraft was a response to the strains of a time of profound change, marked by immense political and religious conflict. Although witch beliefs had been a feature of European culture since the Dark Ages, the Church managed to keep the situation under control until the turmoil of the sixteenth and seventeenth centuries, when the practice of labeling Church heretics as witches became popular and the witchhunt craze became a terrifying fact of history. Naturally, the Salem witchhunt of 1692 is of the greatest interest to Americans, but Salem's 200 arrests and 19 executions pale in comparison with the approximately 500,000 people who were executed in Europe during the fifteenth, sixteenth, and seventeenth centuries after having been convicted of witchcraft.

Ethnographic reports on witchcraft and sorcery dominate the literature, but other forces of evil are also responsible for much unjust suffering. One such power, but certainly not the only one, is the evil eye—widely known in the Middle East, parts of Europe, Central America, and Africa, areas characterized by Islamic and Judeo-Christian as well as so-called pagan religious traditions. The evil eye was believed to be a voluntary power brought about by the malicious nature of the possessor, on the one hand, or an involuntary but still dangerous, uncontrolled power, on the other. Strangers, dwarfs, old women, certain types of animals, menstruating women, and people with one eye have been often viewed as being particularly dangerous. Children and farm animals, the most precious of one's possessions, were thought most vulnerable to the evil eye, which could cause various disasters to occur immediately or in the future, particularly by asserting control over the victim. A variety of protective measures have been prescribed to ward off the evil eye. Glass evil eyes and various shaped metal amulets, for example, are sold to tourists and residents alike in modern Greece. Plants, certain avoidance actions, colors, and magical words and gestures have also at different times and places been felt to be effective against the evil eye.

In addition to the evil eye, anguish can be created by malicious ghosts, spirit possession, attacks by enemy shamans, curses of the envious, and the spells of evil magicians and other specialists who have learned how to manipulate power to harm others. Each of these causes harm and creates fear in a community and as such is an index of social strain; however, each may also function positively by allowing individuals to blame supernatural agencies rather than kinsmen and neighbors for illness or misfortunes that befall them.

In societies where no other explanations are available or satisfactory, belief in witchcraft, sorcery, and other forces of evil still accounts for the occurrence of disease, death, injustice, and other unpleasant and tragic events. In the lead article of this chapter, Jeffrey Burton Russell provides a historical approach to witchcraft, distinguishing between simple sorcery, diabolical witchcraft of late medieval and early modern Europe, and the pagan revival of the twentieth century. In the second article, Phillips Stevens, Jr., explores various social, clinical, and judicial implications of witchcraft beliefs in contemporary Western urban communities. Harry Eastwell updates previous research on "Voodoo Deaths," arguing that some Australian aborigine deaths by magic or sorcery, resembling classic cases of "Voodoo death," may be more accurately diagnosable as orthodox medical conditions. In the fourth article, I. M. Lewis investigates the cluster of imagery and metaphor surrounding cannibalism and demonstrates that accusations of cannibalism are closely linked to witchcraft accusations. Michael Buonanno discusses how the evil eye, normally associated with cultures far from the United States, effects Italian immigrants in and around Buffalo, New York. The final article, by Edward J. Moody, is about witchcraft in contemporary United States. Through his fieldwork with a group of Satanists in San Francisco, Moody shows how some people use witchcraft today to help them understand the world in which they live and to help them adjust to their personal inadequacies.

References

Cannon, Walter B.
  1942 "Vodoo Death." *American Anthropologist* 44: 169–81.

Evans-Pritchard, E. E.
  1937 *Witchcraft, Oracles and Magic Among the Azandi.* Oxford: Clarendon Press.

Kluckhohn, Clyde
  1967 *Navaho Witchcraft.* Boston: Beacon Press (first published, 1944).

Kluckhohn, Clyde, and Dorothea Leighton
  1962 *The Navaho.* Cambridge, Mass.: Harvard University Press (first published, 1946).

Mair, Lucy
  1969 *Witchcraft.* New York: McGraw–Hill.

Shehu, U.
  1975 *Health Care in Rural Areas.* AFRO Technical Papers, No. 10.

Warner, W. Lloyd
  1964 *A Black Civilization: A Study of an Australian Tribe,* rev. ed. New York: Harper Torchbooks.

Witchcraft

Jeffrey Burton Russell

In this article Jeffrey Burton Russell provides a historical review of ideas about witchcraft, pointing out that three quite different phenomena have been called witchcraft: simple sorcery, diabolical witchcraft of late medieval and early modern Europe, and the pagan revival of the twentieth century. After a discussion of sorcery throughout the world, Russell turns to European witchcraft and describes how the Christian concept of the devil transformed the idea of the sorcerer into that of the witch, giving us the concept of diabolical witchcraft. Russell examines four major elements in the historical development of European witchcraft: simple sorcery, Christian heresy, scholastic theology, and the Inquisition. He then analyzes the social and religious dynamics behind the "great witch craze" of the period from 1450 to 1700, and the article ends with a discussion of neopaganism, or modern witchcraft. Most scholars would have trouble denying Russell's conclusion that witchcraft is such a diverse subject no single approach—theological, historical, mythological, psychological, sociological, or anthropological—can completely explain the phenomenon.

"Witchcraft" by Jeffrey Burton Russell. From *The Encyclopedia of Religion*, Mircea Eliade, Editor-in-Chief. Volume 15, pages 415–423. Copyright © 1987 by Macmillan Publishing Company, a Division of Macmillan, Inc. Reprinted by permission of the publisher.

The term *witchcraft* embraces a wide variety of phenomena. The word *witch* derives from the Old English noun *wicca*, "sorcerer," and the verb *wiccian*, "to cast a spell." The original concept of witchcraft is sorcery, a web of beliefs and practices whose purpose is to manipulate nature for the benefit of the witch or the witch's client. Three quite different phenomena have been called witchcraft. The first is simple sorcery, which is found worldwide in almost every period and every culture. The second is the alleged diabolical witchcraft of late medieval and early modern Europe. The third is the pagan revival of the twentieth century. This article will distinguish sharply among these three phenomena, because the connections between them are tenuous and few.

Simple Sorcery

The simplest sorcery is the mechanical performance of one physical action in order to produce another, such as performing sexual intercourse in a sown field to assure a good harvest or thrusting pins into an image to cause an injury. However, sorcery often goes beyond the merely mechanical to invoke the aid of spirits. Thrusting pins into the image of a god is usually intended to release latent divine power rather than to cause harm, but such power may also be sought by direct appeal. For example, if a member of the Lugbara tribe of Uganda was injured, he went to the shrines of his dead ancestors and invoked their aid. The distinction between the magical invocation of a god and religious prayer to a god is not clear, but the tendency of magic is to attempt to compel, or at least assure, the god's assistance, whereas the tendency of religion is to implore or beseech his cooperation.

Simple sorcery, which can also be called low magic, is usually practiced by the uneducated and unsophisticated. It assumes a magical worldview, implicitly and preconsciously, in distinction to the sophisticated magical worldview of high magicians such as astrologers and alchemists, whose philosophy is often highly structured. High magic is quite different from low magic, or simple sorcery, and has never been called witchcraft. The magical worldview professed explicitly by the high magicians and held implicitly by many sorcerers is a belief in a coherent universe in which all the parts are interrelated and affect one another. In such a universe a relationship exists between individual human beings and stars, plants, minerals, and other natural phenomena. Both science and magic make this assumption, but where science looks for empirically demonstrable connections, magic assumes a nexus of occult, hidden connections. High magic resembles natural science; simple sorcery resembles technology. A sorcerer fertilizes his field by slitting a rooster's throat over it at midnight, a technologist by spreading steer excrement on it at dawn.

The thought processes of sorcery are intuitive rather than analytical. They often spring from an emotionally charged experience that becomes a critical incident in one's life. In a rage you curse someone who has offended you; shortly afterward the person dies; you are filled with sensations of power and guilt; henceforth you are convinced that certain powers are available to you. Empirical methodology ignores such critical events because they cannot be verified by repetition, but societies whose worldviews are not empirical regard such events as direct and convincing evidence.

The Azande of the southern Sudan distinguished three types of sorcery. One was a benevolent magic involving oracles, diviners, and amulets; it was aimed at promoting fertility and good health and at averting evil spells. This benevolent magic was an accepted means of achieving justice in Zande society. The second kind of sorcery was aimed at harming those whom one hated or resented, perhaps for no just cause. A means of distorting or unbalancing justice, it was condemned as antisocial. The third kind was peculiar to the Azande: possession of *mangu*, an internal spiritual power that a male Azande could inherit from his father and a female from her mother. Those possessing *mangu* held meetings at night at which they feasted and practiced magic; they used a special ointment to make themselves invisible; they sent out their spirits to seize and eat the souls of their victims; they had sexual relations with demons in the form of animals. They represented

essential evil and were a source of terror to the other Azande. Yet the Azande used them as helpful scapegoats; every misfortune befalling the Zande community or an individual Azande could be blamed upon the dreaded *mangu*.

Sorcery ordinarily fills certain societal functions. In some societies it merges with public religion, and a priest or priestess may perform ritual acts to make rain, ripen the harvest, procure peace, or ensure victory in war. When such acts are performed publicly and for the public good, they are as close to religion as they are to magic and are generally considered to have a positive social function. But when they are performed privately and for private purposes, they are often regarded with suspicion. The Voodoo cults of Haiti and the Macumba cults of Brazil both make formal distinctions between public religious sorcery and private sorcery; the latter is condemned. The distinction between public and private magic often becomes the most unusual distinction between "good" and "bad" magic.

Sorcery may have a variety of social functions: to relieve social tensions; to define and sustain social values; to explain or control terrifying phenomena; to give a sense of power over death; to enhance the solidarity of a community against outsiders; to provide scapegoats for community disasters; even to supply a kind of rough justice. Private sorcery has the additional functions of providing the weak, powerless, and poor with a putative way of obtaining revenge. In periods of great social tension, such as plague or defeat in war, recourse to sorcery tends to grow more common and more intense. In such situations the witches themselves may become the scapegoats for a community whose magic has failed. Under such circumstances of tension, anthropologists have observed, sorcery can often be dysfunctional, exacerbating and prolonging social tensions rather than relieving them.

Witch doctors, medicine men, or *curanderos* are sorcerers who by definition have a positive function in society, for their business is to cure victims of the effects of malevolent magic. Individuals consult witch doctors to obtain relief from disease or other misfortunes attributed to witchcraft; tribal and village authorities summon them to combat drought or other public calamities. Dances or other rituals, such as those performed by the *ndakó-gboyá* dancers of the Nupe tribe, serve to detect and repel witches and evil spirits. The *ndakó-gboyá* dancers wore tall, cylindrical disguises and identified sorcerers by nodding these weird shapes at them. Such protective sorcery assumes special social importance in times of famine, war, or other severe stress in the community.

Sorcery is less a well-defined body of beliefs and actions than a general term covering marked differences in perceptions among societies and within a given society over time. Among the Nyakyusa of Tanzania it was believed that malevolent sorcerers might be of either sex. They were often accused of eating the internal organs of their neighbors or drying up the milk of cattle. The Pondo of South Africa usually thought witches to be women whose chief crime was having sexual intercourse with malevolent spirits. One reason for the difference is that the Nyakyusa were sexually secure but nutritionally insecure and so expressed their insecurities in terms of food, whereas the Pondo were more insecure sexually and so expressed their fears in sexual terms. The function of witchcraft has changed over time among the Bakweri of Cameroon. Before the 1950s the Bakweri were threatened by poverty and a low fertility rate, and they translated these threats into widespread fear of sorcery. In the 1950s their economic status improved radically owing to a boom in the banana crop. The new prosperity occasioned first a cathartic purging of suspected sorcerers and then a decline in accusations and a relative period of calm. In the 1960s bad economic conditions returned, and fear of sorcery revived.

Patterns of sorcery exist in virtually all present societies and have existed in virtually all past societies. The classical Greco-Roman and Hebrew societies from which Western civilization sprang entertained a great variety of sorcery, from public rituals that melded with religion to the activities of the hideous hags described by the classical poet Horace. Clothed in rotting shrouds, with pale and hideous faces, bare feet, and disheveled hair, they met at night in lonely places to claw the soil with their taloned fingers and invoke the gods of the underworld. The Greeks made theoretical distinctions among three varieties of magic. The highest was *theourgia*, a kind of public liturgy "working things pertaining to the gods [*theoi*]," in which magic and religion blended. *Mageia* was the next variety; its practitioners worked technical magic

privately to help themselves or their clients. *Goēteia* was the lowest form; "howlers" of incantations and mixers of potions, its practitioners were crude, ignorant, and widely feared.

The sorcery of most cultures involved incantations supposed to summon spirits to aid the sorcerer. In many societies the connection between sorcery and the spirits was not explicitly formulated. But in both Greco-Roman and Hebrew thought the connection was defined or elaborated. The Greeks believed that all sorcerers drew upon the aid of spirits called *daimones* or *daimonia*. A Greek "demon" could be either malevolent or benevolent. It could be almost a god (*theos*), or it could be a petty spirit. In the thought of Plotinus (205–270 CE) and other Neoplatonists, the demons occupied an ontological rank between the gods and humanity. The Hebrews gradually developed the idea of the *mal'akh*, originally a manifestation of God's power, later an independent spirit sent down as a messenger by God. In Greek translations of Hebrew, *mal'akh* became *angelos*, "messenger." Christians eventually identified "angels" with the Greek "demons" and defined them as beings ontologically between God and humanity. But a different element gained influence through the apocalyptic writings of the Hellenistic period (200 BCE–150 CE): the belief in evil spirits led by Satan, lord of all evil. The idea had limited precedents in earlier Jewish thought but gained prominence in the Hellenistic period under the influence of Iranian Mazdaism, or Zoroastrianism. Under such influence the Christians came to divide the Greek *daimones* into two groups, the good angels and the evil demons. The demons were supposed to be angels who, under Satan's leadership, had turned against God and thereby become evil spirits. Sorcerers sought to compel spirits to carry out their will, but angels under God's command could not be compelled; thus it was supposed that one practicing sorcery might well be drawing upon the aid of evil demons. This was the central idea of the second main variety of witchcraft, the alleged diabolism of the late medieval and Renaissance periods in Europe.

European Witchcraft

Although simple sorcery had always existed, a new kind of diabolical witchcraft evolved in medieval and early modern Europe. The Christian concept of the devil transformed the idea of the sorcerer into that of the witch, consorter with demons and subject of Satan. Since 1880 this kind of diabolical witchcraft has been subject to four major schools of interpretation. The first, rooted in classical nineteenth-century liberalism, perceived witchcraft as an invention of superstitious and greedy ecclesiastics eager to prosecute witches in order to augment their power and wealth. The second school, that of Margaret Murray, argued that witchcraft represented the survival of the old pagan religion of pre-Christian Europe. This religion (which never existed in the coherent form she believed) she supposed to be the religion of the majority of the people down into the seventeenth century, although subject to constant persecution by the Christian authorities. Murray's theory had great influence from the 1920s through the 1950s; unsupported by any credible evidence, it is now rejected by all scholars. The third school emphasizes the social history of witchcraft, seeking to analyze the patterns of witch accusations in Europe much as anthropologists have done for other societies. The fourth school emphasizes the evolution of the idea of witchcraft from elements gradually assembled over the centuries. Most scholars currently belong to one or the other of the last two schools.

Historical Development

The first element in diabolical witchcraft was simple sorcery, which existed in Europe as it did elsewhere. It persisted through the period of the witch craze and indeed has persisted to the present. Without this fundamental element, witchcraft would not have existed. The second, related aspect was the survival of pagan religion and folklore in Christian Europe, or rather the demonstrable survival and transmutation of certain elements *from* paganism. The Canon Episcopi, a legal document of the Frankish kingdom issued about AD 900, condemns "wicked women . . . who believe that they ride out at night on beasts with Diana, the pagan goddess. . . . Such fantasies are thrust into the minds of faithless people not by God but by the Devil." The wild ride with Diana (the classical name applied to the Teutonic fertility goddess Hilda, Holda, or Bertha) was a form of the "wild hunt," a troop of spirits following a male or female Teutonic deity. Such spirits were believed to ride

out at night blowing their horns and striking down any human that had the temerity or ill fortune to encounter them.

Another element in the development of diabolical witchcraft in Europe was Christian heresy. The classical formulation of witchcraft had been established by the fifteenth century. Its chief elements were (1) pact with the Devil, (2) formal repudiation of Christ, (3) the secret nocturnal meeting, (4) the ride by night, (5) the desecration of the Eucharist and the crucifix, (6) orgy, (7) sacrificial infanticide, and (8) cannibalism. Each of these elements derived from one or another charge made against medieval heretics. Heresy became the medium through which sorcery was linked with the Devil. At the first formal trial of heretics in the Middle Ages, at Orléans in 1022, the accused were said to hold orgies underground at night, to call up evil spirits, to kill and cremate children conceived at previous orgies and use their ashes in blasphemous parody of the Eucharist, to renounce Christ and desecrate the crucifix, and to pay homage to the Devil. The history of such charges goes at least as far back as the court of Antiochus IV Epiphanes of Syria (176–165 BCE), who made similar accusations against the Jews; the pagan Romans used them against the Christians, and the early Christians used them against the gnostics. An early eleventh-century pedant must have resurrected the charges from patristic accounts of gnostic heresy and applied them to the Orléans group, applying the archetypal thinking common in the Middle Ages: a heretic is a heretic, and whatever one heretic does another must also do. Thus the *idea* of heresy, more than any actual heresy itself, became the basis for the connection of heresy with witchcraft. Some later heretical groups, such as the sect of the Free Spirit, also were accused of similar diabolical crimes. Not all heretics were so charged, however. On the whole the accusations were limited to those who had some connection with dualism, the doctrine that not one but two eternal principles existed. One evil and one good, the two principles struggled for control of the cosmos. Dualist influence on most medieval heresies was indirect, but upon Catharism it was both direct and pronounced.

Catharism was a dualist heresy imported into western Europe from the Balkans in the 1140s. Strong in southern France and northern Italy for well over a century, it dominated the culture of Languedoc and the Midi in the years around 1200; it was suppressed by the Albigensian crusade and eradicated by the Inquisition. The Cathari believed that matter, and the human body in particular, were creations of the evil god, whose intent was to hold the spirit imprisoned in the "filthy tomb of the flesh." The evil god is Satan, lord of this world, ruler of all material things and manipulator of human desires for them. Money, sex, and worldly success were the domain of the Devil. These doctrines brought the Devil closer to the center of attention than he had been since the time of the Desert Fathers a thousand years earlier. If only to refute Catharist theories, scholastic theologians had to give the devil his due. The Catharist designation of Satan as the lord of the things of this world may also have led some who desired those things in the direction of Satan worship.

Scholastic theology was the next major element in the formation of the witch concept. Tradition going back to the early church fathers had suggested that the Christian community, which formed the mystical body of Christ, was opposed by an opposite group forming the mystical body of Satan and consisting of pagans, heretics, Jews, and other unbelievers. It was not only the right but the duty of the Christian to struggle against this evil host. Saints' lives and legends of the intense struggles of the desert fathers against demonic forces kept this tradition alive, and it was reinforced by Catharist dualism. In the twelfth through fourteenth centuries the Scholastics developed the tradition of the body of Satan, refined its details, and supplied it with a rational substructure. They extended the Devil's kingdom explicitly to include sorcerers, whom they considered a variety of heretic. Simple sorcerers had become, in the dominant scholastic thought of the later Middle Ages, servants of Satan.

The link between sorcerers, heretics, and Satan was the idea of pact. The notion of pact had been popularized in the eighth century by translations of the sixth-century legend of Theophilus. In this story, Theophilus was a clergyman who sold his soul to the Devil in exchange for ecclesiastical preferment. He met the Devil through a Jewish magician and signed a formal pact with "the evil one" in order to fulfill his desires. The Scholastics derived a number of sinister ideas from the legend of Theo-

philus. Their theory transformed the person making the pact from a relatively equal contracting party to an abject slave of Satan who abjured Christ, did feudal homage to "the dark lord," and kissed his master's genitals or backside in token of his submission. The Scholastics also broadened the idea of the pact to include implicit as well as explicit consent. One did not actually have to sign a contract to be a member of Satan's army; anyone—heretic, sorcerer, Jew, Muslim—who knowingly opposed the Christian community, that is, the body of Christ, was deemed to have made an implicit pact with the Devil and to number among his servants.

The shift from Platonic to Aristotelian philosophy in the thirteenth and fourteenth centuries encouraged the process of demonizing the witches. Platonic thought allowed for the existence of a natural, morally neutral magic between divine miracle and demonic delusion; but Aristotelianism dismissed natural magic and denied the existence of occult natural forces. If no natural magic existed, it followed that wonders were worked either through divine miracle or demonic imposture. Magicians compel or exploit supernatural powers, and since God and the angels cannot be compelled or exploited, the powers with which sorcerers deal must be demonic, whether they know this explicitly or not. Thus scholastic logic dismissed simple sorcery as demonic witchcraft.

Theology, then, made a logical connection between witchcraft and heresy. Heresy is any persistently held belief counter to orthodox doctrine. One who used demons serves the Devil rather than God, and if one serves the devil, one acknowledges that correct theology involves serving the Devil rather than God: this was the worst imaginable heresy.

The final element in the transformation of sorcery into diabolical witchcraft was the Inquisition. The connection of sorcery with heresy meant that sorcery could be prosecuted with much greater severity than before. Late Roman laws against sorcery were extremely severe, but during the early Middle Ages simple sorcery, or natural magic, was treated with relative leniency. Often it was ignored; when detected, it might bring no more than a fairly stiff penance. Elements of simple sorcery were incorporated into Christian practice, as seen in the combination of Christian prayer and pagan spells commonly said by parish priests in England during the tenth and eleventh centuries. Penalties for heresy, on the other hand, were severe. Suppression of heresy in the earlier Middle Ages was inconsistent, but in 1198 Innocent III ordered the execution of those who persisted in heresy after having been convicted and excommunicated. Between 1227 and 1235 a series of decrees established the papal Inquisition. In 1233 Gregory IX accused the Waldensian heretics, who were in fact evangelical moralists, of Satan worship. In 1252 Innocent IV authorized the use of torture by the Inquisition, and Alexander IV (1254–1261) gave it jurisdiction over all cases of sorcery involving heresy. Gradually almost all sorcery came to be included under the rubric of heresy.

The Inquisition was never well organized or particularly effective; in fact, most cases of witchcraft were tried before the secular courts. Nonetheless the Inquisition provided one essential ingredient of the witch craze: the inquisitors' manuals. These manuals told inquisitors what signs of Satanism to look for, what questions to ask, and what answers to expect. Having obtained the answers they expected by using torture or the threat of torture, the inquisitors duly entered the answers in formal reports, which then added to the body of "evidence" that witches flew through the air, worshiped the Devil, or sacrificed babies. It is unlikely that no one in the period ever practiced Satanism, but it is even more unlikely that any widespread Satanism existed. The great majority of the accused were innocent, at least of diabolism.

The Witch Craze

The number of executions for witchcraft was measured in the hundreds until the end of the mid-fifteenth century, but from 1450 to 1700—the period of the Renaissance and the origins of modern science—a hundred thousand may have perished in what has been called the great witch craze. The witch craze can be explained by the dissemination, during a period of intense social unrest, of the intellectual elements summarized above by the Inquisition, the secular courts, and above all the medium of the sermon. The popularity of the sermon in the later Middle Ages and in the Reformation explains how beliefs about witches spread in a period when the leading intellectual movements, such as nominalism and humanism, downplayed or even ignored witchcraft. For example, the mystic

Johannes Tauler, who was capable of great theological sophistication, was also capable of exploiting lurid demonology in his sermons in order to impress his didactic message upon his congregations. The invention of the printing press did its part in spreading the evil. In 1484 Pope Innocent VIII issued a bull confirming papal support for inquisitorial proceedings against the witches, and this bull was included as a preface to the *Malleus maleficarum* (The Hammer of Witches), a book by two Dominican inquisitors. Published in 1486, the *Malleus* went into many editions in many languages, selling more copies in Protestant and Catholic regions combined than any other book except the Bible. The *Malleus* colorfully detailed the diabolical, orgiastic activities of the witches and helped persuade public opinion that a cosmic plot directed by Satan threatened all Christian society.

Fears of cosmic plots increased in periods of high social tension. The fifteenth and sixteenth centuries witnessed a growth of eschatological anxiety, a widespread belief that the Antichrist, the return of the Savior, and the transformation of the world were at hand. As the religious split between Catholicism and Protestantism widened during the sixteenth century and flared up into religious warfare, eschatological fears deepened. Catholics saw the Protestants as soldiers of Satan sent to destroy the Christian community; Protestants viewed the pope as the Antichrist. Terror of witchcraft and prosecution of witches grew in both Catholic and Protestant regions, reaching heights between 1560 and 1660, when religious wars were at their worst. No significant differences distinguished Catholic from Protestant views of witchcraft. The Protestants, who rejected so many of the accretions of doctrine in the Middle Ages, accepted beliefs about witches almost without modification. Luther declared that all witches should be burned as heretics in league with Satan; persecutions in the regions ruled by the Calvinists were comparable to those in Catholic and Lutheran areas. Millions were persecuted and tens of millions terrified and intimidated during one of the longest and strangest delusions in history. The craze was restricted almost exclusively to western Europe and its colonies. Since diabolism is virtually meaningless outside a Christian conceptual framework, it could not spread to non-Christian areas. Although the Eastern Christian church shared the same beliefs in the powers of

Satan as the Western church, it experienced no witch craze. The absence of the witch craze in the Eastern church illustrates the hypothesis that for a craze to break out, three elements are required: (1) the appropriate intellectual structure; (2) the mediation of that structure from the elite to the people at large; (3) marked social tension and fear.

Skeptics such as Johann Weyer (fl. 1563) and Reginald Scot (fl. 1584), who wrote against belief in witchcraft, were rare and were often rewarded for their efforts by persecution; Weyer, for example, was accused of witchcraft himself. More typical of the period were the works of the learned King James I of England and VI of Scotland (d. 1625). Personally terrified of witches, James encouraged their prosecution, wrote a book against them, encouraged the statute of 1604 against pact and devil-worship, and commissioned a translation of scripture (the Authorized Version or King James Bible) that deliberately rendered certain Hebrew words (such as *kashshaf*) as "witch" in order to produce texts such as "Thou shalt not suffer a witch to live," which supported the king's design of suppressing witchcraft legally. In 1681 Joseph Glanvill was still able to publish a popular second edition of a work supporting belief in diabolical witchcraft. But by that time the craze was beginning to fade. Cartesian and scientific thought had no room for witchcraft; ecclesiastical and civil authorities agreed that witch prosecutions had got out of hand; and European society was settling down to two centuries (1700–1900) of relative peace and prosperity. The greatest outburst in those centuries was the French Revolution; it occurred in an intellectual context (the Enlightenment) in which revival of witch beliefs was impossible. European society found other rationales by which to demonize aristocrats, Jews, communists, capitalists, imperialists, or whoever was selected as an object of hatred. The date of the last execution for witchcraft in England was 1684, in America 1692, in Scotland 1727, in France 1745, and in Germany 1775.

Witchcraft and Society

The most important social function of the belief in diabolical witchcraft was scapegoating. Sometimes this process was conscious and cynical, as when Henry VIII added witchcraft to the list of charges trumped up against Anne Boleyn. Much more often it was unconscious. If one is impotent, or one's crops fail, or one becomes ill, it helps to blame a witch, not only because it relieves one of guilt but also because the belief that a witch has caused one's problem gives one the illusion of being able to solve them. If God or fate has caused your illness, you may have no remedy; if a witch caused it, then you may recover once the witch has been found and punished.

Another function of the belief in the existence of witchcraft was to promote the cohesion of Christian communities by the postulation of a powerful external foe. Witches thus served a purpose similar to that of external enemies in modern warfare, for they united the people against a common threat.

Historians have noted correlations between witch accusations and social position. Persons between the ages of forty and sixty were most commonly accused; the accused had fewer children than normal; children were seldom accused of witchcraft but were often believed to be its victims; people accused of witchcraft had been previously accused of other crimes more frequently than normal, especially offensive language, lying, theft, and sex offenses. Chronic grumbling, abrasive personality, quarreling, and cursing also increased one's chances of being accused. The social status of accused witches was usually low or lower middle, though sometimes magistrates, merchants, and other wealthy persons were involved. Anyone connected with medicine, especially midwives, was prone to suspicion, because illness and death could so easily be blamed upon witchcraft.

The most striking social correlation is between witchcraft and women. Although in certain areas and for brief periods of time more men were accused than women, the opposite has almost always been true, and over the entire history of the witch craze women outnumbered men by at least three to one. In New England, for example, 80 percent of the accused were women. In the sixteenth century many more women were living alone than men. Given the patriarchal structure of European society at the time, a woman living alone without the support of father or husband had little influence and little legal or social redress for wrongs. Such women sometimes struck back at society with clandestine crimes such as arson or sorcery, which were difficult to detect. They also naturally tended to grumble or curse more than persons having effective influence in society. A physically weak, socially isolated, financially destitute, and legally powerless old woman could hope to deter only with her spells. But the explanation lies only partly in specific social conditions. The misogyny underlying the association of women with witchcraft sprang from deep and ancient psychological roots. C. G. Jung, Mircea Eliade, Wolfgang Lederer, and others have commented on the powerful ambivalence of the feminine in religions, mythologies, and literatures dominated by males. The male view of the archetypal feminine is tripartite: she is the sweet, pure virgin; she is the kindly mother; she is the vicious, carnal hag. From the twelfth century, Christian society developed a compelling symbol incarnating to first two types in the Blessed Virgin Mother of God. As the power of the symbol of the Virgin Mother grew, the shadow side, the hag symbol, had to find outlet for its corresponding power. In ancient polytheistic religions the dark side of the female archetype had been integrated with the light side in the images of morally ambivalent goddesses such as Artemis. Split off from the positive side of the archetype, the Christian image of the hag became totally evil. In the period of the witch craze, this one-sided image was projected upon human beings, and the witch, no longer simply a sorceress, became the incarnation of the hag. Other androcentric assumptions in male-dominated religions encouraged the connection. God, the chief power of good, was imagined in masculine terms, and so the devil, the chief power of evil, was supposed to be masculine also. Since it was believed that the Devil's followers submitted to him sexually, it was naturally supposed that they should be women, some of whom described their intercourse with the Devil in lurid detail.

The outbreak of witch trials in Salem, Massachusetts, during 1692 has been the subject of careful social analysis. Although the first hanging of a witch in New England occurred in 1647, it was at Salem in 1692, when the craze was already fading in Europe, that the colonies produced their most spectacular series of witch trials, in which nineteen persons were executed. After a group of little girls became hysterical while playing at magic, their elders suggested that they might be the victims of a spell, and the witch hunt began. At the time, Salem village was in the throes of a long dispute concerning the church. An unpopular minister, John Bayley, was succeeded by a controversial one, Samuel Parris, in 1689, just at the time when England was

undergoing a revolution and the lines of authority were blurred. The villagers split into factions supporting and opposing Parris, and, since no structured means of expressing dissent existed, its release took the form of vituperation and slander.

The outbreak was the violent expression of deeply felt moral divisions; the moral divisions were generated by the quarrel over the governance of the church, and the quarrel over governance was exacerbated by strongly felt neighborhood and family problems. Salem was a small, premodern village in which everyone knew everyone else, a situation that encouraged people to correlate unfortunate events with unpopular individuals and to blame them for their misfortunes. Intensely religious to a degree seldom paralleled in Europe at the time, the New England Puritans could not view the strife in their village in purely natural, personal, political terms. They interpreted it in religious terms, as a manifestation of the cosmic struggle between Christ and Satan, good and evil. The tradition of belief in the existence of witchcraft was a vehicle perfectly adapted to the expression of such assumptions. Many towns and villages had political controversies without becoming centers of the witch craze; clearly such controversies do not automatically produce witch accusations and cannot be considered their cause. Most sophisticated scholars give full weight to the history of religious concepts and avoid simplistic correlations between external phenomena and witch beliefs. Disasters and controversies can produce witch accusations only in the presence of certain value systems. But such social tensions, once those value systems are there, can provoke the outbreak of a witch persecution.

Modern Witchcraft

The eighteenth and nineteenth centuries in Europe, with their secularism, scientism, and progressivism, were not conducive to witch beliefs of any kind. Yet already in the nineteenth century the basis had been laid for a new permutation, which became the third main variety of witchcraft: neopaganism. Franz-Josef Mone, Jules Michelet, and other writers of the mid-nineteenth century suggested that European witchcraft was really a widespread fertility cult surviving from pre-Christian paganism. Such arguments influenced anthropologists and folklorists at the turn of the century, such as James Frazer, Jessie Weston, and Margaret

Murray. A fraudulent document entitled *Aradia: The Gospel of the Witches* was published by Charles Leland in 1899. Allegedly evidence that witchcraft was the survival of a fertility cult, *Aradia* influenced Murray and other twentieth-century anthropologists. Meanwhile, interest in the occult gained fashion among intellectuals and poets such as Algernon Blackwood and Charles Baudelaire. By the early part of the twentieth century, occultism enjoyed a certain popularity, especially among dandies and bohemians, and magicians such as Aleister Crowley, who styled himself "the Great Beast," attracted a following. Their doctrines were a mixture of high magic, low sorcery, affected Satanism, hedonism, dubious historical and philosophical arguments, and mere irony.

The occult tradition of Crowley merged with the spurious fertility-cult anthropology of the followers of Margaret Murray during the 1940s and 1950s to produce a new phenomenon. Around the time that the famous literateur Robert Graves was writing his imaginative and wholly unreliable *White Goddess* (1948) about an alleged worldwide cult of the earth and moon goddess, modern witchcraft was being created in the mind of an Englishman named Gerald Gardner. According to his followers, Gardner, who was born in 1884, was initiated into the ancient religion in 1939 by a witch of the New Forest named Old Dorothy Clutterbuck. In fact, Gardner had invented the religion on the basis of his reading of the Murrayites and Aleister Crowley, and his experiences in occult organizations such as the Hermetic Order of the Golden Dawn and Crowley's Order of the Temple of the Orient. Gardner's claim to be the mediator of an ancient religion was spurious, but he launched a growing religious movement that has gained many adherents, especially in Anglo-Saxon countries. Whatever its origins, it has become a small religious movement in its own right.

The overall world numbers of the witches must be fewer than a hundred thousand. There are numerous schismatic groups. The tenets of witchcraft as it has evolved include a reverence for nature expressed in the worship of a fertility goddess and (sometimes) a god; a restrained hedonism that advocates indulgence in sexual pleasures so long as such indulgence hurts no one; the practice of group magic aimed (usually) at healing or other positive ends; colorful rituals; and release from guilt and sexual inhibitions. It rejects diabolism and even belief in the Devil on the grounds that the existence of the Devil is a Christian, not a pagan, doctrine. It offers a sense of the feminine principle in the godhead, a principle almost entirely forgotten in the masculine symbolism of the great monotheistic religions. And its eclectic paganism promotes a sense of the variety and diversity of the godhead.

This modern neopaganism has few connections with simple sorcery, and virtually none with diabolism. Diabolism has in fact almost ceased to exist in the late twentieth century, though a few self-styled and self-conscious Satanists can be found here and there. Among other problems, Satanism suffers from a glaring contradiction: in order to worship Satan, the Satanists redefine him as good according to their own ritualistic and hedonistic views. Simple sorcery, on the other hand, continues to flourish worldwide. *Curanderos* in Mexico and the American Southwest still practice healing with herbs and charms. Fear of sorcerers persists as widely as sorcery itself. In Germany those who suspect that they are the victims of malevolent sorcery still call upon the *Hexenbanner*, professional witch doctors who sell remedies, spells, and countermagic to protect their clients from witchcraft.

Sometimes sorcery has been transmuted by conceptions taken from Christianity or other more sophisticated religions. Voodoo, for example, is a syncretistic religion pieced together from West African religions, sorcery, Christian religion, and folklore. It has become the real religion of many of the people of Haiti, including those who are nominally Catholic. Voodooists worship *lwa* ("spirits") whom the Catholics claim are demons; the Voodooists claim that the *lwa* are morally ambiguous and can be summoned for good or ill. Voodoo practices are in the shadowy area between religion and magic: it is difficult to define the Voodooists' address to their spirits as either prayer or magical incantation. Yet Voodooists themselves distinguish between religion, which is good, and sorcery, which is always evil whether worked mechanically or with the help of the *lwa*. Voodoo sorcery, a mixture of European and African elements, includes incantations, spells, the use of images, rain making, and a cult of the dead.

In syncretistic cults such as Haitian Voodoo and the Macumba cult of Brazil, it is difficult to distinguish native from Christian elements, particularly because a similarity of themes worldwide seems to precede any cultural diffusion. One of the most surprising aspects of the study of witchcraft is that African, Asian, and European witchcraft all postulate the following: witches are usually female and often elderly; they meet at night, leaving their bodies or changing their shapes; they suck the blood or devour the internal organs of their victims; they kill children, eat them, and sometimes bring their flesh to the secret assemblies. Witches ride through the air naked on broomsticks or other objects; they have familiar spirits; they dance in circles; they hold indiscriminate orgies; they seduce sleeping people. The similarities go beyond the possibility of coincidence or cultural diffusion; the most likely explanation is that such ideas have an archetypal ground in the psychic inheritance shared by all humanity.

Conclusions

Witchcraft will continue to be examined theologically, historically, mythologically, psychologically, anthropologically, and sociologically. No single approach can completely explain the phenomenon; even together they do not seem to provide full understanding of such a diverse subject. Witchcraft dwells in the shadowy land where the conscious and unconscious merge, where religion, magic, and technology touch dimly in darkness. Its forms are so varied that it cannot be said to represent any one kind of quasi-religious expression. Modern, neopagan witchcraft is a naive, genial, nature religion. Simple sorcery is usually located across the border into magic yet is frequently combined with religion in two important ways: it is often incorporated into the liturgy of public religion; its charms and spells are often amalgamated into prayers. The Anglo-Saxon clergy of the tenth and eleventh centuries, for example, christianized charms by taking over from wizards the right to say them and then introducing Christian elements into them. By incorporating the sign of the cross or an invocation of the Trinity into a pagan charm, the clergy legitimized the magic. They argued that everything that occurred resulted from God's power and will, and that the use of herbs and charms simply drew upon benevolent forces that God had appointed in nature. It was essential to use them reverently, with the understanding that they were God's and that whatever one accomplished through them was achieved only by appeal to him.

Simple sorcery could be malevolent as well as benevolent. Malevolent sorcery, practiced for private, unjust purposes, was universally condemned. But in late medieval and early modern Europe, evil sorcery merged with diabolism, the result being a different dimension in the religious meaning of witchcraft. This dimension is that of transcendent, transpersonal, or at least transconscious evil.

The sense of the witch as a manifestation of an uncontrollable, superhuman force of evil is not peculiar to Christianity. The Azande, for example, considered the witch a superhuman force of evil. The witch is often on the border between mortal and spirit; she expresses the same characteristics as the Lilitu of the Sumerians, the Lilith of the Hebrews, and the *ranggada* of Malaysia, evil spirits that roam the world at night sucking blood, killing babies, and seducing sleeping men. In many societies the witch is supposed to be a wholly evil being. In Christianity, with its belief in a supernatural power of evil, the witch became a human associate of the devil, closely associated with demons and occasionally indistinguishable from them. The witch came to be seen as a pawn of Satan, a tool used in his efforts to destroy humanity and block God's plan of salvation. Thus the witch in Christianity was a minor symbol of that transpersonal evil of which Satan was the major symbol.

Many people feel that evil exists in the world to a degree far beyond what one would expect in nature, and many are not satisfied by the tradional theodicy argument that evil arises from free will (which God creates for the greater good). We observe people performing monstrous acts of destruction and cruelty against their own self-interest as well as against that of the community; and we sense in ourselves monstrous urges transcending anything that we might consciously desire. Thus a power of evil seems to exist that exceeds our own personal limitations, ignorance, and sin. This brooding, pervasive power, whose purpose is to corrupt and destroy the cosmos, may be perceived as coming from an external being, or it may be felt to operate from within the soul. In either case it transcends the conscious, and, as Jung observed, one might as well call it the devil. The witch, melding the two archetypes of human hag and evil demon, is a powerful metaphor whose power may be diminished from time to time but is unlikely to disappear.

Some Implications of Urban Witchcraft Beliefs

Phillips Stevens, Jr.

In this selection Phillips Stevens explores various social, clinical, and judicial implications of witchcraft beliefs in contemporary urban communities. He expresses dismay at the failure of modern communities to recognize sorcery and witchcraft as social problems, and observes that it is the misunderstanding of such phenomena, rather than the actual beliefs, that proves to be disruptive to society. Students will need to look carefully at Stevens's important distinction between sorcery and witchcraft, a key element in understanding American popular sentiment toward "witchcraft." Reminding the reader that there is a common agreement among many researchers that charges of witchcraft increase with the intensity of social stress, Stevens examines the relationships between witchcraft and stress caused by urban life, especially stress experienced by recent arrivals from rural or different cultural backgrounds (the "culturally marginal"). Drawing on data from specific hexing cases in western New York and Ontario, Stevens also discusses the clinical and judicial implications of the problem.

Reprinted from *New York Folklore*, Vol. 8, nos 3–4 (Winter 1982), pp. 29–42, by permission of the New York Folklore Society and the Editor of *New York Folklore*.

Beliefs in phenomena variously termed "witchcraft" are timeless and universal, found at all stages of recorded human history and in all societies, and at all levels of society, today. They have become a popular topic in the U.S., but they are generally either dismissed as "superstition," relegated to "the occult," or wrapped up in fantasy; or they are condemned and suppressed —as they have been for centuries—by organized religion. It is, therefore, not generally appreciated that they are very real, very serious, and immediate, for a great many people; indeed, those who profess *not* to believe in witchcraft constitute a tiny minority of the world's peoples. And such skeptics are acting from individual, not cultural, convictions. This paper demonstrates and discusses some social, clinical, and judicial implications of witchcraft beliefs in urban communities today. The extent of such beliefs in well-established cultural communities is seldom recognized by social researchers, because victims of hexing have access to anti-witchcraft and curative agencies. But for recent migrants and others who are not well integrated into urban social networks, witchcraft beliefs can have unfortunate implications. General observations are illustrated by data from specific cases of hexing encountered in western New York and southern Ontario.

Sorcery and Witchcraft as Social Problems

Witchcraft beliefs persist—indeed, as we shall see, they can intensify—within contemporary urban populations, but they receive little sympathetic attention by academic, clinical, judicial, theological, or popular agencies. This is especially unfortunate when it is recognized that *sorcery and witchcraft are social problems*. They are not addressed to, nor do they invoke, any "super-natural" agency, nor do they fall within modern popular categories of the "paranormal" or "occult." There are, to be sure, within all religious traditions, mythological explanations of the origins of evil, including accounts of Faustian alliances between mortals desirous of temporal wealth and power and supernatural beings who use such people as their terrestrial agents. But such traditions themselves assert that once such powers, be they mystical (witchcraft) or magical (sorcery), are implanted in human society they are transmitted socially (or congenitally) to subsequent generations. Witchcraft and sorcery are social problems, conceived by and perpetrated within society, and it is through social agencies that relief from them is obtained.

Such beliefs are extremely widespread and deeply rooted, particularly within the American urban environment where they can develop urgent implications. But they tend to remain covert, for two principal reasons: (1) within specific cultural populations anti-witchcraft and curative mechanisms operate and are available to persons who are well integrated into such socio-cultural networks, and such mechanisms are adequate during times when the degree of social stress remains within generally tolerable limits; and (2) little sympathy for such belief systems is to be found within "mainstream" institutions, to which the traditional cultural populations are ultimately subordinate.

Paradoxically, it is often the general misunderstanding of such beliefs, rather than the beliefs themselves, which is the more divisive or disruptive to society. People in whose lives sorcery and witchcraft are real and active but who are not sufficiently integrated into a cultural system to avail themselves of effective anti-witchcraft mechanisms, and who at the same time perceive little sympathy within mainstream institutions, may be left frustrated, victimized, psychologically damaged, or perhaps even victims of "the Voodoo Death" syndrome (Cannon 1942, 1957).

And adding to the general misunderstanding and resultant callous treatment of the problem is the lack of consensus on meanings of terms applied to what may be related or totally distinct phenomena. Anthropologists are generally—though by no means universally—agreed that *sorcery* is evil magic, involving the learned use of objects or words and believed to operate according to the classic principles of sympathy elucidated in 1890 by Sir James George Frazer in *The Golden Bough*, whereas *witchcraft* is the belief in an evil extra-somatic ("psychic" or "mystical") power vested in certain individuals which operates without recourse to magic. But American popular sentiment, being largely heir to Christian attitudes developed during the Middle Ages, still subsumes under "witchcraft," sorcery, any association with Satan, and all those nefarious traffickings and dabblings condemned in Deuteronomy (18:10–12). Hence, for example, a lecture titled "Sorcery, Witchcraft, and Inter-Personal Conflict" which I was scheduled to present to a local suburban teachers' conference was cancelled at the last minute because some influential members of the school board objected to having such topics discussed among the teachers of their children. And members of Wicca and other "neo-pagan" organizations have experienced some difficulties simply because they call themselves witches, even though Margot Adler (*Drawing Down the Moon*) and a few other representatives of "The Craft" have publicly denied any recognition of Satan (or Christ), or practice of evil, and have delineated the principal tenets of their religion through various widely available media.

What is meant by "witchcraft" in this paper, unless otherwise specified, is sorcery, the most common referent of the term today. Sorcery is evil sympathetic magic, the manipulation of objects and/or the uttering of words with intent to bring about that which is symbolically communicated or enacted in the rite. Sorcery works according to Frazer's "law of sympathy:" things or actions which resemble others, either extant or expected, can have a causal relationship with those other things or actions. The "resemblance" is most commonly symbolic, and symbols are culturally assigned, often to material things or verbal utterances which have no intrinsic resemblance to that which is desired. Their meanings—often no more than the perpetrator's general malice toward the recipient of the hex—are culturally understood. The victim's own psychology, strengthened by the beliefs in the efficacy of magic held by those close to him, does the rest. He may either assign the cause of a real or perceived misfortune to the alleged hex, or he may experience genuine physical discomfort after "knowing" that he has been hexed. A "cure" is effected by reversing that psychology; i.e., convincing the victim and, of course, his supportive social network, that the magical act has been nullified, or counteracted (Prince 1982; Tivnan 1979).

This, really, is all the researcher needs to know about the way sorcery works. Theoretically, magic in primitive society operates according to a fairly sophisticated set of ideas about the way the cosmos works, constituting what might be called "primitive physics," involving the actions of natural forces and the notion that the speed, efficiency, and direction of these forces can be influenced by sympathetic human action. Increasing speed and/or efficiency of the forces along their pre-determined paths is the theoretical premise underlying good magic; slowing or stopping or alternating the direction of the forces is the basis for evil magic, or sorcery. This latter action is dangerous. Although the skilled sorcerer is presumed to be able to control the deflected forces, he can err; and no one knows what havoc might result by thus tampering with the natural order of things—and this partly accounts for the fact that sorcery is clandestine activity. The fact of the sorcerer's selfish or malicious intent, making his activities anti-social, accounts for its illegality. These underlying theoretical premises probably cannot be elucidated by most urban folk today, but understanding them as they obtain within the traditional cultures from which most urban dwellers are derived strengthens my earlier observations that sorcery is a *social* problem. If left alone, the forces of nature will operate in smooth, systematic order. The natural order is good. Social magic aims to help it along, to make it somehow better. Sorcery, conducted solely by people, invoking no supernatural intermediary, disrupts the natural order.

Witchcraft, in its historical and ethnological sense, is less common on the American urban scene, but variants of it are nevertheless strong among certain American Indian groups, and peoples of Mediterranean, Eastern European, and Latin American derivation. "Evil Eye" beliefs are among the most common of such variants. Witchcraft is the belief in an evil, extra-somatic power, often involuntary, originally of supernatural origin either evil (as the witches of medieval Europe were agents of Satan) or as a good power corrupted by the people to whom it was entrusted, as is often the case in African mythology. The power enables the bearer to change form or to project malign direction

into another body which becomes his *alter ego*, to fly, and to influence the natural order directly, without magical means. The power develops only in some people, but why them and not others is not known; therefore, under certain conditions almost anyone might be suspect. Patterns of suspicion in "normal" times, are accurately predictable by the social researcher who has a good understanding of the social system (Gluckman 1944). Such suspicions most commonly follow patterns of tension or conflict.

This elaboration has been included here because of the general misunderstanding of these phenomena among the public and among social researchers. Any researcher working for long in an urban setting is bound to encounter some variation of them, although without some preparation he may not recognize it, or its social or cultural significance. But the point of this paper is not to discuss what witchcraft is, but rather to emphasize that not only does it persist in the urban environment, but in some cases it can increase in intensity; and it can develop implications for which mainstream social institutions are unprepared, and about which there is little or no discussion in the literature.

The Stress of Urban Life

The fundamental premise upon which this paper is based is now accepted as axiomatic among investigators of witchcraft: that allegations of witchcraft increase with intensity of social stress (Seelye 1956). To this I will add some others, which I hope will be accepted, for now, without evidence of testing by scientific method. These are: (1) that life in a multicultural urban environment is stressful; (2) that the stress of urban life is great for recent arrivals from a rural background; (3) that stress is compounded when the cultural background of such immigrants differs from that of the "mainstream;" and (4) that the nature of rural-urban or trans-cultural migration causes disruption to the point of fragmentation of traditional cultural systems, intensifying to a critical point the degree of stress experienced by some. The results of such stress can most often be identified as culture shock, the symptoms of which might include regression to and embracing with neurotic fervor selected elements of belief from the culture left behind (Furnham and Bochner 1982; Oberg 1960). In such a state, a person who has ascribed his misfortune to the evil influence of others projected by means of witchcraft, and cannot obtain treatment satisfactory within his cultural framework, can suffer severe psychological damage; at worst, he can fall victim to the syndrome of "Voodoo Death" (Eastwell 1982; Lex 1974; Lester 1972; Richter 1957). My fourth premise needs some elaboration before we can go further.

Most recent immigrants to the city could be described as "culturally marginal." Only partially acculturated, they have brought with them some beliefs and values from their traditional culture, but certain needs which developed there cannot be accommodated in their new surroundings. They are neither fully of the old nor fully integrated into the new. Most find supportive networks in cultural communities (unfortunately termed "ethnic neighborhoods") established by older migrants which help their adjustment. But kinship and other social ties retained or newly established are tenuous; urban life, primarily because the only medium of exchange is money, has a way of sharply limiting and inexorably reducing traditional forms of social networks. Some newcomers are therefore unwelcome, for hard practical reasons, even though there exists a cultural community into which they might seem to assimilate easily. In most cultural communities complete cultural systems are operative, which include voluntary associations and institutions for the satisfaction of most basic cultural needs. Specifically, stress-reduction mechanisms like anti-witchcraft and curative agencies are available. For some migrants, however, access to these services is not available. To take a recent, though extreme, example: hospitals in Dade County, Florida, in 1981 and 1982 encountered a staggering number of cases of hexing among Caribbean, particularly Haitian, "boat people," some serious, for which their clinicians were woefully unprepared (*New York Times* 1981). Such recent arrivals come with the reality of witchcraft, exacerbated by economic deprivation and culture shock. One both preys upon and feeds the other. Uneducated, unemployed, separated from traditional support groups and unable to assimilate, the immigrants become victims of an intensifying vicious cycle of disorientation, fear, and helplessness.

I have been involved with several such cases. None has been nearly as severe as those recently encountered among Caribbean refugees, but the histories of most of them show remarkably similar patterns, and they will serve to illustrate the general principles I have discussed above. They also have implications for which neither the social researcher, nor mainstream clinicians nor members of the judiciary, are prepared. In the remainder of this paper I shall discuss some of these cases and their significance. Space will not permit lengthy detailing of the cases nor full analyses of their implications, which is just as well because, as will become clear, they raise problems for which the available data offer no easy resolutions. But they are problems which have previously unrecognized implications for transcultural research and understanding.

A number of persons in western New York and southern Ontario who have believed themselves victims of hexing personally contacted me for help, following my commentary on the subject of witchcraft in various television and radio interviews and newspaper articles. To deal with these cases I developed a method which I have called, without much novelty, "anthropological intervention." In some cases my method has had positive clinical implications, as conventional psychotherapy had been unsuccessful. In 1978 and 1979 I became peripherally involved with the celebrated Gail Trait murder case, because a belief in witchcraft was initially alleged to have influenced the defendant's behavior. This case revealed that beliefs in witchcraft could have complicated and potentially serious judicial implications for which most clinical and legal practitioners, and anthropologists, are unprepared.

Clinical Implications

I was aware of one general guidebook to cross-cultural counseling (Pedersen 1976) and another has recently appeared (Sue 1981), but for guidance specific to witchcraft cases one can only attempt to glean from the few and disparate case studies published in specific professional journals (Cappannari *et al.* 1975; Galvin and Ludwig 1961; Golden 1977; Johns Hopkins 1967; Leininger 1973; Lewis 1977; Michaelson 1972; Raybin 1970; Snell 1967; Tinling 1967; Warner 1977; Wintrob 1973). My method of approach involved two basic premises, both based in sound anthropology. My primary operating premise was that there exists a profound risk in attempting to interpret belief systems engendered in and structured by one cultural framework, through models of "reality" and principles of etiology developed from the perspective of another. In cases of attributions of the causes of physiological or psychological ailments to the practice of sorcery, at least since Senter's 1947 advice to the psychiatric profession (Senter 1947), it has been increasingly widely recognized that the most effective treatment is that worked within a framework that is culturally familiar to the patient, if such treatment can begin early enough—that is, before any serious and debilitating pathological syndrome has developed. I would add the strong caveat that any thought of converting the patient to an alternate mode of "reality" ought to be postponed during the treatment process, which should also include a substantial period of monitoring during recovery.

The basis for my secondary operating premise was that there are only two ways to deal effectively with the power of a hex: (1) to have it voluntarily withdrawn by the perpetrator, or (2) to nullify it, deflect it, or return it directly to its source by counter-magic. In either case, of course, the patient must be satisfied of the efficacy of the method. I was not prepared to attempt either of these two methods, and the nature of most of my cases made seeking the aid of a folk practitioner inadvisable. My clients were first attracted to me principally because they had limited or no access to, or unhappy experiences with, folk practitioners; and they respected me during therapy because I was able knowledgeably and objectively to explain the principles of magic, on the one hand in general terms in a public context, then individually and specifically. So I was able to adopt a third approach: to attempt to convince the client that the hex was ineffectual, either because it had atrophied and lost its power, or that it had been implied but never actually activated in the first place; and whatever symptoms the client was experiencing at the time of consultation with me could be effectively treated by conventional medical means including, if indicated, psychotherapy.

I have selected three cases for presentation, in summary form, here. They represent the range of efficacy of my method, from dramatically successful to discouragingly ineffective. The second case necessitated the enlistment of sympathetic psychiatric assistance. The third case was complicated

by manifestations of severe psychosis, which made anthropological intervention premature.

Mrs. B. She was a black Barbadian woman who had left Bridgetown in 1969 at the age of 17 to work as a nursemaid for a family in Ontario. After 17 months she moved to Toronto to live with a girl friend and to take a clerical job. For the next two years, and after her marriage in 1973 to a Jamaican factory worker, she experienced a great variety of unpleasant emotional and physical symptoms, specifically and increasingly centering upon problems in her genital area which made sexual activity uncomfortable for both partners. Consultations with physicians and psychiatrists gave only temporary relief, and she and her husband concluded that she had been hexed by a jilted boyfriend in Bridgetown. With the cause of her problems thus identified to her satisfaction, she clung to and elaborated upon it with consuming intensity. She recalled her farewell party when he had given her something strange-tasting to drink, and she retrieved letters from relatives which mentioned inquiries he had made about her. Strongest of all was her recollection that he had asked to keep a pair of her underpants, "so that he could still feel close to me;" she became convinced that he still kept this item and was using it to work sorcery against her. This belief explained, in classic principles of contagious sympathetic magic, all of her sexual problems. Her former lover did not want her "to make it" with any other man.

When she came to me in February 1977, Mrs. B. had sought the help of folk practitioners, by proxy, in Brooklyn, "Long Island," and "California," who had confirmed her suspicions of sorcery. She had experienced real gynecological problems, including a blocked Fallopian tube and an ovarian cyst; these further strengthened her conviction that her former boyfriend wanted not only to spoil her sex life, but to render her barren as well.

I asked for time to consult "a learned doctor at a great university" who had much experience with her sort of case. I was able subsequently to convince her that if her boyfriend had hexed her, the spells had long since weakened and died; he could not still be "working" with her underpants because his current steady girlfriend (Mrs. B. had informed me of her) would not tolerate this; he could not possibly have placed spells on her ovaries or Fallopian tubes because this sort of detailed knowledge of the internal female anatomy was beyond his understanding as a primary school leaver; and that she should trust her gynecologist. She had successful surgery, she and her husband entered marital therapy together, and in February 1978 she telephoned to announce that she was pregnant.

Mrs. H. This was an American black woman, raised in rural Alabama, who moved to Buffalo with her husband in 1952, when she was 20. She had four grown children when she and her husband separated, in 1966. Thereafter she experienced a number of work-related physiological and psychological problems, and consulted a physician who prescribed medication, but her problems recurred.

At some point during this period she read a novel which involved "voodoo" and hexing, and she began to read extensively on witchcraft in the public library. She analyzed segments of her own history, and after a time she concluded that she was being bewitched. She had suspected fellow workers in the plant where she was employed, recalling certain suspicious glances, conversations abruptly terminated when she approached, positions on the production line changed for no good reason. She had similarly suspected neighbors, relatives, members of her church. She had finally settled on her estranged husband as the evil-doer. She recalled vignettes of her past: that from their childhood her children had "acted up" during the full moon, their favorite pet had been a black cat, she had difficulty persuading them to attend Sunday school. Her husband had not been willing to support her wishes that the children receive a Christian education, and he himself had been reluctant to attend church with her. He had been "out" one or two evenings per week; he did not smell of alcohol when he returned, but he would not say where he had been. She recalled, now with suspicion, many peculiarities in his behavior, and in certain incidents following their separation she found stronger indications that he was working evil magic against her. She remembered that sometimes his support checks arrived in envelopes that were stained in ways that should not occur during routine postal handling. Sometimes after he had been to her house to fix something she noticed traces of strange dust in doorways, on stairs, and in the kitchen and bathroom. Once a lightbulb he had replaced had been smeared with "a brown sub-

stance" that gave off a noxious smoke shortly after it had been switched on.

She came to me after seeing a television show on which I had been interviewed in January 1977 (the same show Mrs. B. had seen). She was quite determined and explicit about what she wanted from me. Her husband had placed various hexes on her which were causing headaches, dizziness, and sleeplessness, so that she would inevitably have to quit whatever job she had. She wanted the hexes removed and, if possible, re-directed at him.

Mrs. H. was an intelligent and well-read woman. She was convinced that local spiritualists and "two-headed doctors" were quacks. She had a reverential respect for "scientific method," to which I was able to appeal. I pointed out that hexing was only one possible explanation for her physical problems and for the incidents she had interpreted as evidence of hexing; there were others, and these others were far more likely. Furthermore, the indications were that if evil magic was at work, and if her husband was the perpetrator, he was very inefficient at root work; from her readings she herself knew of far more effective methods which he could have used. Any spells he might have placed on her by his methods were so weak as to have been extremely short-lived. I was able to recommend her to a psychiatrist of a West African nationality whom I had apprised of our relationship and my approach, and she entered into reluctant, although eventually successful, therapy with him.

Mrs. P. A third, and the least successful of all my cases, involved a Polish woman of 60 in Lackawanna, who contacted me in November 1977 after having read a Halloween newspaper interview. She was married to a steelworker of Czechoslovak background who was bedridden from an industrial accident in the mid-1960s. Her first husband lived in Houston. Mrs. P. had constructed a confused chronology of events since her recollection of an incident in the early 1960s when her first husband reappeared one day accompanied by a strange little man who cast the Evil Eye upon her. Her second husband's accident, the death of a brother-in-law in an auto accident, and a host of other misfortunes including her own deteriorating sense of control and physical well-being, were all attributable to that incident. Her relatives abhorred discussion of

" the evil" that possessed her, and associated with her only infrequently. A "faith-healer" gave her an envelope of white powder for $300, and was untraceable thereafter. A psychiatrist whom she had contacted earlier assured me that she was severely psychotic and needed urgent therapy; my methods might be effective after she had regained some mental stability. I arranged an appointment with a Polish-speaking psychiatrist with whom I had consulted; but she refused to meet with him, and as I had informed her that I would not attempt to cure her by magical means, which was what she wanted, I had to give up her case.

Mrs. B's entry into Canada was eased by her close association with the family who had befriended her and her family in Barbados. Her problems began when she left her Canadian hosts. Most of her early symptoms were ascribable to a severe case of culture shock, which disoriented her to the point that when an explanation which had validity within her traditional cultural background was offered, she grasped and clung to it with neurotic intensity. It might be said that her beliefs in witchcraft served a positive function for her. All her energies now focused on this, and with her husband's patient support she found stability in this apparently regressive and dysfunctional belief system. Her early symptoms, many of which were very unpleasant, cleared up, and when the case came to me I had only her belief in her former boyfriend's hex to deal with.

Although she had been an urban dweller for 25 years, Mrs. H. was also isolated, probably due to problems in her own personality, from social and cultural networks in the black community. During the earlier years she maintained stability through familial relationships. Her problems developed, and intensified, following her separation from her family. She regressed to and focused upon a belief system which had been very real in the rural Alabama environment of her childhood, but her pride in her intelligence made her distrustful of traditional healers. For apparently similar personality reasons, Mrs. P. was isolated from effective culturally-supportive social networks. She found some stability in clinging to a belief which was culturally relevant to her and her husband's eastern European backgrounds, but which was substantiated in an incident which was quite clearly the product of her own neurotic fantasies. She did attempt to seek relief through what she considered to be traditional means, but she was victimized, and her psychosis intensified.

Each of these three women had sought clinical help through "mainstream" agencies and each had been dissatisfied. The traditional cultural beliefs to which they regressed held that magic could be countered by magic, and provided no preparation for the lengthy analysis required of conventional psychological therapy. Similarly, the medical position on the clinical implications of hexing is generally intolerant.

The three cases discussed above are those of persons whose cultural backgrounds differ from that of mainstream institutions and who are not well integrated into traditional networks; I have called them "marginal" and have focused my discussion upon them. It should not, however, be assumed that magical or supernatural explanations for misfortunes are unique to such persons. Two of my cases involved white middle-class persons who had become convinced that Satan was influencing their lives. Both had high school diplomas. One completed junior college, the other secretarial school. The first, a 37-year-old Roman Catholic of Italian ancestry, was unaware that his own parish priests were potentially good sources of counsel. The other, a Protestant woman, aged 28, of German descent, had been diagnosed as chronic paranoid schizophrenic. (She claimed to have received 11 such diagnoses! I was able to confirm that at least five doctors had treated her for this disease, since her early teens.) She was obliged to stop by a neighborhood clinic weekly to receive medication, but she claimed never to have been informed that her auditory hallucinations, which she identified as Satanic voices, were experiences typical of this syndrome. Clearly, these people's ascriptions of their problems to the work of the devil derives from their own cultural heritage, and such ascriptions were not made hastily, but long after symptoms developed and efforts at obtaining satisfactory treatment had been made.

Such cases receive notice when they are associated with bizarre, violent, or criminal behavior (*New Haven Register* 1981); but persons who believe themselves so afflicted are surely more numerous than is generally recognized. And, reflective of the growing acceptability of "supernatural" or "occult" explanations at all levels of society, such cases are very probably increasing. Most of them are very probably amenable to patient sympathetic treatment of the sort I utilized for my clients, in which the collection of case histories includes eliciting data on cultural beliefs, and in which the nature of those beliefs helps to structure the specific therapeutic approach taken.

Judicial Implications

The fact that this whole business could have legal implications came to me quite suddenly on July 18, 1978, when I was telephoned in Washington, D.C., by a reporter from a Buffalo newspaper. The paper's headlines the day before had suggested, "'Voodoo Curse' May be Linked to 4 Stabbings" (*Buffalo Evening News*). Mrs. Gail Trait had methodically butchered her four children with kitchen cutlery the evening of the 16th, and a police lieutenant had reported that "family members had told him Mrs. Trait thought she was under a voodoo curse." The reporter had hoped to build a story on witchcraft-related crimes, stimulated by an article in a Rochester paper on July 14, which was headlined, "'Witchcraft' Called a Reason for Fatal Firebombing. Police Say Family Believed a Spell Was Cast" (*Times-Union*). The story was not pursued and the witchcraft element was played down in the press thereafter, and Mrs. Trait was remanded for psychiatric examination.

She was incarcerated for a year, during which time she received anti-psychotic medication, and was interviewed extensively by three court-appointed psychiatrists. The reports of all three doctors show clearly that Mrs. Trait was quite obsessed with ideas of sorcery, "voodoo," "roots," and demon possession. Two reports saw her as psychotic and not responsible for her behavior at the time of the crime, and diagnosed chronic paranoid schizophrenia. Mrs. Trait was judged competent to stand trial, and her case came to court in the late summer of 1979. In August a representative of the Erie County District Attorney's office telephoned me, saying that his office feared that Mrs. Trait's defense counsel would bring up the alleged "voodoo hex," and they wanted to be prepared. "How widespread is this voodoo business?" and "Is there anything to it?" were among his questions. But Mrs. Trait's trial progressed with no

mention of witchcraft, and in spite of the pre-trial psychiatric testimony, it concluded in the Spring of 1980 with a finding of guilty of eight counts of murder.

The Trait case raises some very disturbing questions, for which neither the psychiatric nor, certainly, the legal professions are prepared. Since Seventeenth-century New England courts denied the admissibility of "spectral evidence," there have been few precedents for defense of criminal acts based on beliefs in the supernatural. I have found no reported modern cases in this country in which beliefs in witchcraft formed the basis for a defense (Lewis 1958; Williams 1949, 1961). In retrospect, it is just as well that such a defense was not pursued in the Trait case. Mrs. Trait's ultimate fate, specifically the nature of her institutionalization, would probably not have been different; but a complicated anthropological and legal dilemma would certainly have developed.

Many of my clients were culturally marginal people. All had been at least partially acculturated, and had fallen back on explanations recovered from their cultural heritage after sporadic efforts at achieving relief through other means had failed. But after having focused on their cultural explanations, such persons receive little sympathy from either acculturated *or* traditional friends; relatives may not want to get involved, probably for reasons, unspoken, of fear of contagion; and doctors use Western methods and tend to dismiss such beliefs as superstitions, infantile regressions, or paranoid fantasies. Such people may become desperate in their obsession, and become vulnerable to fraudulent—and expensive—promises of magical cures, as in the case of Mrs. P. Or they may resort to criminal acts. Gail Trait was possessed by evil, she told her psychiatrists, and she despatched her children to God to save them from similar possession.

It is such people that the practitioner of "anthropological intervention" is best able to help, although, as my data show, he may be of some help to people who are well integrated in a cultural system. But in attempting to provide such help, certain unforeseen problems may develop, problems with complicated and far-reaching implications. The clinical implications are becoming more widely recognized. Judicial implications, however, are potentially so complicated as to require careful thought and detailed examination of resources which are not available at the time of this writing. But given contemporary urban social problems, and the directions of popular sentiment, it seems to me that mainstream practitioners *and* social researchers must be far more amenable to the recognition of the nature and strength of cultural beliefs and of their validity within the cultural traditions which generate them.

Voodoo Death and the Mechanism for Dispatch of the Dying in East Arnhem, Australia

Harry D. Eastwell

Among the Murngin of Australia, if a person commits a particularly heinous act—incest, for example—a possible response may be punishment by sorcery. The perpetrator may have a supernatural curse leveled at him and as a result shortly sicken or die. Cases of illness or death caused by witchcraft or sorcery are common in the ethnographic literature, with many documented accounts coming from aboriginal Australia. Several terms have been applied to this phenomenon—"psychosomatic," "magical," "psychogenic"—but "voodoo death" appears to be the most popular usage. In a classic article, Walter Cannon (1942) reasoned in physiological terms that a victim of sorcery may experience fear to the extent that he or she will die from the prolonged shock. W. Lloyd Warner (1964) believed a person who fell victim to a sorcerer's witchcraft could become ill or die because the community withdrew its support from the already "half-dead" person. Although Cannon's and Warner's theories on the subject have prevailed over the years, Harry D. Eastwell, a senior lecturer in psychiatry at the University of Queensland, Australia, provides in this article a much-needed update. Professor Eastwell does not deny the role of sorcery in "voodoo deaths"; rather, he takes issue with explanations that place the mechanism of the illness or death on "psycho-physiological reactions." It is Eastwell's belief that sorcery-induced phenomena such as those described in this article are more accurately diagnosable as orthodox medical conditions—specifically, dehydration by confiscation of fluids. With this explanation, Eastwell believes much of the mystique of voodoo death will fade.

Reproduced by permission of the American Anthropological Association from the *American Anthropologist*, Vol. 84, no. 1 (March 1982), pp. 5–17.

PIONEER ARNHEM ANTHROPOLOGIST W. LLOYD Warner, working with the "Murngin" people in and around Milingimbi Mission in 1926–29, thought that social practices involving direct suggestion caused certain deaths. In *A Black Civilization* he describes this sequence:

> The attitude is taken that the man is "half-dead" and will shortly die. The effect on a suggestible individual . . . is sufficient to set up certain psychophysiological reactions which tend to destroy him. Pressure is then applied through the mortuary rites which perform the function of attempting to remove him from the society of the living to that of the dead, further destroying his desire to live and frequently bringing about his ultimate death. [1958: 9]

Together with other sections of Warner's account, this statement is regarded by Landy (1975) as a most useful description of the involvement of the social system in voodoo death which it helps define. Another early Arnhem anthropologist, Donald Thompson, also believed that suggestion could kill. He records: " . . . to the individual the prediction of death is sufficient ultimately to bring it to pass" (1939: 20).

The term "voodoo death" is time-hallowed, although Yap (1974) prefers "thanatomania," but also uses "psychosomatic" or "magical," and Lex (1974) uses "death by suggestion" but considers "psychocultural" as more appropriate. "Psychogenic" is also used, as by Lewis (1977). By implying a nonphysical cause, all these terms beg the question as to the mode of death, which characteristically occurs among native peoples after putative sorcery, from taboo violation, or while anticipating avengers. Barber (1961) notes the scarcity of satisfactorily documented case material, and Lewis comments that "it would require very special circumstances to be able to provide such information" (1977: 136). He concludes that most reports are anecdotal, not having been observed first-hand. Thus it has always been difficult to study actual cases scientifically, and this problem may become more acute in the future. Because medical services are now within call, to observe in Australia today is to intervene.

It is the nature of Warner's "psycho-physiological reaction," the mechanism of death, which is under debate. The classic contribution is by physiologist W. B. Cannon (1942), who uses Warner's descriptions. Cannon's conclusions are summarized by ethnopsychiatrist P. M. Yap, who defines voodoo death as "progressive psychophysiological disorganization with surgical shock from terror in catastrophic situations" (1974: 95), thus dispelling any ambiguity lingering around the term. Yap here follows Cannon in implicating dysfunction of the autonomic nervous system, translating this concept as "surgical shock," which is a well-known clinical entity associated with many conditions other than surgery, and which is often terminal. The autonomic nervous system adjusts the body to emotional stimuli, of which hearing the prediction of one's own imminent demise is an extreme example. Other forceful proponents of an autonomic cause are Richter (1957) and Lex (1974). Lewis stresses the inconclusive aspect of this work of Cannon, Richter, and Lex: "[this] area of the subject is uncertain, holding a morbid fascination to find if it is true or not" (1977: 111).

Alternatively, the psychology of voodoo death is stressed by other authors, without specifying precisely the bodily mode of death. Thus Engel (1971) coined the term "giving up—given up complex" for the mental state involved. Lester (1972) describes it as hopelessness or helplessness, reinforced by social process. Another school of thought rejects the whole concept of psychogenic death. Barber (1961) favors physical illness or poison, but admits the possibility of terminal dehydration. Clune (1973), in a short comment unsupported by cases, also believes that poisoning is the mechanism, but this is criticized by Yap (1977), who regards it unlikely to be used by relatively unsophisticated peoples. Medical anthropologist G. Lewis is also skeptical:

"Is it really the case that healthy people have died in a day, or three days, because they know they were victims of sorcery? Who has seen this happen with his own eyes? Is there no explanation for it but sorcery?" (1977: 111). In the face of discord and questioning, Yap (1977) appeals for concrete findings from ethnologists and medical field-workers that can be appraised critically.

Deaths in Times of Transition

Local Whites refer to this region with no roads to the outside world as "a backwater within a backwater," but White imperialism is nevertheless pervasive. In the northeast there is a small mining community, Nhulunbuy, where the hotel acts as a magnet for Aboriginal men on drinking sprees. The administration of the area is from the state capital, Darwin (population 50,000), 650 km. west of Nhulunbuy. Here the White coroner records and scrutinizes the details of each death. The Aboriginal population centers around five ex-mission settlements and one government settlement, each with 500 to 1,000 people. More traditional life styles are preserved in the 30 or so small outstations in the bush (populations from about 30 to 70). These are on clan territory and are an Aboriginal reaction to White encroachments. The total Aboriginal population is approximately 6,000.

Materially, White technology drastically changes death practices. Bush vehicles and aircraft now transport corpses and are then ritually decontaminated. At one settlement there are two mobile freezers, one for each moiety, so the corpse can be preserved in the deceased's house while distant relatives forgather (Reid 1979), some of them hiring aircraft for the journey. Above all, the behavior of relatives and health caretakers around the dying person is an amalgam of custom and intruding modern medical interventions, the latter increasingly carried out by trained Aboriginal health workers. White nurse practitioners organize small clinics at centers of over 200 people, and the Flying Doctor makes routine visits. The missionary pastor commonly sits on the sand with the dying patients. The juxtaposition of cultures makes the events under discussion more outstandingly incongruous and more difficult to describe with the minimum of bias.

Method

Since 1969 I have collected data during visits that were primarily for the purpose of conducting psychiatric clinics among the people. During the years 1970–76, I spent six weeks in the field; in other years I made two visits of two weeks each. The data were compiled from patients' medical records kept at the bush hospitals and outstation clinics, and from 15 Aboriginal health workers; 12 females and 3 males who were mostly in their 30s. All came from different clans: they were selected widely to gain community acceptance for their unsupervised work at night and weekends when, among other tasks, they attend the dying. They were not particularly acculturated, and most were not Christians. I have known many of them for a couple of years, some for a decade. All found these topics about death highly distasteful. All female informants were questioned in groups of two or three. Five spoke of the deaths of close relatives in the recent past. All responses were in Aboriginal English, and where relevant, these are recorded verbatim. Older male informants were deliberately not sought out for two reasons: they found the topics even more disagreeable, regarding the discussion as personally ominous, and the language problem was greater.

The Sorcery Syndrome: A Forerunner of Voodoo Death?

The third most common "psychiatric" syndrome in East Arnhem is a gross fear state. Fear of death from sorcery is the dominant symptom, with intense agitation and restlessness, gross sleeplessness and increased vigilance at night, terror, sweating, and other physiological accompaniments of fear. Many patients attempt to arm themselves with guns, knives, or spears, or to flee to the protection of Whites. Illusory misperceptions are common, such as hearing malefactors prowling outside their huts. The syndrome is similar whether or not sorcery has actually been performed; it is the belief of the patient and the patient's kin that establishes the diagnosis. It is treated pragmatically using tranquilizing drugs, with or without referral to traditional healers. Commonly, the syndrome exists for some weeks before diagnosis and treatment; because sorcery is suspected, it is not immediately referred for Western treatment. The syndrome understandably refuses to fit readily into Western classificatory molds. I treated 39 such East Arnhem patients between 1969 and 1980; all but 1 were men. The syndrome is a reaction to specific life events that conform to the ethnographic situations preceding classical voodoo death, as listed in Table I. Most commonly, the evidence for sorcery is the sudden death of a clan relative, where all clan members regard themselves endangered by sorcery; when one patient recovers, another clan member may show the same symptoms. Three patients showed the overwhelming extent of their fear by an unusual autonomic reaction—marked protrusion of the eyeballs with widely dilated pupils. All these patients can be considered prime risks for voodoo death because of the ethnographic precipitants and because of the extreme autonomic reaction (Table I).

Only two patients died; their cases will be considered individually. The first died three months after the onset of his symptoms. He was 27 years old in 1973, and his father was accused of a mistake in a ceremony. His family moved to Numbulwar to minimize the sorcery risk. The son feared retribution, becoming so tremulous that he could not place tranquilizing tablets in his mouth and his pupils were widely dilated from autonomic activity. He died in the company of his parents, an Aboriginal health worker, and his tribal practitioner, in a panic attack with froth issuing from his mouth, similar to the description of one of Cannon's cases. A chest radiograph one month before death was normal. Arguments for the reality of voodoo death are not advanced in this case, because the patient suffered from a syndrome of psychosexual infantilism with a hormonal basis, with sex characteristics very poorly developed. This may have predisposed him to sudden death under stress, possibly because of abnormality of the adrenal glands, which mediate responses to stress as well as male sexual characteristics.

The second fatality was a 20-year-old Numbulwar man, newly married to an attractive girl. Within months of his marriage in 1979 he began losing weight and became impotent. He was dismayed when his wife began consorting with a rival who had been interested in her in the past but who had not negotiated successfully for her. The patient was more dismayed when his parents, seeking to

Table 1   EVIDENCE OF SORCERY

Life Event Precipitating Fear-of-Sorcery Syndrome	Number of Patients
Sudden death of close clan relative	8
Serious illness of close clan relative	5
Disputes over acquisition of second or third wives	5
Promiscuity with married women	5
Life-threatening accident to patient (motor vehicle, electric shock, lightning strike)	3
Dispute with wife's lover	2
Promiscuity by sons	1
Murder of opponent in interclan spear fight	1
Unwitting desecration of ceremony ground	1
Ceremonial "mistakes" by father	1
Severe physical illness	1
Tribal healers accused of causing deaths	2
Unknown (precipitants not investigated)	4
	39

explain his obvious physical decline, asserted that his rival was ensorcelling his beer. When referred for treatment, he was a well-developed case of the syndrome described above, convinced that nothing could save him. At this time, medical tests at the settlement clinic suggested an alternative explanation for his physical decline: kidney function was failing. He was transported by Flying Doctor aircraft to Darwin for treatment in a fully equipped hospital, where the diagnosis was chronic nephritis and treatment involved correcting the imbalance of chemicals in his body by intravenous therapy, with tubes inserted into veins, mouth, and bladder. In his frightened state he misinterpreted these tubes into and out of his body, fearing that his vital essence was draining away through them, a recurrent Aboriginal fear in this situation. He escaped from the hospital, borrowed air fare, and returned home to the care of his parents who were already making plans to avenge his death. Here his kidney failure was complicated by heart failure, and he died one month after the initial diagnosis. (The young wife remarried the rival after the unseemly lapse of only four months. Thereupon the patient's

uncles, who lived on a large island off the coast, hired an aircraft to mount a revenge expedition to Numbulwar. The new husband was wounded but escaped with his life, and the uncles retired with honor, reboarded their aircraft, and headed back home.)

In these 39 syndrome cases both patient and relatives expected death, but when it did occur it was explainable by orthodox Western medicine. These data cannot be used to argue that terror can never cause death, but its rarity here poses significant questions. It implies we may have adopted the native belief system too readily and unquestioningly that in accepting sorcery as a sufficient cause. Fear states such as this Arnhem example are widely distributed among native peoples. The Latin American variant, *susto*, meaning "fright," is mentioned by Rubel (1964) as not being associated with dramatic death. Despite Lewis's familiarity with sorcery cases during his two years in New Guinea, he also found the absence of dramatic deaths noteworthy: "I did not witness illnesses or deaths more devastating and intrinsically mysterious than illnesses and deaths I had seen in English hospitals" (1977: 112). As Western medical services extend into regions where voodoo deaths were reported, so the possibility diminishes of detecting a death in which psychosocial factors operate to the exclusion of physical causes. The two cases already described would serve as good models of voodoo death if the physical substratum remained undisclosed. From his study of historical and ethnographic sources, Ellenberger (1965) elaborates the concept of psychogenic death into rapid and slow varieties. The above cases conform to his rapid variety and to his Australo-Melanesian type which is characterized by paralyzing fear. This is contrasted with his Polynesian type, in which the emotion of shame is predominant.

Voodoo Death Averted

To establish the cause of voodoo death in bodily terms, a series of victims should be examined just prior to death. Cannon recommends a set of simple but valuable observations to test the validity of his theory, for example: "The pulse towards the end would be rapid and thready. The skin would be cool and moist" (1942: 180). That such observations are not available attests to the difficulty of examining even isolated cases. In practical terms of fieldwork, once the sequence is set in motion, the major difficulty in making observations is lack of preexisting rapport with the relatives who must tolerate the intrusion and potential intervention of the observer. The voodoo death sequence of Warner where "all the members of the society act in a manner exactly opposite to the ordinary" (1958: 9) was interrupted in the following two cases.

G., an unmarried mother aged 24, lived in a tribally oriented outstation 30 km. from Milingimbi. She refused marriage to a tribal elder and his third wife, and there was speculation, even expectation, that he would retaliate with sorcery because he had paid the bride price, which could not now be repaid. In 1974, her mother, an attractive widow, decided to remarry, threatening to end G.'s notably dependent relationship with her. G. was supported by her mother's welfare payments, which would cease when she remarried. G. responded to these twin threats of losing mother and losing financial support with a series of dramatic hysterical trances, treated first by a tribal practitioner. These trances

were misinterpreted by her relatives as evidence of sorcery from her spurned husband. After one trance, they responded by commencing the ancestral songs, withdrawing from her, and restricting her water. This was an effort to salvage her soul, which would then be available to animate later generations of her clan, as Warner describes. Hearing of these events, the White nurse at Milingimbi demanded that G. be brought to her clinic. After two days G. was carried in, close to death from dehydration, with a fungal growth in her mouth from the drying up of salivary flow. At that time she was anuric (experiencing kidney failure from severe dehydration), a state akin to Yap's "surgical shock." She was beyond help in the bush and was flown to the Darwin Hospital, 450 km. away, against the wishes of relatives who acted as if she were dead already and so should remain near clan territory. In the hospital she was still anuric, clear evidence of dehydration, despite intravenous fluids given in the bush. After lengthy resuscitation in hospital, hysterical blindness remained, easily interpreted as reaction to her recent victim status. I examined the patient in the hospital and took her full history later from her mother at Milingimbi. Her sight recovered in four months and she is presently quite well. It is clear that had this patient died, the mode of death would have been dehydration.

M. of Yirrkala was 35 years old in 1972 when he suffered a radiographically demonstrated artery occlusion to the brain (the basis of a severe stroke). This occurred while he was dancing in a ceremony, clear evidence of sorcery. A year later I found him lying in the sun, socially isolated, with chanting relatives withdrawn to the shade of a nearby hut. Against the wishes of relatives, but at his own request, he was removed by air to Darwin Hospital 650 km. away. He drank copiously before boarding the plane. In the hospital I treated him with major tranquilizing drugs. After a good recovery he chose not to return to Yirrkala for one year for fear of further "singing" (his own word). For him this was a year of lonely existence in Darwin, so he relented and returned to his clan. He died at his clan outstation one month later but the circumstances are unknown. The precipitant of the previous mortification is known in this case: his stroke induced disinhibited behavior in which he made sexual advances to his caretaker, a classificatory mother.

The death of M. of Milingimbi (born 1929, died 1955) is recounted here, not because of relevance to the dehydration hypothesis, but because it provides additional information about the relatives' reactions, necessary for the presentation of a more complete model of the voodoo death sequence. The information comes from her medical file and from the White nurse who was in attendance. Three weeks before death, relatives began chanting her clan songs, wailing in grief, and withdrawing from her, saying that she was "dead," the sequence described by Warner. She attended the clinic daily in an agitated state, spending most of her time in the company of White nurses, a most un-Aboriginal behavior, which is otherwise observed only in the fear state described above. She was not immediately diagnosed as pregnant but she went into labor and delivered a small, stillborn baby of perhaps 24 weeks gestation. She remained in postpartum care because of grossly disturbed behavior unrelated to any signs of fever, in which she screamed repeatedly and attacked White staff. Then three days postpartum, a fever of 39°C was recorded and she died with copious frothing of saliva and mucus. Her relatives then arranged burial within hours, while her body was still warm, with no chanting or rites. Her brother asked the White linguist to write to absent relatives giving the time of death as three weeks previously, the time when the chanting and wailing was heard. From the Aboriginal viewpoint, the cause of death was sorcery by a cowife, using the patient's urine patch. From the Western viewpoint, the sudden rise of temperature preceding death is typical of a well-known complication of childbirth, abnormal blood clots in the lung, which occurs with greatest frequency two to four days postpartum, as here, and with a temperature of the order recorded. This does not imply that psychosomatic factors were completely absent. The case is included as "voodoo death averted" because her death in the manner described probably preempted the usual voodoo death sequence with terminal dehydration had she returned to her relatives.

A model for mortification in voodoo death can now be presented. The relatives and victim conclude that sorcery-induced death is inevitable. The relatives withdraw, wailing in grief, and the songs begin. The victim is socially dead and fluid is withheld. After death there is no wailing and burial

takes place promptly, for fear of the victim's trickster spirit, the *mokwuy*.

The Psychosocial Sequence for the Dispatch of the Dying

The predeath events surrounding certain old, enfeebled patients are described in this section. The majority of the patients have diagnosable medical conditions that sooner or later will cause death. All are regarded by relatives as loosely integrating body and soul. It is the concern for timely salvage of the soul that precipitates the sequence. Because of the difficulty of recording a series of voodoo deaths, it is proposed to argue by analogy, with the inference that if the mode of expediting bodily dying can be established in these cases, then it is likely that the same holds for voodoo death. The conclusion is that dehydration from confiscation of fluids is the common factor and the ultimate cause of death. The components of the sequence follow.

Beginning the Funeral Rites

Health-worker informants are adamant that chanting is requested by the dying person. H., a Rembarrnga woman, says: "Sick person asks his sons to start that singing." This is not always so, as Warner implies, because in the two cases cited previously where voodoo death was averted, and in the one following, the victims were not expecting the songs to begin and it was against their wishes, but they were powerless to prevent the sequence from continuing. These cases conform closely to the situation that Warner and Cannon discuss. Some local Whites mistakenly believe that the rites themselves are meant to hasten death, as mentioned by Reid (1979). That the rites alone are not a major factor is shown by the large number of patients who recover after the chants are begun, as Reid also notes. These recovering patients sometimes dismiss their mourners with some vexation, a comment on the power ascribed to the sequence, of which the songs are harbingers.

J. (born 1925, died 1976) was a man from the Arnhem bush. He underwent lengthy hospital stays in Darwin for leprosy, which became complicated by failure of major organs. When nothing more could be done, hospital authorities discharged him on November 29 to his clan outstation where it was expected he would live for a few weeks or months. He himself anticipated renewing associations with brothers, sons, ex-wives, and seeing for the last time places in the bush of significance to him (so stated to hospital staff). Relatives hired a small plane to take him to the nearest airstrip, Ramangining. He alighted unassisted from the plane to confront a situation he was totally unprepared for. As witnessed by resident anthropologist J. P. Reser, his clansmen were chanting his ancestral songs, and they remained at a distance from the plane. This is an example of Warner's "looking at the man as one already dead" (1958: 241). J. was conveyed back by truck to his outstation, where he died within three days, on December 2.

The Acquiescence of the Dying

"The victim on his part reciprocates this feeling" (that his proper position is in the world of the dead) (Warner 1958: 242). Once the mortification gains momentum, when the body is regarded as weakly animated by the spirit of a guiding forefather, the patient develops a fatalistic acceptance of death. Health worker H. comments that her grandmother said emphatically in the vernacular, "This is time for me to die." Many patients are still capable of walking for nourishment if they so desired, but medical aid is rejected from this point on, and death occurs within days. Engel's complex of "giving up—given up" applies to this psychological state rather better than Lester's "hopelessness or helplessness." The ideology of clanship in Arnhem includes the concept of recycling the individual soul through future generations of the clan. This implies a quality of timelessness to individual life which aids the acceptance of death. Terminal patients often show great relief once the rites have begun, as White nurses comment.

The components of this psychosocial sequence are summed up by the senior nurse discussing a death at Yirrkala in 1972, of a woman I examined.

Maku was an old widow, probably in her late 50s. After a vertebra collapsed (probably from tuberculosis) she was hospitalized for bedrest. We did not think she would die. One morning an old man appeared and said he dreamt she was going to die. He brought singers and dancers who began outside but she was left alone in the room. From that time she was not given water

and we were asked not to help her. The health workers did what the old man ordered. Her tongue was misshapen from thirst and she died the next day. There was running water in the hospital room but she made no attempt to reach it, although she could have if she tried.

This sequence was encountered again in a death at Galiwinku in 1978. G. was born in the bush around 1930 and became the second of four wives, with five grown children. When infection supervened on her chronic lung disease she became bedridden but was not considered moribund. She was moved on her blanket into the open where she remained day and night, until her death three days later. To the local missionary she said: "This is time for me to die." Relatives requested the White nurse to discontinue antibiotic injections. Twenty people were sitting in the shade 5 m. away. While she was still alert, one of her sons delivered a large bolt of red cloth in which her body was to be wrapped. This was ceremoniously placed beside her on the blanket. At this time the songs were begun and all fluid was withdrawn for her last two days. The cause of her death was listed as dehydration, not chest infection.

These three cases show an element of isolation by the relatives which brings them closely into line with the voodoo death sequence. This factor with its negation of lifelong social bonds must suggest strongly to the dying person the role he or she is expected to play.

The Death Mechanism: Dehydration by Confiscation of Fluids

With the establishment of this mechanism, much of the mystique of voodoo death will fade, at least for Arnhem. In this permaheat region which is 12° south latitude, where day temperatures below 27°C occur only once or twice a year, deaths were observed to take place 24 to 36 hours after total restriction of fluids. The deaths range from a desirable euthanasia where the sequence prevents prolonged dying, to an occasional avoidable death. In this circumstance the term "senilicide" is appropriate, signifying active intervention by the relatives in the confiscation of fluids. Jones and Horne (1972) believe that dehydration is the cause of similar deaths in the Australian Western Desert, but their case material, gathered from White nurses, is not given in detail. Two Melanesian voodoo deaths from dehydration are recorded in the literature (Barber 1961: Simon et al. 1961). Cannon quotes his medical correspondent W. E. Roth of Queensland, Australia, who says of the victim: " . . . he will actually lie down to die . . . even at the expense of refusing food and succour within his reach" (1942: 172). Other commentators record the refusal of food without specifically mentioning fluid: Gelfand's reliable African account is an example (1957: 539), as is Elkin's Arnhem case of 1956 (1977: 153). Cannon himself mentions of the victim: "In his terror he refuses both food and drink, a fact which many observers have noted . . ." (1942: 176), and he quotes a Spanish Civil War death from "malignant anxiety" in which: "The lack of food appears to have attended lack of water for the urine was concentrated . . ." (1942: 180).

In Arnhem, the health workers are explicit that fluid is actually confiscated. Health worker H. states, "We take that water away from him—no need for water or food. We just don't give food or water." P., a Burada clanswoman living in Galiwinku: "The relatives say no more water." Male health worker D. of the Warramirri at Galiwinku: "If real close up finish, take water away so spirit goes." M., a Djapu woman at Yirrkala: "We take the water and food from the sick one." They reveal that it is a common practice which can be discussed openly.

Deaths at Two Settlements

Recent deaths at the compact settlement of Millingimbi, population 700, are well documented for two reasons. First, the nurse practitioner has been resident for nearly 30 years; she knows all the aged, and personally ministers to them at their deaths. Second, because Aboriginal houses have no refrigeration to store milk drinks, a system of distributing them to the dying has been arranged. When a container is used, it is returned to the clinic where it is refilled and sent back to the patient again. Thus the regularity of refilling gives some check on probable fluid intake. Between 1978 and mid-1980 there were eight deaths of patients over the age of 50, with terminal dehydration observed in seven, and brief case descriptions of these follow.

L., female, was born about 1915 and led a healthy life until an episode of heart failure devel-

oped, which would normally respond to therapy allowing a prolongation of life. The Flying Doctor was hopeful of recovery but finally annotated her medical file: "I cannot be held responsible if relatives refuse to give my patient food or fluid." The last note in her file reads: "Not eating or drinking. Deceased."

D., female, was born about 1926. She suffered from the common obstructive airways disease, not necessarily fatal. Toward the end of her life she lived in the household of her son, a traditional healer. She was befriended by White staff members for many years. One of them, a graduate teacher, had this to say of her last illness: "Her relatives became upset when I gave fluids and her son threatened to knock me down. Later she herself became negativistic and refused water. She died of thirst." White concern had been increased by the patient's role in caring for an eight-year-old waif not directly related to her.

M., male, was born about 1922. He was a traditional painter on bark, which brought him an adequate income. Eventually he developed severe heart failure, which required hospital treatment away from his home, but which he refused. The senior nurse commented: "He would have died anyhow, but he was not given water for his last 24 hours." This was the most prompt death in the series, and one which was unquestionably a desirable euthanasia.

D., male, born about 1892, showed great tenacity for life, recovering from repeated chest infections. He was a sought-after informant as one of the last men to remember the annual visits of Indonesian traders to this coast. Warner mentions him by name. He was mentally alert up to his final year when senility supervened. The senior nurse commented on his mode of death: "His mouth was so dry, and the milk container left unused in the same room."

M., male, born about 1917, suffered from lung cancer. He died within days of receiving news of the death of his favorite son. The file reads: "Sept. 12: Told about son's death, deteriorating. Sept. 13: Fluid intake—minimal oral. Has not passed urine. Sept. 14: Died." The psychological aspect of "giving up—given up" was particularly prominent.

D., female, born about 1911, is mentioned in Warner as the femme fatale of the day. She later became a respected traditional healer. She suffered from obstructive airways disease but her last days were marked by temporary recovery when fluids were given by nurses. The file reads: "Aug. 28. More alert. Taking drinks when offered. Aug. 30. Flying Doctor orders intravenous fluids. 2 litres given. Sept 2. Refused fluids. Sept. 7. Died." Initially ambivalent about the prospect of death, she later became resigned and succumbed when additional relatives gathered.

D., male, born around 1900. Warner mentions him as embarking on a political career in which he acquired eight wives. Five of these were sitting at a respectful distance from him in his dying days. His physical disease was prostate cancer. "May 16: No fever. Given only very small amounts of fluid. May 18: Very little water. May 20: No fever. Died." The aspect of euthanasia with the prevention of suffering was paramount in his case. Three hundred people attended his funeral, with burial five days after death.

The Darwin coroner's conclusions are quoted for the following two deaths in 1978 at the remote Lake Evella settlement of 300 people. The first was D., male, born about 1915, who was in unskilled employment until his final illness, which was a potentially treatable heart ailment. The coroner recorded this finding: "He continued to refuse food and would drink only sips of water. He deteriorated rapidly and deceased." The second was M., female, born about 1920. She was reported to the nurse as suffering from diarrhea, but no evidence for this could be found. The coroner concluded: "While her condition improved she became reluctant to eat and drink and refused further medical treatment. Her condition stabilized but due to her refusal to eat or drink she gradually wasted away, deceasing June 19th." The coroner's findings were more detailed than usual for tribal deaths for the following reason. The only White nurse at this outpost became alarmed when he observed the confiscation of fluids from patients whom he judged capable of recovery. He gave sufficient evidence in writing to enable the coroner to absolve him from responsibility in these deaths.

Ritual Nullification of the Thirst Drive

According to Yap (1977), voodoo death takes place too rapidly to be due to dehydration, but he refers

to no case material. The most rapid death reported here is that of M. from Milingimbi, 1978, when death took place in 24 hours in the absence of any fluid intake. Lex (1974) concedes that dehydration may sometimes be a factor, but she takes the view that autonomic dysfunction prevents the victim swallowing fluid or absorbing it. The evidence of the health workers is that fluid is actively withheld to expedite dying, and this also applied to the two cases in which voodoo death was averted. This confiscation of fluids explains the observed dehydration more parsimoniously; Lex's hypothesis regarding difficulty in swallowing is not a major factor, but in terminal dehydration it is true that water cannot be absorbed without aggravating the imbalance of minerals and salts in the body fluids. Among these people there is the cultural rationalization that the mortified individual is animated only by the spirit of the forefather, which does not require fluid: "It is then too late for food or drink." This ideology explains why some relatives actively promote dehydration while others passively allow it to occur. A unitary hypothesis for voodoo death is not proposed: what is proposed is that psychological factors are secondary to the basic physical process of dehydration, but both are involved. The continuing concept of voodoo death as caused by suggestion, that is, by the victim's belief in sorcery and the conviction of the victim's own demise, speaks to total involvement in his or her assumptive world. The notion of the psychological causation has persisted because "it would seem to show such final and tragic evidence of true belief" (Lewis 1977: 139).

The social behavior of beginning the obsequies while the patient-victim is alert defines the role of the dying person and prescribes the person's behavior. The ancestral songs in which he or she silently participates become self-referential, and the induced mental state of "giving up—given up" is sufficient to suppress the physiological drive for fluid. It allows dehydration its final action and prevents active efforts to obtain fluid. In this fatalistic state of mind the person truly regards death as a rite of passage and is oriented to the next world. Significantly, as the health workers say, it is a "water world and has spirits in it," in the depths of the clan waterhole. As Warner says "[he] returns to his totemic well, and the circle is complete" (1958: 5).

The Cannibal's Cauldron

I. M. Lewis

In this article, excerpted from I. M. Lewis's book,
Religion in Context: Cults and Charisma, *the
author investigates the cluster of imagery and
metaphor surrounding cannibalism and demonstrates
that accusations of cannibalism are closely linked
with witchcraft accusations. Ritual cannibalism, the
most common setting of cannibalism, functions both
to commemorate the deceased and to reflect the
hostility between groups. Lewis also maintains that
the ritual closely associates eating with sexuality.
Replete with overtones of power, supernatural and
political, cannibalism has, not surprisingly, survived
in the imagery of mankind.*

AS WILLIAM ARENS (1979) HAS PERSUASIVELY ARGUED,
anthropologists are often remarkably casual and
uncritical in their treatment of reports of cannibalism in exotic cultures. Disregarding the usual
methodological prerequisite of firsthand observation—enshrined in the Malinowskian fieldwork manifesto—our accounts of cannibalism all
too frequently rely on secondhand reports. Such
lack of scholarly rigor regularly leads to the confusion and conflation of the idea or ideology of
cannibalism with its actual practice. Hence, many
modern anthropological studies inadvertently
tend to entrench and further legitimize deep-
seated Eurocentric assumptions concerning the
prevalence of cannibalism in tribal societies. Although few of the anthropologists involved here
would see it in this light, they thus implicitly
maintain the tradition of Freud, who in his magnificent cosmic fable *Totem and Taboo* ([1913];
1950) casually introduced cannibalism to embel-
lish his theory of primordial incest. In the
Freudian version of the Oedipus myth, once liberated by the murder of their tyrannical rebellious sons, being "cannibal savages," celebrated
the event by *eating* him. The subsequent regularly performed ritual slaughter and eating of the
totemic animal, which replaced the murdered father, commemorated and replicated the original
act of parricidal cannibalism. According to Freud
(1950: 142) these hypothetical events marked the
crucial turning point in man's evolutionary development—the beginning . . . of social organization, of moral restrictions and of religion."

In fact, the application of the derogatory label
"man-eater" is one of the most widely distributed methods by which the members of one
group or community dissociate and distance
themselves from outsiders beyond the pale. Cannibalism, however, *pace* Arens (1979: 145*ff*), is
much more than merely a matter of labeling and
stigmatizing disparaged groups and individuals.
The ideology of man-eating provides a pregnant

Reprinted from *Religion in Context* (1986), pp. 63–77.
Reprinted with the permission of Cambridge University Press and the author.

cluster of imagery and metaphor to express the exercise and experience of power, domination, and subjection which may be realized in different forms in particular historical and cultural contexts. The appellation "cannibal" is not merely an appropriate term of contempt for uncouth subjects at the bottom of the political hierarchy or on the edge of the civilized world. It may be applied equally appropriately by the victims of oppression to designate their superiors. The designation "cannibal" can thus convey a sense of impotence and desperation and is consequently not always flattering to its user. Again, the term may be employed reciprocally between antagonistic parties of equal status and rank. In this chapter we explore this inherently double-edged imagery, arguing that both in theory and in practice cannibalism ultimately derives its perennial fascination and pervasive evocative power from intimate physical experiences common to all human beings. Although psychoanalytic insights may be helpful here, it is thus unnecessary, *pace* Epstein (1979), to invoke particular childhood traumas or culturally specific child-rearing practices in order to understand the phenomenon.

The orthodox anthropological approach to the social dynamics of witchcraft, which we sought to expand in the previous chapter, assumes a disinterested (if not disbelieving) external perspective that concentrates upon the accusation and the *accuser* rather than upon the *accused* witch. In the case of cannibalism, an inadvertent personal experience of the author's—shared with Arens and others—reverses the equation and so provides serendipitous food for thought. Traveling in the remote Ndembu countryside of western Zambia (then Northern Rhodesia) in the late 1950s, I personally experienced and still vividly recall the suspicion and fear with which lonely African pedestrians responded to offers of lifts in my Land Rover. Their stock reaction was to disappear swiftly into the nearby bush. The explanation for this rather striking avoidance behavior, I discovered, was the assumption, widely prevalent in central Africa at that time, that many Europeans were vampire-men who sucked the blood and ate the flesh of innocent Africans. Similar concepts about cannibalistic Europeans flourished with varying degrees of intensity in east Africa (see Friedland 1960), southern Africa, and in the Congo, where during the Belgian period in

Leopoldville the white vampire was known as the "man with the lamp." Around the same time (1958) an unsuspecting European firm in the Belgian Congo marketed canned meat in cans with labels depicting chubby, smiling African babies. The product was not an unqualified success.

A similarly mixed reception greeted the appearance in Northern Rhodesia during this period of cans of cheap meat designed for the local African work force market and labeled "For African Consumption" (see Fraenkel 1959). The ill-fated British plan to form a multiracial Central African Federation joining Northern Rhodesia and Nyasaland (now Malawi) to white-settler dominated Southern Rhodesia (Zimbabwe) had aroused deep and widespread suspicion and alarm among the African population. Africans accustomed to the relatively benign paternalistic colonial administrations of Northern Rhodesia and Nyasaland feared that the proposed federation would involve an extension to their territories of the pattern of white supremacy characteristic at that time of Southern Rhodesia. Since the majority of the population were cultivators, there was particularly acute anxiety that traditional land rights would be endangered by an influx of European farming interests from Southern Rhodesia (Watson 1958; Epstein 1958, 1979). In such an atmosphere of mistrust, and with the failure of African political pressure to prevent the establishment in 1953 of the Federation (doomed to collapse six years later under the weight of African opposition), rumors quickly spread in Northern Rhodesia that the meat marked "For African Consumption" contained human flesh specially doctored to break down African resistance to the unpopular policy of federation. Seeking to counter such fears, a European district commissioner on the Northern Rhodesian copper belt publicly consumed the meat to prove that it was harmless. This demonstration almost certainly had the paradoxical effect of confirming rather than allaying general African fears that Europeans were cannibals. Nor was African public opinion on this issue likely to be disabused by the conviction, about this time, in a European court in Nyasaland, of an African accused of trying to sell two well-fattened children to a European for his Christmas dinner.

In some parts of Africa, as in other European colonies, it appears possible to trace a link between this view of Europeans as cannibalistic bloodsuckers and blood donation campaigns. Sometimes these ideas are (or were) associated through the color red, with European-introduced fire services and fire stations (while still novel) acquiring a sinister reputation as centers for extracting and collecting the African blood believed to be consumed by Europeans to sustain their vitality (Friedland 1960). Similarly, in Northern Rhodesia rural health campaigns involving blood tests have sometimes precipitated outbreaks of panic, during which consumption of tinned tomato juice by Europeans has been taken as further proof of their lust for blood. More recently, in southern Africa as a whole, it does not require much imagination to grasp the further medical confirmation of these ideas provided by reports of Dr. Christian Barnard's transplant surgery, utilizing in some cases hearts from African bodies to give new life to whites.

In the more distant past, there is direct evidence that African fears about the vampire propensities of Europeans are also in part a reflection of the slave trade. And it is ironic to note that both the Arabs and the Europeans involved in this traffic appear to have spread rumors accusing each other of practicing cannibalism. Such allegations naturally helped to reinforce and extend the existing indigenous belief in the reality of cannibalism, associating it, in particular, with rapacious invaders.

These factors, however, do not alone suffice to explain how Africans came to suspect Europeans of being cannibals. To understand this fully we have to set cannibalism in context as part of a wider constellation of ideas concerning mystical power in general and witchcraft in particular. It is obviously significant that Europeans were believed by Africans not only to indulge in cannibalism but also to practice witchcraft. From an African perspective, it was largely *because* Europeans were seen as witches that they were liable to be suspected of practicing cannibalism. Witches, as we know, employ sinister forces to achieve selfish ends to the disadvantage of virtuous citizens and neighbors. Success—in the "limited good" witchcraft scenario (cf. Foster 1965)—is at the expense of others. The witch, consequently, inevitably becomes endowed with all the antisocial vices that are the counterparts of corresponding social virtues. Hence the inverted witch stereotype includes all manner of sexual perversion, incest, and the ultimate denial of

human sociability and commensality—cannibalism. "Witches eat people," as the Nso of Cameroon (Kaberry 1969), the Shona of Zimbabwe (Crawford 1967), and many other peoples succinctly state. Indeed, the statement, "A witch is a cannibal," is one of the more widely current minimum definitions of the witch role.

Those who define the epitome of evil in this way also believe that the mystical forces that so enable ambitious, unscrupulous individuals to achieve more than their fair share of life's good things can, in other contexts, be used positively in the general interest. As we emphasized in the previous chapter, what anthropologists regularly translate from other cultures by the English term "witchcraft" (or the French "*sorcellerie*") is, on closer inspection, typically ambiguous. Those whom English anthropologists describe as socially approved "witch doctors" because of their expertise in combating and countering illicit witchcraft usually owe their success to causing what they cure. Here the negative side empowers the positive side which legitimates it. The "python power" of the Nyakyusa both provides the basis of witchcraft and empowers the positive righteous indignation of the village elders to defend the local community against external threat. Similarly, as we saw, the mystical force that enables the elders among the Tiv of Nigeria to uphold morality and protect their community is equally the source of malevolent witchcraft. A Tiv witch seeks to obtain selfish aims at the expense of others, and to secure success nourishes his *tsav* on a diet of human flesh—cannibalism again becoming a critical element in the definition of "witch." In precisely the same vein, unpopular Amazonian shamans are denounced as "witches" practicing cannibalism against their own people—aggressive shamanic power in the Amazon generally being associated with the anaconda and jaguar (Lévi-Strauss 1966; Reichel-Dolmatoff 1971; Hugh-Jones 1980; Colajanni 1982; Seymour-Smith 1984).

So too accusations of abuse of power (implying, as we have seen, witchcraft) leveled today against African government ministers and chiefs may include the denunciation "cannibal" (cf. MacCormack 1983). Here we need again recall the equivocal nature of power and its mystical implications. What was typically involved was essentially control over the ruler's subjects and lands, whose fecundity was affected by the chief's mystical energies, which had always to be protected and maintained at the requisite level of effectiveness. In Africa, as elsewhere, leaders were expected to have sex appeal. There was always some connection, however concealed, between such political sexuality and the fertility of people and land. The Bemba of Zambia illustrate these themes with unusual directness. Their kings, members of the ruling clan (whose totem is the maneating crocodile), were expected regularly to perform ritual sexual intercourse with their wives in order to promote the prosperity of their land and its inhabitants (Richards 1968).

It is against such traditional attitudes toward power (which, as Balandier remarks, is never completely emptied of religious content) that we should understand the conviction, widespread in colonial Africa, that Europeans were cannibalistic witches. The superior military and material technology of the white man, the sources of which were unfamiliar and often mysterious; his miraculous healing medicines; the Christian religion, which underpinned his moral superiority and helped him to maintain law and order in adverse conditions: all these inevitably suggested that the European possessed a unique store of mystical power. If some aspects of European colonial rule were perceived as beneficial, others were not; and, here as elsewhere, the exercise of authority always engendered some resentment against the rulers. What is involved here is more complex than simply colonial exploitation.

African suspicions concerning the sinister roots of European power received additional support from the way in which European colonial administrations and missions reacted to traditional African beliefs in witchcraft (and sorcery). Proclaiming that witches did not exist, European administrations had typically made it illegal for Africans to accuse or punish suspected witches. Legislation proscribing witchcraft accusations was introduced throughout British Africa. The Southern Rhodesia Witchcraft Suppression Act of 1899 is a typical example from the region that is our primary focus here. The act is primarily concerned to prevent "imputations" of witchcraft, as the following extracts indicate:

In this Act "witchcraft" includes the "throwing of bones," the use of charms and other means or devices adopted in the practice of sorcery.

Whoever imputes to any other person the use of

non-natural means in causing any disease in any person or animal or in causing any injury to any person or property, that is to say, whoever names or indicates any other person as being a wizard or witch shall be guilty of an offense and liable to a fine not exceeding two hundred dollars or to imprisonment for a period not exceeding three years, or to whipping not exceeding twenty lashes or to any two or more of such punishments.

Whoever, having so named and indicated any person as a wizard or witch, is proved at his trial under section three to be by habit and repute a witch doctor or witch finder shall be liable, on conviction, in lieu of the punishment provided by section three to a fine not exceeding five hundred dollars or to imprisonment for a period not exceeding seven years or to whipping not exceeding thirty-six lashes or to any two or more of such punishments.

As Gordon Chavunduka, the first black African professor of sociology at the University of Zimbabwe, observes, the aim of this act is not to punish witches but those who expose witches (by making witchcraft accusations), and consequently in rural Zimbabwe it is regarded today as a "very unjust piece of legislation" (Chavunduka 1980: 130). In a similar fashion, in French Africa, the *Code Penal Indigene* and later the *Code Napoleon* outlawed witchcraft accusations (cf. Alexandre 1974). The effect, of course, of such colonial legislation and its implementation in administrative (and sometimes "native") courts was to *protect* witches and to suppress legitimate means of exposing witchcraft. For those believing in witchcraft the obvious conclusion to draw was that the European rulers were on the side of the witches—and hence, indeed, given all the other aspects of their political superiority, "super-witches." This seems to me the most potent factor in the train of circumstantial evidence leading to the ascription of cannibalistic witchcraft to Europeans (including unsuspecting anthropologists).

It is ironic that those who do not believe in witchcraft should as a result be suspected of practicing it. Cannibalism, on the other hand, is often not practiced by those believed by anthropologists to be cannibals. This strange anthropological paradox, which despite their close connection treats witchcraft and cannibalism so differently, reflects the outright disbelief with which reports of witchcraft are usually received, in contrast to the reception usually accorded reports of cannibalism. The stock anthropological response to the juxtaposition of the two is very revealing. Firmly believing that witchcraft does not exist, anthropologists are likely to dismiss as pure fantasy reports of acts of cannibalism in a witchcraft context. In other contexts, the response to reports of cannibalism is often much less critical.

This intriguing contrast in emphasis and interpretation can be seen in what still remains the most comprehensive and subtle anthropological analysis of witchcraft—Evans-Pritchard's magisterial work on the Azande of the southern Sudan and Congo. If the reality of witchcraft is unacceptable to Evans-Pritchard, there is no question of the reality of accusations of witchcraft, since these can be readily observed and the associated diagnostic rituals and alleviating procedures recorded in minute detail. The famous Zande distinction (to which we have already referred) between "sorcery" as an objective physical technique and "witchcraft" as a psychic force, also happens to accord with Evans-Pritchard's Eurocentric, objective bias. This distinction, in turn, appears to have led Evans-Pritchard to emphasize the unintentional, unpremeditated aspects of Zande witchcraft as an unconscious phenomenon at the expense of the conscious, deliberate aspects that are uppermost in the mind of the bewitched accuser. Although he presents detailed evidence for both these contradictory facets, this at least is how the overall picture of Zande witchcraft has usually been "read"; and it is, I suggest, in harmony with the broader distinction between witchcraft and sorcery.

It is not unreasonable to suggest that Evans-Pritchard's own disbelief in witchcraft helps him to investigate with admirable detail and precision the complex issue of Zande skepticism—a topic almost completely ignored in the same author's celebrated account of the theistic beliefs of the Nuer (published after his conversion to the Catholic faith). Confident as he was in discounting the efficacy claimed for witchcraft by the Zande, Evans-Pritchard was more cautious in his assessment of references to Zande cannibalism. Having subjected earlier travelers' allegations to devastating and caustic criticism, he nevertheless felt it imprudent to dismiss them entirely, on the grounds that "there is no smoke without fire" (Evans-Pritchard 1965: 153).

Here, as usual, much turns on the accurate rendering of native statements and so on translation, which, as is well-known, Evans-Pritchard himself saw as the crux of the anthropological endeavor. A more recent study of Zande mystical beliefs by the Austrian anthropologist Manfred Kremser (1981) sheds important new light on this problem. Kremser shows that the term *kawa*, translated into English as "human meat" and usually taken in the Zande literature as evidence of cannibalism, relates primarily to the witchcraft domain. Thus the witch may attack his victim by extracting the latter's life force (*kawa*), putting it in a pot, and typically hanging the pot with its contents on a tree. This is a state of raw suspense. For if this *kawa* is cooked and eaten, the bewitched victim can never recover. If, however, events do not proceed to this irreversible conclusion and the *kawa* remains uncooked and unconsumed, the witch can be persuaded to unbind this life essence from the branch and restore it to the bewitched victim, who is then expected to recover. Curiously, as far as I have been able to determine, Evans-Pritchard's richly documented study of Zande witchcraft does not contain any mention of *kawa* and does not explore this important relationship between the process of witchcraft attack (which he refers to as "vampirism") and cannibalism. This specific linkage, however, is clearly present in a text which in Evans-Pritchard's translation (1937: 35) includes the following passage: "Witches arise and beat their drum of witchcraft. The membrane of this drum is human skin. . . . Their drum call is 'human flesh, human flesh, human flesh.'" Although Evans-Pritchard does not tell us this, it would thus appear that *one* of the sources for the imputation of cannibalism to the Zande rests on the (metaphorical or psychic) consumption of "human flesh" extracted from their victims by witches.

More generally, this contrasting anthropological treatment of witchcraft and cannibalism, and the ironical readiness on the part of some anthropologists to view as cannibals those who are prone to view Europeans in the same light, cannot of course be explained in quite the same terms as our central

African examples. We can understand the anthropological disbelief in witchcraft more easily than the anthropological belief in cannibalism. The functionalist William Arens (1979: 184), appropriately enough, has proposed a functionalist explanation for his colleagues' lingering credulity. The appellation *cannibal*, he argues, continues to have wide exotic appeal. As the study of cannibals, anthropology is thereby made to seem more exciting. At the same time, anthropologists have a professional interest in maintaining their uniquely privileged role as the specially licensed mediators between their Western world and the exotic alien cultures which, through the imputed stigma of cannibalism, help define the boundaries of Western civilization.

I do not dissent at all from this view of the exploitative, entrepreneurial role of anthropology and anthropologists (cf. Lewis 1976: 34). But to claim, as Arens does, that in general the concept "cannibal" primarily functions as a boundary marker or label distinguishing "us" (non-cannibals) from "them" (cannibals) hardly does justice to the relevant data. The suggestion (Arens 1979: 145) that groups of similar culture have *more* need to resort to the distancing (not-us) label "cannibal" is interesting, but not substantiated—and in fact appears unconvincing. Arens seems also to imagine that since witchcraft does not exist (except as a reality of thought) the same applies to the linked concept of cannibalism, which must therefore be accorded the same mythical status. This perspective on cannibalism is clearly biased in the direction of the negative aspects of witchcraft and takes little or no account of mystical ambivalence or positive charisma. To reach a more balanced and comprehensive view, we must acknowledge that when people interpret the actions of others in terms of cannibalism, they are making statements of more pervasive significance than mere intellectual labeling. As Sahlins (1983: 88) cogently puts it: "Cannibalism is always 'symbolic' even when it is real." To proceed further, we should, I believe, pay close attention to body symbolism, recognizing the extent to which the biological functions of the human body provide a fertile matrix for potently charged ("natural") symbols.

In applying this perspective to cannibalism we should begin by noting that its most general cultural context—either as idea or as actual practice —is usually a ritual setting. Here, where a tabooed negative action—eating human flesh—acquires positive force, the ritual consumption of parts of the human body enables the consumer to acquire something of the body's vital energy. Ritual cannibalism (as indeed Arens himself recognizes) is consequently a form of sacrificial communion. Indeed, it is perhaps *the* prototype of sacrificial communion, since as Sahlins maintains (no doubt correctly) "cannibalism exists *in nuce* in most sacrifice." As is well-known, this has very powerful resonance in the Christian Eucharist, where according to the official doctrine communicants consume the bread and wine that through the miracle of transubstantiation becomes the flesh and blood of Christ. The case of cannibal converts to Christianity is thus particularly poignant, as Sahlins, referring to nineteenth-century missionary accounts in the Marquesas, trenchantly observes.

The Trobriand Islanders practiced a more direct and lurid form of commemorative cannibalism than the Eucharist (Malinowski 1929: 133). The body of a deceased man was exhumed and dismembered by his sons and other (nonmatrilineal) relatives. Although, as Malinowski observed, the mourners found this extremely repugnant, they were expected to display their filial piety by sucking the decaying flesh of the corpse they were dismembering. The bones were conserved as relics commemorating the dead, reverently wrapped in dry leaves, and finally deposited on rocky shelves overlooking the sea. With subtle changes of symbolic emphasis, similar practices are reported elsewhere in Melanesia. Until as recently as 1950, for example, the Gimi of the New Guinea highlands practiced what might be called compassionate cannibalism. Women were expected to eat the dead bodies of their men in order to release the latters' individual spirits, freeing them to rejoin the collective body of ancestral forest spirits. According to Andrew Strathern (1982: 125), as they ate the men's bodies women used to sing seductively, "Come to me lest your body rot in the ground. Better it should dissolve inside me." There is a significant emphasis on sexual antagonism and sexuality here, to which we shall return shortly. For in releasing the men's spirits by consuming their bodies, the women are also considered to be exacting vengeance on men for stealing the penislike initiation flutes that the women originally possessed.

This sexual complementarity is further elaborated in the complex mortuary cannibalism of another New Guinea people, the Bimin-Kuskusmin described by Fitzjohn Porter Poole (1983). Here, male agnates honor the dead, counteracting the pollution of the mortuary rites by eating morsels of the (male-substance) bone marrow of the deceased. This ensures the passage of the dead man's spirit to the ancestral underworld and the recycling of his procreative and ritual strength within his patrilineage. Female agnates eat small pieces of lower belly fat (female substance) to enhance their reproductive and ritual powers. Although it is considered particularly disgusting, penis flesh is even presented to the widow, the eating of which is believed to enhance her fertility and bind her productive power to the agnatic kin of the deceased husband. Reciprocally, the ritually active husband of a dead woman is expected to eat a fragment of her sexual organ so as to enhance the fertility of her daughters. In all these funeral contexts, the stress is on ensuring the fertility and continuity of a group weakened by death. On the battlefield, however, Bimin-Kuskusmin warriors add insult to injury, expressing their contempt for defeated foes by eating the feminine portions of their corpses and thus preventing them from achieving full ancestor status (Porter Poole 1983: 15).

This brings us to the classical political context of cannibalism in the agonistic relations between hostile groups, the prime sacrificial victims being war captives or slaves (often similarly recruited). In this vein, Maori cannibalism—well-documented from contemporary nineteenth-century eyewitness accounts—was set in a context of ritual warfare, the consumption of human flesh paralleled that of birds and fish in hunting rituals. Men consumed at cannibalistic feasts were referred to as "fishes," and "first fish" being eaten by a chief who thus acquired control over the land of the vanquished. Victorious Maori chiefs are reported to have increased their *mana* by swallowing the eyes of their enemies. In Fiji during the same period, chiefs of reputedly immigrant origin received tribute in the form of what Sahlins (1983: 80) calls "raw" women and supplied "cooked" men in communion feasts as largesse in return. The resources for this system of noblesse oblige were typically war captives or "internal" aliens in the form of rebels and dissidents. These sacrificial victims, "food for the gods," assumed divine status and were accorded the same

terms of ritual reference as the body of a chief.

The ideas and symbols in play here achieve their most elaborate realization in Amazonian Indian ritual cannibalism. The Tupinamba of Brazil have long provided the locus classicus, known to Western scholars from the extensive, carefully documented sixteenth-century eyewitness accounts of the Portuguese Jesuit missionaries. Although Arens has attempted to discredit this picture of Tupi cannibalism by questioning the evidence in some of the more sensational popular accounts, the cumulative testimony is overwhelming and very convincing, as Donald Forsyth (1983) has recently demonstrated in an impressively rendered reappraisal of the firsthand Jesuit evidence. The picture that emerges in these accounts is that the Tupi practiced ritual cannibalism extensively in the context of war and vengeance raids. Among the Tupinamba, who in common with so many other people married their enemies, a war captive was called a "loved one." Such prisoners, potential affines like the Tupi gods, were feted, provided with unmarried women as companions, and enjoyed luxury prisoner status for extended periods before they were ritually executed and consumed in an often orgiastic communion feast. Thus at the heart of the most sumptuous ritual cannibalism we encounter the theme of sexuality, which is also present in witchcraft. This is no coincidence. I do not think that we can reach any general understanding of the meaning and pervasive appeal of the ideology of cannibalism, and its use in labeling others and in interpreting their activities, unless we take due note of these sexual allusions.

As is well-known, eating and sexuality are closely related modes of intimate social interaction that readily flow together, both literally and metaphorically. In many, perhaps most, languages, including to some extent English, the same or similar expressions are used to refer to eating and making love. Consumed with desire, the lover eagerly seeks to devour the object of his passion. Terms of endearment, likewise, regularly compare the love object to a tempting dainty dish. In the contemporary Western world this equivalence or concurrence of the two modes of commensality—eating and sex—is appropriately reflected in the striking similarity in style and format between gourmet sex manuals and cookbooks. Some sex manuals, indeed, literally set out the stages of amorous play in the form of a menu; and sexual and culinary recipes lie side by side in the pages of journals like *Penthouse* and *Playboy*. Common expressions relating to love and sexual intercourse, such as "conquest" and "match," bear an obvious aggressive charge that is also present in the competitive elements of feasting and hospitality. In some African contexts, political usurpation is said to be represented as a process of seduction with the aid of tempting food. In Fiji, according to Sahlins (1983: 79), a lowly commoner would grovel before a chief with the obeisance, "Eat me." Elsewhere "Be my guest!" is apt to be a challenge as well as an invitation. It is consequently scarcely necessary to refer to love bites, or *vagina dentata*, or indeed to the intermittent Western vogue for oral sex, to evoke the image of Dracula, the pan-human vampire, who so vividly embraces all these themes.

Ernest Jones certainly recognized these parallels when he identified what he termed "oral sadism" in the concept of the vampire. For him this was a "regressive complex," provoked by the repression of normal adult genital sexuality. A typical if tragic illustration at the individual level would presumably be the case of the "cannibal of the Bois de Boulogne," the Japanese student in Paris who confessed to shooting and then eating an attractive Dutch girl who had rebuffed his advances and refused to sleep with him. This is the sort of "abnormal" case that the psychoanalytic anthropologist Georges Devereux (1956) would no doubt characterize as "egodystonic." But a diagnosis of cannibalism, where it is a culturally accepted practice, as "culture dystonic" and hence indicative of general cultural malaise, is unlikely to appeal to the cultural-relativist anthropologist (cf. Geertz 1984). Similarly, Ernest Jones's rigid Freudian schema of evolutionary stages of sexual aggression seems today an excessive piece of psychoanalytic dogma. We surely no longer need to invoke the ideas of "regression" and "repression" to acknowledge a more flexible framework in which the different modes of sexuality interpenetrate and flow into each other. From this perspective, linked as they are to oral and genital sexual aggression, the ideas of consumption, ingestion (see Porter Poole 1983), engulfment, and mastery clearly constitute potent symbols of power. Rooted in the universal human experiences of suckling, engaging in sex, and eating, these motifs provide the most pervasive thematic and emotional matrix for everything that pertains to the general phenomenon of cannibalism. It is therefore hardly surprising that, even when the practice of cannibalism has disappeared or has never existed, the *idea* of man-eating should survive as a latent force always capable, so long as beliefs in mystical power are sustained, of being evoked in myth and popular fantasy. The problem is not, as Arens (1979: 139) claims, that of explaining why people attribute cannibalism to their neighbors and enemies, but rather of understanding those cultures in which cannibalism is (or was) actually practiced as an integral part of ritual life. Here, as usual in the analysis of cultural forms, we may discern general thematic patterns associated with symbolic meanings recurring in similar ritual contexts. To attribute these, or other aspects of institutionalized culture, to such simple materialist "causes" as protein deficiency (Marvin Harris 1977), is in my opinion patently absurd.

Becoming White: Notes on an Italian-American Explanation of Evil Eye

Michael Buonanno

Although the belief in evil eye is commonly associated with societies far from the continental United States, Michael Buonanno illustrates the presence of this malevolent power among Italian immigrants in and around Buffalo, New York. These traditions of belief are traced from sections of Italy to America, but not without changes, and are best represented by the jettatore *(the outsider), and the* strega *(the witch). Unlike classic definitions of the witch, the* strega *is the widow, the barren wife, or the recluse. Both the* jettatore *and the* strega *function, in part, to remind Italian-Americans of the obstacles to their smooth acculturation into the new culture, that is, obstacles to their being viewed as Americans, or, as they put it, "to becoming white."*

Reprinted from *New York Folklore*, Vol. X, nos. 1–2 (Winter–Spring 1984), pp. 39–53, by permission of the New York Folklore Society and the Editor of *New York Folklore*.

IN THE COURSE OF AN EXPLORATION OF EVIL EYE beliefs in and around Buffalo, New York, it became apparent to me that the beliefs were somehow involved in the process of acculturation. This involvement centered upon the evil eye victim. There seemed to be two categories of victim existing side-by-side in the same communities. The first included such individuals as the unbaptized child, the preadolescent, the bride and groom. The second was comprised entirely of those individuals making the transition from Italian to American society. This transition was often described in the economic terms of success and failure, but the notion of passing in and out of the Italian-American community was ever present. No matter what the category of victim, the preferred method of curing the evil eye involved explicit references to baptism into the Roman Catholic Church. Thus, "unbaptized child" became the metaphoric equivalent to "immigrant." Perhaps the situation was best summed up by the informant who said "Evil eye was something we believed in before we were white." He did not mean before we started acting like Americans, but before we were looked upon as Americans. Here was an ideal of acculturation which considered the attitudes of both the societies involved, Italian and American, and which could be understood as a function of the belief in evil eye. The function is not simply that of acculturation; it is more properly that of becoming white.

Evil Eye and the Distribution of Power

Evil eye is an attribute. He who "has the evil eye" (*tiene il malocchio*) casts a malevolent power into an object simply by gazing upon it. This malevolent power is referred to as envy (*invi-*

dia). Once cast, envy acts as a disease. If the object is a plant it will wither; if it is a cow it will go dry. Headache, impotency, and fever are some of the symptoms of envy once cast into a human object. There is the suggestion in the Italian-American explanation of evil eye that the object, once victimized, becomes dangerous. Thus, it will be said of the evil eye victim that he too "has the evil eye."

In actuality, anyone is capable of envy. A woman will add, *"Dio benedica"* ("God bless you"), after complimenting a newborn child, in recognition that compliments are often the thin veil of envy. Incantations, gestures, and amulets are sufficient to ward off this mundane type of envy; but there are times when envy becomes personified. He who has the evil eye becomes defined. Apotropaic precautions lose their efficacy and the community is thrown into turmoil. Two notable personifications of envy in the Italian-American explanation of evil eye are the *jettatore* and the *strega*.

The *jettatore* is thought to have its origins in Naples. He is a mysterious and often authoritative figure whose mere presence disorders the world. Giuseppe Pitrè speaks of a Sicilian *jettatore* "whose glance was considered so fatal that at his death the rumor spread that he died because, while walking down Corso Garibaldi, he just happened to look in a large mirror displayed in a store-window." (Pitrè 1981: 132–133).

Willa Appel has found the jettatore to be a pervasive danger to the peasants of the Apulia region of southern Italy. There the peasants will divert him from his malevolent task by strewing scraps of newspaper around the matrimonial bed. "Being only half-literate, like peasants themselves," the *jettatore* will spend the entire night trying to read the bits of news (Appel 1979: 26).

Appel sees in the *jettatore* an idiom for ambiguity within the social structure. For instance, the Neapolitan *jettatore* of the eighteenth and nineteenth centuries was modeled after the intellectual who attempted to reconcile Illuministic ideals with a feudalistic order (pp. 23–24), while today's Apulian *jettatore* is modeled after the peasant who cannot achieve the consumeristic ideals of industrialized society (p. 26).

The Italian-American *jettatore* is not clearly related to a particular class, but an amorphous perception of authority relative to his victim is implicit in his description; thus, he is overtly related to the Neapolitan *jettatore*. His major attribute, however, is that he exists outside of the Italian-American community, the suggestion being that ambiguity becomes the metaphoric equivalent of the ambivalence experienced by Italian-Americans faced with the prospect of acculturation.

But the more pervasive personification of envy in Italian-American explanations of evil eye is the *strega*, or witch. She seems no longer to be the blood-sucking fiend who creeps from her husband's bed and prowls throughout the night. She is instead the widow, the "barren" wife, the recluse. She is like the Apulian *jettatore* in that she is integrated into, and represents, her own community.

A two-fold source of danger emerges from Italian-American explanations of evil eye. The *strega* is a constant reminder of those factors which keep the immigrant from effecting a smooth transition from Italian to American society: the inability to learn the new language, the temptation to withdraw into the relative security of the Italian-American community. The *jettatore* expresses the recognition that there are obstacles to effective acculturation beyond those represented by the *strega*, obstacles which occur outside of the Italian-American community.

Just as there exist individuals who are animated by the power of envy, individuals who are socially polluting; so there exist individuals who are animated by the power of grace, individuals who are purifying to society. These later individuals are referred to as *Comare*, Godmother. Their power of grace is bestowed upon them by Jesus Christ through the interlocution of his Mother, Mary.

Comparatico, or Godparenthood, is an essential relationship to the Italian-American. Both the *Comare* (Godmother) and the *Compare* (Godfather) accompany their Godchild to the baptismal font. Both are responsible for that child's spiritual and physical well-being from that time on. When a woman becomes *Comare* to the community her obligations are extended. Midwives are referred to as *Comare* because they administer the rite of baptism to the newborn child. An especially close friend is referred to as *Comare* because she is relied upon for the most intimate type of assistance. When a man becomes *Compare* to the community his obligations are subject to an extension similar to that of the *Comare's*; this extension will be discussed later.

In the context of this paper *Comare* means healer, specifically spiritual healer of those who have been victimized by the evil eye. My ideas about the *Comare* were largely formulated through discussion with Lucia, who immigrated to the United States over sixty years ago from a small farming village near Naples. She had been in the United States nearly ten years before she became *Comare*. Lucia may have a special right to the curing ritual employed against evil eye. Her patron saint, Santa Lucia, when about to be ravaged by her wicked brother, San Aniello, tore her own eyes from her head. She was instantly presented with a new pair of glorified eyes by an angel of the Lord, and she was given the gift of curing the evil eye. I should note that there is occasionally the perception that evil eye arises from San Aniello, "the wicked saint." For instance, if a pregnant woman or her husband works on December fourteenth, San Aniello's day, their child may be born with the evil eye.

Lucia cleanses the evil eye victim by drawing envy out of his body and replacing it with Christ's grace. She does this by means of a purifying ritual which symbolically re-enacts the patient's baptism into the Roman Catholic Church. The importance of baptism to the Italian-American is underscored by the following selection from Phyllis Williams' *South Italian Folkways in Europe and America* (1938).

The finding of godparents proved a difficult problem to the Maturo family during the depression following 1929. Successive births made it increasingly difficult to find friends or relatives willing to take this responsibility in a large family, especially in one on relief. When the last baby was eight weeks old and no godparents had been found, the situation became the talk of the neighborhood. The unbaptized child was a direct invitation to the Evil Eye. It was therefore loaded with amulets, and its father borrowed a large set of cowhorns from a butcher cousin to nail over the door inside his home.

The child developed a slight cold. Its parents in desperation let it be known that the baby was dying of pneumonia . . . a young brother of the father and the boy's fiancee came forward and permitted the baptism to take place in proper

form. The baby rapidly grew better, and the parents announced that its recovery was due to the beneficial effects of the ceremony (Williams 1969: 95).

The unbaptized child is the model of ambiguity within the evil eye context. He has been "separated" from his mother's womb, but not "incorporated" into the Christian community. He is perceived to be in constant danger and, as may be expected, to be a source of danger. Only the transitional imagery provided by the rite of baptism will define him, secure his position within the Christian community, render him harmless and out of harm's way.

Perhaps the best means of understanding the significance of the interplay between the powers, grace and envy, are offered by Mary Douglas in her book *Purity and Danger* (1966). As the following passage will illustrate, spiritual powers are often reflective of the social system and its inherent or formulative strengths and weaknesses.

Where the social system explicitly recognizes positions of authority, those holding such positions are endowed with explicit spiritual power; controlled, conscious, external and approved — powers to bless or curse. Where the social system requires people to hold dangerously ambiguous roles, these persons are credited with uncontrolled, unconscious, dangerous, disapproved powers — such as witchcraft and evil eye. In other words, where the social system is well-articulated, I look for articulate powers vested in the points of authority; where the social system is ill-articulated, I look for inarticulate powers vested in those who are a source of disorder. I am suggesting that the contrast between form and surrounding non-form accounts for the distribution of symbolic and psychic powers; external symbolism upholds the explicit social structure and internal, unformed psychic powers threaten it from the nonstructure (Douglas 1966: 99).

The condition which gives rise to the personification of envy is one in which ambiguity is pervasive. Such is the immigrant condition. The immigrant is caught between two societies: the Italian, which is reconstructed in his community, and the American, which surrounds the community in which he lives. He is much like the unbaptized child. He is the initiate involved in a peculiar rite of passage. The condition which permits the pursuance of Christ's grace is one of articulation. The *Comare* is clearly defined in her capacity. Her power is sought when all others fail.

The Evil Eye Warning

Any explanation of evil eye carries a warning. It is not so much "beware envy," as "beware the arousal of envy." The *strega* and the *jettatore* have little (if any) control over their power. The victim, on the other hand, can avoid their gaze by maintaining a certain profile. Thus, before discussing the *Comare*'s cure, I will consider the *strega* and the *jettatore* in regard to their victim.

The *strega*, with her inability to bear children and her withdrawal from society, conforms to an old formula for evil eye in rural societies throughout the Mediterranean region; yet there is something more to her characterization in the Italian-American explanations. Her reclusiveness makes the stronger statement. She does not necessarily retire to the comfort of her own home, but to the confines of her own community. She shrinks back from the society whose language and behavior she does not understand and in so doing she forfeits any pretensions she may have to the "American Dream."

Among Lucia's neighbors there was a *strega* who would march up and down the sidewalk, brandishing a huge stick, and chasing children into the street (where they belonged). Sidewalks, in her estimation, were for the elderly. Her face was so red and her hooked nose so prominent that she gained the nickname "Tanto," a reference to a stereotypic characterization of the Lone Ranger's sidekick. Once, when Lucia's grandson was shooting firecrackers off in the railroad yard above their house, "Tanto" became convinced that he had a gun. As the grandson descended from the tracks, "Tanto" came running down the street. "Lucia, Lucia! He's got a gun!" she cried. Lucia watched in horror as "Tanto" thrust her hands into the boy's pocket and searched for the gun. She dragged her grandson back into the house, traced a cross in olive oil on his forehead, and forced some salt (the *salis sapientis* of baptism) between his lips. As the boy did not fall ill she deemed no cure necessary, but a year or so later as the boy passed through adolescence and his nose began to grow Lucia expressed the wish that she had performed the cure, fearing that her grandson had been cursed with Tanto's nose.

The *strega* does not want to see her buffer zone diminished and it is supposed that she must envy those that have learned the new language, have dealings outside of the community, and will someday make their homes in one of the sparkling developments on the outskirts of town. It follows that the predominant description of her victim is he or she who appears to partake in the "American Dream": the factory-worker, the shopkeeper, the secretary.

Lucia had a client who had landed a secretarial position. Her first order of business was to purchase the clothes and cosmetics that her American peers had taken always for granted, that she had always lacked. Within a few weeks she was building quite a wardrobe but she was also stricken with an incessant headache.

Week after week she appeared in Lucia's kitchen, seeking a cure for her malady. She secreted amulets beneath her new blouses; yet relief was always temporary and she was forced to resign her secretarial post. She is an exceptional case and Lucia never, before or after, experienced such a failure in her profession. Yet this client is typical of the description of the victim in the Italian-American explanation of evil eye.

If the *strega* were to be the only possible source of danger, then evil eye would be a relatively easy belief to understand. But another, possibly greater, danger comes into play when the Italian-American steps out of his neighborhood. It is often the amorphous danger of envy, but it becomes personified as the *jettatore*. The most salient features of this source of danger are that it exists outside of the Italian-American community and that when personified it is applied to some person of authority, relative to the victim.

A man trying to cross the road was forced back onto the curb by a Lincoln Continental. The driver leered out the car window and stepped on the accelerator. The pedestrian scratched his genitals and flashed a *mano cornuto*. He claimed that the driver was a known *jettatore* who worked at City Hall and that his own quick reflexes had saved him a serious illness. The pedestrian was just opening his own business in a non-Italian neighborhood and had reason to beware the evil eye.

The two-fold nature of danger allows us to draw

correlations between the belief in evil eye and the process of acculturation. The first obstacle to acculturation occurs within the Italian-American community. This obstacle is represented by the *strega*. The inability to understand and adjust to American society and the danger of withdrawal into the Italian-American community are made explicit. The second obstacle to acculturation occurs outside of the community. The *jettatore* represents mainstream American society.

This obstacle is clarified by the notion that the *jettatore* stands in both a spiritual power and physical authority position to his victim. Here is the formulative notion of a power structure which considers the Italian-American to be an uninvited participant in the acculturation process. The significance of this two-fold source of danger is clarified when the victim is taken into consideration. Just as the *strega* and *jettatore* are incomplete in their characterizations as barren wretches envying the fecundity of others; so the victim is incomplete in his characterization as unbaptized child, preadolescent boy, bride or groom. The *strega* as recluse and the *jettatore* as outsider are complemented by the victim as he or she who is making the transition from Italian to American society. The victim's transition may be stated in the economic terms of success and failure, but the notion of transition is the more potent imagery. Thus, we can look to Victor Turner's discussion of transitional ritual to understand the primary idiom for the acculturation process in the Italian-American context.

Turner maintains that beyond separating an initiate from one social position and incorporating him into another, transitional ritual effects an interstitial mediation between the two positions during which the initiate's condition is one of liminality. The liminal entity is one who is "betwixt and between the positions assigned and arrayed by law, custom, convention, and ceremonial (Turner 1969: 95)." As such he is perceived to be ambiguous and polluting. Something of the ambiguity of the evil eye victim must be recognized to be akin to the ambiguity of the unbaptized child. Thus, baptismal imagery dominates the evil eye cure (and to some extent apotropaic measures taken against the evil eye). The implication is that the evil eye cure is a means of rearticulating the patient's position within the social structure. Baptism once incorporated him into the Christian community. Baptismal imagery will now incorporate him into a community that can act as his ally during the acculturation process. The *Comare* is recognized to be the proper purveyor of the evil eye cure, precisely because of its baptismal imagery. The curing ritual was first presented to Santa Lucia, Lucia's patron saint. Therefore, Lucia is sought out to perform the evil eye cure.

The Evil Eye Cure

Lucia traces a cross in olive oil on the foreheads of both her patient and herself. She again dips her finger into the tin of oil and carefully shakes three drops into a dishpan of water. For each drop she offers the cross. *"In nome del Padre e del Figlio e dello Spirito Santo."* If the oil beads the illness is of the mundane sort, but if it slicks the illness is the result of envy and a cure must be effected. Nine times Lucia recites the *Ave Maria*.

> Hail Mary full of grace
> the Lord is with thee
> Blessed art thou among women
> and blessed is the fruit of thy womb,
> Jesus.
>
> Holy Mary
> Mother of God
> pray for us sinners
> now and at the hour of our death.
> Amen.

With each recitation she shakes a drop of oil into the water. With her ninth recitation she adds an incantation, the purpose of which is to chase away the envy.

I do not know Lucia's incantation. To reveal it without the proper intent is to ruin its efficacy. It may be revealed to only two people during her lifetime, and this only at midnight on Christmas Eve. Here, instead, are two incantations obtained by Phyllis Williams. Both are of Italian origin.

> Occhio morto, occhio tristo
> ti seguito coll'acqua, olio
> e Gesù Cristo.
>
> Eye of death, Evil Eye,
> I am following you with water,
> Oil and Jesus Christ (Williams 1969: 156).
>
> Santa Rosalia,
> l'acqua veniva.
> C'era una donna,

mal'occhio teneva.
Passò nostro Signore
con palma d'oliva in mano.
L'acqua fece seccare,
L'erba fece malagnare,
a quattro cantoni spumicava.
Padre, Figlio e Spirito Santo.

Saint Rosalie,
The water came flowing.
There was a woman,
Who had the evil eye.
Our Lord passed by
With an olive palm in his hand.
He made the water dry up,
The grass he made to wither,
Cast it to the four corners (of the earth).
Father, Son and Holy Spirit (Williams 1969: 155).

The divination must again be undertaken to determine whether the cure has been effected. This time, if the oil beads the water is thrown outside the house in a spot where it will pose no danger, but if it slicks the water will be poured down the kitchen sink and the cure repeated. The implication is that if the cure is effected the envy is contained in the water, if not it remains within the patient.

Willa Appel has observed that in certain parts of Italy the "polluted" water is poured upon a crossroads in a deliberate attempt to unload the envy upon some unaware passerby. In effect, Appel observes, "the original victim of the evil eye becomes the next *jettatore* (Appel 1976: 26)." This turnabout sheds light upon the nature of the spiritual powers, grace and envy. They are not so much two different things as they are two extremes of the same thing. Indeed, the *Comare* is commonly perceived to be as able in the use of envy as she is in the use of grace. Lucia never fails to display a mischievous grin when the word *strega* arises in conversation. She understands the two-sided nature of spiritual power. Mary Magdalene was the most wretched sinner and because of this condition most benefitted by Christ's grace. Of her, Jesus says, "Her sins which are many, are forgiven; for she loved much: but to whom little is forgiven, the same loveth little (Luke 7:47; King James Version).

The divination/cure process is rich in allusions to baptism into the Roman Catholic Church. Thus, Lucia is firmly defined in her capacity as *Comare*. Yet, the ritual can also be viewed as a reenactment and prefiguration of the entire spiritual develop-

ment of the patient. For instance, the drawing of the cross in oil on the foreheads references baptism, confirmation, and the last rite. Thus, the act might imply initiation into the Christian community, adulthood, and the Kingdom of God simultaneously.

The dropping of oil into water is another reference to baptism but with an elaborate twist. Lawrence DiStasi (1981) argues that olive oil is the symbolic equivalent to "soul-substance." If it maintains proper tension (i.e., the oil beads upon the water) the soul is maintaining its proper function as link between body and spirit. If, on the other hand, proper tension is broken (i.e., the oil slicks) body and spirit are unbound. The result is sickness. DiStasi sees in this instance an elaboration on the ancient belief in soul-loss (DiStasi 1981: 46–48).

The recitation of the Hail Mary represents a special instance within the divination/cure process. It is involved in the immediate pursuance of Christ's grace through the Interlocution of his mother, Mary. Here is the suggestion that just as Mary acts as Interlocutor for the *Comare*; so the *Comare* acts as Interlocutor for her patient (i.e., the *Comare* becomes, like Mary, "full of grace"). Given the nature of this relationship we might suppose that the *Comare* fills her patient with grace. In other words, envy is drawn out of the body and the "space" left behind is filled with grace. This process involves a spiritual uplifting of both the *Comare* and her patient. Together they remove themselves from a polluted world and partake in an almost sensual relationship with the Lord.

Thus, we find in the evil eye context an important idiom for differentiation of psychic from symbolic power. Psychic power is "masculine." The *jettatore* needs no explanation in his conformance to this rule. The *strega*, on the other hand, is "like man" in her inability to bear children (as did Mary). Symbolic power is "feminine." Obviously the *Comare* conforms to this rule but there are other occasions when grace comes into play. Julian Pitt-Rivers speaks of "a young man of markedly effeminate manner and dress named Rafael" who, for a short time, offered serious competition to the traditional (i.e., female) healers of the Andalusian village of "Alcalá." "Others may have their grace" Rafael claimed "but my grace is of the holy spirit itself (Pitt-Rivers 1961: 192)." In this case Rafael had to be "like woman" to be believably embued with grace.

The delineation of psychic and symbolic power in the evil eye context allows us to appreciate the authority the *Comare* enjoys within a traditionally patriarchal structure. It is her duty to order ambiguity and thus lessen pollution. This duty entails an elaboration of the social fabric, one in which women take the lead. Pollution, which exists as an idiom for social anxiety (in our case, that brought about through the process of acculturation), imposes a reorganization of society which will alleviate anxiety (i.e., ease the acculturation process). If anxiety is alleviated we must assume that the reorganization was a healthy one. If anxiety persists we can expect only disintegration of the social fabric.

Evil Eye and Patronage

The Italian-American explanation of evil eye should be considered a phenomenon indigenous to America. Perhaps the best paradigm to exonerate such a claim is that provided by Ward Goodenough in *Culture, Language, and Society* (1981). The Italian-American "culture pool" (p. 111) of the early twentieth century appears to have contained various evil eye explanations ranging from vague impressions on one end of the spectrum to highly elaborate complexes of belief and activity on the other. At some point these various explanations became Italian-American; that is to say, they gained a function particularized to America. The *strega* became the dominant personification of envy, while the *jettatore* retains that position in those regions of Italy that still maintain an evil eye belief. Perhaps the assumption that the Italian-American explanation of evil eye is a direct import from Italy, dying with those who carried it to America, arises from the mistaken notion that the belief in evil eye is to be found throughout the *Mezzogiorno*, the southern portion of Italy. Indeed, Charlotte Gower Chapman was surprised to discover that the people of Milocca (a peasant commune in western Sicily) had never even heard of the evil eye (Chapman 1971: 205).

Goodenough explains that "the role . . . an element within the culture pool plays in the conduct of activities—as well as its chance of continuing as a part of the pool—is liable to change, as the society's members make different choices among such elements as ways of thinking and acting that seem suitable for accomplishing their purposes and grati-

fying their wants (Goodenough 1981: 116)." In other words, the elaboration or abandonment of an element within the "culture pool" is dependent upon that element's social function. It is essential to understand the Italian-American explanation of evil eye as a phenomenon indigenous to America. Without that understanding there is no basis to postulate a function particularized to America.

The function of the Italian-American explanation of evil eye was the recognition and removal of the obstacles to acculturation. Recognition was addressed by the power of envy. The *strega* evoked the necessity for the Italian-American to adjust to a new society, while the *jettatore* evoked an element within that society which considered the Italian-American to be an intruder. Removal was addressed by the power of grace. The *Comare* taught her patient the efficacy of Interlocution.

We left the male counterpart to the *Comare* back at the baptismal font. He is the *Compare*, or Godfather. He borrowed the *Comare*'s method of Interlocution and transposed it from a spiritual to an economic sphere of influence. Thus, many of the external obstacles to acculturation were removed.

The Italian-American *Compare* is neither the Sicilian *Mafiosa*, nor the Neapolitan *Cammorrista*. In form, he is more closely related to the rural *padrone*, or patron, of Italy (Ianni 1972: 47). This *padrone* was the go-between for peasant and landowner. Garrison and Arensberg have seen in the apotropaic precautions employed against evil eye a type of veneration on the part of the peasant for the *padrone* (Garrison and Arensberg 1976: 294). Appel, on the other hand, has seen in the evil eye cure the desire on the part of the peasant to usurp the *padrone*'s position (Appel 1976: 26). Evil eye seems an accommodating belief, structuring itself to any given situation. Thus, both interpretations could be correct. The point to be made here is that the belief in evil eye is visibly related to the ideal of patronage. That relation is made explicit in the Italian-American explanation of evil eye. The evil eye cure and patronage are the same act played out in two separate spheres of influence: one spiritual, the other physical.

In closing, we should be alerted to the danger involved in considering the Godfather's method of Interlocution a direct import from Italy. It is the same danger that arises from considering the Italian-

American explanation of evil eye to be the same as the Italian. It negates the possibility of assigning the Godfather a function particularized to America (i.e., that of acculturation). Such a negation is a self-serving denial of American culpability in the resurgent ideal of patronage. For as long as it persists, we will ask "How white are we?" The informant mentioned at the beginning of this paper answers "We're not white yet. They just let us think we are." If it is the belief in evil eye that allows us to define who "they" are and how to overcome "their" obstacles, there may still be a *jettatore* loose in this forbidding land.

Urban Witches

Edward J. Moody

Starting in the mid-1960s, contemporary America began to witness a revival of witchcraft. In this article, Edward J. Moody examines a particular offshoot of witchcraft known as Satanism. As might be expected, the Satanic belief system described by Moody is the opposite of Christianity. Using the participant-observation research technique common to anthropological field investigation, Moody joined a group of Satanists in San Francisco, California, and sought answers to such questions as why people join the group, why Satanists persist in spite of their denouncement and persecution, and what benefits do they derive from membership. Interestingly, unlike witchcraft proper, where the witch may practice white (good) or black (bad) magic, the Satanists believe all magic is black magic. White or altruistic magic does not exist for the Satanist. Although brief mention is made in the article to the Satanist's leader, the so-called Prince of Darkness or, as he is sometimes known, the "Black Pope of Satanism," there is no reference to any prolonged interview with him. However, John Fritscher's fascinating interview with the high priest and founder of the Church of Satan, Anton Szandor La Vey, is recounted in Chapter 10 of this book.

Reprinted from *Conformity and Conflict: Readings in Cultural Anthropology*, 3rd ed. (Boston, 1977), pp. 427–37, by permission of the author.

EVERY FRIDAY EVENING JUST BEFORE MIDNIGHT, A group of men and women gathers at a home in San Francisco; and there, under the guidance of their high priest, a sorcerer or magus sometimes called the "Black Pope of Satanism," they study and practice the ancient art of black magic. Precisely at midnight they begin to perform Satanic rituals that apparently differ little from those allegedly performed by European Satanists and witches at least as early as the seventh century. By the dim and flickering light of black candles, hooded figures perform their rites upon the traditional Satanic altar—the naked body of a beautiful young witch—calling forth the mysterious powers of darkness to do their bidding. Beneath the emblem of Baphomet, the horned god, they engage in indulgences of flesh and sense for whose performance their forebears suffered death and torture at the hands of earlier Christian zealots.

Many of these men and women are, by day, respected and responsible citizens. Their nocturnal or covert practice of the black art would, if exposed, make them liable to ridicule, censure, and even punishment. Even though we live in an "enlightened" age, witches are still made a focus of a community's aggression and anxiety. They are denounced from the pulpit, prosecuted to the limit of the law, and subjected to extra-legal harassment by the fearful and ignorant.

Why then do the Satanists persist? Why do they take these risks? What benefits do they derive from membership in a Satanic church, what rewards are earned from the practice of witchcraft? What indulgences are enjoyed that they could not as easily find in one of the more socially acceptable arenas of pleasure available in our "permissive" society?

The nearly universal allegation of witchcraft in the various cultures of the world has excited the interest of social scientists for years and the volume of writing on the topic is staggering. Most accounts of witchcraft, however, share the common failing of having been written from the point of view of those who do not themselves practice the black art. Few, if any, modern authors have had contact with witches, black magicians, or sorcerers, relying instead on either the anguished statements of medieval victims of inquisition torture, or other types of secondhand "hearsay" evidence for their data. To further confuse the issue, authoritative and respected ethnologists have reported that black magic and witchcraft constitute an imaginary offense because it is impossible—that because witches cannot do what they are supposed to do, they are nonexistent.

Witches and Magicians

But the witches live. In 1965 while carrying out other research in San Francisco, California, I heard rumors of a Satanic cult which planned to give an All-Hallows Eve blessing to a local chamber of horrors. I made contact with the group through its founder and high priest and thus began over two years of participant-observation as a member of a contemporary black magic group. As a member of this group I interacted with my fellow members in both ritual and secular settings. The following description is based on the data gathered at that time.

The witches and black magicians who were members of the group came from a variety of social class backgrounds. All shades of political opinion were represented from Communist to American Nazi. Many exhibited behavior identified in American culture as "pathological," such as homosexuality, sadomasochism, and transvestism. Of the many characteristics that emerged from psychological tests, extensive observations, and interviews, the most common trait, exhibited by nearly all Satanic novices, was a high level of general anxiety related to low self-esteem and a feeling of inadequacy. This syndrome appears to be related to intense interpersonal conflicts in the nuclear family during socialization. Eighty-five percent of the group, the administrative and magical hierarchy of the church, reported that their childhood homes were split by alcoholism, divorce, or some other serious problem. Their adult lives were in turn marked by admitted failure in love, business, sexual, or social relationships. Before entering the group each member appeared to have been battered by failure in one or more of the areas mentioned, rejected or isolated by a society frightened by his increasingly bizarre and unpredictable behavior, and forced into a continuing struggle to comprehend or give meaning to his life situation.

Almost all members, prior to joining the group, had made some previous attempt to gain control over the mysterious forces operating around them. In order to give their environment some structure, in order to make it predictable and thus less anxiety-provoking, they dabbled in astrology, the Tarot, spiritualism, or other occult sciences, but continued failure in their everyday lives drove them from the passive and fatalistic stance of the astrologer to consideration of the active and manipulative role of sorcerer or witch. In articles in magazines such as *Astrology* and *Fate*, the potential Satanist comes into direct contact with magic, both white and black. Troubled by lack of power and control, the pre-Satanist is frequently introduced to the concept of magic by advertisements which promise "Occult power . . . now . . . for those who want to make real progress in understanding and working the forces that rule our Physical Cosmos . . . a self-study course in the practice of Magic." Or, Ophiel will teach you how to "become a power in your town, job, club, etc.," how to "create a familiar [a personal magic spirit servant] to help you through life," how to "control and dominate others." "The Secret Way" is offered free of charge, and the Esoteric Society offers to teach one how herbs, roots, oils, and rituals may be used, through "white magic," to obtain love, money, power, or a peaceful home. They will also teach one self-confidence and how to banish "unwanted forces." The reader is invited to join the Brotherhood of the White Temple, Inc.; the Monastery of The Seven Rays (specializing in sexual magic); the Radiant School; and numerous other groups that promise to reveal the secrets of success in business, sex, love, and life—the very secrets the potential or pre-Satanist feels have eluded him. Before joining the group, the pre-Satanist usually begins to perform magic ceremonies and rituals whose descriptions he receives for a fee from one of the various groups noted above, from magical wholesale houses, or from occult book clubs. These practices reinforce his "magical world view," and at the same time bring him in contact with other practitioners of the magical arts, both white and black.

Although most of the mail-order magic groups

profess to practice "white" magic—benevolent magic designed only to benefit those involved and never aggressive or selfish, only altruistic—as opposed to "black," malevolent, or selfish magic, even white rituals require ingredients that are rare enough so they can be bought only at certain specialty stores. These stores, usually known to the public as candle shops although some now call themselves occult art supply houses, provide not only the raw materials—oils, incenses, candles, herbs, parchments, etc.—for the magical workings, but serve as meeting places for those interested in the occult. A request for some specific magic ingredient such as "John the Conqueror oil," "Money-come powder," "crossing" powder, or black candles usually leads to a conversation about the magical arts and often to introductions to other female witches and male warlocks. The realization that there are others who privately practice magic, white or black, supports the novice magician in his new-found interest in magical manipulation. The presence of other witches and magicians in his vicinity serves as additional proof that the problems he has personally experienced may indeed be caused by witchcraft, for the pre-Satanist has now met, firsthand, witches and warlocks who previously were only shadowy figures, and if there are a few known witches, who knows how many there might be practicing secretly?

Many witches and magicians never go beyond the private practice of white or black magic, or at most engage in a form of magic "recipe" swapping. The individual who does join a formal group practicing magic may become affiliated with such a group in one of several ways. In some cases he has been practicing black magic with scant success. Perhaps he has gone no further than astrology or reading the designs on the ancient Tarot cards, a type of socially acceptable magic which the leader of the Satanic church disparagingly calls "god in sport clothes." But the potential Satanist has come to think of the cosmos as being ordered, and ordered according to magical—that is, imperceptible—principles. He is prompted by his sense of alienation and social inadequacy to try to gain control of the strange forces that he feels influence or control him and, hearing of a Satanic church, he comes to learn magic.

Others join because of anxiety and inadequacy of a slightly different nature. They may be ho-

mosexual, nymphomaniac, sadist, or masochist. They usually have some relatively blatant behavioral abnormality which, though they personally may not feel it wrong, is socially maladaptive and therefore disruptive. As in many "primitive " societies, magic and witchcraft provide both the "disturbed" persons and, in some cases, the community at large with a ready and consistent explanation for those "forces" or impulses which they themselves have experienced. Seeking control, or freedom, the social deviants come ultimately to the acknowledged expert in magic of all kinds, the head of the Satanic church, to have their demons exorcised, the spells lifted, and their own powers restored.

Others whose problems are less acute come because they have been brought, in the larger religious context, to think of themselves as "evil." If their struggle against "evil" has been to no avail, many of the individuals in question take this to mean that the power of "evil" is greater than the power of "good"—that "God is dead"—and so on. In their search for a source of strength and security, rather than continue their vain struggle with that "evil" force against which they know themselves to be powerless, they seek instead to identify themselves with evil, to join the "winning" side. They identify with Satan—etymologically the "opposition" —and become "followers of the left-hand path," "walkers in darkness."

Finally, there are, of course, those who come seeking thrills or titillation, lured by rumors of beautiful naked witches, saturnalian orgies, and other strange occurrences. Few of these are admitted into the group.

Black Magic

For the novice, initial contact with the Satanists is reassuring. Those assisting the "Prince of Darkness" who heads the church are usually officers in the church, long-term members who have risen from the rank and file to positions of trust and authority. They are well-dressed, pleasant persons who exude an aura of confidence and adequacy. Rather than having the appearance of wild-eyed fanatics or lunatics, the Satanists look like members of the middle-class, but successful middle-class. The Prince of Darkness himself is a powerfully built and striking individual with a shaven head and black, well-trimmed beard. Sitting among the implements of magic, surrounded by books that contain the "secrets of the centuries," he affirms for those present what they already know: that there is a secret to power and success which can and must be learned, and that secret is black magic.

All magic is black magic according to the Satanists. There is no altruistic or white magic. Each magician intends to benefit from his magical manipulation, even those workings performed at someone else's behest. To claim to be performing magic only for the benefit of others is either hypocrisy—the cardinal sin in Satanic belief—or naiveté, another serious shortcoming. As defined by the Satanists, magic itself is a surprisingly common-sense kind of phenomenon: "the change in situations or events in accordance with one's will, which would, using normally accepted methods, be unchangeable." Magic can be divided into two categories: ritual (ceremonial) and nonritual (manipulative).

Ritual, or "the greater magic," is performed in a specific ritual area and at a specific time. It is an emotional, not an intellectual act. Although the Satanists spend a great deal of time intellectualizing and rationalizing magic power, they state specifically that "any and all intellectual activity must take place *before* the ceremony, not during it."

The "lesser magic," nonritual (manipulative) magic, is, in contrast, a type of transactional manipulation based upon a heightened awareness of the various processes of behavior operative in interaction with others, a Satanic "games people play." The Satanist in ritual interaction is taught to analyze and utilize the motivations and behavioral Achilles' heels of others for his own purposes. If the person with whom one is interacting has masochistic tendencies, for example, the Satanist is taught to adopt the role of sadist, to "indulge" the other's desires, to be dominant, forceful, and even cruel in interaction with him.

Both the greater and the lesser magic is predicated upon a more general "magical" world view in which all elements of the "natural world" are animate, have unique and distinctive vibrations that influence the way they relate to other natural phenomena. Men, too, have vibrations, the principal difference between men and inanimate objects being that men can alter their pattern of vibrations, sometimes consciously and at will. It is the manipulation and the modification of these vibrations,

forces, or powers that is the basis of all magic. There are "natural magicians," untrained and unwitting, manipulators of magic power. Some, for example, resonate in harmony with growing things; these are people said to have a "green thumb," gardeners who can make anything grow. Others resonate on the frequency of money and have the "Midas touch" which turns their every endeavor into a profit-making venture. Still others are "love magnets"; they automatically attract others to them, fascinate and charm even though they may be physically plain themselves. If one is a "natural magician," he does some of these things unconsciously, intuitively, but because of the intellectual nature of our modern world, most people have lost their sensitivity to these faint vibrations. Such individuals may, if they become witches, magicians or Satanists, regain contact with that lost world just as tribal shamans are able to regain contact with another older world where men communicated with animals and understood their ways. It is this resensitization to the vibrations of the cosmos that is the essence of magical training. It takes place best in the "intellectual decompression chamber" of magic ritual, for it is basically a "subjective" and "non-scientific" phenomenon.

Those who have become members of the inner circle learn to make use of black magic, both greater and lesser, in obtaining goals which are the antithesis of Christian dogma. The seven deadly sins of Christian teaching—greed, pride, envy, anger, gluttony, lust, and sloth—are depicted as Satanic virtues. Envy and greed are, in the Satanic theology, natural in man and the motivating forces behind ambition. Lust is necessary for the preservation of the species and not a Satanic sin. Anger is the force of self-preservation. Instead of denying natural instincts the Satanist learns to glory in them and turn them into power.

Satanists recognize that the form of their ritual, its meanings, and its functions are largely determined by the wider society and its culture. The novitiate in the Satanic cult is taught, for example, that the meaning of the word "Satan" etymologically is "the opposition," or "he who opposes," and that Satanism itself arose out of opposition to the demeaning and stultifying institutions of Christianity. The cult recognizes that had there been no Christianity there would be no Satanism, at least not in the form it presently takes, and it maintains that much of the Satanic ritual and belief is structured by the form and content of Christian belief and can be understood only in that larger religious context. The Satanists choose black as their color, not white, precisely because white is the symbol of purity and transcendence chosen by Christianity, and black therefore has come to symbolize the profane earthy indulgences central to Satanic theodicy. Satanists say that their gods are those of the earth, not the sky; that their cult is interested in making the sacred profane, in contrast to the Judeo-Christian cults which seek to make the profane sacred. Satanism cannot, in other words, be understood as an isolated phenomenon, but must be seen in a larger context.

The Satanic belief system, not surprisingly, is the antithesis of Christianity. Their theory of the universe, their cosmology, is based upon the notion that the desired end state is a return to a pagan awareness of the mystical forces inhabiting the earth, a return to an awareness of their humanity. This is in sharp contrast to the transcendental goals of traditional Christianity. The power associated with the pantheon of gods is also reversed: Satan's power is waxing; God's, if he still lives, waning. The myths of the Satanic church purport to tell the true story of the rise of Christianity and the fall of paganism, and there is a reversal here too. Christ is depicted as an early "con man" who tricked an anxious and powerless group of individuals into believing a lie. He is typified as "pallid incompetence hanging on a tree." Satanic novices are taught that early church fathers deliberately picked on those aspects of human desire that were most natural and made them sins, in order to use the inevitable transgressions as a means of controlling the populace, promising them salvation in return for obedience. And finally, that substantive belief, the very delimitation of what is sacred and what is profane, is the antithesis of Christian belief. The Satanist is taught to "be natural; to revel in pleasure and in self-gratification. To emphasize indulgence and power in this life."

The opposition of Satanists to Christianity may be seen most clearly in the various rituals of greater magic. Although there are many different types of rituals all aimed at achieving the virtues that are the inverted sins of the Christian, we shall examine briefly only two of these: blasphemy and the invocation of destruction. By far the most famous of Satanic institutions, the Black Mass and other forms of ritual blasphemy serve a very real and necessary function for the new Satanist. In many cases the exhortations and teachings of his satanic colleagues are not sufficient to alleviate the sense of guilt and anxiety he feels when engaging in behavior forbidden by Judeo-Christian tradition. The novice may still cower before the charismatic power of Christian symbols; he may still feel guilty, still experience anxiety and fear in their presence. It is here that the blasphemies come into play, and they take many forms depending on the needs of the individuals involved.

A particular blasphemy may involve the most sacred Christian rituals and objects. In the traditional black Mass powerful Christian symbols such as the crucifix are handled brutally. Some Black Masses use urine or menstrual flow in place of the traditional wine in an attempt to evoke disgust and aversion to the ritual. If an individual can be conditioned to respond to a given stimulus, such as the communion wafer or wine, with disgust rather than fear, that stimulus's power to cause anxiety is diminished. Sexuality is also used. A young man who feared priests and nuns was deliberately involved in a scene in which two witches dressed as nuns interacted with him sexually; his former neurotic fear was replaced by a mildly erotic curiosity even in the presence of real nuns. The naked altar—a beautiful young witch—introduces another deliberate note of sexuality into a formerly awe-inspiring scene.

By far the most frequently used blasphemy involves laughter. Awe-inspiring or fear-producing institutions are made the object of ridicule. The blasphemous rituals, although still greater magic, are frequently extremely informal. To the outsider they would not seem to have any structure; the behavior being exhibited might appear to be a charade, or a party game. The Satanists decide ahead of time the institution to be ridiculed and frequently it is a Christian ritual. I have seen a group of Satanists do a parody of the Christmas manger scene, or dress in clerical garb while performing a satire of priestly sexual behavior. The target of blasphemy depends upon the needs of the various Satanists. If the group feels it is necessary for the well-being of one member, they will gladly, even gleefully, blaspheme anything from psychiatry to psychedelics.

In the invocation of destruction black magic

reaches its peak. In some cases an individual's sense of inadequacy is experienced as victimization, a sense of powerlessness before the demands of stronger and more ruthless men. The Satanic Bible, in contrast to Christian belief, teaches the fearful novice that "Satan represents vengeance instead of turning the other cheek." In the Third Chapter of the Book of Satan, the reader is exhorted to "hate your enemies with a whole heart, and if a man smite you on one cheek, SMASH him on the other . . . he who turns the other cheek is a cowardly dog."

One of the most frequently used rituals in such a situation is the Conjuration of Destruction, or Curse. Contrary to popular belief, black magicians are not indiscriminately aggressive. An individual must have harmed or hurt a member of the church before he is likely to be cursed. Even then the curse is laid with care, for cursing a more powerful magician may cause one's curse to be turned against oneself. If, in the judgment of the high priest and the congregation, a member has been unjustly used by a non-Satanist, even if the offender is an unaffiliated witch or magician, at the appropriate time in the ritual the member wronged may step forward and, with the aid and support of the entire congregation, ritually curse the transgressor. The name of the intended "sacrifice" is usually written on parchment made of the skin of unborn lamb and burned in the altar flame while the member himself speaks the curse; he may use the standard curse or, if he so desires, prepare a more powerful, individualistic one. In the curse he gives vent to his hostility and commands the legions of hell to torment and sacrifice his victim in a variety of horrible ways. Or, if the Satanist so desires, the High Priest will recite the curse for him, the entire group adding their power to the invocation by spirited responses.

The incidence of harmful results from cursing is low in the church of Satan because of two factors: first, one does not curse other members of the church for fear that their superior magic might turn the curse back upon its user; second, victims outside the congregation either do not believe in the power of black magic or do not recognize the esoteric symbols that should indicate to them they are being cursed.

On only one occasion was I able to see the effect of a curse on a "victim." A member attempted to

use the church and its members for publicity purposes without their permission. When the leader of the group refused to go along with the scheme, the man quit—an action that would have normally brought no recrimination—and began to slander the church by spreading malicious lies throughout San Francisco social circles. Even though he was warned several times to stop his lies, the man persisted; so the group decided to level the most serious of all curses at him, and a ritual death rune was cast.

Casting a death rune, the most serious form of greater magic, goes considerably beyond the usual curse designed to cause only discomfort or unhappiness, but not to kill. The sole purpose of the death rune is to cause the total destruction of the victim. The transgressor's name is written in blood (to the Satanist, blood is power—the very power of life) on special parchment, along with a number of traditional symbols of ceremonial magic. In a single-minded ritual of great intensity and ferocity, the emotional level is raised to a peak at which point the entire congregation joins in ritually destroying the victim of the curse. In the case in question, there was an orgy of aggression. The lamb's-wool figurine representing the victim was stabbed by all members of the congregation; hacked to pieces with a sword, shot with a small calibre pistol, and then burned.

A copy of the death rune was sent to the man in question, and every day thereafter an official death certificate was made out in his name and mailed to him. After a period of weeks during which the "victim" maintained to all who would listen that he "did not believe in all that nonsense," he entered the hospital with a bleeding ulcer. Upon recovery he left San Francisco permanently.

In fairness, I must add that the "victim" of the curse had previously had an ulcer, was struggling with a failing business, and seemed hypertense when I knew him. His knowledge of the "curse" may have hastened the culmination of his difficulties. The Satanic church, however, claimed it as a successful working, a victory for black magic, and word of it spread among the adherents of occult subculture, enhancing the reputation of the group.

Conclusion

Contemporary America is presently undergoing a witchcraft revival. On all levels, from teenagers to octogenarians, interest in, or fear of, witchcraft has increased dramatically over the past two years. It is hardly possible to pass a popular magazine rack without seeing an article about the revival of the black arts. Covens and cults multiply, as does the number of exorcisms and reconsecrations. England, France, Germany, and a host of other countries all report a rebirth of the black art. Why? Those who eventually become Satanists are attempting to cope with the everyday problems of life, with the here and now, rather than with some transcendental afterlife. In an increasingly complex world which they do not fully understand, an anxiety-provoking world, they seek out a group dedicated to those mysterious powers that the sufferers have felt moving them. Fearful of what one witch calls "the dark powers we all feel moving deep within us," they come seeking either *release* or *control.* They give various names to the problems they bring, but all, anxious and afraid, come to the Satanic cult seeking help in solving problems beyond their meager abilities. Whatever their problem—bewitchment, business failure, sexual impotence, or demonic possession—the Satanists, in the ways I have mentioned and many more, *can* and *do* help them. Witchcraft, the witches point out, " is the most practical of all beliefs. According to its devotees, its results are obvious and instantaneous. No task is too high or too lowly for the witch." Above all, the beliefs and practices provide the witch and the warlock with a sense of power, a feeling of control, and an explanation for personal failure, inadequacy, and other difficulties.

Moreover, a seeker's acceptance into the Inner Circle provides a major boost for his self-esteem; he has, for the first time, been accepted into a group as an individual despite his problems and abnormalities. Once within the Inner Circle that support continues. The Satanic group is, according to the cultural standards of his society, amoral, and the Satanist frequently finds himself lauded and rewarded for the very impulses and behavior that once brought shame and doubt.

Each Satanist is taught, and not without reason, that the exposure of his secret identity, of the fact that he is a powerful and adequate black magician, means trouble from a fearful society. Therefore, in keeping with the precepts of lesser magic, he learns to transform himself magically by day (for purposes of manipulation) into a bank clerk, a businessman, or even a college professor. He wears the guise and plays the role expected by society in order to manipulate the situation to his own advantage, to reach his desired goals. Members of society at large, aware only of his "normal" role behavior and unaware of the secret person within, respond to him positively instead of punishing him or isolating him. Then, in the evening, in the sanctity of his home, or when surrounded by his fellow magicians, he reverts to his "true" role, that of Satanic priest, and becomes himself once again. Inadequate and anxious persons, guilty because of socially disapproved impulses, are accepted by the Satanists and taught that the impulses they feel are natural and normal, but must be contained within certain spatial and temporal boundaries—the walls of the ritual chamber, the confines of the Inner Circle.

7

Demons, Exorcism, Divination, and Magic

Demons, spirits, ancestors, and gods all exist as realities in the human mind, and possess the power to harm and harass the living. Good and evil are counter-balanced in every society through a variety of rituals and other forms of protection; yet this balance is inevitably broken by human weaknesses and transgressions that invite the evil nature of supernatural agents. The malicious acts of these agents inflict pain and anguish on the innocent as well as on those deserving of punishment. Although all supernaturals can possess an individual and cause an unending variety of harm, the most commonly known agent of possession is the demon. Demons may aid their human consorts from time to time, but generally they are seen as being responsible for diseases, injuries, or a myriad of major and minor personal and group disasters. More powerful than mere humans, they are also generally believed to be less powerful than gods and ancestral spirits (Collins 1978: 195).

Tsham mask from Tibet.

Possession by demons is ordinarily considered dangerous, but this is not always the case. For the Aymara Indians of Bolivia, for example, possession results in serious consequences for the victims and their community, whereas among the Haitians it is actively sought at Voodoo ceremonies in order to obtain the supernatural knowledge of the spirits. Haitians, however, conceive of both good and evil spirits, and all fear possession by the latter.

The functions of possession commonly go unnoticed, overshadowed as they are by the dramatic expressive actions of the possessed and those in attendance. Stanley and Ruth Freed (1964: 71) showed that spirit possession in a north Indian village functioned primarily to relieve the individual's intropsychic tensions while simultaneously giving the victim the attention and sympathy of relatives and friends. The possession itself and its overt demonstration was only a vehicle for these functions. Even rules designed to avoid demons, such as the *jinns* of Islamic countries, can promote individual self-discipline and propriety in behavior, both, as Howells has pointed out, desirable qualities (1962: 202).The prohibitions promoted to avoid *jinns* do direct behavior toward socially approved goals, but despite these positive functions, the fact remains that demons cause suffering and pain to members of both Western and non-Western societies and every society is forced to cope with their devious nature.

Exorcism—the driving away of evil spirits such as demons by chanting, praying, commanding, or other ritual means—occurs throughout the world and is invoked when an evil spirit has caused illness by entering a person's body. (A belief in exorcism assumes a related belief in the power of ritual to move an evil spirit from one place to another.) Although the idea that foreign objects can enter the body and cause illness has been widespread, it was especially prevalent among American Indians, where curers, shamans, and sometimes a specialist known as a "sucking doctor," had the ability to remove these materials by such techniques as rubbing and kneading the patient's body, gesturing over the diseased area, or directly sucking out the evil object. Shamans, because of the "trick" aspect of their rituals, are especially well versed in the intricacies of exorcism

as a means of removal of disease-causing objects. Typically, a sleight-of-hand maneuver is used to show the patient that the harmful substance has been removed.

William Howells (1962: 92–94) has described several techniques used around the world for exorcising evil spirits and diseases: using sweat-baths, cathartics, or emetics to flush out the offending spirits; trephining; manipulating and massaging the body; sucking-out of the disease objects; scraping or sponging the illness off the body; reciting magical spells, coaxing, or singing songs to lure the spirit away; tempting the spirit to evacuate the body by laying out a sumptuous meal for it; keeping the patient uncomfortable, sometimes by administering beatings, so the spirit will be discontented with the body and want to depart; building a fire under the patient to make it uncomfortably warm for the spirit; placing foul-smelling, overripe fruit near the patient; and scandalizing the demon by having the patient's naked wife jump over the patient.

There is considerable evidence to support the belief that trephination among pre-Columbian Peruvians was a supernatural-based method of exorcism. A technique of skull surgery, trephining involved cutting a hole in the skull with a type of small saw or knife known as a trephine. Although the primary reason for the procedure was generally believed to be the physical easing of pressure on the brain, the supernatural reasons for the practice cannot be overlooked.

Until the recent popularity of movies, television shows, and novels about possession by demons, the American public was largely unaware that exorcism has been practiced throughout the history of Western religions. Somewhat alarming to many Americans was the realization that the Catholic church continued to approve exorcisms in twentieth-century America. The following seventeenth-century conjuration was recited by priests in order to exorcize evil spirits from troubled houses. The words may be different, as are the names for the supernatural beings referred to, but the intent of the conjuration is identical to incantations uttered by religious specialists in preliterate societies during exorcism rites for similar purposes:

I adjure thee, O serpent of old, by the Judge of living and the dead; by the Creator of the world who hath power to cast into hell, that thou depart forthwith from this house. He that commands thee, accursed demon, is He that commanded the winds and the sea and the storm. He that commands thee, is He that ordered thee to be hurled down from the height of heaven into the lower parts of the earth. He that commands thee is He that bade thee depart from Him. Hearken, then, Satan, and fear. Get thee gone, vanquished and cowed, when thou art bidden in the name of our Lord Jesus Christ who will come to judge the living and the dead and all the world by fire. Amen. (Crehan 1970: 873)

William James saw religion as the belief in an unseen order. If one important aspect of religion is helping believers to come to know that unknown, it then follows that divination is important to religion. Divination means learning about the future or about things that may be hidden. Although the word itself may be traced to "divinity," which indicates its relationship to gods, the practice of divination belongs as much to magic as it does to religion proper. From the earliest times, human beings have wanted to know about such climatic changes as drought and heavy rainfall. Without scientific information to help predict natural events, early humans looked for "signs" in the flight of birds, or the entrails of small animals, or perhaps the positions of coals in a fire or pebbles in a stream. To this day the methods of divination in the world's cultures are far too varied and numerous to mention here. However, John Collins (1978: 56–58), following a classification scheme conceived by H. J. Rose, has listed ten basic varieties of divination techniques:

1. *Dreams*, probably the most prevalent form of divination, with the dream's meaning either obvious or requiring analysis.

2. *Presentiments*, a more personal type of divination in which an individual develops a feeling, or presentiment, about something.

3. *Body actions*, such as sneezing, twitching, and hiccuping, which may be interpreted as predictions of rainfall, good or bad luck, drought, or some other particular event.

4. *Ordeals*, painful and often life-threatening tests that a person suspected of guilt may be forced to undergo, such as dipping a hand into hot oil, swallowing poison, or having a red-hot knife

blade pressed against some part of the body. Although the ordeal is usually used to help resolve conflict situations, the likelihood that an innocent person may be found guilty is potentially as great as "divining" the actual guilty individual.

5. *Possession* by spirits, enabling the diviner better to reveal the future by discovering hidden knowledge.

6. *Necromancy*, similar to possession, a technique of seeking "signs" from spirits of the dead, or perhaps by close observation of a corpse.

7. *Animal types*, a form of divination in which knowledge is derived either from the observation of living animals or from the inspection of the entrails of dead animals.

8. *Mechanical types*, a form of divination (the most comprehensive category of all) that involves seeking answers by manipulating an innumerable number of objects (for example, a sandal flipped in the air may be interpreted as meaning yes if it lands on its sole, no if on the straps).

9. *Nature types*, in which answers are determined by looking for signs in nature (for example, a particular pattern of mushrooms in the ground, the way leaves tumble from a tree, astrological signs such as the position of the stars and moon).

10. *Miscellaneous divination*, a large category including divination techniques that do not fit into the previous types (for example, death always strikes in threes).

Up to this decade controversy has surrounded the definition of magic and religion by anthropologists. Only recently have they come close to agreement that the dichotomy is a false one or that, if a dichotomy does exist, its ramifications are not significant to the study of the practitioners of each. Both magic and religion deal directly with the supernatural, and our understanding of the cultural applications of each provides deeper insights into the world view of the people practicing them.

Magic is usually divided into types, depending on the techniques involved. For example, Frazer distinguished "imitative magic," in which the magician believes that the desired result could be achieved by imitation, from "contagious magic," in which materials or substances once in contact with the intended victim are used in the magical attack. Other scholars would include "sympathetic magic," a form of magic in which items associated with or symbolic of the intended victim are used to identify and carry out the spell. Obviously, sympathetic magic contains elements of both imitative and contagious magic.

These forms of magic, still in use today, have been important methods of reducing anxiety regarding problems that exceeded the ability of people to understand and control them, especially because of a lack of technological expertise. Divination, special formulas and incantations, spells and curses, all are considered magical, and all can be used for good or evil. Since these activities are learned, they should be differentiated from witchcraft, which is considered innate and, most believe, uncontrollable.

It is logical to assume that non-Western reliance on explanations of events in terms of magic, sorcery, and witchcraft is a natural outcome of a lack of scientific training. But it is equally important to note that Westerners also rely on religious beliefs, with faith playing a strong role in determining actions and behaviors in our daily lives. Our ethnocentrism still blinds us to the similarities between ourselves and our fellow humans in the underdeveloped regions of the world. The great questions concerning the human condition are asked by all peoples, and despite the disparate levels of technology our sameness is demonstrated by the universality of religion.

In the first article of this chapter, June Nash describes the relationship of Bolivian miners with the Devil and other spirits residing in the mines. E. Mansell Pattison's article is concerned with the widespread renewal of social interest in the supernatural, mystical, magical, and "irrational" in contemporary Western society. The article is a good choice for this chapter because of its focus on exorcism, demonology, and possession. Eugene Mendonsa shows how divination acts as a social control mechanism among the Sisala of northern Ghana. The Malinowski essay is a classic analysis of the distinction preliterate peoples make between magic and science. In the last article, George Gmelch cleverly applies Malinowski's ideas on magic and science to modern baseball.

References

Collins, John J.
1978 *Primitive Religion*. Totowa, N.J.: Littlefield, Adams and Co.

Crehan, J. H.
1970 "Exorcism." In Richard Cavendish, ed., *Man, Myth and Magic*, Vol. 7, pp. 869–73. London: BPCC/Phoebus Publishing.

Freed, Stanley A., and Ruth S. Freed
1964 "Spirit Possession as Illness in a North Indian Village." *Ethnology* 3: 152–71.

Howells, William
1962 *The Heathens*. Garden City, N.Y.: Doubleday.

Devils, Witches, and Sudden Death

June Nash

In this article June Nash describes the dangerous and frightening workaday world of Bolivian tin miners as they ply their trade one-half mile deep in the high Andean plateau of Bolivia. In this fearful world they have found a spiritual ally in the Devil, or Tio (uncle). Because Tio controls the mines, revealing veins of ore at his whim, the miners must venerate him. In addition to the omnipresent images of Tio, there are other spirits in the shafts: Awiche, a positive force who can temper the evil of Tio, and Virida, a consort of Tio who has the power to make men lose their minds. Shortly after Professor Nash visited the mines, three workers were killed in a mine explosion, thus necessitating the holding of a k'araku, a ceremonial banquet of sacrificed animals. During the ceremony, Tio will be offered coca and alcohol and be recognized as the true owner of the mine (the ch'alla ceremony). Nash's article is a poignant reminder of the power of the Devil, and in the rituals that the miners have constructed to turn his destructive power into the positive force of increasing the ore yield and providing a safer place to work.

TIN MINERS IN THE HIGH ANDEAN PLATEAU OF Bolivia earn less than a dollar a day when, to use their phrase, they "bury themselves alive in the bowels of the earth." The mine shafts—as much as two miles long and half a mile deep—penetrate hills that have been exploited for more than 450 years. The miners descend to the work areas in open hauls; some stand on the roof and cling to the swaying cable as the winch lowers them deep into the mine.

Once they reach their working level, there is always the fear of rockslides as they drill the face of the mine, of landslides when they set off the dynamite, of gas when they enter unfrequented areas. And added to their fear of the accidents that have killed or maimed so many of their workmates is their economic insecurity. Like Wall Street brokers they watch international price quotations on tin, because a difference of a few cents can mean layoffs, loss of bonuses, a cut in contract prices—even a change of government.

Working in the narrow chimneys and corridors of the mine, breathing the dust- and silicate-filled air, their bodies numbed by the vibration of the drilling machines and the din of dynamite blasts, the tin miners have found an ally in the devil, or Tio (uncle), as he is affectionately known. Myths relate the devil to his pre-Christian counterpart Huari, the powerful ogre who owns the treasures of the hills. In Oruro, a 13,800-foot-high mining center in the western Andes of Bolivia, all the miners know the legend of Huari, who persuaded the simple farmers of the Uru Uru tribe to leave their work in the fields and enter the caves to find the riches he had in store. The farmers, supported by their ill-gained wealth from the mines, turned from a virtuous life of tilling the soil and praying to the sun god Inti to a life of drinking and midnight revels. The community would have died, the legend relates, if an Inca maiden, Nusta, had not descended from the sky and taught the people to live in harmony and industry.

Despite four centuries of proselyting, Catholic priests have failed to wipe out belief in the legend, but the principal characters have merged with Catholic deities. Nusta is identified with the Virgin of the Mineshaft, and is represented as the vision that appeared miraculously to an unemployed miner.

The miners believe that Huari lives on in the hills where the mines are located, and they venerate him in the form of the devil, or Tio. They believe he controls the rich veins of ore, revealing them only to those who give him offerings. If they offend the Tio or slight him by failing to give him offerings, he will withhold the rich veins or cause an accident.

Miners make images of the Tio and set them up in the main corridors of each mine level, in niches cut into the walls for the workers to rest. The image of the Tio varies in appearance according to the fancy of the miner who makes him, but his body is always shaped from ore. The hands, face, horns, and legs are sculptured with clay from the mine. Bright pieces of metal or burned-out bulbs from the miners' electric torches are stuck in the eye sockets. Teeth are made of glass or crystal sharpened "like nails," and the mouth is open, gluttonous and ready to receive offerings. Sometimes the plaster of Paris masks worn by the devil dancers at Carnival are used for the head. Some Tios wear embroidered vests, flamboyant capes, and miners' boots. The figure of a bull, which helps miners in contract with the devil by digging out the ore with its horns, occasionally accompanies the image, or there may be *chinas*, female temptresses who are the devil's consorts.

The Tio is a figure of power: he has what everyone wants, in excess. Coca remains lie in his greedy mouth. His hands are stretched out, grasping the bottles of alcohol he is offered. His nose is burned black by the cigarettes he smokes down to the nub. If a Tio is knocked out of his niche by an extra charge of dynamite and survives, the miners consider him to be more powerful than others.

Another spirit present in the mines but rarely represented in images is the Awiche, or old woman. Although some miners deny she is the Pachamama, the earth goddess worshiped by farm-ers, they relate to her in the same way. Many of the miners greet her when they enter the mine, saying, "Good-day, old woman. Don't let anything happen to me today!" They ask her to intercede with the Tio when they feel in danger; when they leave the mine safely, they thank her for their life.

Quite the opposite kind of feminine image, the Viuda, or widow, appears to miners who have been drinking *chicha*, a fermented corn liquor. Miners who have seen the Viuda describe her as a young and beautiful *chola*, or urbanized Indian, who makes men lose their minds—and sometimes their paychecks. She, too, is a consort of the devil and recruits men to make contracts with him, deluding them with promises of wealth.

When I started working in Oruro during the summer of 1969, the men told me about the *ch'alla*, a ceremonial offering of cigarettes, coca, and alcohol to the Tio. One man described it as follows:

"We make the *ch'alla* in the working areas within the mine. My partner and I do it together every Friday, but on the first Friday of the month we do it with the other workers on our level. We bring in banners, confetti, and paper streamers. First we put a cigarette in the mouth of the Tio and light it. After this we scatter alcohol on the ground for the Pachamama, then give some to the Tio. Next we take out our coca and begin to chew, and we also smoke. We serve liquor from the bottles each of us brings in. We light the Tio's cigarette, saying 'Tio, help us in our work. Don't let any accidents happen.' We do not kneel before him as we would before a saint, because that would be sacrilegious.

"Then everyone begins to get drunk. We begin to talk about our work, about the sacrifices that we make. When this is finished, we wind the streamers around the neck of the Tio. We prepare our *mesas* [tables of offerings that include sugar cakes, llama embryos, colored wool, rice, and candy balls].

"After some time we say, 'Let's go.' Some have to carry out those who are drunk. We go to where we change our clothes, and when we come out we again make the offering of liquor, banners, and we wrap the streamers around each others' necks. From there on, each one does what he pleases."

I thought I would never be able to participate in a *ch'alla* because the mine managers told me the men didn't like to have women inside the mine, let alone join them in their most sacred rites. Finally a friend high in the governmental bureaucracy gave me permission to go into the mine. Once down on the lowest level of San José mine, 340 meters below the ground, I asked my guide if I could stay with one of the work crews rather than tour the galleries as most visitors did. He was relieved to leave me and get back to work. The men let me try their machines so that I could get a sense of what it was like to hold a 160-pound machine vibrating in a yardwide tunnel, or to use a mechanical shovel in a gallery where the temperature was 100°F.

They told me of some of their frustrations—not getting enough air pumped in to make the machines work at more than 20 percent efficiency and constant breakdowns of machinery, which slowed them up on their contract.

At noon I refused the superintendent's invitation to eat lunch at level O. Each of the men gave me a bit of his soup or some "seconds," solid food consisting of noodles, potatoes, rice, and spicy meat, which their wives prepare and send down in the elevators.

At the end of the shift all the men in the work group gathered at the Tio's niche in the large corridor. It was the first Friday of the month and the gang leader, Lino Pino, pulled out a bottle of fruit juice and liquor, which his wife had prepared, and each of the men brought out his plastic bag with coca. Lino led the men in offering a cigarette to the Tio, lighting it, and than shaking the liquor on the ground and calling for life, "Hallalla! Hallalla!"

We sat on lumps of ore along the rail lines and Lino's helper served us, in order of seating, from a little tin cup. I was not given any priority, nor was I forgotten in the rounds. One of the men gave me coca from his supply and I received with two hands, as I had been taught in the rituals aboveground. I chewed enough to make my cheek feel numb, as though I had had an injection of novocaine for dental work. The men told me that coca was their gift from the Pachamama, who took pity on them in their work.

As Lino offered liquor to the Tio, he asked him to "produce" more mineral and make it "ripen," as though it were a crop. These rituals are a continuation of agricultural ceremonies still practiced by the farmers in the area. The miners themselves are the sons or grandsons of the landless farmers who were recruited when the gold and silver mines were reopened for tin production after the turn of the century.

A month after I visited level 340, three miners died in an explosion there when a charge of dynamite fell down a shoot to their work site and exploded. Two of the men died in the mine; the third died a few days later in the hospital. When the accident occurred, all the men rushed to the elevators to help or to stare in fascinated horror as the dead and injured were brought up to level O. They carried the bodies of their dead comrades to the social center where they washed the charred faces, trying to lessen the horror for the women who were coming. When the women came into the social center where the bodies were laid out, they screamed and stamped their feet, the horror of seeing their husbands or neighbors sweeping through their bodies.

The entire community came to sit in at the wake, eating and drinking in the feasting that took place before the coffins of their dead comrades. The meal seemed to confirm the need to go on living as well as the right to live.

Although the accident had not occurred in the same corridor I had been in, it was at the same level. Shortly after that, when a student who worked with me requested permission to visit the mine, the manager told her that the men were hinting that the accident had happened because the gringa (any foreign-born, fair-haired person, in this case myself) had been inside. She was refused permission. I was disturbed by what might happen to my relations with the people of the community, but even more concerned that I had added to their sense of living in a hostile world where anything new was a threat.

The miners were in a state of uneasiness and tension the rest of that month, July. They said the Tio was "eating them" because he hadn't had an offering of food. The dead men were all young, and the Tio prefers the juicy flesh and blood of the young, not the tired blood of the sick older workers. He wanted a k'araku, a ceremonial banquet of sacrificed animals.

There had not been any scheduled k'arakus since the army put the mines under military control in 1965. During the first half of the century, when the "tin barons"—Patiño, Hochschild, and Arayamao —owned the mines, the administrators and even some of the owners, especially Patiño, who had risen from the ranks, would join with the men in sacrificing animals to the Tio and in the drinking and dancing that followed. After nationalization of the mines in 1952, the rituals continued. In fact, some of the miners complained that they were done in excess of the Tio's needs. One said that going into the mine after the revolution was like walking into a saloon.

Following military control, however, the miners had held the ritual only once in San José, after two men had died while working their shift. Now the Tio had again shown he was hungry by eating the three miners who had died in the accident. The miners were determined to offer him food in a k'araku.

At 10:30 P.M. on the eve of the devil's month, I went to the mine with Doris Widerkehr, a student, and Eduardo Ibañez, a Bolivian artist. I was somewhat concerned about how we would be received after what the manager of the mine had said, but all the men seemed glad we had come. As we sat at the entry to the main shaft waiting for the yatiris, shamans who had been contracted for the ceremony, the miners offered us chicha and cocktails of fruit juice and alcohol.

When I asked one of the men why they had prepared the ritual and what it meant, his answer was:

"We are having the k'araku because a man can't die just like that. We invited the administrators, but none of them have come. This is because only the workers feel the death of their comrades.

"We invite the Pachamama, the Tio, and God to eat the llamas that we will sacrifice. With faith we give coca and alcohol to the Tio. We are more believers in God here than in Germany or the United States because there the workers have lost their soul. We do not have earthquakes because of our faith before God. We hold the crucifix to our breast. We have more confidence before God."

Most miners reject the claim that belief in the Tio is pagan sacrilege. They feel that no contradiction exists, since time and place for offerings to the devil are clearly defined and separated from Christian ritual.

At 11:00 P.M. two white llamas contributed by the administration were brought into level O in a company truck. The miners had already adorned the pair, a male and a female, with colored paper streamers and the bright wool earrings with which farmers decorate their flocks.

The four yatiris contracted for did not appear, but two others who happened to be staying at the house of a miner were brought in to perform the ceremony. As soon as they arrived, the miners took the llamas into the elevator. The male was on the right and the female to his left, "just the same as a marriage ceremony," one miner commented. Looking at the couple adorned with bright streamers and confetti, there was the feeling of a wedding.

Two men entered the elevator with the llamas and eight more climbed on top to go down to level 340. They were commissioned to take charge of the ritual. All the workers of 340 entered to participate in the ceremony below and about 50 men gathered at level O to drink.

At level 340 the workers guided the yatiris to the spot where the accident had occurred. There they cast liquor from a bottle and called upon the Tio, the Awiche, and God to protect the men from further accidents—naming all the levels in the mine, the various work sites, the different veins of ore, the elevator shaft, and the winch, repeating each name three times and asking the Tio not to eat any more workers and to give them more veins to work. The miners removed their helmets during this ritual. It ended with the plea for life, "Hallalla, hallalla, hallalla." Two bottles of liquor were sprinkled on the face of the rock and in the various work places.

The yatiris then instructed the men to approach the llamas with their arms behind their backs so that the animals would not know who held the knife that would kill them. They were also told to beg pardon for the sacrifice and to kiss the llamas farewell. One miner, noting what appeared to be a tear falling from the female's eye, cried and tried to comfort her. As the men moved around the llamas in a circle, the yatiris called on the Malkus (eagle gods), the Awiche, the Pachamama, and finally the Tiyulas (Tios of the mines), asking for their care.

The female llama was the first to be sacrificed. She struggled and had to be held down by two men as they cut her jugular vein. When they disemboweled her, the men discovered that she was pregnant, to which they attributed the strength of her resistance. Her blood was caught in a white basin.

When the heart of the dying llama had pumped out its blood, the yatiri made an incision and removed it, using both his hands, a sign of respect when receiving an offering. He put the still palpitating heart in the basin with the blood and covered it with a white cloth on which the miners placed k'oa—an offering made up of herbs, coca, wool, and sweets—and small bottles of alcohol and wine.

The man in charge of the ceremony went with five aides to the site of the principal Tio in the main corridor. There they removed a piece of ore from the image's left side, creating a hole into which they put the heart, the blood, and the other offerings. They stood in a circle, their heads bent, and asked for safety and that there be no more accidents. In low voices, they prayed in Quechua.

When this commission returned, the yatiris proceeded to sacrifice the male llama. Again they asked the Tio for life and good ore in all the levels of the mine, and that there be no accidents. They took the heart, blood, k'oa, and bottles of alcohol and wine to another isolated gallery and buried it for the Tio in a place that would not be disturbed. There they prayed, "filled with faith," as one commented; then returned to the place of the sacrifice. The yatiris sprinkled the remaining blood on the veins of ore.

By their absorption and fervid murmuring of prayers, both young and old miners revealed the same faith and devotion. Many of them wept, thinking of the accident and their dead companions. During the ritual drinking was forbidden.

On the following day those men charged with responsibility for the ritual came to prepare the meat. They brought the two carcasses to the baker, who seasoned them and cooked them in large ovens. The men returned at about 1:15 P.M. to distribute the meat. With the meat, they served chicha. Some sprinkled chicha on the ground for the Pachamama, saying "Hallalla," before drinking.

The bones were burned to ashes, which were then offered to the Tio. The mine entrance was locked shut and left undisturbed for 24 hours. Some remarked that it should be closed for three days, but the company did not want to lose that much time.

During the k'araku the miners recognize the Tio as the true owner of the mine. "All the mineral that comes out from the interior of the mine is the 'crop' of the devil and whether one likes it or not, we have to invite the Tio to drink and eat so that the flow of metal will continue," said a young miner who studied evenings at the University of Oruro.

All the workers felt that the failure of the administrators to come to the k'araku indicated not only their lack of concern with the lives of the men but also their disregard of the need to raise productivity in the mine.

When the Tio appears uninvited, the miners fear that they have only a short time to live. Miners who have seen apparitions say the Tio looks like a gringo—tall, red-faced, with fair hair and beard, and wearing a cowboy hat. This description hardly resembles the images sculptured by the miners, but it does fit the foreign technicians and administrators who administered the mines in the time of the tin barons. To the Indian workers, drawn from the highland and Cochabamba farming areas, the Tio is a strange and exotic figure, ruthless, gluttonous, powerful, and arbitrary in his use of that power, but nonetheless attractive, someone to get close to in order to share that power. I was beginning to wonder if the reason I was accepted with such good humor by the miners, despite their rule against women in the mines, was because they thought I shared some of these characteristics and was a match for the devil.

Sickness or death in the family can force a man in desperation to make a contract with the devil. If his companions become aware of it, the contract is destroyed and with it his life.

The miners feel that they need the protection of a group when they confront the Tio. In the ch'alla and the k'araku they convert the power of the Tio into socially useful production. In effect, the rituals are ways of getting the genie back into the bottle after he has done his miracles. Security of the group then depends upon respect toward the sacrificial offering, as shown by the following incident told me by the head of a work gang after the k'araku:

"I know of a man who had a vein of ore near where the bones of the sacrificial llama were buried. Without advising me, he made a hole with his drill and put the dynamite in. He knew very well that the bones were there. On the following day, it cost him his life. While he was drilling, a stone fell and cut his head off.

"We had to change the bones with a ceremony. We brought in a good shaman who charged us B$500 [about $40], we hired the best orchestra, and we sang and danced in the new location where we laid the bones. We did not work in that corridor for three days, and we spent all the time in the *ch'alla*."

Often the miners are frightened nearly to death in the mine. A rock falls on the spot they have just left, a man falls in a shaft and is saved by hitting soft clay at the bottom, a tunnel caves in the moment after a man leaves it—these are incidents in a day's work that I have heard men say can start a *haperk'a*, or fear, that can take their lives.

A shaman may have to be called in to bring back the spirit that the Tio has seized. In one curing, a frightened miner was told to wear the clothing he had on when the Tio seized his spirit and to enter and give a service to the Tio at the same spot where he was frightened. The shaman himself asked the Tio to cure his patient, flattering him, "Now you have shown your power, give back his spirit."

The fear may result in sexual impotency. At one of the mines, Siglo XX, when there is full production, a dynamite blast goes off every five minutes in a section called Block Haven. The air is filled with smoke and the miners describe it as an inferno. Working under such tension, a shattering blast may unnerve them. Some react with an erection, followed by sexual debilitation. Mad with rage and fear, some miners have been known to seize a knife, the same knife they use to cut the dynamite leads, and castrate themselves. When I visited Block Haven, I noticed that the Tio on this level had a huge erection, about a foot long on a mansized figure. The workers said that when they find themselves in a state of impotency they go to the Tio for help. By exemplifying what they want in the Tio, they seek to repair the psychic damage caused by fear.

After feasting on the meat of the llamas and listening to stories of the Tio, I left the mine. The men thanked me for coming. I could not express the gratitude I felt for restoring my confidence in continuing the study.

Shortly thereafter I met Lino Pino returning from a fiesta for a miraculous saint in a nearby village. He asked me if I would be *madrina* at his daughter's forthcoming confirmation, and when I agreed, his wife offered me a tin cup with the delicious cocktail she always prepares for her husband on the days of the *ch'alla*, and we all had a round of drinks.

Later, when I knelt at the altar rail with Lino and his daughter as we received the wafer and the wine, flesh and blood of another sacrifice victim, I sensed the unity in the miners' beliefs. The miraculous Virgin looked down on us from her marbelized, neon-lit niche, her jewelled finger held out in benediction. She was adequate for that scene, but in the mine they needed someone who could respond to their needs on the job.

In the rituals of the *ch'alla* and the *k'araku* the power of the Tio to destroy is transformed into the socially useful functions of increasing mineral yield and giving peace of mind to the workers. Confronted alone, the Tio, like Banquo's ghost makes a man unable to produce or even to go on living. Properly controlled by the group, the Tio promises fertility, potency, and productivity to the miners. Robbed of this faith, they often lose the faith to continue drilling after repeated failure to find a vein, or to continue living when the rewards of work are so meager. Knowing that the devil is on your side makes it possible to continue working in the hell that is the mines.

Psychosocial Interpretations of Exorcism

E. Mansell Pattison

E. Mansell Pattison, a professor of psychiatry and human behavior, begins this article with an examination of the contemporary interest in demonology and exorcism in Western society. Agreeing with Claude Lévi-Strauss, Pattison observes that primitive ideas of reality result in a more coherent and cohesive model of the world than do Western scientific explanations. He traces the present renewal of interest in demonology and exorcism in contemporary scientific cultures to certain social situations that support an oppressive social structure. Pattison believes modern psychiatry's failure to provide meaning and understanding of reality has caused people to abandon the psychoanalyst in favor of the exorcist. The author demonstrates how modern psychoanalytic psychotherapy is like exorcism, discusses the differences between "scientific healers" and "folk healers," and analyzes the implications for psychotherapeutic practice.

Reprinted from the *Journal of Operational Psychiatry*, Vol. 8, no. 2 (1977), pp. 5–19, by permission of the author and the University of Missouri-Columbia, Department of Psychiatry.

"The power of magic defeats the demons of scientific technology" (advertisement for the movie "Wizards," 1977).

THIS PAPER IS CONCERNED WITH THE WIDESPREAD renewal of social interest in the supernatural, mystical, magical, and "irrational" in contemporary western society. This is reflected in the rapid shift among young people from the iconoclastic social activism of the 1960s toward an internal personal quest for peace and meaning in the 1970s. This latter quest is seen in the popularity of non-conventional religiosity, mystical experience, and eastern philosophies. The tip of the iceberg of this social revolution of consciousness is our manifest fascination with demonology and exorcism.

Corollary to society in general, the mental health professions have begun to closely examine the beliefs and practices of indigenous healers. Therefore, my inquiry begins with the general social phenomenon and leads into a comparative examination of "scientific healers" versus "folk healers" and the implications for psychotherapeutic practice.

Naturalistic Versus Supernaturalistic Systems

Our western views of health and illness, cause and effect, reality and fantasy are, of course, the product of an evolving construction and explanation of reality, in large part determined by the empirical rationalism of experimental science, its adoption by medicine, and thence to psychiatry. The western mode of thought and its construction of reality has often been the measure against which all other cultural constructions of reality were assessed; while so-called primitive cultures were considered to be unrealistic, irrational, simplistic, and naive. From this point of view, it seems absurd that sophisticated western people should evince interest, much less belief, in magical, mystical, and metaphysical ideas that western culture has long since given up for more realistic views and explanations of the world. In particular the belief in demons, possession, and exorcism seems especially atavistic.

What the western mind does not see, is that western science and its construction of reality is terribly fragmented. The naturalistic system of the world of the west, rooted in the empirical rationalism of latter day humanism, provides proximate and limited explanations of isolated fragments of human life. It fails to provide western mankind with a cohesive picture of human life. Further, without ontological grounding it does not provide a rationale, nor purpose, nor meaning to life. The optimistic world view of 19th-century scientific humanism has become the 20th-century world view of cynicism, despair, existential ennui and a cosmos of the absurd.

Sartre states the dilemma of modern western man succinctly:

> The existentialist . . . thinks it very distressing that God does not exist, because all possibility of finding values in a heaven of ideas disappears along with him. . . . Everything is permissible if God does not exist, and as a result man is forlorn, because neither within him nor without does he find anything to cling to. . . . We find no values or commands to turn to which legitimize our conduct. So, in the right realm of values, we have no excuse behind us, nor justification before us. We are alone, with no excuses.

Or consider the conclusion of psychoanalyst Allen Wheelis:

> At the beginning of the modern age science did, indeed, promise certainty. It does no longer. Where we now retain the conviction of certainty we do so on our own presumption, while the advancing edge of science warns that absolute truth is a fiction, is a longing of the heart, and not to be had by man. . . . Our designations of evil are as fallible now as they were ten thousand years ago; we simply are better armed now to act on our fallible vision.

My point is that the superiority of western consciousness and the western construction of reality as a mode of existence has failed to be demon-strated. That western empirical technology has achieved greater creature comforts and longevity of life is indisputable, but what of the quality, meaning, and value of life?

These considerations only briefly intimate the conclusion that in the west we have entered a new age of irrationalism. Yet at the same time, we continue to misinterpret other world views of reality.

As Lévi-Strauss has demonstrated so well in *The Savage Mind*, so-called primitive constructions of reality provide a much more coherent, cohesive, and explanatory model of the world and human behavior than does the western scientific construction of the cosmos. Science does not provide a very comprehensive description and explanation of human behavior. *The Savage Mind* had an explanation and intervention for everything.

Foster has compared naturalistic versus supernaturalistic systems of thought about health and illness. He finds that naturalistic systems (western) view misfortune and illness in atomistic terms. Disease is unrelated to other misfortune, religion and magic are unrelated to illness; and the principal curers lack supernatural or magical powers, for their function is solely an instrumental technical task performance. On the other hand, supernaturalistic systems integrate the totality of all life events. Illness, religion, and magic are inseparable. The most powerful curers are astute diagnosticians who employ both technical and symbolic means of therapeusis.

Early students of supernaturalistic systems of healing such as Ackerknecht and Rivers emphasized the particular magical beliefs and rituals of shamans and other folk healers; thus they overlooked the complex integrated view of nature and mankind, and the complex refined distinctions that were made between different kinds of misfortunes, their causes, and cures.

Loudon comments:

> This reduces the study of health and disease to studies of witchcraft, sorcery, magic, and in general curative or socially readjustive ritual practices, with herbalist and empirically rational treatment and prophylaxis as residual categories.

In brief, supernaturalistic systems encompass the totality of life, which integrates man and nature. Careful ethnographic studies of folk healers reveal a complex and sophisticated description of reality, in which there is indeed differentiation between accidents, distortions of natural process such as malformed fetus, hazards such as snake-bites, psychosomatic disorders, and existential disorders of impaired human relations. Similarly, within the supernaturalistic system there are a range of interventions practiced by a variety of healers with skills suitable to the curing of the misfortune.

In sum, I have attempted to illustrate that the distinction between the naturalistic and the supernaturalistic is not so wide a gulf as we might suppose. Our rationalistic culture is absurd and irrational; while the supernaturalistic cultures possess a sophisticated, coherent construction of reality, with attendant differentiated diagnostic and therapeutic concepts. The fundamental difference may lie rather in our differing construction of what reality is.

Demonology as Part of Supernaturalism

Beliefs in demonology, possession, and exorcism can be adequately interpreted only within the framework of supernaturalistic systems. Anthropologist Erika Bourguignon has organized the variety of trance behaviors and associated beliefs into convenient chart form, as shown in Figure 1. As illustrated, the same phenomena can be explained in either naturalistic or supernaturalistic systems. And also evident is that demon possession is only one sub-type of many concepts of man and spirits.

Abundant ethnographic data have shown that although there may be widespread tacit acceptance and private belief in demonology, the actual practice of witchcraft and experience of possession states is limited. That is, the particular emergence of demon possession and exorcism can be shown to relate to rather particular socio-cultural milieux. The general conclusion is that the eruption of demonology is coincident with social situations where there is an oppressive social structure, a loss of trust in the efficacy of social institutions, and a seeming inability to cope with the evils of the social structure. In this situation, then, we see the personification of social evil in evil demons, and a displaced social protest in the form of accusations of witchcraft and personal experiences of possession. Being possessed of social evil is personified, while accused, accuser, and exorcist act out the symbol-

ization of the social dilemma in safely displaced form, since active social protest and reform seem impossible.

For example, Bourguignon finds the distribution of demonic possession in folk societies to be correlated with conditions of social oppression and stagnation. Wijesinghe, et al. report a high incidence of possession in a low status sub-community of Sri Lanka; and Carstairs and Kapur note that in an Indian community it was in the most oppressed case that they found possession.

Socio-cultural studies have thus emphasized the social dynamics that produce demonology. Yet at the same time we must account for the psychological dimensions which have played such a large part in typical psychiatric interpretations of demonology.

Freud stated the classic psychological formulation: "The states of possession correspond to our neuroses. . . . The demons are bad and reprehensible wishes." But this interpretation reduces demonology to nothing but individual neurosis, and may lead to the conclusion that the actors in the drama of demonology are dealing with individual neuroses.

In contrast the eminent medical historian George Rosen observes:

> Witch hunting expresses a dis-ease of society, and is related to a social context. . . . To be sure, some individuals involved in witch trials were mentally and emotionally disordered. Most of those involved were not. In part, their reactions were learned, in part, they conformed because of fear-producing pressures.

Similarly the historian Russell concludes:

> But it will not do to assume that the witches were on the whole mentally ill. They were responding to human needs more universal than those of individual fantasy: universal enough to be described in terms of myth. . . . The phenomenon of witchcraft, whether we are talking about the persecutors or the witches, was the result of fear, expressed in supernatural terms in a society that thought in supernatural terms, and repressed by a society that was intolerant of spiritual dissent. In most respects a variety, or at least an outgrowth, of heresy, witchcraft was one manifestation of alienation.

We cannot gainsay that the belief and practice of demonology was not and is not a defensive and

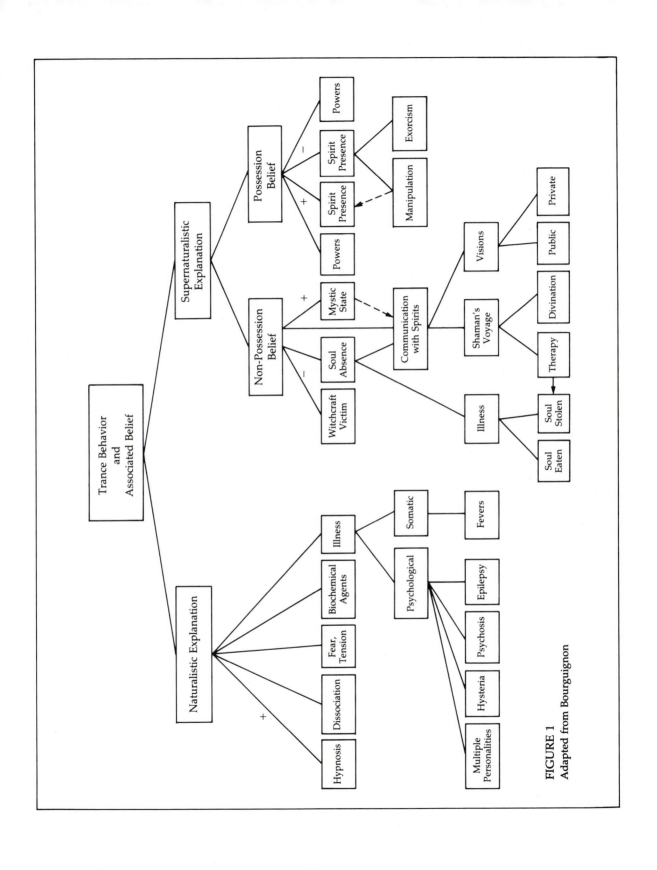

FIGURE 1
Adapted from Bourguignon

adaptive psychological maneuver. But from the viewpoint of culture this is not neurosis. As Spiro says: "There is a third category of defense mechanisms—culturally constituted defenses—which are not only not disruptive of, but rather serve to perpetuate, the socio-cultural system."

Robert LeVine has pointedly synthesized the issue by describing a *psychosocial* interpretation of demonology. That is, within the general culture of belief there will be degrees of potential, for more or less individuals, to act out the beliefs of demonology. And where the general belief of demonology is culturally no longer a modal belief, only those with specific psychological propensities (i.e., neurotic) are likely to use such beliefs in their ego defense.

With this summary at hand, we can now see that Freud and other psychiatric observers could readily reduce demonology to nothing but neurosis, for they were observing persons acting out beliefs not modal to the culture. But where demonology is modal, we must look beyond neurosis for our understanding.

Contemporary Demonology

With an understanding of the social conditions which give rise to demonology, it is possible to see that contemporary social conditions are ripe in the western world for the re-emergence of supernaturalistic belief systems, and even demonology. Society has been perceived as oppressive, trust in social institutions has disintegrated, social protest has been realistically dangerous, and a mood of helpless impotence has emerged. New hope, new meaning, and new purpose can be seen in the myriad of supernaturalistic systems now gaining devotees. So it should not surprise us that the evil society should again be personified and symbolized in demonology.

In his analysis of medieval demonology the Spanish anthropologist Baroja notes that western rationalism ousted the belief in witchcraft from its place in the collective consciousness of man, to survive only in the marginal circles of cranks and neurotics. Yet he finds us coming full circle with the breakdown of rationalism:

> We are in a better position nowadays to appreciate the feelings of the people involved, who discovered one day that they had a devilish

power in them, or were subject to the devilish power of a close enemy who had lived near them for years, watching and hating. For ours is no period of calm, with an optimistic view of public morality and religious philosophy and beliefs. It is an age of existentialism and an existentialist way of life, which leads man to break down the barriers and conventions and face up to his own angst.

Following along the existential consciousness of our day is the stark sense of alienated and singular responsibility for everything. Historian Judith Neaman finds it not surprising that psychiatry is becoming more biological just at the time when our society is becoming more metaphysical. She recalls that in every culture hyper-rationalism has been followed by a renewal of supernaturalism. For with the rationalism and ultimately the existentialism comes too much responsibility—too much to bear. Psychiatry brought man from outer reality into himself and only himself, and left man there. Neaman concludes:

> The legacy of the Middle Ages was the increasing interiorization of the self and a concomitant increase in responsibility for human action. These ideas were consummated in the twentieth century belief that we are responsible not only for our own actions but also for our own guilts, fears, and obsessions. The fantasy of the 1970s has been a wish to return to an age of exorcism.

Bourguignon similarly finds: "There is a wish to find alternative ways of living; and thus not only modify the society, but to modify the self."

Thus, we see that rather than unexpected, it is most consonant with history that supernaturalism and demonology should again appear in our time. The nadir of scientific psychiatry offers least to western man in terms of meaning, and people turn from the psychoanalyst to the exorcist.

Psychoanalytic Demonology

The demons out there that possessed us, have been gradually deanthropomorphized. Healing which was exorcism of the personal spirit became gradually more an exorcism of bad thoughts and feelings. Pattison et al. found that modern seekers of faith healing seek a spiritual cure of the self, which is but a step from the final abstraction of evil into pure thought in Christian Science, where evil, misfortune and illness exist only in thought and have no reality.

But demonology has been resurrected in new form in the object relations theory of psycho-analysis. Possession is not to be left behind, but only redefined. We are possessed of good and bad objects—ego introjects. So we find twentieth cen-tury demonology interpreted by Fairbairn thusly:

It is to the realm of these bad objects . . . that the ultimate origin of all psychopathological developments is to be traced; for it may be said of all psychoneurotic and psychotic patients that, if a True Mass is being celebrated in the chancel, a Black Mass is being celebrated in the crypt. It becomes evident, accordingly, that the psychotherapist is the true successor to the exorcist, and that he is concerned, not only with the "forgiveness of sins," but also with "the casting out of devils."

From the same object-relations theory, Hender-son concludes that the therapist is not successor to the exorcist, just different in technique:

The religious view of emotional pain contains an important if imperfect truth which has been too long disregarded. The psychotherapist differs from the exorcist not so much in theory, although his terminology is different, but in his belief that the therapeutic process to be effective is apt to require a more painstaking process to dissolve the persecuting forces.

This quote is interesting from several points of view, which all reflect typical western cultural biased assumptions. One, that the supernatural description of possession is less accurate than the naturalistic. Two, that folk healers are less pains-taking than psychoanalysts. Three, that psy-chotherapy, western style, is more efficacious than folk healing. These assumptions are clearly chal-lenged in the volumes cited in the bibliography; here I wish only to highlight the above assump-tions, which lead to the next issue.

Modes of Relations Between Scientific and Folk Healers

In our time it has become fashionable to talk about providing psychotherapy to ethnic and minority groups, the poor and the working class, and the application of western psychotherapy to other cul-tures. But the limits of application of western style psychotherapy have yet to be clearly determined. Up to this point most of such interest has led to the notion of developing working relations between scientific psychotherapists and indigenous folk healers. Again what those working relations should or can consist of, remains vaguely defined. I propose that there are three current modes of working relations.

The first mode is *cooperation*. This mode is fre-quently found in developing countries where west-ern psychiatrists establish friendly cooperative relations with native healers. Each retains his own assumptive world view, provides treatment within separate spheres of action, and transfers or triages mutual clients between each other. Carstairs and Kapur and Kiev have documented many examples of this type.

The second mode is *syncretistic*. That is, there is an attempt to functionally use indigenous healers as part of the psychiatric mental health care system. This mode functionally fuses two worlds of exis-tence that have no necessarily logical relation. In this view the indigenous healer becomes coopted as a new style mental health "para-professional."

The third mode is *collaborative*. Here I have in mind a working relationship that involves sharing and participating in two worlds of consciousness and action.

In some cases documented by Carstairs and Kapur western psychotherapists have gradually given up western psychiatry and become healers within the folk tradition. It is hard to live in two worlds! Even to begin to move into collaborative modes requires real immersion into non-western modes of existence. Jilek and Jilek describe their efforts:

"We found it is possible to bridge the cultural gap by first making oneself known to the people through participation in the activities of the non-western community. We strove to inform ourselves on the belief system, myths, rituals, social customs and organizations; we attended feasts, social, religious and political functions, seeking discussion with leading community figures and traditional healers."

In sum, I suggest that the popular enthusiasm to "work with the natives" does not do justice to the profound differences in consciousness and con-struction of reality involved. It would appear that we are just beginning to appreciate the culture-boundedness of our western psychiatric thinking.

A Case Study

To illustrate some issues raised thus far, the following case from my own experience highlights the psychological meaning of possession and the function of exorcism from a comparative therapeutic view.

This experience occurred during a period when I served as the psychiatric consultant to the public Health Service Clinic serving the Yakima Indian reservation. The Yakima are located on several thousand acres of farming and lumbering land in central Washington amidst the rich agricultural Yakima valley. As on many Indian reservations, these Indian people live in close proximity to white Western culture. Although they have relatively good economic resources, life on the reservation is isolated from the world in which it is located. The reservation culture is in the midst of cultural disintegration. The "long hair" Indians cling to the traditional Yakima mores, while their middle-aged children flounder in bewilderment, not part of the white culture, not part of the Indian. Meanwhile the grandchildren attend the local white schools and watch television in the homes of their grandparents. Here in the middle of two cultures we find our case.

Upon arrival at the reservation one snowy December morning, the young public health doctor grabbed me for an emergency consultation. He had been called to the home of an Indian family the previous night to see an adolescent girl. The family stated that she was crying, frightened, incoherent, running around the house in a state of panic. He reported that upon arrival at the home he found the girl incoherent, babbling, agitated, muttering about ghosts and stated that she was afraid of dying. He gave her an intramuscular injection of chlorpromazine which calmed her down, and she went to sleep. He made a diagnosis of acute schizophrenic psychosis. Since I was due to arrive the next day, he requested that the family bring the girl to the clinic for my evaluation and recommendation for further treatment.

Precisely at the appointed time, the mother and daughter appeared. I had worked on the reservation for several years at this time, and was known

to the Indian people. I had found good rapport and little difficulty in establishing working relationships with my Indian clientele. But this was a different situation from my usual clinical consultations. Both mother and daughter were sullen, guarded, withdrawn. The girl was a pretty, well developed, adolescent, thirteen years old. She was dressed like a typical high school girl. But she hunched herself over, eyes downcast, speaking in barely audible tones. With great difficulty and much patience her story was told.

The problems began the prior August when Mary (her pseudonym) had gone off to a week-long summer camp for Indian girls, sponsored by the local O.E.O. program. One night, as children are wont to do at a summer camp, after lights were out and the counselors were in bed, Mary and several of her girl friends went sneaking out of their cabin to frolic in the moonlight among the tall fir trees. As they ran about in the moonlight they looked up in the trees and saw human figures. These ghost-like figures drifted down from the trees, and the girls recognized them as their tribal ancestors. The girls talked to the ghosts and the ghosts talked to the girls. But after a few minutes the girls became frightened, ran back to their cabin, jumped into bed, and hid under their covers.

All seemed safe now. Except for Mary. A ghost followed her into the cabin, jumped on her as she lay in bed, and tried to choke her. She fought and struggled against the ghost, she gasped for breath, she screamed for help. The counselors came running into the cabin, but they could not calm her. Mary was sure the ghosts would kill her, she sobbed and screamed. Finally, the counselors bundled her up in a car and drove back home to the local hospital. When seen in the emergency room she was still in an agitated state and was given an intramuscular tranquilizer shot before being taken home to her parents.

The stage was set, and the pattern from then on to December was rather routine. Mary would go off to high school everyday with ratted hair and teenie-bopper clothes. She would participate in her daily high school activities like any teenager. She was on the honor roll, was a cheerleader, and a student body officer. But when she came home a different Mary appeared. She combed her hair into long Indian braids. She put on long-skirted traditional Indian clothes, and wandered about the house as if in a daze. She would see ghosts at the window and cry out in startled fright. She went walking in the fields and saw blood on the ground. She thought the ghosts had killed one of her girl friends. She thought the ghosts would attack and kill her younger brothers and sisters. She would become so frightened and worried that at times she would cry, and scream, and run around the house. At times the parents could not calm her, and they would take her to the hospital for a shot to calm her down. But the next morning she would always get up and go to school like a normal adolescent girl.

The mother and the girl had no explanation for this behavior. They were bewildered. The mother turned to me and asked what I, as a psychiatrist, thought of this behavior. Was her daughter crazy? What I observed was a withdrawn sullen girl. But she spoke in a coherent manner; she was logical and realistic in her conversation with me. I stated that I did not know what this all meant, but perhaps the mother might have some ideas.

The mother said she had heard that psychiatrists did not believe in religion. Did I believe in religion? I told her that I thought religion was very important in the lives of people. Did I believe that she had been healed? I told her that many people experience healing, and that she too might have had a healing experience. She smiled, relaxed and leaned toward me. Look at my face! Do you see any scars? No, I don't. Well, my father healed me. Do you believe that? Yes. Well he was a witchdoctor; he used to care for the whole tribe. And when I was a girl I fell in a fire and burned my face. And he made a pack of mud with his spittle, and anointed my face and said his prayers. And said I would be healed and have no scars. He said I would have a beautiful face. Do you think he was right? Is my face beautiful? Yes.

The mother was satisfied. She sat back. Then she tensed up again. Doctor? Yes? Should I say this? Maybe I shouldn't. I've never talked about this before. My daughter doesn't know about this. I've never told her. Well. You see, my father, the witchdoctor, he told me that his powers would be passed on when he died. But not to his children, not to me. His powers would be passed on to his grandchildren. And the oldest, this daughter, this girl, would have his powers.

By this time my thoughts about the clinical situation had been stirred. Do you think that Mary's experience has something to do with your father? Oh yes, she answered. But we don't talk about those things anymore, because, you know, we're Presbyterians now, and people don't believe in witchcraft anymore. But what if they did, I asked. How would you handle something like this?

The mother was now animated, and the daughter was listening intently. Well, we knew what to do. You see, in the old times, when someone was going to be given the powers of the spirits, was to be given the gifts of the witchdoctor, you had to struggle with the spirits. You had to prove you could rule them. Well, what would you do? I asked. Oh, there's nothing we can do. If this were the old times we would just open the door and let Mary wander out of the house at night. And she would go out and meet the spirits. And she would have to fight with them. And then she would come back with the powers . . . or maybe we would just find her out there after a few days, but that's the way it happens. . . .

I see, Well, what do you think about this now? Since this is not the old days, what do you think might be the best way to help Mary now?

Well, you know doctor, I've been thinking about that. You can't really practice much as a witchdoctor these days. It might be better if Mary were a Presbyterian and didn't accept the gift her grandfather left her.

Well, how would you work that out?

You see, doctor, we have to get rid of the spirits. We have to tell them that Mary doesn't want to fight with them. And then they'll go away and leave her alone. And she'll be O.K.

H'm. Well what do you have to do?

Oh, I don't know how to do that.

Who does?

Oh, Grandma does. She and some of the other old women know the ceremony. We all have to get together. And we would dress Mary up in the ceremonial dress, and we have to have prayers, and offerings, and we would anoint her, and say the prayers . . .

Lest I leave the reader in suspense, at the end of one of the most fascinating experiences in my professional life, I reached an agreement with Mary and her mother. We agreed that it was not appropriate for Mary to attempt to achieve the mantle of power her grandfather had bequeathed her. That would be looking backward. So we agreed that

Mary should renounce the legacy and look forward to becoming part of the modern world. The mother agreed to call the grandmother and see if she and the other tribal women could conduct a ritual of exorcism that night. I would return in one month. They agreed to see me again at that time.

Now it was January. With some trepidation I awaited their arrival. They came early! They were delighted to see me. I was a great doctor. They had followed my advice. The ceremony of exorcism had been conducted. It had been successful. Mary was healed.

Indeed, since that night of exorcism, the strange behavior had disappeared. The mother was happy, Mary was happy, I was happy. Because of my ongoing contact with this tribe, I had the opportunity to follow this family for many months thereafter. Mary remained healthy and happy. No more was she bothered. In contrast to her mien that first cold snowy December morning, when I saw her thereafter she was bright and bouncy, talkative and enthusiastic, like any other energetic adolescent girl beginning to become a woman.

Some Religious Observations

As I listened to this story, I thought of an Old Testament story that was almost identical, and I thought of the universality of human experience.

In the following passage, we read of Jacob wrestling with the angel of the Lord, in order to obtain power over the spirits:

> "And Jacob was left alone; and there wrestled a man with him until the breaking of the day. And when he saw that he prevailed not against him, he touched the hollow of his thigh; and the hollow of Jacob's thigh was out of joint, as he wrestled with him. And he said, Let me go, for the day breaketh. And he said, I will not let thee go, except thou bless me. And he said unto him, What is thy name? And he said, Jacob. And he said, Thy name shall be called no more Jacob, but Israel: for as a prince hast thou power with God and with men, and hast prevailed. . . . And Jacob called the name of the place Peniel: for I have seen God face to face, and my life is preserved . . . and he halted upon his thigh. (Genesis 32:24–3l)

What is remarkable is that over a span of perhaps six thousand years and over three continents we find the same interpretation. The man gains power over spirits by fighting with the spirits. If man wins, he then has special powers, he can command the spirits. He is a shaman, a healer, a witchdoctor. But it is a dangerous business, for to acquire the special powers requires a mortal combat. Jacob won, but he was crippled for life. And as for Mary, she feared her own death, or that of her siblings, if they got in the way of the combat.

In this case, we have the reenactment of an age-old saga: Man in quest of power over the forces of his life.

Some Psychodynamic Observations

Although we have limited clinical material, we may rough out the following possible interpretations. The mother presents herself as the favored daughter of her father. Father heals her, using his spittle (semen?). Mother continues to frame her acceptability as a person around her external appearance, her beauty, her sexuality. She asks for acceptance as a desirable object from the therapist (father symbol). Daughter Mary appears on the scene at the time of adolescence as a maturing woman, hence competitor to mother. Mother does not give approval to daughter to become a sexually mature woman, for that poses a threat to mother. Mary projects the disapproving mother into the hallucinatory ghost object who would kill her. But also the projected forbidden object is the father figure who lies upon her in bed—the incestuous father. Mary wanders in the field and finds blood in the fields (menstrual blood?) where her girl friend was killed. While the sibling competitive rivalry between mother and daughter is projected onto the fear of Mary's siblings being killed by the spirits.

The conflict is resolved. The mother is reaffirmed in her role as woman. She in turn, in concert with her own mother, participates in a symbolic ritual which gives daughter, mother, granddaughter the sanction and approval to mature, to grow up, to become a sexually mature woman. Daughter Mary is no longer a competitive rival, seeking to gain the exclusive rights and affections of the witchdoctor grandfather (oedipal father). So mother can now allow daughter Mary to become a woman in her own right. Result: daughter no longer acts out the mother-daughter conflict.

A Trans-Cultural Perspective

Our observations are in concert with the work of Melford Spiro who has shown how one can look at various possession states and methods of healing from both the Western psychodynamic perspective and from the cultural perspective of the indigenous healer. It is of note that, in Spiro's work on possession, the most common conflict was sexual conflict. Spiro notes that the dissociative state of possession deals with the fear of retaliation, which is certainly true in this case.

But given the fact that we deal with a dissociative state, can we consider this an abnormal state? Here we have an instance in which the particular psychodynamic of family life was acted out in a pattern provided by the culture. Within the culture set, the behavioral pattern exhibited by Mary was not unusual nor unexpected. In fact, she acted out the cultural norm.

In this instance we can note that the diagnosis of acute schizophrenia is understandable, but inappropriate. However, the family itself was caught in an interesting and pathetic cultural bind. If they had been living within the traditional Indian culture, they would have followed the prescribed patterns of response. We may assume that the deviant behavior would have been appropriately resolved. However, the family was caught between two cultures, between two belief systems. And so the family was immobilized. The behavior of the patient, Mary, was congruent with the belief system of the old culture, while the treatment of the hospitals was congruent with the new belief system.

What provided a significant intervention in this impasse was a sanction by a scientific professional psychotherapist to an indigenous cultural healer. And that collaborative support enabled this natural system to function and to restore a person to function.

A psychodynamic interpretation of this case intervention might include the possibility of a "transference cure." In this instance the mother experiences reaffirmation of her beauty, her wholeness, her person, from the psychiatrist (witchdoctor-transferential father). She need not feel threatened by her daughter's emerging sexuality, for mother is still the favored one. Then too, the psychiatrist (transference father symbol) enlists the aid of

mother (herself now the successful oedipal competitor) to help daughter grow up. And this is allowed because daughter will not be stronger than mother.

Although these psychodynamic speculations may be appropriate and accurate, I do not think that one can conclude that this explains the total interaction.

In my opinion, these psychoanalytic motifs may indicate why this particular intervention was so rapidly catalytic of a therapeutic resolution. The psychodynamic cards were stacked in my favor.

On the other hand, the family had sought medical treatment on many occasions before they came to see me. The medical interventions could have been given the same symbolic ascriptions, which I propose were ascribed to me. And the failure of medical treatment, or the knowledge of the tribal beliefs could have resulted in the family going ahead and conducting the exorcism ceremonies. Yet they have not ostensibly even thought about exorcism.

If this family were fully participant in the Western thought world of the psychiatrist, then I would have considered a typical family therapy model of intervention. But this family was not in my thought world—it only looked like they were thinking and living within the Western scientific tradition of medicine. Indeed, they themselves were only conscious of their Western world thought and beliefs. Whether one can consider this solely an intra-psychic repression is an interesting problem. My own inclination is to conclude that this family had a higher than usual level of repressive defense structures. But also that idiosyncratic family style was reinforced by the transitional Indian culture in which they live, in which repression of the "old" belief systems is built into the experiential world of living on the reservation.

I seriously doubt that a scientific style psychotherapy intervention would have been of any value at all. Not that one cannot conduct rather typical psychotherapy with Indians living on the reservation. For I did conduct a great deal of straightforward psychodynamic interpretive psychotherapy. But the problem of Mary and her mother was embedded in the traditional Indian belief system. I think that psychotherapy with either Mary or her mother around other issues might have been possible and appropriate within the Western scientific frame of thought. But with the acting out of the problem within the framework of the traditional Indian belief system, in order to conduct a scientific psychotherapy, one would have to translate the whole problem from one belief system to another belief system.

The alternative which I followed was to take the traditional Indian belief system for real. To accept the interpretation of cause and effect within that system for real also. And to support an intervention within that system that would indeed be real.

Healing Symbols and the Future

It has long been recognized that there are many similarities if not identities between the western psychotherapist and the folk healer. Jerome Frank has elegantly summarized the non-specific *extrinsic* factors common to all psychotherapeutic healers; while Prince has recently reviewed evidence for the fact that there are common *intrinsic* self-healing factors in the client, which any healer may catalyze. Thus, there may be common extrinsic and intrinsic factors in psychotherapy regardless of the particular cultural context, language, or belief system. Thus, it might seem that moving across cultural systems of belief would be relatively simple, if one could make the necessary translations and understand the idioms.

But I propose that the matter of therapeutic healing is more profound than just the extrinsic factors of healing alluded to above. We see clearly in the healing rituals of folk healers a rich symbolization. What we do not see so clearly is that western psychotherapy is also a healing ritual with its own symbols.

Symbols are vital aspects of our existence. As Rollo May notes:

> The symbol draws together and unites
> experience. It bridges the inescapable antinomies
> of life—conscious and unconscious, reason and
> emotion, individual and society, history and the
> present. . . . A symbol is real and efficacious only
> to those who commit themselves to it.

It is noteworthy that in folk society, anthropologists such as Turner and Lévi-Strauss, have shown that the healing rituals symbolize not only personal conflict and resolution, but at the same time mirror the cultural conflict and its resolution. The symbols of the rituals unite the person and his culture. The

client and the healer both communicate effectively through the symbolic modes which are given them in their culture.

Now Perry London has pointed out that all psychotherapies have three common elements: (1) a theory of the nature of man, (2) a superordinate moral code, (3) healing techniques which symbolically evoke a healing transformation in accord with the first two elements.

In this light I suggest that western modes of psychotherapy are extremely limited to a small segment of our current society—at least as widely practiced. Henri Ellenberger notes the sub-cultural consciousness within which psychotherapy has been symbolized:

> By the end of the nineteenth century the upper
> classes could no longer be content with the
> existing method of hypnotic and suggestive
> therapy and demanded a new, nonauthoritarian
> psychotherapy that would explain to the patient
> what was going on in his own mind.

And again:

> One had to find a psychotherapy for educated
> people; it would be a non-authoritarian method,
> which would keep personal liberty intact, explain
> to the patient what was going on in his own
> mind, and guarantee that all the methods
> employed acting only through his own psyche.

Furthermore, it is widely recognized that the linguistic verbal content of psychotherapy may not be the most pertinent aspect of therapy, but rather there is a therapeutic transaction that symbolizes rationalistic construction of reality for "psychotherapeutic man." I find it interesting that the most recent symbolic-linguistic study of psychotherapy is aptly titled "The Structure of Magic."

In his history of psychotherapy, Jan Ehrenwald begins with the magical encounter (which is symbolization) and leads us finally to encounter groups (which, too, is symbolization). Is the history of psychotherapy then not linear but circular?

Returning to Ellenberger, he concludes his magnum opus aware of the fact that the history and evolution of psychotherapy may be circular, for he says:

> The dynamic psychotherapist is thus dealing . . .
> with psychic realities. . . . But what exactly are
> psychic realities? . . . there are many kinds of
> psychic realities, and they often are contradictory
> and incompatible with each other, though

endowed with the same character of certainty for those who are working with them. . . . The coexistence of two mutually incompatible approaches to the cognition of the human psyche shocks the scientist's yearning for unity.

Western psychoanalytic psychotherapy, I submit, has emerged as a healing ritual, based upon a particular western rationalistic, deterministic, and empiricist image of man. It has its own existentialist morality. And its therapeutic technique symbolizes this modern reality. Martin Grotjahn, the eminent psychoanalyst grasps this latter point well in his most recent book, "The Voice of the Symbol." Therein Grotjahn describes psychoanalytic technique as fundamentally a process for symbolizing reality:

> He seeks the outline of the future in which "free creative symbol integration" will fulfill the only demand, the only duty which man has to life: to live to the fullest capacity of his potential, to experience life with all his courage, to become literate in terms of understanding himself and to integrate his unconscious with his intelligence.

The problem inherent in Grotjahn's description of psychoanalytic symbolizing is his assumption that Freud was the first to discover a method for understanding the symbol and the unconscious and thereby create a symbolizing therapy that integrates conscious man with unconscious realities of his socio-cultural development.

I suggest that the same discovery and process of integrating symbolization can be found in the therapies of indigenous folk healers. I believe the ethnographic evidence indicates that we have sold the folk healers short. We have interpreted their therapies solely as simple-minded magic rituals; whereas the potency and efficacy of their therapies may be every bit as efficacious with their culture as psychoanalytic therapy is in our culture. And perhaps with the same failures, as well!

In turn, there seems to be an almost romantic fascination with folk healers today. But belief in supernatural demonology and exorcism is not an unmixed blessing, even if supernatural rites of exorcism may be effective. For the particular forms of supernaturalism that become distilled as witchcraft and demonology contain a virulent disguise of the social ills of the society, and invite the acting out of personalized destructiveness.

Thus, Geoffrey Parrinder concludes:

"Belief in witchcraft is one of the great fears from which mankind has suffered. It has taken its toll literally in blood. . . . Witchcraft must be symbolic. It is a belief which helps to interpret and canalize the disease of society . . . (witchcraft beliefs) resolve certain conflicts or problems: but I did not say that this is a good solution. The aggression invited by witchcraft beliefs is as harmful as anything a society can produce in the way of disruptive practices; the relief offered by witch-hunting and witch-punishing is no more than temporary and their capacity to allay anxieties no more illusory: for if witchcraft beliefs resolve certain fears and tensions, they also produce others . . . the kind of remedy which both becomes a drug and poisons the system."

The personalization of social evil into demonology is the transformation to be avoided, not supernaturalism.

Paul Pruyser states it well: "The great question is: if illusions are needed, how can we have those that are capable of correction, and how can we have those that will not deteriorate into delusions." Similarly, Becker says: "If men live in myths and not absolutes, there is nothing we can do or say about that. But we can argue for nondestructive myths."

It is appropriate now, to examine the future of psychoanalytic western psychotherapy, both in relation to other folk healing systems and unto itself.

First, I have alluded to the data which allow us to conclude that psychoanalytic psychotherapy is part of a mythic system of western man, that its view of man, its morality, and its symbolizing techniques are relevant and efficacious only within the symbolizing mythic culture out of which it has developed. Therefore, we face a major task of re-evaluating the structure and future of the interface between this symbolizing psychotherapy and other cultural views of man and the attendant symbolizing therapies of those cultures. Even within western culture there are widely divergent sub-cultures, such as the various religious associations of America for whom the psychoanalytic construction of reality is by no means easily made relevant. I only make passing note of the many modifications of psychotherapy underway today in America to provide effective therapeutic services to other than the educated well-to-do intelligentsia of America.

Second, let us turn to the future of psychoanalytic psychotherapy itself. As we have seen, psychoanalysis and its derivative dynamic therapies are an integral part of the scientific epoch of western civilization—the time of the humanistic rational man.

As noted herein, we live in the twilight of the scientific age—we have moved on to the age of existential man. Accordingly, it is not surprising that there is widespread disillusionment with the psychoanalytic model of man.

S. K. Pande, a non-western psychiatrist, observes how the western cosmology created "deficits in the Western way of life . . . negative psychological implications . . . and Western psychotherapy, especially the psychoanalytic model, as a symbolic and substantive undertaking to correct them." But the psychoanalytic model becomes increasingly irrelevant as a symbolically effective force as it addresses a vanishing breed of humanistic rational men. Indeed irrational man, or at least existential man, is creating a new view of man, a new morality, and therefore new symbolizing therapeutic techniques, as represented in the existential psychotherapies, the humanistic psychotherapies, and direct experiential encounters of sundry form.

In all of this we are gradually becoming aware of the fact that the ontological underpinnings of any psychotherapy is critical to its relevance, acceptance, and efficacy. Psychotherapy in the western world is indeed a supernaturalistic system, that parades itself as a naturalistic system. Consider the trenchant observations of Ernest Becker:

> Often psychotherapy seems to promise the moon: a more constant joy, delight, celebration of life, perfect love, and perfect freedom . . . psychotherapists are caught up in modern culture and forced to be part of it. Commercial industrialism promised western man a paradise on earth, . . . that replaced the paradise in heaven of Christian myth. And now psychology must replace them both with the myth of paradise through self-knowledge. This is the promise of psychology, and for the most part psychotherapists are obliged to live it and embody it.

At issue is the fact that over history and centuries of time, folk healers, the psychotherapists of societies and cultures were unabashedly part of the supernaturalistic system. Thus, they moved easily between the treatment of accident, illness, misfortune, interpersonal conflict and existential malaise. But as Ellenberger has so nicely illustrated, the

historical development of western psychotherapy has led it to a fragmented, isolated, and naturalistic position within society. The crisis of modern psychiatry is reflected in the fact that medical science cannot provide a belief system to live by, nor can psychiatry as a branch of medicine. Thus, we see a return of "psychiatry to medicine"—as a limited enterprise. Meanwhile, the psychotherapeutic side of psychiatry has been increasingly vulnerable to competing systems and persons each offering discipleship.

The problem is this: that the *atomization* and *particularization* of misfortune in western society leads to the *fragmentation* of healing. We have a seeming paradox. We see that psychotherapeutic healing deeply involves ideology, belief, and symbolization of reality. Yet in western society we have attempted to create a non-ideological, belief-free psychotherapy. I suggest that psychotherapy in the west has survived thus far because it has been based on a covert belief system. As we have unmasked that covert belief system, psychotherapists are now making unabashed pitches for their method of psychotherapy, which is a belief system.

Again Becker pertinently observes:

> Now there are only three ways, I think, that psychology itself can become an adequate belief system. One of them is to be a creative genius as a psychologist and to use psychology as the immorality vehicle for oneself—as Freud and subsequent psychoanalysts have done. Another is to use the language and concepts of psychotherapy in much of one's waking life, so that it becomes a lived belief system . . . this is one of the reasons that psychotherapy has moved away from the Freudian intellectual model to the new experiential model. . . . The third and final way is merely an extension and sophistication of this. It is to take psychology and deepen it with religious and metaphysical associations so that it becomes actually a religious belief system with some breadth and depth. At the same time, the psychotherapist himself beams out the steady quiet power of transference and becomes the guru-figure of religion.

In conclusion, the symbolizing power of psychoanalytic psychotherapy is waning as the society out of which it sprang changes. I suggest that psychoanalytic psychotherapy is a supernaturalistic system of belief. (In this case the God and cosmos of science.) But its ontological grounding, its fundamental commitment to humanistic rational man, its method of experimental empiricism, is melting away. We can see the truth pointed out sometime ago by the French anthropologist Lévi-Strauss, that the psychoanalyst and the shaman are structurally the same. Both engage in powerful rituals that are symbolizing exercises of their culture. *Both are exorcists.*

My interpretation of all the foregoing data is that the reemergence of demonology and exorcism in our current society is symptomatic of an ontological crisis in western society. Psychoanalytic psychotherapy is losing its symbolic power because the society no longer strongly invests in the symbols of a scientific cosmos. And where the symbols have lost their power, the accompanying techniques become vapid. Accordingly, we see the search for a new cosmos, a new symbolic integration of life, and new healers invested with therapeutic powers because they participate in the new symbolization. One solution is regressive, a return to the ancient forms and symbols of demonology. Another solution, that of a scientific psychotherapy has been tried and is failing because of loss of its symbolic community and the erosion of its ontology. I propose that the future may produce psychotherapies that are much more explicit in their ontology; that there will be a delineation of the limited goals of treatment that can be offered by psychiatry as a universal science; that the more overarching existential problematics of life may well be addressed within a diversity of socio-culturally specific psychotherapeutics, which are part of specific supernaturalistic communities.

It appears to me that western psychotherapy has engaged in the self illusion that we offer a culture-free, value free, ideology-free cure, under the universal rubric of mental health. But a philosopher Joseph Margolis acutely observes:

Psychotherapy, then, is primarily concerned with a technical goal, the preservation and restoration of mental health; nevertheless its own development leads it, inevitably, to take up the role of moral legislator.

Thus, it may be that we are on the edge of a new interpretation of psychotherapy. The notion of a scientific psychotherapy may be a chimera. The challenge for tomorrow is to explore the relationship between universalistic dimensions of psychotherapy which are naturalistic and particularistic dimensions of psychotherapy that must be supernaturalistic, naturalistic.

Summary

This study started with an exploration of the current social interest in demonology and exorcism in western society. We have seen that beliefs in demonology are part of a larger supernaturalistic cosmology. However, acting out of demonology beliefs occurs only in times where there is social oppression and loss of social integration. Modern demonology can be seen to be part of the social repudiation of the scientific determinism of rational man, coincident with the rise of existential irrationalism. The practice of exorcism is but one example of the powerful use of symbolic transformations in healing rituals. Seen in terms of symbolic actions, psychoanalytic psychotherapy is also a practice of exorcism. This leads us then to examine the symbolic systems of society that incorporate both the client and the healer. It is seen that western psychotherapy is just as much a part of its culture as other healing systems. We close with an eye to the future, can there be a psychotherapy that is not supernaturalistic?

Characteristics of Sisala Diviners

Eugene Mendonsa

*Divination is a mystical technique for acquiring
knowledge about past, present, or future events that
is unobtainable using ordinary explanatory methods.
Rituals of divination have a vast variety. The
Azande use at least four different oracles to gain
information and answers without the use of
empirical data. Unlike the use of oracles by the
Azande, the Sisala divination techniques stress the
power and intervention of ancestors in their daily
lives. Mendonsa demonstrates that for the Sisala,
divination is a customary method of communicating
with the ancestors, who are thought to control the
power of the universe and who use this power to
afflict the living. It is through necromancy that the
Sisala can determine the cause of and remedy for
problems originating with ancestors. To a lesser
degree the Sisala use other forms of divination
techniques, but contact with the ancestors is of
primary importance and illustrates the roles of
ancestors and divination as mechanisms of social
control.*

Reprinted from *The Realm of the Extra-Human: Agents
and Audiences*, World Anthropology Series (The
Hague, 1976), pp. 179–95, by permission of the author and Mouton Publishers (Division of Walter de
Gruyter and Co.).

Sisala Social Structure

THE SISALA LIVE MAINLY IN THE TUMU DISTRICT
in northern Ghana. The environment is African
savanna, which is primarily bush, due to the
relatively low population density. The Sisala
show cultural uniformity with the other tribes of
the Ashanti hinterland, that is, they are patrilineal, with a social structure of the Guinea type,
and they practice hoe horticulture to produce a
subsistence diet of millet, sorghum, maize,
yams, and rice. Cattle are kept in small numbers
for sacrificial purposes and bridewealth.

Agnatic descent is the keystone of Sisala social structure. Their society is divided into a
number of patri-clans (*-viara*), which form localized ritual units having a common interest. The
clan is an exogamous unit made up of several
villages or sometimes village segments. The village (*tang* or *jang*) is the important focal point of
identification for an individual. Patrilocal residence dictates, therefore, a divided sense of
identification for the women, while men remain
firmly rooted in their natal villages. A village is
normally divided into a series of lineages (*jechiking*) which are arranged to form two reciprocal
burial groups—that is, the village is divided in
two. While the entire village considers itself to be
one body of kinsmen, kinship increases in intensity as the units of the segmentary system become smaller, and therefore the reciprocal burial
groups are felt to be "brother" groups. The lineage (*jechiking*) is the important corporate unit. It
is the subsistence-residential homestead or
walled enclosure normally inhabited by an agnatic extended family. This unit is further divided
into compounds or yards (*kaala*) made up of joint
families who farm together. Each *kaala* is divided
into houses (*diasang*) and rooms (*dia*). In this
segmentary system the developmental cycle is a
continual enlargement of the single room (*dia*),
through marriage and childbirth, into higher-order

units which may eventually result in fission and a repetition of the process.

Today the Isalung-speakers are governed by a paramount chief (the *Tumukuoro*) and various village chiefs (*kuoro*), of whom twelve are divisional chiefs. This system was initiated by the British during their colonial efforts in northern Ghana, and although these political units did not correspond to traditional ones, they have since become realities. The most important precolonial political unit was the village (*jang*), under the leadership of the village *tinteintina* (custodian of the earth) and the elders (*nihising*). Because there were no "chiefs," the *tinteintina* wielded politico-ritual power based on his control of the ancestral shrines. Today the village chief (*kuoro*) has taken on the political functions, while the *tinteintina* has remained concerned with ritual matters such as the fertility of the earth and the fecundity of women.

Sisala society is a gerontocracy, and life is a series of age-based stages or grades. There are two important rites of passage for a man or woman, namely, marriage (*jaanung*) and death (*suunung*). The first allows the passage from the status of small boy (*henmie*) or girl (*hantolowie*) to adult (*niwang*). This transition is further enhanced when the marriage produces living offspring. The second rite of passage comes at a person's death, necessitating the performance of elaborate funerary rites marking passage from the status of elder (*nihiang*) to that of a remembered ancestor (*lelung*).

Kinds of Sisala Divination

For the Sisala, divination is not so much a way of knowing the future, as a way of knowing *fa fa*—that is, knowing which occult entity has afflicted them—although it can also be used to determine whether affliction lies ahead. There are five major ways in which this is accomplished: (1) necromancy, (2) ordeal, (3) throwing cowries, (4) fairy-calling, and (5) traditional divination.

Necromancy

If a death is thought to be due to witchcraft, the members of the family in which the death has occurred may perform necromancy at the funeral. In former times this involved three men carrying the dead body on their shoulders; it was thought that as the men wandered around the crowded

funeral, the body would point out the dead person's killer. However, during colonial times the British stressed immediate burial of the body, and now the Sisala have substituted for the body a bundle of ebony sticks tied with the cover cloth of the dead person. If this bundle does not point out an individual who is responsible for the death, it may point to a shrine. This type of divination is practiced infrequently, and is most likely to be performed when the person has died mysteriously, e.g., by drowning or in the bush.

Ordeal

Ordeals are infrequent, possibly owing to the low level of witchcraft accusation but also because the Sisala prefer a less public means of sanction. Many times I noticed that persons would avoid taking their grievances to a public forum or ordeal. At first I thought this was a function of their guilt, but soon I learned that the Sisala prefer private means to public means. One day I was sitting with the *nihiang nihiang* [oldest man] of Bujan, and we were discussing the fact that his son's wife had had one *cedi* stolen while at the Tumu market. I suggested that she swear by the rain (*gmiese duong*) in order to punish the thief or force him to come forward, but everyone present was shocked at the suggestion. The *nihiang nihiang* explained that the Sisala do not like to do such things, and when I asked why this was so, he related a story:

> A long time ago in Kasana [a Kasena village to the north] an old woman had just pounded some *dawa-dawa* flour, and a woman of another lineage came and took part of it. When the old lady returned to discover the theft, she swore by the rain, calling it to kill the thief. Meanwhile the thief had put some of the flour in every cooking pot in her lineage. Every lineage member ate of it except one man who had just gone to the farm. The rain sent the lightning and killed all the lineage members except the one man at the farm. This is why we now hesitate to swear by the rain, although we don't taboo it. The Kasena still do this frequently, but we do not. Even if a chicken were to eat some of the flour, the rain would kill it. Many innocent people can die from such an act.

Nevertheless, some people do swear by the rain to discover a hidden thing, since doing hidden things (*luore*) is considered bad and is akin to witchcraft—as indicated by the word *luore*, which is cognate with the word for stomach, *luorung*, which is the seat of witchcraft. Since witchcraft is such a bad thing, some people feel justified in swearing by the rain to find a witch, but more commonly a sacrifice will be made on the earth shrine to determine whether a given individual is a witch.

The scorpion ordeal is another form of divination. It is usually used to divine a petty theft or some other minor delict—e.g., a man may determine which of his wives put her hand into his compound granary (*viribalung*). Suspects are lined up and the scorpion is allowed to crawl over their arms, and the sting is both the proof and the punishment. When persons are accused of a petty crime, they often expose themselves to a kind of ordeal. When confronted, a person may deny the deed and add, "If I am guilty, let a snake bite me." The Sisala greatly fear the bite of a snake, and also believe that such a bite is often a punishment by the ancestors.

Although these institutions have judicial functions, they can be viewed as divinatory devices as well. Reynolds (1963: 121) has pointed out that an ordeal can be considered a legal device when administered to one person, whereas it is a divinatory device when several persons are involved. Yet there is an element of divination even in an accusation of witchcraft. A ritual formula is allowed to stimulate an answer from the occult world, and this is precisely what the traditional diviner does when he divines. When looking at divination, one should therefore consider the entire range of devices used to receive feedback from *fa fa* [the occult world].

Throwing Cowries

Diviners who throw cowrie shells (*vuge ari mowribie*) are also known and consulted, but this practice is not indigenous to the Sisala and has probably diffused into the Sisala area from the Islamic peoples to the north. There are relatively few Sisala who actually practice this kind of divination. Mostly cowrie-shell-throwers are found in the northwest section of Sisala-land, which is more heavily influenced by Islamic culture, and they are strangers who practice as wandering diviners. Many of the Sisala who practice throwing cowries are innovators who have made several earlier attempts to achieve prestige by nontraditional means. In my experience, the same individuals who have tried throwing cowries have also tried calling

fairies—which is also a practice that has been borrowed from the neighboring Awuna and Kasena to the north. Pagan Sisala who consult traditional diviners tend to look down on cowrie-throwing as less reliable than traditional divination, and traditional diviners have told me that if their verdict was too different from that of a cowrie-thrower, the latter would die from ancestral anger. Cowrie-throwers are sometimes consulted if they happen to be passing through the village—e.g., when a Wangara cowrie-thrower came through Bujan, many persons consulted him merely because he was there, and they hoped he would tell them something good. In general, however, when a Sisala suffers an affliction, he will seek out the traditional diviner to ascertain the occult cause. Cowrie-throwers are not viewed as being in the same class. One informant (a diviner) told me the following story, which is biased, but nonetheless reflects a general feeling:

> The divining bag [of the traditional diviner] came from God. It was here prior to those who throw cowries and who only profess to see things. Anyone can become a cowrie-thrower by going to another cowrie-thrower and asking to share his medicine. His face is washed with the medicine after he pays a fee, and he can start throwing cowries.

Fairy-Calling

The fairy-caller (*kantonngo yirang*) is a relatively recent introduction from the neighboring Awuna-Kasena peoples. There are only a few Sisala men who have learned this technique of divining, and the technique does not seem to be gaining much ground. Of the 272 Sisala males I interviewed about their consulting habits, only 7.3 percent had ever been to a fairy-caller in their entire lifetime, while 86 percent had consulted a traditional diviner at least once in the month prior to the interview. It is commonly held that Sisala men do not know the proper technique for calling fairies, therefore those who wish to consult a fairy-caller often make a rather long journey across the border into Upper Volta to do so. Some of the Sisala fairy-callers have fallen into outright disrepute as fakes and charlatans, and the people speak of them with contempt. They are usually individuals of some drive, who greatly desire public recognition, but who lack any traditional role in the public eye. Some fairy-callers even try throwing cowries as well.

The Sisala say that in former times (*fa fa*) there were no fairy-callers among them, although there have always been fairies (*kantonngo*). Fairies are beings of the wild, that dwell in trees or in the rivers of the bush. They are perceived as having access to both *fa fa* and *lele* [ancestors], and they can communicate with God and bring these messages back to man. At times they capture a man while he is walking through the bush and teach him secrets of one kind or another. But the Sisala have never had any way of initiating contact with the fairies, and have remained in a position of passively waiting for the fairies to communicate with them. The Awuna-Kasena, on the other hand, have developed a technique whereby the diviner calls the fairies, who then communicate by voice with assembled clients. Several persons consult such a diviner each night, and he calls the fairies to come into a dark room and speak to each of them about their troubles or wishes. The fairy-caller is the link between man and the fairies, and the fairies are the link with God (*Wia*), whereas the traditional diviner is a link with the ancestors (*lele*).

The institution of calling fairies is most widespread among those Sisala who live to the north and border on the Awuna-Kasena; Sisala people there tend to consult fairy-callers more often, and Islam is more entrenched there. Moslems use fairy-callers as a means of divining the wishes of Allah. Most of the Sisala men who have attempted to learn to call fairies live in these northern clans. The institution does not greatly affect the Sisala to the south—for example, the Crocodile Clan forbids any of its members from becoming a fairy-caller, although it is not taboo to consult one. Needless to say, traditional diviners are quite scornful of fairy-callers, and one frequently hears a diviner make reference in the course of his divining to "those fairy-callers who make so much noise."

Traditional Divination

A traditional diviner (*vugura*) is a man who occupies an accepted, traditional status in Sisala society. Neither the fairy-caller nor the cowrie-thrower has such a status. The office of diviner was instituted by God for the sake of the ancestors, who have perpetuated divination as a means of maintaining control over the living and thereby insuring the continuity of the moral order. It is the link *par excellence* with the occult world, and is the method most used when affliction strikes.

Myth of Origin

The first diviner was thought to have descended from God shortly after man descended to earth via the baobab tree. God gave shrines to men, but men did not understand what their function was nor did they know how to sacrifice on them, therefore affliction abounded in those first days (e.g. children were continually sick, wives died in childbirth, crops failed). God saw that man was confused, and sent down the diviner to help man in the proper use of shrines.

The first diviner was the chief of all diviners, the black ant (*chungchusunung*), which today remains a symbol of divination. The black ant is seen as being similar to God, and therefore serves as a link with God. When a diviner tells someone that he must "apologize to God" or to "pray to God," the person will be instructed to take items (e.g. three kola nuts and fifty cowries) to do so. If the decision is left to the client, he can do one of two things: he can take the objects to a black anthill and leave them on top of it, or he can take them to a real diviner. Also, when people purchase medicine from a medicine man (*dalusungtina*), they must throw away any remaining medicine on a black anthill—which is symbolic of returning the medicine to God. Black ants are like God because both are omnipresent, and both are dangerous if certain precautions are not taken. Black ants never sleep, and anyone who has walked through the African bush at night with a torch focusing on a black anthill has noticed that the ants are busy at work. Black ants are also very strong, and can destroy an entire millet harvest in one night if it is not properly protected. One informant made the following statement:

> Black ants are like God and Moslems. Have you ever seen a pile of millet after black ants have finished with it? They enter, and leave nothing but the chaff. That is what Moslems do, too.

Myth (*namaka*) explains that it was God who sent down the black ant to instruct the first human diviners in the beginning, and black ants taught the diviners to teach the people the purpose of their shrines. Man had received the blacksmith shrine prior to the divining shrine, and yet he did not know how to use it to prevent affliction; because he had no way of knowing when to sacrifice on it, affliction was rampant in the land.

Myth relates that God gave the divining shrine to man so that he could have a link with the occult world. It allowed man to communicate with *fa fa*, and provided a feedback mechanism. When affliction struck, man had some way of knowing the occult reason behind the affliction, and, more importantly, he had a mechanism for ameliorating the affliction through shrine sacrifice. The Sisala verbalize this as a link with God (*Wia*), but it must be emphasized that this is somewhat misleading, because when they say this they are using God as a general symbol of *fa fa*—an occult mythical state which includes not only *Wiajang* [God's village], which is in the sky, but also *lelejang* [the ancestor's village], which is in the earth, as well as the "mystical" side of all shrines, rivers, rocks, trees, and farms. The diviner deals with the whole range of occult entities, but most consultations reveal an ancestral cause of affliction. The Sisala do not always verbalize about the ancestors as causative agents, but will do so if pressed; and they may substitute the word "God" or "shrine"—e.g. "a shrine has afflicted me," or "God has done it."

The Power of the Ancestors

Almost every consultation deals directly or obliquely with the power of the ancestors as guardians of the moral order. Much of the work of Meyer Fortes among the nearby Tallensi has pointed to this power in the daily lives of the living. Cultures in northern Ghana exhibit a pattern of ancestor worship, and the Sisala are no exception. The following two cases illustrate the importance of the ancestors and the belief in their power.

My informant said:

In the village of Pulima a man named Baton decided to go to Tumu. He went to the lineage of Tokurojang and told lies, saying that he was asked by the elders of his compound to collect twenty *cedis* in bridewealth from Baduong. He collected this money and went home, but when he returned home he did not inform anybody, and spent the whole amount himself.

In about three months' time, when the people of Pulima came to collect the bridewealth (*hajarikiaa*), they were told that Baton had already collected it. The members of Tokurojang informed the Pulima party that Baton had said that the Pulima elders had sent him to fetch the money for them. The Pulima elders returned immediately to their village and confronted Baton with the facts. They asked him if he had done this thing but he denied it. The elders could not prove him guilty, so they dropped the matter. Not long afterwards Baton became seriously ill, and his parents went from place to place trying to find medicines to cure him. None of the medicines worked, and they finally took him to the government health center in Tumu where he was given many injections, but he still did not recover. On the way home from the health center he died, and his body was taken home and buried.

The elders came together and called in a diviner. They consulted to know the cause of death. They asked if he was killed by the ancestors because he went to Tumu and told lies. It was determined that this was the case, and Baton's father was required to bring a cow, goat, and sheep to sacrifice at the ancestor (*lele*) shrine. If they had not done this, the ancestors would have brought great harm to the family (lineage) of Baton in the future. Because he told lies, he was killed by the ancestors.

Another informant related the following account:

At Tuorojang in Tumu there was a young man named Cedu. He caught a goat that was for the ancestor of his house (*dia*), and killed it to sell the meat. When the day came for the sacrifice, the elders searched for the goat so that they could kill it at the *lele* shrine. They could not find it, and asked to know who might have caught the goat. They could not decide who had taken the goat, so they caught another and used it for the sacrifice instead. During the sacrifice, the elders begged the ancestors to forgive them for not sacrificing the proper goat. The elders asked the ancestors to find and punish the thief. After the sacrifice, when all the elders had gone to their various houses, they heard that Cedu had died. They summoned a diviner to determine the cause of death, and found that Cedu had been the thief. He had been killed by the ancestors because he was the person who stole the goat which belonged to the ancestors. Cedu's father was required to bring a cow to be sacrificed to the ancestors so that they might not do further harm to the family in the future.

These two cases clearly illustrate that the Sisala believe the ancestors have the power of affliction. When an individual goes contrary to the moral order, he stands the chance of suffering the wrath of the ancestors. In both of these cases a wrong was discovered and the ancestors were called upon to afflict the deviant. When a serious affliction befell a person who might have been the culprit, the elders consulted a diviner to determine whether this had been the case. Divination is the only method whereby the living can determine the actions of the ancestors, and by linking an affliction and a delict, divination reinforces belief in the power of the ancestors.

Affliction and Death Divination

In both of the above cases, death divination revealed that the ancestors had been the cause of death. Other afflictions, such as illness and accident, can also be caused by the ancestors, but death is the ultimate affliction.

After death, two consultations take place. The first is called *vuge na yoho* [literally, "divine to see the funeral"], and takes place before the funeral, as soon after death as possible; but since it is best to call a diviner from another village in cases of death determination, sometimes a day passes before this divination takes place. If the deceased was the lineage elder, his heir will consult; if not, the *jechikintina* will consult just outside the lineage gateway (*peke*) in the shade area (*biling*). This is the only divining session that is held out of doors, as a public affair which anyone may attend, although, unless the death was an unusual one, usually only the family and close friends do attend. The primary function of this consultation is to determine whether the upcoming funeral will be free from conflict and quarrel—that is, whether it will be a "cool funeral" (*yoho fiala*). At this time the family may also ask the occult cause of death (although most omit the question until the second consultation after the funeral); this is usually done only if the family suspects witchcraft or poisoning. In any case, the main reason for this initial consultation is to determine whether any sacrifices need to be

performed prior to the funeral to ensure that no conflict will erupt there. After the funeral, a second consultation takes place, which is called *vuge ne wi la siti suung suri* [literally, "divine to uncover the truth about death"]. This usually takes place shortly after the funeral. Some persons postpone making the second consultation for a week or so, but it should not be put off for long. Whereas the first consultation is public, the second is private, and is attended only by the lineage elders of the death lineage. Again, the *jechikintina* calls in an outside diviner and consults to know the occult cause of death, which nearly always involves the ancestors—that is, some delict is uncovered and used as a rationale of death. It may be determined that the ancestors became enraged at some breach of the norm and caused the death. Once the cause of death is known, it is determined what ritual remedies and sacrifices need to be performed. In addition, the lineage consults to know whether the death has "brought anything our way"—e.g. has the soul of the dead man decided to come back into a newborn child of the lineage; has the funeral been pleasing to the ancestors; has any shrine been defiled during the course of the funeral; has the soul (*dima*) of the dead man been successfully incorporated into the village of the ancestors (*lelejang*)? In essence, then, this consultation is performed to clear away any lingering ritual obligations resulting from the death, and to provide an explanation of the death, as well as a means of rectifying any wrongdoing.

Reasons for Consulting a Diviner

The harshness of life leads people to consult diviners quite frequently, although most clients go to a *dalusuntina* [owner of medicine] first, and only when "medicine" fails is a diviner contacted.

Table 1 shows that the modal number of consultations during the month prior to the interview was two, and only 14 percent of the population had not consulted a diviner during that period.

In an environment where almost no scientific medicine exists, it is not surprising that one of the main concerns of the Sisala is health. Table 2 shows that the modal reason for consulting a diviner is illness. Of the sample interviewed, 38 percent said that illness was their motivation, while another 15 percent of the troubles that led to consultation (e.g.

Table 1 NUMBER OF TIMES A DIVINER WAS CONSULTED IN THE PREVIOUS MONTH

Consultations	0	1	2	3	4	5	6	7	8	9+	Totals
No. of clients	37	71	90	36	22	6	3	2	1	3	271
Percent	14	26	33	13	8	2	1	1	0	1	100

insomnia, childbirth, infertility, and death) were health-related. Clearly over half of the persons who consult diviners do so because of a health problem which is occurring at the time of the consultation. The Sisala say, "We do not consult by heart," meaning that a Sisala man does not consult a diviner unless there is an affliction, and the affliction is usually an immediate one.

The belief in occult causation, and especially in the power of the ancestors, is the primary motivation to consult and the *raison d'être* of divination. These beliefs exist in a milieu where scientific medicine is difficult to obtain, and where traditional medicine is often ineffective. The majority of the population takes refuge in traditional divination, which provides them with a ritual outlet when empirical ones are lacking or fail. Many Sisala admit the superiority of the "white man's medicine" and readily use it when it is available, but when it is not, or when it and/or their own medicines fail, they consult to determine the occult cause of the affliction. Once that is determined, they are provided with a ritual course of action, whereas they had no course of action before.

Fallibility of Divination

The Sisala have a saying: "Diviners tell lies and people die, and they tell lies and the people live," which indicates that there are powers greater than divination. Diviners are fallible because fate (*Wia ne longe*—literally, "what God brings down") is something that a diviner cannot always know. One informant explained that diviners may tell you certain things to do "to have life," but when a person's time to die comes, diviners are useless.

Several factors enter into the belief in the fallibility of diviners. First, it is common knowledge that some diviners are better at their art than others and can communicate with the occult world more effectively. Bascom (1941: 52) also notes this tendency in Ifa divination when he says:

> The diviners themselves admit that some of their number may not be able to answer all questions, and it is to be noted that in placing the blame on the individual's lack of knowledge of Ifa, they shift it from the system itself.

Second, some diviners are believed to tell outright lies to get gain. Third, a diviner's shrine may

Table 2 REASONS FOR CONSULTING A DIVINER

	No Answer	Journey	Marriage	Child-Naming	Illness	Insomnia	Childbirth	Dreams	Wife Infertility
No. of clients	25	32	33	4	102	12	18	3	7
Percent	9	12	12	1	38	4	8	1	3

	Death	To See Future	Conflict in Compound	Death of Animals	To Foretell Outcome of Harvest	General Trouble	Total
No. of clients	3	3	4	1	1	10	271
Percent	1	1	1	0	0	4	100

Table 3 NUMBER OF CONSULTATIONS BY DIVINERS IN THE MONTH PRIOR TO THE INTERVIEW

Consultations	0	1	2	3	4	5	6	7	8	9	10	11	12	13	14	15	16	Total
Diviner																		
Number	12	1	6	10	8	1	5	0	1	0	1	0	9	4	2	0	2	62
Percent	18	2	10	16	13	2	8	0	2	0	2	0	15	6	3	0	3	100
Sisala male																		
Number	37	71	90	36	22	6	3	2	1	3	0	0	0	0	0	0	0	271
Percent	14	26	33	13	8	2	1	1	0	1	0	0	0	0	0	0	0	100

lose power (*dolung*) if he does not sacrifice on it periodically, or if one of the ancestors who previously owned it is angry with him. Fourth, tradition relates that diviners have been imperfect even in the past, and since *fa fa* is a pattern for the present, even imperfection in *fa fa* is carried into the present world of the living.

Diviners are well aware that people do not consider their pronouncements as final, and they often add a rider to the pronouncement, such as: "If I have spoken the truth, you will hear of a funeral soon" (a very ambiguous statement, and a highly probable event to predict in western Africa). I have many times heard Sisala, by circular, *ex-post-facto* thinking, justify a diviner's pronouncement because such an event transpired. Because a diviner is not considered infallible, more than one is consulted about an important matter. The second consultation is a check on the first, and if the first diviner's edict is confirmed by a second consultation, it is considered to be valid, so that no more

divining is needed. However, if the second diviner contradicts the first one, then the client seeks a third diviner to try and match up the third edict with one of the other pronouncements, in which case the inconsistent one will be ignored. In fact, most clients use an institutionalized technique called *dachevung* to test a diviner's edict. Although I was unable to find a suitable translation for the word *dachevung*, roughly it means "he heard some things." Once a client has "heard some things" from one diviner, he does not have to go through another complete consultation to check the validity of the proclamation. He may merely go to a diviner and tell him that he wants to have *dachevung*. This method of divining is much quicker than a normal consultation, and is used only to confirm or reject another diviner's edict, because with *dachevung* the diviner does not have to open his bag and go through all of its contents; he merely uses a wand. This method is also called *a ga purung* [literally, "to steal the bag"]. The client squats before the diviner

Table 4 SHRINE OWNERSHIP BY DIVINERS AND BY PAGAN MALES

Number of Shrines	0	1	2	3	4	5	6	7	Total
Diviner									
Number	0	7	10	12	25	5	4	0	62
Percent	0	12	16	19	39	6	6	0	100
Pagan male									
Number	62	25	29	59	78	6	6	6	271
Percent	23	9	11	22	29	2	2	2	100

Table 5 FARTHEST CITY VISITED BY DIVINERS AND BY NON-DIVINERS

	No Answer	Tumu	Wa/Bolga	Tamale	Kumasi	Accra	Total
Diviner							
Number	0	11	12	6	24	9	62
Percent	0	18	19	10	39	15	100
Non-diviners							
Number	6	15	55	54	98	33	261
Percent	2	6	21	21	38	13	100

and presents silent alternatives in the form of marks on the floor or in the dirt. The diviner points the wand toward one mark or the other without knowing what they mean. For example, if the first diviner has told the client that his affliction was due to a quarrel with his elder brother, he will present that as one possibility. If the second diviner chooses that possibility (without knowing what it is), the client will be satisfied that the first diviner was telling the truth and the *dachevung* will come to an end. The following is an account of a *dachevung*:

> The client entered the room of the diviner and indicated that he would like to have a *dachevung* conducted. He squatted before the diviner and made two marks on the dirt floor. In his mind he had assigned the edict of the first diviner to one of the marks, while the other mark stood for the negation of that edict (he told me this afterwards). When he made the marks he said:
> "What has brought me from the house this morning?"
> Diviner: "This." (The wand pointed to one of the marks.)
> At this point the client made several more marks in silence and said: "What is inside it?"
> Diviner: "This."
> Client (making new marks): "I've put it down."
> Diviner: "No!" (This was an attempt on the part of the client to get the diviner to contradict himself.)
> Client: "I've stolen it."
> Diviner: "This is what you have stolen."

This type of consultation takes only a few minutes, whereas a normal consultation can take up to an hour.

Although the Sisala are aware that, for one reason or another, diviners do not always tell the whole truth, they view divination as the only legitimate mechanism whereby they can receive feedback from the ancestors. Since diviners are not infallible, and since they are considered the best means of receiving such feedback from the occult world, a client wishing to consult about an important matter may travel some distance to consult an alien, and therefore unbiased, diviner (see also Colson 1970). This diviner is alien only in the sense that he is a stranger, and hence is thought to be less prejudiced than a local diviner. He is normally a Sisala diviner, although Kasena diviners and fairy-callers are also consulted. In any case, he operates within a similar cultural framework as a local diviner.

Divination is a powerful mechanism for the release of anxiety in Sisala society. In a society where illness is unchecked by modern medicine, where wells can go dry or water holes dry up, where crop success is at the mercy of the elements, divination provides answers in a world of questions. Even Moslems, Christians, and the educated elite find it difficult indeed, when faced with affliction, to resist the "concreteness" of divination. More than once I have been sitting with a diviner and had an educated Christian enter the room to consult. In one case I had had a conversation the previous week with this very Christian in which he had passed divination off as a mere superstition of "uneducated pagans," yet when faced with the severe illness of his wife, he resorted to the ways of his forefathers. I have seen men who were very depressed at the onset of the consultation leave happy and content with what they had learned. On the other hand, a consultation may increase one's anxiety, as in the case of a man whose worst suspicions are confirmed. But there is almost always a

Table 6   SEX OF DIVINERS

	No Response	Male	Female	Total
Number of respondents	1	54	7	62
Percent	2	87	11	100

ritual outlet provided by divination for the release of anxiety. Almost no consultation ends without the client having been instructed to avoid a "danger" before consulting the diviner, but only afterward does the client have means to avoid it. Therefore, even though many consider diviners to be fallible, it is the traditional method *par excellence* of dealing with dangers, problems, and affliction. Also, the internal structure of the institution of divination is ordered so that it copes with this fallibility. Indeed, the belief in fallibility may be partly responsible for the continued existence of divination. Concerning the repeated consultation of many diviners, Horton (1967: 167) says:

> What is notable in all this is that the client never takes his repeated failures as evidence against the existence of the various spiritual beings named as responsible for his plight, or as evidence against the possibility of making contact with such beings as diviners claim to do. Nor do members of the community in which he lives ever try to keep track of the proportion of successes to failures in the remedial actions based on their beliefs, with the aim of questioning these beliefs. At most, they grumble about the dishonesty and wiles of many diviners, whilst maintaining their faith in the existence of some honest, competent practitioners.

In spite of the belief in fallibility, it must be pointed out that diviners themselves consult each other frequently. In fact, Table 3 shows that they do so more frequently than the average pagan male. Sisala diviners, like their Yoruba counterparts (Bascom 1941: 52–53), believe in divination as a means of communicating with the occult world, and regu-larly perform postdivinatory sacrifices in an effort to appease the ancestors and thereby avoid or eliminate an affliction.

Diviner Characteristics

Persons who become diviners tend to be traditional, conservative individuals who are oriented toward the past and who adhere to the ways of the ancestors—the true path (*wenbiing titi*). A comparison of shrine ownership by diviners as against pagan males highlights this conservatism (see Table 4).

Also, diviners appear to be more conservative in that they utilize other diviners more often than do non-diviners (it is also true that they do not have to pay the fee). Table 3 shows that Sisala males have a mode of two consultations per month, whereas the diviners have a mode of three consultations, and many consult as often as twelve times per month.

Diviners also appear to have traveled slightly less than non-diviners (see Table 5). Disinclination to travel is an indication of conservatism.

Most diviners are males, but some very old women, who "are like men because they can no longer bear children," do practice divination (see Table 6).

My sample included no diviners below the approximate age of twenty, and the greatest number of diviners were between the ages of thirty and forty (see Table 7).

Divining is not a full-time occupation (see Table 8). Most diviners are full-time farmers, who take clients in the early morning hours before they go to their farms, and sometimes (but rarely) at night.

Table 7   AGE OF DIVINERS

	20–30	31–40	41–50	51–60	61–70	71–80	81–90	Total
Number of respondents	12	21	15	8	1	3	2	62
Percent	19	34	24	13	2	5	3	100

Table 8   OCCUPATION

	None*	Farmer	Trader	Hunter	Laborer	Educated	Total
Diviner							
Number	8	51	2	0	0	1	62
Percent	13	82	2	0	0.	2	99
Non-diviner							
Number	7	224	2	3	26	6	268
Percent	3	83	1	1	10	2	100

Summary

While the Sisala have other kinds of divination, the traditional method predominates. The institution of divination provides a customary way of communicating with the ancestors who control the power of the universe. Ancestors use this power to afflict the living, and divination allows the living to determine the cause and to remedy this affliction. Most diviners are males, and the rest are old women and therefore have shown their support for the gerontocratic order. Diviners appear to be traditionalists who have inherited a position in the social order which functions to orient the Sisala toward the "true path" of the ancestors. Divination, therefore, acts as a social control mechanism. Deviant behavior is handled in the context of affliction-divination-sacrifice. Affliction leads a client to consult a diviner, who provides an institutionalized occult cause, as well as a sacrificial remedy, to his problem. Thus, divination is a conservative mechanism which reinforces the established social order, and it is not surprising to find that ordinarily Sisala diviners are older males who own a higher than average number of shrines, who have had little travel experience, and who tend to engage in farming rather than non-farming economic pursuits.

Rational Mastery by Man of His Surroundings

Bronislaw Malinowski

Rare is the anthropology course that sometime during the semester is not directed to the thought and writings of Bronislaw Malinowski (1884–1942). This world-famous Polish anthropologist was trained in mathematics, but shifted his interests to anthropology after reading Sir James Frazer's The Golden Bough. *Malinowski's field work in the Trobriand Islands of Melanesia influenced the direction of anthropology as an academic discipline. He is recognized as the founder of functionalism, an anthropological approach to the study of culture that believes each institution in a society fulfills a definite function in the maintenance of human needs. His major works include* Crime and Customs in Savage Society *(1926),* The Sexual Life of Savages *(1929), and* Coral Gardens and Their Magic *(1935). Malinowski was professor of anthropology at the University of London from 1927 until his death in 1942. In this classic article Malinowski asks two important questions: do pre-literate people have any rational mastery of their surroundings; and can primitive knowledge be regarded as a beginning or rudimentary type of science, or is it merely a crude hodgepodge devoid of logic and accuracy?*

Reprinted from *Magic, Science and Religion* (New York: Doubleday, 1955), pp. 25–35, by permission of the Society for Promoting Christian Knowledge.

THE PROBLEM OF PRIMITIVE KNOWLEDGE HAS BEEN singularly neglected by anthropology. Studies on savage psychology were exclusively confined to early religion, magic, and mythology. Only recently the work of several English, German, and French writers, notably the daring and brilliant speculations of Professor Lévy-Bruhl, gave an impetus to the student's interest in what the savage does in his more sober moods. The results were startling indeed: Professor Lévy-Bruhl tells us, to put it in a nutshell, that primitive man has no sober moods at all, that he is hopelessly and completely immersed in a mystical frame of mind. Incapable of dispassionate and consistent observation, devoid of the power of abstraction, hampered by "a decided aversion towards reasoning," he is unable to draw any benefit from experience, to construct or comprehend even the most elementary laws of nature. "For minds thus orientated there is no fact purely physical." Nor can there exist for them any clear idea of substance and attribute, cause and effect, identity and contradiction. Their outlook is that of confused superstition, "pre-logical," made of mystic "participations" and "exclusions." I have here summarized a body of opinion, of which the brilliant French sociologist is the most decided and competent spokesman, but which numbers besides, many anthropologists and philosophers of renown.

But there are dissenting voices. When a scholar and anthropologist of the measure of Professor J. L. Myres entitles an article in *Notes and Queries* "Natural Science," and when we read there that the savage's "knowledge based on observation is distinct and accurate," we must surely pause before accepting primitive man's irrationality as a dogma. Another highly competent writer, Dr. A. A. Goldenweiser, speaking about primitive "discoveries, inventions and improvements"—which could hardly be attributed to any pre-empirical or pre-logical mind—affirms that "it would be unwise to ascribe to the primitive mechanic merely a passive part in the origination of inventions. Many a happy thought must have crossed his mind, nor was he wholly unfamiliar with the thrill that comes from an idea effective in action." Here we see the savage endowed with an attitude of mind wholly akin to that of a modern man of science!

To bridge over the wide gap between the two extreme opinions current on the subject of primitive man's reason, it will be best to resolve the problem into two questions.

First, has the savage any rational outlook, any rational mastery of his surroundings, or is he, as M. Lévy-Bruhl and his school maintain, entirely "mystical"? The answer will be that every primitive community is in possession of a considerable store of knowledge, based on experience and fashioned by reason.

The second question then opens: Can this primitive knowledge be regarded as a rudimentary form of science or is it, on the contrary, radically different, a crude empiry, a body of practical and technical abilities, rules of thumb and rules of art having no theoretical value? This second question, epistemological rather than belonging to the study of man, will be barely touched upon at the end of this section and a tentative answer only will be given.

In dealing with the first question, we shall have to examine the "profane" side of life, the arts, crafts and economic pursuits, and we shall attempt to disentangle in it a type of behavior, clearly marked off from magic and religion, based on empirical knowledge and on the confidence in logic. We shall try to find whether the lines of such behavior are defined by traditional rules, known, perhaps even discussed sometimes, and tested. We shall have to inquire whether the sociological setting of the rational and empirical behavior differs from that of ritual and cult. Above all we shall ask, do the natives distinguish the two domains and keep them apart, or is the field of knowledge constantly swamped by superstition, ritualism, magic or religion?

Since in the matter under discussion there is an appalling lack of relevant and reliable observations, I shall have largely to draw upon my own material, most unpublished, collected during a few years'

field work among the Melanesian and Papuo-Melanesian tribes of Eastern New Guinea and the surrounding archipelagoes. As the Melanesians are reputed, however, to be specially magic-ridden, they will furnish an acid test of the existence of empirical and rational knowledge among savages living in the age of polished stone.

These natives, and I am speaking mainly of the Melanesians who inhabit the coral atolls to the N.E. of the main island, the Trobriand Archipelago and the adjoining groups, are expert fishermen, industrious manufacturers and traders, but they rely mainly on gardening for their subsistence. With the most rudimentary implements, a pointed digging-stick and a small axe, they are able to raise crops sufficient to maintain a dense population and even yielding a surplus, which in olden days was allowed to rot unconsumed, and which at present is exported to feed plantation hands. The success in their agriculture depends—besides the excellent natural conditions with which they are favored—upon their extensive knowledge of the classes of the soil, of the various cultivated plants, of the mutual adaptation of these two factors, and, last not least, upon their knowledge of the importance of accurate and hard work. They have to select the soil and the seedlings, they have appropriately to fix the times for clearing and burning the scrub, for planting and weeding, for training the vines of the yam plants. In all this they are guided by a clear knowledge of weather and seasons, plants and pests, soil and tubers, and by a conviction that this knowledge is true and reliable, that it can be counted upon and must be scrupulously obeyed.

Yet mixed with all their activities there is to be found magic, a series of rites performed every year over the gardens in rigorous sequence and order. Since the leadership in garden work is in the hands of the magician, and since ritual and practical work are intimately associated, a superficial observer might be led to assume that the mystic and the rational behavior are mixed up, that their effects are not distinguished by the natives and not distinguishable in scientific analysis. Is this so really?

Magic is undoubtedly regarded by the natives as absolutely indispensable to the welfare of the gardens. What would happen without it no one can exactly tell, for no native garden has ever been made without its ritual, in spite of some thirty years of European rule and missionary influence and well over a century's contact with white traders. But certainly various kinds of disaster, blight, unseasonable droughts, rains, bush-pigs and locusts would destroy the unhallowed garden made without magic.

Does this mean, however, that the natives attribute all the good results to magic? Certainly not. If you were to suggest to a native that he should make his garden mainly by magic and scamp his work, he would simply smile on your simplicity. He knows as well as you do that there are natural conditions and causes, and by his observations he knows also that he is able to control these natural forces by mental and physical effort. His knowledge is limited, no doubt, but as far as it goes it is sound and proof against mysticism. If the fences are broken down, if the seed is destroyed or has been dried or washed away, he will have recourse not to magic, but to work, guided by knowledge and reason. His experience has taught him also, on the other hand, that in spite of all his forethought and beyond all his efforts there are agencies and forces which one year bestow unwonted and unearned benefits of fertility, making everything run smooth and well, rain and sun appear at the right moment, noxious insects remain in abeyance, the harvest yields a superabundant crop; and another year again the same agencies bring ill luck and bad chance, pursue him from beginning till end and thwart all his most strenuous efforts and his best-founded knowledge. To control these influences and these only he employs magic.

Thus there is a clear-cut division: there is first the well-known set of conditions, the natural course of growth, as well as the ordinary pests and dangers to be warded off by fencing and weeding. On the other hand there is the domain of the unaccountable and adverse influences, as well as the great unearned increment of fortunate coincidence. The first conditions are coped with by knowledge and work, the second by magic.

This line of division can also be traced in the social setting of work and ritual respectively. Though the garden magician is, as a rule, also the leader in practical activities, these two functions are kept strictly apart. Every magical ceremony has its distinctive name, its appropriate time and its place in the scheme of work, and it stands out of the ordinary course of activities completely. Some of them are ceremonial and have to be attended by the whole community, all are public in that it is known when they are going to happen and anyone can attend them. They are performed on selected plots within the gardens and on a special corner of this plot. Work is always tabooed on such occasions, sometimes only while the ceremony lasts, sometimes for a day or two. In his lay character the leader and magician directs the work, fixes the dates for starting, harangues and exhorts slack or careless gardeners. But the two roles never overlap or interfere: they are always clear, and any native will inform you without hesitation whether the man acts as magician or as leader in garden work.

What has been said about gardens can be paralleled from any one of the many other activities in which work and magic run side by side without ever mixing. Thus in canoe building empirical knowledge of material, of technology, and of certain principles of stability and hydrodynamics, function in company and close association with magic, each yet uncontaminated by the other.

For example, they understand perfectly well that the wider the span of the outrigger the greater the stability yet the smaller the resistance against strain. They can clearly explain why they have to give this span a certain traditional width, measured in fractions of the length of the dugout. They can also explain, in rudimentary but clearly mechanical terms, how they have to behave in a sudden gale, why the outrigger must be always on the weather side, why the one type of canoe can and the other cannot beat. They have, in fact, a whole system of principles of sailing, embodied in a complex and rich terminology, traditionally handed on and obeyed as rationally and consistently as is modern science by modern sailors. How could they sail otherwise under eminently dangerous conditions in their frail primitive craft?

But even with all their systematic knowledge, methodically applied, they are still at the mercy of powerful and incalculable tides, sudden gales during the monsoon season and unknown reefs. And here comes in their magic, performed over the canoe during its construction, carried out at the beginning and in the course of expeditions and resorted to in moments of real danger. If the modern seaman, entrenched in science and reason, provided with all sorts of safety appliances, sailing on steel-built steamers, if even he has a singular tendency to superstition—which does not rob him of his knowledge or reason, nor make him altogether prelogical—can we wonder that his savage colleague, under much more precarious conditions, holds fast to the safety and comfort of magic?

An interesting and crucial test is provided by fishing in the Trobriand Islands and its magic. While in the villages on the inner lagoon fishing is done in an easy and absolutely reliable manner by the method of poisoning, yielding abundant results without danger and uncertainty, there are on the shores of the open sea dangerous modes of fishing and also certain types in which the yield greatly varies according to whether shoals of fish appear beforehand or not. It is most significant that in the lagoon fishing, where man can rely completely upon his knowledge and skill, magic does not exist, while in the open-sea fishing, full of danger and uncertainty, there is extensive magical ritual to secure safety and good results.

Again, in warfare the natives know that strength, courage, and agility play a decisive part. Yet here also they practice magic to master the elements of chance and luck.

Nowhere is the duality of natural and supernatural causes divided by a line so thin and intricate, yet, if carefully followed up, so well marked, decisive, and instructive, as in the two most fateful forces of human destiny: health and death. Health to the Melanesians is a natural state of affairs and, unless tampered with, the human body will remain in perfect order. But the natives know perfectly well that there are natural means which can affect health and even destroy the body. Poisons, wounds, burns, falls, are known to cause disablement or death in a natural way. And this is not a matter of private opinion of this or that individual, but it is laid down in traditional lore and even in belief, for there are considered to be different ways to the nether world for those who died by sorcery and those who met "natural" death. Again, it is recognized that cold, heat, overstrain, too much sun, overeating, can all cause minor ailments, which are treated by natural remedies such as massage, steaming, warming at a fire and certain potions. Old age is known to lead to bodily decay and the explanation is given by the natives that very old people grow weak, their oesophagus closes up, and therefore they must die.

But besides these natural causes there is the enormous domain of sorcery and by far the most cases of illness and death are ascribed to this. The line of distinction between sorcery and the other causes is clear in theory and in most cases of practice, but it must be realized that it is subject to what could be called the personal perspective. That is, the more closely a case has to do with the person who considers it, the less will it be "natural," the more "magical." Thus a very old man, whose pending death will be considered natural by the other members of the community, will be afraid only of sorcery and never think of his natural fate. A fairly sick person will diagnose sorcery in his own case, while all the others might speak of too much betel nut or overeating or some other indulgence.

But who of us really believes that his own bodily infirmities and the approaching death is a purely natural occurrence, just an insignificant event in the infinite chain of causes? To the most rational civilized men health, disease, the threat of death, float in a hazy emotional mist, which seems to become denser and more impenetrable as the fateful forms approach. It is indeed astonishing that "savages" can achieve such a sober, dispassionate outlook in these matters as they actually do.

Thus in his relation to nature and destiny, whether he tries to exploit the first or to dodge the second, primitive man recognizes both the natural and the supernatural forces and agencies, and he tries to use them both for his benefit. Whenever he has been taught by experience that effort guided by knowledge is of some avail, he never spares the one or ignores the other. He knows that a plant cannot grow by magic alone, or a canoe sail or float without being properly constructed and managed, or a fight be won without skill and daring. He never relies on magic alone, while, on the contrary, he sometimes dispenses with it completely, as in fire-making and in a number of crafts and pursuits. But he clings to it, whenever he has to recognize the impotence of his knowledge and of his rational technique.

I have given my reasons why in this argument I had to rely principally on the material collected in the classical land of magic, Melanesia. But the facts discussed are so fundamental, the conclusions drawn of such a general nature, that it will be easy to check them on any modern detailed ethnographic record. Comparing agricultural work and magic, the building of canoes, the art of healing by magic and by natural remedies, the ideas about the causes of death in other regions, the universal validity of what has been established here could easily be proved. Only, since no observations have methodically been made with reference to the problem of primitive knowledge, the data from other writers could be gleaned only piecemeal and their testimony though clear would be indirect.

I have chosen to face the question of primitive man's rational knowledge directly: watching him at his principal occupations, seeing him pass from work to magic and back again, entering into his mind, listening to his opinions. The whole problem might have been approached through the avenue of language, but this would have led us too far into questions of logic, semasiology, and theory of primitive languages. Words which serve to express general ideas such as *existence, substance,* and *attribute, cause* and *effect,* the *fundamental* and the *secondary;* words and expressions used in complicated pursuits like sailing, construction, measuring and checking; numerals and quantitative descriptions, correct and detailed classifications of natural phenomena, plants and animals—all this would lead us exactly to the same conclusion: that primitive man can observe and think, and that he possesses, embodied in his language, systems of methodical though rudimentary knowledge.

Similar conclusions could be drawn from an examination of those mental schemes and physical contrivances which could be described as diagrams or formulas. Methods of indicating the main points of the compass, arrangements of stars into constellations, co-ordination of these with the seasons, naming of moons in the year, of quarters in the moon—all these accomplishments are known to the simplest savages. Also they are all able to draw diagrammatic maps in the sand or dust, indicate arrangements by placing small stones, shells, or sticks on the ground, plan expeditions or raids on such rudimentary charts. By co-ordinating space and time they are able to arrange big tribal gatherings and to combine vast tribal movements over extensive areas. The use of leaves, notched sticks, and similar aids to memory is well known and seems to be almost universal. All such "diagrams" are means of reducing a complex and unwieldy bit of reality to a simple and handy form. They give man a relatively easy mental control over it. As such are they not—in a very rudimentary form no

doubt—fundamentally akin to developed scientific formulas and "models," which are also simple and handy paraphrases of a complex or abstract reality, giving the civilized physicist mental control over it?

This brings us to the second question: Can we regard primitive knowledge, which, as we found, is both empirical and rational, as a rudimentary stage of science, or is it not at all related to it? If by science be understood a body of rules and conceptions, based on experience and derived from it by logical inference, embodied in material achievements and in a fixed form of tradition and carried on by some sort of social organization—then there is no doubt that even the lowest savage communities have the beginnings of science, however rudimentary.

Most epistemologists would not, however, be satisfied with such a "minimum definition" of science, for it might apply to the rules of an art or craft as well. They would maintain that the rules of science must be laid down explicitly, open to control by experiment and critique by reason. They must not only be rules of practical behavior, but theoretical laws of knowledge. Even accepting this stricture, however, there is hardly any doubt that many of the principles of savage knowledge are scientific in this sense. The native shipwright knows not only practically of buoyancy, leverage, equilibrium, he has to obey these laws not only on water, but while making the canoe he must have the principles in his mind. He instructs his helpers in them. He gives them the traditional rules, and in a crude and simple manner, using his hands, pieces of wood, and a limited technical vocabulary, he explains some general laws of hydrodynamics and equilibrium. Science is not detached from the craft, that is certainly true, it is only a means to an end, it is crude, rudimentary, and inchoate, but with all that it is the matrix from which the higher developments must have sprung.

If we applied another criterion yet, that of the really scientific attitude, the disinterested search for knowledge and for the understanding of causes and reasons, the answer would certainly not be in a direct negative. There is, of course, no widespread thirst for knowledge in a savage community, new things such as European topics bore them frankly and their whole interest is largely encompassed by the traditional world of their culture. But within this there is both the antiquarian mind passionately interested in myths, stories, details of customs, pedigrees, and ancient happenings, and there is also to be found the naturalist, patient and painstaking in his observations, capable of generalization and of connecting long chains of events in the life of animals, and in the marine world or in the jungle. It is enough to realize how much European naturalists have often learned from their savage colleagues to appreciate this interest found in the native for nature. There is finally among the primitives, as every field worker well knows, the sociologist, the ideal informant, capable with marvelous accuracy and insight to give the *raison d'être*, the function and the organization of many a simpler institution in his tribe.

Science, of course, does not exist in any uncivilized community as a driving power, criticizing, renewing, constructing. Science is never consciously made. But on this criterion, neither is there law, nor religion, nor government among savages.

Baseball Magic

George Gmelch

In the preceding article, Malinowski observed that in the Trobriand Islands magic did not occur when the natives fished in the safe lagoons but when they ventured out into the open seas: then the danger and uncertainty caused them to perform extensive magical rituals. In the following article, anthropologist George Gmelch demonstrates that America's "favorite pastime" is an excellent place to put the test to Malinowski's hypothesis about magic. Anyone who has watched baseball, either at a ballpark or in front of a television set, is aware of some of the more obvious rituals performed by the players; but Gmelch, drawing upon his own experiences as a one-time professional baseball player, provides an insider's view of the rituals, taboos, and fetishes involved in the sport.

Reprinted by permission of the author.

ON EACH PITCHING DAY FOR THE FIRST THREE months of a winning season, Dennis Grossini, a pitcher on a Detroit Tiger farm team, arose from bed at exactly 10 A.M. At 1 P.M. he went to the nearest restaurant for two glasses of iced tea and a tuna fish sandwich. Although the afternoon was free, he changed into the sweat shirt and supporter he wore during his last winning game, and one hour before the game he chewed a wad of Beech-Nut chewing tobacco. During the game he touched his letters (the team name on his uniform) after each pitch and straightened his cap after each ball. Before the start of each inning he replaced the pitcher's rosin bag next to the spot where it was the inning before. And after every inning in which he gave up a run he would wash his hands.

I asked him which part of the ritual was most important. He responded, "You can't really tell what's most important so it all becomes important. I'd be afraid to change anything. As long as I'm winning, I do everything the same. Even when I can't wash my hands [this would occur when he had to bat], it scares me going back to the mound. . . . I don't feel quite right."

Trobriand Islanders, according to anthropologist Bronislaw Malinowski, felt the same way about their fishing magic. Among the Trobrianders, fishing took two forms. In the inner lagoon, fish were plentiful and there was little danger; on the open sea, fishing was dangerous and yields varied widely. Malinowski found that magic was not used in lagoon fishing, where men could rely solely on their knowledge and skill. But when fishing on the open sea, Trobrianders used a great deal of magical ritual to ensure safety and increase their catch.

Baseball, the American national sport, is an arena in which the players behave remarkably like Malinowski's Trobriand fishermen. To professional baseball players, baseball is more than a game. It is an occupation. Since their livelihood depends on how well they perform, they use magic to try to control or eliminate the chance and uncertainty built into baseball.

To control uncertainty, ex-San Francisco Giant pitcher Ron Bryant added a new stick of bubble gum to the collection in his bulging back pocket after each game he won. Jim Ohms, my teammate on the Daytona Beach Islanders in 1966, used to put another penny in the pouch of his supporter after each win. Clanging against the hard plastic genital cup, the pennies made an audible sound as the pitcher ran the bases toward the end of a winning season. Fred Caviglia, former Kansas City minor-league pitcher, used to eat the same food before each game he pitched.

Whether they are professional baseball players, Trobriand fishermen, soldiers, or farmers, people resort to magic in situations of chance, when they believe they have limited control over the success of their activities. In technologically advanced societies that pride themselves on a scientific approach to problem solving, as well as in simple societies, rituals of magic are common. Magic is a human attempt to impose order and certainty on a chaotic, uncertain situation. This attempt is irrational in that there is no causal connection between the instruments of magic and the desired consequences of the magical practice. But it is rational in that it creates in the practitioner a sense of confidence, competence, and control, which in turn is important to successfully executing a specific activity and achieving a desired result.

I have long had a close relationship with baseball, first as a participant and then as an observer. I devoted much of my youth to the game and played professionally as a first baseman for five teams in the Detroit Tiger organization over three years. I also spent two years in the Quebec Provincial League. For additional information about baseball magic, I interviewed 28 professional ballplayers and sportswriters.

There are three essential activities in baseball—pitching, hitting, and fielding. The first two, pitching and hitting, involve a great deal of chance and are comparable to the Trobriand fishermen's open sea; in them, players use magic and ritual to increase their chances for success. The third activity, fielding, involves little uncertainty, and is similar to the Trobriander inner lagoon; fielders find it unnecessary to resort to magic.

The pitcher is the player least able to control the

outcome of his own efforts. His best pitch may be hit for a home run, and his worst pitch may be hit directly into the hands of a fielder for an out or be swung at and missed for a third strike. He may limit the opposing team to a few hits yet lose the game, or he may give up a dozen hits and win. Frequently pitchers perform well and lose, and perform poorly and win. One has only to look at the frequency with which pitchers end a season with poor won-lost records but good earned run averages (a small number of runs given up per game), or vice versa. For example, in 1977 Jerry Koosman of the Mets had an abysmal won-lost record of 8 and 20, but a competent 3.49 earned run average, while Larry Christenson of the Phillies had an unimpressive earned run average of 4.07 and an excellent won-lost record of 19 and 6. Regardless of how well he performs, the pitcher depends upon the proficiency of his teammates, the inefficiency of the opposition, and caprice.

An incredible example of bad luck in pitching occurred some years ago involving former Giant outfielder Willie Mays. Mays intentionally "dove for the dirt" to avoid being hit in the head by a fastball. While he was falling the ball hit his bat and went shooting down the left-field line. Mays jumped up and ran, turning the play into a double. Players shook their heads in amazement—most players can't hit when they try to, but Mays couldn't avoid hitting even when he tried not to. The pitcher looked on in disgust.

Hitting is also full of risk and uncertainty—Red Sox outfielder and Hall of Famer Ted Williams called it the most difficult single task in the world of sports. Consider the forces and time constraints operating against the batter. A fastball travels from the pitcher's mound to the batter's box, just 60½ feet, in three to four tenths of a second. For only three feet of the journey, an absurdly short 2/100ths of a second, the ball is in a position where it can be hit. And to be hit well, the ball must be neither too close to the batter's body nor too far from the "meat" of his bat. Any distraction, any slip of a muscle or change in stance can throw a swing off. Once the ball is hit, chance plays a large role in determining where it will go—into a waiting glove, whistling past a fielder's diving stab, or into the wide-open spaces. While the pitcher who threw the fastball to Mays was suffering, Mays was collecting the benefits of luck.

Batters also suffer from the fear of being hit by a pitch—specifically, by a fastball that often travels at speeds exceeding 90 miles per hour. Throughout baseball history the great fastball pitchers—men like Sandy Koufax, Walter Johnson, Bob Gibson, and currently Nolan Ryan of the California Angels—have thrived on this fear and on the level of distraction it causes hitters. The well-armed pitcher inevitably captures the advantage in the psychological war of nerves that characterizes the ongoing tension between pitcher and hitter, and that determines who wins and loses the game. If a hitter is crowding the plate in order to reach balls on the outside corner, or if the batter has been hitting unusually well, pitchers try to regain control of their territory. Indeed, many pitchers intentionally throw at or "dust" a batter in order to instill this sense of fear (what hitters euphemistically call "respect") in him. On one occasion Dock Ellis of the Pittsburgh Pirates, having become convinced that the Cincinnati Reds were dominating his team, intentionally hit the first three Reds' batters he faced before his manager removed him from the game.

In fielding, on the other hand, the player has almost complete control over the outcome. Once a ball has been hit in his direction, no one can intervene and ruin his chances of catching it for an out. Infielders have approximately three seconds in which to judge the flight of the ball, field it cleanly, and throw it to first base. Outfielders have almost double that amount of time to track down a fly ball. The average fielding percentage (or success rate) of .975, compared with a .250 success rate for hitters (the average batting percentage), reflects the degree of certainty in fielding. Compared with the pitcher or the hitter, the fielder has little to worry about. He knows that in better than 9.7 times out of 10 he will execute his task flawlessly.

In keeping with Malinowski's hypothesis about the relationship between magic and uncertainty, my research shows that baseball players associate magic with hitting and pitching, but not with fielding. Despite the wide assortment of magic—which includes rituals, taboos, and fetishes—associated with both hitting and pitching, I have never observed any directly connected to fielding. In my experience I have known only one player, a short-

stop with fielding problems, who reported any ritual even remotely connected with fielding.

The most common form of magic in professional baseball is personal ritual—a prescribed form of behavior that players scrupulously observe in an effort to ensure that things go their way. These rituals, like those of Malinowski's Trobriand fishermen, are performed in a routine, unemotional manner, much as players do nonmagical things to improve their play: rubbing pine tar on the hands to improve a grip on the bat, or rubbing a new ball to make it more comfortable and responsive to the pitcher's grip. Rituals are infinitely varied since ballplayers may formalize any activity that they consider important to performing well.

Rituals usually grow out of exceptionally good performances. When a player does well he seldom attributes his success to skill alone. Although his skill remains constant, he may go hitless in one game and in the next get three or four hits. Many players attribute the inconsistencies in their performances to an object, item of food, or form of behavior outside their play. Through ritual, players seek to gain control over their performance. In the 1920s and '30s sportswriters reported that a player who tripped en route to the field would often retrace his steps and carefully walk over the stumbling block for "insurance."

The word "taboo" comes from a Polynesian term meaning prohibition. Failure to observe a taboo or prohibition leads to undesirable consequences or bad luck. Most players observe a number of taboos. Taboos usually grow out of exceptionally poor performances, which players often attribute to a particular behavior or food. Certain uniforms may become taboo. If a player has a poor spring training season or an unsuccessful year, he may refuse to wear the same number again. During my first season of professional baseball I ate pancakes before a game in which I struck out four times. Several weeks later I had a repeat performance, again after eating pancakes. The result was a pancake taboo—I never ate pancakes during the season from that day on. Another personal taboo, against holding a baseball during the national anthem (the usual practice for first basemen, who must warm up the other infielders), had a similar origin.

In earlier decades some baseball players believed that it was bad luck to go back and fasten a missed buttonhole after dressing for a game. They simply left missed buttons on shirts or pants undone. This taboo is not practiced by modern ballplayers.

Fetishes or charms are material objects believed to embody supernatural powers that aid or protect the owner. Good-luck fetishes are standard equipment for many ballplayers. They include a wide assortment of objects: horsehide covers from old baseballs, coins, bobby pins (Hall of Fame pitcher Rube Waddell collected these), crucifixes, and old bats. Ordinary objects acquire power by being connected to exceptionally hot batting or pitching streaks, especially ones in which players get all the breaks. The object is often a new possession or something a player finds and holds responsible for his good fortune. A player who is in a slump might find a coin or an odd stone just before he begins a hitting streak, attribute an improvement in his performance to the influence of the new object, and regard it as a fetish.

While playing for Spokane, a Dodger farm team, Alan Foster forgot his baseball shoes on a road trip and borrowed a pair from a teammate. That night he pitched a no-hitter, which he attributed to the borrowed shoes. After he bought them from his teammate, they became a prized possession.

During World War II, American soldiers used fetishes in much the same way. Social psychologist Samuel Stouffer and his colleagues found that in the face of great danger and uncertainty soldiers developed magical practices, particularly the use of protective amulets and good-luck charms (crosses, Bibles, rabbits' feet, medals), and jealously guarded articles of clothing they associated with past experiences of escape from danger. Stouffer also found that prebattle preparations were carried out in a fixed "ritual" order, much as ballplayers prepare for a game.

Because most pitchers play only once evey four days, they perform rituals less frequently than hitters. The rituals they do perform, however, are just as important. A pitcher cannot make up for a poor performance the next day, and having to wait three days to redeem oneself can be miserable. Moreover, the team's win or loss depends more on the performance of the pitcher than on any other single player. Considering the pressures to do well, it is not surprising that pitchers' rituals are often more complex than those of hitters.

A 17-game winner last year in the Texas Ranger organization, Mike Griffin, begins his ritual preparation a full day before he pitches, by washing his hair. The next day, although he does not consider himself superstitious, he eats bacon for lunch. When Griffin dresses for the game he puts on his clothes in the same order, making certain he puts the slightly longer of his two outer, or "stirrup," socks on his right leg. "I just wouldn't feel right mentally if I did it the other way around," he explains. He always wears the same shirt under his uniform on the days he pitches. During the game he takes off his cap after each pitch, and between innings he sits in the same place on the dugout bench.

Steve Hamilton, formerly a relief pitcher for the Yankees, used to motion with his pitching hand as he left the mound after an inning. He would make a fist, holding it at arm's length by his side, and pull it upward, as if he were pulling a chain—which is what the announcers used to call it. Tug McGraw, relief pitcher for the Phillies, slaps his thigh with his glove with each step he takes leaving the mound at the end of an inning. This began as a means of saying hello to his wife in the stands, but has since become a ritual. McGraw now slaps his thigh whether his wife is there or not.

Many of the rituals pitchers engage in—tugging their caps between pitches, touching the rosin bag after each bad pitch, smoothing the dirt on the mound before each new batter or inning (as the Tigers' Mark Fidrych does)—take place on the field. Most baseball fans observe this behavior regularly, never realizing that it may be as important to the pitcher as actually throwing the ball.

Uniform numbers have special significance for some pitchers. Many have a lucky number, which they request. Since the choice is usually limited, pitchers may try to get a number that at least contains their lucky number, such as 14, 24, 34, or 44 for the pitcher whose lucky number is 4. Oddly enough, there is no consensus about the effect of wearing number 13. Some pitchers will not wear it; others, such as Oakland's John "Blue Moon" Odom and Steve Barber, formerly of the Orioles, prefer it. (During a pitching slump, however, Odom asked for a new number. Later he switched back to 13.)

The way in which number preferences emerge varies. Occasionally a pitcher requests the number of a former professional star, hoping that—in a form of imitative magic—it will bring him the same measure of success. Or he may request a favorite number that he has always associated with good luck. Vida Blue, formerly with Oakland and now playing for San Francisco, changed his uniform number from 35 to 14, the number he wore as a high-school quarterback. When the new number did not produce the better pitching performance he was looking for, he switched back to his old number.

One of the sources of his good fortune, Blue believed, was the baseball hat he had worn since 1974. Several American League umpires refused to let him wear the faded and soiled cap last season. When Blue persisted, he was threatened with a fine and suspension from a game. Finally he conceded, but not before he ceremoniously burned the hat on the field before a game.

On the days they are scheduled to appear, many pitchers avoid activities that they believe sap their strength and therefore detract from their effectiveness, or that they otherwise generally link with poor performance. Many pitchers avoid eating certain foods on their pitching days. Some pitchers refuse to walk anywhere on the day of the game in the belief that every little exertion subtracts from their playing strength. One pitcher would never put on his cap until the game started and would not wear it at all on the days he did not pitch. Another had a movie taboo. He refused to watch movies on the day of the game. And until this season Al Hrabosky, recently traded from the St. Louis Cardinals to the Kansas City Royals, had an even more encompassing taboo: Samsonlike, he refused to cut his hair or beard during the entire season—hence part of the reason for his nickname, the "Mad Hungarian."

Many hitters go through a series of preparatory rituals before stepping into the batter's box. These include tugging on their caps, touching their uniform letters or medallions, crossing themselves, tapping or bouncing the bat on the plate, swinging the weighted warm-up bat a prescribed number of times, and smoothing the dirt in the batter's box.

Rocky Colavito, a colorful home-run hitter active in the 1950s and '60s, used to stretch his arms behind his back and cross himself when he came to the plate. A player in the Texas Ranger organization draws a triangle in the dirt outside the batter's box, with the peak pointing toward center field. Other players are careful never to step on the chalk lines of the batter's box when standing at the plate.

Clothing, both the choice of clothes and the order in which they are put on, is often ritualized. During a batting streak many players wear the same clothes and uniforms for each game and put them on in exactly the same order. Once I changed sweat shirts midway through the game for seven consecutive games to keep a hitting streak going. During a 16-game winning streak in 1954 the New York Giants wore the same clothes in each game and refused to let them be cleaned for fear that their good fortune might be washed away with the dirt. Taking this ritual to the extreme, Leo Durocher, managing the Brooklyn Dodgers to a pennant in 1941, spent three and a half weeks in the same black shoes, gray slacks, blue coat, and knitted blue tie.

The opposite may also occur. Several of the Oakland A's players bought new street clothing last year in an attempt to break a 14-game losing streak. Most players, however, single out one or two lucky articles or quirks of dress rather than ritualizing all items of clothing. After hitting two home runs in a game, infielder Jim Davenport of the San Francisco Giants discovered that he had missed a buttonhole while dressing for the game. For the remainder of his career he left the same button undone.

A popular ritual associated with hitting is tagging a base when leaving and returning to the dugout during each inning. Mickey Mantle was in the habit of tagging second base on the way to or from the outfield. During a successful month of the season one player stepped on third base on his way to the dugout after the third, sixth, and ninth innings of each game. Asked if he ever purposely failed to step on the bag he replied, "Never! I wouldn't dare. It would destroy my confidence to hit." A hitter who is playing poorly may try different combinations of tagging and not tagging particular bases in an attempt to find a successful combination.

Another component of a hitter's ritual may be tapping the plate with his bat. A teammate of mine described a variation of this in which he gambled for a certain hit by tapping the plate with his bat a fixed number of times: one tap for a single, two for a double, and so on. He even built in odds that prevented him from asking for a home run each time at bat. The odds of hitting a home run with four taps were one in 12.

When their players are not hitting, some managers will rattle the bat bin, the large wooden box containing the team's bats, as if the bats were asleep or in a stupor and could be aroused by a good shaking. Similarly, some hitters rub their hands or their own bats along the handles of the bats protruding from the bin, presumably in hopes of picking up some power or luck from bats that are getting hits for their owners.

There is a taboo against crossing bats, against permitting one bat to rest on top of another. Although this superstition appears to be dying out among professional ballplayers, it was religiously observed by some of my teammates a decade ago. And in some cases it was elaborated even further. One former Detroit minor leaguer became quite annoyed when a teammate tossed a bat from the batting cage and it landed on top of his bat. Later he explained that the top bat might steal hits from the lower one. In his view, bats contained a finite number of hits, a sort of zero-sum game or baseball "image of limited good." For Pirate shortstop Honus Wagner, a charter member of baseball's Hall of Fame, each bat contained only a certain number of hits and never more than 100. Regardless of the quality of the bat, he would discard it after its 100th hit.

Hall of Famer Johnny Evers, of the Cub double-play trio Tinker to Evers to Chance, believed in saving his luck. If he was hitting well in practice, he would suddenly stop and retire to the bench to "save" his batting for the game. One player told me that many of his teammates on the Asheville Tourists in the Class A Western Carolinas League would not let pitchers touch or swing their bats, not even to loosen up. The traditionally poor-hitting pitchers were believed to contaminate or weaken the bats.

Food often forms part of a hitter's ritual repertoire. Eating certain foods before a game is supposed to give the ball "eyes," that is, the ability to seek the gaps between fielders after being hit. In hopes of maintaining a batting streak, I once ate chicken every day at 4 P.M. until the streak ended. Hitters—like pitchers—also avoid certain foods that are believed to sap their strength during the game.

There are other examples of hitters' ritualized behavior. I once kept my eyes closed during the national anthem in an effort to prolong a batting streak. And a teammate of mine refused to read anything on the day of a game because he believed that reading weakened his eyesight when batting.

These are personal taboos. There are some taboos, however, that all players hold and that do not develop out of individual experiences or misfortunes. These taboos are learned, some as early as Little League. Mentioning a no-hitter while one is in progress is a widely known example. It is believed that if a pitcher hears the words "no-hitter," the spell will be broken and the no-hitter lost. Until recently this taboo was also observed by sports broadcasters, who used various linguistic subterfuges to inform their listeners that the pitcher had not given up a hit, never mentioning "no-hitter."

Most professional baseball coaches or managers will not step on the chalk foul lines when going onto the field to talk to their pitchers. Cincinnati's manager Sparky Anderson jumps over the line. Others follow a different ritual. They intentionally step on the lines when they are going to take a pitcher out of a game.

How do these rituals and taboos get established in the first place? B. F. Skinner's early research with pigeons provides a clue. Like human beings, pigeons quickly learn to associate their behavior with rewards or punishment. By rewarding the birds at the appropriate time, Skinner taught them such elaborate games as table tennis, miniature bowling, or to play simple tunes on a toy piano.

On one occasion he decided to see what would happen if pigeons were rewarded with food pellets every 15 seconds, regardless of what they did. He found that the birds tended to associate the arrival of food with a particular action—tucking the head under a wing, hopping from side to side, or turning in a clockwise direction. About 10 seconds after the arrival of the last pellet, a bird would begin doing whatever it had associated with getting the food and keep it up until the next pellet arrived.

In the same way, baseball players tend to believe

there is a causal connection between two events that are linked only temporally. If a superstitious player touches his crucifix and then gets a hit, he may decide the gesture was responsible for his good fortune and follow the same ritual the next time he comes to the plate. If he should get another hit, the chances are good that he will begin touching the crucifix each time he bats and that he will do so whether or not he hits safely each time.

The average batter hits safely approximately one quarter of the time. And, if the behavior of Skinner's pigeons—or of gamblers at a Las Vegas slot machine—is any guide, that is more often than necessary to keep him believing in a ritual. Skinner found that once a pigeon associated one of its actions with the arrival of food or water, sporadic rewards would keep the connection going. One bird, which apparently believed hopping from side to side brought pellets into its feeding cup, hopped 10,000 times without a pellet before it gave up.

Since the batter associates his hits at least in some degree with his ritual touching of a crucifix, each hit he gets reinforces the strength of the ritual. Even if he falls into a batting slump and the hits temporarily stop, he will persist in touching the crucifix in the hope that this will change his luck.

Skinner's and Malinowski's explanations are not contradictory. Skinner focuses on how the individual comes to develop and maintain a particular ritual, taboo, or fetish. Malinowski focuses on why human beings turn to magic in precarious or uncertain situations. In their attempts to gain greater control over their performance, baseball players respond to chance and uncertainty in the same way as do people in simple societies. It is wrong to assume that magical practices are a waste of time for either group. The magic in baseball obviously does not make a pitch travel faster or more accurately, or a batted ball seek the gaps between fielders. Nor does the Trobriand brand of magic make the surrounding seas calmer and more abundant with fish. But both kinds of magic give their practitioners a sense of control—and an important element in any endeavor is confidence.

8

Ghosts, Souls, and Ancestors: Power of the Dead

Religions universally promise believers that there is life after death. Although the worship of ancestors is not universal, a belief in the immortality of the dead occurs in all cultures. There is variation among cultures in the degree of interaction between the living and the dead, however, as well as in the intensity and concern a people may have for the deceased. Eskimos are never free of anxieties about ghosts, while Pueblo Indians are seldom bothered by them; the Plains Indians of North America constructed elaborate ghost beliefs, while the Siriono of South America, although believing in ghosts, paid little attention to them.

Perhaps humans have some basic need that causes us to believe in ghosts and to worship ancestors: to seek verification that although the mortal body may die, the soul survives after death. The nineteenth-century sociologist Herbert Spencer speculated that the beginnings of religion were in ancestor worship—the need for the living to continue an emotional relation-

Ivory pendant mask from Benin, Nigeria.

ship with their dead relatives. A major problem with Spencer's argument is that many societies at the hunting-and-gathering level do not practice ancestor worship. The Arunta of Australia, for example, worshiped their totemic plants and animals, but not their human ancestors. This objection to Spencer's belief notwithstanding, ancestor worship does remind the living of a vital continuing link between the living and the dead.

One writer has pointed out that two major attitudes are widely held about the dead: that they have either left the society or remain as active members (Malefijt 1968: 156–59). In societies that separate the dead from the living social group, any possibility of the dead returning is regarded as undesirable because they could disrupt the social order and the daily routine of life. In such cultures, Malefijt believes, the dead are likely to be greatly feared, and an elaborate belief system—a cult of the dead—is constructed and practiced in order to separate them from the living. The primary function of cults of the dead is to aid the survivors in overcoming the grief they may feel about the dead. Such cults are not found in societies where the dead are seen as active members of the group; instead, funeral ceremonies are undertaken with the hope the deceased will return to society in their new status. These beliefs, according to Malefijt, result in the development of ancestor cults instead of cults of the dead.

Ancestor cults and the ritual that surrounds them may also be seen as an elaboration of cults of the dead. The Bantu of Africa, for example, outline distinct ancestral deities for each lineage and clan. All of these ancestral gods are gods to their living relatives, but not to individuals who belong to other kinship organizations. Further elaboration of Bantu ancestor worship may be seen in Bantu beliefs about the supernatural beings believed to head their royal clans. Gods of such royal clans are worshiped by the entire kingdom, not just the royal clan itself.

The study of ancestor worship among American and British anthropologists has emphasized the connection between the identity and behavioral characteristics of the dead, on one hand, and the distribution and nature of their authority in both domestic and political domains of the society, on the other (Bradbury 1966: 127). Although the belief in ghosts of ancestors is universal, the functions ancestors play vary greatly among societies. It is also clear that variations in ancestor worship are directly related to social structure and that this relationship is not based on mere common religious interests alone: rather, the structure of the kin group and the relationships of those within it serve as the model of ancestor worship (Bradbury 1966: 128). Among the Sisala of Ghana, for example, only a select number of Sisala elders, based on their particular status and power within the group, can effectively communicate with the ghosts of ancestors (Mendonsa 1976: 63–64). In many other parts of the non-Western world, non-elder ritual specialists, such as heads of households, are responsible for contacting the ancestors. A cross-cultural study of fifty societies found that where important decisions are made by the kin group, ancestor worship is a high probability (Swanson 1969: 97–108).

Many, but certainly not all, non-Western societies believe ancestors play a strong and positive role in the security and prosperity of their group, and anthropological data is full of these kinds of examples. It is important, however, to recognize that ancestors are but one of several categories of spirits whose actions directly affect society. John S. Mbiti's study of East and Central Africa shows that the status of spirits may change through time. Ancestor spirits, the "living dead," are those whose memory still exists in the minds of their kin, and who are primarily beneficial to the surviving relatives. When the living dead are forgotten in the memory of their group and dropped from the genealogy as a result of the passing of time (four or five generations), they are believed to be transformed into "nameless spirits," non-ancestors, characterized as malicious vehicles for misfortune of all kinds (1970). In keeping with Mbiti's model, the Lugbara of Uganda recognize two types of dead. The first group, simply called "ancestors," comprises nameless, all deceased relatives; these are secondary in importance to the recently deceased, called "ancestor spirits" or "ghosts," who can be invoked by the living to cause misfortune to befall those whose acts threaten the solidarity of the kin group (Middleton 1971: 488).

Clearly spirits, ghosts, and ancestors are often given unique statuses in the afterlife, and are viewed as having different functions and effects on the living. In many respects the relationship of fear and responsibility of elders toward ancestors is mirrored by the son-father relationship among the living. The ancestral world in many cases is an extension or model of the real world. The supernatural status of the ancestors exhibits major differences, for although one can argue to a point with an elder, no one questions the wisdom and authority of an ancestor.

The power of the dead is an important aspect of religion and social control. If, for example, a Lugbara man threatened the solidarity of the clan or lineage in any of a number of ways, the elder may invoke ghosts to punish the troublemaker (Middleton 1971: 488–92). Without doubt this veneration of the ancestors and the fear of their power functions importantly to help control many societies. Interestingly, ancestor worship also contributes to the conservative nature of those cultures where it is practiced. Typically, dead ancestors do not smile favorably on any kind of change in the cultures of their living relatives. Because ghosts are capable of severely punishing an earthly mortal desirous of change, the force for conformity is strong.

Not all societies assign power to ancestors. In many cultures, North America included, a high god (monotheism) or gods (polytheism) exert authority over the living, punishing those who violate religious tenets, rules that often are duplicated in civil law and serve as the bases of appropriate social behavior. In these groups ancestor cults and worship of the deceased are not found, although the spiritual nature of ancestors and belief in the afterlife persevere.

Among peoples where the deceased are believed to take an active role in society, the living are understandably concerned with the welfare of ancestors. Customs are established to assure the comfort of the dead in their life after death. Most commonly, rituals carried out at funerals, burials, and in some cases reburial or cremation, insure that loved ones arrive safely at what the living believe is the proper abode of the dead. The care taken in preparing the deceased for the afterlife is an important reinforcement of the society's customs and an expression of unity among its members. Participation helps insure that the same care can be expected to be given at the time of one's own death. Beyond this motivation, however, the power to rain down misfortunes is a major reason for carefully following customs surrounding the preparation, interment, and propitiation of the dead. No one wants to be subjected to supernatural punishment by vengeful and angry ghosts.

To most people in Western culture the word "ghost" brings forth an image of a disembodied spirit of a dead person swooping through dark halls, hovering frighteningly over a grave, or perhaps roaming aimlessly through damp woods. Typically, the ghost is observed wearing white sheets—an image that undoubtedly arises from the shroud or winding sheet used to wrap the corpse for its placement in the grave. There is a wide variety of shapes available to would-be ghosts, however. Some are transparent; some are lifelike apparitions of their former selves; others appear with horribly gaunt, empty faces, devoid of eyes and lips. Not all ghosts take a human or even vaguely human shape: horses frequently appear in phantom form, as do dogs and large birds, and ghost lore is full of accounts of ghost trains, stagecoaches, and, of course, such phantom ships as the Flying Dutchman.

Very few peoples do not support the idea of a separate spirit world—a land of the dead. It is to this other world that souls will travel and, once there, will rest in eternal peace. At some point in history, however, the notion arose that not all souls deserved an easy trip to a blissful spiritual world. Murder victims, miscreants, and evil people, for example, might become ghosts doomed to wander the earthly world. Inadequate funerals also might give rise to restless ghosts: thus, the attention paid by cultures everywhere to meticulously preparing and dressing the corpse for burial, and to placing gifts, food, and weapons in the grave or at the gravesite to enhance the spirit's journey to the place of eternal rest.

In the first article of this chapter, Shirley Lindenbaum explores the problem of why some New Guinea societies show little interest in ghosts and sorcery, while others seem preoccupied with both. The granting of the first gun permits to another New Guinea group and the resulting formation of a cult is the subject of the article by William Mitchell. Mitchell shows how the cult's belief in vengeful spirits helps them understand why they sometimes experience unsuccessful hunting. In the third selection, Karen McCarthy Brown examines the practice of Voodoo in Haiti, pointing out that despite the distorted popular version we see all too frequently in the mass media, it is a legitimate religious practice of 80 to 90 percent of Haitians. Gino Del Guercio's article, "The Secrets of Haiti's Living Dead," serves as a companion piece to Brown's more broadly based discussion of Voodoo. Del Guercio recounts the research of Wade Davis, who believes that zombies do exist in Haiti, but are actually "the living drugged" rather than "the living dead." In the final selection, Peter Metcalf compares American and Berawan funeral rites. As Metcalf learned to see Berawan funerary customs as natural, American treatment of the dead began to seem exotic.

References

Bradbury, R. E.
1966 "Fathers, Elders, and Ghosts in Edo Relig-
ion." In Michael Banton, ed., *Anthropological Approaches to the Supernatural*, pp. 127–53. London: Tavistock Publications, Ltd.

Malefijt, Annemarie de Waal
1968 *Religion and Culture: An Introduction to Anthropology of Religion.* New York: Macmillan.

Mbiti, John S.
1970 *African Religions and Philosophies.* Garden City, N.Y.: Doubleday.

Mendonsa, Eugene L.
1976 "Elders, Office-Holders and Ancestors Among the Sisala of Northern Ghana." *Africa* 46: 57–64.

Middleton, John
1971 "The Cult of the Dead: Ancestors and Ghosts." In William A. Lessa and Evon Z. Vogt, eds., *Reader in Comparative Religion: An Anthropological Approach*, 3rd ed., pp. 488–92. New York: Harper and Row.

Sorcerers, Ghosts, and Polluting Women: An Analysis of Religious Belief and Population Control

Shirley Lindenbaum

Concentrating on three important components of New Guinean culture, Shirley Lindenbaum here analyzes the roles that sorcery, ancestral ghosts, and female pollution play in maintaining social structural integrity. Emphasis on varying ecological conditions led her to the construction of a continuum in which groups could be located and compared in terms of the relative importance they placed on these elements. Taking a structural-functional approach, her data and the resulting model clarify why some groups differ so radically in their beliefs surrounding incest, adultery, chastity, and the relative importance of witches, sorcerers, and ghosts, in enforcing the institutionalization of male-female relationships and reproduction.

Reprinted from *Ethnology*, Vol. 11 (1972), pp. 241–53, by permission of the author and the Department of Anthropology, University of Pittsburgh.

THE PROBLEM OF WHY SOME NEW GUINEA SOcieties evince little interest in sorcery while others seem preoccupied with sorcery as an explanation for disease and death has been examined in recent publications. (Hogbin 1958; Lawrence and Meggitt 1965; Lindenbaum 1971). Analyses have focused on the structural features of society. It has been suggested that sorcery accusations are a necessary means of easing tension between individuals who lack the security of membership in solidary groups. Sorcery also acts as a mechanism whereby permanently settled descent groups maintain their identity in the absence of wars for economic aggrandizement (Lawrence and Meggitt 1965: 17). It has been noted that these theories do not account for the absence of a great interest in sorcery among the Mae Enga and the Ngaing, and it was suggested that these peoples have an alternate means of channelling aggression through warfare and ceremonial exchange (Lawrence and Meggitt 1965: 18). This paper continues the discussion, but relates the presence of sorcery to ecological variables. The polluting woman is also seen to inhabit a particular form of social and material environment; an examination of the interaction of the two accounts for her presence.

Enga and Fore

Two societies in the Highlands of New Guinea illustrate the variations which exist at each end of the range; the Enga in the West and the Fore in the East. It has been noted that Enga, for instance, believe misfortune and death to be the result of attacks by malicious ghosts of the dead rather than by living sorcerers. Enga, moreover, do not simply fear ghosts in general; they fear male ancestral ghosts. As the degree of danger is judged more serious—such as the death of a socially important victim or an epidemic of illness— Enga turn from appeasing particular domestic ghosts to the placation of all the ancestral ghosts of a clan. There is, as Meggitt (1965b: 131) points out, an isomorphism of the structures of the lineage system and the religious system. A hierachical order runs through them both.

Fore beliefs about the etiology of disease also reflect structural features of their society. Fore use the idea of sorcerers rather than of ancestral ghosts to define the boundaries of their social groups and to maintain their internal cohesion. The composition of South Fore political groups provides the bases for mutual mistrust. The political unit of widest span, the parish, is an aggregate of people residing on a defined territory. Parish membership is not based on common descent; rather, the parish may be described as a temporary coalition of factions united by a common desire for security and defense. The parish section is similarly a residential rather than a genealogical unit. The smallest parish subdivision, the "people of a place," is based on genealogical criteria, although the permitted adoption of outsiders disqualifies it as a strictly unilineal group. The social system at all levels is thus characterized by flexibility and expediency. Every parish includes immigrants who have fled conflict in their original parish. Newcomers are readily incorporated, given gardening land, and if necessary are bound to their new co-residents by ties of fictional kinship. The ambiguity felt about the loyalty of people with ties to an outside parish is expressed in sorcery beliefs and activities. Sorcery is thus a political institution peculiarly suited to the organizational problems of South Fore society. Fore do not enjoy the comfort of genealogical unity, and sorcery discussions are endemic (Lindenbaum 1971).

I wish to argue here that the choice between ancestral ghosts or sorcerers as an explanation for death from disease may be ecologically determined. If disease is considered to result from the anger of ancestors, the society in which such a religious belief is held is one in which there is population pressure on scarce resources. The implication is that members of the society regard disease sent by one's own former kinsmen as an acceptable

form of population control. Enga typify this position. Enga land is scarce, and the relative scarcity of arable land is a significant determinant of the rigidity of lineage structure in the society. Enga religion is also one in which agnatic ghosts are believed to control the fertility of the land and the people (Meggitt 1965b: 105–131). Disease and death are attributed to angry ghosts. This philosophical viewpoint appears to be a Malthusian acceptance of the realities of the Enga man-land ratio.

Fore, on the other hand, do not hold such beliefs. They have ample land for a small population. Their problems are not focused on restricting the access of outsiders to group resources. The opposite is the case—how to maintain group strength in the face of aggressive neighbors. South Fore groups readily admit newcomers and provide them with fertile land. Fore view illness and death as an attack by jealous enemy sorcerers who not only endanger the viability of small groups, but who may be attempting to wipe out the entire society. The presence of *kuru*, a fatal neurological disorder which mainly kills women, gives rise to realistic fears for survival, expressed in terms of the assault of particularly malignant sorcerers.

Illness and Death

The hypothesis may be illustrated by examining the behavior provoked by illness and death in Enga and Fore societies. Meggitt (1965b: 113) describes Enga response to the illness and death of an adult man. The victim's brothers or sons kill a pig and give its essence to the ghost they think is causing the misfortune, distributing the meat to both maternal and paternal kinsmen. If the sick man does not recover, his agnates consult a diviner to locate the identity of the angered ghost, and again kill pigs to propitiate the ghost. If the victim is an important person, all the men of his patrilineage, with pigs contributed by subclan and even parallel subclan members, may perform a ritual to placate the ancestral ghosts of a clan. The clan fertility stones are rubbed with pig grease. If the patient then dies, his relatives mourn briefly and publicly. Close relatives of the deceased slice their ear lobes or cut off finger joints. For the next two or three weeks the immediate family members do not tend their pigs or gardens. They subsequently return to everyday life after holding a feast.

The Enga response thus appears to be controlled and orderly. The source of attack is assumed to come from within the group itself—not a disrupting idea for Enga. It is assumed that an invisible agnatic ghost attacks the internal agnatic spirit of the victim, and at the same time injures the victim's maternally acquired flesh and vitality. Both paternal and maternal kinsmen are thus offered pork in compensation for their loss. Enga attempt to avert the loss of an important man by ceremonial treatment of the clan fertility stones, but the death itself elicits only a brief, public mourning period. The family's loss of a productive member is indicated by injury to body extremities, an important mutilation of the domestic group but not of the body of the lineage. The family group, in a realistic acknowledgment of its decreased size, does not attempt to increase its food production for the following two or three weeks. Meggitt (1965a: 187) also notes that the deaths of women and children are rarely the subject of inquiry.

Fore response to illness and death is markedly more excited. Sorcery accusations arise over the severe illness or death of any adult male or female. Most sorcery accusations occur between men residing in different parish groups. The location of a sorcery challenge thus indicates the extent of mutual distrust felt by allies and neighbors; if an accusation occurs within parish borders, it signals the possibility of incipient political fission. Sorcery challenges are therefore socially disruptive, particularly as the sorcerer is assumed to be within a close range. In the past, sorcery challenges led to fighting and migration; now charges and counter-charges are adjudicated in indigenous courts and cases heard by the Administration.

Fore do not accept severe illness with equanimity. Much day-to-day behavior is concerned with preventing a sorcerer from acquiring the material he needs for attack. Men, women, and children make use of deep pit latrines for feces and food scraps. They also hide hair cuttings and nail parings. Women, in particular, scrupulously eliminate menstrual blood, the emissions from childbirth, and an infant's umbilical cord; that is, they conceal evidence of their fertility in response to the high incidence of *kuru*, a sex-biased disease. Fore use the image of the human body to make symbolic statements about the body politic (Douglas 1966). They monitor substances entering and issuing from the body; the small South Fore groups fear population decline resulting from social intermingling. South Fore both protect the body's boundaries and police the borders of their social groups (Lindenbaum 1972).

When an adult falls ill, Fore resort to a variety of cures, part of which involves a divination test to reveal the identity of the sorcerer. Opossum meat, an environmental mediator, is used as an oracle to screen suspected groups, and after many tests the malicious actor is finally identified. Relatives of the victim try to persuade or threaten the sorcerer to reverse his actions, to remove his hidden sorcery materials, and to allow the patient to recover. This acrimonious political activity, in the case of *kuru* victims, may last for a year or more. The victim's supporting group, her husband, and his kinsmen and friends, are also involved in expensive, time-consuming visits to foreign curers who live outside Fore territory.

At this point the patient may die. In the past, most deceased persons were eaten. Rules of the cannibal consumption of dead bodies are somewhat undefined, because cannibalism was a relatively late custom in Fore society and has been forbidden since the mid 1950s. In general, however, body parts were distributed along the same lines as were traditional death payments in pork and valuables—large payments to matrilateral kinsmen and smaller payments to age-mates and classificatory brothers and friends. That is, kinship cannibalism among the Fore appears to underline the recognition of responsibility for loss to those who generated the body and to those who see themselves as its equivalents.

Little ideology was associated with the consumption of dead bodies. If the body was buried, the Fore say "the ground ate him"; that is, bodies fertilize the ground. Dismemberment of a corpse for consumption was carried out in a kinsman's garden. The association between cannibalism and fertility has also been noted by Berndt (1962: 271). Kinship cannibalism among the Fore suggests that a society in biological decline may attempt regeneration by eating itself. A wife expects to eat her husband's buttocks and penis (Berndt 1962: 273). It may be significant that South Fore society has a marked imbalance in the sex ratio; *kuru* decimates adult women, and women were in the main the cannibals. In contrast, cannibalism is repugnant to the Enga (Meggitt 1965b: 120). Cannibalism does occur, according to Enga, among demons who inhabit the inhospitable forest. Some demons with an appetite for human flesh eat solitary bush travelers; others appear as snakes to abduct men from the men's houses, or as sexually appealing women whose false promises of wealth lead to property dissipation and dementia (Meggitt 1965b: 122). For Enga, fertility and cannibalism present the same kinds of danger.

The responses to epidemic illness in Enga and Fore societies are markedly different. If Enga are troubled by an increase in the death rate of children or important men, or by an increase in the incidence of disease, they turn their attention to clan ghosts. The same response is elicited by a sudden rise in the death rate of pigs, or by a clan-wide crop failure, resources on which man depends (Meggitt 1965b: 114). To deal with this threat, they perform rituals which require peace to be observed among neighboring clans. During part of the rituals, a bachelor and a spinster sit on the roof of a cult house which protects the clan stones. The ancestral ghosts are believed to have temporarily removed their potency from men and land, withdrawing into the stones. Each clansman is offered a fragment of pork fat bespelled in the presence of the ancestral ghosts. Married men may eat it; bachelors may only smell the fat. Black opossums, used in another part of the ritual, are offered to the oldest men of the clan, but some refuse to eat, fearing it may hasten their deaths. For a month or two following the rituals, clansmen should not copulate or prepare new gardens; such activities would, it is said, "antagonize the ancestors." The cult house may be left to disintegrate, or neighboring clans may be invited to destroy it. This contest to destroy the cult house generates much ill will against the triumphant clan, which boasts its superiority (Meggitt 1965b: 114–120).

The rituals may be interpreted as a cultural mechanism by which Enga accept a population or a subsistence loss. The performance of the rituals requires a truce amongst warring clans, a regulation which precludes further depletion of numbers. Although the purpose of the rituals is ostensibly to restore the good humor of ancestral ghosts so that they will cease meting out punishment in the form of illness and death, the central actors are persons whose generative powers are recognized to be tem-

porarily inactive—bachelors and spinsters—as are the generative powers of the clan stones. Nor does the impetus of the ritual seem to suggest great renewal of fertility. Indeed, Meggitt (1965b: 118) comments that "the propitiatory rituals . . . are not thought to be immediately efficacious . . . it is assumed that revitalization of the clan and its land may take some time." Ritual symbolism seems to have more to do with death, and a recognition of temporary stasis, than with renewed fertility. Some old men are afraid to eat the large black opossums which may propel them beyond life to join the body of ancestors. For one or two months following the rituals there is a ban on copulation and new gardening of which the ancestors might disapprove—an indication that there will be no new additions to society and no provision for them.

In similar rituals held by Western Enga, ceremonies surround the clan pool (Meggitt 1965b: 118–119). Again the theme is a separation of men and women, the use of a pair of bachelors as central actors, and a temporary ban on copulation and gardening. The young boys selected to participate in the clan pool rituals are moreover considered inducted into the bachelors' association, which prescribes prolonged avoidance of contact with women.

Thus the response to epidemic illness or unusual loss of life and resources results in ceremonies which do not emphasize fertility, or symbolize creative behavior. Rather, the depletion of clan membership is publicly accepted in a number of ceremonies whose content emphasizes instead the spacing of men and women, the importance of men whose sexual capacities are socially constrained, and an acceptable stasis in the relationship between men and land. Enga clans appear to repair damaged relationships with the ghosts of their ancestors lest they decline in relation to similar groups. The clan which successfully demolishes the cult house—a symbol of withdrawn fertility—threatens others with its suggestion of superiority and imbalance.

Fore response to illness is another matter. Fore rituals concern protection and unity; groups close their ranks against the sorcerer. Annual ceremonies are observed for the safety of children and pregnant women. Infants and future mothers eat special foods, and receive a share of the feast before other women and all men. The ceremonies are held if there is news of infant illness in surrounding

areas, or at the beginning of the dry season, presumably a time of increased sickness. During the
early 1960s, the South Fore responded dramatically
to the high incidence of *kuru* among the population. From November, 1962, to March, 1963, mass
meetings took place almost daily throughout the
entire region. Men from hostile parishes faced each
other in compact opposing groups and demanded
an end to *kuru* sorcery and the mending of the
male-female sex imbalance. Reputed sorcerers
made public confessions of their past activities;
men sought to purge themselves of ill feeling in a
context of beneficial ritual forces at a time when
mutual suspicion and hostility were disrupting social life. To the often expressed fears of extinction
through the loss of the reproductive capacity of the
women was now added the fear of internal disorder so great that society itself was felt to be endangered. Persuasive orators gave moral discourses on
good behavior and appealed to those sorcerers
who had not come forward to relinquish all future
activities. The meetings had a formal, ritual quality
in seating arrangement, orderly speechmaking,
and food distribution. Sometimes they culminated
in peacemaking rituals that signaled an end to hostile action. Men clapped hands and poured water
on *kuru* victims—symbolic actions common to ceremonies calling for a truce between enemies,
whether warriors or sorcerers.

Ritual emerged as a device by which the society
attempted to create an illusion of unity. Orators
recalled a golden past of supposedly less divisive
times when their ancestors were not troubled by
kuru. Men, they said, must halt their present inter-
group strife and realize that they are one people.
They named little-known all-inclusive groups to
which they said they belonged. The meetings
sought to redefine and enlarge the moral boundaries of the assembled groups. To survive the
epidemic, the Fore thus offered the fiction of a
united community.

Sorcerers, the Fore noted, had plainly exceeded
the concept of self-limitation that men recognize in
wartime. In the past, peace ceremonies were arranged when the toll of deaths met a certain limit of
propriety. Fore accused sorcerers of aiming to eliminate all women, of perpetrating a crime against
society, a breach of the natural order. Women of
the host group were present to listen to the discussion, sometimes angrily taking part. At some

meetings, borrowing symbolism from recent mission exposure, men pledged their commitment to
the future by washing their right hands in soapy
water and raising the purged hand for all to see.
They promised thenceforth, to forego sorcery.

The Fore image of society, then, is that of a body
under attack. Illness, like warfare, endangers the
viability of small groups whose cohesion is constitutionally unsound. Fore therefore attempt to enlarge their moral boundaries to avert further loss.
Debates emphasize renewal, a new order, a society
without sorcerers.

For the Enga, interpretation of disease as a form
of ghost attack is an acknowledgment that the
attack is coming from within one's own political
group. It is internal and invisible, and not subject to
identification in living human form. A population
or resource reduction caused by the ancestors is
socially acceptable; they are assumed to have the
proper balance in mind. On the other hand, when
Fore interpret disease as a consequence of attack by
sorcerers they assume that aggression is coming
from known living enemies outside the viable
political units. It is unacceptable, and the ritual
underlines this. The choice between the two interpretations is related to the man-resource ratio.

Sorcery is therefore a political instrument
whereby antagonistic political groups recognize
and adjust to a competitive advance or decline in
strength. In societies where sorcery is an overwhelming issue—Tangu (Burridge 1960: 122), Dobu
(Fortune 1963: 312), and Fore—epidemic disease
has created alarming population problems. Sorcerers in these societies not only kill people; they are
also wife stealers. Men are in competition for the
sexual productivity of the women. Sorcerers are
thus predators of the scarcest resource. This throws
into relief other New Guinea societies where sorcery is not a central issue, but where the predominant theme is fear of women and their powers of
contamination. The concept of female pollution in
the latter societies would therefore appear to be a
cultural regulator impressing on men their need to
keep distant from the women.

Female Pollution

In a paper on female pollution in New Guinea,
Meggitt (1964) outlined a complex of social attitudes and practices characteristic of certain parts of
the Highlands. Meggitt (1964: 219) pointed out,

without suggesting any causal sequence, that certain attitudes and practices clustered together.

We might expect, therefore to find the notion of female pollution emphasized in societies where affinal groups are seen—for whatever reason—as inimical to one's own group, but absent or of little significance where marriages usually occur between friendly groups. Moreover, as a logical extension of this argument, associations devoted to male purification, seclusion, or initiation should be more sharply defined among the former. Finally, it follows that where male-female hostility exists in societies of the second category—those favouring inter-marriage among friendly groups—it will differ markedly from that of the first category.

He defined a regional variation in the phenomenon, noting two main kinds of intersexual conflict or opposition, the "Mae type" and the "Kuma type," reflecting the Western and Central Highlands social arrangements. The Mae reflect the anxiety of prudes to protect themselves from contamination by women, the Kuma the aggressive determination of lechers to assert control over recalcitrant women (Meggitt 1964: 221). In addition, Meggitt noted that Eastern Highlands societies appear to display both sets of characteristics simultaneously or in parallel form.

The argument pursued here would add causality to the analysis. The idea of female pollution is used as a cultural whip in societies where available resources are endangered by further population increase. Pollution is of less concern (Eastern Highlands) or absent (Central Highlands) where population expansion is not an environmental threat and is generally desired. Fear of pollution is a form of ideological birth control. Fear of female contamination thus declines with the introduction of new technologies and food sources.

Enga, Kaulong, and Sengseng are New Guinea societies with the most acute fear of female pollution yet recorded (Meggitt 1964; Goodale and Chowning 1971). Enga pressure on resources and pollution fears are well documented (Meggitt 1965a, 1965b), fears that lead to male postponement of marriage and to conflict over the need for heirs (Meggitt 1964: 210). Kaulong and Sengseng, neighboring societies in the Passismanua Census Division of Southwest New Britain, also live in a taxing environment, one subject to rapid flooding. Shift-

ing taro cultivation is a major subsistence activity, while "at least 60% of the food consumed comes from the forest" (Goodale and Chowning 1971: 3). The "lack of any strong demarcation of sex roles in basic subsistence," noted as an unusual feature of New Guinea societies, suggests the need for an equal labor contribution by both men and women. Fear of female pollution and male avoidance of marriage are "one of the most distinctive aspects of Passismanua culture" (Goodale and Chowning 1971: 6). Kaulong and Sengseng males, like Enga, marry late. Some avoid sexual union until their 60s, and permanent bachelors are allowed a place of prestige in society. Until Mission and Administration interference, widows were strangled and buried 24 hours after the death of their husbands, thus seriously limiting their reproductive years. Kaulong and Sengseng manifest no strong desire for heirs, and practice infanticide. Belief in the contaminating powers of women, together with certain socially accepted behavioral manipulations, appears to have resulted in an effective cultural barrier to human reproduction. The population density of two to three persons per square mile is reported to have been held constant for many generations (Goodale and Chowning 1971: 2).

In Enga, Kaulong, and Sengseng societies the cultural sanctions against sexual congress are expressed in biological terms. An Enga husband refrains from frequent copulation, equating the loss of semen with a depletion of male vitality. Overindulgence will "dull his mind and leave his body permanently exhausted and withered" (Meggitt 1964: 210). The Enga bachelor, who should remain chaste, is kept from socially disapproved sexual congress by the belief that contact with a menstruating woman "will, in the absence of countermagic sicken a man and cause persistent vomiting, turn his blood black, corrupt his vital juices so that his skin darkens and wrinkles as his flesh wastes, permanently dull his wits, and eventually lead to a slow decline and death" (Meggitt 1964: 207). That is, socially approved sexual congress within marriage is a biological danger; sexual contact outside the severe limits imposed by society leads to premature withering of the society.

Kaulong and Sengseng similarly resort to threats of biological disaster to enforce behavioral compliance. Shortly after her husband's death, a widow should be strangled by a close male kinsman—her son, brother, or father (Goodale and Chowning 1971: 8). The widow goads the reluctant murderer by suggesting that his restraint is based on a desire to copulate with her (Goodale: personal communication). This is not only a taunt of incest, but also an open reference to sex which is an affront in this prudish culture. The feeling of guilt is sufficient to force the murderer's hand. Enga, Kaulong, and Sengseng thus appear to be telling us their problems. For Enga, to contemplate nonapproved sexual activity leads to the dispatch of the actor. Kaulong and Sengseng males face a similar threat to their health; in addition, a male who fails to carry out a socially approved execution is contemplating an improper addition to society.

People are also telling us something of their problems by the way they mix or separate sex and the staple crop. Enga men, with magic to protect them from female pollution, copulate with their wives in the bush. Moreover, a husband "should not enter his gardens on the day he copulates, lest the female secretions adhering to him blight his crops" (Meggitt 1964: 210). Nor should he attempt to cook meat on that day, for it would spoil. In addition, Enga believe the menstrual blood destroys the *Acorus calamus* plants men use for wealth, pig, and war magic. Enga thus fear that increased female fertility would upset the delicate balance between men and their resources. Fore males, in contrast, purchase love magic to enchant the women they desire, and they copulate in the gardens.

Initiation

Initiation and bachelor associations also differ markedly in the Eastern and Western Highlands. The theme of Enga initiation rites concerns the shielding of males "from femininity, sexuality and impurity" (Meggitt 1964: 123). The men's behavior is prudish; they refrain from looking at each other's sexually provocative body areas and keep their conversations free of reference to sex or natural functions. Boys enter the bachelor associations when they are fifteen or sixteen, and remain members until marriage at a modal age of 25 to 27 (Meggitt 1965a: 86). The rituals require bathing to purify the youths from female influence, and ceremonies to keep alive the *Acorus* plants, the joint heritage of the subclan. A bachelor who breaks the sex rules prescribing chastity endangers not only his own health but also the welfare of the bachelors of the entire subclan. The iris plant would consequently die. Subclan members then beat the wayward youth and demand from him pig compensation "for the injury he has done them." The subclan thus exerts strong sanctions against unregulated additions to its size.

Courtship ceremonies in Enga society are "drearily proper gatherings," unlike the licentious functions in other parts of the Highlands, and girls attend with their chaperones (Meggitt 1964: 212). The playful culmination, where girls seize favored bachelors, is "not a betrothal" but a sign of willingness to pursue future acquaintance. The bachelors use the left hand to touch the penis throughout the unmarried period, thus keeping it from the fertilizing dangers of the right hand which has had contact with women (Meggitt 1964: 223–224). The bachelors themselves, the purificatory rituals, and the bog-iris leaves are all referred to as *sanggai*, "that which is hidden." That which is hidden would seem to be the penis, a fact recognized by the frustrated women who exert no restraint on public reference to sex, and taunt men about the smallness of their penises (Meggitt 1964: 214, 210).

The stress throughout the ceremonies is on male chastity and the aggregation of clan groups. The rituals culminate in a potentially explosive period, as the bachelors in each clan group shout mutually aggressive and boastful songs at other clans. Their earlier songs indicate the problems and ultimate dangers in Enga society; they tell of the shortage of the bog-iris plants for the many bachelors of the clan, and their dreams of territorial conquest (Meggitt 1964: 215).

Fore initiation is another matter. The ceremonies emphasize fertility and stress the rapid maturity of the youths. Rituals center on symbolic and imitative biological reproduction. In place of the bog-iris, which must be protected by the chastity of the bachelors, Fore men in seclusion reveal a pair of flutes, one male and one female. For men the flutes are a symbol of their virility, but the women refer to them as "flute-women" or co-wives (Berndt 1962: 70). Like the flutes, age-mates in Fore society are ideally pictured as matched pairs, men with an interest in the same women. The two must protect each other in life and are pledged to avenge each other's death. They are sexual confidants, and each has the right to inherit the other's widow (Lindenbaum and Glasse 1969).

The flutes are thus potent symbols of fertility, and during rituals are rubbed with pig blood, as are the male and female participants. Pig blood is also splashed on the earth. The ritual also requires that the youths undergo forced nose-bleeding, an imitative menstruation (Berndt 1962: 65–73, 104), believed to strengthen them and hasten maturity. Moreover, the same nose-bleeding ritual is performed for girls to strengthen them after menstruation and childbirth and before marriage (Berndt 1962: 106). This illuminates the danger men fear most. It seems that women represent two different kinds of danger in the Eastern and Western Highlands. Enga men fear women for the dangers of excess fertility. Fore men fear sexual inadequacy in the face of aggressively demanding females. Fore fear for their powers of reproduction; men and women alike must protect and increase their fertility with rituals which celebrate the physiological events of menstruation and childbirth (Berndt 1962: 105). Male-female relationships in the Eastern Highlands express complementarity rather than conflict (cf. Newman 1964: 265–266).

The tone of Fore society would shock the Enga. Male initiation ceremonies include men dressed as women, enacting scenes of copulation as a lesson on the dangers of adultery (Berndt 1962: 103). Female initiation presents women dressed as men, causing vaginal bleeding with mock coitus (Berndt 1962: 106). Fore women's songs, predictably, do not include frustrated reference to penises the size of tiny mushrooms (Meggitt 1964: 214) but extol the irresistible attraction of the penis-flutes (Berndt 1962: 70). Erotic farces are also frequently enacted, dramatizing incidents from myth or everyday life (Berndt 1962: 148).

Fore boys undergo initiation at a tender age (Berndt 1962: 106 photo) and continue until past adolescence. Participation in the rituals, however, does not rule out sexual adventure. Rather the ceremonies stimulate an interest in sex and carry the message that society awards prestige to the sexually active male. Moral rules during initiation stress protection of the political unit by aggressive behavior in both war and sex (Berndt 1962: 110), while negative lessons deal emphatically with stealing property and adultery, thefts which endanger internal solidarity. The negative lessons are hardly effective, for adultery is a common source of conflict. Berndt (1962: 328–380) records 107 indigenous court hearings among Fore and their neighbors. Most cases concern adultery, and there was no case of homicide. Punishment in one adultery case required the forced re-enactment of the crime by the adulterous pair, after which the husband received a compensation payment and also kept his wife. In contrast, Enga beat adulterous wives and then transfer them to the adulterer in return for a compensation payment of pigs, a scarce resource.

Although Fore may talk about female pollution, they lack the Enga sense of horror. Premarital and extra-marital affairs abound, and Fore are cavalier in their approach to incest. Faced with a shortage of women, South Fore redefine classificatory sisters as marriageable partners; the new wife's father then becomes a mother's brother, and her brothers the husband's cross-cousins (Glasse 1969: 29–30).

Conclusion

Gross differences thus emerge in the relationship of men to women throughout New Guinea. It may be possible to construct a continuum whereby Enga, Kaulong, and Sengseng typify societies in which the man-resource ratio is unusually high, giving rise to a certain cultural complex. Here death from disease is accepted as the punishment of ancestral spirits, pollution ideas limit the meeting of men and women during their fertile years, and there is an emphasis on male chastity. Other cultural features also seem to cluster at this end of the spectrum: a severe attitude towards incest and a view that adulterers are no great threat. Cannibalism in these societies is considered repulsive to the living, but may occur among ogres and other inhabitants of the pantheon.

At the other end of the spectrum are societies where population increase is desired—Fore, Daribi, Tangu, Dobu, Bena-Bena, and Orokaiva. Here disease is interpreted as an external attack by sorcerers, pollution ideas are not strenuously used to curb the access of men to women, the incest rule may be loosely observed, adultery is the serious theft of a scarce resource, and cannibalism may be present as a form of symbolic self-generation.

Few societies are found at these extremes. Kyaka, for instance, who are neighbors of the Enga but with a lower population density, have a cultural complex that includes malicious ghosts of the dead, together with a fertility goddess and more emphasis on sorcery (Bulmer 1965: 132–161). It is suggested that witches appear in the middle of the continuum, where population densities rise, altering the ratio of people to resources. Witches are not connected with the important survival issues but are concerned with the lesser dangers of infant mortality, small property less, and constitutional conflicts. Important survival issues are left to gods or to sorcerers.

A New Weapon Stirs Up Old Ghosts

William E. Mitchell

In the following article, William E. Mitchell describes the Wape shotgun cult, a belief and behavioral system that sprang up in New Guinea after the introduction of guns to the area in the late 1940s and early 1950s. Mitchell tells how Wape villagers pool their money to collectively purchase a shotgun, and then select a candidate from within their ranks to take the firearm test administered by officials. If the applicant is successful, a permit is issued and the individual must agree to shoot game for his village. Of special interest for this chapter is the role of ancestral ghosts in the system. Among the Wape, the dead are believed not only to protect the living from harm but also to supply them with meat and punish anyone who may have wronged them. Thus, a dead male relative becomes an invaluable aide to the hunter. The author shows how the cult's belief in vengeful spirits helps them understand why they sometimes experience unsuccessful hunting.

Reprinted with permission from *Natural History*, Vol. 82, no. 10 (December 1973), pp. 75–84. Copyright the American Museum of Natural History, 1973.

WHEN, IN 1947, THE FRANCISCAN FRIARS WENT to live among the nearly 10,000 Wape people of New Guinea, the principal native weapons were bone daggers and the bow and arrow. Even then, game was scarce in the heavily populated mountains where the Wape live, and the killing of a wild pig or a cassowary, New Guinea's major game animals, was an important village event. The Wape live in the western part of the Sepik River Basin. Their small villages lie along the narrow ridges of the Torricelli Mountains, above the sago palm swamps where women process palm pith, the Wape staff of life.

Today the Wape hunter's principal weapon is still the bow and arrow and game is even scarcer, This is partially the result of a new addition to the hunter's armory—the prosaic shotgun—which has had a profound moral impact on Wape village life.

The first guns were brought into this area in the late 1940s and early 1950s by missionaries, traders, and Australian government officials. Although natives were not permitted to own guns, they could use them if employed by a white man to shoot game for his table. This was a very prestigious job.

In 1960, government regulations were changed to permit natives to purchase singleshot shotguns. At first only a few Wape men, living in villages close to the government station and helpful to government officials, were granted gun permits. Eventually more permits were issued, but today, in hopes of preserving the remaining game, one permit is issued for every 100 people.

Within ten years of the granting of the first gun permits, a belief and behavioral system had evolved around the shotgun. It was based on traditional Wape hunting lore but had distinctive elaborations stemming from native perceptions of the teachings of government officials and missionaries. For descriptive purposes I call this system of formalized beliefs and ritual the "Wape shotgun cult." It is one of several Wape ceremonial cults, but the only one originating after contact with Europeans. Although the specific practices of the shotgun cult vary from village to village, the underlying beliefs are the same.

In creating the shotgun cult the Wape faced the challenge of adapting an introduced implement to their culture. Unlike steel axes and knives, which replaced stone adzes and bamboo knives, the shotgun has never replaced the bow and arrow. The shotgun is a scarce and expensive machine. This, together with the European sanctions imposed upon its introduction, places it in a unique position, both symbolically and behaviorally, among the Wape.

The cult is a conservative institution. It breaks no new cognitive ground by challenging established Wape concepts. Instead it merges traditional hunting concepts with European moral teachings to create a coherent system. The cult upholds traditional beliefs, accepts European authority, and most important, provides an explanation for unsuccessful hunting.

In 1970, my family and I arrived in Lumi, a small mountain settlement, which is the government's subdistrict headquarters in the middle of Wapeland. For the next year and a half, we lived in the village of Taute, near Lumi. There my wife and I studied Wape culture.

Taute, which has a population of 220, is reached by narrow foot trails, root strewn and muddy, passing through the dense, damp forest. The low houses—made of sago palm stems and roofed with sago thatch—are scattered about in the sandy plaza and among the coconut palms and breadfruit trees along the ridge. Towering poinsettias, red and pink hibiscus, and multicolored shrubs contrast with the encircling forest's greens and browns. A few small latrines perch on the steep slopes, concessions to Western concepts of hygiene. In the morning, flocks of screeching cockatoos glide below the ridge through the rising mists. When the breadfruit trees are bearing, giant fruit bats flop across the sky at dusk.

Since the mid-1950s the Franciscan friars have maintained off and on, a religious school in Taute. There, Wape boys are instructed by a native catechist in Catholicism, simple arithmetic, and Melanesian Pidgin. A priest from Lumi visits the village several times a year, and the villagers, Catholic and heathen alike, are proud of their affiliation with the Franciscans and staunchly loyal to them. But their Catholicism is nominal and superficial—a scant and brittle frosting that does not mask their own religious beliefs, which dominate everyday life.

The ethos of Wape society is oriented around sacred curing rituals. Whereas some Sepik cultures aggressively center their ceremonial life around headhunting and the raising of sturdy and brave children, the Wape defensively center theirs in the ritual appeasement of malevolent ghosts and forest demons, who they believe cause sickness. Most men belong to one of the demon-curing cults where, once initiated as priests, they are responsible for producing the often elaborate curing ceremonies for exorcising the demon from the afflicted.

The little money that exists among the Wape is earned primarily by the men, who work as two-year contract laborers on the coastal and island copra plantations. Because of the lack of money to buy canned meats, the scarcity of game, and the paucity of fish in the mountain streams, the protein intake of the Wape is exceedingly low. The most common meal is sago dumplings and boiled leaves. Malnutrition is common among youngsters, and physical development is generally retarded. According to studies by Dr. Lyn Wark, a medical missionary who has worked widely among the Wape, the average birth weight of the Wape baby is the lowest recorded in the world. Correspondingly, secondary sex characteristics are delayed. For example, the mean age for the onset of menses is over eighteen years.

Before contact with Westerners, Wape men were naked and the women wore short string skirts. Today most men wear shorts and the women wear skirts purchased from Lumi's four small stores. To appear in a semblance of European dress, however meager or worn, is a matter of pride and modesty to both sexes. "Savages" do not wear clothes, but white men and those who have been enlightened by white men do. In this sense, the Wape's Western-style dress represents an identification with the politically and materially powerful white man. The identification is with power; it is an ego-enhancing maneuver that permits the Wape to live with dignity, even though they are subservient to Western rule and influence. The tendency of the Wape to identify with, and incorporate, the alien when it serves to preserve their culture will help us to understand how they have woven diverse cultural strands into the creation of the shotgun cult.

From the first day I arrived in Taute, the men repeatedly made two urgent requests of me. One was to open a store in the village, saving them the difficult walk into Lumi; the other was to buy a shotgun to help them kill game. This was the least, they seemed to indicate, a fair-minded and, in Wape terms, obviously rich neighbor should do. One of the hardest things the anthropologists in the field must learn is to say "no" to deserving people. To be stingy is almost to be un-American, but we had come half-way around the world to learn about the Wape way of life, not to introduce stores and shotguns that would alter the established trading and hunting patterns.

After several months the people of the major Taute hamlets, Kafiere, where we lived, and Mifu, a ten-minute walk away, each decided to buy a group-owned shotgun. The investment was a sizable forty-two Australian dollars; forty dollars for the gun, and two dollars for the gun permit. Each hamlet made a volunteer collection from its members and I, as a fellow villager, contributed to both guns. A week later the villagers purchased the guns from one of the Lumi stores, and I began to learn about the shotgun's ritual and moral importance to the Wape. The villagers were already familiar with the significance of the shotgun for they had purchased one several years before. The cult ended, however, when the gun broke.

The shotgun, like Melanesian Pidgin, is associated by the Wape with Europeans and modernity. Not surprisingly, Pidgin is favored for shotgun parlance. The licensed gunman is not only called *sutboi* ("shootboy") but also *laman* ("law man"), the latter a term that connotes his official tie to European law and government as perceived by the villagers.

When a candidate for a gun permit appears before the government official in Lumi, he is examined orally on the use of firearms, then given an unloaded shotgun and tested on his handling knowledge. Under the direct and questioning gaze of the examining official, candidates sometimes become flustered. One inadvertently aimed the gun first toward the wife of the assistant district

commissioner and then toward a group of observers. His examination ended ignominiously on the spot.

If the candidate passes the test and the examining official approves of his character, he is then lectured on the use of the gun: only the candidate can fire it, he must willingly shoot game for his fellow villagers, and the gun must be used exclusively for hunting. He is strongly warned that if any of these rules are broken or if there is trouble in the village, he will lose the gun and the permit and will be imprisoned.

The candidate's friends and the inevitable audience are present for the lecture. Here, as in many spheres of native life, the official's power is absolute, and the Wape know this from long experience. Guns have been confiscated or destroyed without reimbursement and gunmen have been jailed.

The official's charge to the candidate is willingly accepted. Henceforth, he will never leave the village without carrying his gun. He is now a *laman*, and he has the gun and permit, printed entirely in English, to prove it.

The government official's strong sanctions against village quarrels are motivated by his fear that the gun might be used in a dispute among villagers. The sanctions are further upheld by the missionaries' and catechists' sermons against quarreling and wrongdoing as they attempt to teach the Christian doctrine of brotherly love. The message the villagers receive is this: To keep the white man's gun, they must follow the white man's rules. This the Wape do, not in servile submission, but with some pride because the presence of the gun and the public focus on morality mark the village as progressive and modern. The licensed gunman, therefore, is not only the guardian of the gun but of village morality as well.

Rain or shine, he is expected to go into the forest without compensation to hunt for his fellow villagers, who give him cartridges with some personal identifying mark upon them. After a gunman makes a kill, the owner of the cartridge receives the game and distributes it according to his economic obligations to others. But the gunman, like the bow and arrow hunter, is forbidden to eat from the kill; to do so would jeopardize further successful hunting.

In the hamlet of Kafiere, the clan that had

contributed the most money toward the gun and on whose lands the most game was to be found appointed Auwe as gunman. But Auwe's wife, Naiasu, was initially against his selection. Her previous husband, Semer, now dead several years, had been Kafiere's first *sutboi* and she argued that the heavy hunting responsibilities of a *sutboi* took too much time, forcing him to neglect his own gardening and hunting obligations.

When Auwe first requested a gun permit he was turned away. The villagers believed that the ghost of Naiasu's dead husband, Semer, had followed Auwe to Lumi and influenced the examining official against him. Semer's ghost was acting to fulfill Naiasu's wish that her young son, now Auwe's stepson, would have a stepfather who was always available. This was the first of many stories I was to hear about the relationship between ghosts and the gun. When Auwe returned to Lumi for a second try, he passed the examination and was given the official permit.

The hamlet now had its own gun and hunting could begin in earnest. The first step was an annunciation feast called, in Pidgin, a *kapti* ("cup of tea"). Its purpose was to inform the villagers' dead ancestors about the new gun. This was important because ancestral ghosts roam the forest land of their lineage, protecting it from intruders and driving game to their hunting descendants. The hunter's most important hunting aide is his dead male relatives, to whom he prays for game upon entering his hunting lands. The dead remain active in the affairs of the living by protecting them from harm, providing them with meat, and punishing those who have wronged them.

The small sacrificial feast was held in front of Auwe's house. Placing the upright gun on a makeshift table in the midst of the food, Auwe rubbed it with sacred ginger. One of Auwe's elderly clansmen, standing and facing his land, called out to his ancestors by name and told them about the new gun. He implored them to send wild pigs and cassowaries to Auwe.

Several men spoke of the new morality that was to accompany hunting with a gun. The villagers should not argue or quarrel among themselves; problems must be settled quietly and without bitterness; malicious gossip and stealing were forbidden. If these rules were not obeyed, Auwe would not find game.

In traditional Wape culture there is no feast analogous to the *kapti*. Indeed, there are no general community-wide feasts. The *kapti* is apparently modeled on a European social gathering.

For the remainder of my stay in Taute, I followed closely the fortunes of the Taute guns and of guns in nearby villages as well. All seemed to be faced with the same two problems: game was rarely seen; and when seen, was rarely killed. Considering that a cartridge belongs to a villager, not the gunman, how was this economic loss handled? This presented a most intriguing and novel problem for there were no analogs to this type of predicament within the traditional culture. By Wape standards, the pecuniary implications of such a loss, although but a few Australian shillings, could not graciously be ignored by the loser. At the very least the loss had to be explained even if the money for the cartridges could not be retrieved.

Now I understood the concern about the ancestral ghosts. If the hunter shot and missed, the owner of the fired shells was being punished by being denied meat. Either he or a close family member had quarreled or wronged another person whose ghost-relative was securing revenge by causing the hunter to miss. This, then, was the functional meaning of the proscription against quarreling. By avoiding disputes, the villagers were trying to prevent the intervention of ancestral ghosts in human affairs. In a peaceful village without quarrels, the gunman could hunt undisturbed by vengeful ghosts chasing away game or misrouting costly shells.

Although a number of factors in European culture have influenced the shotgun cult, the cult's basic premise of a positive correlation between quarreling and bad hunting is derived directly from traditional Wape culture. In bow and arrow hunting, an individual who feels he was not given his fair share of a hunter's kill may punish the hunter by gossiping about him or quarreling openly with him. The aggrieved person's ancestral ghosts revenge the slight by chasing the game away from the offending hunter or misdirecting his arrows. But this is a private affair between the hunter and the angered person; their quarrel has no influence upon the hunting of others. And it is rare for an issue other than distribution of game to cause a ghost to hinder a bowman's success. The hunter's prowess is restored only when the angered person performs a brief supplication rite over the hunter.

This, then, is the conceptual basis for the tie between quarreling and bad hunting. Originally relevant only to bow and arrow hunting, it was then broadened to accommodate the government's pronouncements about the shotgun and keeping the village peace. And it applies perfectly to the special circumstances of shotgun hunting. Because the shotgun is community owned and many villagers buy cartridges for it, the villagers are identified with both the gun and the gunman. As a proxy hunter for the villagers, the gunman is potentially subject to the ghostly sanctions resulting from their collective wrongs. Thus gun hunting, unlike bow and arrow hunting, is a community affair and the community-wide taboo against quarrels and personal transgressions is the only effective way to prevent spiteful ghosts from wrecking the hunt.

No village, however, even if populated by people as disciplined and well behaved as the Wape, can constantly live in the state of pious peace considered necessary for continuous good gun hunting. When the hunting is poor, the gunman must discover the quarrels and wrongs within the village. After having identified the individuals whose ancestral ghosts are sabotaging the hunting, the gunman must also see to it that they implore the ghosts to stop. Embarrassed by the public disclosure, they will quickly comply.

The common method for detecting points of friction within the village is to bring the villagers together for a special meeting. The gunman will then document in detail his misfortunes and call on the villagers to find out what is ruining the hunting. If confessions of wrongdoing are not forthcoming, questioning accusations result. The meeting, beginning in Pidgin, moves into Wape as the discussion becomes more complex and voluble. It may last up to three hours; but even if there is no resolution, it always ends amiably—at least on the surface. For it is important to create no new antagonisms.

The other technique for locating the source of the hunting problem is to call in a professional clairvoyant. As the villagers must pay for his services, he is usually consulted only after a series of unsuccessful meetings. Clairvoyants have replaced the shamans, who were outlawed by the government and the mission because they practiced sorcery and ritual murders. The Wape do not consider a clairvoyant a sorcerer; he is a man with second

sight who is experienced in discovering and treating the hidden causes of intractable problems. As such, shotguns are among his best patients.

Mewau, a clairvoyant from a neighboring village, held a "shotgun clinic" in Taute to examine the Mifu and Kafiere guns. For about an hour he examined the two guns and questioned the villagers. Then he declared the reasons for their misfortune.

Kapul, a dead Mifu shaman, was preventing the Mifu gun from killing game because a close relative of the gunman had allegedly stolen valuables from Kapul's daughter. Because of the family ties between the gunman and the thief, Kapul's ghost was punishing the gunman.

The Kafiere gun, Mewau declared, was not able to find game because a widow in the village felt that her dead husband's clan had not previously distributed game to her in a fair way. By interfering with the Kafiere gun, her husband's ghost was punishing his clan for the neglect of his family.

Once the source of trouble is named, there are several possible types of remedial ritual depending upon the seriousness of the situation. For example, the circumstances surrounding the naming of the husband's ghost were considered serious, and a *kapti* was held to placate him. Another, simpler ritual involves the preparation of taro soup, which the gunman consumes. But the simplest, commonest remedial rite is the supplication ritual without sacrificial food offerings, a ritual in which I became involved.

Mifu's gunman had shot a pig with one of his own cartridges but did not give me the small portion due me as a part owner of the gun. Partly as a test to see if my ancestors counted for anything in Taute and partly because I did not want to let this calculated slight go unchallenged, I, in typical Wape fashion, said nothing to the gunman but gossiped discreetly about his selfishness. The gunman continued to hunt but had no further success. When his bad luck persisted, a meeting was called to find out the reason. The gunman asked me if I was angry because I had not been given my portion of the pig. When I acknowledged my anger, he handed the shotgun to me and I dutifully spoke out to my ancestors to stop turning the game away from the gun.

But the gunman still had no success in the hunt, and the villagers decided there were other wrongs as well. The search for the offending ghosts continued. Eventually the villagers became so discouraged with the Mifu gun that they stopped giving cartridges to the gunman. The consensus was that a major undetected wrong existed in the hamlet, and until it was uncovered and the guilty ghost called off, hunting with the gun was senseless and extravagant. Thus the propriety of a remedial rite is established if there is success on the next hunt. The system is completely empirical: if no game is seen or if seen, is not killed, then the search for the wrong must continue.

Wape people are generally even tempered, and their villages, in contrast to many in New Guinea, strike the newcomer as almost serene. But the social impact of the guns at this time was pervasive, and life in Taute literally revolved around the guns and their hunting fortunes. Whereas the villagers previously had kept to their own affairs, they now became embroiled in meeting after meeting, seeking out transgressions, quarrels, and wrongdoing. As the gunman continued to have bad luck, his efforts to discover the cause became more zealous. A certain amount of polarization resulted: the gunman accused the villagers, the men accused the women, and the adults accused the young people of hiding their wrongs. And a few who had lost many cartridges wondered if the *sutboi* was keeping the game for himself. But no one ever suggested that he was an inexperienced shotgun hunter. The gunman was generally considered to be blameless; in fact, the more game he missed, the more self-righteous he became and the more miscreant the villagers.

Six months of poor hunting had gone by; the villagers felt that the only recourse left to them was to bring a bush demon named *mani* into the village from the jungle for a festival. The *mani's* small stone heart is kept enshrined in a rustic altar in a corner of Kafiere's ceremonial house and after a kill the animal's blood is smeared upon it. The *mani* will reward the village with further kills only if he is fed with blood. *Mani* is the only spirit, other than ghosts, who can cause both good and bad hunting depending upon the way he is treated. Soon after the shotgun arrived in Taute, the gunman and some other men left their homes to sleep in the men's ceremonial house to keep *mani's* stone heart warm. They thought *mani*, in appreciation, would send game to the gunman.

When little game was killed, the villagers decided on the hunting festival. In a special house outside of the village, men constructed the great conical mask that depicts *mani*. For several weeks they worked to cover the mask's frame with the spathes of sago palm fronds painted with designs traditional to *mani*. Finally, a priest of the *mani* cult, wearing a 20-foot-high mask festooned with feathers and leaves, pranced into the village to the thunderous beat of wooden drums.

For the next week and a half men from other villages who wished us well came and joined in the all-night singing of the *mani* song cycle. In the morning, if the weather was clear, *mani* led the bow and arrow hunters and the gunman to the edge of the village and sent them on their way to hunting success. But in spite of the careful attentions the villagers directed toward *mani*, he rewarded them with only one wild pig. The villagers became openly discouraged, then annoyed. Finally the hunters, disgusted and weary from numerous long futile hunts, and other men, their shoulders sore and bloody from constantly carrying the heavy mask around the plaza, decided that *mani* was simply taking advantage of them; all of their hard work was for nothing. Disgusted, they decided to send *mani* back to his home in the forest.

One late afternoon the *mani* appeared in the plaza but he did not prance. He walked slowly around the plaza, stopping at each house to throw ashes over himself with his single bark cloth arm. The villagers said he was in mourning because he had to leave by dusk and would miss the company of men. Silently the people watched the once gay and graceful *mani* lumber out of the village. The men and boys followed him into the forest. Then the gunman split open the mask, to insure the spirit's exit and eventual return to his forest home, and hurled it over the edge of the cliff into the bush below.

A few months after the *mani* hunting festival, the shotgun cult as I had known it in Taute ceased to function. All but one of the able young men of the hamlet of Kafiere went off to work on a coastal plantation for two years. With no young men, the ceremonial activities of the hunting and curing cults were suspended and the fault-finding meetings halted until their return. The drama and excitement of the previous months had vanished with the men.

Voodoo

Karen McCarthy Brown

It is likely that no other topic in this book is as misunderstood as Voodoo. Movies, television, and novels have been merciless in delivering to the public a highly distorted picture of what is a legitimate religious practice of 80 to 90 percent of the people of Haiti. In this article, Karen McCarthy Brown explains that Voodoo, or Vodou according to Haitian Creole orthography, is an African-based, Catholic-influenced religion. She also points out the differences between urban and rural Voodoo, and discusses African and Roman Catholic influence in the development of the religion. In addition, Brown discusses Voodoo spirits, Voodoo ceremonies, and the relationship of magic to Voodoo. The article concludes with some comments on the massive emigration of Haitians, mostly to Miami, New York, or Montreal, where Voodoo ceremonies are carried on in storefronts, rented rooms, and apartments.

VOODOO, OR *VODOU* (ACCORDING TO OFFICIAL HAItian Creole orthography), is a misleading but common term for the religious practices of 80 to 90 percent of the people of Haiti. A mountainous, poverty-stricken, largely agricultural country of approximately six million people, Haiti has a land area of 10,700 square miles that covers the western third of the island of Hispaniola, which it shares with the Dominican Republic. The term *voodoo* (or *hoodoo*, a derivative) is also used, mostly in a derogatory sense, to refer to systems of sorcery and magic or to specific spells, or charms, emanating from such systems, which are for the most part practiced by the descendants of the African slaves brought to the Western Hemisphere.

Outsiders have given the name *Voodoo* to the traditional religious practices of Haiti; only recently, and still to a very limited extent, have Haitians come to use the term as others do. The word can be traced to *vodu* ("spirit" or "deity") in the language of the Fon peoples of Dahomey (present-day Benin). In contemporary Haiti, *vodou* refers to one ritual style or dance among many in the traditional religious system. Haitians prefer a verb to identify their religion: they speak of "serving the spirits."

Sensationalized novels and films, as well as spurious travelers' accounts, have painted a highly distorted picture of Haitian religion. It has been incorrectly depicted as magic and sorcery that involves uncontrolled orgiastic behavior and even cannibalism. These distortions are undoubtedly attributable to racism and to the fear that the Haitian slave revolution sparked in predominantly white nations. Haiti achieved independence in 1804, thus becoming a black republic in the Western Hemisphere at a time when the colonial economy was still heavily dependent on slave labor.

Voodoo is an African-based, Catholic-influenced religion that serves three (not always clearly distinguished) categories of spiritual beings: *lemò*, *lemistè*, and *lemarasa* (respectively, "the dead," "the mysteries," and "the sacred twins"). While certain Voodoo prayers and invocations preserve fragments of West African languages, Haitian Creole is the primary language of Voodoo. Creole (*Kreyol* in the orthographical system employed in this article) is the first and only language of 80 percent of contemporary Haitians; it has a grammatical structure influenced by West African languages and a largely French vocabulary.

Although many individuals and families regularly serve the Voodoo spirits without recourse to religious professionals, Voodoo does have a loosely organized priesthood, open to both men and women. The male priest is called *oungan* and the female, *manbo*. There are many different types of Voodoo ritual, including individual acts of piety, such as the lighting of candles for particular spirits, and large feasts, sometimes of several days' duration, which include animal sacrifice as part of a meal offered to the spirits. Energetic drumming, singing, and dancing accompany the more elaborate rituals. In the countryside, rituals often take place outdoors on family land that has been set aside for the spirits. On this land there is often a small cult house, which houses the Voodoo altars. In the cities, most rituals occur in the *ounfò* ("temple"). Urban altars are maintained in *jèvo*, small rooms usually off the *peristil*, which is the central dancing and ritualizing space of the temple.

The goal of Voodoo drumming, singing, and dancing is to *chofe*, that is, to "heat up," the situation sufficiently to bring on possession by the spirits. As a particular spirit is summoned, a devotee enters a trance and becomes that spirit's *chwal* ("horse"), thus providing the means for direct communication between human beings and the spirits. The spirit is said to ride the *chwal*. Using that person's body and voice, the spirit sings, dances, and eats with the people and offers them advice and chastisement. The people, in turn, offer the spirit a wide variety of gifts and acts of obeisance whose goal is to placate the spirit and ensure his or her continuing protection.

There are marked differences in Voodoo as it is practiced throughout Haiti, but the single most important distinction is that between urban and rural Voodoo. The great majority of Haiti is agricultural, and the manner in which peasants serve the spirits is determined by questions of land tenure

and ancestral inheritance. Urban Voodoo is not tied to the land, but the family connection persists in another form. Urban temple communities become substitutes for the extended families of the countryside. The priests are called "papa" and "mama"; the initiates, who are called "children of the house," refer to one another as "brother" and "sister." In general, urban Voodoo is more institutionalized and more elaborate than its rural counterpart.

African Influence

Haiti's slave population was largely built up in the eighteenth century, a period in which Haiti supplied a large percentage of the sugar consumed in Western Europe. Voodoo was born on the sugar plantations out of the interaction among slaves who brought with them a wide variety of African religious traditions. But, due to inadequate records, little is known about this formative period in Voodoo's history. There are, however, indications that Voodoo played a key role in the organization of the slave revolt (Leyburn, 1941), as it apparently did in the downfall of President Jean-Claude Duvalier in February 1986.

Three African groups appear to have had the strongest influence on Voodoo: the Yoruba of present-day Nigeria, the Fon of Dahomey (present-day Benin), and the Kongo of what are now Zaire and Angola. Many of the names of Voodoo spirits are easily traceable to their African counterparts; however, in the context of Haiti's social and economic history, these spirits have undergone change. For example, Ogun among the Yoruba is a spirit of ironsmithing and other activities associated with metal, such as hunting, warfare, and modern technology. Neither hunting nor modern technology plays a significant role in the lives of Haitians. Haiti does, however, have a long and complex military history; thus the Haitian spirit Ogou is a soldier whose rituals, iconography, and possession-performance explore both the constructive and destructive uses of military power, as well as its analogues within human relations—anger, self-assertion, and willfulness.

Africa itself is a powerful concept in Voodoo. Haitians speak of Gine ("Guinea") both as their ancestral home, the continent of Africa, and as the watery subterranean home of the Voodoo spirits. Calling a spirit *frangine* (lit., "frank Guinea," i.e., truly African) is a way of indicating that the spirit is good, ancient, and proper. The manner in which an individual or a group serves the spirits may also be called *frangine*, with similar connotations of approval and propriety.

Roman Catholic Influence

The French slaveholders were Catholic, and baptism was mandatory for slaves. Many have argued that slaves used a veneer of Catholicism to hide their traditional religious practices from the authorities. While Catholicism may well have functioned in this utilitarian way for slaves on the plantations, it is also true that the religions of West Africa, from which Voodoo was derived, have a long tradition of syncretism. Whatever else Catholicism represented in the slave world, it was most likely also seen as a means to expand Voodoo's ritual vocabulary and iconography. Catholicism has had the greatest influence on the traditional religion of Haiti at the level of rite and image, rather than theology. This influence works in two ways. First, those who serve the spirits call themselves Catholic, attend Mass, go to confession, and undergo baptism and first communion, and, because these Catholic rituals are at times integral parts of certain larger Voodoo rites, they are often directed to follow them by the Voodoo spirits. Second, Catholic prayers, rites, images, and saints' names are integrated into the ritualizing in Voodoo temples and cult houses. An active figure in Voodoo is the *pretsavan* ("bush priest"), who achieves his title by knowing the proper, often Latin, form of Catholic prayers. Though neither a Catholic nor a Voodoo priest, he is called into the Voodoo temple when the ritualizing has a significant Catholic dimension.

Over the years, a system of parallels has been developed between the Voodoo spirits and the Catholic saints. For example, Dambala, the ancient and venerable snake deity of the Fon peoples, is worshiped in Haiti both as Dambala and as Saint Patrick, who is pictured in the popular Catholic chromolithograph with snakes clustered around his feet. In addition, the Catholic liturgical calendar dominates in much Voodoo ritualizing. Thus the Voodoo spirit Ogou is honored on 25 July, the feast day of his Catholic counterpart, Saint James the Elder.

Bondye, the "Good God," is identified with the Christian God and is said to be the highest, indeed the only, god. The spirits are said to have been angels in Lucifer's army whom God sent out of heaven and down to Gine. Although the spirits may exhibit capricious behavior, they are in no sense evil. Rather, they are seen as intermediaries between the people and the high god, a role identical to the one played by the so-called lower deities in the religions of the Yoruba and Fon. Bondye is remote and unknowable. Although evoked daily in ordinary speech (almost all plans are made with the disclaimer "if God wills"), Bondye's intervention is not sought for most of life's problems. That is the work of the spirits.

The Catholic church of Haiti has sometimes participated in the persecution of those who follow Voodoo. However, the last "antisuperstition campaign" was in the 1940s, and currently there is an uneasy peace between Voodoo and the Catholic church. Until quite recently, the Catholic clergy routinely preached against serving the spirits, and those who served routinely remarked, "That is the way priests talk." Most Catholic events have a simultaneous Voodoo dimension that the Catholic church for the most part ignores. Since Catholicism is the official religion of Haiti and the church has been to some extent state-controlled, the degree to which Voodoo has been tolerated, or even encouraged has been at least partly a function of politics. For instance, Haitian presidents Dumarsais Estime (1946–1950) and François Duvalier (1957–1971) were known for their sympathy with Voodoo.

Voodoo Spirits

The Voodoo spirits are known by various names: *lwa* (from a Yoruba word for "spirit" or "mystery"), *sint* ("saints"), *mistè* ("mysteries"), *envizil* ("invisibles"), and, more rarely, *zanj* ("angels"). In the countryside, the spirits are grouped into *nanchon* ("nations"). Although no longer recognized as such by Haitians, the names of the Voodoo spirit nations almost all refer to places and peoples in Africa. For example, there are *nanchon* known as Rada (after the Dahomean principality Allada), Wangol (Angola), Mondon (Mandingo, Ibo, Nago (the Dahomean name for the Ketu Yoruba and Kongo. In rural Voodoo, a person inherits responsibilities to one or more of these *nanchon* through maternal and paternal kin. Familial connections to the land, where the *lwa* are said to reside in trees, springs and wells, also determine which spirits are served.

In urban Voodoo, two *nanchon*, the Rada and the Petro, have emerged as dominant largely by absorbing other *nanchon*. Rada and Petro spirits contrast sharply in temperament and domain. The Rada spirits are *dous* ("sweet") and known for their wisdom and benevolence. The Petro spirits were probably named for the Spanish Voodoo priest Dom Petro; they show a marked Kongo influence and are considered *cho* ("hot"), and their power is stressed. Each spirit group has drum rhythms, dances, and food preferences that correspond to its identifying characteristics. For example, Dambala, the gentle Rada snake spirit, is said to love *orja*, a syrup made from almonds and sugar. His worshipers perform a sinuous spine-rippling dance called *yanvalou*. By contrast, the Petro rhythm, played for such rum-drinking spirits as Dom Petro and Tijan Petro, is energetic and pounding, and the accompanying dance is characterized by rapid shoulder movements.

The Voodoo View of the Person

In Voodoo teachings the human being is composed of various parts: the body, that is, the gross physical part of the person, which perishes after death, and from two to four souls, of which the most widely acknowledged are the *gro bonanj* and the *ti bonanj*. The *gro bonanj* ("big guardian angel") is roughly equivalent to consciousness or personality. When a person dies the *gro bonanj* survives, and immediately after death it is most vulnerable to capture and misuse by sorcerers. During possession, it is the *gro bonanj* that is displaced by the spirit and sent to wander away from the body, as it does routinely during sleep. The *ti bonanj* ("little guardian angel") may be thought of as the conscience or the spiritual energy reserve of a living person and, at times, as the ghost of a dead person. Each person is said to have one spirit who is the *mèt-tet* ("master of the head"). The *mèt-tet* is the major protector and central spirit served by that person, and it is that spirit that corresponds to the *gro bonanj*. Because the *gro bonanj* is the soul that endures after death and because it is connected to a particular *lwa*, a person who venerates the ances-

tors inherits the service of particular spirits. In addition to the master of the head, each person has a small number of other *lwa* with whom there is a special protective connection. There is a rough parallel between the characters of the spirits and those of the people who serve them. Thus the language of Voodoo is also a language for categorizing and analyzing the behavior of groups and individuals. For example, when an individual, family, or temple is described as worshiping in a mode that is *Rada net*, ("straight *Rada*"), a great deal is also being said about how that person or group functions socially.

Voodoo and the Dead

In both urban and rural Haiti, cemeteries are major ritual centers. The first male buried in any cemetery is known as the Baron. Baron's wife is Gran Brijit, a name given to the first female buried in a cemetery. Every cemetery has a cross either in the center or at the gate. The cross is known as the *kwa Baron* ("Baron's cross"), and this is the ritualizing center of the cemetery. Lighted candles and food offerings are placed at the foot of Baron's cross. In addition, many rituals for healing, love, or luck that are performed in the rural cult houses or the urban temples are not considered complete until the physical remnants of the "work" are deposited at crossroads or at Baron's cross, which is itself a kind of crossroads marking the intersection of the land of the living and the land of the dead.

Haitians make a distinction between *lemò* ("the dead") and *lemistè* ("the mysteries"). Within Voodoo, there are rituals and offerings for particular family dead; however, if these ancestral spirits are seen as strong and effective, they can, with time, become *mistè*. The group of spirits known as the *gèdè* are not ancestral spirits but *mistè*, and their leader is the well-known Baron Samdi, or Baron Saturday. In and around Port-au-Prince, the capital of Haiti and its largest city, the *gèdè* are the object of elaborate ritualizing in the cemeteries and Voodoo temples during the season of the Catholic Feast of All Souls, or Halloween.

The *gèdè* are not only spirits of death but also patrons of human sexuality, protectors of children, and irrepressible social satirists. Dances for *gèdè* tend to be boisterous affairs, and new *gèdè* spirits appear every year. The satirical, and often explicitly sexual, humor of the *gèdè* levels social pretense. Appearing as auto mechanics, doctors, government bureaucrats, Protestant missionaries, and so forth, the *gèdè* use humor to deal with new social roles and to question alienating social hierarchies.

Voodoo Ceremonies

In rural Voodoo, the ideal is to serve the spirits as simply as possible because simplicity of ritual is said to reflect real power and the true African way of doing things (Larose, 1977). In practice, rural ritualizing tends to follow the fortunes of the extended families. Bad times are said to be due to the displeasure of the family spirits. When it is thought to be no longer possible to satisfy the spirits with small conciliatory offerings, the family will hold a large drumming and dancing feast that includes animal sacrifice.

Urban Voodoo, by contrast, has a more routine ritualizing calendar, and events tend to be larger and more elaborate. Ceremonies in honor of major spirits take place annually on or around the feast days of their Catholic counterparts and usually include sacrifice of an appropriate animal—most frequently a chicken, a goat, or a cow. A wide variety of ceremonies meet specific individual and community needs: for example, healing rites, dedications of new temples and new ritual regalia, and spirit marriages in which a devotee "marries" a spirit of the opposite sex and pledges to exercise sexual restraint one night each week in order to receive that spirit in dreams. There is also a cycle of initiation rituals that has both public segments and segments reserved for initiates. The latter include the *kanzo* rituals, which mark the first stage of initiation, and those in which the adept takes the *asson*, the beaded gourd rattle that is the symbol of the Voodoo priesthood. Certain rituals performed during the initiation cycle, such as the *brule zen* ("burning of the pots") and the *chire ayzan* ("shredding of the palm leaf") may also be used in other ritual contexts. Death rituals include the *desounen*, in which the *gro bonanj* is removed from the corpse and sent under the waters, and the *rele mò nan dlo* ("calling the dead up from the waters") a ritual that can occur any time after a period of a year and a day from the date of death. Good-luck baths are administered during the Christmas and New Year

season. Many of the rituals of urban Voodoo are performed in rural Haiti as well.

Annual pilgrimages draw thousands of urban and rural followers of Voodoo. The focal point of events, which are at once Catholic and Voodoo, is usually a Catholic church situated near some striking feature of the natural landscape that is believed to be sacred to the Voodoo spirits. The two largest pilgrimages are one held for Ezili Dantò (Our Lady of Mount Carmel) in mid-July in the little town of Saut d'Eau, named for its spectacular waterfall, and one held for Ogou (Saint James the Elder) in the latter part of July in the northern town of Plain du Nord, where a shallow pool adjacent to the Catholic church is sacred to Ogou.

Voodoo and Magic

Serge Larose (1977) has demonstrated that magic is not only a stereotypic label that outsiders have applied to Voodoo, but also a differential term internal to the religion. Thus an in-group among the followers of Voodoo identifies its own ritualizing as "African" while labeling the work of the out-group as *maji* ("magic"). Generally speaking, this perspective provides a helpful means of grasping the concept of magic within Voodoo. There are, however, those individuals who, in their search for power and wealth, have self-consciously identified themselves with traditions of what Haitians would call the "work of the left hand." This includes people who deal in *pwen achte* ("purchased points"), which means spirits or powers that have been bought rather than inherited, and people who deal in *zombi*. A *zombi* may be either the disembodied soul of a dead person whose powers are used for magical purposes, or a soulless body that has been raised from the grave to do drone labor in the fields. Also included in the category of the left hand are secret societies known by such names as Champwel, Zobop, and Bizango. These powerful groups use magic not for personal gain but to enforce social sanctions. Wade Davis (1985) claims that *zombi* laborers are created by judgments of tribunals of secret societies against virulently antisocial persons.

The "work of the left hand" should not be confused with more ordinary Voodoo ritualizing that also has a magical flavor, such as divination, herbal healing, and the manufacture of charms for love or luck, or for the protection of the home, land, or person. Much of the work of Voodoo priests is at the level of individual client-practitioner interactions. Theirs is a healing system that treats problems of love, health, family, and work. Unless a problem is understood as coming from God, in which case the Voodoo priest can do nothing, the priest will treat it as one caused by a spirit or by a disruption in human relationships, including relations with the dead. Generally speaking, cures come through a ritual adjustment of relational systems.

Voodoo in the Haitian Diaspora

Drought and soil erosion, poverty, high urban unemployment, and political oppression in Haiti have led to massive emigration in the last three decades.

Voodoo has moved along with the Haitians who have come to the major urban centers of North America in search of better life. In Miami, New York, and Montreal, the cities with the greatest concentrations of Haitian immigrants, Voodoo ceremonies are carried on in storefronts, rented rooms, and high-rise apartments. North American rituals are often truncated versions of their Haitian counterparts. There may be no drums, and the only animals sacrificed may be chickens. However, it is possible to consult a *manbo* or *oungan* in these immigrant communities with ease, and the full repertoire of rituals is found there in one form or another. Even the pilgrimages are duplicated. On 16 July, rather than going to the mountain town of Saut d'Eau to honor Ezili Dantò, New York Haitians take the subway to the Italian-American Church of Our Lady of Mount Carmel in the Bronx.

The Secrets of Haiti's Living Dead

Gino Del Guercio

Recounting the experience of Wade Davis, author of
The Serpent and the Rainbow, *Gino Del Guercio
points out Davis's startling discovery that zombies
do indeed exist in Haiti; however, rather than being
"the living dead," they are actually the "living
drugged." Haitian secret societies use the threat of
zombification to control deviant activity, and for the
rural population this punishment is regarded as
more severe than death. The secret was unlocked by
ethnobotanist Davis, who recognized that the
symptoms brought on by fish poisoning in Japan
were identical to those experienced by victims of
so-called zombification in Haiti. Davis shows that
zombies cannot be dismissed as folklore, nor are they
the living dead. It is important to note here that
serious controversy continues to surround the Davis
thesis. William Booth's review article, "Voodoo
Science" (*Science *240: 274–77 [April 18, 1988])
cites scholars who question Davis's findings.*

Reprinted from *Harvard Magazine*, January-February
1986, pp. 31–37. Copyright © 1986 *Harvard Magazine*.
Reprinted by permission.

FIVE YEARS AGO, A MAN WALKED INTO L'ESTÈRE, A
village in central Haiti, approached a peasant
woman named Angelina Narcisse, and identified
himself as her brother Clairvius. If he had not
introduced himself using a boyhood nickname
and mentioned facts only intimate family members knew, she would not have believed him.
Because, eighteen years earlier, Angelina had
stood in a small cemetery north of her village and
watched as her brother Clairvius was buried.

The man told Angelina he remembered that
night well. He knew when he was lowered into
his grave, because he was fully conscious, although he could not speak or move. As the earth
was thrown over his coffin, he felt as if he were
floating over the grave. The scar on his right
cheek, he said, was caused by a nail driven
through his casket.

The night he was buried, he told Angelina, a
voodoo priest raised him from the grave. He was
beaten with a sisal whip and carried off to a
sugar plantation in northern Haiti where, with
other zombies, he was forced to work as a slave.
Only with the death of the zombie master were
they able to escape, and Narcisse eventually
returned home.

Legend has it that zombies are the living
dead, raised from their graves and animated by
malevolent voodoo sorcerers, usually for some
evil purpose. Most Haitians believe in zombies,
and Narcisse's claim is not unique. At about the
time he reappeared, in 1980, two women turned
up in other villages saying they were zombies. In
the same year, in northern Haiti, the local peasants claimed to have found a group of zombies
wandering aimlessly in the fields.

But Narcisse's case was different in one crucial respect; it was documented. His death had
been recorded by doctors at the American-
directed Schweitzer Hospital in Deschapelles.
On April 30, 1962, hospital records show, Narcisse walked into the hospital's emergency room

spitting up blood. He was feverish and full of aches. His doctors could not diagnose his illness, and his symptoms grew steadily worse. Three days after he entered the hospital, according to the records, he died. The attending physicians, an American among them, signed his death certificate. His body was placed in cold storage for twenty hours, and then he was buried. He said he remembered hearing his doctors pronounce him dead while his sister wept at his bedside.

At the Centre de Psychiatrie et Neurologie in Port-au-Prince, Dr. Lamarque Douyon, a Haitian-born Canadian-trained psychiatrist, has been systematically investigating all reports of zombies since 1961. Though convinced zombies were real, he had been unable to find a scientific explanation for the phenomenon. He did not believe zombies were people raised from the dead, but that did not make them any less interesting. He speculated that victims were only made to *look* dead, probably by means of a drug that dramatically slowed metabolism. The victim was buried, dug up within a few hours, and somehow reawakened.

The Narcisse case provided Douyon with evidence strong enough to warrant a request for assistance from colleagues in New York. Douyon wanted to find an ethnobotanist, a traditional-medicines expert, who could track down the zombie potion he was sure existed. Aware of the medical potential of a drug that could dramatically lower metabolism, a group organized by the late Dr. Nathan Kline—a New York psychiatrist and pioneer in the field of psychopharmacology—raised the funds necessary to send someone to investigate.

The search for that someone led to the Harvard Botanical Museum, one of the world's foremost institutes of ethnobiology. Its director, Richard Evans Schultes, Jeffrey professor of biology, had spent thirteen years in the tropics studying native medicines. Some of his best-known work is the investigation of curare, the substance used by the nomadic people of the Amazon to poison their darts. Refined into a powerful muscle relaxant called D-tubocurarine, it is now an essential component of the anesthesia used during almost all surgery.

Schultes would have been a natural for the Haitian investigation, but he was too busy. He recommended another Harvard ethnobotanist for the assignment, Wade Davis, a 28-year-old Canadian pursuing a doctorate in biology.

Davis grew up in the tall pine forests of British Columbia and entered Harvard in 1971, influenced by a *Life* magazine story on the student strike of 1969. Before Harvard, the only Americans he had known were draft dodgers, who seemed very exotic. "I used to fight forest fires with them," Davis says. "Like everybody else, I thought America was where it was at. And I wanted to go to Harvard because of that *Life* article. When I got there, I realized it wasn't quite what I had in mind."

Davis took a course from Schultes, and when he decided to go to South America to study plants, he approached his professor for guidance. "He was an extraordinary figure," Davis remembers. "He was a man who had done it all. He had lived alone for years in the Amazon." Schultes sent Davis to the rain forest with two letters of introduction and two pieces of advice: wear a pith helmet and try ayahuasca, a powerful hallucinogenic wine. During that expedition and others, Davis proved himself an "outstanding field man," says his mentor. Now, in early 1982, Schultes called him into his office and asked if he had plans for spring break.

"I always took to Schultes's assignments like a plant takes to water," says Davis, tall and blond, with inquisitive blue eyes. "Whatever Shultes told me to do, I did. His letters of introduction opened up a whole world." This time the world was Haiti.

Davis knew nothing about the Caribbean island—and nothing about African traditions, which serves as Haiti's cultural basis. He certainly did not believe in zombies. "I thought it was a lark," he says now.

Davis landed in Haiti a week after his conversation with Schultes, armed with a hypothesis about how the zombie drug—if it existed—might be made. Setting out to explore, he discovered a country materially impoverished, but rich in culture and mystery. He was impressed by the cohesion of Haitian society; he found none of the crime, social disorder, and rampant drug and alcohol abuse so common in many of the other Caribbean islands. The cultural wealth and cohesion, he believes, spring from the country's turbulent history.

During the French occupation of the late eighteenth century, 370,000 African-born slaves were imported to Haiti between 1780 and 1790. In 1791, the black population launched one of the few successful slave revolts in history, forming secret societies and overcoming first the French plantation owners and then a detachment of troops from

Napoleon's army, sent to quell the revolt. For the next hundred years Haiti was the only independent black republic in the Caribbean, populated by people who did not forget their African heritage. "You can almost argue that Haiti is more African than Africa," Davis says. "When the west coast of Africa was being disrupted by colonialism and the slave trade, Haiti was essentially left alone. The amalgam of beliefs in Haiti is unique, but it's very, very African."

Davis discovered that the vast majority of Haitian peasants practice voodoo, a sophisticated religion with African roots. Says Davis, "It was immediately obvious that the stereotypes of voodoo weren't true. Going around the countryside, I found clues to a whole complex social world." Vodounists believe they communicate directly with, indeed are often possessed by, the many spirits who populate the everyday world. Vodoun society is a system of education, law, and medicine; it embodies a code of ethics that regulates social behavior. In rural areas, secret vodoun societies, much like those found on the west coast of Africa, are as much or more in control of everyday life as the Haitian government.

Although most outsiders dismissed the zombie phenomenon as folklore, some early investigators, convinced of its reality, tried to find a scientific explanation. The few who sought a zombie drug failed. Nathan Kline, who helped finance Davis's expedition, had searched unsuccessfully, as had Lamarque Douyon, the Haitian psychiatrist. Zora Neale Hurston, an American black woman, may have come closest. An anthropological pioneer, she went to Haiti in the Thirties, studied vodoun society, and wrote a book on the subject, *Tell My Horse*, first published in 1938. She knew about the secret societies and was convinced zombies were real, but if a powder existed, she too failed to obtain it.

David obtained a sample in a few weeks.

He arrived in Haiti with the names of several contacts. A BBC reporter familiar with the Narcisse case had suggested he talk with Marcel Pierre. Pierre owned the Eagle Bar, a bordello in the city of Saint Marc. He was also a voodoo sorcerer and had supplied the BBC with a physiologically active powder of unknown ingredients. Davis found him willing to negotiate. He told Pierre he was a representative of "powerful but anonymous interests in New York," willing to pay generously for the priest's services, provided no questions were asked. Pierre agreed to be helpful for what Davis will only say was a "sizable sum." Davis spent a day watching Pierre gather the ingredients—including human bones—and grind them together with mortar and pestle. However, from his knowledge of poison, Davis knew immediately that nothing in the formula could produce the powerful effects of zombification.

Three weeks later, Davis went back to the Eagle Bar, where he found Pierre sitting with three associates. Davis challenged him. He called him a charlatan. Enraged, the priest gave him a second vial, claiming that this was the real poison. Davis pretended to pour the powder into his palm and rub it into his skin. "You're a dead man," Pierre told him, and he might have been, because this powder proved to be genuine. But, as the substance had not actually touched him, Davis was able to maintain his bravado, and Pierre was impressed. He agreed to make the poison and show Davis how it was done.

The powder, which Davis keeps in a small vial, looks like dry black dirt. It contains parts of toads, sea worms, lizards, tarantulas, and human bones. (To obtain the last ingredient, he and Pierre unearthed a child's grave on a nocturnal trip to the cemetery.) The poison is rubbed into the victim's skin. Within hours he begins to feel nauseated and has difficulty breathing. A pins-and-needles sensation afflicts his arms and legs, then progresses to the whole body. The subject becomes paralyzed; his lips turn blue for lack of oxygen. Quickly—sometimes within six hours—his metabolism is lowered to a level almost indistinguishable from death.

As Davis discovered, making the poison is an inexact science. Ingredients varied in the five samples he eventually acquired, although the active agents were always the same. And the poison came with no guarantee. Davis speculates that sometimes instead of merely paralyzing the victim, the compound kills him. Sometimes the victim suffocates in the coffin before he can be resurrected. But clearly the potion works well enough to make zombies more than a figment of Haitian imagination.

Analysis of the powder produced another surprise. "When I went down to Haiti originally," says Davis, "my hypothesis was that the formula would contain *concombre zombi*, the 'zombie's cucumber,' which is a *Datura* plant. I thought somehow *Datura* was used in putting people down." *Datura* is a powerful psychoactive plant, found in West Africa as well as other tropical areas and used there in ritual as well as criminal activities. Davis had found *Datura* growing in Haiti. Its popular name suggested the plant was used in creating zombies.

But, says Davis, "there were a lot of problems with the *Datura* hypothesis. Partly it was a question of how the drug was administered. *Datura* would create a stupor in huge doses, but it just wouldn't produce the kind of immobility that was key. These people had to appear dead, and there aren't many drugs that will do that."

One of the ingredients Pierre included in the second formula was a dried fish, a species of puffer or blowfish, common to most parts of the world. It gets its name from its ability to fill itself with water and swell to several times its normal size when threatened by predators. Many of these fish contain a powerful poison known as tetrodotoxin. One of the most powerful nonprotein poisons known to man, tetrodotoxin turned up in every sample of zombie powder that Davis acquired.

Numerous well-documented accounts of puffer fish poisoning exist, but the most famous accounts come from the Orient, where *fugu* fish, a species of puffer, is considered a delicacy. In Japan, special chefs are licensed to prepare *fugu*. The chef removes enough poison to make the fish nonlethal, yet enough remains to create exhilarating physiological effects—tingles up and down the spine, mild prickling of the tongue and lips, euphoria. Several dozen Japanese die each year, having bitten off more than they should have.

"When I got hold of the formula and saw it was the *fugu* fish, that suddenly threw open the whole Japanese literature," says Davis. Case histories of *fugu* poisoning read like accounts of zombification. Victims remain conscious but unable to speak or move. A man who had "died" after eating *fugu* recovered seven days later in the morgue. Several summers ago, another Japanese poisoned by *fugu* revived after he was nailed into his coffin. "Almost all of Narcisse's symptoms correlated. Even strange things such as the fact that he said he was conscious and could hear himself pronounced dead. Stuff that I thought had to be magic, that seemed crazy. But, in fact, that is what people who get *fugu*-fish poisoning experience."

Davis was certain he had solved the mystery. But far from being the end of his investigation,

identifying the poison was, in fact, its starting point. "The drug alone didn't make zombies," he explains. "Japanese victims of puffer-fish poisoning don't become zombies, they become poison victims. All the drug could do was set someone up for a whole series of pyschological pressures that would be rooted in the culture. I wanted to know why zombification was going on," he says.

He sought a cultural answer, an explanation rooted in the structure and beliefs of Haitian society. Was zombification simply a random criminal activity? He thought not. He had discovered that Clairvius Narcisse and "Ti Femme," a second victim he interviewed, were village pariahs. Ti Femme was regarded as a thief. Narcisse had abandoned his children and deprived his brother of land that was rightfully his. Equally suggestive, Narcisse claimed that his aggrieved brother had sold him to a *bokor*, a voodoo priest who dealt in black magic; he made cryptic reference to having been tried and found guilty by the "masters of the land."

Gathering poisons from various parts of the country, Davis had come into direct contact with the vodoun secret societies. Returning to the anthropological literature on Haiti and pursuing his contacts with informants, Davis came to understand the social matrix within which zombies were created.

Davis's investigations uncovered the importance of the secret societies. These groups trace their origins to the bands of escaped slaves that organized the revolt against the French in the late eighteenth century. Open to both men and women, the societies control specific territories of the country. Their meetings take place at night, and in many rural parts of Haiti the drums and wild celebrations that characterized the gatherings can be heard for miles.

Davis believes the secret societies are responsible for policing their communities, and the threat of zombification is one way they maintain order. Says Davis, "Zombification has a material basis, but it also has a societal logic." To the uninitiated, the practice may appear a random criminal activity, but in rural vodoun society, it is exactly the opposite—a sanction imposed by recognized authorities, a form of capital punishment. For rural Haitians, zombification is an even more severe punishment than death, because it deprives the subject of his most valued possessions: his free will and independence.

The vodounists believe that when a person dies, his spirit splits into several different parts. If a priest is powerful enough, the spiritual aspect that controls a person's character and individuality, known as *ti bon ange*, the "good little angel," can be captured and the corporeal aspect, deprived of its will, held as a slave.

From studying the medical literature on tetrodotoxin poisoning, Davis discovered that if a victim survives the first few hours of the poisoning, he is likely to recover fully from the ordeal. The subject simply revives spontaneously. But zombies remain without will, in a trance-like state, a condition vodounists attribute to the power of the priest. Davis thinks it possible that the psychological trauma of zombification may be augmented by *Datura* or some other drug; he thinks zombies may be fed a *Datura* paste that accentuates their disorientation. Still, he puts the material basis of zombification in perspective: "Tetrodotoxin and *Datura* are only templates on which cultural forces and beliefs may be amplified a thousand times."

Davis has not been able to discover how prevalent zombification is in Haiti. "How many zombies there are is not the question," he says. He compares it to capital punishment in the United States: "It doesn't really matter how many people are electrocuted, as long as it's a possibility." As a sanction in Haiti, the fear is not of zombies, it's of becoming one.

Davis attributes his success in solving the zombie mystery to his approach. He went to Haiti with an open mind and immersed himself in the cultrue. "My intuition unhindered by biases served me well," he says. "I didn't make any judgments." He combined this attitude with what he had learned earlier from his experiences in the Amazon. "Schultes's lesson is to go and live with the Indians as an Indian." Davis was able to participate in the vodoun society to a surprising degree, eventually even penetrating one of the Bizango societies and dancing in their nocturnal rituals. His appreciation of Haitian culture is apparent. "Everybody asks me how did a white person get this information? To ask the question means you don't understand Haitians—they don't judge you by the color of your skin."

As a result of the exotic nature of his discoveries, Davis has gained certain notoriety. He plans to complete his dissertation soon, but he has already finished writing a popular account of his adventures. To be published in January by Simon and Schuster, it is called *The Serpent and the Rainbow*, after the serpent that vodounists believe created the earth and the rainbow spirit it married. Film rights have already been optioned; in October Davis went back to Haiti with a screenwriter. But Davis takes the notoriety in stride. "All this attention is funny," he says. "For years, not just me, but all Schultes's students have had extraordinary adventures in the line of work. The adventure is not the end point, it's just along the way of getting the data. At the Botanical Museum, Schultes created a world unto itself. We didn't think we were doing anything above the ordinary. I still don't think we do. And you know," he adds, "the Haiti episode does not begin to compare to what others have accomplished—particularly Schultes himself."

Death Be Not Strange

Peter A. Metcalf

In this article Peter A. Metcalf compares American and Berawan funeral and mortuary rites and shows why Western practices so shocked the Berawan. To the Berawan we trap the deceased in a suspended condition between life and death, producing evil, not beneficent spirits. "For the Berawan, America is a land carpeted with potential zombies." Metcalf's field work not only explains the fate of the Berawan dead and demonstrates their beliefs to be as coherent and reasonable as any, but also draws attention to the exotic nature of American funerary practices. His comparison reminds us that our level of ethnocentrism both leads us to view the beliefs of others as illogical and sometimes reprehensible and causes us to ignore our own death rituals and practices.

THE POPULAR VIEW OF ANTHROPOLOGY IS THAT it is concerned with faraway places, strange peoples, and odd customs. This notion was neatly captured by a nineteenth-century wit who described the field as "the pursuit of the exotic by the eccentric." In recent decades many anthropologists have tried to shake this image. They see the exotic as dangerously close to the sensational and, therefore, a threat to the respectability of a serious academic discipline. They argue that anthropology has solid theoretical bases, and that some anthropologists routinely work in cities right here in America. And they are right. Nevertheless, anthropologists are as much involved with the exotic as ever, and I think that this concern actually works to scholarship's advantage.

This continuing involvement is a result of the characteristic *modus operandi* of anthropologists. First, we seek out the exotic, in the sense of something originating in another country or something "strikingly or excitingly different," as my *Webster's* puts it. Second, we try to fit this alien item—culture trait, custom, piece of behavior—into its social and cultural context, thereby reducing it to a logical, sensible, even necessary element. Having done that, we feel that we can understand why people do or say or think something instead of being divorced from them by what they say, think, or do.

Sir James Frazer, whose classic study of primitive religions *The Golden Bough*, was first published in 1890, provides an excellent example of the eccentric in pursuit of the exotic. For him, the process of reducing the mysterious to the commonplace was the very hallmark of scientific progress. Like many anthropologists of his time, Frazer assumed that some societies were superior and others inferior, and that anthropology's main task was to describe how the latter had evolved into the former. To Frazer, Europe's technological achievements were proof of social, intellectual, and moral superiority. The dominance of the West represented the triumph of science, which in Frazer's evolutionary schema, superseded even the most rational of world religions. Science's clear light was to shine far and wide, driving superstition, the supernatural, and even God himself back into shadows and dimly lit corners.

But Frazer might have found a second aspect of the anthropological *modus operandi* less to his taste. In the course of making sense of someone else's behavior or ideas, we frequently begin to observe our own customs from a new angle. Indeed, this reflexive objectivity is often acclaimed as one of the great advantages of our methods and cited as a major justification for the long, expensive physical and psychic journeys that we make, seeking out societies far removed from our own cultural traditions. Less often remarked upon, however, is that the exotic possesses its own reflexive quality. As we learn to think of other people's ways as natural, we simultaneously begin to see our own as strange. In this sense, anthropologists import the exotic, and that, I suppose, puts us on the side of the angels.

An incident that occurred about four years ago during my fieldwork in north-central Borneo brought home to me the depth and subtlety of anthropologists' involvement with the exotic. I was working with the Berawan, a small tribe comprising four communities, each made up of several hundred people living in a massive wooden longhouse. The four longhouses stand beside the great rivers that are the only routes into the interior of Borneo. Berawan communities live on fish and on rice planted in clearings cut anew in the rain forest each year. In the late nineteenth century, which was a stormy period of tribal warfare, each longhouse was a fortress as well as a home, and the Berawan look back with pride on the military traditions of that era.

Among the things that interested me about the Berawan were their funeral rites, which involve what anthropologists call "secondary burial," although the Berawan do not usually bury the dead at all. Full rites consist of four stages: the first and third involve ritual preparation of the corpse; the second and fourth make up steps in storage of the remains. The first stage, lasting two to ten days, consists of rites performed immediately after death. During the second stage, the bereaved family stores the corpse in the longhouse or on a simple platform in the graveyard. This storage lasts at least eight months and sometimes for several years if the close kin cannot immediately afford to complete the expensive final stages. Third, if the corpse has been in the graveyard, the family brings it back to the longhouse, where it is kept for six to ten days, while the family lavishly entertains guests who have been summoned from far and wide. Finally, the remains are removed to a final resting place, an impressively proportioned mausoleum.

Within this four-part plan, details of the corpse's treatment vary considerably. During the first storage stage, the family may place the corpse in a large earthenware jar or in a massive coffin hewn from a single tree trunk. For secondary storage, the family may use a valuable glazed jar or the coffin left over from the first stage. During the third-stage rites, the family may take out the bones of the deceased and clean them. As the corpse decomposes, its secretions may be collected in a special vessel. Some neighbors of the Berawan reportedly consume liquids of decomposition mixed with rice—a variety of endocannibalism.

For anthropologists, this intimate interaction with the corpse is certainly exotic. For Americans not professionally trained in the niceties of cultural relativism, Berawan burial is no doubt disgusting: keeping corpses around the house, shuttling them between the graveyard and the longhouse, storing them aboveground instead of burying them, manipulating the bones, and, to Western eyes, paying macabre attention to the process of decay itself. My Berawan informants were aware that some phases of their ritual bothered Europeans. They soon learned, moreover, that I had a lot of questions about their funerals. One of the pleasures of working in Borneo is that people soon begin to cross-examine their interviewer. They are as curious about the stranger as he or she is about them. So before long, they began to quiz me about the death ways of my country.

On one memorable occasion, during a lull in ritual activity, I responded to one of these questions by outlining American embalming practices—the treatment of the corpse with preservative fluids and its display in an open coffin. I was well into my story, concentrating on finding the right words to describe this unfamiliar topic, when I became aware that a sudden silence had fallen over my audience. They asked a number of hesitant questions just to be sure that they had understood me correctly and drew away from me in disgust when they found that they had. So shocked were they that I had to backtrack rapidly and change my story. The topic was never broached again.

At the time, I did not understand why American embalming practices had so unnerved the Berawan. Now, having thought about the meaning of Berawan death rituals, I think that I do understand.

The death rituals of central Borneo early attracted the interest of explorers and ethnologists. In 1907, Robert Hertz, a young student of French sociologist Emile Durkheim, wrote an essay about these rites that has become a classic. Never having set foot in Borneo, Hertz relied on the accounts of travelers. Had he not been killed during the First World War, he might well have undertaken first-hand research himself. Nevertheless, his analysis is still routinely cited in discussions and comparisons of funeral customs. Yet, oddly, Hertz's central thesis has received very little attention. Hertz hypothesized that peoples who practice secondary burial have certain beliefs about the afterlife, namely, that the fate of the body provides a model for the fate of the soul.

Since Hertz did not know of the Berawan, they provided me with an appropriate test case for his hypothesis. I collected data on everything related to Berawan death rites: the people involved, mourning practices, related rituals, myths and beliefs, and so on. I also pressed my informants for interpretations of rituals. All the material I accumulated revealed a consistent set of ideas very similar to those described by Hertz. The Berawan believe that after death the soul is divorced from the body and cannot reanimate the already decaying corpse. However, the soul cannot enter the land of the dead because it is not yet a perfect spirit. To become one of the truly dead, it must undergo a metamorphosis. As the body rots away to leave dry bones, so the soul is transformed slowly into spirit form. As the corpse is formless and repulsive until putrefaction is completed, so the soul is homeless. It lurks miserably on the fringes of human habitation and, in its discomfort, may affect the living with illness. The third stage of the mortuary sequence, which Hertz called the "great feast," marks the end of this miserable period. The soul finally passes to the land of the dead, and the mortal remains of the deceased join those of its ancestors in the tomb.

But before this happy conclusion is reached, the hovering soul is feared because it may cause more death. Even more dread surrounds the body itself, caused not by the process of rotting, for that releases the soul of the deceased from the bonds of the flesh, but by the possibility that some malignant spirit of nonhuman origin will succeed in reanimating the corpse. Should this occur, the result will be a monster of nightmarish mien, invulnerable to the weapons of men, since it is already dead.

I once witnessed an incident that dramatically demonstrated how real is the Berawan fear of reanimated corpses. Toward sunset, a group of mourners and guests were chatting casually beside a coffin that was being displayed on the longhouse veranda in preparation for primary storage. Suddenly there was a tapping sound, apparently from inside the coffin. The noise could have come from the house timbers, contracting in the cool of the evening, but the people present saw a different explanation. After a moment of shock, the women fled, carrying their children. Some panic-stricken men grabbed up what weapons were handy, while others tied up the coffin lid with yet more bands of rattan. Calm was not restored until later in the evening when a shaman investigated and declared that nothing was amiss.

We can now see why American mortuary practices so shock the Berawan. By delaying the decomposition of corpses, we commit a most unnatural act. First, we seem to be trying to trap our nearest and dearest in the unhappiest condition possible, neither alive nor in the radiant land of the dead. Second, and even more perverse and terrifying, we keep an army of undecomposed corpses, each and every one subject to reanimation by a host of evil spirits. For the Berawan, America is a land carpeted with potential zombies.

After a couple of years of field work, and an application of the ideas of Hertz and others, I can offer a relatively full account of Berawan death ways: what they express about Berawan notions of life and death; how they are manipulated by influential men in their struggles for power; how they relate to their sense of identity, art forms, and oral history. Meanwhile, I have also explored the literature on American death ways—and have found it wanting. For the most part, it is restricted to consideration of psychological variables—how people react to death, either the possibility of their own or that of close relatives and friends. None of these studies begins to explain why American funerals are the way they are; why they differ from British funerals, for instance.

Jessica Mitford, author of *The American Way of Death*, tried to explain the form that American funerals take by arguing that they are a product of the death industry's political power. But Mitford's theory does not explain the tacit support that Americans give to this institution, why successive immigrant groups have adopted it, or why reform movements have failed.

I have tried to relate American practices to popular ideas about the nature of a fulfilling life and a proper death. Despite these intellectual efforts, I am left with a prickly sense of estrangement. For, in fact, I had spared my Berawan friends the more gruesome details of embalming: replacement of the blood with perfumed formaldehyde and other chemicals; removal of the soft organs of the chest and abdomen via a long hollow needle attached to a vacuum pump; injection of inert materials. I did not mention the American undertaker's elaborate restorative techniques: the stitching up of mutilated corpses, plumping out of emaciated corpses with extra injections of waxes, or careful cosmetic care of hands and face. Nor did I tell the Berawan about the padded coffins, grave clothes ranging in style from business suits to negligees, and other funeral paraphernalia. Had I explained all this, their shock might have been transformed into curiosity, and they might have reversed our roles of social scientist and informant.

In the meantime, something of their reaction has rubbed off on me. I have reduced the celebrated mortuary rites of remote and mysterious Borneo to a kind of workaday straightforwardness, only to be struck by the exotic character of an institution in our very midst.

9

Old and New Religions: The Search for Salvation

Anthropologists have long studied cultural stability and change and agree that all cultures have continuous change, although the rate of change can vary dramatically. Whereas American society has an unmatched cultural dynamism, other cultures change so gradually as to appear static. The types and rates of cultural changes are functions of many factors originating from within the society itself or from external pressures and influences.

Internal conditions affecting the rate of change include the relative degree of cultural receptivity to new ideas, the amount of freedom of inquiry and competition, the degree of cultural elaboration, the population size and density, the presence of innovators and inventors, and—perhaps most important—the degree of harmony between cultural and social values. Among the external conditions affecting culture change, the degree of contact with other groups is the outstanding factor (Malefijt 1968: 329).

Protective mask from the Sepik River region, New Guinea.

What anthropologists have discovered is that religious change occurs for the same reasons as general culture change and, as is the case with change generally, religious change is both continuous and universal.

One of the most dramatic classes of change, and one that has strong religious content, is what Anthony F. C. Wallace termed "revitalization movements": "a deliberate, organized, conscious effort by members of society to construct a more satisfying culture" (1956: 265). This chapter presents three examples of revitalization movements (Wallace writes of nativism and revivalism and Worsley of cargo cults), and Wallace (1956) outlined several other major types of revitalization movements that are clearly religious in nature (vitalistic movements, millenarian movements, and messianic movements). It is important to recognize that these kinds of cultural change phenomena are not mutually exclusive; several may be at work within a single society at any one time, all simultaneously contributing to change in the cultural gestalt. Wallace's article, for example, combines nativism and revivalism, but there are cases in which these types of changes in a single society are accompanied by messianic and millenarian movements as well. All revitalization movements have in common a reactionary character; all are the result of real or imagined conditions that create a demand for change.

Wallace's categories and definitions have been broadly accepted. Nativistic movements are characterized by a strong emphasis on the elimination of alien persons, customs, values, and material from the "mazeway," which Wallace defines as the mental image an individual has of the society and its culture, as well as of his own body and its behavior regularities, in order to act in ways to reduce stress at all levels of the system. Revivalistic movements emphasize the readoption of customs, values, and even aspects of nature in the mazeway of previous generations. Cargo cults emphasize the importation of alien values, customs, and material into the mazeway, these being expected to arrive, metaphorically, as a ship's cargo. Vitalistic movements also emphasize the importation of alien elements into the mazeway, although not via a cargo mechanism. Millenarian movements emphasize changes in the mazeway through an apocalyptic world transformation en-

gineered by the supernatural. Messianic movements emphasize the actual participation of a divine savior in human flesh in bringing about desired changes in the mazeway (1956: 267). (This categorization of revitalization movements, however, is only one of many schemes used by ethnographers, and as John Collins has noted, "any such scheme, basically, is merely a device to initiate thought and comparison" [1978: 137]).

The religious nature of revitalization in the non-Western world, particularly in Melanesia, is made clear not only by the expectation of a messiah and the millennium in some of the movements, but also by the very structure of movement phenomena, in which prophets play an indispensable role. I. C. Jarvie maintains that the religious character of these movements may be explained by the fact that traditional institutions are not able to adopt and respond to social changes, and that the only new organizational system offered these societies by European colonialists is Christianity. Melanesians, for example, have learned more about organization from religion than from any other foreign institution, and it is logical for them to mold revitalization movements in religious form in order to accommodate, indeed combat, the impact of Eurpean society (1970: 412–13).

Revitalization in the broad sense of bringing new vigor and happiness to society is certainly not restricted to traditional groups or to the religious realm. Edward Sapir, for example, spoke of cultures "genuine" and "spurious": in the former, individuals felt well integrated into their culture, and in the latter they experienced alienation from the mainstream of society. Examples of attempts to change Western cultures abound. Political and economic conditions have frequently moved modern prophets to seek power to change, sometimes radically, the institutional structure and goals of society.

Throughout the readings in this chapter, reference is frequently made to cults and sects. These are terms that have been used in the anthropology and sociology of religion to describe particular types of religious organizations. Typically, the word *church* is applied to the larger community's view of the acceptable type of religious organization, whereas the term *sect* is used to refer to a protest group. Sects are generally small, express defiance of the world, or sometimes withdrawal from the world. Sect members are strict believers who usually experience some sort of conversion experience before becoming members. Bryan Wilson (1959, 1961) has described four different types of sects based on their ideologies: (1) the conversionist sect is hopeful of converting others; (2) the adventist sect anticipates a drastic divine intervention; (3) the introversionist sect is very pious and eager to develop its inner spirituality; and (4) the gnostic sect possesses esoteric religious knowledge. The word *cult* is not as clearly defined as sect and church, and appears to refer to a more casual, loosely organized group. Cults seem to have a fluctuating membership whose allegiance can be shared with other religious organizations. (It is well to remember, however, that the terms *church*, *sect*, and *cult* are best seen as scholarly descriptions of ideal, theoretical concepts).

During the last decade this country has witnessed an immense growth in the number of religious cults. The Children of God, Hare Krishna, the followers of Bhagwan Shree Rajneesh, the Maharaj Ji's Divine Light Mission, and, of course, the largest and most controversial group of all, the Reverend Sun Myung Moon's Unification Church, are a few examples of groups that have attracted thousands disenchanted with traditional religious organizations. The history of the world is replete with examples of new religious groups springing to life as spiritually dissatisfied peoples seek alternatives to traditional religious organizations.

What appeal do these movements have for people? What social forces underlie the development and rapid growth of religious movements? Many sociological and psychological analyses have attempted to answer these important questions (see especially Glock and Stark, 1965; Eister, 1972; Zaretsky and Leone, 1974; Talmon, 1969). Briefly, these studies draw a picture of people who have become attracted to cults because of such lures as love, security, acceptance, and improved personal status. Unstable and rapidly changing social and political situations in contemporary technological countries also provide a rich seedbed for the emergence and blossoming of religious movements. Charles Y. Glock (1964) has listed five types of deprivation that may result in the establishment of a new sect or that may lead individuals to join one: (1) *economic* deprivation, which is suffered by people who make less money, have fewer material goods, and are financially beholden to others; (2) *organismic* deprivation, which applies to those who may exhibit physical, mental, and nutritional problems; (3) *ethical* deprivation, which grows out of a perceived discrepancy between the real and the ideal; (4) *psychic* deprivation, which can result in the search for meaning and new values (and which is related to the search for closure and simplicity); and (5) *social* deprivation, which results from a society's valuation of some individuals and their attributes over others.

The articles in this chapter have been selected to demonstrate how religion can help people living in cultures undergoing sudden and disruptive social change. The selections also show the wide extent of ritual used by religious groups in their quest and deep longing for holiness. Anthony F. C. Wallace describes revivalistic and nativistic movements, using as examples the Ghost Dance of 1890 among certain North American Indian tribes and the Paliau Movement in the Admiralty Islands. Peter Worsley points out that throughout history people who have felt themselves to be oppressed and deceived have always been ready to pour their hopes and fears into a belief in a coming golden age. Worsley's article describes a cargo cult, a revitalization movement among the peoples of New Guinea and adjacent islands. Mary Lee Daugherty discusses serpent handlers in West Virginia, who base their particular religious practice on the Gospel of Mark: "they shall speak with new tongues; they shall take up serpents."

In the final article, "Rajneeshpuram: The Boom and Bust of a Buddhafield," James Myers describes the story of Bhagwan Shree Rajneesh, a controversial Indian spiritual leader with a worldwide following. The focus of the selection is on the political and religious dynamics involved in the rise and fall of a Rajneesh-inspired commune in eastern Oregon during the years 1981 to 1985.

References

Collins, John J.
  1978 *Primitive Religion*. Totowa, N.J.: Rowman and Littlefield.

Eister, Allen
  1972 "An Outline of a Structural Theory of Cults." *Journal for the Scientific Study of Religion* 11: 319–33.

Glock, Charles Y.
  1964 "The Role of Deprivation in the Origin and Evolution of Religious Groups." In R. Lee and M. E. Marty, eds., *Religion and Social Conflict*. New York: Oxford University Press.

Glock, Charles Y., and Rodney Stark
  1965 *Religion and Society in Tension*. Chicago: Rand McNally.

Jarvie, I. C.
  1970 "Cargo Cults." In Richard Cavendish, ed., *Man, Myth and Magic*, pp. 409–12. New York: Marshall Cavendish Corporation.

Malefijt, Annemarie de Waal
  1968 *Religion and Culture: An Introduction to Anthropology of Religion*. New York: Macmillan.

Sapir, E.
  1924 "Culture, Genuine and Spurious." *American Journal of Sociology* 29: 401–29.

Talmon, Yonina
  1969 "Pursuit of the Millennium: The Relation Between Religious and Social Change." In Norman Birnbaum and Gertrude Lenzer, eds., *Sociology and Religion: A Book of Readings*. Englewood Cliffs, N.J.: Prentice-Hall.

Wallace, A. F. C.
  1956 "Revitalization Movements." *American Anthropologist* 58: 264–81.

Wilson, Bryan R.
  1959 "Role Conflicts and Status Contradictions of the Pentecostal Minister." *American Journal of Sociology* 64: 494–504.
  1961 *Sects and Society: A Sociological Study of the Elim Tabernacle, Christian Science, and Christadelphians*. Berkeley, Calif.: University of California Press.

Zaretsky, Irving S., and Mark P. Leone, eds.
  1974 *Religious Movements in Contemporary America*. Princeton, N.J.: Princeton University Press.

Nativism and Revivalism

Anthony F. C. Wallace

As a social movement, nativism and revivalism have the goal of reconstituting a way of life that has been destroyed for one reason or another and retaliating against the group responsible for the loss. In this selection Anthony F. C. Wallace explores the history of the concept, the four major schools of thought concerning the conditions under which these movements arise, and the current status of research that seeks to explain them. Finally, Wallace offers two examples of revivalistic and nativistic movements: the Ghost Dance of 1890 among the Plains Indians of North America and the Paliau movement in the Admiralty Islands of Melanesia following World War II. Wallace's article is an excellent selection to show how people use religious principles to cope with a cultural crisis that has prevented them from achieving a more satisfying culture.

NATIVISM AND REVIVALISM ARE TWO FORMS OF social movements. Like several other forms of social movements—such as millenarianism, cargo cults, and utopian communities—revivalism and nativism have been considered to be aspects of the same class of phenomena. This larger class has been termed "revitalization movement" and has been defined as a conscious, deliberate, organized effort on the part of some members of a society to create a more satisfying culture. In revivalism, the aim of the movement is to return to a former era of happiness, to restore a golden age, to revive a previous condition of social virtue. In nativism, the aim of the movement is to purge the society of unwanted aliens, of cultural elements of foreign origin, or of both. Frequently, a movement is both revivalistic and nativistic.

The term nativism has also been used to refer not to social movements but to a widespread attitude in a society of rejection of alien persons or culture. In this second sense of the term, nativism is a form of utopian thought (Mannheim 1929–1931). It is thus comparable to such popular beliefs as faith in the existence of a land without evil, or in the ultimate arrival of a messiah or mahdi, or in the coming of a millennium or of the ancestors with cargo. All of these beliefs are pervasive "myth-dreams" (Burridge 1960), which suffuse a society or culture area over considerable periods of time; but although the code of a movement may incorporate such a myth-dream, the myth-dream, as well as the general social policy, of nativism, millennial expectation, revivalistic nostalgia, etc., does not in itself constitute a movement.

Natural History

Revivalistic, nativistic, and other kinds of revitalization movements have been generally observed to go through certain processual stages. These stages, if effectively fulfilled, are characterized by the initiation of certain functional tasks without which the movement cannot achieve its aim, the transformation of society. Manifestly, all movements do not complete the cycle, sometimes because the movement is suppressed by force, because its millenarianism or messianic hopes are disappointed, or because it cannot attract or retain a sufficient membership. The successful movement, however, passes through the following stages:

1. Premovement phase.

(a) *Steady state*. The society is satisfied with itself; no major group is experiencing sufficient stress or is sufficiently disillusioned to be seriously interested in radical change.

(b) *Period of increased individual stress*. As a consequence of one or more of many possible circumstances—depression, famine, conquest by an alien society, acculturation pressures, or whatever leads to the awareness of a growing discrepancy between life as it is and life as it could be (and is for someone else)—growing numbers of people experience psychological and physical stress.

(c) *Periods of cultural distortion*. As increasing numbers of individuals, singly and in small groups, find their situation both intolerable and without hope of relief by the use of available, culturally sanctioned means, they turn to idiosyncratic or systematically deviant means. This period of anomie (Merton 1949) leads to the distortion of the cultural fabric by the institutionalization of such socially dysfunctional customs as drug and alcoholic addictions, organized crime, excessive corruption of officials, mob violence, sabotage, and vandalism, etc.

2. Movement phase.

(d) *Prophetic formulation of a code*. A prophet formulates a code, frequently (in religious movements) as a result of a vision in which he is instructed by supernatural beings and in which he and his people are promised salvation if the instructions are followed. The code defines what is wrong with the existing culture, delineates a goal that is described as better than the existing culture (if not utopian), and outlines a cultural transfer, by the use of which the people can move

from the bad existing culture to the good future culture.

(e) *Communication*. The prophet preaches his revelation to the people, promising salvation to the convert and to the society if his code is accepted.

(f) *Organization*. Special disciples and then mass followers join the prophet. As the number of members in the group increases and as the complexity of the mission grows, a division of labor develops. Different disciples take over the responsibility for various aspects of the movement's activities.

(g) *Adaptation*. The movement will encounter resistance from vested interests. These must be either defeated in political or military combat or converted; sometimes conversion is accomplished by making modifications in the code that will remove the fears of the reluctant.

(h) *Cultural transformation*. As the whole, or a controlling portion, of the population comes to accept the new code, the system of cultural transfer, and perhaps even the goal culture, is instituted.

3. Postmovement phase.

(i) *Routinization*. Once the cultural transformation has been accomplished, or is well under way, the organizational structure is divested of executive control of many spheres of the culture and contracts, maintaining responsibility only for the maintenance of doctrine and for the performance of ritual. It thus ceases to be a movement and becomes, in effect, a church or a political party.

(j) *Steady state*. Once the cultural transformation has been accomplished and the movement's organization has been routinized in its activities, a new steady state may be said to exist. Even if the professed aim of the movement was revivalistic, this new state will almost certainly be different from the initial steady state. Now the cycle is ready to begin again.

History of the Concept

Anthropological interest in revivalistic and nativistic movements can be considered to have begun with the work of Lewis Henry Morgan. In his book

League of the Iroquois (1851), which is considered to be the first systematic ethnography of a primitive people, Morgan devoted considerable space to a study of the New Religion of Handsome Lake. This was a religious movement , beginning in 1799, that was only mildly nativistic and even more mildly revivalistic, but it did represent an effort to rebuild a healthy way of life among the reservation Iroquois of New York state. Following Morgan's work, the next major contribution was James Mooney's study of the Ghost Dance among the Plains Indians (Mooney 1896). The Ghost Dance was both enthusiastically revivalistic and vehemently nativistic.

Comparable phenomena were soon reported by anthropologists working in other parts of the world. In 1923 Williams published his study of the Vailala Madness, a cargo cult among a native people in New Guinea. Later workers have described other cargo cults in the Melanesian area and in general found them, as Williams found the Vailala Madness, to be revivalistic in native theory (in that the followers of the cult believe that they are restoring a golden age in which they will be reunited with their ancestors, and to be nativistic in social policy (in that whites are to be driven away). But inasmuch as the "cargo" is composed principally of European goods, and native goods and rituals are abandoned, both the nativistic and revivalistic aspects of cargo cults are qualified by a strong motive toward acculturation.

By the 1940s, it was possible to recognize that what were then generally called "nativistic movements" occurred within almost all of the areas of primitive culture known to anthropologists, among North and South American Indians, African Negroes, the peoples of the Pacific, and the tribal peoples of Europe and Asia as well. (The only major culture area in which revitalization movements are not known to have occurred on a wide scale is the aboriginal culture area of Australia and Tasmania.) In 1943 Ralph Linton published a brief paper on nativistic movements that served to establish the phenomenon as a special topic in anthropological studies of culture change.

Because communication among the various social science disciplines has been fitful, anthropological workers did not at first take full cognizance of studies of comparable movements by sociologists, historians, Biblical scholars, classicists, and classical archeologists. Sociologists have been concerned with such contemporary social movements in complex societies as the Father Divine cult in urban areas of the United States; historians have dealt with millenarian movements and utopian communities of the past, with major anti-Western movements in Africa (e.g., the Mahdi in Sudan) and in Asia (e.g., the Taiping Rebellion), and with the origins of the great religious and political movements in both Western and Oriental traditions; Biblical scholars have studied the origin of Christianity as a social movement; and classicists and classical archeologists have investigated the new religion of Ikhnaton in ancient Egypt and the pre-Christian Essene cult memorialized by the Dead Sea scrolls. These materials, together with anthropological observations, now make possible sophisticated field and historical studies as well as generalizations about the phenomenon of rapid culture change.

Schools of Thought

Concerning the conditions under which these movements arise, there would seem to be four major schools of thought.

The Absolute Deprivation Theory

Perhaps the most common, and least sophisticated, theory is the view that absolute deprivation, in the sense of a low material standard of living, leads to dissatisfaction with the *status quo* and eventually to the adoption of a revolutionary ideology. This viewpoint, in political application, leads to a "bread and circuses" theory of social control. Mere material deprivation, however, does not inevitably prompt the deprived to revolt: on the one hand, under some circumstances, such as war, both civilian and military personnel may maintain high morale while hungry, cold, and uncomfortable; on the other hand, the response to extreme deprivation, as in concentration camps, may be profound apathy, dependence, and suggestibility. Furthermore, it may be empirically observed that social movements sometimes occur not in the least fortunate class or nation, nor in the most, but in a middle station.

The Acculturation Theory

Many nativistic and revivalistic movements have occurred among tribal peoples in contact with

European civilization. This has sometimes led to the impression that acculturation pressure leads directly to fanatical social movements. This pressure, it is implied, produces a state of "culture shock," in which the tribal people experiences a sort of collective hysterical syndrome characterized by ecstatic, but unrealistic, commitment to a utopian social movement. The nature of the trauma inflicted by the higher civilization upon the lower may be conceived as the imposition of a competitive way of life, or as the requirement of an unfamiliar pattern of culture, or simply as interference with tradition. The code of the movement will, it is argued, represent some sort of compromise between withdrawal from, and approach to, the higher civilization. Although this viewpoint has merit as far as it goes, its relevance appears to be restricted largely to tribal populations in culture-contact situations; and even here it is only a partial explanation, since it fails to account for many kinds of social responses to acculturation pressure which are not fanatical, hysterical, or unrealistic at all, such as rationalistic political and economic movements or wholesale adoption of major portions of the higher culture.

The Social Evolutionary Theory

Scholars working in the tradition of social criticism and analysis founded by Karl Marx have pointed out that in many revivalistic and nativistic movements it is possible to discern the expression of social protest by disadvantaged classes or groups. Furthermore, the historical significance in a program of social evolution of a given kind of movement may be defined by Marxian theory. Thus, millenarian movements in early modern European history and the Taiping Rebellion in nineteenth-century China have been interpreted as premature popular protests against oppressive social conditions, and the cargo cult in Melanesia as an early, naive, supernaturalistic effort to overturn a social order that can be effectively challenged only by a more rational revolution. As Worsley (1957) has indicated, the organization and tactics of even primitive social movements can be usefully analyzed by applying the Marxist model of revolutionary procedure. The rigid application of a class-revolutionary model in an evolutionary perspective, however, can obscure both general sociopsycho-

logical principles and also particular local and temporal conditions.

The Relative Deprivation Theory

The most generally acceptable theory of revivalistic, nativistic, and other types of revitalization movement would seem to be one that recognizes, on the one hand, the influence of local and temporal circumstances and, on the other, the effect of a situation of increasing discrepancy between level of aspiration and level of realization. This theory has been called the "relative deprivation theory" (Aberle 1962). According to this view, the *content* of the movement, as expressed in the code promulgated by the prophet or other leaders, will be determined by the cultural materials locally available at the time, including in particular the myth-dream, the traditional customs of the society, and the customs of the society that may be exerting the acculturation pressure. The *occurrence or nonoccurrence and timing* of the movement will be determined by the degree of disillusionment of a significant number of members of the society with the way of life now available to them. This disillusionment must be based on an awareness of extreme discrepancy between some available image of the good life and the prevailing image of life as it is. The good life will be conceived as the life of a happier past era if present circumstances contrast unfavorably with nostalgic memory, or it will be conceived as the life of another group (a higher class, an acculturating alien society, or a foreign nation). The good life, however, generally is defined not only as a materially more comfortable existence but also as a life with self-respect and the respect of significant others. The precise moment at which the movement crystallizes is difficult to predict, and even the content is not easy to foretell in detail, because these features will be heavily determined by the knowledge, personality, and circumstances of the prophet and other leaders of the movement. Paradoxically, individual variability in society thus plays a crucial role in determining the nature and timing of a movement whose motivation derives from widespread social and cultural conditions.

Current Status of Research

There now exists a considerable literature describing nativistic, revivalistic, and similar kinds of movements, and, in view of the commonness of the phenomenon, there will be no dearth of future studies. Comparative analysis and theory, however, are slight in quantity and uneven in quality. Because there is no general consensus concerning the classification of movements, it is difficult to relate the definitive characteristics of the various types of movements to other classes of phenomena. Thus, a principal research need is the establishment of a taxonomy of social movements. Even though such a taxonomy will very likely require modification as experience with its use reveals inadequacies, it will serve to focus research problems more effectively than in the present system, which is a combination of culture area types (e.g., Melanesian cargo cults, South American *terre sans mal* migrations, Judaeo-Christian Messianic movements), and nonindependent general attributes (e.g., revivalism, nativism, millenarianism).

The technical problem in establishing a reasonable classification of revitalization movements is the same as in most areas of the social sciences: there are so many variables of interest that the inclusion of all of them in one taxonomic matrix generates a very large number of classes, each defined by a large number of criteria. Thus the investigator is forced to choose between a simple rule-of-thumb typology convenient to his own interests but of little value as an absolute classification, or a complex classification, too cumbersome for convenient use as a typology and too demanding for general use as a guide to observation. Until this problem is solved, this area of investigation, like many others in the social sciences, must remain imprecise.

Among the research questions of particular interest in the current state of understanding, the following may be mentioned.

(1) *Psychological processes*. It has been often observed that new codes formulated by prophets have a paranoid quality and that in the case of religious movements they often occur in hallucinatory visions. To what extent do "psychopathological" processes actually occur in prophets in the genesis and development of such movements? In particular, to what extent and under what conditions are the prophets and leaders of the movement necessarily dependent upon paranoid and hallucinogenic modes of thought? It has also been observed that the behavior of followers has a sug-

gestible, even hysterical, quality. Is the hysterical conversion process a necessary feature of successful social movement?

(2) *Cultural processes*. Successful revitalization movements are able to induce coordinated change in large areas of culture in a short period of time. To what extent does evolutionary culture change depend upon this rapid process, as opposed to slower processes of invention, diffusion, and acculturation? What is the relative importance of cultural syncretism and of radical innovation?

(3) *Social processes*. The social structure of revitalization movements is often inadequately described. What are the relationships among the members of the movement, and between them and nonmembers (including both potential converts and enemies)? To what extent are these relationships determined by available cultural models, and to what extent are they developed in response to the exigencies of the movement itself?

Examples

Finally, two examples of revivalistic and nativistic movements may suffice to convey the quality of these phenomena.

The Ghost Dance of 1890

Among the Plains Indians of North America during the last quarter of the nineteenth century, a religious movement emerged under the leadership of the prophet Wovoka (Mooney 1896). The central tenets of the prophet's teaching were both revivalistic and nativistic: the existing world was soon to be destroyed by fire, flood, and upheaval, and in the holocaust the intruding whites would be annihilated, and along with them those Indians who followed their ways. Salvation, however, was assured for those who participated in certain prescribed dances, who led pure lives, and who abandoned white customs and returned to Indian ways. The new world, which was to follow the apocalypse, would see America returned to the surviving "Ghost Dance" followers and to their Indian ancestors, who would lead together lives of virtue and happiness. The Ghost Dance swept across the Plains and into neighboring culture areas, with various modifications from place to place. Although the Ghost Dancers planned no violence, American frontier settlers and military authorities feared an armed uprising. These suspicions led directly to the notorious massacre at Wounded Knee, in which U.S. troops killed a band of Sioux Indians who had fled their reservation after the "medicine man," Sitting Bull, was shot while resisting arrest. Indian interest in the Ghost Dance subsided gradually in the face of white hostility and the failure of the millennium to arrive.

The Paliau Movement in the Admiralty Islands

Following World War II, the Manus, a coastal people residing near New Guinea in the Australian Trust Territory, developed a new religious, political, and economic system under the leadership of a secular prophet named Paliau (Schwartz 1962). The Paliau movement was not a cargo cult and did not aim at the categorical expulsion of all whites. It was nativistic, however, to the extent that the movement sought to secure for Melanesians a greater degree of economic and political sovereignty than they had hitherto enjoyed under either the Japanese or Australian administrations. The "New Fella Fashion," as the movement was termed in pidgin, dispensed with many of the traditional religious beliefs and observances, reorganized the settlement pattern and economy, and proposed new standards of family organization, political structure, and economic activity. In effect, the Paliau movement was an effort by a native population to bring itself into the main stream of world cultural development by a rationally conceived reorganization of its entire culture. Although Australian authorities were suspicious of Paliau, and his movement suffered administrative setbacks, and although a short-lived cargo cult temporarily interrupted its progress, the Paliau movement has survived and contributed substantially to the furtherance of the general aims of the Trust Territory itself: the development of self-respecting, self-supporting, and self-governing native communities linked to the rest of the modern world by mutually satisfying economic and political ties (Mead 1956).

Cargo Cults

Peter M. Worsley

A cargo cult, one of the several varieties of revitalization movements, is an intentional effort on the part of the members of society to create a more satisfying culture. Characteristic of revitalization movements in Melanesia, but not restricted to that area, cargo cults function to bring scattered groups together into a wider religious and political unity. These movements are the result of widespread dissatisfaction, oppression, insecurity, and the hope for fulfillment of prophecies of good times and abundance soon to come. Exposure to the cultures and material goods of the Western world, combinations of native myth with Christian teachings of the coming of a messiah, and belief in the white man's magic—all contributed to the New Guinean's faith that the "cargo" would soon arrive, bringing with it the end of the present order and the beginning of a blissful paradise. Worsley's article depicts a movement that often was so organized and persistent as to bring government work to a halt. Cargo cult movements still occur in Melanesia, where they are often intermixed with other types of revitalization movements.

PATROLS OF THE AUSTRALIAN GOVERNMENT VENturing into the "uncontrolled" central highlands of New Guinea in 1946 found the primitive people there swept up in a wave of religious excitement. Prophecy was being fulfilled: The arrival of the Whites was the sign that the end of the world was at hand. The natives proceeded to butcher all of their pigs—animals that were not only a principal source of subsistence but also symbols of social status and ritual preeminence in their culture. They killed these valued animals in expression of the belief that after three days of darkness "Great Pigs" would appear from the sky. Food, firewood, and other necessities had to be stockpiled to see the people through to the arrival of the Great Pigs. Mock wireless antennae of bamboo and rope had been erected to receive in advance the news of the millennium. Many believed that with the great event they would exchange their black skins for white ones.

This bizarre episode is by no means the single event of its kind in the murky history of the collision of European civilization with the indigenous cultures of the southwest Pacific. For more than one hundred years traders and missionaries have been reporting similar disturbances among the peoples of Melanesia, the group of Negro-inhabited islands (including New Guinea, Fiji, the Solomons, and the New Hebrides) lying between Australia and the open Pacific Ocean. Though their technologies were based largely upon stone and wood, these peoples had highly developed cultures, as measured by the standards of maritime and agricultural ingenuity, the complexity of their varied social organizations, and the elaboration of religious belief and ritual. They were nonetheless ill prepared for the shock of the encounter with the Whites, a people so radically different from themselves and so infinitely more powerful. The sudden transition from the society of the ceremonial stone ax to the society of sailing ships and now of airplanes has not been easy to make.

After four centuries of Western expansion, the densely populated central highlands of New Guinea remain one of the few regions where the people still carry on their primitive existence in complete independence of the world outside. Yet as the agents of the Australian Government penetrate into ever more remote mountain valleys, they find these backwaters of antiquity already deeply disturbed by contact with the ideas and artifacts of European civilization. For "cargo"—Pidgin English for trade goods—has long flowed along the indigenous channels of communication from the seacoast into the wilderness. With it has traveled the frightening knowledge of the white man's magical power. No small element in the white man's magic is the hopeful message sent abroad by his missionaries: the news that a Messiah will come and that the present order of Creation will end.

The people of the central highlands of New Guinea are only the latest to be gripped in the recurrent religious frenzy of the "cargo cults." However variously embellished with details from native myth and Christian belief, these cults all advance the same central theme: the world is about to end in a terrible cataclysm. Thereafter God, the ancestors, or some local culture hero will appear and inaugurate a blissful paradise on earth. Death, old age, illness, and evil will be unknown. The riches of the white man will accrue to the Melanesians.

Although the news of such a movement in one area has doubtless often inspired similar movements in other areas, the evidence indicates that these cults have arisen independently in many places as parallel responses to the same enormous social stress and strain. Among the movements best known to students of Melanesia are the "Taro Cult" of New Guinea, the "Vailala Madness" of Papua, the "Naked Cult" of Espiritu Santo, the "John Frum Movement" of the New Hebrides, and the "Tuka Cult" of the Fiji Islands.

At times the cults have been so well organized and fanatically persistent that they have brought the work of government to a standstill. The outbreaks have often taken the authorities completely by surprise and have confronted them with mass opposition of an alarming kind. In the 1930's, for example, villagers in the vicinity of Wewak, New Guinea, were stirred by a succession of "Black King" movements. The prophets announced that the Europeans would soon leave the island, abandoning their property to the natives, and urged their followers to cease paying taxes, since the government station was about to disappear into the sea in a great earthquake. To the tiny community of Whites in charge of the region, such talk was dangerous. The authorities jailed four of the prophets and exiled three others. In yet another movement, that sprang up in declared opposition to the local Christian mission, the cult leader took Satan as his god.

Troops on both sides in World War II found their arrival in Melanesia heralded as a sign of the Apocalypse. The G.I.'s who landed in the New Hebrides, moving up for the bloody fighting on Guadalcanal, found the natives furiously at work preparing airfields, roads and docks for the magic ships and planes that they believed were coming from "Rusefel" (Roosevelt), the friendly king of America.

The Japanese also encountered millenarian visionaries during their southward march to Guadalcanal. Indeed, one of the strangest minor military actions of World War II occurred in Dutch New Guinea, when Japanese forces had to be turned against the local Papuan inhabitants of the Geelvink Bay region. The Japanese had at first been received with great joy, not because their "Greater East Asia Co-Prosperity Sphere" propaganda had made any great impact upon the Papuans, but because the natives regarded them as harbingers of the new world that was dawning, the flight of the Dutch having already given the first sign. Mansren, creator of the islands and their peoples, would now return, bringing with him the ancestral dead. All this had been known, the cult leaders declared, to the crafty Dutch, who had torn out the first page of the Bible where these truths were inscribed. When Mansren returned, the existing world order would be entirely overturned. White men would turn black like Papuans, Papuans would become Whites; root crops would grow in trees, and coconuts and fruits would grow like tubers. Some of the islanders now began to draw together into large "towns"; others took Biblical names such as "Jericho" and "Galilee" for their villages. Soon they adopted military uniforms and began drilling. The Japanese, by now highly unpopular, tried to dis-arm and disperse the Papuans; resistance inevitably developed. The climax of this tragedy came when several canoe-loads of fanatics sailed out to attack Japanese warships, believing themselves to be invulnerable by virtue of the holy water with which they had sprinkled themselves. But the bullets of the Japanese did not turn to water, and the attackers were mowed down by machine-gun fire.

Behind this incident lay a long history. As long ago as 1857 missionaries in the Geelvink Bay region had made note of the story of Mansren. It is typical of many Melanesian myths that became confounded with Christian doctrine to form the ideological basis of the movements. The legend tells how long ago there lived an old man named Manamakeri ("he who itches"), whose body was covered with sores. Manamakeri was extremely fond of palm wine, and used to climb a huge tree every day to tap the liquid from the flowers. He soon found that someone was getting there before him and removing the liquid. Eventually he trapped the thief, who turned out to be none other than the Morning Star. In return for his freedom, the Star gave the old man a wand that would produce as much fish as he liked, a magic tree and a magic staff. If he drew in the sand and stamped his foot, the drawing would become real. Manamakeri, aged as he was, now magically impregnated a young maiden; the child of this union was a miracle-child who spoke as soon as he was born. But the maiden's parents were horrified, and banished her, the child, and the old man. The trio sailed off in a canoe created by Mansren ("The Lord"), as the old man now became known. On this journey Mansren rejuvenated himself by stepping into a fire and flaking off his scaly skin, which changed into valuables. He then sailed around Geelvink Bay, creating islands where he stopped, and peopling them with the ancestors of the present-day Papuans.

The Mansren myth is plainly a creation myth full of symbolic ideas relating to fertility and rebirth. Comparative evidence—especially the shedding of his scaly skin—confirms the suspicion that the old man is, in fact, the Snake in another guise. Psychoanalytic writers argue that the snake occupies such a prominent part in mythology the world over because it stands for the penis, another fertility symbol. This may be so, but its symbolic significance is surely more complex than this. It is the "rebirth" of the hero, whether Mansren or the Snake, that exercises such universal fascination over men's minds.

The nineteenth-century missionaries thought that the Mansren story would make the introduction of Christianity easier, since the concept of "resurrection," not to mention that of the "virgin birth" and the "second coming," was already there. By 1867, however, the first cult organized around the Mansren legend was reported.

Though such myths were widespread in Melanesia, and may have sparked occasional movements even in the pre-White era, they took on a new significance in the late nineteenth century, once the European powers had finished parceling out the Melanesian region among themselves. In many coastal areas the long history of "blackbirding" —the seizure of islanders for work on the plantations of Australia and Fiji—had built up a reservoir of hostility to Europeans. In other areas, however, the arrival of the Whites was accepted, even welcomed, for it meant access to bully beef and cigarettes, shirts and paraffin lamps, whisky and bicycles. It also meant access to the knowledge behind these material goods, for the Europeans brought missions and schools as well as cargo.

Practically the only teaching the natives received about European life came from the missions, which emphasized the central significance of religion in European society. The Melanesians already believed that man's activities—whether gardening, sailing canoes, or bearing children—needed magical assistance. Ritual without human effort was not enough. But neither was human effort on its own. This outlook was reinforced by mission teaching.

The initial enthusiasm for European rule, however, was speedily dispelled. The rapid growth of the plantation economy removed the bulk of the able-bodied men from the villages, leaving women, children, and old men to carry on as best they could. The splendid vision of the equality of all Christians began to seem a pious deception in face of the realities of the color bar, the multiplicity of rival Christian missions and the open irreligion of many Whites.

For a long time the natives accepted the European mission as the means by which the "cargo" would eventually be made available to them. But they found that acceptance of Christianity did not bring the cargo any nearer. They grew disillusioned. The story now began to be put about that it was not the Whites who made the cargo, but the dead ancestors. To people completely ignorant of factory production, this made good sense. White men did not work; they merely wrote secret signs on scraps of paper, for which they were given shiploads of goods. On the other hand, the Melanesians labored week after week for pitiful wages. Plainly the goods must be made for Melanesians somewhere, perhaps in the Land of the Dead. The Whites, who possessed the secret of the cargo, were intercepting it and keeping it from the hands of the islanders, to whom it was really consigned. In the Madang district of New Guinea, after some forty years' experience of the missions, the natives went in a body one day with a petition demanding that the cargo secret should now be revealed to them, for they had been very patient.

So strong is this belief in the existence of a "secret" that the cargo cults generally contain some ritual in imitation of the mysterious European customs which are held to be the clue to the white man's extraordinary power over goods and men. The believers sit around tables with bottles of flowers in front of them, dressed in European clothes, waiting for the cargo ship or airplane to materialize; other cultists feature magic pieces of paper and cabalistic writing. Many of them deliberately turn their backs on the past by destroying secret ritual objects, or exposing them to the gaze of uninitiated youths and women, for whom formerly even a glimpse of the sacred objects would have meant the severest penalties, even death. The belief that they were the chosen people is further reinforced by their reading of the Bible, for the lives and customs of the people in the Old Testament resemble their own lives rather than those of the Europeans. In the New Testament they find the Apocalypse, with its prophecies of destruction and resurrection, particularly attractive.

Missions that stress the imminence of the Second Coming, like those of the Seventh Day Adventists, are often accused of stimulating millenarian cults among the islanders. In reality, however, the Melanesians themselves rework the doctrines the missionaries teach them, selecting from the Bible what they themselves find particularly congenial in it. Such movements have occurred in areas where missions of quite different types have been dominant, from Roman Catholic to Seventh Day Adventist. The reasons for the emergence of these cults, of course, lie far deeper in the life-experience of the people.

The economy of most of the islands is very backward. Native agriculture produces little for the world market, and even the European plantations and mines export only a few primary products and raw materials: copra, rubber, gold. Melanesians are quite unable to understand why copra, for example, fetches thirty pounds sterling per ton one month and but five pounds a few months later. With no notion of the workings of world-commodity markets, the natives see only the sudden closing of plantations, reduced wages and unemployment, and are inclined to attribute their insecurity to the whim or evil in the nature of individual planters.

Such shocks have not been confined to the economic order. Governments, too, have come and gone, especially during the two world wars: German, Dutch, British, and French administrations melted overnight. Then came the Japanese, only to be ousted in turn largely by the previously unknown Americans. And among these Americans the Melanesians saw Negroes like themselves, living lives of luxury on equal terms with white G.I.'s. The sight of these Negroes seemed like a fulfillment of the old prophecies to many cargo cult leaders. Nor must we forget the sheer scale of this invasion. Around a million U.S. troops passed through the Admiralty Islands, completely swamping the inhabitants. It was a world of meaningless and chaotic changes, in which anything was possible. New ideas were imported and given local twists. Thus in the Loyalty Islands people expected the French Communist Party to bring the millennium. There is no real evidence, however, of any Communist influence in these movements, despite the rather hysterical belief among Solomon Island planters that the name of the local "Masinga Rule" movement was derived from the word "Marxian"! In reality the name comes from a Solomon Island tongue, and means "brotherhood."

Europeans who have witnessed outbreaks inspired by the cargo cults are usually at a loss to understand what they behold. The islanders throw away their money, break their most sacred taboos, abandon their gardens, and destroy their precious livestock; they undulge in sexual license, or, alternatively, rigidly separate men from women in huge communal establishments. Sometimes they spend days sitting gazing at the horizon for a glimpse of the long-awaited ship or airplane; sometimes they dance, pray and sing in mass congregations, becoming possessed and "speaking with tongues."

Observers have not hesitated to use such words as "madness," "mania," and "irrationality" to characterize the cults. But the cults reflect quite logical and rational attempts to make sense out of a social order that appears senseless and chaotic. Given the ignorance of the Melanesians about the wider European society, its economic organization and its highly developed technology, their reactions form a consistent and understandable pattern. They wrap up all their yearning and hope in an amalgam that combines the best counsel they can find in Christianity and their native belief. If the world is soon to end, gardening or fishing is unnecessary; everything will be provided. If the Melanesians are to be part of a much wider order, the taboos that prescribe their social conduct must now be lifted or broken in a newly prescribed way.

Of course the cargo never comes. The cults nonetheless live on. If the millennium does not arrive on schedule, then perhaps there is some failure in the magic, some error in the ritual. New breakaway groups organize around "purer" faith and ritual. The cult rarely disappears, so long as the social situation which brings it into being persists.

At this point it should be observed that cults of this general kind are not peculiar to Melanesia. Men who feel themselves oppressed and deceived have always been ready to pour their hopes and

fears, their aspirations and frustrations, into dreams of a millennium to come or of a golden age to return. All parts of the world have had their counterparts of the cargo cults, from the American Indian Ghost Dance to the Communist-millenarist "reign of the saints" in Münster during the Reformation, from medieval European apocalyptic cults to African "witch-finding" movements and Chinese Buddhist heresies. In some situations men have been content to wait and pray; in others they have sought to hasten the day by using their strong right arms to do the Lord's work. And always the cults serve to bring together scattered groups, notably the peasants and urban plebeians of agrarian societies and the peoples of "stateless" societies where the cult unites separate (and often hostile) villages, clans, and tribes into a wider religio-political unity.

Once the people begin to develop secular political organizations, however, the sects tend to lose their importance as vehicles of protest. They begin to relegate the Second Coming to the distant future or to the next world. In Melanesia ordinary political bodies, trade unions and native councils are becoming the normal media through which the islanders express their aspirations. In recent years continued economic prosperity and political stability have taken some of the edge off their despair. It now seems unlikely that any major movement along cargo-cult lines will recur in areas where the transition to secular politics has been made, even if the insecurity of prewar times returned. I would predict that the embryonic nationalism represented by cargo cults is likely in future to take forms familiar in the history of other countries that have moved from subsistence agriculture to participation in the world economy.

Serpent-Handling as Sacrament

Mary Lee Daugherty

*In this article Mary Lee Daugherty discusses
serpent-handlers in West Virginia. The author,
raised in the area she writes about, maintains that
the handling of serpents as a religious act reflects the
geographic and economic harshness of the
environment in which the snake-handlers live.
Professor Daugherty has been studying religious
behavior and beliefs throughout Appalachia as well
as West Virginia. It is a mark of her professional
ability that she has been allowed by the members of
several Holiness-type churches to conduct her
research. Although many people in this country are
appalled at the thought of religious behavior that
encourages the handling of poisonous snakes and the
drinking of such poisons as strychnine and lye, West
Virginia's defeat of a 1966 bill that would have made
serpent-handling illegal serves as an indication of
religious freedom in the United States.*

Reprinted from *Theology Today*, Vol. 33, no. 3 (October 1976), pp. 232–43, by permission of the author
and Princeton Theological Seminary.

"And he [Jesus] said unto them, Go ye into
all the world, and preach the gospel to
every creature. He that believeth and is
baptized shall be saved; but he that
believeth not shall be damned. And these
signs shall follow them that believe; In my
name shall they cast out devils; they shall
speak with new tongues; they shall take up
serpents; and if they drink any deadly
thing, it shall not hurt them; they shall lay
hands on the sick, and they shall recover."

—Mark 16:15–18 (AV)

THE SERPENT-HANDLERS OF WEST VIRGINIA WERE
originally simple, poor, white people who
formed a group of small, independent Holiness-
type churches. Serpent-handlers base their particular religious practices on the familiar passage
from the "long-conclusion" of the Gospel of
Mark. (They are unaware of the disputed nature
of this text as the biblical scholars know it.)

The handling of serpents as a supreme act of
faith reflects, as in a mirror, the danger and
harshness of the environment in which most of
these people have lived. The land is rugged and
uncompromisingly grim. It produces little except
for coal dug from the earth. Unemployment and
welfare have been constant companions. The
dark holes of the deep mines into which men
went to work every day have maimed and killed
them for years. The copperhead and rattlesnake
are the most commonly found serpents in the
rocky terrain. For many years mountain people
have suffered terrible pain and many have died
from snake bite. Small wonder that it is considered the ultimate fact of faith to reach out and
take up the serpent when one is filled with the
Holy Ghost. Old timers here in the mountains,
before the days of modern medicine, could only
explain that those who lived were somehow
chosen by God's special mercy and favor.

Today serpent-handlers are experiencing, as are other West Virginians, great economic improvement. Many now live in expensive mobile homes that dot the mountain country side. They purchase and own among their possessions brand new cars and modern appliances. Many of the men now earn from twelve to eighteen thousand dollars a year, working in the revitalized mining industry. Most of the young people are now going to and graduating from high school. I know of one young man with two years of college who is very active in his church. He handles serpents and is looked upon as the one who will take over the pastor's position sometime in the future. What the effect of middle-class prosperity and higher education will be among serpent-handlers remains to be seen. It may be another generation before the effects can be adequately determined.

Knowing serpent-handlers to be biblical literalists, one might surmise that they, like other sects, have picked a certain passage of Scripture and built a whole ritual around a few cryptic verses. While this is true, I am persuaded, after years of observation, that serpent-handling holds for them the significance of a sacrament.

Tapestry paintings of the Lord's Supper hang in most of their churches. Leonardo da Vinci's *Last Supper* is the one picture I have seen over and over again in their churches and in their homes. But in West Virginia, the serpent-handlers whom I know personally do not celebrate the Lord's Supper in their worship services. It is my observation and hypothesis that the ritual of serpent-handling is their way of celebrating life, death, and resurrection. Time and again they prove to themselves that Jesus has the power to deliver them from death here and now.

Another clue to the sacramental nature of lifting up the serpents as the symbol of victory over death is to be observed at their funerals. At the request of the family of one who has died of snake bite, serpents may be handled at a funeral. Even as a Catholic priest may lift up the host at a mass for the dead, indicating belief that in the life and death of Jesus there is victory over death, so the serpent-handlers, I believe, lift up the serpent. Of course, none of this is formalized, for all is very spontaneous. But I am convinced that they celebrate their

belief that "in the name of Jesus" there is power over death, and this is what the serpent-handling ritual has proved to them over and over again. This is why I believe they will not give up this ritual because it is at the center of their Christian faith, and in West Virginia, unlike all the other States, it is not illegal.

Many handlers have been bitten numerous times, but, contrary to popular belief, few have died. Their continued life, and their sometimes deformed hands, bear witness to the fact that Jesus still has power over illness and death. Even those who have not been bitten know many who have, and the living witness is ever present in the lives of their friends. If one of the members should die, it is believed that God allowed it to happen to remind the living that the risk they take is totally real. Never have I heard any one of them say that a brother or sister who died lacked faith.

The cultural isolation of these people is still very real. Few have traveled more than a few miles from home. Little more than the Bible is ever read. Television is frowned upon; movies are seldom attended. The Bible is communicated primarily through oral tradition in the church or read at home. There is little awareness of other world religions. Even contacts with Roman Catholics and Jews are rare. Most of their lives revolve around the local church where they gather for meetings two or three times a week.

When one sees the people handling serpents in their services, the Garden of Eden story immediately comes to mind. In the Genesis story, the serpent represents evil that tempts Adam and Eve and must be conquered by their descendants. But the serpent means something far different to West Virginia mountain people; it means life over death. There is never any attempt to kill the snake in Appalachian serpent-handling services. Practitioners seldom kill snakes even in the out of doors. They let them go at the end of the summer months so that they may return to their natural environment to hibernate for the winter. They catch different snakes each spring to use in their worship services. When you ask them why, they tell you quite simply that they do not want to make any of God's creatures suffer. The serpent is always handled with both love and fear in their services, but it is never harmed or killed. Handlers may be killed from bites, but they will not kill the snake.

Neither do they force the handling of serpents on any who do not wish to do so.

The snake is seldom handled in private, but usually in the community of believers during a church service. Members may encourage each other to take the risk, symbolically taking on life and testing faith. Their willingness to die for their beliefs gives to their lives a vitality of faith. Handlers usually refuse medicine or hospital treatment for snake bite. But they do go to hospital for other illnesses or if surgery is needed. In the past, they usually refused welfare. They revere and care for their elderly who have usually survived numerous snake bites. Each time they handle the serpents they struggle with life once more and survive again the forces that traditionally oppressed mountain people. The poverty, the unemployment, the yawning strip mines, death in the deep mines have all been harsh, uncontrollable forces for simple people. The handling of serpents is their way of confronting and coping with their very real fears about life and the harshness of reality as experienced in the mountains in years gone by and, for many, even today.

Yet in the face of all this, they seek to live in harmony with nature, not to destroy it or any of its creatures, even the deadly serpent. It is only with the Holy Ghost, however, that they find the sustenance to survive. They live close to the earth, surrounded by woods, streams, and sky. Most live in communities of only a few hundred people or less.

The deep longing for holiness of these Appalachian people stands out in bold relief in the serpent-handling ritual of worship. The search for holiness is dramatized in their willingness to suffer terrible pain from snake bite, or even death itself, to get the feeling of God in their lives. The support of their fellow Christians is still with them. In their experience, God may not come if you don't really pray or ask only once. The person in the group who has been bitten most often and who has suffered the most pain or sickness is usually the leader. While it is the Holy Ghost who gives the power, those who have survived snake bite do get recognition and praise for their courage and their faith from the group. They have learned to cope with their anxieties by calling upon the name of Jesus and the power which he freely offers. Support is given to each member through the laying on of hands in healing ceremonies, through group prayers, and through verbal affirmations, such as: "Help her Jesus," "Bless him, Lord," "That's right, Lord." Through group support, anxiety about life is relieved. They feel ennobled as God becomes manifest in their midst.

The person of the Holy Ghost (they prefer this to Holy Spirit), enables them not only to pick up serpents, but to speak in tongues, to preach, to testify, to cure diseases, to cast out demons, and even to drink strychnine and lye, or to use fire on their skin when the snakes are in hibernation during the winter months. In these dramatic ways, the mountain folk pursue holiness above all else. They find through their faith both meaning and encouragement. Psychological tests indicate that in many ways they are more emotionally healthy than members of mainline Protestant churches.

Having internalized my own feelings of insecurity and worthlessness for many years because I was "no count" having been born from poor white trash on one side of my family, I have in my own being a deep appreciation and understanding of the need of these people to ask God for miracles accompanied with spectacular demonstrations. Thus they are assured of their own worth, even if only to God. They have never gotten this message from the outside world. They know they have been, and many still are, the undesirable poor, the uneducated mountain folk, locked into their little pockets of poverty in a rough, hostile land. So the Holy Ghost is the great equalizer in the church meeting. One's age, sex, years of schooling are all of less value. Being filled with the Holy Ghost is the only credential one needs in this unique society.

The Holy Ghost creates a mood of openness and spontaneity in the serpent-handling service that is beautiful to behold. Even though there is not much freedom in the personal lives of these people, there is a sense of power in their church lives. Their religion does seem to heal them inwardly of aches and pains and in many instances even of major illnesses. One often sees expressions of dependence as men and women fall down before the picture of Jesus, calling aloud over and over again, "Jesus . . . Jesus . . . Jesus . . ." The simple carpenter of Nazareth is obviously a person with whom mountain people can identify. Jesus worked with his hands, and so do they; Jesus was essentially, by our standards, uneducated, and so are they; Jesus came from a small place, he lived much of his life out of doors, he went fishing, he suffered and was finally done in by the "power structure," and so have they been in the past and often are today.

As I think about the mountain women as they fall down before the picture of Jesus, I wonder what he means to them. Here is a simple man who treated women with great love and tenderness. In this sense, he is unlike some of the men they must live with. Jesus healed the bodies of women, taught them the Bible, never told jokes about their bodies, and even forgave them their sexual sins. In the mountains, adultery is usually punished with beatings. Maybe it should not surprise us that in a State where the strip miners have raped the earth that the rape of the people has also taken place, and the rape of women is often deeply felt and experienced. Things are now changing, and for this we can be grateful.

In the serpent-handlers' churches, the Bible usually remains closed on the pulpit. Since most older members cannot read very well and have usually felt shy about their meager education, they did not read the Bible aloud in public, especially if some more educated people were present. They obviously read the Bible at home, but most remember it from stories they have heard. The Bible is the final authority for everything, even the picking up of serpents and the drinking of poison. It is all literally true, but the New Testament is read more often than the Old Testament.

In former years, their churches have given these poor and powerless people the arena in which they could act out their frustrations and powerless feelings. For a short time, while in church, they could experience being powerful when filled with the Holy Ghost. Frustrated by all the things in the outside world that they could not change, frustrated by the way the powerful people of the world were running things, they could nevertheless run their own show in their own churches. So they gathered three or four times a week, in their modest church buildings, and they stayed for three to five hours for each service. On these occasions, they can feel important, loved, and powerful. They can experience God directly.

I am always struck by the healing love that emerges at the end of each service when they all seem to love each other, embrace each other, and give each other the holy kiss. They are free from restrictions and conventions to love everyone. Sometimes I have the feeling that I get a glimmer of what the Kingdom of God will be like as we kiss each other, old and young, with or without teeth, rich and poor, educated and uneducated, male and female. So I have learned much and have been loved in turn by the serpent-handlers of West Virginia. As they leave the church and go back to their daily work, all the frustrations of the real world return, but they know they can meet again tomorrow night or in a few days. So they have faith, hope, and love, but the greatest message they have given to me is their love.

There are thousands of small Holiness churches in the rural areas of West Virginia. While four-fifths of all Protestants are members of mainstream denominations, no one knows just how many attend Holiness churches. Membership records are not considered important to these people, and although I personally know of about twenty-five serpent-handling churches, there may be others, for those in one church often do not know those in another. They laugh and make jokes about churches that give you a piece of paper as you enter the door, telling you when to pray and what to sing. They find it difficult to believe that you can "order around" the worship of the Holy Ghost on a piece of paper.

Those who make up the membership of the serpent-handling churches are often former members of other Holiness churches or are former Baptists or Methodists. In the Holiness churches, the attainment of personal holiness and being filled with the Spirit is the purpose and goal of life. Members view the secular world as evil and beyond hope. Hence they do not take part in any community activities or social programs.

Fifty-four percent of all persons in the state of West Virginia still live in communities of 1,000 people or less. Freedom of worship is the heritage of the Scotch-Irish, who settled these mountains

200 years ago. In more recent times, among Holiness groups there were no trained ministers. So oral tradition, spontaneous worship, and shared leadership are important.

Holiness church members live by a very strict personal code of morality. A large sign in the church at Jolo, W. Va., indicates that dresses must be worn below the knees, arms must be covered, no lipstick or jewelry is to be worn. No smoking, drinking, or other worldly pleasures are to be indulged in by "true believers." Some women do not cut their hair, others do not even buy chewing gum or soft drinks. For years, in the mountains, people have practiced divine healing, since medical facilities are scarce. Four counties in West Virginia still do not have a doctor, nurse, clinic, dentist, or ambulance service.

In a typical serpent-handling church service, the "true believers" usually sit on the platform of the church together. They are the members who have demonstrated that they have received the Holy Ghost. This is known to them and to others because they have manifested certain physical signs in their own bodies. If they have been bitten from snakes, as many have, and have not died, they have proved that they have the Holy Ghost. And those who have been bitten many times, and survived, are the "real saints." The "true believers" also demonstrate that they have the Holy Ghost by speaking in tongues, by the jerking of their bodies, and by their various trance-like states. They may dance for long periods of time or fall on the floor without being hurt. They may drink the "salvation cocktail," a mixture of strychnine or lye and water. They may also speak in tongues or in ecstatic utterances. Usually this is an utterance between themselves and God. But sometimes members seek to interpret the language of tongues. They lay their hands upon each other to heal hurts or even serious illnesses such as cancer. They sometimes pass their hands through fire. I have witnessed this activity and no burn effects are visible, even though a hand may remain in the flame for some time. A few years ago, they picked up hot coals from the pot bellied stoves and yet were not burned. They apparently can block out pain totally, when in a trance or deep into the Spirit of God.

One woman who attended church at Scrabble Creek, W. Va., experienced, on two occasions, the stigmata as blood came out of her hands, feet, side and forehead. This was witnessed by all present in the church. When asked about this startling experience, she said that she had prayed that God would allow people to see through her body how much Jesus suffered for them by his death and resurrection.

A local church in the rural areas may be known as "Brother So and So's" or "Sister So and So's" church to those who live nearby, but the sign over the door will usually indicate that the church belongs to Jesus. Such names as "The Jesus Church," "The Jesus Only Church," "The Jesus Saves Church," and "The Lord Jesus Christ's Church" are all common names. The churches do not belong to any denomination, and they have no written doctrines or creeds. The order of the service is spontaneous and different every night. Everyone is welcome and people travel around to each other's churches, bringing with them their musical instruments, snakes, fire equipment, poison mixtures, and other gifts.

Often the service begins with singing which may last thirty to forty-five minutes. Next, they may all pray out loud together for the Holy Ghost to fall upon them during the service. Singing, testifying, and preaching by anyone who feels God's spirit may follow. Serpents then will be handled while others are singing. It is possible that serpents will be handled two or three times in one service, but usually it is only once. Serpents are only handled when they feel God's spirit within them. After dancing ecstatically, a brother or sister will open the box and pull out a serpent. Others will follow if there are other snakes available. If only one or two serpents are present, then they may be passed around from believer to believer. Sometimes a circle may be made and the snakes passed. I have only once seen them throw snakes to each other. Children are kept far away.

There is much calling on the name of Jesus while the serpents are being handled, and once the "sacrament" is over, there is a great prayer of rejoicing and often a dance of thanksgiving that no one was hurt. If someone is bitten, there is prayer for his or her healing and great care is taken. If the person becomes too ill to stay in the church, he or she may be taken home and believers will pray for the person for days, if necessary. Even if the person does not die, and usually he or she doesn't, the person is usually very sick. Vomiting of blood and swelling are very painful. Some persons in the churches have lost the use of a finger or suffered some other deformity. But in many years of serpent-handling, I believe there are only about twenty recorded deaths.

The symbolism of the serpent is found in almost all cultures and religions, everywhere, and in all ages. It suggests the ambiguity of good and evil, sickness and health, life and death, mortality and immortality, chaos and wisdom. Because the serpent lives in the ground but is often found in trees, it conveys the notion of transcendence, a creature that lives between earth and heaven. And because it sheds its skin, it seems to know the secret of eternal life.

In the Bible, the serpent is most obviously associated with the Adam and Eve temptation (Gen. 3:1–13), but we also read of the sticks that Moses and Aaron turned into snakes (Ex. 7:8–12), and of Moses' bronze serpent standard (Num. 21:6–9). The two entwined snakes in the ancient figure of the caduceus, symbolizing sickness and health, has been widely adopted as the emblem of the medical profession. And sometimes in early Christian art, the crucifixion is represented with a serpent wound around the cross or lying at the foot of the cross (cf. John 3:14). Here again good and evil, life over death, are symbolized.

In early liturgical art, John the Evangelist was often identified with a chalice from which a serpent was departing, a reference to the legend that when he was forced to drink poison, it was drained away in the snake. Among the early Gnostics, there was a group known as Ophites who were said to worship the serpent because it brought "knowledge" to Adam and Eve and so to all humanity. They were said to free a serpent from a box and that it then entwined itself around the bread and wine of the Eucharist.

But, of course, this ancient history and symbolic lore are unknown to the mountain serpent-handlers of West Virginia, and even if they were told, they probably would not be interested. Their own tradition is rooted in their literal acceptance of what they regard as Jesus' commandment at the conclusion of Mark's Gospel. The problems of biblical textual criticism, relating to the fact that these verses on which they depend are not found in the best manuscript evidence, does not bother them. Their Bible is the English King James Version, and they know through their own experience that their faith in the healing and saving power of Jesus has been tested and proven without question. In any case, their ritual is unique in church history.

What the future holds for the serpent-handlers, no one can tell. Although the young people have tended to stay in their local communities, the temptation in the past to move out and away to find work has been very great. Now many of the young people are returning home as the mining industry offers new, high-paying jobs. And a new era of relative economic prosperity is emerging as the energy problem makes coal-mining more important for the whole Appalachian area. In the meantime, serpent-handling for many mountain people remains a Jesus-commanded "sacrament" whereby physical signs communicate spiritual reality.

Honor Thy Father Moon

Berkeley Rice

Reverend Sun Myung Moon's Unification Church, the most controversial psychoreligious cult of the several that mushroomed across the United States in the last decade, described vividly here by Berkeley Rice, still holds the allegiance of thousands of Americans. Rice explores the major tenets of the religion, its appeal to certain youth, and why, in terms of growth, wealth, organization, and discipline, it is the most controversial manifestation of the new evangelism. Considered both fraud and saint, the Reverend Moon utilizes a training system, not unlike that of other new sects, which offers to the initiate the strength of an unbreachable family, the removal of worldly cares, and a path to salvation.

Reprinted with permission from *Psychology Today Magazine* (January 1976), pp. 36–47. Copyright 1976 (P T Partners, L. P.).

HELLFIRE, DAMNATION, SALVATION! THE MESsiah is here. Sun Myung Moon has come from Korea to save our country, and thousands of young Americans have left their homes and schools to join his evangelical crusade, one of several religious cults that have mushroomed in the last decade. Thousands of other youths have joined Hare Krishna, the Children of God, the Jesus People, and the Maharaj Ji's Divine Light Mission. Hundreds of others have attached themselves to lesser-known sects, gurus and mystics.

In a time of recession and turmoil, the cults are a growth industry, their leaders successful entrepreneurs of salvation for the young. None of these new psychoreligious cults threatens to sweep the country, and probably none commands more than 5,000 full-time members. But in a country in which many of the young have recently tripped out on drugs and radical politics, the cults have become a new opiate for the youth of the 70s.

In terms of growth, wealth, organization and discipline, the Reverend Moon's Unification Church is the hottest and most controversial manifestation of the new evangelism. Founded in Korea in 1954 as The Holy Spirit Association for the Unification of World Christianity, it now claims a worldwide membership of 500,000 to two million, based mainly in Korea and Japan, with a modest following in Europe. Moon moved his headquarters to America in 1973 because he believes it to be God's chosen land, and possibly because it looked like promising territory. It has been. This article concentrates on the movement's activities in the United States.

Starting with only a few hundred members in 1970, the Unification Church now claims a U.S. following of 10,000 to 30,000, with a core of 2,000 to 10,000 full-time members. The movement now takes in about $10 million a year from fund raising and contributions. It is difficult for any outsider to measure its size or wealth with full confidence, since the numbers vary wildly from one supposedly official estimate to another. As of the fall of 1975 the Church operated 120 communal recruiting and fund-raising centers in cities across the country, with recruiting teams covering 150 college campuses. Teams of Moon's missionaries bring word of the new Messiah to the heathen in other parts, and a Church-run publishing company spreads his message in pamphlets, paperbacks and leaflets.

Professional "Deprogrammers"

Moon has been denounced as a religious fraud and hustler, an antichrist who threatens established Christianity. He has also been accused of manipulating and ripping off the innocent young "Moonies" who serve him. His recruiters have left behind a trail of irate or hysterical parents who claim he has stolen their children and brainwashed them into conversion and slavery.

Many parents have tried to rescue their sons and daughters from Moon's communes, but often the kids can't be found, or refuse to come home. Some parents have hired professional "deprogrammers" to kidnap their children and free them from Moon's spell. Some have sued the Church for holding the youths against their will, a charge difficult and humiliating to prove when the kids swear they prefer Moon's Family to their own.

Many other parents either approve of or don't seem to mind their children joining Moon's movement. Some feel it may be better than drugs or drifting aimlessly around the country. Others look with favor upon it as a Christian youth movement, without understanding exactly what the members do or believe.

While Church members easily accept Moon's theology as revealed truth, outsiders tend to find it a mind-boggling mixture of Pentecostal Christianity, Eastern mysticism, anticommunism, pop psychology and metaphysics. According to *Divine Principle*, Moon's book of revelations, God intended Adam and Eve to marry and have perfect children, thereby establishing the Kingdom of Heaven on Earth. But Satan, embodied in the snake, seduced Eve, who in turn passed her impurity on to Adam, bringing about the Fall of Man.

God then sent Jesus to redeem mankind from sin, but Jesus blew it too. He died on the cross before he could marry and father a new race of perfect children. The time has now come for a second Christ who will finally fulfill God's original plan. Moon doesn't identify the new Messiah, but like Moon, He just happens to have been born in Korea in 1920.

A short, stocky, moon-faced man of great energy, this 55-year-old millionaire industrialist-evangelist remains unfamiliar to most Americans. He speaks little English, grants almost no interviews, and makes infrequent public appearances at Unification rallies and banquets, usually surrounded by a phalanx of husky Moonie bodyguards. Since Moon addresses his American followers only in Korean, outsiders cannot understand his charisma, which depends mostly on his dynamic delivery and the members' belief in his semidivinity.

Since settling in the U.S., Moon has lived near Tarrytown, N.Y., in a $620,000 25-room mansion overlooking the Hudson River, with his wife, seven children, and a personal staff of 35 Moonies. The estate was called "Exquisite Acres" by the brassiere tycoon who built it; Moon has renamed it "East Garden"—a Garden of Eden for the new Adam from the East.

When not looking after his religious and corporate affairs, Moon spends a good deal of time out fishing on his 50-foot cabin cruiser, *New Hope*. Church officials bristle at criticisms of Moon's luxury. "Why must a religious leader be an ascetic?" one of them responded recently. "Look at the Pope." When I raised the issue with Farley Jones, a 29-year-old Princeton graduate who handles the Church's press relations, he said, "Followers of many religions honor their spiritual leader with physical comforts worthy of the dignity of his position. I trust the Reverend Moon's relationship with God, so I don't object to his lifestyle."

Moon's dealings with God began soon after his birth in North Korea. "From childhood I was clairvoyant," Moon once told his followers. "I could see through people, see their spirits." When he was 12 he began praying for "extraordinary things," and must have caught God's attention. On an Easter Sunday morning when Moon was 16, he had a vision in which Jesus appeared and told him to "carry out my unfinished task."

THE QUOTATIONS OF SUN MYUNG MOON

"I am your brain."

"What I wish must be your wish."

"My mission is to make new hearts, new persons."

"Of all the saints sent by God, I think I am the most successful one."

"The time will come . . . when my words will almost serve as law. If I ask a certain thing it will be done."

"The whole world is in my hand, and I will conquer and subjugate the world."

"By putting things in order, we can accomplish God's will. All obstacles to this world must be annihilated."

"Our strategy is to be unified into one with ourselves, and with that as the bullet we can smash the world."

Shining Dragon

Moon prepared for his divine mission by carrying on visionary chats with other prominent Biblical figures, and studying religious sects and cults then popular in Japan and Korea. In 1946 he began preaching his own version of Messianic Christianity, and gradually attracted a small, devoted following. He also changed his name from Yong Myung (Shining Dragon) Moon to a more celestial Sun Myung (Shining Sun) Moon. Moon, in Korean, means moon.

As his sect grew, Moon ran afoul of the authorities. He was excommunicated by the Presbyterian Church in 1948 and arrested various times by the police—on morals charges according to his Korean critics; for anticommunist activities according to Moon. Church legend tells how Moon was imprisoned, tortured and starved, yet shared his faith and his food with fellow inmates. Upon his escape or release in 1950 he led a band of followers on the mountainous trek to South Korea. He demonstrated his supernatural strength by carrying a crippled comrade on his bicycle—400 miles on the handlebars, according to one account; 600 miles on his back, according to another.

Reestablished in the South at the end of the Korean War, Moon founded the Unification Church, which has flourished under the military dictatorship of General Park Chung Hee.

Since moving to the United States in 1973, Moon has proclaimed his new age of Christianity at lectures, banquets and mass rallies in every major city in the country, culminating in a rally at New York City's Madison Square Garden in 1974. This spring he hopes to gather 250,000 people at a rally in Yankee Stadium.

Moon's crusades feature performances of the Korean National Folk Ballet, a Korean children's dance troupe called the "Little Angels," the New Hope Singers and a rock group called "Sunburst."

As a build-up for the Garden rally, 2,000 Moonies (about half flown in from Japan and Europe) spent weeks thrusting out leaflets on crowded street corners, and plastering virtually every bare wall in the city with posters announcing the coming of Sun Moon.

"Kung-Fu Tantrum"

In a two-hour speech punctuated by kicks, jumps, karate chops and tears (one reporter called it a "kung-fu tantrum") the Reverend Moon spewed forth a torrent of hellfire and brimstone in Korean, which was translated by a heavily accented Korean interpreter as Moon stood smiling beatifically. Moon told of the fall of man, recounted the history of Christianity, warned of the approaching apocalypse and announced the arrival of a second Christ who would offer the world one last chance at salvation. "You can be the citizens of the Kingdom of Heaven if you meet the coming Messiah," he told a packed audience that thinned considerably before he finished. "He is your hope . . . and the only hope of America and this world." As usual, Moon stopped just short of actually proclaiming himself the Messiah, but he left little doubt in anyone's mind.

At other rallies the Unification Church's President Neil Salonen holds forth. Salonen, 30, is a smooth New Yorker who managed a psychiatric hospital in Washington, D.C. before his life was "transformed" by Sun Moon. Salonen tells Americans how the country is going to hell because of all the crime, suicide, alcoholism, divorce, sex, drug abuse, college radicals and foreign communists. He says God has sent the Reverend Moon to the U.S. to solve these problems, and to "mobilize an ideological army of young people . . . to unite the world in a new age of faith."

The immediate goal of the crusades, rallies and street-corner evangelism is the recruitment of new members for the movement. Wherever the clean-cut, smiling Moonies can find them—on city streets or college campuses—they engage young Americans in discussions of the state of the country or their souls. As one U.C. official told me, "If someone's lonely, we talk to them. There are a lot of lonely people walking around."

The discussions almost invariably end with an invitation to an introductory lecture at the nearest Unification center. After these lectures come invitations to other lectures and dinners at the center. Along with dinner, potential converts get a diet of relentlessly hearty friendship from the brothers and sisters of what soon becomes the Family instead of the Church.

Those attracted to Moon's Family or his religion get invited next to a weekend "workshop" devoted to further study and friendship. The weekends follow an exhausting and rigidly structured pattern with little time for sleep and none for private reflection. Recruits get a daily dose of six to eight hours of mind-numbing theology based on Moon's *Divine Principle*. By the final lecture they learn that God has sent Sun Moon to save the world in general, and themselves in particular.

After each lecture, recruits and Moonies join in small discussion groups to answer questions but also to explore any personal problems, and to offer comforting attention. The rest of the days are filled with group activities: calisthenics, meals, sports, and lots of singing and praying. After dinner, and often lasting well past midnight, there's more group singing and praying, with testimony by Moonies of how they came to find peace, purpose, love and joy in the Family. Never left alone, the recruits are encouraged to pour out their hearts to their new brothers and sisters. Many do.

By Sunday night the conversion process turns hard-sell, with each recruit pressed to make a commitment to a week-long workshop, the next stage in the initiation process. About one out of four does. Those who don't often receive phone calls or visits afterward by Moonies who don't give up easily.

No Time for Relatives

For most of those who sign up for the seven-day workshop, the next stop is the Church's training headquarters at Tarrytown, N.Y., about 90 miles up the Hudson from New York City. Tarrytown is big time. Indoctrination there becomes more serious, the study more rigorous, and the life more spartan than that of the cadets just down the river at West Point. The program leaves neither time nor opportunity for contacting relatives or friends on the outside.

At the end of the week comes the pressure for commitment to full-time membership in the Family. The recruits reach this moment of decision worn out from lack of sleep, numbed by the endless lectures, cut off from the advice of family or friends, and softened up by the embracing warmth of the group. "It was like being taken care of," one ex-Moonie recalled. "The people were very friendly, and you really thought they did love you. . . . Also, I was kind of afraid of going out into the world. . . . It was an escape from the outside world." Some seem to have been ready for just such a commitment. "I've been looking for something like this for years," one told me. "It answers all the questions I was asking."

About half of those who complete the week-long seminar join the movement. Some join as "followers," remaining at their jobs or at school, and working evenings or weekends on Church projects. Some contribute part of their salaries. Those who join as a full-time members either move into a local commune or stay at Tarrytown and go on to increasingly intense seminars of three to 16 weeks.

During their first few months in the movement, new members often get phone calls or letters from parents or friends, urging them to drop out or at least come home to talk it over. Those who even waver, or who consider leaving are often told that their parents and others who oppose the Church are acting on behalf of Satan. A few do eventually drop out, but usually over the strenuous objections of their leaders. An evening of intense prayer and guidance frequently brings such wayward sheep back to the fold.

Once they move in, new members often give what possessions they have to the Church. While this rarely involves much money, some wealthy converts have donated considerable sums. At Tarrytown or the communal centers, the Moonies no longer need money anyway. The Church takes care of all their daily needs, from toothpaste to trousers. Except for a few senior officials, every member who needs a new pair of shoes or eyeglasses has to ask the local director or team leader for the money to buy them. Directors of the bigger centers sometimes buy up large lots of nearly identical clothes for their resident members, thereby increasing the degree to which groups of smiling Moonies look as though they were cloned rather than recruited.

Life in a Moonie commune offers a welcome refuge to those unwilling or unable to face the daily frustrations of life on the outside: no drugs, no drinks, no sex, no money, no problems, no choices, no decisions. From the team leader's cheerful "Rise and shine!" in the sexually segregated dormitories to the last group songs and prayers at midnight, the Moonies rarely have to think for themselves. Full of religious fervor and new-found purpose, they follow orders and perform chores with gusto.

When not out recruiting, fund raising or working for the movement's various commercial enterprises, Moonies spend most of their remaining hours in group prayer. While they sometimes pray to God, they frequently pray to "Father." I asked one church official who "Father" was, and he replied, "Reverend Moon." One ex-Moonie feels the Church uses prayer as a means of emotional control over its members. "Everyone else is praying, like 'Heavenly Father, help us, help us. Oh, we're so lost Father.' They tell you that in order to reach God, you have to scream as loud as you can, and work up emotionally. . . . You're supposed to pray so fervently that you cry."

Spiritual Highs

I once watched a few dozen Moonies kneel in prayer at "the holy rock" at Tarrytown. It got the title because Moon often stands on it to preach. Most were crying, some sobbing, as they prayed loudly and independently, but with the same general plea: "Father, oh Father, please help us." Some jerked spasmodically, in spiritual transport, like participants in a voodoo ceremony.

Those who observe Moonies closely often notice a glassy, spaced-out look in their eyes, which, combined with their everlasting smiles, makes them look like tripped-out drug freaks. Many are

indeed on a high, but they are tripping out on God, not drugs. Some of that glassy-eyed look may also be attributable to lack of sleep.

Like the Unification Church, the other religious cults also produce highs without the aid of drugs or liquor. The Jesus People urge potential converts to "turn on with Jesus," or to "take a trip with Jesus." The Hare Krishna movement advertises: "Stay high forever." The mother of a Child of God gave this description of her son's cult-mates: "Their eyes are fully dilated, and they glitter. . . . Although they talk to you, and they smile at you, you don't feel that it's the whole person."

To learn how the Church creates such spiritual fervor I visited the Tarrytown training center recently with Michael Warder, a 29-year-old Stanford graduate who joined the Church seven years ago and now serves as its director of training. The center occupies a former Catholic seminary the Church purchased a few years ago for $1.5 million.

As we toured the buildings and grounds at Tarrytown, I saw dozens of Moonies servicing the center's cars and vans, preparing meals for hundreds of trainees, and doing all the chores involved in running a sizable education institution.

Wherever we went in the buildings, photos of Moon smiled down on us. In one office I met a spry, gray-haired lady of 67 who was led into the movement in 1974 by her son. She admits to having been negative at first, "but once I saw the light I quit my job, sold my house, and joined the Church." When I asked her what her son had been doing before he joined, she replied, "Spacing out. He didn't know what to do with his life." In another office I met a girl who said she'd been "a strong hippie radical at Berkeley" where she spent two years at college. "I didn't like the world the way it was. I wanted to change it. I had tried several Christian groups, and the Guru Maharishi. This was the first movement I tried that offered real answers."

Warder and I tried to look in on the three-week and six-week groups, but they were both away recruiting or fund raising as part of their training. The four-month trainees spend about one month out fund raising, but we found them at Tarrytown just as their afternoon session began with several stirring hymns and a prayer to "Father" Moon for the "strength to understand his teaching."

The 120 well-dressed novitiates then sat through

a four-hour lecture on predestination, which they followed attentively, taking notes in detail. When I asked if four hours without a break wasn't a bit long for such a topic, a staff member sitting next to me explained, "That is part of our training."

Diverting Energies

As I had noticed at other Church activities, the male and female members sat on separate sides of the hall. Warder explained that all activities at Tarrytown and other Church centers are carefully segregated by sex. "We find that way everyone feels more comfortable in their study and in their search for the truth. As soon as they're mixed you find the boys and girls begin thinking about other things."

The Chuch's puritan attitudes toward sex govern every minute of the training and lives of its members. Perhaps as a way to divert libidinal energies, group leaders encourage various forms of asexual but segregated physical contact: touching, massaging, backslapping and general horseplay.

In one of the Reverend Moon's "Master Speaks" training lectures, he warned the young men and women against holding hands or even sitting next to each other because it might lead to sin: "You must keep your purity and chastity. You must think of it as more valuable, more important than your own life. . . . Purity is something like a blossom before it is opened. So before you are blessed, you must be like a blossom shut tight, and bear the fragrance deep within you."

Before they can become eligible for marriage, Moonies must put in seven years of faithful service to the Church and even then they need Moon's personal approval. Eligible members may propose mates of their own choice, but Moon makes the final selection, often pairing couples completely unknown to each other.

As a generous and efficient father, Moon likes big weddings. Last year, at an all-day affair held in a Seoul sports arena, he married 1,800 member couples from 24 countries, including 70 couples from the United States.

As in the outside world, marriage does not bring immediate bliss. Newlywed Moonies must live separate and celibate lives for at least 40 days, and up to three years for younger members, which allows them time to achieve a proper level of spiritual perfection. Even after the period of enforced

celibacy, Church couples tend to live as brothers and sisters in the Family, rather than as husband and wife. By enforcing celibacy and permitting only the distant prospect and eventual facade of marriage, Moon's movement follows a long tradition of American communes. The successful ones generally encouraged free love or enforced celibacy, thereby preventing the formation of family units that could threaten the cohesiveness of the communal family and the authority of its leader [see "Individualism Busts the Commune Boom" by Laurence Veysey, *pt*, December 1974].

In addition to warnings on the evils of sex, trainees at Tarrytown receive a heavy indoctrination in the dangers of communism. According to Moon, communism equals satanism, and every good Christian should be willing to give up his life to fight it anywhere in the world, particularly in defense of South Korea, the movement's "Fatherland."

Since he arrived in America, Moon has continued to mix politics with his religion. The Church has a political affiliate in Washington, D.C. called the Freedom Leadership Foundation (FLF), dedicated to "ideological victory over communism in the United States." The FLF's rallies, seminars, lectures and publications stress America's moral obligation to provide military and economic support for General Park's government in South Korea.

God Chose Nixon

Like his competitor Billy Graham, the Reverend Moon has demonstrated considerable flair for political publicity. With bipartisan agility he has had his picture taken (and used repeatedly in Church publications) with Senators Hubert Humphrey, Edward Kennedy, Strom Thurmond and James Buckley.

When Richard Nixon was under siege during the final months of his presidency, Moon, acting upon what he called direct instructions from God, took out full-page ads in major newspapers across the country urging public support of the President. Blending piety and patriotism, Moon proclaimed: "This nation is God's nation. The office of the President of the United States is therefore sacred. . . . God has chosen Richard Nixon to be President of the United States."

The following month Moon mobilized 1,000 of

the faithful for a Washington prayer fast and vigil in the President's support. They marched on Capitol Hill carrying signs that read: "PRAY FOR NIXON" and "GOD LOVES NIXON."

Except for their anticommunist indoctrination, most Moonies seem uninterested in politics. Besides, few have much time or energy left over from fund raising and recruiting. During much of their life in the family, the brothers and sisters put in grueling dawn-to-dusk days peddling candles, peanuts, dried flowers or anything else the Church feels will inspire donations.

Moonies work in pairs at street corners or shopping plazas; others go out in teams selling door to door in suburban neighborhoods. When asked what they're raising money for, they give vague or misleading answers like "Christian youth work," "youth counseling," or "a drug-abuse program."

The young solicitors rarely mention the Church or Sun Moon. They are polite, but remarkably persistent. Success at fund raising becomes a test of devotion to the Church. Team leaders send their troops off in the morning with songs, prayers and pep talks, encouraging competition among each other and with other teams. Stoked up like Marine recruits for a bayonet drill, the Moonies charge out and work the streets with a fervor no profit motive could ever inspire. Those who fail to meet a respectable daily quota often spend the evening praying for God's help the following day.

Except for the spartan food, clothing and shelter it provides for its members, the Church seems to invest most of its funds in real estate. It bought the former Columbia University Club in New York for $1.2 million, for its national headquarters, and owns another $10 million worth of property along the Hudson River.

In addition to its real-estate holdings, the movement also runs cottage industries in dozens of communes around the country, with members turning out candles and other items used for fund-raising drives. The Church also owns and operates other member-run commercial enterprises: a ranch, gas station, printing company, travel agency, landscape service, home-cleaning service and tea house. While these hardly amount to a financial empire, they grow fast on tax exemptions and free labor.

From similarly modest beginnings, Moon has built up a $15 million-a-year industrial conglom-erate in Korea, drawing largely on churchmembers' labor. His factories turn out heavy machinery, titanium, paint, pharmaceuticals, marble vases, and shotguns.

"He Has a Right"

Current plans call for U.S. distribution of a ginseng tea produced in Korea by Moon's Ilhwa Pharmaceutical Co. An old Oriental favorite brewed from a powdered root, Moon's ginseng tea reputedly "lowers blood sugar, prevents degeneration of human cells, and stimulates the gonads." It sells for $24 for seven ounces, and tastes like boiled chalk.

To arouse consumers in this country, Moon has hired a high-priced public-relations firm (whose other accounts include General Motors, Gulf and Exxon) to promote his tea and to repair the Church's image in the U.S., which even its own officials admit is pretty bad.

Newspapers around the country have run stories about tearful parents who have tried in vain to free their children from Moon's cult; ex-Moonies have appeared on televised press conferences to denounce the Church for brainwashing them into conversion and turning them against their parents. Rabbi Maurice Davis, of White Plains, N.Y., has formed a national organization of several hundred parents who have lost their children to Sun Moon and other religious cults.

"Moon's theology is nonsense," says Rabbi Davis, "but he has a right to preach whatever nonsense he wants. What I hold against the Moon movement is that they take kids and treat them as things. They use the kids as slaves, as workers. They don't really care about these kids, and they do nothing to make the world better."

Church officials often argue they are making the world better by getting wayward youths off drugs and away from crime. But few of their recruits look like ex-junkies, and most come from middle-class schools and homes rather than crime-ridden ghettos. For all its talk about crime, drugs, alcohol and other social ills, the movement runs few programs aimed at solving such problems, or at helping non-members. Most of its resources are directed inward, producing more money and more members, who in turn will recruit more members and raise more money. Rather than helping society, the movement siphons off the energy and idealism of its members. When I asked one official how this would benefit society, he replied, "we can change the world by changing men's hearts." When I countered that such a policy would solve society's problems only if everyone joined the Unification Church, he smiled.

Americans may not all join the Unification Church, but many are joining its competitors, which share similar policies and practices. The Children of God also spend much of their time selling various articles and soliciting donations, turning all receipts over to their leader Moses David. The movement is often accused of "brainwashing," and teaches recruits to regard anyone who challenges it as an agent of the devil. "They give you the answers for everything," one ex-member recalled. "The leader does your thinking for you."

Pattern of Vulnerability

The 5,000-member Hare Krishna Society is run by a successful businessman from India, who, like Moon, has organized his followers into a band of devoted fund raisers willing to live a life of ascetic denial. Membership requires insulation from the outside world, surrender of prior identity, strict standards of dress and behavior, and a great deal of group chanting which helps create the high. Instead of drugs, sex, or personal pleasure, the members substitute dedication, endurance, and self-sacrifice.

Psychologists who have studied the Jesus People movement found a pattern of vulnerability among the members. On a personality test they scored significantly lower than average on self-confidence and personal adjustment. The conversion process at Jesus People communes follows a rigid pattern, involving subtle and overt pressure, and a rewarding warmth, and acceptance from new "brothers" and "sisters" upon conversion. Converts must make a total commitment, and give up all material possessions and outside contacts with family or friends.

The charge of "brainwashing" deserves attention. Much of what happens to Moon's converts during the weekend and week-long initiation workshops does follow the classic steps of brainwashing: isolating them from all past and outside contacts; surrounding them with new instant comrades and a new authority figure; wearing them down physically, mentally and emotionally; then "programming" them with new beliefs and pressuring them into total commitment.

But the term brainwashing implies force and captivity, conditions that do not apply to Moon's recruits. Church members may use heavy-handed emotional or psychological pressure, but they do not force anyone to join or believe. While one might question the independence of a convert's mind, no one has proven the Church holds its members against their will. It might be fairer to use the term conversion instead of brainwashing. If conversion requires the suspension of critical faculties, at least the Moonies do so willingly.

In his classic study of *The Varieties of Religious Experience*, William James described religious conversion in a manner strikingly similar to the tales told by Moonies. James wrote that conversion occurs most often among those beset by a "sense of incompleteness and imperfection," and frequently during a "state of temporary exhaustion." He told how conversion brings "a new level of spiritual vitality" in which "new energies and endurances are shown. The personality is changed, the man *is* born anew . . . perceiving truths not known before," a sense of peace and harmony in themselves and in the world.

Instant Salvation

Through a process of self-selection Moon's movement probably attracts only those youths already seeking some form of total commitment. Many Moonies have been drifting from cults to communes for years, sampling the spiritual fare like diners at a smorgasbord. The Church may be capitalizing on their loneliness, but it can hardly be blamed for their vulnerability. However remarkable the experience seems to the convert and his family, James described it as essentially an "adolescent phenomenon, incidental to the passage from the child's small universe to the wider intellectual and spiritual life of maturity."

While one can commiserate with parents whose children leave home to join religious cults, it's hard to condone the desperate attempts to recover the children by kidnapping and deprogramming, a process openly based on the techniques of brainwashing. Youths of legal age have a right to practice any religion they choose. Whether or not their choice is wise has nothing to do with their right to exercise it. Eighteen-year-olds who join the U.S. Marines may be using equally rash judgment, and their boot-camp training subjects them to group discipline, exhaustion and "brainwashing" that match anything that the Moonies endure. One could easily question the judgment of grown-ups who seek instant salvation in such socially acceptable adult cults as TM, Arica, est, primal therapy, or encounter groups.

While its critics describe the Unification Church as authoritarian, Church leaders prefer to call their approach "loving and parental." They may be right. To thousands of young Americans threatened by the approach of life as an adult, Moon's Family offers the security of perennial childhood. To lonely young people drifting through cold, impersonal cities, it offers instant friendship and communion, a sense of belonging. To college students suffering the rigors of academic competition, it offers an egoless life of cooperative group spirit. To those troubled by personal problems with drugs or sex, it offers a drugless, sexless world of militant puritanism. To those troubled by our materialistic society, it offers a life of disciplined asceticism. To those who have no faith in the traditional institutions of society, it offers the comfort of belief. To those hungering for truth and meaning in a complicated world, it offers simple answers.

Critics may call Moon's movement a religious fraud, and accuse it of exploiting innocent youths but, except for those who drop out, most Moonies seem genuinely happy in their service to Moon and the Church. In exchange for their labor, devotion and commitment, the Church has given them a home, a family, and a purpose. Critics may call that exploitation or slavery, but the Moonies consider it a bargain. No more problems, no more hassles, no more doubts. Just honor thy Father Moon.

Rajneeshpuram: The Boom and Bust of a Buddhafield

James E. Myers

Most of the world knows Bhagwan Shree Rajneesh for his collection of ninety-three Rolls-Royces, his outrageous mockery of the Great Faiths, his free-swinging attitudes toward sex (earning him the media nickname, "the Swami of Sex"), and the controversies that follow his every move. In this selection James Myers provides us with an account of the guru, his disciples, and the movement known as Rajneeshism. After a description of life at the Bhagwan's commune at Poona, India, Myers focuses on the rise and fall of Rajneeshpuram, or "Rancho Rajneesh," the controversial commune that the Bhagwan inspired in Eastern Oregon. Myers also provides several reasons for the collapse of the commune and brings us up-to-date on the Bhagwan and the movement. Readers will want to compare Rajneeshpuram and the Bhagwan with Jonestown and the Reverend Jim Jones, as there are similarities but also monumental differences.

This selection was written for this volume and appears here in print for the first time.

RELIGIOUS UTOPIAN MOVEMENTS AND "CULTS" HAVE always been a part of the American scene. Through recessions and inflations, depressions and economic booms, war and peace, they have had a visible role in our social theater, usually subjected to the slings and arrows of a suspicious, if not outright hostile, audience of mainstream Americans.

The mass media has often struggled to sate the enormous appetite Americans have for devouring accounts of the latest or strangest cult. The spicier the serving, the tastier the meal, with lurid descriptions of aberrant sexual practices, accounts of internal strife or tales of intrigue and conflict between leaders being especially tempting to the public palate. The academic press long ago joined the popular press in this pursuit, as scholars and students alike worked to fathom the meaning of cults, sects, utopian groups, messiahs, or anything else resembling a new religious movement.

It was in response to this national craving that huge numbers of journalists, social scientists, theses-burdened graduate students, and religious writers descended upon the peaceful rolling range land of Eastern Oregon between 1981 and 1985. Joined by thousands of others—the seekers, the curious, the tourists (although the latter were discouraged), they gawked their way through the streets, buildings, and fields of what was an amazing newly incorporated city located about 120 miles southeast of Portland and about 20 miles from the nearest paved road. This, of course, was Rajneeshpuram, or "Rancho Rajneesh," a 64,000-acre commune that sprang up, flourished, and withered in the space of four troubled years.

Accounts of the rise and decline of the Rajneeshee and their charismatic leader, Bhagwan Shree Rajneesh, are now legion: the Bhagwan's vastly popular free-swinging ashram (a religious commune and therapy center) in Poona, India; his move to the United States in 1981; the political takeover of the little town of Antelope, Oregon; the development of Rancho Rajneesh; the bitter skirmishes between the commune and several levels of county, state, and national governments; the allegations and eventual convictions of some Rajneeshee for such crimes as immigration fraud, attempted murder, poisoning, purposefully inducing a salmonella epidemic, wiretapping, bugging, and arson. In addition, there was the recruiting of street people to provide voter clout in an important election; the Bhagwan's ninety-plus Rolls-Royces; the antics of Ma Anand Sheela, the gun-lugging second-in-command and acknowledged "mother" of the commune; and, of course, the eventual collapse of what the Bhagwan himself had fondly dubbed the "Buddhafield."

Rajneesh-watchers disagree about whether or not Rajneeshism is actually a religion. In a 1983 booklet the Bhagwan himself announced it so (although a few years later he would repudiate the declaration):

> Rajneeshism is not a religion like Christianity, Hinduism, Mohammedanism, Buddhism, etc. It simply shows a poverty of language—to be exactly true, Rajneeshism is a religionless religion.
>
> In other words, it is a kind of religiousness, not a dogma, cult or creed but only a quality of love, silence, meditation and prayerfulness. Hence it can never end. (Academy of Rajneeshism, 1983: 58)

It is virtually impossible, however, to discuss Rajneeshism without making reference in one way or another to the religious world. For this reason, the man, his disciples, and the movement as a whole will be regarded as religious entities in the account that follows.

Freedom Through Sex: The Poona Experience

Chandra Mohan Jain was born in 1931, in a small town in India. His parents were successful cloth merchants who preferred to call the future Bhagwan, "Raja," or Rajneesh. After being disenrolled from one college (ostensibly for annoying his professors with pesky questions), the young Rajneesh eventually graduated from another in 1955. He received a master's degree in Philosophy in 1957 and taught at the University of Jabalpur from 1958 to 1966. Quitting his teaching job in 1966, Rajneesh supported himself by giving public lectures, many of which centered around the notion that the basic energy of sex was divine and must not be repressed, a notion that resulted in his being referred to as the "Swami of Sex."

In the fall of 1970, Rajneesh founded the Neo-Sannyas International Movement, the beginning of a spectacular enterprise that would be labeled at various times a new religion, a utopian movement, a human potential movement, and, of course, a cult. Whatever the label, by 1984 the worldwide operation included 500 Rajneesh Meditation Centers, 50 ashrams, 12 neo-Sannyas communes, hundreds of small businesses, and 40 Zorba the Buddha restaurants (Braun: 206). Rajneesh himself placed his flock at "half a million" in 1984 and "one million" in 1985 (Gordon: 150), a quite bloated, unrealistic figure according to most observers. Ma Anand Sheela and the Rajneesh Foundation International (1983: 12) proclaimed 350,000. Gordon, citing figures from several Sannyasin who had access to the mailing lists, concludes that a worldwide figure of 40,000 "initiated Sannyasins" should be considered as tops (1987: 150).

In 1971, Rajneesh added "Bhagwan" to his name, a word meaning "God" or "Blessed One" (chosen from a list of possible titles drawn up by a disciple who knew Sanskrit), and in 1974 the movement began building an ashram in Poona, India, a university city of 856,000 people, seventy-five miles southeast of Bombay. By now one of the most popular, if not controversial, of the Indian spiritual masters, the Bhagwan had attracted several thousand devotees, most of whom were drawn from the wealthy and educated classes of both India and the West. Indeed, whereas in 1975 only two Western therapies were offered at the ashram, four years later the number had jumped to sixty, including "almost every booth in the entire holistic New-Age marketplace" (FitzGerald, Sept. 22, 1986: 82). That many of the therapies combined an appealing blend of Eastern religion and Western pop psychology apparently proved to be irresistible to

---

BHAGWAN SHREE RAJNEESH SPEAKS

"Jesus Christ was a crackpot. He was trying to save the whole world. He couldn't save himself."

"Only retarded and utterly mediocre people can believe in God."

"True religion is a luxury which can come only after one's survival needs are met."

"Any religion that is concerned with death is wrong, and all religions are concerned with death."

"The major world religions are the cunning strategies of clever people trying to exploit you."

"Priests and politicians are responsible for keeping poverty alive."

"Stop giving Nobel Prizes to criminals like Mother Theresa."

"I have loved many women. Perhaps no man has loved so many women. In the beginning I used to keep count, but I've lost track."

"I am the best showman in the whole history of mankind."

---

many Westerners, as upwards of 30,000 visitors in 1981 poured into the ashram to hear the Bhagwan's ideas of total freedom (Carter: 158).

Rajneesh's timing and teachings were perfect for the historical moment. Just when the peace movement and the student unrest of the early 1970s were petering out, he appeared on the mystic scene as an exciting and provocative guru. Whatever attraction the numerous and controversial therapies held for the seekers, there can be no denial of the sexual lure. Sexuality was a meditation in and of itself, and religions that suppressed it were perverted, or so pronounced the guru. One individual who was caught up in the Poona excitement in 1978, but never formally joined, told me as he reflected on the experience ten years later, "I know for a fact I had gonads for brains in those years. My gonads drove me out of college, my gonads placed me in Poona, and my gonads told me Bhagwan's teachings were beautiful."

The idea that humans could be free only by acknowledging their sexual nature did not go unnoticed by the Poona townspeople. Gordon (1987: 43–44) tells of the sexual effect the female disciples had on the local Indian males:

The sannyasin women, with their round hips and swinging breasts, their nipples and pubic hair pushing against the fronts of their dresses, drive the postpubescent, puritannical, sex-starved Indian males mad. Young men on foot and scooters stare and jeer and occasionally pinch or grab them from behind as if breasts and buttocks were so many fruits in the market.

Braun (1984: 95) argues that the Bhagwan felt sex was a pathway to God, a necessary first step that would simmer down, even fizzle out, and eventually allow one to reach enlightenment. Quoting the Bhagwan:

My whole effort here is to make you bored with sex, only then can you become interested in God, never otherwise. . . . A repressed person remains obsessed with sex, so I say have all the sex that you can have and you soon will be finished with it. And when you are finished with it and sex loses all meaning, that will be a great day, a great moment in your life. (Braun: 95)

Predictably, the media fixed its sights on the zeal and overt delight in which the disciples and seekers worked their way through the necessary first stage of having all the sex they could have, while giving no attention to those who may have "finished with it." To ascribe Rajneeshism's success to a sexual attitude alone, however, is to ignore the movement's great appeal and success through its offerings of mysticism, materialism, meditation, therapy techniques, and social and spiritual goals.

A central feature of Rajneesh's key to spiritual satisfaction was a type of dance he called "Dynamic Meditation." Consisting of five stages that carried the individual from a frantic active period (accompanied by shouts of the Sufi mantra "hoo") to a final stage of relaxed silence, it is perhaps best described by Carter, as "a combination of vigorous 'jazzercise' with a 'primal' followed by a period of quiet passive meditation" (1987: 158). Of course, frenzied dancing as a vehicle to enhance a spiritual emotion is not unusual as a form of religious behavior. Sufi twirling, the foot-stomping, arm-swinging gyrations of certain pentecostal sects, and the energetic possession-seeking dancing of Voodoo come immediately to mind.

James S. Gordon, a Harvard-trained psychiatrist and a specialist in the study of "new religions," is the author of an insightful book entitled, *The Golden*

Guru: The Strange Journey of Bhagwan Shree Ranjneesh. Although Gordon is a devotee of some of Rajneesh's teachings, including "Dynamic Meditation," he could never quite bring himself to take *sannyas* ("joining-up"). Gordon believes that Rajneesh's huge success with his followers was due to his skillful use of various devices to "enhance the psychological and psychohistorical fit between him and his disciples":

> In discourses and darshans Rajneesh also used hypnotic techniques to bypass his disciples' conscious defenses, to win their assent to his words, and to enhance their transference to him. He created confusion and elaborated paradoxes and contradictions, which baffled their rational minds and the habitual ways they looked at themselves and the world. He used his voice, varying the volume and pace of speech, punctuating, modifying his words with his hands and eyes, even with his stillness. As his disciples listened and watched, their minds slowed. They followed the winding discursive thread of his stories the way the eye follows the motions of a tiny falling feather. In trance they were more receptive and suggestible.
>
> In Poona and later in Rajneeshpuram, Rajneesh used other devices as well to heighten his effectiveness and his listeners' receptivity: barriers to entry (sniffers and guards); identification bracelets; elaborately staged entrances and exits; repetitive music; sentimental songs; a bare setting; the raised place of his chair and the increasing remoteness of his person; absolute silence. One came to Rajneesh as if in procession to a temple deity. And, like all great performers, Rajneesh played the crowd, multiplying the power of his words and his presence by the attention his audience payed to him; augmenting, as any charismatic leader must, the power of those who were attributing power to him, as if in a continual and continually recharged circuit (Gordon 1987: 235).

In spite of the popularity of the Poona ashram, this phase of the Rajneesh movement was drawing to a close, as Indian authorities and the general public began to respond to the burgeoning number of stories about sexual orgies, prostitution, drug use, violence-prone therapy techniques and a multitude of other sensational charges. FitzGerald (Sept. 22, 1986: 83) lists several cases of rape, a broken leg, and several broken arms as examples of "therapeutic" violence at the Poona ashram. With the move-

ment's public relations in a quickening state of deterioration and the cancellation of the Ashram's tax-exempt status by the Indian government, there was talk among the leadership of a move to the United States. On May 31, 1981, the Bhagwan abruptly left India. Only a few disciples were alerted. The official explanation for the relocation was the Bhagwan's ill health and the better health services offered in the United States.

Seeing Red in Oregon

The guru's first residence in the United States was a castle in Montclair, New Jersey, which had been purchased by Ma Anand Sheela in the spring of 1981. In July 1981, the Bhagwan's chief aides quietly bought the Big Muddy Ranch in Eastern Oregon for six million dollars (1.5 million dollars in cash). Within a few months, a small commune of 150 to 170 people had been established at the ranch; in May 1982, they voted to become incorporated as Rajneeshpuram ("the City of the Lord of the Full Moon"). This move allowed the group to avoid, at least temporarily, Oregon's strict land-use laws.

Soon, the Rajneeshee began buying up property in Antelope, a nearby hamlet whose residents were quickly outnumbered in population by the newcomers. By winning the race for mayor and being elected to five of six city council seats, the commune was able to fill all the little town's public positions with fellow sannyasins. When the town's taxes soon tripled, most of the old-timers moved out in anger. Antelope's general store was converted into a Zorba the Buddha Restaurant, and nudity was legalized in the public park (making Antelope the first Oregon city to adopt such a measure). The town itself was renamed Rajneesh.

Meanwhile, back at the Ranch, things were jumping. When the Big Muddy Ranch was originally purchased by one of the Rajneesh corporations, anxious Oregonians were told the development would be small-scale and low-key—perhaps forty residents who would plant a few acres of sunflowers. Within two years, the number of permanent residents had jumped from forty to eight hundred, all followers of Bhagwan. Sporting a new name, "Swami" for the men, followed by a name selected by the Bhagwan, and "Ma" for the women, followed by a name chosen by the Bhagwan, disciples proudly wore a *mala*, a necklace of 108 beads with a locket containing a picture of Bhagwan. They also wore clothing in the color of their choice—varying shades of pink, orange, and red. To the Rajneeshee, the colors represented sunlight, life, and a growing consciousness; to the Oregonians, the colors more fittingly reflected an increasing sense of rage at what was happening before their eyes.

Under the leadership of the Bhagwan and Ma Anand Sheela, a powerful aide to the Guru during the Poona years and now his chief secretary, the Ranch flourished. Since work was seen as "meditation" by the Bhagwan, the sannyasin happily contributed free labor throughout twelve-hour work days. One sannyasin, who had lived on the ranch for four months in 1984, told me how inspired she became on her first night at the ranch:

> I had just arrived. It was 10:00 PM on a bitterly cold December night and there were women climbing around on the top of this big building constructing a roof. You could see their red clothes in the floodlights. It was a beautiful and moving sight that is still with me today.

It was this inspiration and commitment that so quickly got the Ranch's development underway: a 1.5 million dollar earthen dam was constructed, along with a 45-acre reservoir holding 350 million gallons of water. More than three thousand acres were planted in crops. A sophisticated sewage treatment plant was built, and numerous projects initiated to control erosion problems. Permanent buildings were constructed, along with residential quadraplexes, a shopping mall, restaurants, stores, offices, and the five-wing Rajneesh International Meditation University. Soon would come townhouses, A-frame lodges, a hotel, casino, and disco. The commune had a police force ("Peace Force"), a fire department, a medical clinic, and an airport with five aircraft, including three "Air Rajneesh" DC-3's.

One of the Bhagwan's management policies at the Ranch involved the placement of women in key power positions. Referred to by some as a "ma-archy" or the "ma-system," the commune's organization was administered mostly by female department heads and coordinators. (The "chief" mom was clearly Ma Sheela, who had joined the movement in 1973 at the age of twenty-three and had quickly become the Bhagwan's secretary, confidante, and spokeswoman.) The Bhagwan's views should not be interpreted as standard-issue feminism, however. Women, he claimed, were more suited to the role of leadership in part because their sense of intuition was finer than men. Moreover, as he once explained to his disciples,

> "The open secret is that you can be free only if you have put too many women around you. Then they are so concerned with each other that they leave you absolutely alone. . . . Their jealousies, their envies are enough to keep them occupied" (FitzGerald: Sept. 22, 1986: 94).

The Rajneeshee's vast amount of accomplishment in Oregon in so brief a time were hardly reminiscent of the struggling hippie communes that had dotted the Western states a decade earlier. Nor could such spectacular development have sprung from a poverty-espousing assembly of Hare Krishna or the poorly educated, unskilled collection of people who followed the Reverend Jim Jones to Guyana. The Rajneeshee were a truly distinctive group. A University of Oregon survey (Littman *et al.* 1984) described their average age as about thirty-four in 1983, 80 percent of whom came from middle-class or upper-middle class backgrounds and enjoyed a median income of $20,000 to $30,000 a year before coming to Rancho Rajneesh. Their fathers were professionals and businessmen, a factor largely responsible for 83 percent of the group having attended college. Indeed, two-thirds held bachelor's degrees (compared to 17 percent for Oregonians in general), and an amazing 12 percent had earned doctorates. Of those holding college degrees, 22 percent were in psychology or psychiatry. Doctors, lawyers, professors, teachers, musicians, dancers, and skilled craftspeople joined architects, actors, psychotherapists, social workers, and others to form a remarkable roster. FitzGerald (Sept. 22, 1986: 71) was being less than fair when she referred to the ranch as "the ultimate Me Generation boarding school." After all, the disciples were educated, intelligent, motivated, skillful, committed—a perfect set of attributes for a group of people confronted with the challenge of converting an arid wasteland into a Garden of Eden.

Indeed, commitment, the *sine qua non* of all utopian efforts, was as visible as the malas around their necks. In a commune, the ideal concept of living has to coincide with the cold, hard facts of day-to-day reality. Kanter (1972: 64) puts it succinctly: "In Utopia, for instance, who takes out the garbage?" Like other mundane tasks, taking out the garbage was not a problem for the committed Rajneeshee. Of the several measures Kanter (1972) describes for achieving "commitment," sacrifice, investment, community, renunciation, and mortification (the submission of self to social control), only two were missing at the commune: celibacy and a specific theology.

In addition to their commitment to the Bhagwan, the Rajneeshee were in other ways different from the population of a "typical" American town. After several research trips to Rajneeshpuram, Carter (1987: 160) reflected on what features of an "ordinary" town were missing:

> There were no children in residence, though a few were housed in Antelope. There were very few people over the age of 40 and almost no one was impaired. Most residents were in the 25–35 year range. In April, 1984, White Americans predominated, with most others of Northern European derivation (Germany, Switzerland, Holland, England, and some white Rhodesians and South Africans) and a small minority of Eastern Indians. Also startling was the lack of diversity in housing, commercial activities and publicly available facilities. Exclusive ownership by Rajneesh Corporations meant that housing was uniform. The usual small town varieties of churches were absent as well as many businesses (grocers, automobile dealers, hardware, etc.). Outside magazines, newspapers, books or television were not publicly available, media were virtually restricted to Rajneesh produced messages. No gasoline was readily available to passers-through. While a hotel suggests public services, access was limited to those willing to undergo rigorous security checks and sign away normal legal rights. The town was an exclusive (almost reclusive) total society with restricted outsider contact, limited to catering to spiritual and therapeutic needs of well-to-do "seekers." Routine tourists or travelers were discouraged.

The World Celebration at the Ranch

In July 1983, fifteen thousand people from around the world arrived at Rajneeshpuram to celebrate the movement's second annual World Celebration. By plane, car, and bus, red-clad true-believers and seekers swarmed onto the ranch to participate in a seven-day extravaganza of "Dynamic Meditation" dancing, therapy sessions, recreation, and enlightenment. It was a time to live and appreciate the commune's official theme of "love, lightness, and laughter."

The visiting red people and the other celebrants were greeted at the Visitor's Center by bright and attractive young women called "Twinkies," a cutesie play-on-words title based on their job as "hostesses." It was the Twinkies' job to act as guides to the never-ending stream of visitors (the Rajneeshpuram Chamber of Commerce claimed that in 1984, a hundred thousand visitors toured the ranch at two dollars a head) and to deal with the press. The latter job was becoming increasingly difficult as the conflict between the Rajneeshee and an increasingly hostile outside world intensified.

At $500 a person for tent accommodations, each of the faithful could stroll over to the great open-sided 2.2-acre Buddha hall and join a throng of other devotees. Although the Bhagwan was not speaking these days (he had entered into a "silent period" in his life), admiring sannyasin could listen to his audiotapes and drink in the ambrosia of his presence as he sat mute on the stage for hours at a time. The uncontested highlight of each day of the celebration was the Bhagwan's afternoon drive-by. A regular feature of everyday Rancho Rajneesh life, the drive-by occurred at precisely 2:00 PM and resulted in sannyasin dashing from their worksites to line the streets of Rajneeshpuram as the Bhagwan cruised slowly by in one of his celebrated Rolls-Royces. With armed security forces alongside and an Air Rajneesh chopper hovering noisily overhead, some of the faithful kneeled, some bowed low, and all gazed in loving admiration during the slow but seemingly all-too-swift passage. Many stayed longer than a week, paying $1,100 for three weeks or $3,000 for a three-month stay. This is a lot of money, but, then, the building and upkeep of a Buddhafield is not a cheap operation. By 1983, two years after coming to Oregon, the Rajneeshee had dumped 50 million dollars into the Ranch. By October 1985, the total would reach 200 million dollars.

Of the multi-millions spent at the ranch, nothing caught the outside world's attention as much as the fleet of Rolls-Royces. There were almost as many reasons given for the Bhagwan's car collection as there were cars. For those on the outside, the Rolls-Royces were largely viewed as offensive. The feeling of much of the world was reflected in the statement by one source in India who observed that "the money spent on 70 Rolls-Royces could take care of 700 families in India for the rest of their lives." (*The Oregonian*, June 30, 1985: 25). That the Rajneeshee enjoyed their master's display of wealth was evidenced by a popular bumper sticker at the ranch: "Jesus Saves. Moses Invests. Bhagwan Spends."

The festival was a success beyond any of the planners' dreams. Kirk Braun, a journalist sympathetic to the Rajneeshee, complained that while "official" Oregon ignored the economic significance of fifteen thousand visitors to a small commune in the midst of their dusty outback, the state's Department of Tourism and governor were heaping accolades on two businessmen for their efforts in bringing conventions of "several hundred" people to the state (1984: 195).

Rumblings at the Ranch

Not all was love, lightness, and laughter for the regulars at the Ranch, however. FitzGerald (Sept. 22, 1986: 96) found it extraordinary that these well-educated people did not notice "warning signals" that were evident even during the first two years and that should have indicated something was amiss. First, there was an intense fund-raising drive, during which Ma Sheela traveled around the world soliciting contributions. Sannyasin were asked to donate their pocket money, the rings off their fingers, the watches off their wrists, and were even encouraged to write home to parents for money. There was over-crowding that put a premium on toilets, showers, and living quarters (at its peak in 1984, five to six thousand people were living on the ranch), and the "total commitment" that strongly discouraged temporary absence. In addition, there was the premium placed on long hours of work, the lack of contact with outsiders, and the geographical isolation of the ranch.

Somewhat of a stir occurred in the spring of 1984, when disciples were encouraged to help build an arsenal of handguns and semiautomatic weapons, including Uzi carbines and Galil assault rifles. Taking note of the arms collection, FitzGerald (Sept. 22, 1986: 97) observed that some disciples might lay their life on the line for the commune, but others "would see a clear alternative in the hot tubs of Mill Valley" (a Marin County community north of San Francisco).

It was also at this time that the Bhagwan began to speak again, eventually making three public announcements that had dramatic and unsettling effects on his disciples, not only at the Ranch but around the world. Ever since mid-1981, when the Bhagwan had entered into his "silent retreat," the group had been relying for the most part on Ma Anand Sheela for information. The first announcement was made in late 1981 and declared Rajneeshism a religion. Two years later, the Bhagwan codified his remarks on Rajneeshism as a religion in a booklet entitled, *Rajneeshism: An Introduction to Bhagwan Shree Rajneesh and His Religion*. Later, in 1985, he would repudiate the codification, claiming the booklet was the work of overzealous disciples. The second announcement, in September 1983, again through Ma Sheela, predicted an apocalypse brought about by natural catastrophes and nuclear war sometime between 1984 and 1999. This proclamation caused even more sannyasin to pour into the already overcrowded ranch. The third announcement came in March 1984, when Ma Sheela delivered the Bhagwan's reflections on AIDS. Predicting two-thirds of the world would succumb to the disease, he urged that strict precautions be undertaken by his followers. Quickly, the Rajneesh Medical Corporation issued a series of guidelines designed to protect the group: oral and anal sex were out, gloves and condoms were in. Dishes were to be rinsed in bleach, while toilet seats and telephones were to be sprayed with alcohol. Gordon (1987: 131) observed that "the feast of fucking was over. The time for fasting had come." All of this, however, amounted to mere nagging discomforts compared to the major problems that were settling over the Oregon commune and would soon lead to its demise.

The Collapse

As has often been the case with communes in the United States, Rajneeshpuram collapsed while still in its fledgling development. After such an astounding beginning, what factors led to its fall? Although the movement was never free from conflict or controversy, the following problems were of sufficient magnitude to eventually bust what followers called the Buddhafield's "special flow of energy" and force its dissolution.

Violation of Immigration Laws

The Immigration and Naturalization Service (INS) had never relaxed its tenacious grip on Bhagwan Shree Rajneesh. Because he had entered the United States on a limited medical visa, his only hope of a prolonged stay was by achieving legal recognition as a religious leader. Because the group seesawed on this matter frequently and openly—stating one time that Rajneeshism was a religion, another time denying it as such—this avenue was easily closed by the INS. The INS also charged that the Bhagwan and his followers were running a sham marriage operation by arranging marriages of American members with foreign members, thus maximizing the number of foreign sannyasins in the United States. These, and thirty-plus other counts of conspiring to violate immigration laws, eventually resulted in the Bhagwan pleading guilty to two false statement charges and being slapped with a fine of $400,000 and a ten-year suspended sentence.

Violation of Land-Use Laws

Another major problem was the commune's obvious thwarting of Oregon's rigid land-use laws. A powerful environmentalist group known as the 1000 Friends of Oregon led a strong, persistent, and often controversial attack against the Rajneeshee attempt to incorporate Rajneeshpuram. The 1000 Friends successfully argued that the commune was building a city in a rural-use-only zone. Although the Rajneeshee lost out on this critical issue, they were not without support from unbiased people who followed the skirmish and concluded the commune received shameful treatment from the various levels of government involved in the land-use decisions.

The "Share-A-Home" Program

In the late summer of 1984, Oregonians were enraged as word spread that the Bhagwan's followers were importing thousands of "street people" to the Ranch in order to increase the Rajneeshee voting power in the November elections. It would have been impossible to find a solitary non-commune-dwelling Oregon resident who really bought the claim that the importing of the "street people" was just another example of Bhagwanian humanitarianism. Carter (1987:161) observed that recruiters traveled through major American cities offering meals, beer, cigarettes, and a place to sleep; eventually, approximately four thousand indigents signed up for the "Share-A-Home" program. As might be expected, there was immediate conflict between the street people and the Ranch regulars. The commune could not for long sustain the predictable conflict between the degree-laden devotees of an Eastern master with three-score Rolls-Royces, on the one hand, and a collection of the homeless from the streets of Chicago, New York, Miami, Houston, and Los Angeles. Within a week over half the recruits had forsaken their rations of free beer and cigarettes and checked out of the commune. Some were simply bused off the ranch and deposited in one Oregon town or another, a practice that left Oregonians screaming until their faces turned as red as their antagonists' clothing. The "Share-A-Home" program and its negative effect on the non-commune citizenry amounted to a gargantuan public relations blunder by the Rajneeshee.

"Being Outrageous"

The Rajneeshee's delight in deriding and provoking their less-sophisticated rural Oregon neighbors and the state's political leaders must also be mentioned as a factor in their downfall (the sannyasin loved to describe such behavior as "being outrageous"). Condoned and used by Bhagwan himself—when he was speaking—the practice was widespread among the commune members, but reached its undeniable perfection in the pronouncements of Ma Anand Sheela. Shortly after the group's arrival at the Big Muddy Ranch and subsequent takeover of Antelope, Ma Sheela commented at a City Council meeting that the local students looked "retarded" and observed that a local woman was responsible for the death of her husband. Although the man had died in a hunting accident, Ma Sheela opined that he had shot himself because his wife "was screwing around with another man" (FitzGerald: Sept. 29, 1986: 93). In an interview with writer Frances FitzGerald she referred to the Antelope citizens as "your average day-to-day bigots. Their brains are in the fifteenth century" (Sept. 29, 1986: 94). That Ma Sheela was President of the Rajneesh Foundation International and a highly visible spokeswoman for the group—appearing frequently on national television and with regularity in the newspapers—her references to Oregonians as "red necks," "monkeys," and "hicks," along with press pictures of her "giving the finger" to an adversary or posing with her .357 Magnum sidearm did little to smooth the boiling waters.

Carter (1987: 169) singles out such "intention to offend" as a primary reason the Rajneesh communes in Poona and Oregon were rejected. Noting that Bhagwan Shree Rajneesh is a tantric guru, more specifically, a "left-handed" tantric guru, Carter reasons that the outrageous behavior simply followed a tradition—one of violating the value system of surrounding populations. Unfortunately for the movement, such offensive behavior proved to be intolerable to outsiders.

Schafer (1987: 31) argues persuasively that the group's delight in angering Oregonians was a tactical ploy designed to "promote antipathy from the outside for the sake of building internal unity," and concludes that the practice eventually helped cause the commune's downfall. Not that the Oregonians were slouches when it came to responding in kind. Bhagwan jokes abounded, as did snickering references to the "Poontang" ashram (the Poona Center), the "Crotch Guru," the "Old Bag of Worms," "cultists," "zombies," "red clones," and "satanists."

Departure of "The Gang"

The most serious blow to the Ranch came on September 14, 1985, when the commune members awakened to discover that Ma Anand Sheela and three other commune leaders had fled in the night to Switzerland. Ten other leaders were to follow the next day. Breaking his silence, the Bhagwan came out swinging, asserting that Sheela and "her gang" were all along responsible for such heinous crimes as the attempted poisonings of seven people (including his personal physician, dentist, and the Jefferson County district attorney), the masterminding of a 1984 outbreak of salmonella in the area, the bugging of his bedroom and other facilities at the ranch, wiretapping, and the torching of the Wasco County Planning Office.

The Departure of the Bhagwan

The Bhagwan and his remaining close advisors moved quickly to restore a semblance of order and calm at the ranch, but the damage was irreversible. On Sunday night, October 27, 1985, the Bhagwan

and six associates chartered two Learjets to fly them from the ranch. As in the Poona getaway four years earlier, few disciples were involved in the departure. The eventual destination was Bermuda, but when they landed at the Charlotte, North Carolina, airport they were arrested by federal customs agents. The media was alive with accounts of the story, especially the Learjets and their cargo of Bhagwan's white-upholstered throne, $58,000 in cash, a box loaded with jewel-encrusted watches, and a .38-caliber Smith and Wesson revolver. After pleading guilty of trying to avoid prosecution, the Bhagwan paid his fine and left for India with his seventy-two-year-old mother, who had come to visit him in Oregon. More than five hundred red-garbed sannyasin would be on hand to greet him when he landed at the airport in New Delhi, chanting "Our hero is back".

Ironically, the day the Bhagwan was arrested at the Charlotte airport, the West German police had nabbed Ma Anand Sheela and two others who had fled from Oregon with her, at a Black Forest resort hotel. Pleading guilty to immigration fraud, wiretapping, attempted murder, first- and second-degree assault, arson, and involvement in the salmonella poisoning escapade, Sheela would be sentenced to four and a half years in a California prison after a plea-bargaining agreement on several charges. (She had been facing the prospect of two twenty-year and two ten-year sentences to run concurrently.)

There was a brief flurry of excitement among the stunned sannyasin about the possibility of keeping the ranch in operation, but the Bhagwan's absence and the freezing of the commune's bank accounts foretold an imminent closure. A sannyasin would later tell me, "It would have been useless. The place simply could not have existed without Bhagwan. He was everything. There was nothing without him." By Christmas 1985, most of the sannyasin had dispersed, some returning to prior jobs, others operating Rajneesh-oriented businesses, still others going back to their pre-Ranch homes in hopeful anticipation of a Phoenix-like resurrection of their beloved Buddhafield.

Aftermath

Today, a small caretaking crew and administrative staff remain on the Ranch, overseeing the sale of equipment and the hoped-for sale of the Ranch itself. Although the assessed value of the property was 65 million dollars, the initial advertised price was 40 million dollars. By July 1986, the asking price had dropped to 28.5 million dollars. As of January 1988, much of the ranch had been dismantled and sold, but the ranch acreage and large buildings remained for sale at 26 million dollars.

And what of the much-discussed ninety-three Rolls-Royces? Eighty-five of them were purchased by a Dallas, Texas, car dealer for nearly seven million dollars; he later complained that he was having trouble selling many of them because they were either painted in wild metallic-flake colors or bedecked with symbols inspired by Bhagwan's teachings.

Why did so many intelligent, highly educated, seemingly independent, thinking people reared in a democratic tradition give themselves spiritually and intellectually to the autocracy and "outrageousness" that flourished at Rajneeshpuram? The literature offers the following: Schafer (1987) likes the dynamics of "psychic surrender": that is, the investment of trust in Bhagwan was so great that sannyasin abandoned their critical thinking. Gordon (1987: 59) also builds on the idea of surrender, reasoning that the phenomenon caused the disciples to lower their everyday protective barriers and recreate "the kind of symbiotic dependency that the infant has on its mother." Benderly (1988: 70) figures it was the Bhagwan's sheer power that was responsible. Braun (1984: 72) believes it was a matter of unconditional commitment. FitzGerald (Sept. 29, 1986: 124) concludes that the disciples followed the system because they were "taking responsibility without taking responsibility at all"—they had

"clear consciences" because their all-knowing and trusted guru was responsible for everything that occurred. Carter (1987: 170) thinks the movement's practice of "deprogramming" is important in understanding the phenomenon: in "deprogramming" disciples rid themselves of "prior socialization, normative rules and guidelines for behavior."

Most accounts of the breakup agree that the Ranch financial records were in sound order and that the administrative staff had set about immediately to pay the Ranch's debts and square its accounts with individual sannyasins who had loaned money to the Rajneesh Foundation. Whether the latter was actually done is not known at this date.

Shortly after Rajneesh's return to India the government began to cancel the visas of his non-Indian close associates. Perhaps because of this and numerous other negative signals from the Indian government, he decided to embark on a "world tour." After a short spell in Crete, an enraged Greek Orthodox Church quickly pressured the Greek government to expel him. Germany and Italy refused his request for entry, as did Switzerland, Great Britain, Spain, and Sweden and a half-dozen other countries. He eventually was granted entry to Uruguay, where he remained briefly—then on to Jamaica, Pakistan, and once again, where it all started, Poona.

It would not be wise to bet that the Bhagwan is washed-up as a spiritual leader. The strength and continuing devotion of his followers worldwide, plus his past personal history and that of his movement for the twenty years of its existence, strongly indicate that Rajneeshism, in one form or another, will continue to be.

10

The Occult: Paths to the Unknown

The occult, from the Latin *occulere*, meaning to conceal, is a non-specific term for things magical and mystical—a kind of esoteric knowledge available only to those initiated into the secrets of acquisition. As the authors of the following selections make clear, the study of the occult properly falls into the realm of the study of magic, witchcraft, and religion. In addition, the tremendous recent interest in the occult has made it a worthy subject for study. Wuthnow (1978) cites evidence that the occult has become an even more popular supernatural belief than is the belief in God. The popularity of the occult serves as an index of social strain, of rebellion against tradition, and of the need for small-group reinforcement.

This chapter emphasizes occult practices in contemporary America and demonstrates that even Western groups seek wisdom and knowledge unavailable through science or established religions. The articles incorporated here will also demonstrate that occult practices in America appear to many to be more exotic in nature than the traditional religious practices of members of non-Western societies.

Goat mask of a modern witch high priestess.

Most attempts at determining how believers in the occult feel about religion are met with difficulty. Some occultists see themselves as philosophers, whereas others describe themselves as scientists or even as religious practitioners—the latter in spite of the usual disdain occultists have for the teachings of established religions. In regard to this point, Harriet Whitehead (1974: 561) believes the rejection by occultists of Christian theodicy does not mean a denial of Christian morality, for there is evidence that contemporary occult publications reflect a "generalized" Christian morality. What is being rejected by the occultists, according to Whitehead, is the doctrine of atonement and the belief that the unrepentant will be cosigned to some sort of eternal punishment. Whitehead sums up the basis of American occultism in the following way:

> Occultism seeks to reunite the separate pieces of the intellectual, emotional, and apprehensional jig-saw puzzle by surveying and abstracting from all the traditions that address themselves to the task of *understanding* things, whether this understanding be directed at practical mastery or a passive acceptance. Occultism posits an underlying singular Truth, the search for which cannot be confined to a particular style and the content of which cannot exclude any dimension of human experience, however "irrational" it may seem (Whitehead 1974: 587).

As is the case with all religions, occultists have developed systems of beliefs that guide true believers, but because occult practices appear exotic to most observers, they are viewed with skeptical interest and suspicion. Astrology is the most popular and accepted of the occultist traditions in the Western world. The growing popularity of witchcraft, however, and the fact that witchcraft is still well embedded in traditional beliefs in various parts of the pre-industrial world, offer an opportunity for cross-cultural comparison (see Chapter 5 on "Witchcraft, Sorcery, and Other Forces of Evil").

Modern witches, according to Frank Smyth, "refer to their religion as 'wicca,' the feminine form of an Old English word, 'wicce,' meaning a witch, possibly a derivative of the verb 'wiccian,' to practice witchcraft. Wicca is a largely urban cult. . . . In common with more orthodox religions, wicca has worship as its main object, but the additional element of magic lends the cult an illicit and undoubtedly attractive aura" (Smyth 1970: 1866). Wicca has a matriarchal character, and while in most cases both men and women are referred to as witches, local organizations of witches, called covens, are made up of more women than men. Indeed, the high priestess is symbolic of the mother goddess and not dissimilar to the Virgin Mary; the mother goddess is the principal deity of witchlore. Wicca is basically a fertility cult with its great festivals geared to the seasons (Smyth 1970: 1866). The elements of sexuality that sometimes appear as part of initiation and the symbolic or actual intercourse of members have brought wicca into disrepute in many quarters, but the explanation that it is a fertility cult has been used as a justification for these acts. Whatever the accusations made or answers given, it has provided the media with tantalizing copy.

The popular press in this country typically portrays believers in the occult as a single group. This is an incorrect assessment. Marcello Truzzi (1974: 628–32) provides a more accurate analysis of the occult by dividing practitioners into three broad categories. At the first level are people whose involvement in the occult is minimal—who do not see themselves as occultists per se but as concerned individuals interested in explaining such strange occurrences as flying saucers, assorted land and sea monsters, and various parapsychological phenomena. Typically their activities are characterized by an absence of mysticism, supernaturalism, and anti-scientific thought; in fact, scientific support for their beliefs is highly valued. On Truzzi's second level of occultism are people who seek to understand mysterious causal relationships between events—who express an interest, for example, in numerology, sun-sign astrology, and palmistry. Knowledge gained at this level is more likely to be *a*scientific or *extra*-scientific rather than *anti*-scientific. Truzzi's third level of occultism is concerned with those complex belief systems—witchcraft, Satanism, ritual magic, and other mystical traditions—that combine elements from the first two levels. Third-level believers often question or contradict scientific validation of an event or relationship, and thus may see themselves as competitors to science. Truzzi concludes that although some occult believers exist in "pure form," most are a combination of all three types.

This final chapter is a departure from the preceding ones in that every article is based on American society. This is because the subject matter, the occult, constitutes a set of beliefs and practices that become distinctive only in cultures steeped in a scientific tradition of problem-solving. What the scientific world regards as occult would possibly constitute a "correct" system of knowledge or of technical arts in a non-Western culture. The formulas, the spells, the paraphernalia, the reliance upon the supernatural—all aspects of the occult world—fall quite acceptably into a culture that relies on magic as a logical system of explaining events or getting something done.

There can be no doubt that from the very beginning a cloud of controversy has hung over occultism. Yet, through all the controversy its appeal has attracted scholars, scientists, and philosophers, as well as the general public. Freud at one time was fascinated by certain numerological theories, but apparently discarded them as well as the entire subject of occultism. The conflict between Freud and Jung over the occult is caught in the following quotation from Jung (1961: 150):

> I can still recall vividly how Freud said to me, "My dear Jung, promise me never to abandon the sexual theory. This is the most essential thing of all. You see, we must make a dogma of it, an unshakeable bulwark." He said that to me with great emotion, in the tone of a father saying, "and promise me this one thing, my dear son: that you will go to church every Sunday." In some astonishment I asked him, "A bulwark —against what?" To which he replied, "Against the black tide of mud"—and here he hesitated for a moment, then added—"of occultism."

Margaret Mead's article is an excellent selection to open the chapter. Mead defines the occult and offers some reasons why so many people are fascinated by forms of wisdom that originated in Babylonia and ancient Egypt and by beliefs and practices known in Europe in the Middle Ages and earlier. Barry Singer and Victor Benassi also examine the popularity of the occult in an age of science, and then speculate about the social mechanisms that may have given rise to the recent widespread interest in the occult. John

Fritscher believes that what witches say about themselves is more revealing than what non-witches say about them. Accordingly, Fritscher presents the personal revelations of Anton Szandor LaVey, high priest and founder of the Church of Satan in San Francisco. Marcello Truzzi assesses the rising tide of occultism in the United States. Truzzi, who has done extensive research on contemporary occultism, concludes that for most Americans the interest in the occult is a leisure-time activity and a fad of popuar culture rather than a serious religious movement.

In the final article, New Age disciples such as Shirley MacLaine are discussed in terms of their particular advocacies, which range from the spiritual to the sometimes farcical. Oho Friedrich's encyclopedic discussion includes most of those elements in the so-called New Age movement that have captured the imaginations of millions in their search for health, enlightenment, and joy.

References

Jung, C. G.
    1961 *Memories, Dreams, Reflections.* New York: Vintage Books.

Smyth, Frank
    1970 "Modern Witchcraft." In Richard Cavendish, ed., *Man, Myth and Magic*, Vol. 14, pp. 1865–70. New York: Marshall Cavendish Corporation.

Truzzi, Marcello
    1974 "Towards a Sociology of the Occult: Notes on Modern Witchcraft." In Irving I. Zaretsky and Mark P. Leone, eds., *Religious Movements in Contemporary America*, pp. 628–45. Princeton, N.J.: Princeton University Press.

Whitehead, Harriet
    1974 "Reasonably Fantastic: Some Perspectives on Scientology, Science Fiction, and Occultism." In Irving I. Zaretsky and Mark P. Leone, eds., *Religious Movements in Contemporary America*, pp. 547–87. Princeton, N.J.: Princeton University Press.

Wuthnow, R.
    1978 *Experimentation in American Religion.* Los Angeles: University of California Press.

The Occult: On the Edge of the Unknown

Margaret Mead

Margaret Mead's knowledge of Western society serves as the basis for her explanation of the popularity of the occult among contemporary youth. Providing a number of sociological and psychological explanations for the phenomena, Mead advocates a combination of the abilities of open-minded scientists and open-minded occultists to gain entry to the unknown through experiments carried out in an atmosphere of skeptical but meticulously careful exploration. She rejects the value of extremists of either camp in this attempt to contact other intelligences in the universe, and argues for expansion of knowledge of our own human capacities and senses.

HOW DO YOU DEFINE THE OCCULT?

I asked a group of my students that question not long ago. Their answers were both knowledgeable and puzzling—and very different from what they would have been only a few years ago.

All of them—somewhat to my surprise—said correctly that the occult has to do with things kept "secret" or "hidden" from those not initiated, and with the mysterious and perhaps the supernatural. But their examples encompassed the ancient and the modern, the East and the West; they included subjects nowadays studied by scientists, and other subjects believed to be beyond the reach of empirical science as we understand it today. They ranged from astrology and alchemy to witchcraft, from medieval cabalism to modern Theosophy, from Taoism to Yoga, from geomancy to numerology, from palm reading and fortune telling with tarot cards to clairvoyance and telekinesis and telepathy, from the magical to the mystical. Altogether it was an extraordinary mélange of ideas, beliefs, practices and forms of both prescientific and scientific exploration and explanation, held together by the idea of mystery and of some relationship to what we call the supernatural.

None of the students rejected the idea of the occult out of hand, and the diversity of the subjects mentioned suggests the paths on which their curiosity had taken them and, further, the extent to which the idea of the occult has captured the imagination not just of these students but of so many of their generation.

Why should this be? How is it that so many of our young people are fascinated by forms of wisdom that originated long ago in Babylonia and ancient Egypt, by conceptions of life and arts developed in the distant past in China and India, by beliefs and practices known in Europe in the Middle Ages and earlier?

It is certainly strange and unexpected that in a generation that belongs by birth to the space age, so many young people have turned away from the sciences that have made possible the world they live in and the extraordinary expansion of our knowledge about our universe. Instead there are, all around the world, very large numbers of young people who spend long, solitary hours in silent meditation; others who gather in groups to chant mystical syllables in monotonous, dreamlike repetition; others who concentrate on learning complex and difficult body disciplines; and still others who scan numbers minutely to work out the relationship between the day and the hour of their birth and the astrological potentialities of a day on which they propose to make a journey or marry or take an examination.

How can we explain all this?

It is useful, I think, to bear in mind that since the earliest times and in the simplest cultures of which we have any knowledge, members of human societies have tried to understand the past—where they came from and who they are and how the world came to be as it is—and to discover how to predict the future so as to order their lives more safely. And as far as we know, this kind of striving often has been a compound of two very different things: careful, accurate observations of the part of the world in which a people lived, and imaginative explanations of *why* and *how* that often were closer to dreams than anything we think of as science.

People have observed the movements of the sun and the moon, the configurations of the fixed stars, the motions of the visible planets, the changing seasons, the migrations of birds or whales or salmon or the monthly appearance of fish over the reef. They have mused on the way sleepers seem to leave their inert bodies and travel to far places, and on the way a person's shadow grows and shrinks and dances in the flickering firelight; and they have concluded that there must be some part—perhaps more than one part—of the self that is separable from the body and may have existed before birth and may endure after death. And some peoples have solved, with a belief in an endlessly turning circle of reincarnation, the problem of life and death in which past and future are linked. But however differently human beings have tried to explain what they could observe, thinking about

our relationship to the cosmos has been a distinctive, universal human activity.

Through long ages, workable knowledge slowly accumulated and was passed from one people to another—as, for instance, the idea of zero treated as a number passed from Hindu to Arabian and finally to European mathematicians in the later Middle Ages, making modern mathematics possible. But almost invariably ancient wisdom was embedded in magical, religious or ideological systems. Such systems enfolded the knowledge that made it possible, for instance, for the ancient Egyptians to work out quite accurately the length of the solar year or, using simple geometric principles, to measure land accurately and design great structures such as the pyramids.

Sometimes an element has escaped from its magical matrix, but without losing a kind of aura of the mysterious, the marvelous. There is, for example, the number 7. This was the number of the luminaries in the sky (the sun, the moon and the five visible planets) that were observed in their courses by the ancient Babylonians and were believed to control the fate of all human beings. So 7 became embedded as a key number in astrology, but it also broke free of its matrix and time and again has been associated in a marvelous way with great things. So we have Rome built on seven hills; we have the seven seas and the Seven Wonders of the World, the seven ages of man, the seven deadly sins, the seventh heaven, where, according to Islamic belief and the cabala, God and the most exalted angels live. There is also the seventh son (or the seventh son of the seventh son), variously believed to be gifted with healing powers or to be clairvoyant or telepathic or simply lucky, and among Gypsies the seventh daughter who always tells true fortunes.

People can get into a fine state of confusion over beliefs like those that relate numbers to the events of life. And their belief that there is a real relationship can easily affect their expectations and their acts, and so the outcome of events. The belief that 13 is an unlucky number, a number that foreshadows disaster, is still potent enough to cause a hand to slip, a bolt to be left unfastened, a mission to fail on the 13th day. Yet the Thirteen Colonies stood together against England to form a new country.

When people go back through degraded superstition and the veils of a religious symbolism to trace a magic number or a whole number system to its oldest matrix, there is a very good chance that they will feel they are finding out something secret and wonderful, something that puts them in touch with the deep wisdom of the ancients, something that can give them power too. And they may begin to think that numbers matter—like the Pythagoreans, who built a kind of religion on the belief that the essence of all things is number and that the most complex ideas could be expressed as relations between numbers.

Tracing back such a philosophical conception of how the universe is constructed and how human beings are related to the universe and one another, people may easily come to endow numbers (or, equally, some other set of emotionally highly charged symbols) with extraordinary powers. And when they find that there is working knowledge embedded in such a matrix (for the Pythagoreans were innovative mathematicians as well as philosophers and religious cultists), they may well take it as proof that the special view of the universe, the religious belief, also is "true."

This is, it seems to me, one important ingredient in the current fascination with the occult. And because so many of these old beliefs have been superseded as obsolete, outlawed religiously, or politically (sometimes, 1,000 or more years ago), driven underground and carried through generations by tiny groups or carried in writings buried in obscure libraries and rediscovered by accident, there is also the fascination of secretly resuscitating and secretly joining with others in practices known only to an initiated few. This identifies the practitioner at one and the same time as an individual who is different and as someone who belongs to a group with a unique identity. In a world in which individuals continually see themselves classified anonymously as one in a category of thousands —or millions—the search for personal identity can become crucial to survival.

But there is another aspect to the search that guides modern young people in their choices of what to look for in ancient beliefs and practices. Modern science and its application—for example in medicine—has become increasingly impersonal and detached from the problems that beset individuals as they grow and mature, suffer disappointment and loss and try to find satisfaction and happiness—or simply health and quiet. So in their search for some alternative life-style a great many young people turn to those occult beliefs and disciplines in other cultures—Chinese or Indian, Japanese or Persian in origin—that promise both a greater understanding of one's own self and some sense of unity between one's private, personal self and the infinite, impersonal universe. In the predicament in which these young people find themselves, the familiar disciplines of Christianity and Judaism have become bonds to be cast off and only the unfamiliar disciplines of Zen or Yoga or one of the new cultist groups have the imaginative power to give them access to their own minds and bodies and a sense of participation in some larger, spiritual whole.

This is, I think, a use of the occult that is quite different from anything in the past, for it is a specific response to needs unmet in our very troubled present. For many it has great fascination; for some it is a way out of the present.

However, there are also points of real contact between certain ideas of great importance in the occult—telepathy, for example—and the thinking of scientists whose experiments have taken these ideas to the very edge of science. Here the extraordinary engineering capacities of scientific instruments are being brought to bear in more and more refined ways to explore and characterize the infinitely small and the vastly distant, the extremely delicate and the extremely complex. With the use of infrared photography and under certain conditions, today we can take a picture of a car that was parked in a parking space yesterday; we can "look" at the land surface of Mars; we can "see" with the radio telescope unimagined distances into the universe. And on this growing edge of knowledge, scientists are devising experiments that may— almost certainly *will*—give us, in time, new insight into the powers attributed to seers and clairvoyants, to those who have the power to "see" auras, to communicate with plants, to dream or visualize events outside the bounds of time.

Instead of a world in which scientists, who have been by definition unbelievers in all that the great religions have ever claimed, are divided by a deep unbridgeable gulf from blind believers, who insistently reject all that science has learned, we are in the process of discovering a middle ground. Here the most open-minded scientists and the most open-minded believers in occultism can meet to plan and carry out experiments in an atmosphere of expectant, skeptical but also meticulously careful exploration. We are living on the edge of the unknown not only in terms of possible communication with other intelligences somewhere in the universe but also with renewed and greatly expanded knowledge of our own human sensibilities and capacities.

In can be said that in some sense we have come full circle. And it may be that among those young people who seem to be lost in some unreal relationship to the magical thinking or the miraculous beliefs of the past, there will be some who will shake themselves loose of inappropriate beliefs, past and present, and will help to shape a world society in which women and men know what human beings in the past could see only through a glass darkly, know only in part.

Occult Beliefs

Barry Singer
Victor A. Benassi

In the following article Barry Singer and Victor A. Benassi maintain, as did Mead, the social and scientific importance of understanding the occult; although they show these beliefs to be based on psychological and sociological rather than on rational determinants, they do not totally reject their validity. According to Singer and Benassi, media distortion, social uncertainty, and the deficiencies of human reasoning seem to be the basis of occult beliefs. They also maintain that occult phenomena are a possible index of fluctuations in religious belief or social dislocation. The article addresses the question of the origins and mechanism of the individual's occult beliefs and speculates about the social mechanisms that may have given rise to the recent widespread involvement with the occult.

Reprinted from *American Scientist*, Vol. 69, no. 1 (1981), pp. 49–55, by permission of the authors and the Scientific Research Society.

WHY IS AN UNDERSTANDING OF OCCULT BELIEFS scientifically and socially important? One reason is their current prevalence in Western societies. Occult beliefs have increased dramatically in the United States during the last two decades (Freedland 1972; Godwin 1972). Far from being a "fad," preoccupation with the occult now forms a pervasive part of our culture. Garden-variety occultisms such as astrology and ESP have swelled to historically unprecedented levels (Eliade 1976). Belief in ESP, for instance, is consistently found to be moderate or strong in 80–90 percent of our population (Gallup 1978; Polzella et al. 1975); in one survey it ranked as our most popular supernatural belief, edging out belief in God in strength and prevalence (Wuthnow 1978). Ouija boards overtook Monopoly as the nation's best-selling board game in 1967.

As indexed by audience tallies and book sales, more exotic occultisms such as spoon bending, the Bermuda Triangle, biorhythms, psychic healing, and hauntings have also increased dramatically in variety and popularity since the early 1960s. Von Däniken's book *Chariots of the Gods?*, a vivid account of ancient astronauts' bestowing their technology and spermatozoa upon human beings, has become the best-selling book of modern times. Occult beliefs are salient not only among the lay public, but also among college students, including those at some of our science-oriented campuses. The occult trend shows no signs of diminishing.

The current high level and strength of occult beliefs, which at least implicitly constitute a challenge to the validity of science and to the authority of the scientific community, may be a cause for our concern. This growing trend is also intrinsically of scientific interest as a psychological and sociological phenomenon. The psychological mechanisms involved in occult beliefs may represent more dramatic forms of some mundane pathologies of reasoning. To the extent that occult and mundane beliefs have similar determinants, the study of occult beliefs, which are at the outer limits of irrationality, may throw light on more ordinary reasoning pathologies.

From a sociological point of view, the occult phenomenon is of interest as a possible index of fluctuations in religious belief or social dislocation. Moreover, the study of occult beliefs may further our understanding of scientific belief systems as they are explicitly constructed to compensate for the cognitive shortcomings which characterize many occult beliefs. This article will address the question of the origins and mechanisms of the individual's occult beliefs, a topic which psychological research is beginning to illuminate. We will also speculate about the social mechanisms that may have given rise to the recent widespread involvement with the occult.

Let us make clear at the outset of this discussion that we do not assume the beliefs and practices termed "occult" or "paranormal" to be totally without validity. They seem rather to span a range from the objectively unsupportable at present to the demonstrably absurd. Therefore, to the extent that such beliefs are held widely and strongly, they are probably based on psychological and sociological rather than rational determinants.

A variety of methodological cautions are appropriate in this inquiry. It is likely that differing occult beliefs have different determinants. Evidence suggests, for instance, that those occult beliefs which are institutionalized and are organized around a social community of believers may serve functions similar to those of traditional religions, whereas other beliefs cluster with factors related to escapist entertainment, such as interest in fantasy and science fiction (Bainbridge 1978). Still others may be personally insignificant beliefs acquired desultorily through media misinformation. Determinants may contribute differently at various levels of strength of a particular belief. Further, it has been shown for astrology and spiritualism, for instance, that several disparate demographic populations tend to entertain these beliefs for differing reasons (Jahoda 1969; Robbins et al. 1978)

Research on occult beliefs has not reached the scope and precision necessary to address these complexities in full. A complete account of the rise in occult beliefs will have to explain the concomitant rise of such beliefs in other industrialized na-

tions for which data are available (Jahoda 1969), and probably should also account for recent social movements which appear correlated with the occult trend, such as the development of a youth counterculture and the recent spread of pentacostal and charismatic religions through a considerable portion of the world. Social science has provided a number of plausible explanations for these social trends, but little relevant data. However, we believe we can identify at present a number of causal or contributing factors involved in occult beliefs, keeping in mind the strictures discussed above.

Media Promotion of the Occult

It is not clear how great a role promotion by the popular media played in starting the occult inflation of the early 1960s. The present treatment of the occult by the media, however, may account for much of the near universality of belief. The public is chronically exposed to films, newspaper reports, "documentaries," and books extolling occult or pseudoscientific topics, with critical coverage largely absent. Our most trusted and prestigious sources of information are no exception. When the layperson hears about New Zealand UFOs from Walter Cronkite or reads about new frontiers in psychic healing in a front-page article in the *Los Angeles Times* (1977), he has prima facie reasons for believing such phenomena valid. Such uncritical coverage may be due in part to the inherent difficulties of science reporting in a popular medium. However, media coverage of the occult may sometimes be deceptive and monetarily motivated. It is our impression that the public is not aware of the extent to which First Amendment privileges permit such practices. The public seems to trust the printed word implicitly.

Research has consistently shown that people attribute most of their occult beliefs to the popular media and/or to personal experiences (Evans 1973). In a survey of several hundred college students, we were surprised to find that "scientific media" was also listed as a source of occult beliefs—more frequently than popular media, personal experience, personal faith, or logical arguments. When the students were asked afterwards to list examples of the scientific media in question, however, not one mentioned even a single genuinely scientific source. Instead, *Reader's Digest* and the *National*

Enquirer were occasionally cited as "scientific media," as were such films as *The Exorcist* and *Star Wars* (i.e. "the Force"). Television "documentaries" were also frequently mentioned, with the documentary "Chariots of the Gods?" being the single most frequently cited "scientific" source. Scientists have recently brought lawsuits against the television networks in protest of misleading occult documentaries. In response, the networks have claimed that their pro-occult coverage was formerly billed as "entertainment" rather than as a "documentary," and that the public can and does make this discrimination. Our evidence does not support these claims.

Although scientists who wish to rebut paranormal claims are sometimes denied access to the media, it also seems to be true that scientists have not extended themselves to gain media access and to issue public rebuttals. Those few scientists who do visibly protest may thus be perceived as stodgy and prejudiced isolates who have not yet climbed on the bandwagon of scientific acceptance of the occult. In addition, scientists have generally not cared to monitor or rebut occult claims issuing from their own academic institutions. Uncritical courses on occult topics are frequently found in the extension division of even our most reputable universities. In our experience the public invariably perceives the university as having then placed its stamp of approval upon the occultism, perhaps as having an entire department devoted to the topic, and understands that the extension instructor is "on the faculty."

The promotion of the occult by the popular media probably serves to heighten the general cognitive "availability" of the occult as an explanatory category in the culture. Puzzling events for which explanations might otherwise be conceived in terms of scientific phenomena or of fraud may tend to be explained as paranormal phenomena when the media bring this category so obtrusively to our attention.

Cognitive Biases and Heuristics

With occult beliefs currently so prevalent as to constitute, perhaps, part of what it means to be human, we might be justified in speculating on the basic quirks inherent in human psychological structure that support such beliefs. Current research in an area of cognitive psychology termed "cognitive biases and heuristics" has revealed deficits in human inference so universal and so stubborn that they can plausibly account for many of our errant beliefs, including occult ones. This recent spate of research, focusing on human problem-solving and judgmental processes, has resulted in an unflattering portrait of intuitive human reasoning (Nisbett and Ross 1980).

Briefly stated, the findings are that when presented with an array of data or a sequence of events in which they are instructed to discover an underlying order, subjects show strong tendencies to perceive order and causality in random arrays, to perceive a pattern or correlation which seems a priori intuitively correct even when the actual correlation in the data is counterintuitive, to jump to conclusions about the correct hypothesis, to seek and use only positive or confirmatory evidence, to construe evidence liberally as confirmatory, to fail to generate or to assess alternative hypotheses, and, having thus managed to expose themselves only to confirmatory instances, to be fallaciously confident of the validity of their judgments (Jahoda 1969; Einhorn and Hogarth 1978). In the analyzing of past events, these tendencies are exacerbated by selective memory and by failure to appreciate the pitfalls of post hoc analyses.

As an illustration of these tendencies, Wason (1960) asked subjects to try to discover a rule he had in mind for generating series of three numbers, where an example of the rule was the series "2, 4, 6." Subjects were to discover the rule by generating their own three-number series and receiving feedback on whether or not each series was an instance of the rule in question. The correct rule was "Any ascending sequence of whole numbers." Subjects typically generated sequences, such as "8, 10, 12, 14, 16, 18, etc.," repeatedly, for the duration of the experiment. They then expressed the rule as, for instance, "Even numbers increasing by two," and, having been consistently confirmed, were highly confident that this rule was the correct one.

When a judgment involves data that are probabilistic or minimally complex, people behave as if they do not possess the concept of probability, basing their estimates on a simple enumeration of positive instances rather than on the ratio of positive to negative instances. In addition, they adopt simplifying judgmental heuristics which can easily result in misconceptions (Tversky and Kahneman 1974). Thus, an instance is judged to be a number of a larger class on the basis of whether or not it seems intuitively to "represent" that class, rather than on the basis of the known number of times the instance in fact falls either in or out of the class; or hypotheses are chosen simply on the basis of their "availability," circumstances which have made them more vivid or salient. For instance, personal experience is more potent in influencing judgments than is abstract data (Nisbett and Ross 1980). When tested in experimental situations, scientists and mathematicians as well as laypersons have displayed the above tendencies (Kahneman and Tversky 1973; Mahoney 1976).

On the whole, then, our everyday intuitions do not seem to serve us well in the understanding of probabilistic or complex patterns in our environment. Under what circumstances will such cognitive biases and limitations lead to occult beliefs? Given that through media or other influences occult ideas are highly available in the culture, and given that there is a tendency to trust intuitive rather than scientific judgments, Marks and Kammann (1979), Myers (1980), and Singer (in press) have shown how occult beliefs can easily be acquired and supported through our cognitive biases and heuristics. For instance, due to our cognitive quirks it is predictable that we will notice and be impressed by the coincidence of a dream and an external event, will overlook the disconfirming instances of failures to match our dreams with reality, and will have difficulty appreciating the concept of random occurrence as an explanation for the coincidences. Even when informed that such matches are predicted to occur occasionally on the basis of the large number of opportunities for dreams and external events to coincide by chance, we fail to appreciate intuitively the mathematics of rare events. A rare event is seen as one that seldom occurs, regardless of the number of opportunities for its occurrence. As a result of our natural tendency to misunderstand the probabilities involved in a match of dreams and reality, the hypothesis of clairvoyance is apt to be a more intuitively compelling explanation for such an occurrence than the concept of chance.

As another example of cognitive bias, an event that seems mysterious, or difficult to explain through ordinary causes, will seem to us to "represent" a mysterious cause. When an abandoned ship is found floating intact off the coast of Florida, causes such as freakish weather, geysers, or sharks are often dismissed because they seem too rare and therefore inherently unlikely. An explanation in terms of some malevolent occult force in the Bermuda Triangle, however, seems intuitively to represent or "fit" the event better. The representativeness heuristic thus fails entirely to consider the very large number of opportunities for rare but natural causes to determine the event.

In the "illusion of control," another common cognitive fallacy, a random process such as rolling of dice is perceived as under personal control to the extent that it seems to incorporate elements of skill. At Long Beach we have shown (Benassi et al. 1979) that subjects who were permitted practice sessions or active physical involvement in a dice-rolling task reported greater belief in their ability to produce psychokinesis than subjects who were instructed to "influence" the dice but were not permitted such involvement.

Experiments which have attempted to encourage disconfirmation of occult or illusory beliefs by motivating subjects to think through their judgments more carefully or by providing blatant disconfirmatory input have uniformly revealed an astonishing resistance to change of such beliefs. Marks and Kammann (1979), in attempting to reduce the impression of validity of generalized personality descriptions, provided subjects with negatively toned, highly specific, and inherently unlikely statements about their personality, but found only a slight reduction of belief in their accuracy.

In a series of experiments (Benassi and Singer, in press; Benassi et al., in press) we arranged for an amateur magician to perform three psychic-like stunts—blindfold reading, teleportation of ashes, and mental bending of a metal rod—in front of six introductory psychology classes. Under one condition, the instructors skeptically introduced the performer as an alleged psychic, and under the other as an amateur magician. Belief was assessed through written feedback from the students to the performer. We expected to demonstrate a difference in occult belief depending on the introductory descriptions, but found instead that three-quarters of the subjects in both conditions believed strongly that the performer was psychic; more than a few, in fact, displayed an agitated conviction that the performer was an agent of Satan.

We then added a third condition in which the instructors quite emphatically repeated six different times that the performer was an amateur magician and that the students would be seeing only tricks, and not psychic phenomena. A written check attested that the students had heard and understood their instructors. This manipulation succeeded in reducing the occult belief, but only to the level where 50 percent of the class believed the performer to be psychic.

In follow-up studies with other subjects we provided neutral written descriptions of the performer and asked for an assessment of whether the performer was genuinely psychic. Again we found a majority of subjects judging that he was. We then asked whether magicians could also perform such stunts as described, and do so in identical fashion, and found near-unanimous agreement that they could; when asked how many people who performed such stunts were likely to be fakes and magicians, instead of genuine psychics, students agreed that the vast majority were likely to be tricksters and magicians. Finally, we asked students to re-estimate the likelihood that the particular performance described was in fact psychic, in light of the information they themselves had just generated. Once again the performer was judged to be psychic.

Such astonishing stubbornness of illusory and occult beliefs is typical rather than exceptional (Nisbett and Ross 1980). There may be several reasons for this intransigence. First, our intuitive reasoning errors may be like visual illusions. At some abstract level we may suspect that our perceptions are in error, but the error remains just as intuitively compelling. To the extent that we get "lost in the details" of a mental problem, as was probably the case with our subjects who watched or read about our magic act above, the problem becomes increasingly difficult to reason about abstractly. Second, to the extent that our cognitive structuring of our environment is "theory-driven," interpreted through a personal hypothesis, we may be all but blind to any evidence disconfirming our theory.

Finally, in the laboratory reasoning tasks described above, our subjects may not be strongly motivated to reason and behave at their rational best. If we had told them that they must reason accurately or be taken out and shot in the morning, they might have performed better. It may be that occult beliefs, both in the laboratory and in everyday life, surface mainly when they entail little personal cost to the believer. The following section discusses such motivational factors in occult beliefs.

Environment and Motivation

Studies in the laboratory and in naturalistic settings have indicated that, in general, superstitions (including occult beliefs) are likely to form under two conditions: environmental uncertainty (roughly conceived as the product of the unpredictability and the magnitude of an event) and low "cost" of the superstition (Jahoda 1969). The erroneous belief may thus alleviate feelings of helplessness and anxiety under uncontrollable or unpredictable circumstances, and in this sense may be functional. Superstitions seldom supplant or intrude upon rational, empirical approaches, where such approaches will serve. In his classic example, the anthropologist Malinowski (1954) described the Trobriand islanders as showing no superstitious bahavior when fishing in their lagoon, where the task was routine and the returns relatively certain, but much superstitious behavior when fishing in the open sea, a more uncertain and dangerous enterprise.

As a modern example, Gmelch (1978) has recently documented the plethora of superstitions surrounding batting (a highly uncertain activity) in baseball, and the absence of superstitions in fielding, where skill and practice can virtually guarantee success. Similarly, Malinowski noted superstitious ritual in the launching of South Sea canoes and the impressive development of the science of navigating them. The islanders had done all they could empirically and rationally in developing their sailing practices, and the added superstitious behavior "cost" little and probably allayed their anxiety. Malinowski has pointed out furthermore that the supernatural and the empirical were typically emphatically compartmentalized from each other: "The body of rational knowledge and the body of magical lore are incorporated each in a different tradition, in a different social setting, and in a different type of activity" (pp. 86–87). This deliberate distinguishing of the non-rational may serve to validate, through contrast, the general validity of rational approaches.

In inspecting modern occultisms, we find that most offer an alleged ability to increase predictability and control, especially under uncertain circumstances. Thus, Tarot cards, clairvoyance, or astrology allow us to "know" the future; biorhythms and psychic healing allow us to regulate our often capricious bodies and health. It is further clear that occultisms in this category "cost" little and do not make many demands on our lives. Despite their often fervidly avowed beliefs in psychic healing, the clients of a psychic surgeon do not go to the "healer" as their first choice, but usually after all else has failed; nor do law enforcement agencies seek the aid of psychics before they have attempted traditional police methods.

Moreover, as with superstitions in South Seas cultures, the occultisms are compartmentalized. On the personal level, people seem easily able to be less than rational in their occult beliefs while being hard-headed where rational approaches are strategic. We are willing to use astrology in determining our partners for social dating, because nothing else seems to work well, but would not contemplate trusting to the stars if we were making legal and financial arrangements with these same partners. On the societal level, and particularly in America, limited and scaled involvement with the occult may be achieved through commercialization—packaging of the occult as a commodity in graduated quantities. Thus, many occult beliefs seem to be instances of superstitious or magical thought patterns. Cognitive heuristics and biases may serve as a mental substructure which leads to and rationalizes the maintenance of such beliefs, while the circumstances under which they are maintained may be defined by how dearly they cost us.

An explanation in terms of environmental determinants for the rise in occult beliefs since the early 1960s must show that, like other superstitions, occult beliefs increase as a function of environmental uncertainty, and that uncertainty has in fact increased in the last two decades. To begin with, we do have evidence that many occult beliefs are a function of shifting levels of environmental uncertainty. For example, Hyman and Vogt (1979) have

shown that the practice of water dowsing was more prevalent in locations where finding water was difficult, and Sales (1973) has found that astrology beliefs increased in the United States during the years of the Depression. Lamar Keene (1976, pp. 70–71), who was once a famous and fraudulent medium, writes: "All mediums would agree. . . . Wars, depressions, personal and national disasters spell prosperity for us. The present economic stresses in the United States are good news for mediums."

There is also evidence that environmental uncertainty in the United States and other Western countries has increased markedly since the early 1960s.

Constructing a working definition of variables such as "environmental uncertainty" at the level of a society is a decidedly complex and ambiguous task. Like the subjects in our experiments, we can find confirming evidence through post hoc analyses, depending on how assiduously we search for it and on the liberality of our interpretations. It is clear, however, that social change, which may have resulted from or given rise to feelings of uncertainty, has been marked since 1960. The past two decades have seen a decline of membership in the traditional religions in the United States and Europe, through not a decline in private religious belief; increased membership in fundamentalist, charismatic, and pentacostal religions; a proliferation of cults, paganism, and Eastern religions; a 29 percent rise in belief in the Devil; the development of a youth counterculture; disruption of traditional patterns in marriage and the family; a feminist movement; an alternative lifestyles movement and change in sexual ethics; the development of a drug culture; and the rise of a "human potential movement" (Glock and Bellah 1976; Wuthnow 1976).

These social trends overlap with the occult belief trend not only in time, but also in structural characteristics and in populations (Gallup 1976; Greeley 1975; Jahoda 1969; Johnson 1979; Wuthnow 1978). The evidence thus suggests that social trends may have caused, or may share causes with, the rise in occult beliefs. A long and unpopular war, political assassinations, and other events of the turbulent 1960s may have contributed to such trends. Other plausible determinants of these social changes include the recent increase in the youth population cohort, a long-term economic decline dating from 1965, and a devaluing of conventional meaning systems through the rising influence of social science. Thus, the prima facie case for an increase in environmental uncertainty since the early 1960s, while only partially substantiated in concrete detail, is a strong one.

Beit-Hallahmi (unpubl.) has pointed out that occultisms are not the only form of magical belief that has recently increased. The *National Enquirer*, which has become one of the best-selling newspapers in the United States, features articles not only on UFOs and ESP, but also on various miracle discoveries in health, dieting, cure of disease, and getting rich quickly. Whether such ideas are labelled "occult" is somewhat arbitrary, but they have similar superstitious qualities.

We have so far neglected to consider a category of occult beliefs that do make demands on believers' lives and extract heavy costs of belief. Occultisms such as Scientology, Theosophy, Satanism, and UFO cults resemble religions rather than ordinary superstitions, and there is evidence that they serve needs usually associated with religions, such as affiliation, moral direction, and an occasion for profound emotion (Bainbridge and Stark 1980). Such belief systems often demand total commitment, monetary and otherwise, from their members.

An explanation for the recent proliferation of such cults is then best couched in terms of developments in American religious practices. Stark and Bainbridge, at the University of Washington, have provided such an explanation, along with compelling documentation. A marked decline in membership in traditional religions over the past two decades has coincided with their theological retreat toward a more abstract, less personal deity, and with an orientation of these religions toward civil rights and other secular concerns, with consequently less investment in individual parishioners' needs (Bainbridge and Stark 1980; Stark and Bainbridge, in press; Glock and Bellah 1976). However, private belief in and need for the supernatural has not declined, and thus we infer that there has been a large population pool available for conversion to new, unorthodox religions, including those of the occult variety. In support of this interpretation, Bainbridge and Stark (1980) have found a negative correlation between membership in organized occult groups or reports of mystic psychic experiences, and membership in traditional religions.

In general, we do not adopt superstitions or fall prey to cognitive biases in areas where empirical approaches bear fruit and where illusory beliefs would be costly. As Sagan (1979, p. 93) observes, "A people going to war may sing over their spears in order to make them more effective. If there ever have been people who felt they could defeat an enemy in war merely by singing and who therefore dispensed with spears, we have not heard of them; they were, undoubtedly, all dispatched."

In areas where judgments under uncertainty are important, we self-consciously avoid biases and fallacies. Thus, we have institutionalized elements of the scientific method, including meticulous weighing of alternative hypotheses, into police work, criminal law, and medical diagnosis. Under conditions of uncertainty, and where the cost of illusory belief is low, however, superstitions will surface and will be maintained through the aid of our somewhat faulty cognitive apparatus. In the last two decades it has become socially permissible to entertain occult beliefs as well as many other deviant beliefs and values, and conventional meaning systems and social orders have changed rapidly, perhaps generating widespread feelings of uncertainty and occult beliefs in the process. In addition, occultisms in the form of religious cults have moved into the void created by the recent decline of traditional religions.

Deficiencies in Science Education

There remains the question of how people maintain occult beliefs in the face of contravening scientific opinion. Granted that the popular media present a distorted picture, and that dependence upon our intuitive cognitions can also result in occultisms. The public nevertheless does seem to recognize that science emphatically rejects most occultisms. The layperson usually accepts scientific opinion unquestioningly, even when it is strikingly counter to his own intuitive understandings, as in the case of the atomic structure of matter or the astronomy of the solar system. Why are occult beliefs an exception to this customary deference to scientific authority?

One general explanation rests on the observation that people seem adept at compartmentalizing incongruent beliefs. We can comfortably live with disparate scientific, religious, and common sense approaches to different beliefs, and employ the belief approach most suitable to the personal need at hand. Personal needs which support occult beliefs may include, for instance, a need to assert the validity of one's own common-sense judgment vis-à-vis scientific "authority," needs for feelings of control and predictability, and a need for affiliation with a religious community. If the need to maintain an irrational belief outweighs any cost associated with maintaining it, the fact that the belief is not rational or scientifically supportable does not usually enter the equation. If cognitive dissonance does occur in maintaining an occult belief in spite of scientific debunking, any number of simple rationalizations, such as "Scientists are prejudiced about paranormal phenomena," will serve to reduce the cognitive tension. It is thus not really inexplicable that widespread occult beliefs exist within our most scientifically advanced societies.

Nevertheless it is our impression that the occult trend cannot be attributed wholly to innate cognitive flaws and emotional needs, but that current practices in the field of science education itself facilitate the rationalizing and compartmentalizing of occult beliefs. We have examined three major aspects of this problem.

First, from elementary school through graduate training, science seldom seems to be taught as a cognitive tool, a way of reaching deeper understanding of our environment. It is taught instead as a set of facts and concepts to be acquired by the same rote methods used in other academic subjects (Godfrey 1979). Even at graduate schools, research methodology appears to be taught as a set of advanced laboratory techniques, specific to the subject matter at hand. From elementary school onward the student does not seem to learn about the validity of scientific approaches vis-à-vis his intuitive understandings, but is simply heavily socialized to accept certain counterintuitive facts—the earth is round and rotates, matter is structured atomically—as items of culturally given common sense. Science is taught in the context of a specific, often technical subject matter, such as chemistry or botany; religious claims, occult claims, everyday problems are seldom examined in the science classroom. The student is thus encouraged to compartmentalize science as a set of facts or at best a dry,

technical methodology within a limited number of narrow domains, and to trust his intuitions in the larger spheres remaining. The occult is then naturally viewed as outside the domain of science, to be apprehended intuitively instead.

Second, many occult claims could be countered with even an elementary knowledge of scientific facts, but even elementary knowledge may be largely lacking. Morison (1969) has questioned whether science has in fact had any effect in raising the cognitive sophistication of the lay public above prehistoric levels, and suggested as one test asking people whether all objects fall at the same rate. We have tested hundreds of college sophomores over the past several years (Singer, in press) with the problem of estimating the duration of flight of a 4-lb and a 2-lb lead weight dropped simultaneously from the same 16-ft height. Over half the students gave different estimates for the flight durations of the two weights. Fifteen percent gave estimates in the range of 4–50 seconds, perhaps envisioning them floating down like paper airplanes. On the same test we found that over half the students did not know that water in a tipped glass remains level, and many believed that islands float in the ocean and that the moon remains fixed in the sky over them, but is only visible at night. This is not a useful armamentarium for evaluating occult claims.

Third, many students have the impression that science is entirely subjective and unable to assess or predict the validity of ideas, apparently on the basis of limited exposure to philosophers such as Polanyi, Hansen, and Kuhn. In presenting perspectives on science in our classrooms, we have perhaps overdone the critical view of the validity of our knowledge. In a series of paradoxical confusions, students attribute more empirical validity to philosophy than to science itself, and the fact that science "changes its mind" is regarded as a totally discrediting weakness. We do not read these philosophers as subscribing to the total subjectivity of science, and we do not believe they would subscribe to such a position. It would seem a service to speak more plainly and more assertively about science's track record.

One benefit of studying the mechanisms of occult beliefs is that we can thereby highlight the characteristics of science, considered as a belief process. That is, we can look at science as a cognitive system deliberately constructed to avoid or compensate for the mechanisms involved in occult beliefs. For instance, we can say that science in theory trusts data and distrusts intuition, generates alternative hypotheses, systematically attempts disconfirmation of favored hypotheses, uses mathematically calculated probabilities, and conscientiously engages in self-examination to determine whether values and motives are influencing beliefs. The question then arises whether the compensatory mechanisms of science are as comprehensive and effective as is feasible. Although the scientific enterprise is obviously successful, we have evidence that its compensatory mechanisms are not complete.

Einhorn and Hogarth (1978), Mahoney (1976), and Kahneman and Tversky (1973) have all found confirmatory cognitive biases, at a level approaching that of a layperson's, in scientists and mathematicians who were administered simple conceptual problems. Recent work in the psychology of science, particularly that of Mahoney (1976) and Mitroff (1974), has demonstrated the operation of confirmatory bias in actual scientific processes. In our own discipline, psychology, we have seen numerous cases of scientists operating in ways which seem intuitively correct to them on the basis of their personal experience, though objectively contraindicated. For example, scientifically trained clinicians continue to rely on personal interviews and clinical judgment in prediction and diagnosis of mental illness, despite twenty years of consistent evidence that simple actuarial techniques are more predictive (Dawes 1979).

Some scientists develop occult beliefs. Surveys have indicated, for example, that over half the natural and social scientists in the United States believe ESP to be established or likely (*Psychology Today* 1978: Wagner and Monnet 1979) and are either unaware of the small fraction of research psychologists who hold such a view, or convinced that their own intuitive understandings are somehow more correct than the scientific ones in this case. In addition, now as throughout the history of science there is a sprinkling of scientists, including eminent ones, who have been duped by the fraudulent practices of "psychics."

The evidence just presented raises the question of the locus of the norms of science and the mech-

anisms by which they are maintained. It is quite possible, for instance, that scientific rules of belief formation operate primarily at a system level. Such rules may affect scientists' cognitive behavior or public statements under particular contingencies as enforced by the scientific community, but this public attitude may not be completely internalized by the scientist as an individual. There may be tensions between the beliefs uttered by the scientist as a professional person operating within a professional community and those entertained by him as a private person who is still humanly prone to the flaws of intuition. Such tensions may substantively affect the conduct of science or the formation of scientific belief.

How should the scientific community respond to the upsurge of popular interest in the occult? The interest in occultism and pseudoscience may in fact be dangerously distracting from rational solutions to social problems and corrosive to rationality, as some scientists have feared. It seems to us, however, that occult beliefs are more symptomatic of dislocating social trends than causal of them, and that they are usually compartmentalized well enough that they do not in themselves corrupt a practical rationality, any more than does a monotheistic faith or a belief that Moses parted the Red Sea. The most serious side effect of occult beliefs may be that they are inherently discrediting of science, although the evidence does not indicate that this outcome has been realized. While recent public disaffection with science and technology is often mentioned as a stimulus to occult belief, hard evidence for such disenchantment is lacking (Marshall 1979). Further, correlational studies have more often than not found no relation between negative feelings toward science and occult beliefs (Wuthnow 1978).

The most convincing rationale for a scientific response to the occult preoccupation may simply be scientific self-integrity. The following steps seem appropriate: issuing rebuttals to fraudulent or unsubstantiated occult claims—far from being beneath our dignity; this can be considered a compelling social responsibility; increasing the availability to the media of scientific expertise on the occult; helping the public recognize which media sources speak with scientific authority and which do not; treating occult concepts in science education, including perhaps, introductory text-books; examining policies relating to occult courses and concepts that appear in the name of a university, and relating to the selection of books and films for public school reading and science classes; and reorienting science education so that science becomes more personal, more life-oriented, and more easily apprehended as a highly useful mode of inquiry.

Straight from the Witch's Mouth

John Fritscher

John Fritscher's article presents the thoughts of Anton Szandor LaVey, the founder and high priest of the Church of Satan in San Francisco. Although LaVey's personal theology, the basis of Satanism, has attracted few to the church, the exotic nature of his views has drawn the attention of many. LaVey, author of the Satanic Bible, *maintains that Satanism is the reverse of Christian values: that God is evil and the Prince of Darkness good, and that Lucifer will ultimately triumph over the Christian God. LaVey's scathing attacks on would-be Satanists are an enlightening exposé of other occultists, pseudo-occultists, and miscellaneous pretenders who profit from what he considers the true religion—a theology that requires anarchy and chaos before Satanic morality can prevail.*

Reprinted from *Popular Witchcraft* by John Fritscher (Bowling Green, Ohio, 1972), pp. 89–90 and 107–123, by permission of the author and Bowling Green University Popular Press.

As men's prayers are a disease of the will, so are their creeds a disease of the intellect.

Emerson, *Self-Reliance*

WITCH-HUNTING THESE DAYS IS A SNAP. IN FACT, new inquisitors have it easy since witches advertise. Where advertisement is lacking, as the manager of the local occult bookstore. If he is not a witch, he'll know who is. Check out the backwater boutiques and the slightly-off campus shops with window signs reading "Occult Records." Catch up on occult symbolism and casually confront anyone wearing mystic insignia during a rock concert. (The median age of witches has lowered drastically. Crones are out.) Read the classifieds of the local college newspaper or the advertising in the local TV guides (free for the taking at supermarkets). Clip addresses from the Wanton Ads of the Underground Press or from overground tabloids like *The National Enquirer.*

Let your fingers do the walking through the Bell System's Yellow Pages (pop culture's surest and handiest index): check listings for astrologers, astrology schools, and palmists. In every instance, ask the persons listed what they think about witchcraft. (What they're advertising is often not what they're selling. Witches advertise as palmists because of Dis(ney)-crimination against witches. After all, in the popular mind what does a witch do? *Witch* is too indirect a come-on. Palmist, *astrologer, numerologist* are titles specific of what the consumer expects and will get.) In any group of seven or more people, interrupt the conversation to ask, "Has anyone here any American Indian blood?" Always there will be someone. Try the same with: "Does anyone here know a witch?" Once a witch is found, ask for a referral to his or her friends in the Craft. If all else fails, join a psychic encounter group or better yet the Psychic Club of Dayton, Ohio. For ten dollars this club, which advertises itself as the place "where witches and warlocks abound," will give you—besides what you deserve—an astro-twin pen pal, a Free Location Service for correspondence with others with the same interests, and a one year subscription to the Psychic Club Bulletin. In the last analysis, witches like beauty and smut are in the eye of the beholder. What they say about themselves though at times repetitious is often more revealing than what we say.

◇　◇　◇

Anton Szandor LaVey, High Priest and Founder of The Church of Satan; San Francisco, California

I don't feel that raising the devil in an anthropomorphic sense is quite as feasible as theologians or metaphysicians would like to think. I have felt His presence but only as an exteriorized extension of my own potential, as an alter-ego or evolved concept that I have been able to exteriorize. With a full awareness, I can communicate with this semblance, this creature, this demon, this personification that I see in the eyes of the symbol of Satan—the goat of Mendes—as I commune with it before the altar. None of these is anything more than a mirror image of that potential I perceive in myself.

I have this awareness that the objectification is in accord with my own ego. I'm not deluding myself that I'm calling something that is disassociated or exteriorized from myself the godhead. This Force is not a controlling factor that I have no control over. The Satanic principle is that man willfully controls his destiny; if he doesn't, some other man—a lot smarter than he is—will. Satan is, therefore, an extension of one's psyche or volitional essence, so that that extension can sometimes converse and give directives through the self in a way that mere thinking of the self as a single unit cannot. In this way it *does* help to depict in an externalized way the Devil per se. The purpose is to have something of an idolatrous, objective nature to commune with. However, man has connection, contact, control. This notion of an exteriorized God-Satan is not new.

My opinion of succubi and incubi is that these are dream manifestations of man's coping with guilt as in the case of nocturnal emissions with a succubus visiting a man or of erotic dreams with an incubus visiting a woman. This whole idea of casting the blame off one's own sexual feelings onto convenient demons to satisfy the Church has certainly proved useful in millions of cases. When the priest is confronted one morning by a parishioner holding a stiffened nightshirt, a semen-encrusted nightgown, the priest can tell him about this "terrible" succubus who visited him in the night. They proceed to exorcise the demon, getting the parishioner off the sexual hook and giving the priest a little prurient fun as he plays with the details of its predication on some pretty girl in the village. This, on top of it all, leaves the girl suspect of being a witch.

Naturally the priest can keep his eyes open as to who fits the succubi descriptions that he's heard in the confessional. Of course, the concept of incubi and succubi has also been used by people who have engaged in what they would consider illicit sexual relations. More than one lady's window has been left open purposely for the incubus to enter—in the form of some desirable male. This can then be chalked up the next day to demonic possession. All these very convenient dodges have kept Christianity and its foibles alive for many hundreds of years.

The birth of a satanic child is another manifestation of the need to extend the Christ-myth of the virgin birth to an antithetical concept of a demonic birth, a Devil-child. *Rosemary's Baby* wasn't the first to use this age-old plot. The Devil's own dear son or daughter is a rather popular literary excursion. Certainly the Devil walks in the sinews and marrow of a man because he is the representation of fleshy deity. Any animal heritage, any natural predilections, any real human attributes would be seen in the personification of the Devil. Consequently the Devil would have offspring and be proud of them, antithetic as they are to Christianity. Instead of being ashamed the child was conceived in sin and baptized out of sin, the Devil revels in the lust-conception of his child. This child would be involved much more magically than one who was the by-product of an environment that sought to negate at first opportunity the very motivating force—carnal desire—that produced him.

Religious artists' desexualizing of the birth process (Christ coming out of the bowels of Mary) has caused women to suffer childbirth pains much more than they need to because of the age-old collective unconsciousness that they must suffer this and the periodic suffering that comes every 28 days. Both these attempts to stamp out or discredit what is in the animal world the most passionate feelings when the animal comes into heat at that time of the month. The "curse" of the menstrual cycle is a manufactured thing, manufactured by society that recognizes this period as one of great desire. Automatically, we have over-emphasized its pains, tensions, turmoil, cramps. This taboo is not just Christian. Women have been placed in huts outside many villages. Every culture has thought she'd cause more jealousy and turmoil at this time because of this increase in her passions. Male animals fight more when the female is in heat. Having been a lion tamer, I know even the females are more combative at this time.

Christianity has put women at this time in more need of self-recrimination. This is the big difference between tribal customs and Christian: in the tribe, the woman is considered bleeding poison; in Christianity the woman is not only considered taboo, but she has to endure her pain as a "moral" reminder of her morality and guilt. The primitive woman can give birth relatively painlessly and return to the fields. She goes through the physical act, but not through the moral agonies of the Christian woman. Such is the compounding of guilt. This kind of hypocrisy is my enemy number one.

I don't think young people can be blamed too much for their actions and antics. Although they coat their protests in ideological issues, I think what they resent most is not the actions of older adults, but the gross hypocrisy under which adults act. What is far worse than making war is making war and calling it peace and love and saying it's waged under the auspices of God or that it's the Christian thing to do. Onward, Christian soldiers and all that. I think that the worst thing about Christianity is its gross hypocrisy which is the most repugnant thing in the world to me. Most Christians practice a basic Satanic way of life every hour of their waking day and yet they sneer at somebody who has built a religion that is no different from what they're practicing, but is simply calling it by its right name. I call it by the name that is antithetical to that which they hypocritically pay lip service to when they're in church.

Take for example, the roster of people executed for witchcraft in the Middle Ages. They were unjustly maligned because they were free-thinkers, beautiful girls, heretics, Jews, or people who happened to be of a different faith than was ordained. They were mercilessly tortured and exterminated without any thought of Christian charity. The basic lies and propaganda of the Christian Fathers added to the torment of the people. Yet the crime in today's streets and the mollycoddling of heinous criminals is a byproduct of latter-day Christian charity. Christian "understanding" has made our city streets unsafe. Yet helpless millions of people, simply because they were unbelievers or disbelievers, were not "understood." They were killed. It's not right that a mad dog who is really dangerous should be "understood" and those who merely dissent from Christianity should have been killed. At the Church of Satan we receive lots of damning letters from people condemning us in the most atrocious language. They attest they are good Christians; but they are full of hate. They don't know if I'm a good guy or a bad guy. They only know me by the label they've been taught: that Satanism is evil. Therefore they judge me on the same basis those people did in the thirteenth through sixteenth centuries. These very same people hardly ever get worked up over a murderer.

I think, in short, that Christ has failed in all his engagements as both savior and deity. If his doctrines were that easily misinterpreted, if his logic was that specious, let's throw it out. It has no place. It is worthless to a civilized society if it is subject to gross misinterpretation. (I'm not just protesting the "human element" in Christianity the way Christians do when something goes wrong with their system. I void the whole of the system that lends itself to such misinterpretation.) Why the hell didn't the writers mean what they said or say what they meant when they wrote that stupid book of fables, the Bible? This is the way I feel about it.

Anybody who takes up the sanctimonious cult of white light is just playing footsy with the Christian Fathers. This is why the bane of my existence are these white witches, white magicians, people who'd like to keep their foot in the safety zone of righteousness. They refuse to see the demonic in themselves, the motivations Satan's Majesty and Nature has placed inside them for their terrestrial goal. Materialism is part of Satanism, but a right kind of materialism. Everyone wants to acquire. The only thing wrong with money is it falls into the wrong hands. This makes it a curse, a disadvantage rather than an advantage. The marketplace is full of thieves. Easy wealth may be something would-be Faustian Satanists would like to get ahold of. In my experience people have come to me after I had opened doors for them. They come back wanting to know how to turn "it" off as they have more troubles than they had before. Once I offer to people what they think they want, given a week to think it over, they get cold feet. Success is a threat. Threatened by success, most people show their true colors. They show they need a god or an astrological forecast to really lay the blame on for their own inadequacy in the threatening face of imminent success.

Man needs religion, dogma, ritual that keeps him exteriorized outside of himself to waylay his guilt and inadequacy. Men will always, therefore, search for a god. We should, however, be men in search of man. The man in search of God is the masochist: he is the world's masochist. There are more than we imagine.

In the beginning I may not have intended Satanism to evolve into an elitist movement. But experience has taught me that Satanism can be a mass movement insofar as its basic pleasureseeking premise is concerned. You build a better mousetrap, and people are going to flock to it. A pleasure principle is going to be more popular than a pleasure denying. I can't help attracting the masses. As for the people who practice a truly Satanic way of life, you can't expect the masses to transcend mere lipservice to the pleasureseeking principle and get into the magical state of the Absolute Satanist. The Absolute Satanist is totally aware of his own abilities and limitations. On this self-knowledge he builds his character.

The Absolute Satanist is far removed from the masses who look for Satanic pleasure in the psychedelics of the headshops. We Satanists are magically a part of all this surface. I realize what my magical lessons have done, the things I've stumbled upon. We necessarily spawn our neo-Christian masses seeking their sense of soma through pills and drugs. Certainly I don't oppose this for other people who get stoned out of their minds. When they do this, the more material things there will be for me and my followers since all those people who freaked themselves out on drugs will be satisfied with their pills and will move off to colonies based on drugs. The rest of us, the Materialists, will inherit the world.

Actually, I'm very much opposed to drugs from a magical point of view, from a *control* point of view. I feel drugs are antithetical to magic. The pseudo-Satanist or pseudo-witch or self-styled mystic who predicates his success on a drug revelation is only going to succeed within his drugged peer group. His miracles go no farther than his credibility. This type of witchery is limited. This, I say, despite the fact that the druggies are no longer just a marginal group, but are a very large subculture which threatens to be the New Spirituality or the New Mysticism or the New Non-Materialism. They don't realize the whole concept of witchery is manipulation of other human beings. Druggies are not manipulative witches. To manipulate someone you've got to be able to relate to that someone. Their idea of witchery is not witchcraft so much—in the sense of witchery being manipulative magic—as witchery equalling revelation of a spiritual nature. Their superego gets developed through the use of drugs. This superego can be the earmark of a new world of drones who, through soma, would attain superegos which allow them while so controlled to think they have superiority over those really enjoying the fruits of the earth. This is why as the leader of the Satanic movement I have to examine these popular movements in the culture from a very pragmatic point of view.

The point is there will always be, among the masses, substitutes for the real thing. A planned way of life—not drugs—gets the materialist what he wants. There's nothing wrong with color TV and cars in the garage as long as the system which provides them respects law and order—a terribly overworked term. But as long as people don't bother other people, then I think this is an ideal society. I'm in favor of a policeman on every corner as long as he doesn't arrest people for thinking their own way or for doing within the privacy of their own four walls what they like to do.

We haven't been hassled too much by the law because we have so many policemen in our organization. I'm an ex-cop myself. I worked in the crime lab in San Francisco and I've maintained my contacts. They've provided for me a kind of security force. But all in all we have a very clean slate. We are very evil outlaws in theological circles, but not in civil.

How could we murder? We—unlike Christians—have a real regard for human bodies. The Satanist is the ultimate humanist. The Satanist realizes that man can be his own worst enemy and must often be protected against himself. The average man sets up situations for himself so he can be a loser. We Satanists have ancient rituals which exorcise these needs for self-abasement before they happen. We wreck Christians' tidy little dreams. When you have somebody rolling orgasmically on the floor at a revival meeting claiming an ecstasy, you tell them they're having a "forbidden" orgasm and they hate you for enlightening them. You've robbed them of their "succubus," of their freedom from guilt. They push their evilness on to us. In this sense, then, we are *very* evil.

I needn't send my child to a private school. Why should I when children are, in fact, all Satanists. She has no trouble at school. Ironically enough, the majority of our members are that often-attacked silent middle class. At least fifty percent of our members have children; the other fifty percent are not rebels, but they're not losers.

I was very liberal in my younger years. I would have been thrown into prison during the McCarthy purge had I been of any prominence. I was ultra-liberal, attending meetings of the Veterans of the Spanish Civil War, the Abraham Lincoln Brigade, the Revisionist Movements of Israel's founding. This was all very liberal at the time. I was always for civil rights. I had Negro friends when Negro friends weren't fashionable. A man should be judged on his accomplishments, his kindness and consideration for others. A certain planned form of bigotry may be a little healthy. I mean, if a person is the worst that his race has produced, he should be prevented from using his race unless he is a credit to his race, religion, whatever it is.

Martin Luther King was killed because he was an articulate gentleman, concerned about his wife and family. He tried to do things in a mannerly way. A man like that belongs on a pedestal. But these loud baboons—and I choose the term—are nothing but rabblerousers, spewing venom. The more a person has at stake the more he watches his p's and q's. This is my test of a person's sincerity. The public is no judge. The public is not too particular in its choosing of heroes.

I voted for Wallace to act out a magical ritual. I performed it—knowing he would not win, but wishing simply to cast my runes. Wallace's advantage was he would have been helpful in the inert area between action and reaction. The pendulum is swinging. I've been misinterpreted when I've said people like Reagan and Nixon are doing a lot to help Satanism because they are causing tremendous popular reaction whereby we're getting off the hook in Vietnam.

Popular opinion is simply a reaction against the leaders who have made their stand so heinous that the protesters don't realize they're doing exactly what the masters want them to do: they're getting the masters off the hook. The masters are using the old magical technique of allowing the people to think it's their idea. This explains the government's permissive attitude toward protest. The idealists of the early fifties during the McCarthy era were certainly just as against violence; but the Government posture did not lie in that direction so they had to be shut up fast. Currently the show of rebellion is, therefore, a very magical ritual.

The new emphasis will be placed on staging. Life is a game and we'll realize it's a game. Life is not "God's Will." We have to go to the point of no return before we can return. We will get to the point where anybody who is establishment oriented is suspect as being the worst kind of individual. This will happen before we return to a rather safe normality, to a sane discrimination as to who are really the contributing members of society and who are the cancerous tissue.

Satanically speaking, anarchy and chaos must ensue for awhile before a new Satanic morality can prevail. The new Satanic morality won't be very different from the old law of the jungle wherein right and wrong were judged in the truest natural sense of biting and being bitten back. Satanic morality will cause a return to intrigue, to glamour, to seductiveness, to a modicum of sexual lasciviousness; taboos will be invoked, but mostly it will be realized these things are fun.

The various Liberation Fronts are all part of the omelet from which the New Satanic Morality will emerge. Women's Liberation is really quite humorous. Supposedly women were liberated after the Industrial Revolution when they got out of the sweatshops. They're going to defeat themselves because they're not using the ammunition of their femininity to win as women. They're trying to reject their femininity which is their greatest magical weapon.

They're parodying themselves.

Speaking of parody, the historical Black Mass is a parody of a parody. The Black Mass parodies the Christian service which parodies a pagan. Every time a man and woman go to church on Sunday they are practicing a Black Mass by parodying ancient earth rituals which were practiced by their ancestors before they were *inverted* by the Christian Fathers. Our Satanic mass captures the beauty of the self and ritualizes that; the Satanic mass is no parody. It is catharsis. The Women's Libists should simply use their femininity by taking the Devil's name and using it and playing the Devil's game. They should take the stigma that cultural guilt has thrown at them and invert the values, making a virtue in their semantic reversal. This is what we have done in Satanism. What theologians have supplied in stigma, we use as virtue. We therefore have the attraction of the forbidden. This has greatly aided our success.

I know I have been rumored to have cursed Jayne Mansfield and caused her death. Jayne Mansfield was a member of the Church of Satan. I have enough material to blow sky-high all those sanctimonious Hollywood journalists. She was a priestess in the Church of Satan. I have documentation of this fact from her. There are many things I'll not say for obvious reasons. Her lover, who was a decidedly unsavory character, was the one who brought the curse upon himself. There was decidedly a curse, marked in the presence of other people. Jayne was warned constantly and periodically in no uncertain terms that she must avoid his company because great harm would befall him. It was a very sad sequence of events in which she was the victim of her own—as we mentioned earlier—inability to cope with her own success. Also the Demonic in her was crying out to be one thing and her Apparent Self demanded that she be something else. She was beaten back and forth in this inner conflict between the Apparent Self and the Demonic Self. He was black-mailing her. I have definite proof of this. She couldn't get out of his clutches. She was a bit of masochist herself. She brought about her own demise. But it wasn't through what I had done to curse *her*. The curse was directed at *him*. And it was a very magnificent curse.

The dedication of my *Satanic Bible* to Marilyn Monroe and Tuesday Weld was, in Marilyn's case, homage to a woman who was literally victimized by her own inherent witchery potential which was there in her looks. I think a great deal of the female mystique of beauty which was personified in Marilyn's image. In the case of Tuesday Weld it's part of the magical ritual. She is my candidate of a living approximation of these other two women. Unlike them, Tuesday has the intelligence and emotional stability to withstand that which Marilyn Monroe could not. For this reason Tuesday is not in the public eye as much. Her own better judgment has cautioned her not to bite off more than she can chew.

I'd like to point out that another popular American, Ben Franklin, was a rake without question. He was a sensual dilettante. He joined up with the British Hellfire Club. Their rituals came to them from the Templars and other secret societies. We practice some of these same rituals secretly in the Church of Satan. Not only did Ben Franklin influence the activities of the Hellfire Club, his very association sheds some light on the *quality* of members of what would appear to be a blasphemous group of individuals. This proves the Devil is not only a gentleman but a cultured gentleman.

Throughout history the witch most feared is the witch most antithetical to the physical standards. In Mediterranean cultures, anyone with blue-eyes would have been the first to be named as a witch. The black woman Tituba in Salem was antithetical to New England physical standards. Anyone who is dark has an edge because of all the connotations of black arts, black magic, the dark and sinister side of human nature. Tituba probably was not only more feared but also more sought after. She was set apart physically from the rest of the people. She was the magical outsider.

The Church of Satan does not employ males as altars simply because the male is not considered to be the receptacle or passive carrier of human life. He possesses the other half of what is necessary to produce life. Woman is focal as receiver of the seed in her recumbent role as absorbing altar. A male would defeat the purpose of receptor unless he were fitted out with an artificial vagina and were physically and biologically capable of symbolizing the Earth Mother.

We do, however, accept homosexuals. We have

many in the Church of Satan. They have to be well adjusted homosexuals—and there *are* many well adjusted homosexuals who are not on the daily defensive about their sexual persuasion. Many have a great amount of self-realization. Of course, we get the cream of the crop. Since they cannot relate to the basic heterosexuality of the Church of Satan whatever they do must be modified. If the homophile were involved in defining the dogma of our Church it would be very imbalanced for the masses of people with whom we deal. The homophile would very easily like to substitute a male for the female altar. It's a fact that a heterosexual can accept homosexuality more readily than a homosexual can accept heterosexuality. Relating to the existence of the other sex is something that MUST be in evidence. Women cannot be denied their function in our Satanic Church. Needless to add, man-hating women cause us a great lack of sensual scintillation.

My book *The Complete Witch; or What to Do When Virtue Fails* is a guide for witches. It doesn't stress the drawing of pentacles on the floor. It smashes all the misconceptions that women have had, not only about witchery but about their own sexuality. I think of this book like de Beauvoir's *The Second Sex*. Even if a woman is a man-hater, she can use her femininity to ruin that man. This book tells her how to do it. If she wants to enjoy men, this book will open her eyes to a few things.

Sexual fetishes we find natural. Everybody has one. These should be catered to. Sexual deviations are only negative factors when they present an obstacle to one's success. They present an obstacle when they are carried out of the ritual chamber, out of the fantasy room into the world where others will see them disapprovingly.

I must tell you something quite amusing. *Rosemary's Baby* did for us what *The Birth of a Nation* did for the Ku Klux Klan. I never realized what that film could do. I remember reading at the premiere of Griffith's *Birth of a Nation* recruiting posters for the KKK in southern cities. I chuckled because at the premiere of *Rosemary's Baby* there were posters of the Church of Satan in the lobby. Here at the San Francisco premiere there was a great deal of consternation, but the film started an influx of very worthwhile new members. Since *Rosemary* the quality of membership has gone up. Immeasurably.

Since that film with Polanski, I am constantly confronted with scripts by thick-skulled exploitation producers who want me either to be technical advisor or play the role of the Devil or the Satanic doctor in their new films. They think to one-up *Rosemary*. What they don't realize is that *Rosemary's Baby* was popularly successful because it exploded a lot of the preconceptions of Satanism: it didn't chop up the baby at the end. It threw all the crap down the drain and showed the public who was expecting the sensational the real image of the Satanist. It will remain a masterpiece.

The allegory of the Christ child in reverse is simply the birth of the new Satanic Age, 1966. The year 1966 was used in *Rosemary's Baby* because it was our Satanic Year One. The birth of the baby was the birth of Satanism. *Rosemary's Baby* stands foursquare against the popular image of child sacrifice. The role that I played in the picture—the devil in the shaggy suit was not from my point of view anything other than it should have been: man, animal, bestial, carnal nature coming forth in a ritualized way. The impregnation of Rosemary in that dream sequence was to me the very essence of the immodest, the bestial in man, impregnating the virginal world-mind with the reawakening of the animalism within oneself. This impregnation was very meaningful because it spawned literally the Church of Satan. Among all the rituals in the film, this was the big ritual in *Rosemary's Baby*.

These others who want my opinion on their scripts are simply producing more trash of the blood-sacrifice variety. In *Rosemary's Baby*, the girl who went out the window and landed on the pavement died in the pure Satanic tradition. She had made it clear—although the people who saw the film didn't realize it—that she was a loser. Everything she said pointed to it. She'd been kicked around. She'd been on the streets. She'd been on dope. She was obviously the wrong girl to be a carrier. Satan saw her lack of maternal instinct, of winning instinct, of spunk to carry this baby out into the world. She therefore, sort of fell "accidentally" out the window. The end of the film shows Rosemary throw away her Catholic heritage and cherish the devil-child. The natural instinct of Satanism wins over man-made programming.

Even though I have done the consulting for *Mephisto Waltz* for Twentieth Century Fox, that film still has the old elements of witchery. It's going to take a lot to come up with a film that's as much a blasphemy as *Rosemary's Baby*. Polanski's other film *The Fearless Vampire Killers* is like nothing else that's ever been done before in the film world. The film explodes all the puerile Christian myths about vampires. The old professor, sort of a Count Dracula, is shown to be not only the doddering old fool he really is but also the real victim at the end. The fact that all those unfortunate murders took place at Polanski's—his wife Sharon Tate and all the rest— was used by the press to highlight Polanski's interest in witchery and Satanism. The deaths had nothing to do with the films. The Polanskis were simply plagued with hippies and drug addicts. If I were to allow it, my house would be full of the sychophantic loungers. If I neglected them, they'd be paranoid. I would have been put in the same position as those people at Polanski's house had I allowed it. He attracted, as people in Hollywood do, all the creeps, kooks, and crackpots. He wasn't around to stop it or was too nice to put his foot down. He, in a sense, put himself in much the same position as Jayne Mansfield.

Those people that were killed were all freaked out of their minds anyway. They were people who were only a little better than the killers. As far as their warped outlooks on life, their senses of values, it was a case of the blind destroying the blind. Sharon was probably the victim of her environment, but I can't find it in myself to whitewash these people. I know firsthand how the people at the Factory and the Daisy and these other nightclubs behave. They're quite indiscriminate as to the people they take up with.

The devil in *Rosemary's Baby* was depicted as a combination of many anthropomorphic ideals of the bestial man: the reptilian scales, the fur, claws. A combination of animal kingdom. It was not a red union suit with a pitchfork. Nor was it Pan transmogrified by Christians into a cloven-hoofed devil. *The Cloven Hoof* title of our newsletter was chosen precisely for its eclectic image in the popular mind as one of the devil's more familiar and acceptable traits. Cloven-hoofed animals in pre-Christian times had often been considered sacred in their association with carnal desire. The pig, goat, ram— all of these creatures—are consistently associated with the devil. Hence our title.

The truest concept of Satan is not in any one animal but is in man, the evolutionary accomplishment from many animals.

The historical note that Satan has an icecold penis is a very pragmatic thing because when Satan had to service the witches who would come to him to draw from his power at the Sabbaths, he could actually remain erect either with those who stimulated him—that is the magician who portrayed Satan—or until he became expended of his sexual vigor. Naturally then, under his fur cloak or garb he had to strap on something of an artificial nature, a bull's pizzle, a dildo. In the night air, it would cool off. The witches all swore that it was cold. He would have to use something like this to maintain his position as the devil.

It is of interest to me that hippies and Hell's Angels tattoo themselves with the markings of Satanism and other symbols of aggression. Tattooing is an ancient and obscure art. One of the few books on it is called *Pierced Hearts and True Love* by Ebensten. There's also George Burchett's *Memoirs of the Tatooist*. Certainly much needs to be said of the relation of Satanism and witchery to tattooing. We have members that were tattooed long before the Hell's Angels made it fashionable. One man has the Goat of Bathona, the Satanic Goat, tattooed across his back. Beautifully done. The devil-headed eagle is on his chest. Then on each thigh he has the figure of Seth. He's quite spectacular. He has a shaven head and the build of a professional wrestler. He is extremely formidable when he is in ceremony wearing only a black pair of trunks with a very small mask across his eyes. His are very symmetrically contrived attempts at using tattoos for ritualistic purposes.

Witchcraft has a lot of show business in it. Religious ritual after all was the first theater. For this reason, I think, *Dark Shadows* and *Bewitched* are fine. White witches think these TV shows are terrible because they play the witch as a pretty girl who can snap her fingers and get things done. They try to impress the world that a *wicca* is not up to that sort of thing. They try to play that they're an intellectually justified "Old Religion." The popular image of the witch is a gal who can get things done in apparently supernatural ways. Like *I Dream of Jeannie*. Why not take advantage of the glamorized witch? If this has been the very element that has brought witchcraft out of a stigmatized, persecuted stereotype, then why put it down? It is the glamorization of witchcraft that gives the erstwhile white witches the free air in which to breathe. Why knock it?

This gets me to Gerald Gardner, whom I judge a silly man who was probably very intent on what he was doing; he had to open a restaurant and get it filled with customers. He took over a not too successful teashop and turned it into a museum. He had to say he was a research scholar. He got the term *white witch* from a coinage in *Witchcraft's Power in the World Today*. Gardner used the term because witchery was illegal in England at the time. To avoid persecution he opened his museum under the guise of research. He stated he wasn't a witch until the repeal of the laws in 1953. Then he made it very clear he was a white witch. That's like saying, "Well, I'm a good witch. The others are bad witches. So don't persecute me." Gardner did what he had to do, but I don't think he was anymore of an authority on the true meaning of witchcraft than Montague Summers. I think that he simply followed Summers' crappy rituals of circles and "Elohim" and "Adonai." They used the name of Jesus and crossed themselves.

I have broken the barrier. I have made it a little bit fashionable to be a black magician. A lot of them, therefore, are trying to say now that their horned god is not a Devil. It is just a horned god. Well, let me tell you, until five or six years ago they wouldn't even admit to a horned god. Suddenly they like to intimate that perhaps they have made pacts with the Devil. For many years the old Religionists used Albertus Magnus, the Sixth and Seventh Books of Moses, The Book of Ceremonial Magic, crossing themselves as they turned the pages, denying theirs was a Christian based faith. Why in the hell did they use all these accoutrements? White witches are no more than a byproduct of Christianity, or they wouldn't have to call themselves white witches in the first place. I don't think white witches have the courage of their convictions.

I have said that Aleister Crowley had his tongue jammed firmly in his cheek. I think Crowley was a pragmatist. He was also a drug addict. The demons he conjured were the products of a benumbed mind. Basically he was a sweet, kind man who was trying to emancipate himself from the throes of a very strict upbringing. He can't be blamed for anything he did from a psychoanalytical point of view. He wasn't really that wicked of a man. He had to work overtime. All the arbitrary numbers, dogma, and so on of his magical curriculum were constructs he invented to answer the needs of his students. Crowley's greatest wisdom was in his *Book of Lies*. The particular page can be paraphrased: "My disciples came to me, and they asked, Oh Master, give us your secret." He put them off. They insisted. He said it would cost them ten thousand pounds. They paid, and he gave them his words: "A sucker is born every minute." This says more for Crowley than all his other work. His judgment of the popular follower was accurate; most of the public wants gibberish and nonsense. He alluded to this in his numbering of his *Libers* which are not immense volumes but just a few bound sheets of paper. He's saying the real wisdom is about ten lines long.

Like Crowley, Gerald Gardner probably knew a good thing when he saw it and got something going that turned out to be more sanctimonious than it should be. Ray Buckland began the same way. Now he admits to once being part of the more mundane rather than the complete esoteric he was made out to be. Ray Buckland certainly knows a great deal about the occult. He has a good synthesis of the Arts. But sanctimony still comes through. His famous chapter on black magic threatens that if a curse is not performed properly it will return to the sender. He defines things like good and bad, white and black magic for those who—as I say in my *Satanic Bible*—are frightened by shadows. I maintain that good like evil is only in the eyes of the beholder. Ray Buckland has guts, though, to sit in his Long Island home conducting his rituals and not caring what the neighbors think.

I don't know whether Sybil Leek is as big a fool as she sometimes seems, or whether she's laughing up her sleeve. Sybil is a good business woman. I don't want to judge her—if she is a good business woman she knows on which side her bread is buttered! My only complaint with Sybil—and I do know her personally—is she has done nothing to dispel all the crap about black and white witches. If she's after the little old ladies in tennis shoes, fine. But she is a dispenser of misinformation.

Alex Sanders has become more public in proclaiming himself the king of the Witches. He is a dispenser of misinformation too. He's not too bad; in the stifling climate of England he's a forward man among a backward people. He's got a big load. For this I admire him. He's great enough to claim himself King. I don't put much credence in astrology—it's a case of the tail wagging the dog. A competent sorcerer, however, should know his astrology because it is a motivating factor for many people. Sydney Omarr, the popular syndicated astrologer, is basically a level headed guy who sees through a lot of the fraud.

I'll be the first to give Sybil Leek and Louise Huebner and all these people their due. They don't say, "We witches don't want publicity." That takes moxie in a sanctimonious society. They're not like these damn cocktail party witches who can't defend their self-styled reputations when called to do it. These people give me a pain. It's part of being a witch, the ego gratification of being a witch, to want to talk about it in detail in public.

The Occult Revival as Popular Culture: Some Observations on the Old and the Nouveau Witch

Marcello Truzzi

How can the rising tide of occultism in the United States be assessed? In this article Marcello Truzzi observes that the revival of interest in the occult shows how certain religious events can reflect serious social conflict in a culture. After identifying four major categories of occult interest, Truzzi devotes most of his article to an analysis of the two areas that he believes dominate occult interest in this country—astrology and witchcraft-Satanism. Truzzi concludes that for most Americans the involvement in the occult is more a fad of popular culture than a serious religious commitment.

Reprinted from *Sociological Quarterly*, Vol. 13 (Winter 1972), pp. 16–36, by permission of the author and the Midwest Sociological Society, Department of Sociology, Southern Illinois University.

IN HIS CLASSIC ARTICLE ON FASHION, EDWARD SAPIR noted that:

> There is nothing to prevent a thought, a type of morality or an art form from being the psychological equivalent of costuming the ego. Certainly one may allow oneself to be converted to Catholicism or Christian Science in exactly the same spirit in which one invests in pewter or follows the latest Parisian models in dress (Sapir, 1937: 143).

Although religion holds a somewhat exalted position in many of the prominent macro theories of societies (e.g., those of Durkheim, Weber, etc.), it is often a rather mundane phenomenon, satisfying a wide variety of idiosyncratic needs for society's many groups and their members. The functions of a religious phenomenon will often vary for its different actors and audiences, and they need not necessarily reflect a single fundamental fact or crisis of social life. This point is nicely exemplified by Ogden Nash's delightful poem describing the sequential religious affiliations of Mrs. Marmaduke Moore. He reminds us that her changes in religion might result from causes other than those of some set of central social structural origins (e.g., anomie, status inconsistency). Describing her many conversions from Methodism to Bahai, he concluded:

> When seventy stares her in the face
> She'll have found some other state of grace.
> Mohammed may be her Lord and Master
> Or Zeus, or Mithros, or Zoroaster.
> For when a woman is badly sexed,
> God knows what god is coming next.
> Nash, 1945: 12

The revival of interest in the occult and the supernatural is a current example of religious events that some have seen as being of great cultural significance and as reflecting serious social conflicts and strains of macroscopic import. (For good examples of this alienation-argument, see Staude, 1970; Greeley, 1969. For a somewhat similar view, see Harris, 1970.) A wide variety of indicators shows that we are in the midst of a widespread boom of things occult. As *Time* magazine (1968: 42) noted: "A mystical renaissance is evident everywhere, from television to department stores." In late 1969, The *Wall Street Journal* reported that the boom continued and "mysticism is becoming a big business. A New York book store specializing in the occult says sales have zoomed 100% in the past three years" (Sansweet, 1969: 1, for the British counterpart, see Williams, 1970). In 1968, 169 paperback books dealing with occult topics were in print [see *Paperbound Books in Print* (June 1968), under the headings "Psychology: Occult Sciences," "Parapsychology," and "Astrology,"] and, by 1969, the figure had jumped to 519 books (see *Paperbound Books in Print*, October 1969). In 1969, 364 hardback volumes dealt with occultism, which represented an increase both from 261 volumes in 1968 and from 198 volumes in 1967 (Prakken and Shively, 1967, 1968, 1969). A final indicator of this boom has been the sales of Ouija boards. After some forty years of poor sales, companies reported over two million sold in 1967 (Pileggi, 1970: 63), thereby outdistancing the sales of *Monopoly* (Buckley, 1968: 31). (An excellent history of the Ouija and its family can be found in Jastrow, 1962: 129–143. For a discussion of the mechanisms involved, see Rawcliffe, 1959: 134–151; and for an interesting case study, see Wenger and Quarantelli, 1970. On the earlier Ouija board fads, see Sann, 1967: 139–144.)

The revival of occultism has been heavily touted as (and, in large part, certainly does represent) an important part of the current youth culture (see Greeley, 1969; Levin, 1968; and Gams, 1970; and on the concept of "youth culture," see Berger, 1963). Certain facts and assumptions, however, indicate that a broad spectrum of persons has been involved in this boom. My own teaching experiences and the wide variety of magazines now giving space to this subject (from *McCall's* and *The Ladies Home Journal* to *Playboy* and *Esquire*) show that many persons outside the youth culture are interested in the occult. A 1969 survey of *Fate* magazine readers, which then had about 94,000 monthly readers, showed that 88 percent of them were over 34 years old, 37.9 percent being over 55 years old (Consumer Communication Corporation). A 1963 Gallup Poll showed that one in five persons reported some sort of sudden or dramatic "religious or mystic experience." The study further showed no relationship between the respondent's experience and his level of education (Gallup, 1963; for a detailed analysis of this report, see Bourque, 1969; and Bourque and Back, 1968). It is safe to assume that even though they were not sudden or dramatic, a great many other Americans have had comparable religious experiences. It is also likely that even though today's social scientists have only superficially examined the subject, a vast reservoir of magical and superstitious thought exists in the American population. (Such studies of magic in modern America would include Henslin, 1967; Hyman and Vogt, 1967; McCall, 1964; Lewis, 1963; Blumberg, 1963; Whitten, 1962; Vogt and Golde, 1958; Roth, 1957; Vogt, 1956; Simpkins, 1953; Levitt, 1952; Zapf, 1945–1946, and 1945; Belanger, 1944; Weiss, 1944; Passin and Bennet, 1943; Caldwell and Lundeen, 1937; Dudycha, 1933; Hurston, 1931; Grilliland, 1930; Wagner, 1928; Park, 1923; Conklin, 1919; and Shotwell, 1910). These facts and assumptions plus the well-known concern held by the elderly about occultisms relating to healing and survival of bodily death (see Buckner, 1968) indeed indicate that interest in the occult is not an unique phenomenon with the youth culture.

Despite the widespread interest in occultism throughout the population, this current revival seems to be primarily a youth phenomenon. Some facts support this claim. The mass media portray youth as adherents of occultism. Occult bookstores have emerged around the academic campuses. Even many institutions in the nation, including so-called Free-Universities, have offered numerous courses dealing with occult topics.

Empirical research on the prevailing attitudes of the occult among youths is nearly non-existent. During the past three years, my investigations of the national occult scene reveal four rather distinct foci of interest, foci sometimes intersecting but basically quite separate. Three major sources of data provided the basis for my interpretation of the integrated pattern of existing occult belief-systems: extensive readings in the available literature, interviews with hundreds of students, and interviews or exchanged communications with numerous major occult figures, writers, and publishers. The four major foci of occult interest currently dominating the youth culture are (1) astrology, (2) witchcraft-satanism, (3) parapsychology and extrasensory perception, and (4) Eastern religious thought. Classified as a "waste-basket variety," a fifth category encompasses a large number of esoteric items of occult interest, including among others, prophets (Edgar Cayce, Nostradamus, etc.), strange monsters (sea serpents, snowmen, were-wolves, vampires, etc.), unidentified flying objects, and many others. Because the interests in the fifth category either have small scope and influence or are in an actual state of decline, the interests in the four major categories represent the dominant factors or motifs currently in fashion. At times, these four interest-areas do intersect among some believers. (For example, some witches, as Sybil Leek, also believe in astrology.) This, however, is not necessarily the case and indeed is relatively uncommon.

Of the four major foci of occult interest, the first two are most clearly central in the current revival. Parapsychology does not seem to be undergoing any significant increase in popularity. Interest in Eastern religious thought seemingly passed its peak as a topic of mass interest when interest in Zen Buddhism, which the so-called "beat-generation" writers of the 1950's made popular, began to decline (for sociologically relevant works on this subculture, see Regney and Smith, 1961; Moore, 1960; and Feldman and Gartenberg, 1958). Both parapsychology and Eastern religious thought act not as central values in the youth occult world, but as *bolsters* or legitimizing linkages to the broader and more generally accepted cultural areas of science and religion. One becomes receptive to an analysis of witchcraft-satanism with their generally unacceptable magical elements if he remembers two facts. First, the current limits of scientific understanding have been highlighted by the parapsychologists conducting "respectable" laboratory investigations. Second, in the process of establishing their own identity, some proponents of Western philosophical naturalism may have become rather parochial in their own views toward the older and more mystical traditions of the East. I will now devote the rest of this paper to an analysis of these two major foci of occult interest currently

dominating the scene—astrology and witchcraft-satanism.

Astrology

Certain existing indicators of occult preferences clearly reveal the predominant interest in astrology. In 1969, 252 or 68 percent of the 373 books printed on occultism dealt with astrology (Prakken and Shively, 1969). In 1969, 33 of 40 articles dealing with occultism covered the topic of astrology [in *Readers Guide to Periodical Literature* (New York: H. W. Wilson Co.), for January 17, 1969, to January 29, 1970]. Paperbound books on astrology increased from 35 in 1968 to 102 in 1969 (see *Paperbound Books in Print*, October 1969, June 1968). Even the popular press (Time, 1969; Jennings, 1970; Robinson, 1970; and Buckley, 1968) has widely reported the phenomenal growth of interest in this ancient pseudoscience (for good reviews of the scientific repudiation of astrology, see, Bok and Mayakkm, 1941; Thorndike, 1955; Hering, 1924: 18–37; de Camp and de Camp, 1966: 20–31; Lewinsohn, 1962; 90–114; and, especially, Guaquelin, 1970); such interest has become a marketing bonanza. Twenty years ago only about 100 papers carried horoscope columns, but today 1200 of the 1750 daily newspapers regularly carry such columns (Buckley, 1968: 31; and Jennings, 1970: 104). Because of their public endorsement of astrology, a wide variety of celebrities, which range from Hollywood stars (e.g., Marlene Dietrich, Robert Cummings, Susan Hayward), to members of the political (e.g., Ronald Reagan) and intellectual (e.g., Marshall McLuhan) communities, have added to its attractiveness to their admirers. The popular musical *Hair* with its hit song of *Aquarius* and its own well publicized company-astrologist gave special impetus to the movement (Buckley, 1968: 136). The Dell publishing company alone had some 49 horoscope publications in press and sold over 8,000,000 copies of its annual astrological dopesheet in 1969 (Jennings, 1970: 104). About 10,000 full-time and 175,000 part-time astrologers in the United States serve some 40,000,000 persons in their American audience (Jennings, 1970: 154). One only has to look around at the shops in any semiurban community to see astrological recordings, calendars, ashtrays, hairstyles, sweatshirts, and thousands of merchandized items linked to the zodiac. As one leading figure in the occult world, who himself does not endorse astrology, succinctly put it: "The stars may affect no one, but astrology affects everyone" (LaVey, 1968).

How, then, are we to account for the renewed popularity of this ancient and scientifically discredited belief system? No one who is familiar with the rules of scientific evidence or with the history of both astrology and astronomy over the centuries can accept the interpretation of the manifest functions of astrology, that it represents a scientifically true explanation and predictive framework for understanding man and his actions. Of course, some followers of astrology claim acceptance of their "science" for just such reasons. Such rigid scientific justification, however, is rare among the practitioners. Most astrology-believers place their credence in their system for reasons, at least partly, beyond what they themselves see as a legitimate science. To them, the heart of the matter is not that they use science as the basis for their acceptance of astrology as truth but that science must catch up with their truth. We, thus, might look at the latent functions of astrological beliefs, both for the social system (group) in which they exist and for the needs of the social actors involved in the system. One must, however, recognize that the involvements of those "into" astrology are quite varied. One can meaningfully speak of at least three, somewhat oversimplified and "ideal typical," levels of involvement. Each level of involvement manifests somewhat different consequences for the actors.

At the first, most superficial level of involvement, we find the occasional reader of the newspaper and magazine astrology-columns. This person knows next to nothing about the "mechanics" of astrology. From my interviews and preliminary explorations, I found that most of the middle-aged (over 35 years old) population who follow astrology fall into this category. These astrology-followers were largely present before the astrology-revival of these past five years. Because horoscopes do not normally take into account the subject's (client's) exact time and place of birth, those more advanced than are others in astrology perceive this level of astrology-believers as highly superficial. Even the noted newspaper-astrologer, Sidney Omarr, was quoted as conceding that "daily columns provide entertainment rather than enlightenment" (Buckley, 1968: 31). The overwhelming majority of astrol-

ogy-believers fall into this first level. Consideration of the latent functions for the individual involved at the first level would have to take into account the following factors: (1) the familiarity with astrology, its ancient and pervasive character; (2) the quasi-scientific character of astrology that acts as legitimating astrology to those not scientifically critical but personally concerned about the present explorations of the heavens; (3) the usually positive character of astrological advice that makes it ego-boosting; (4) the ego-directed attention of the advice; (5) the element of mystery, of the esoteric that makes the advice exciting and entertaining; (6) the ambiguity of the message that makes it amenable to interpretation and difficult to falsify; and (7) the self-fulfilling nature of many astrological predictions. (This phenomenon may operate in the following way: a person who reads that he is in good spirits becomes so, or a person who reads that he should be cautious acts so and then finds a justifying event.) Some latent functions on the group (societal) level might include the following factors: (1) tension-management of anxieties within the social system; (2) fulfillment of economic goals that the mass merchandising of an astrology-fad affords; and (3) the availability of a cognitive belief-system that transcends science and is "safe" from the sanctions of or overt conflict with the major religions. (This is true today, but it was not always so.)

At the second level of involvement with astrology, we find those people who have some knowledge of the "mechanics" of astrology. These people usually have their own personal horoscopes cast. They do this through a variety of ways, ranging from personal visits with a consulting astrologer to a computer-analysis of their horoscopes. Unlike those in the first level of involvement, the astrology-believers in the second level have some knowledge of the special language and of the astrological reasoning; they are able to speak about other people astrologically. Like those in the first level, most astrology-believers in the second level seek advice and predictions from their excursions into astrology. I have observed that *the astrology-believers in the second level primarily represent those of college-age, and this level has had the greatest relative increase during the current revival.* Some latent functions for the individual involved at the second level might include the following factors: (1) all functions available to those involved at the first level; (2) the enhancement of the *personal* and ego-gratifying character of the involvement; (3) an increased commitment to astrology [by means of the expense and trouble of getting a personal horoscope, by means of a direct interpersonal relation with the astrologer, and by means of a personal investment (dissonance) strongly motivating the person to act upon the belief-system]; and (4) the enhancement of the believer's self-esteem among his friends and colleagues. (This phenomenon operates in the following way: because of its special language, astrology is an excellent topic of conversation; because the believer can direct the substance of astrology to another's ego as well, he gains great interpersonal merit in his interactional process.) Some latent functions on the group (societal) level might include the following factors: (1) all functions available to those involved in the first level; (2) the creation and maintenance of an in-group cohesiveness and an out-group exclusion by means of the special language of astrology; and (3) the presence of a highly interpersonally binding conversational framework that often centers around a highly personal and ego-centric discourse. (Astrology and psychoanalysis both share this and many other common features.)

At the third level of involvement with astrology, we find those people who have become really involved in the literature of the field and usually cast their own horoscopes. Until relatively recently, this level was composed of only a very small number of elderly people; it now consists of many youthful advocates. Persons involved this deeply in astrology are still comparatively few. (For example, the approximately 30,000 students at the University of Michigan have enough interest in astrology to support an occult-astrology bookstore; yet only about 20 such serious adherents are reportedly around that campus.) Unlike those in the first two levels of involvement, the astrology-believers in the third level are not primarily concerned with advice or prediction. For them, astrology represents a highly complex and symbolically deep conceptual scaffolding which offers them a *meaningful* view of their universe and gives them an *understanding* of their place in it. They use astrology as a means of establishing their identity (Klapp, 1969). They usually acknowledge the great difficulties in establishing any predictive statements from astrology. To them, astrology represents a world view far more reminis-

cent of religion than of science. In fact, they most likely speak of their belief-system, not as a science like physics or astronomy, but as an art or as one of the "occult sciences." The latent functions for the individual involved at the third level may well include many of the features found in the first two rather superficial levels of involvement. The major latent function, however, is that the adept astrologer obtains an ideological integration of his self with his perception of the universe. Of course, other benefits may occur. He may, for example, become a leader in his astrology-oriented circle of friends. He may even become a professional astrologer and earn his living from his involvement; for the social actor, however, the central function is that the astrological belief-system operates as a grand conceptual-philosophical scheme. (Because the actor is aware of the consequences of his belief in astrology, this central function may now become manifest, not latent.) On the group (societal) level, this intensity of involvement may well act as a "sacred canopy" (see Berger, 1967) for the social group. Composed of only a few thousand astrology-believers, this level of involvement clearly follows the depiction of the astrological belief-system as a social reaction against the normlessness of modern life. It is at this level of involvement that we see the search for identity and for new sacred elements. We should, however, see these relatively extreme astrology-believers in their true perspective: they represent a very small minority of those involved in the massive revival of interest in astrology. I would argue, in fact, that the vast majority of those involved with astrology, those at the first two levels, take a highly irreverent, almost playful attitude toward astrology. To most of these people, astrology is fun; it is a non-serious, leisure-time element of popular culture, *not* a spiritual searching for Karmic meaning.

Witchcraft and Satanism

Witchcraft and Satanism follow astrology as the second most popular focus of current attention in occultism. The large number of recent popular books and articles dealing with these subjects attests to this upsurge of interest in them. (Often these publications are reprints of much older volumes.) Although witchcraft and Satanism are commonly linked together, they actually represent very different belief-systems, and each has an existing variety of forms.

The alleged difference between so-called *white* versus *black* magic is one major distinction discussed in much of the occult literature. While white magic is supposed to be the use of magic for socially beneficent ends, black magic is supposed to be the use of magic for malevolent ends. Even though some ritual forms of black magic clearly involve calling upon such malevolent forces as the Devil or his demons, most magicians basically view magic as a value-free "technology-of-the-supernatural" (or *super-normal*, a term preferred by many magicians). They believe that their own motives really determine whether their use of magic is for good (white), or for evil (black). Most contemporary witches stress that they perform only white magic (e.g., Leek, 1968: 3–5; or Holzer, 1969: 19) as an attempted antidote for the stereotypes usually portraying them as evil workers of the devil. The distinction between black and white magic is essentially a matter of the user's intent rather than of his technique.

Contemporary witches usually do not consider themselves to be Satanists. Satanism is basically a worship of the Judaeo-Christian Devil, which is, at times, only a symbol and, at other times, very literally real. (Varying degrees of fundamentalism exist among Satanists. For these varieties, see Truzzi, 1972; and Lyons, 1970.) Practitioners in witchcraft do not usually view themselves as an heretical offshoot of Christianity, but Satanists do view themselves, either literally or symbolically (since many Satanists are atheists), as members in league with the Christian's Devil. Most witches perceive witchcraft as a folk tradition of magical beliefs. Many, if not most of them, further perceive it as an ancient, pre-Christian fertility religion that the Christian churches sought to suppress: primarily through the Catholic inquisitions and the Protestant witch trials. They believe that their religion became misrepresented and distorted as an heretical worship of the Devil. [For the early Catholic image, see Kramer and Sprenger, 1948. Most Catholics no longer accept the orthodox picture of the witch, but some Catholic scholars do; e.g., see Pratt, 1915, and Cristiani, 1962. The leading writer presenting the strictly orthodox (medieval) Catholic viewpoint in recent years was the late Montague Summers (1946, 1956, and 1958).] On the other

hand, Satanists do often constitute a kind of inverted Christian sect. (Most of the presently vast literature on Satanism is quite unreliable. Some reliable sources include Hartland, 1921; Spence, 1960: 123–124; Carey, 1941; and Murray, 1962. For the official views of the Church of Satan, centered in San Francisco, see LaVey, 1969. For good historical commentaries, see Carus, 1969; Langston, 1945; Coulange, 1930; and Garcon and Vinchon, 1929. And for the classic occult view on Satanism, see Huysmans, 1958; and Waite, 1896.) Oddly enough, most of history's Satanisms seemed to be direct outgrowths of the Christian churches' misrepresentations of early witchcraft practices. The inquisitors so impressed some individuals with the fantastic and blasphemous picture of Satanism that they apparently decided that they also would "rather reign in hell than serve in heaven."

Several different varieties seem to depict the non-heretical, non-Satanic or white witches. The major division of great importance to the sociologist is between those witches who are individual practitioners and those who belong to organized witch groups or *covens*. Most frequently encountered, the former variety represents the independent or solitary witches. This variety can be further subdivided into two, somewhat oversimplified, classes: (1) one represents those who, having learned the secrets of the art through some special kinship-relation to another solitary witch, practice witchcraft as a culturally inherited art from kin; (2) the other represents those who, having invented their own techniques or having obtained their practices from the occult literature, practice witchcraft as self-designated witches. My investigations show that the vast majority of witches are in the second class: they belong to no organized group and have obtained their knowledge from their readings and conversations with others uninitiated into coven-held secrets. The typical person of this class is a young high-school or college-age girl who, for a variety of reasons, self-designates herself as a witch to her peers; because her status is attractive to her friends but elicits fear in her enemies, it produces many social rewards for her. Yet this type of witch is "illegitimate" in terms of the very criteria that she herself may accept for being a witch. Most of the major works on witchcraft state that before one becomes a true practitioner of the craft, he must obtain initiation into a coven and learn the group (coven) secrets. These secrets, however, are not available in such public works as the occultism-volumes in most public libraries or occult bookstores.

A number of varieties exist among the organized white witch groups. A rather clear division seems to exist between the witch covens formed before and after the 1951 repeal of witchcraft-laws in England or, especially, after the 1954 publication of the late Gerald Gardner's first book on witchcraft (also, see Gardner, 1959, and Bracelin's biography on Gardner, 1960). Gardner's works were very influential in British occult circles, and many contemporary witches, sometimes called Gardnerites, received their credentials through Gardner's Witchcraft Museum on the Isle of Man. The question of legitimacy among British witches is still raging, each accusing the other of concocting his own rituals. *Pentagram: A Witchcraft Review*, the publication of the Witchcraft Research Association in London, prominently featured this debate in its first five issues (for an example of a lively exchange, see issue number 5, December 1965: 18–19). The much publicized witch, Monique Wilson, who with her husband inherited Gardner's museum, has stated that she holds a secret register of covens existing around the world (Wilson, 1968). This, however, seems to include only the Gardnerite covens, which according to Mrs. Wilson, numbered several hundred at that time. In 1969, another well publicized witch, Mrs. Sybil Leek, estimated to me that approximately 300 covens were then operating in the United States. The facts are that covens, especially those in existence before 1951, have little communication with one another. Members sometimes migrate from an area and join or begin a new coven, but no central hierarchy or witchcraft-organization actually exists. Except for Mrs. Wilson and Mrs. Leek, most witches know little about those in the other parts of the country. These women are somewhat unusual because their extensive publicity and travel about the world have brought them into contact with a great many witches wanting interaction with them. It is, therefore, impossible to obtain any sort of accurate estimate of the number of covens now in operation. Because a great number of new covens did begin after 1951, they certainly appear to represent the bulk of the *known* witchcraft-groups about which we read today. Even though more could exist, I did locate three pre-1951 covens in Michigan. I thus estimate that at least 150 such traditional covens probably exist in Great Britain and the United States.

According to Murray, the maximum number of persons in a coven is thirteen: Thus, Great Britain and the United States probably can claim no more than 1950 coven members. These cultists represent a rather small part of the mass market currently devouring the many marketable witchcraft items and books. Coupling the number of coven members with that of the solitary witches (many of whom are really not very serious about witchcraft) still leaves us with a relatively small number of witches in the United States, the maximum being probably less than 3000. Like their interest with astrology, the popular interest of the general public toward this form of occultism is very superficial. From my observations of many people's reactions toward witches during public occasions, I know that most people show interest in meeting a witch for the novelty rather than for any occult enlightenment. Like astrology, witchcraft also represents a play-function for the major portion of its current popular audience.

Like the witches, the Satanists also represent two distinct types of individuals: those acting as solitary agents and those operating in groups. We know next to nothing about the former. If some individuals in the world believe that they have made contractual arrangements with the Devil, then they probably would prefer that this not be widely known: this seems likely, especially if they are really doing evil things. Much diversity exists among the Satanic groups; these groups have at least four major varieties. Probably the least frequent, the first variety represents Satanic groups who follow some non-heretical (to them) interpretation of Christianity in which Satan is perceived as an angel still to be worshipped. These may represent some sort of Gnostic tradition which the members claim to follow.

A second variety about which one can read a great deal in the "soft-core" pornographic literature (e.g., Moore, 1969) consists of sex clubs that incorporate Satanism and some of its alleged rituals. Here we find, as an attraction or embellishment, the celebrated but usually artificial "black mass" (for the best work on this topic, see Rhodes, 1954). Many of these groups are sado-masochist clubs or flagellation societies.

Probably more frequent than the previous two, a third variety of Satanic group is an outgrowth of the current narcotics or "acid-culture" now found in various parts of the country [even though the author seems to confuse it with traditional Satanism, Burke (1970) presents a good description of one of these groups]. Epitomized by the much publicized Charles Manson group that allegedly killed Sharon Tate in 1969, this sort of group has received much publicity. It is, however, much more rare than newspaper headlines would imply. More importantly, most of these groups are almost completely untraditional, and they make up their brand of Satanism as they go along (Burke, 1970; and Kloman, 1970). Like the sex club, their central focus is not occultism at all; in their case, it is narcotics. Ironically enough, many traditional Satanists commonly complain that the sex and acid cultists give a "bad name" to "real Satanism."

Clearly dominant today, the fourth variety of Satanic group consists of members of the Church of Satan in San Francisco. High Priest Anton Szandor LaVey founded this church, which is, in fact, a church, not a cult. Only LaVey knows the exact number of members in the Church of Satan, but on numerous occasions he has stated that over 7000 were contributing members. He gave this figure before mid-1969: since then, LaVey's book *The Satanic Bible* has had national circulation (125,000 copies in its first of now four printings), and two movies that prominently feature the Church of Satan have been released nationally. The figure of 7000 appears reasonable, if not conservative, for several reasons; because LaVey does remarkable public relations work and because *Rosemary's Baby*, the movie with which he was associated, has been a great success, the Church of Satan has received vast international publicity over the past five years.

The church has been remarkably successful during its short life. Although it still depends heavily upon the charisma of its founder, it is hierarchically governed and now has two other churches (Grottos) in the Bay Area plus a number of still secret (to the general public) branches scattered around the country. By the end of 1971, LaVey hopes that Grottos will exist in every state of the Union. At the current rate of growth, achievement of his goal is not impossible. Because contributing members pay an initial fee of twenty dollars for their lifetime membership, the church has a relatively prosperous economic beginning.

Although the Church of Satan believes in the practice of magic, it simply defines magic as "obtaining changes in accordance with one's will." The church perceives magic not as supernatural (i.e., forever scientifically inexplicable), but simply as supernormal (i.e., not yet fully understood by science but amenable to eventual scientific explanation). The church actively rejects spirituality and mysticism of any sort; it espouses an elitist, materialist, and basically atheistic philosophy. Satan constitutes a worship of one's own ego. Unlike most atheisms, the position of the Church of Satan is that these symbolic entities are powerful and indispensable forces in man's emotional life and that these forces are necessary conditions for the success of greater (Ritual) Magic.

In its major features, the Church of Satan takes the position of extreme Machiavellianism and cynical-realism toward the nature of man. It has many philosophical parallels with philosophies as divergent in sophistication as the Superman views of Friedrich Nietzsche and the Objectivist ideals of Ayn Rand. Its major feature, however, is its emphasis upon the importance of myth and magic and upon their impact in a world of people who can still be manipulated through such beliefs and emotions. This Satanist, then, is the *ultimate pragmatist*.

This predominant form of Satanism does not represent a new mysticism at all. It not only denies the existence of anything supernatural or spiritual, but it even condemns any narcotics, hallucinogens, or other agents that might act to separate rational man from his material environment. This Satanist does not seek escape from reality; he wishes full control of reality and is even willing to use all forces—including irrational elements—that help him in achieving his desired ends. Unlike the acid-culture Satanist who seeks identity through mysticism and other levels of "consciousness," this Satanist is very much opposed to the hippie culture of acid and altruism.

Thus, I argue that, like those interested in astrology, the major followers of Satanism represent not a search for a new spiritual meaning, but only a disenchantment with religious orthodoxy.

Conclusion

How are we to assess this rising tide of interest in the occult? I have shown three major facts in this paper. First, the interest in the occult is multidimensional, and it is not the simple, integrated, and consistent "bag" that many, especially the writers in the popular press, have described it to be. Second, many persons involved in the following of today's occultisms are not the simple identity-seeking variety that some have portrayed them to be; these occultisms serve a variety of functions quite apart from offering new normative structures as an escape from alienation for the anomie. Third, most of those involved in supporting the current occult revival have a relatively superficial connection with it, a connection that is usually more one of play than one of seriousness. For most Americans, the involvement in the occult is a leisure-time activity and a fad of popular culture rather than a serious religious involvement in the search for new sacred elements.

Dr. Donald Kaplan has made a very insightful observation about astrology: "It's pop science . . . It has the same contempt, in a playful way, for science that pop art has for academic art" (quoted in Buckley, 1968: 133). I believe that we may even go further and refer to the mass version of occultism as *pop religion*. I would argue that it shows a playful contempt for what many once viewed seriously (and some still view thusly). I further would argue that the current mass interest in occultism represents, in fact, a kind of victory over the supernatural. What we are seeing is largely a demystification-process of what were once fearful and threatening cultural elements. Most significant is the very playfulness in the attitudes of most of the people involved in the occult revival. What were once fearful and awe-inspiring dark secrets known only through initiation into arcane orders are now fully exposed to the eyes of Everyman.

I illustrate this point by the example of the probable contemporary reaction to the allegation that a house in the neighborhood is haunted. Years ago, few would dare enter the house; all would whisper in fear about it. Now, such an allegation would bring a rush of inquisitive teenagers who desire to spend the night there just to see the ghost. Would it be proper to interpret this direct interest as a renewed belief in ghosts? It is precisely because we no longer believe in the fearsome aspects of the occult that we are willing to experiment with them. Most of those who would willingly draw a proper pentagram on the floor to invoke a demon would do so precisely because they do not really believe that some Devil's emissary who might just pluck their souls down to Hell would possibly ever visit them. If we fully believed in demons, we certainly would not want to call them up.

This assessment does not deny that a growth has occurred in the number of true believers in the occult. It also does not deny that other non-occult phenomena, which indicate a growing number of persons seeking new religious meanings, have occurred. Certain factors, however, would alone cause an expected increase in occult activity: (1) the increase in our general population, (2) some disillusionment with the dominant religions, (3) our lack of fear of the occult or an involvement with it, (4) the present lack of social sanctions against involvement with the occult, and (5) the increased saliency of the occult resulting from the revival itself. *I must stress that I am concerned more with the mass character of the occult than with its small but significant minority of serious advocates.* As long as these *mass* phenomena represent a playful and non-serious confrontation with the supernatural elements, they then represent a possible cleansing or purging of the old fears and myths still present in our society. The more we eliminate these old fears and myths, the more we develop a naturalistic rationalism, a scientific view of the universe.

New Age Harmonies

Otto Friedrich

*Describing the "New Age" as a combination of
spirituality and superstition, fad and farce, the
author of this selection reminds us that the elements
the movement comprises—such as faith healing,
fortune telling, and the transmigration of
souls—have been around for centuries. And the
present movement is growing steadily, as evidenced
by popular books on the subject, the number of
specialty stores that deal with the phenomenon, New
Age radio stations, music, magazines, and television
programs. Crystals, therapeutic touch, the Elliott
Wave Theory, astrology, channeling, ancient Mayan
calendars that foretell the end of the world—it's all
here. Led by such varied gurus as Shirley MacLaine,
José Arguëlles, Jack Pursel, J. Z. Knight (who speaks
for the spirit entity 'Ramtha'), and a host of other
spiritual guides who have become famous, and in
many cases wealthy, the followers have eagerly
opened their eyes, ears, and often their pocketbooks
in anticipation of finding health, enlightenment, and
joy.*

"LET US NOT WALK THE PATH OF LIFE IN DARKNESS
but shed your light upon the path so that we
may clearly see the power of your glory forever."
Those words of prayer are the last spoken by Bob
Johnson, 54, a gentle, white-haired man who
practices his spiritual arts in a modest apartment
in mid-town New York City. Now his eyes are
half shut, unseeing, and when he next speaks, in
a strangely clipped Irish accent, he represents a
"tutelage" of spectral beings from Alpha Centauri, the nearest of the stars.

"Greetings from the almighty form of God,"
says the celestial tutelage. "Do you seek our
counsel?"

"Yes," says *Time* Correspondent Mary Cro-
nin.

"Do you have an art?"

"I'm a reporter."

"That is an art of sorts. Do you feel the vibrations now? It may be starting now."

"I'm trying to find out more about the New
Age."

"Always the New Age!"

"Is all this interest in channeling and crystals
a passing fad or something more?"

"It is both: a fad to some, a way of life to
others. We would say there are more true spiritual seekers today."

"What is my mission in life?"

"We feel you will be involved in the process
of bringing the written thought about spirituality
to man. This is a mission. People say there are
accidents, but this is not an accident."

"Can you tell me about one of my past lives?"

"You have been a sailor. A man. You understand the Spanish Armada? You tried to attack
England! You considered it to be a heathen country because they dropped Catholicism."

"What did I learn from that life?"

"To swim very well. You almost lost your life.
Your ship was broken up around the northern
coast of Ireland. You were in the water for days.
It was very painful."

"How do you live up there on Alpha Centauri?"

"We don't have a day, a night. We have never been a human body. We don't speak like this. What is coming through is not our persona. We don't have a personality you could relate to. We manifest a personality so that you may relate to it. You see?"

So here we are in the New Age, a combination of spirituality and superstition, fad and farce, about which the only thing certain is that it is not new. Nobody seems to know exactly where the term came from, but it has been around for several decades or more, and many elements of the New Age, like faith healing, fortune-telling and transmigration of souls, go back for centuries. (Ages, in general, are an uncertain affair. The Age of Aquarius, celebrated in the musical *Hair*, may have started in the 1960s or at the turn of the century or may not yet have begun. Once under way, such astrological ages are supposed to last 2,000 years.)

Though it is hard to say exactly how many Americans believe in which parts of the New Age, the movement as a whole is growing steadily. Bantam Books says its New Age titles have increased tenfold in the past decade. The number of New Age bookstores has doubled in the past five years, to about 2,500. New Age radio is spreading, with such stations as WBMW in Washington and KTWV-FM in Los Angeles offering dreamy light jazz that one listener described as "like I tapped into a radio station on Mars." The Grammys now include a special prize for New Age music (latest winner: Swiss Harpist Andreas Vollenweider). Fledgling magazines with names like *New Age, Body Mind Spirit* and *Brain/Mind Bulletin* are full of odd ads: "Healing yourself with crystals," "American Indian magic can work for you," "How to use a green candle to gain money," "The power of the pendulum can be in your hands," "Use numerology to win the lottery." And, perhaps inevitably, "New health through colon rejuvenation."

If some of those have a slightly greedy tone, the reason is that New Age fantasies often intersect with mainstream materialism, the very thing that many New Age believers profess to scorn. A surprising number of successful stockbrokers consult astrological charts; a yuppie investment banker who earns $100,000 a year talks of her previous life

as a monk. Some millionaires have their own private gurus who pay house calls to provide comfort and advice. Big corporations too are paying attention. "The principle here is to look at the mind, body, heart and spirit," says a corporate spokesperson, who asks that her employer be identified only as a "major petrochemical company." This company provides its employees with regular workshops in stress management; it has hired a faith healer to "read auras" for ailing employees and run her hands over their "fields of energy." Even the U.S. Army has commissioned a West Coast firm to explore the military potentials of meditation and extrasensory perception.

Now come to the ballroom of the New York Hilton, where 1,200 of the faithful have paid $300 apiece to get the word from the New Age's reigning whirling dervish, Shirley MacLaine. To the soothing accompaniment of crystal chimes and distant waterfalls, the star of *Terms of Endearment* leads her new acolytes in meditating on the body's various chakras, or energy points. First comes the spinning red wheel of the base chakra, then the sexual pulsation of the orange chakra, and finally upward to the solar plexus and the visceral emotions of the yellow chakra.

"Feel the cleansing power of the stream of life, the coolness of water . . ." MacLaine purrs. She is wearing a turquoise sweater, violet sweatpants and green ankle-high sneakers, and a sizable crystal dangles from her neck. "There is so much you need to know . . . See the outer bubble of white light watching for you. It is part of you. Let it be. It is showing you itself, that part of God that you have not recognized."

A woman in the audience complains that she has suffered chronic physical pain since childhood. MacLaine is not fazed. "Sometimes people use pain to feel alive," she explains. "Pain is a perception, not a reality." That is a basic New Age doctrine: you can be whatever you want to be.

The doctrine is sometimes a little hard to apply. The woman in the audience (women outnumber the men two to one) does not feel healed. "No one else goes through what I do," she says.

From the back, another small voice says, "I do."

MacLaine moves into a visualization exercise aimed at cleansing the third eye (the one behind the forehead) of negative thought patterns. More questions:

"How do I deal with the vibration of joy and ecstasy that I get when I meet my higher self?" a woman wants to know. "Mine is a naked cupid."

"Ecstasy is a new frequency which we are just beginning to define," MacLaine says. "It is complete surrender and trust, the key words for this new age."

"With all due respect," says another voice, "I don't think you are a god." (That is another New Age doctrine, that everybody is God, co-creator of the universe.)

"If you don't see me as God," says MacLaine, blithe as ever, "it's because you don't see yourself as God."

If this seems to make very little sense, it nonetheless pays handsome dividends. MacLaine's five books of self-exploration and self-promotion have run to more than 8 million copies. Her third volume, *Out on a Limb*, which tells how she discovered the spirit world, became a five-hour TV extravaganza that was aired earlier this year. Her fifth volume, *It's All in the Playing*, published last September and a best seller for more than two months, is mainly about the making of the TV version of Volume 3, including conference/seances on how her astral guides feel about being cast to play themselves on television. And so on.

MacLaine's New York Hilton session was part of a 15-city national tour (estimated earnings: $1.5 million) to spread the New Age gospel. Next year she plans to open Uriel Village, a 300-acre retreat in Baca, Colo., where customers will be able to get weeklong sessions of meditation, past-life regression therapy, and sound and color healing, among other things. "I want this to be all mine, my energy, my control," says MacLaine. "I want a big dome-covered meditation center and a series of dome-covered meeting rooms because spiritual energy goes in spirals. We'll grow all our own food and eat under another dome. I want to turn a profit with this so I can build another center and another. I want to prove that spirituality is profitable."

For all its popularity, the New Age is hard to define. It includes a whole cornucopia of beliefs, fads, rituals; some subscribe to some parts, some to others. Only on special occasions, like the highly publicized "harmonic convergence" in August, do believers in I Ching or crystals gather together with believers in astral travel, shamans, Lemurians and tarot readers, for a communal chanting of om, the Hindu invocation that often precedes meditation. Led on by the urgings of José Argüelles, a Colorado art historian who claimed that ancient Mayan calendars foretold the end of the world unless the faithful gathered to provide harmony, some 20,000 New Agers assembled at "sacred sites" from Central Park to Mount Shasta to—uh—provide harmony.

All in all, the New Age does express a cloudy sort of religion, claiming vague connections with both Christianity and the major faiths of the East (New Agers like to say that Jesus spent 18 years in India absorbing Hinduism and the teachings of Buddha), plus an occasional dab of pantheism and sorcery. The underlying faith is a lack of faith in the orthodoxies of rationalism, high technology, routine living, spiritual law-and-order. Somehow, the New Agers believe, there must be some secret and mysterious shortcut or alternative path to happiness and health. And nobody ever really dies.

Like other believers, many New Agers attach great importance to artifacts, relics and sacred objects, all of which can be profitably offered for sale: Tibetan bells, exotic herbal teas, Viking runes, solar energizers, colored candles for "chromotherapy," and a Himalayan mountain of occult books, pamphlets, instructions and tape recordings. Some of these magical products are quite imaginative. A bearded Colorado sage who calls himself Gurudas sells "gem elixirs," which he creates by putting stones in bowls of water and leaving them in the sun for several hours, claiming that this allows the water to absorb energy from the sun and the stone.

Most New Agers prefer the stones themselves, specifically crystals of all sorts. These are not only thought to have mysterious healing powers but are considered programmable, like a computer, if one just concentrates hard enough. (The most powerful crystals are buried deep under New England, some New Agers believe, because New England was once connected to Atlantis, the famous "lost continent.")

Tina Lucia, a self-styled therapist in Stone Mountain, Ga., uses crystals to treat patients, because "physical problems are manifestations of spiritual problems." Gallbladder ailments, she says, come from a bitterness toward God, and lung trouble from a hatred of one's own body. "All you have to do is release these problems," she says. She uses amethyst, rose and blue quartz, and even black onyx and obsidian. One of her satisfied customers is Annette Manders, who wields a crystal wand that Lucia gave her. "I healed a fungus under my toenail with my wand," says Manders, "and I had a stomach problem that doesn't bother me anymore. The energy is subtle. It's not like you're being zapped."

Another favorite New Age cure for the misfortunes of the body is the therapeutic touch, again an ancient method newly back in fashion. While nobody knows exactly how these quasi-medical techniques work, people generally turn to them because conventional medicine seems so impersonal, costs so much, and fails so often. Greg Schelkun, for example, graduated from Dartmouth and was working for a Boston publisher when he got a chance to go to the Orient with his mother, who was suffering from chronic chills and fevers. In the Philippines she met a healer who laid his hands on her and cured her. The healer also cured Schelkun of migraine headaches, which he had suffered for 15 years. "At the time, I didn't know what was going on," says Schelkun. "All I knew was that the headaches stopped."

Schelkun subsequently spent two years studying with another healer in the Philippines, and now practices his arts in Marin County. A burly, mustachioed man who likes to wear pink oxford-cloth button-down shirts, Schelkun hardly looks like a wizard. "I don't see disease written on a body with flashing neon lights saying 'Here! Here! Here!'" he says. "I place my hands to connect them to their healing source. My hands are able to feel hot spots, cold spots, pain and symptoms of problems in the body. We're not rocks. We're taught in this society to see only reflected light, instead of radiant or inner light."

There is always a danger of quackery in such unorthodox approaches, as orthodox doctors repeatedly warn. But some New Age healers have perfectly standard medical training. Bernie Siegel, for example, is a surgeon who teaches at Yale and has written a new best seller, *Love, Medicine & Miracles*. After years of treating cancer patients, he believes "all disease is ultimately related to a lack of love, or to love that is only conditional, for the exhaustion of the immune system thus created leads to physical vulnerability." Dolores Krieger, an R.N. and a Ph.D., teaches the art of therapeutic touch to nurses at New York University. "The best thing that happens," she says, "is rapid relaxation, the eradication or lessening of pain and the beginning of healing processes."

Another practitioner is a slight, intelligent, no-nonsense woman of 63, who treats ailments as varied as cancer, AIDS and multiple sclerosis in a cluttered studio apartment in Manhattan. A one-time bacteriologist, she had no psychic experiences until after the death of her husband, when she began hearing voices and seeing visions and "thought I was losing my mind." When she began to study these phenomena, she became convinced that unseen doctors were working through her. "I am not a mystical person," she says, "but I have learned to accept many, many things. I know my doctors are geniuses." She has applied her touch to 14 AIDS patients in the past few years and has lost only three so far. "I haven't found any disease that we can't do something for," she says. "Some people have disease for a reason, to learn a lesson in this life or from a past life."

There is no unanimity of New Age belief in anything, but many New Agers do believe in unidentified flying objects, crewed by oddly shaped extraterrestrials who have long visited the earth from more advanced planets, spreading the wisdom that created, among other things, Stonehenge and the pyramids of Egypt. Government officials keep announcing that there are no such things as UFOs, but the National Science Foundation reported last year that 43 percent of the citizenry believe it "likely" that some of the UFOs reported "are really space vehicles from other civilizations." (And where *did* those airstrip-like markings in the Peruvian Andes come from?)

If one can place any faith in Steven Spielberg films like *E.T.* and *Close Encounters of the Third Kind*, the visitors from outer space are benign and friendly folk. But several recently reported episodes have been more sinister. High on the best-seller lists this past summer stood *Communion* by Whitley Strieber, previously known mainly as a writer of fantasies (*The Wolfen, Warday*), who vehemently describes as a "true story" his chilling account of being spirited onto a spaceship by a pack of 3-foot-high "visitors." When they proposed sticking a needle into his brain, he recalls, one of them casually asked him, "What can we do to help you stop screaming?" More scare stories came from

Intruders by Budd Hopkins, a chronicle of 130 people who claim to have been abducted by extraterrestrial visitors and tell tales of being subjected to various degrading medical experiments. On the other hand, the extraterrestrials who turn up in the course of channeling—one of the most popular New Age sports—appear almost unfailingly wise and benevolent.

Come to a rocky meadow on California's Mount Shasta, where a New Zealander named Neville Rowe tells the encircling crowd of 200 (admission: $10) that he speaks with the voice of Soli, an "off-planet being" who has never actually lived on earth. Dressed in a white-peaked cap, purple shirt and purple shoes, Rowe clutches a bottle of Evian water as the voice emerges from him in a rather peculiar British accent. "You are here to express who you are," says Soli. "You are here to search for yourself. The highest recognition you can make is that I am what I am. All that is, is. You are God. You are, each and every one, part of the Second Coming."

Somebody wants to argue. What about murderers? Are they God too?

"Your truth is your truth," says Soli, while his helpers start trying to sell videotapes of his latest incarnation. "My truth is my truth."

Not all the channeled voices are from outer space. Come to the Phoenix Institute in Lexington, Ky., for example, and hear Lea Schultz speak with the voice of somebody called Samuel. "What Lea does," says Tripp Bratton, an official at the institute, "is she calms herself and tunes in to a signal. Everything has a vibration, even if it doesn't have a physical form. Then she becomes animated by the energy on the other end of the 'line.' It's direct telepathic communication." Samuel usually discusses problems he feels are present in the audience and then takes questions: What happened to Atlantis? What happened to the *Challenger*?

Jack Pursel, a former Florida insurance agent living in Los Angeles, squints his eyes and speaks with the voice of Lazaris, a spiritual entity of uncertain origins.

"How old are you?" he is asked.

"In our reality, we have no time," says Lazaris.

"Why are you making your presence known to man?"

"Because you are ready now . . ."

"Is the world about to end?"

"No. In a word, no. This is not the ending. This is the beginning."

Pursel charges customers an average of $700 a year, and he has quite a few customers. "Lazaris is so popular," he says, "that, yeah, a lot of money gets made." But Pursel makes his real money as an art dealer and is opening a second gallery, on Rodeo Drive in Beverly Hills. As for channeling, "it's not a business; it's a labor of love." He adds a dark warning that others are less worthy. "There's some loony tunes out there," he says.

Probably the most celebrated of all current channelers is J. Z. Knight, a handsome ex-housewife in Yelm, Washington, who has performed for thousands at a price of $150 each per session. She speaks for Ramtha, a 35,000-year-old warrior who reports that he once lived on Atlantis. He has even dictated a book, *I Am Ramtha*, published in Portland, Ore., by Beyond Words Publishing and illustrated with photographs of Knight going into a trance on *The Merv Griffin Show*. Sample words of Ramthan wisdom: "Who be I? I am a notorious entity. I have that which is called a reputation. Know you what that is? Controversial, and I do what I say I do. What I am here to do is not to change people's minds, only to engage them and allow the wonderments for those that desire them to come to pass. I have been you, and I have become the other side of what you are . . ."

The sayings of Ramtha have brought Knight substantial rewards, including a luxurious mansion complete with spa, swimming pool, and Arabian horses. A spokesman deprecates talk of her wealth, however, by noting that she pays a staff of 14 and that the tax collectors are insatiable.

Jo Ann Karl is a tall blond who says she was an up-and-coming business executive until she discovered the supernatural seven years ago. She was on a business trip in the Midwest when she first felt herself drifting through space outside her body. She tried to ignore the experience, but it kept recurring. Now she gets $15 a customer for channeling the archangel Gabriel and a spirit named Ashtar.

"The lesson I learned in one of my past lives was about taking risks," says Karl. "I was married to St. Peter. We traveled widely with Jesus, teaching with him. After he was crucified, we continued to teach and travel for several more years, until we were caught by the Romans. Peter was crucified, and I was thrown to the lions, after being raped and pilloried. Now I understand why I've always been afraid of big animals."

Karl's spirit guides had been advising her to go to the Incan empire's sacred Lake Titicaca in Bolivia (the Andes seem to be a favorite way station for UFOs). "They sort of told us we would meet *them*," she says. "I won't believe it until I see them and talk to them and feel the panel on the spaceship. But maybe it is time for people to know they have help." And so, starry-eyed and full of hope, Karl headed southward, and she did catch a distant glimpse of what she took to be a spaceship. "It looked like a whole lot of orange light," she says. "A blast of light spherical in shape. It was big and far away."

This kind of thing inspires some observers to mockery. Garry Trudeau's *Doonesbury* ridiculed the harmonic convergence as an "age where . . . the heavens are in perfect alignment, and finally, after years of anticipation, where Sean Penn is in jail." Some New Age people admit that the movement is so full of eccentrics and profiteers that they even dislike applying the term New Age to their own activities. New York City's Open Center, for example, studiously avoids the label. Founded four years ago by Wall Street Lawyer Walter Beebe, the center runs on a budget of $1.7 million and enrolls 3,000 students a month for a range of 250 one- and two-day workshops and such courses as Aspects of Zen Practice, Internal Kung Fu, and Jungian Symbolism in Astrology.

"We see this movement as a different perspective on life, a holistic view of life," says Ralph White, who teaches philosophy at the center. "It encompasses an enormous spectrum involving the body, mind, and spirit, including an increased awareness of nutrition, the rise in ecological thinking, a change in business perspectives, greater emphasis on preventive medicine, a shift to Jungian philosophy, an emphasis on the individual's intuition. Many people see themselves as living in a pretty meaningless world, and there is a profound cry for meaning. We've seen that tendency in churches, because the way religion is presented traditionally has spoken to our inner selves less and less. People want a living, feeling experience of spirituality. They yearn to get in touch with the soul."

This relatively level-headed approach to spirituality has its attractions in the world of commerce, particularly in the important area of management training. Innovation Associates of Framingham, Massachusetts, charges $15,000 for a four-day seminar designed to strengthen executives' commitment to a common purpose. "We tell them to imagine themselves walking on a beach or a meadow," says the firm's director of consulting services, Joel Yanowitz. "Once we get them in the relaxed state, we ask them to pay attention to new thoughts and to test them against rational information about a situation. We teach them the art of holistic systemic thinking." One major engineering laboratory on the East Coast has established a program, run by a small New York City firm named Hoy Powers & Wayno, that is using meditation, imaging, and techniques of intuitive thought to instill more creativity and leadership in some 400 corporate managers and executives.

Social Psychologist Michael Ray invokes Zen, yoga, and tarot cards when he teaches his course Creativity in Business at the Stanford Graduate School of Business—but he groans at any mention of a New Age. "Our assumption is that creativity is essential for health and happiness in a business career," he says. Business executives have always developed their own methods of clearing the mind. J. P. Morgan used to play solitaire before making an important business decision, Ray points out. Conrad Hilton claimed he relied on intuition to help him decide what prices to bid for properties. "It's not that unusual these days," says Ray, "to see enormously successful, hard-core corporate types doing biofeedback and using crystals." Among those who have participated as guest speakers in Ray's course: Apple Computer Co-Founder Steven Jobs and Discount Broker Charles Schwab.

And what does make the stock market rise and fall? Mason Sexton graduated from Harvard Business School in 1972, went to Wall Street, and decided that all the traditional ways of making predictions were "at best hit or miss." Then he learned of the Fibonacci Ratio, based on the work of a thirteenth-century Italian mathematician, and a modern development of it known as the Elliott Wave Theory, which declares that all advancing markets have five waves up and three waves down.

"But the key to the timing of when these waves will bottom or crest depends very much on astrology," says Sexton, "which is simply the science of understanding the nature of time, since our sense of time depends on the relationship of the earth to the sun and moon. We are getting very close to the end of the primary wave-three rally, which has been in effect since July 1984. Then we will have a primary-wave correction, which will take eight months, representing a decline of 400 to 600 points."

That is what Sexton was saying last August, when he predicted the market would hit its peak late that month. On October 2, he warned: "Any Dow close below 2387 would be a signal to sell all stocks." And he took his own advice, not only selling but also going short.

Incredible? Sexton has 1,500 subscribers who pay $360 a year for his biweekly newsletter of predictions, and many have written to thank him for saving them from Black Monday. Says Marc Klee, who helps manage the $200 million American Fund Advisors: "His techniques are unconventional, to say the least, but I've been working with him three years or so, and his track record is well above average."

One of the most go-getting New Age entrepreneurs is Chris Majer, 36, president of SportsMind, Inc., based in Seattle. As the corporate name indicates, Majer originally worked mainly on athletic training, though his current clients include not only AT&T but also the U.S. Army. Majer started his military efforts in 1982 with an eight-week, $50,000 training program at Fort Hood in Texas. Traditional calisthenics were replaced by a holistic stretching–warm-up–aerobics–cooldown routine. Soldiers practiced visualizing their combat tasks. The results in training test scores were apparently so good that the Army expanded SportsMind's assignment into a yearlong, $350,000 program to help train Green Berets. "They wanted the most far-ranging human-performance program we could deliver," Majer says.

The Green Berets were taught meditation techniques so that they could spend long hours hidden in enemy territory. "They have to be comfortable at a deep level with who they are," Majer says, "not make mental mistakes or they'll give away their position and get killed. People say all this New Age stuff is a bunch of hoo-hoo, but it gets results."

While the idea of New Age Green Berets meditating in the jungle can inspire laughter, it can also inspire a certain concern about the political and social implications of the whole movement. Is it some kind of neoleftist response to the Age of Reagan, or is it an ultrarightist extension of Reaganism? The answer depends somewhat on the answerer's politics. While some see in the New Agers' chants and nebulous slogans a revival of the shaggy '60s, others see the devotion of many New Agers to moneymaking as simply a new variant of yuppieism.

Whether leftist, rightist, or none of the above, the New Age has attracted a fair amount of criticism on philosophical and ethical grounds. "A lot of it is a cop-out, an escape from reality, an anti-intellectual movement denying rationality," says Alan Dundes, a professor of anthropology and folklore at the University of California, Berkeley. "The New Age movement reflects anxieties of one sort or another—the threat of nuclear warfare, the President running a vigilante action out of the White House, nurses accused of killing patients. People look at all this and say, 'If this is the Establishment, then I don't want this. I want something else, something I can trust.' It's people latching onto a belief system to get certainty where there is no certainty."

"It's a religion without being a religion," says Robert J. L. Burrows, publications editor of the evangelical Spiritual Counterfeits Project in Berkeley. "Humans are essentially religious creatures, and they don't rest until they have some sort of answer to the fundamental questions. Rationalism and secularism don't answer those questions. But you can see the rise of the New Age as a barometer of the disintegration of American culture. Dostoyevsky said anything is permissible if there is no God. But anything is also permissible if everything is God. There is no way of making any distinction between good and evil."

Douglas Groothuis, a research associate at a Christian think tank called Probe Center Northwest and author of *Unmasking the New Age*, raises a similar objection. "Once you've deified yourself," he says, "which is what the New Age is all about, there is no higher moral absolute. It's a recipe for ethical anarchy. I see it as a counterfeit religious claim. It's both messianic and millennial."

Though Groothuis is now writing a second

book, *Confronting the New Age*, about the movement's inroads into business and education, it is probably wise to remember that phenomena like the New Age have to some extent been a part of the American scene ever since there was an American scene. Remember the eighteenth-century Shaker leader, Mother Ann Lee, whose followers believed she represented the second coming of Christ. Remember Mary Baker Eddy, severely injured by a fall on the ice, who became cured while reading a passage in St. Matthew and thereafter taught the unreality of all physical ills. Spiritualism was the rage of the 1850s, and a heroine of Henry James' *The Bostonians* went into mesmeric trances to gather recruits for the cause of feminism. Walt Whitman believed in transmigration of the soul—"And as to you Life I reckon you are the leavings of many deaths,/ (No doubt I have died myself ten thousand times before.)"—and so did the practical-minded Thomas Alva Edison.

Remember Madame Blavatsky, who founded the Theosophical Society and revealed the secrets of the universe in *Isis Unveiled*. There were sightings of spaceships in the 1890s, at a time when no American had ever seen an airplane, much less an Apollo rocket, but then as now a century was coming to an end. Mars was once widely believed to be inhabited by little green men, so when Orson Welles declared on the radio in 1938 that space invaders had landed, much of the nation went into a panic. And do not forget *The Search for Bridey Murphy*. Or the fad of talking to plants. *Plus ça change* . . .

"It's important to point out the moral imbecility of what the New Age people are trying to do," says United Methodist Clergyman J. Gordon Melton, director of Santa Barbara's Institute for the Study of American Religion. "But at the same time I wouldn't see it as a threat." Even that, though, is perhaps too harsh a condemnation to serve as the final word on an essentially harmless anthology of illusions.

But Shirley MacLaine is accustomed to slings and arrows. "I think the thrust of this article, aside from bemused sarcasm, is going to be that a lot of people are getting rich on all this," she says, in a fairly successful venture into prophecy. "That seems to be a concern of many journalists. But I would say we all have to decide what we're worth. . . . I think journalists who are investigating belief in the unseen have to adjust the way they are judging the issue of materialism in relation to spirituality. Anything you want to learn costs money in this world."

MacLaine is working hard these days. Aside from all her New Age activities, she is in London to shoot a new John Schlesinger film about a domineering piano teacher. "This character makes Aurora Greenway in *Terms of Endearment* look like a day at the beach," she says. "I'm on the set by 8, and we work till 8, and then I have lines to learn." She has also written a new book, tentatively titled *Going Within*. "It's techniques of meditation, visualization, color therapy, sound therapy, how to work with crystals, how to work with colored jewelry, acupuncture, acupressure, things that have been helpful to me. I can only write about what's happened to me."

In many ways, her life remains much the same as ever. "I live a kind of nomad existence. I like to travel light. I don't wear a lot of jewelry. I travel with one suitcase because I always end up carrying it." In other ways, though, her life is quite different from what it was in her early days of singing and dancing on Broadway, which seem, if one may say so, several lifetimes ago. "It's me that makes things happen to me," she says. "I'm not the leader of this movement. I'm not a high priestess of New Age concepts. I'm just a human being trying to find some answers about what we're doing here, where we came from and where we're going. That search is equal to finding a good script, and maybe it even helps."

So let the final word on the New Age be: om.

Glossary

Acculturation: Culture change occurring under conditions of close contact between two societies. The weaker group tends to acquire cultural elements of the dominant group.

Age-Grade: An association that includes all the members of a group who are of a certain age and sex (for example, a warrior age-grade).

Age-Set: A group of individuals of the same sex and age who move through some or all of the stages of an age-grade together.

Ancestor Worship: A religious practice involving the worship of the spirits of dead family and lineage members.

Animatism: The attribution of life to inanimate objects.

Animism: The belief in the existence of spiritual beings (Tylor's minimal definition of religion).

Anthropomorphism: The attribution of human physical characteristics to objects not human.

Anthropophagy: The consumption of human flesh (cannibalism).

Associations: Organizations whose membership is based on the pursuit of special interests.

Astrology: The practice of foretelling the future by studying the supposed influence of the relative positions of the moon, sun, and stars on human affairs.

Avoidance Rules: Regulations that define or restrict social interaction between certain relatives.

Berdache: A French term for North American Indian transvestites who assume the cultural roles of women.

Bull-Roarer: A flat board or other object that is swung at the end of a cord to produce a whirring sound; commonly used in religious ceremonies around the world.

Bundu: A women's secret society among certain tribes of West Africa (also known as Sande).

Cannibalism: See *Anthropophagy*.

Caste: An endogamus social division characterized by occupational or ritual specialization ascribed by birth.

Ceremony: A formal act or set of acts established by custom as proper to a special occasion, such as a religious rite.

Charisma: A divine gift that endows an individual with the ability to prophesy, perform miracles, and carry out other divinely inspired acts; it often results in a religious following.

Churinga: Sacred objects used by Australian aborigines in a variety of rituals.

Cicatrization: Ritual and cosmetic scarification.

Clan: A unilineal descent group based on a fictive ancestor.

Communitarianism: A secular or religious lifestyle in which groups share beliefs and material goods; these groups are ordinarily isolated from the general population.

Cosmogony: A theory or account of the creation or origin of the world.

Cosmology: Theory or philosophy of the nature and principles of the universe.

Couvade: Culturally prescribed behavior of a father during and after the birth of his child; for example, mimicking the mother's labor pains.

Coven: An organization of witches with a membership traditionally set at thirteen.

Creationism: The doctrine of divine creation. Opposed to evolutionism.

Cult: An imprecise term, generally used as a pejorative to describe an often loosely organized group possessing special religious beliefs and practices.

Cultural Relativism: The concept that any given culture must be evaluated in terms of its own belief system.

Cultural Universals: Aspects of culture believed to exist in all human societies.

Culture: The integrated total of learned behavior that is characteristic of members of a society.

Culture Trait: A single unit of learned behavior or its product.

Curse: An utterance calling upon supernatural forces to send evil or misfortune to a person.

Demon: A person, spirit, or thing regarded as evil.

Diffusion: A process in which cultural elements of one group pass to another.

Divination: The process of contacting the supernatural to find an answer to a question regarding the cause of an event or to foretell the future.

Emic: Shared perceptions of phenomena and ideology by members of a society; insiders' views.

Ethnocentrism: A tendency to evaluate foreign beliefs and behaviors according to one's own cultural traditions.

Ethnography: A detailed anthropological description of a culture.

Ethnology: A comparison and analysis of the ethnographic data from various cultures.

Ethnomedicine: Beliefs and practices relating to diseases of the indigenous peoples of traditional societies.

Ethos: The characteristic and distinguishing attitudes of a people.

Etic: An outside observer's viewpoint of a society's phenomena or ideology.

Exorcism: The driving away of evil spirits by ritual.

Familiar: A spirit, demon, or animal that acts as an intimate servant.

Fetish: An object that is worshipped because of its supernatural power.

Folklore: The traditional beliefs, legends, myths, sayings, and customs of a people.

Functionalism: An analytical approach that attempts to explain cultural traits in terms of the uses they serve within a society.

Ghost Dance: A nativistic movement among several tribes of North American Indians during the late nineteenth century.

Ghosts: Spirits of the dead.

Glossolalia: The verbalizing of utterances that depart from normal speech, such as the phenomenon of "speaking in tongues."

God: A supernatural being with great power over humans and nature.

Hallucinogen: Any of a number of hallucination-producing substances, such as LSD, peyote, ebene, and marijuana.

Holistic: The anthropological approach that emphasizes the study of a cultural and bio-ecological system in its entirety.

Idolatry: Excessive devotion to or reverence for some person or thing.

Incest Taboo: The prohibition of sexual relations between close relatives as defined by society.

Invocation: The act of conjuring or calling forth good or evil spirits.

Legend: A folkloric category that relates an important event popularly believed to have a historical basis although not verifiable.

Magic: A ritual practice believed to compel the supernatural to act in a desired way.

Magic, Contagious: A belief that associated objects can exert an influence on each other—for example, a spell cast using the intended victim's property.

Magic, Imitative: A belief that imitating a desired result will cause it to occur.

Magic, Sympathetic: A belief that an object can influence others that have an identity with it—for example, a bow symbolizes the intended victim.

Mana: A sacred force inhabiting certain objects and people giving them extraordinary power.

Mazeway: Anthony F. C. Wallace's term for an individual's cognitive map and positive and negative goals.

Monotheism: A belief that there is only one god.

Mysticism: A contemplative process whereby an individual seeks union with a spiritual being or force.

Myth: A sacred narrative believed to be true by the people who tell it.

Necromancy: The ability to foretell the future by communicating with the dead.

Neurosis: A mild psychological disorder.

New Age: A loosely used term describing a combination of spirituality and superstition, fad and farce, that supposedly helps believers gain knowledge of the unknown. Largely a North American phenomenon, the movement includes beliefs in psychic predictions, channeling, astrology, and the powers of crystals and pyramids.

Oath: An appeal to a deity to witness the truth of what one says.

Occult: Certain mystic arts or studies, such as magic, alchemy, and astrology.

Ordeal: A ritual method to supernaturally determine guilt or innocence by subjecting the accused to a physical test.

Pantheism: The worship of several gods.

Participant Observation: An anthropological field technique in which the ethnographer is immersed in the day-to-day activities of the community being studied.

Peyote Cult: A cult surrounding the ritual ingestion of any of a variety of mescal cactuses; commonly associated with certain Native American religious beliefs.

Polytheism: See *Pantheism.*

Possession: A trance state in which malevolent or curative spirits enter a person's body.

Primitive: A term used by anthropologists to describe a culture lacking a written language; cultures also characterized by low-level technology, small numbers, few extra-societal contacts, and homogeneity (sometimes referred to as pre-literate or non-literate cultures).

Profane: Not concerned with religion or the sacred; the ordinary.

Prophet: A religious leader or teacher regarded as, or claiming to be, divinely inspired who speaks for a god.

Propitiation: The act or acts of gaining the favor of spirits or deities.

Psychosis: A psychological disorder sufficiently damaging that it may disrupt the work or activities of a person's life.

Reciprocity: A system of repayment of goods, objects, actions, and sometimes money, through which obligations are met and bonds created.

Reincarnation: The belief that the soul reappears after death in another and different bodily form.

Religion: A set of beliefs and practices pertaining to supernatural beings or forces.

Revitalization Movements: According to Wallace, a deliberate, organized, conscious effort by members of a society to construct a more satisfying culture.

Rites of Passage: Ritual associated with such critical changes in personal status as birth, puberty, marriage, and death.

Ritual: A secular or sacred, formal, solemn act, observance, or procedure in accordance with prescribed rules or customs.

Sacred: Venerated objects and actions considered holy and entitled to reverence.

Sacrifice: The ritualized offering of a person, plant, or animal as propitiation or in homage to the supernatural.

Sect: A small religious group with distinctive beliefs and practices that set it apart from other similar groups in the society.

Secular: Not sacred or religious.

Shaman: A religious specialist and healer with powers derived directly from supernatural sources.

Society: A group of people sharing a common territory, language, and culture.

Sorcery: The use of magical paraphernalia by an individual to harness supernatural powers ordinarily to achieve evil ends.

Soul: Immortal or spiritual part of a person believed to separate from the physical body at death.

Structuralism: An anthropological approach to the understanding of the deep, subconscious, unobservable structure of human realities that is believed to determine observable behavior (a leading exponent: Claude Lévi-Strauss).

Supernatural: A force or existence that transcends the natural.

Symbol: An object, gesture, word, or other representation to which an arbitrary shared meaning is given.

Syncretism: A process of culture change in which the traits and elements of one culture are given new meanings or new functions when they are adapted by another culture—for example, the combining of Catholicism and African ancestor worship to form Voodoo.

Taboo: A sacred prohibition put upon certain people, things, or acts that makes them untouchable, unmentionable, and so on (also tabu, tabou, tapu).

Theocracy: Rule by religious specialists.

Totem: An animal, plant, or object considered related to a kin group and viewed as sacred.

Trance: An altered state of consciousness induced by religious fervor, fasting, repetitive movements and rhythms, drugs, and so on.

Transcendence: The condition of being separate from or beyond the material world.

Voodoo: A syncretic religion of Haiti that combines Catholicism and African ancestor worship; sometimes referred to as Tovodun or Vodun.

Witchcraft: An evil power inherent in certain individuals that permits them, without the use of magical charms or other paraphernalia, to do harm or cause misfortune to others.

Zombie: An individual brought to a trance-like state through the administration of a psychotropic drug given secretly, thus bringing the victim under the control of another.

Bibliography

The following bibliography is a compilation of the lists of references or suggested readings that accompanied each article in its original publication. (In some cases, a list of references has been constructed from footnote citations in the original.) We have rendered the citations in as consistent a form as possible, but minor variations in form and content are inevitable because of the varied citation styles of the original publishers.

A few articles were not accompanied by references in their original publication, and accordingly are not included here.

CHAPTER 1
The Anthropological Study of Religion
Religion
Clifford Geertz

REFERENCES

Bettelheim, Bruno
    1954 *Symbolic Wounds: Puberty Rites and the Envious Male*. Glencoe, Ill.: Free Press.

Campbell, Joseph
    1949 *The Hero with a Thousand Faces*. New York: Pantheon.

Devereux, George
    1951 *Reality and Dream: Psychotherapy of a Plains Indian*. New York: International Universities Press.

Eliade, Mircea
    [1949] 1958 *Patterns in Comparative Religion*. New York: Sheed and Ward.

Erikson, Erik H.
[1950] 1964 *Childhood and Society*. 2nd ed. New York: Norton.

Geertz, Clifford
1966 "Religion as a Cultural System." In Michael Banton, ed., *Anthropological Approaches to the Study of Religion*. A.S.A. Monograph No. 3. London: Tavistock Publications Limited.

Hallowell, A. Irving
1955 *Culture and Experience*. Philadelphia: University of Pennsylvania Press.

Kardiner, Abram
1945 *The Psychological Frontiers of Society*. New York: Columbia University Press.

Kluckhohn, Clyde
1944 *Navaho Witchcraft*. Harvard University. Peabody Museum of American Archaeology and Ethnology Papers, Vol. 22, no. 2. Cambridge, Mass.: The Museum.

Lang, Andrew
[1898] 1900 *The Making of Religion*. 2nd ed. New York: Longmans.

Lessa, William A., and Evon Z. Vogt, eds.
1965 *Reader in Comparative Religion: An Anthropological Approach*. 2d ed. New York: Harper.

Lévi-Strauss, Claude
[1958] 1963 *Structural Anthropology*. New York: Basic Books.
[1962] 1966 *The Savage Mind*. University of Chicago Press.

Radcliffe-Brown, A. R.
[1952] 1961 *Structure and Function in Primitive Societies: Essays and Addresses*. Glencoe, Ill.: Free Press.

Róheim, Geza
1950 *Psychoanalysis and Anthropology: Culture, Personality and the Unconscious*. New York: International Universities Press.

Spier, Leslie
1921 *The Sun Dance of the Plains Indians: Its Development and Diffusion*. American Museum of Natural History Anthropological Papers, Vol. 16, part 7. New York: The Museum.

Whiting, John, and Irvin L. Child
1953 *Child Training and Personality: A Cross-Cultural Study*. New York: Yale University Press.

Religious Perspectives in Anthropology
Dorothy Lee

REFERENCES

Barton, R. F.
1946 *The Religion of the Ifugao*. In American Anthropological Association *Memoirs*, No. 65.

Black Elk
1932 *Black Elk Speaks. Being the Life Story of a Holy Man of the Oglala Sioux, as told to John G. Neihardt (Flaming Rainbow)*. New York: William Morrow & Co.

Brown, Joseph Epes
1953 *The Sacred Pipe: Black Elk's Account of the Seven Rites of the Oglala Sioux*. Norman: University of Oklahoma Press.

Firth, Raymond
1940 *The Work of the Gods in Tikopia*. London: Lund, Humphries Co., Ltd.
1950 *Primitive Polynesian Economy*. New York: Humanities Press.

Henry, Jules
1941 *Jungle People*. New York: J. J. Augustin, Inc.

Redfield, Robert, and W. Lloyd Warner
1940 *Cultural Anthropology and Modern Agriculture*. In *Farmers in a Changing World*, 1940 Yearbook of Agriculture. Washington, D.C.: United States Government Printing Office.

Thompson, Laura
1946 *The Hopi Crisis: Report to Administrators*. (Mimeograph).

Vanoverbergh, Morice
1936 *The Isneg Life Cycle*. Publication of the Catholic Anthropological Conference, Vol. 3, no. 2

The Anthropologist's Encounter with the Supernatural
I. M. Lewis
REFERENCES

Bourguignon, Erika, Ed.
1973 *Religion, Altered States of Consciousness and Social Change.* Columbus: Ohio State University Press.

Castaneda, Carlos
1968 *The Teachings of Don Juan.* Berkeley: University of California Press.

Dingwall, Eric J.
1972 "Is Modern Parapsychology a Science?" *Parapsychology Review* (November-December).

Eliade, Mircea.
1951 *Le Chamanisme et les techniques archaïques de l'extase.* Paris: Payot.

Evans-Pritchard, E. E.
1937 *Witchcraft, Oracles and Magic among the Azande.* Oxford: Clarendon Press.
1956 *Nuer Religion.* Oxford: Clarendon Press.

Greenbaum, L.
1973 "Societal Correlates of Possession Trance in Sub-Saharan Africa." In Erika Bourguignon, ed., *Religion, Altered States of Consciousness and Social Change.* Columbus: Ohio State University Press.

Kimball, S. T., and J. B. Watson, eds.
1972 *Crossing Cultural Boundaries.* London: Chandler.

Leach, Edmund
1969 *Genesis as Myth and Other Essays.* London: Cape.

La Barre, Weston
1972 "Hallucinogens and the Shamanic Origins of Religion." In Peter T. Furst, ed., *Flesh of the Gods.* London: Allen & Unwin.

Lewis, I. M.
1971 *Ecstatic Religion*, pp. 66–99, 127–77. London: Penguin Books.
1973 *The Anthropologist's Muse.* London: London School of Economics.

O'Brien, Elmer
1965 *Varieties of Mystic Experience.* London: Mentor-Omega.

Pressel, Esther
1973 "Umbanda in São Paulo: Religious Innovations in a Developing Society." In Erika Bourguignon, ed., *Religion, Altered States of Consciousness and Social Change.* Columbus: Ohio State University Press.

Reichel-Dolmatoff, G.
1972 In Peter T. Furst, ed., *Flesh of the Gods*, pp. 84–113. London: Allen & Unwin.

Van de Castle, Robert L.
1974 "Anthropology and Psychic Research." In Edgar D. Mitchell *et al.*, *Psychic Exploration*, ed. John White. New York: G. P. Putnam.

CHAPTER 2
Myth, Ritual, Symbolism, and Taboo
Genesis as Myth
Edmund R. Leach

REFERENCES

Bartsch, H. W.
1953 "Kerygma and Myth: A Theological Debate." S. P. C. K.

Groddeck, G.
1934 *The World of Man.* C. W. Daniel.

Jakobson, R., and M. Halle
1956 *Fundamentals of Language.* The Hague: Mouton.

Leach, E. R.
1961 "Lévi-Strauss in the Garden of Eden." In *Transactions of the New York Academy of Sciences*, Vol. 23, p. 4.

Lévi-Strauss, C.
1955 "The Structural Study of Myth." In T. A. Sebeok, ed., *Myth: A Symposium.* Bloomington: University of Indiana Press.

Shannon, C., and W. Weaver
1949 *The Mathematical Theory of Communication.* Champaign-Urbana: University of Illinois Press.

Ritual
Max Gluckman

SUGGESTED READINGS

Durkheim, E.
    1933   *The Division of Labour in Society*. New York: Free Press.

Gluckman, M.
    1956   *Custom and Conflict in Africa*. New York: Barnes and Noble.
    1965   *Politics, Law, and Ritual in Tribal Society*. Chicago: Aldine.

Howells, William
    [1948] 1986   *The Heathens*. Salem, Wis.: Sheffield Publishing Company.

Turner, V. W.
    1967   *Forest of Symbols*. Ithaca, N.Y.: Cornell University Press.
    1969   *The Ritual Process*. Chicago: Aldine.

Symbols in African Ritual
Victor W. Turner

REFERENCES

Beattie, J.
    1968   *Africa* 38: 413.

Beidelman, T. O.
    1961   *Africa* 31: 250, 146.
    1966   *Africa* 36: 379.

Calame-Griaule, G.
    1966   *Ethnologie et Language: Le Parole Chez les Dogon*. Paris: Gallimard.

Dieterlen, G.
    1941   *Les Ames des Dogon*. Paris: Institut d'Ethnologie.
    1963   *Le Renard Pale*. Paris: Institut d'Ethnologie.

Douglas, M.
    1955   *Africa* 27: 46.
    1968   *Africa* 38: 16.

Evans-Pritchard, E. E.
    1956   *Nuer Religion*. Oxford: Clarendon Press.

Forde, D., Ed.
    1954   *African Worlds*. London: Oxford University Press.

Gluckman, M.
    1949   In M. Fortes, ed., *Social Structure: Studies Presented to A. R. Radcliffe-Brown*. Oxford: Clarendon Press.

Griaule, M.
    1965   *Conversations with Ogotemmeli*. London: Oxford University Press.

Lévi-Strauss, C.
    1962   *Le Totemisme aujourd'hui*. Paris: Presses Universitaires de France.
    1963   *Structural Anthropology*. New York: Basic.

Morton-Williams, P., W. Bascom, and E. M. McClelland
    1966   *Africa* 36: 406.

Munn, N.
    1969   In R. F. Spencer, ed., *Forms of Symbolic Action*. Seattle: University of Washington Press.

Opler, M. E.
    1945   *American Journal of Sociology* 51: 198.
    1968   *Southwestern Journal of Anthropology* 24: 215.

Richards, A.
    1956   *Chisungu*. London: Faber.

Turner, V. W.
    1961   *Ndembu Divination: Its Symbolism and Techniques*. Manchester, Eng.: Manchester University Press.
    1964   In M. Gluckman, ed., *Closed Systems and Open Minds: The Limits of Naivety in Social Anthropology*. Edinburgh: Oliver & Boyd.
    1966   In M. Banton, ed., *Anthropological Approaches to the Study of Religion*. London: Tavistock.
    1967   *The Forest of Symbols*. Ithaca, N.Y.: Cornell University Press.
    1968   *The Drums of Affliction*. Oxford: Clarendon Press.
    1969a   In R. F. Spencer, ed., *Forms of Symbolic Action*. Seattle: University of Washington Press.
    1969b   *The Ritual Process*. Chicago: Aldine.
    1971   In M. D. Zamora *et al.*, eds., *Themes in Culture*. Quezon City, Philippines: Kayumanggi.

Watson, J. B.
    1964   In J. Gould and W. L. Kolb, eds., *A Dictionary of the Social Sciences*. London: Tavistock.

White, C. M. N.
  1948   *African Studies* 7: 146.

Wilson, M.
  1954   *American Anthropologist* 56: 228.
  1957   *Rituals of Kinship among the Nyakyusa.* London: Oxford University Press.
  1959   *Communal Rituals of the Nyakyusa.* London: Oxford University Press.

Taboo
Mary Douglas

SUGGESTED READINGS

Douglas, Mary
  1966   *Purity and Danger.* New York: Frederick A. Praeger.

Steiner, Franz
  [1956] 1967   *Taboo.* London: Penguin.

You Are What You Eat: Religious Aspects of the Health Food Movement
Jill Dubisch

REFERENCES

Ehrenreich, Barbara, and Deidre English
  1979   *For Her Own Good: 150 Years of the Experts' Advice to Women.* Garden City, N.Y.: Anchor Press/Doubleday.

Geertz, Clifford
  1965   "Religion as a Cultural System." In Michael Banton, ed., *Anthropological Approaches to the Study of Religion.* A.S.A. Monograph No. 3. London: Tavistock Publications Ltd.

Hongladarom, Gail Chapman
  1976   "Health Seeking Within the Health Food Movement." Ph.D. Dissertation: University of Washington.

Kandel, Randy F., and Gretel H. Pelto
  1980   "The Health Food Movement: Social Revitalization or Alternative Health Maintenance System." In Norge W. Jerome, Randy F. Kandel, and Gretel H. Pelto, eds., *Nutritional Anthropology.* Pleasantville, N.Y.: Redgrave Publishing Co.

Kline, Monte
  1978   *The Junk Food Withdrawal Manual.* Total Life, Inc.

Kottak, Conrad
  1978   "McDonald's as Myth, Symbol, and Ritual." In *Anthropology: The Study of Human Diversity.* New York: Random House.

Shryock, Richard Harrison
  1966   *Medicine in America: Historical Essays.* Baltimore: Johns Hopkins University Press.

Wallace, Anthony F. C.
  1966   *Religion: An Anthropological View.* New York: Random House.

Body Ritual Among the Nacirema
Horace Miner

REFERENCES

Linton, Ralph
  1936   *The Study of Man.* New York: D. Appleton-Century Co.

Malinowski, Bronislaw
  1948   *Magic, Science, and Religion.* Glencoe: The Free Press.

Murdock, George P.
  1949   *Social Structure.* New York: Macmillan Co.

CHAPTER 3
Shamans, Priests, and Prophets
Religious Specialists
Victor W. Turner

REFERENCES

Buber, Martin
  [1936] 1958   *I and Thou.* 2nd ed. New York: Scribner.

Callaway, Henry
  1885   *The Religious System of the Amazulu.* Folk-lore Society Publication No. 15. London: Trubner.

Durkheim, Emile
  [1893] 1960   *The Division of Labor in Society.* Glencoe, Ill.: Free Press.

Elwin, Verrier
1955   *The Religion of an Indian Tribe.* Bombay: Oxford University Press.

Evans-Pritchard, E. E.
[1949] 1954   *The Sanusi of Cyrenaica.* Oxford: Clarendon Press.
[1956] 1962   *Nuer Religion.* Oxford: Clarendon Press.

Firth, R. W
1964a   "Shaman." In Julius Gould and William L. Kolb, eds., *A Dictionary of the Social Sciences*, pp. 638–39. New York: Free Press.
1964b   "Spirit Mediumship." In Gould and Kolb, eds., *Dictionary of the Social Sciences*, p. 689. New York: Free Press.

Gelfand, Michael
1964   *Witch Doctor: Traditional Medicine Man of Rhodesia.* London: Harvill.

Herskovits, Melville J.
1938   *Dahomey: An Ancient West African Kingdom.* 2 vols. New York: Harvill.

Howells, William W.
1948   *The Heathens: Primitive Man and His Religions.* Garden City, N.Y.: Doubleday.

Knox, Ronald A.
1950   *Enthusiasm: A Chapter in the History of Religion; With Special Reference to the XVII and XVIII Centuries.* New York: Oxford University Press.

Lessa, William A., and Evon Z. Vogt, eds.
[1958] 1965   *Reader in Comparative Religion: An Anthropological Approach.* 2nd ed. New York: Harper.

Lowie, Robert H.
1954   *Indians of the Plains.* American Museum of Natural History, Anthropological Handbook No. 1. New York: McGraw-Hill.

Nadel, Siegfried F.
1954   *Nupe Religion.* London: Routledge.

Parrinder, Edward G.
1954   *African Traditional Religion.* London: Hutchinson's University Library.

Parsons, Talcott
1963   "Introduction." In Max Weber, *The Sociology of Religion.* Boston: Beacon.

Piddington, Ralph
1950   *Introduction to Social Anthropology.* 2 vols. New York: Frederick A. Praeger.

Richards, Audrey I.
[1940] 1961   "The Political System of the Bembe Tribe: Northeastern Rhodesia." In Meyer Fortes and E. E. Evans-Pritchard, eds., *African Political Systems.* New York: Oxford University Press.

Wach, Joachim
1958   *The Comparative Study of Religions.* New York: Columbia University Press.

Weber, Max
[1922] 1963   *The Sociology of Religion.* Boston: Beacon.

Worsley, P. M.
1957a   "Millenarian Movements in Melanesia." *Rhodes-Livingston Journal* 21: 18–31.
1957b   *The Trumpet Shall Sound: A Study of "Cargo" Cults in Melanesia.* London: MacGibbon and Kee.

The Shaman: A Siberian Spiritualist
William Howells

REFERENCES

Bogoras, W.
1904–09   "The Chuckchee." In *Memoirs of the American Museum of Natural History*, Vol. 11.

Casanowicz, I. M.
1924   "Shamanism of the Natives of Siberia." In *Smithsonian Institution Annual Report.*

Czaplicka, M. A.
1914   *Aboriginal Siberia: A Study in Social Anthropology.*

Evans-Pritchard, E. E.
1937   *Witchcraft, Oracles and Magic among the Azande.* Oxford: Clarendon Press.

Field, Margaret J.
1937   *Religion and Medicine of the Gã People.*

Handy, E. S. Craighill
1927   "Polynesian Religion." Bernice P. Bishop Museum *Bulletin*, No. 34. Honolulu.

Hoernlé, Winifred
1937   In I. Schapera, ed., *The Bantu-Speaking Peoples of South Africa.*

Jochelson, W.
1926   "The Yukaghir and the Yukaghirized Tungus." In *Memoirs of the American Museum of National History*, Vol. 13.
1908   "The Koryak." In *Memoirs of the American Museum of Natural History*, Vol. 10.

Apocalypse at Jonestown
John R. Hall

SUGGESTED READINGS

Cohn, Norman
1970   *Pursuit of the Millennium: Revolutionary Millenarians and Mystical Anarchists of the Middle Ages*. New York: Oxford University Press.

Hall, John R.
1978   *The Ways Out: Utopian Communal Groups in an Age of Babylon*. Boston: Routledge and Kegan Paul.

Kanter, Rosabeth Moss
1972   *Commitment and Community*. Cambridge: Harvard University Press.

Lewy, Gunther
1974   *Religion and Revolution*. New York: Oxford University Press. *San Francisco Examiner* (December 1978).

CHAPTER 4
The Religious Use of Drugs
Drugs
Francis Huxley

SUGGESTED READINGS

Lewin, Lewis L.
1924   *Phantistica: Narcotic and Stimulating Drugs*. New York: Dutton.

Ritual Enemas
Peter T. Furst and Michael D. Coe

Benson, Elizabeth P.
1972   *The Maya World*. New York: Apollo.
1975   *Death and the Afterlife in Pre-Columbian America*. Washington, D.C.: Dumbarton Oaks.

Coe, Michael D.
1966   *The Maya*. New York: Frederick A. Praeger.
1975   *Classic Maya Pottery at Dumbarton Oaks*. Washington, D.C.: Dumbarton Oaks.

Furst, Peter T.
1972   *Flesh of the Gods: The Ritual Use of Hallucinogens*. New York: Frederick A. Praeger.
1976   *Hallucinogens and Culture*. Corte Madera, Calif.: Chandler & Sharp Publishers.
1977   "High States in Culture-Historical Perspective." In Norman E. Zinberg, ed., *Alternate States of Consciousness*. New York: Free Press.

Thompson, J. Eric
1970   *Maya History and Religion*. Norman: University of Oklahoma Press.

The Sound of Rushing Water
Michael Harner

SUGGESTED READINGS

Karsten, R.
1935   "The Head-Hunters of Western Amazonas." In *Commentationes Humanarum Litteraru*. Finska Vetenskaps-Societeten, Vol. 7, no. 1, Helsingfors.

Stirling, M. W.
1938   *Historical and Ethnographical Material on the Jivaro Indians*. U.S. Bureau of American Ethnology *Bulletin 117*. Washington, D.C.: Smithsonian Institution.

Up de Graff, F. W.
1923   *Headhunters of the Amazon: Seven Years of Exploration and Adventure*. London: H. Jenkins.

CHAPTER 5
Ethnomedicine: Religion and Healing

Eyes of the Ngangas: Ethnomedicine and Power in Central African Republic
Arthur C. Lehmann.

REFERENCES

Bahuchet, Serge
   1985   *Les Pygmées Aka et la Forêt Centrafricaine.* Paris: Bibliothèque de la Selaf.

Bibeau, Gillies
   1979   *De la maladie a la guerison. Essai d'analyse systematique de la medecine des Angbandi du Zaire.* Doctoral Dissertation: Laval University.

Bichmann, Wolfgang
   1979   "Primary Health Care and Traditional Medicine—Considering the Background of Changing Health Care Concepts in Africa." *Social Science and Medicine* 13B: 175–82.

Cavalli-Sforza, L. L.
   1971   "Pygmies: An Example of Hunters Gatherers, and Genetic Consequences for Man of Domestication of Plants and Animals." In J. de Grouchy, F. Ebling, and I. Henderson, eds., *Human Genetics: Proceedings of the Fourth International Congress of Human Genetics*, pp. 79–95. Amsterdam: Excerpta Medica.

Feierman, Steven
   1985   "Struggles for Control: The Social Roots of Health of Healing in Modern Africa." *African Studies Review* 28: 73–147.

Green, Edward
   1980   "Roles for African Traditional Healers in Mental Health Care." *Medical Anthropology* 4(4): 490–522.

Hepburn, Sharon J.
   1988   "W. H. R. Rivers Prize Essay (1986): Western Minds, Foreign Bodies." *Medical Anthropology Quarterly* 2 (New Series): 59–74.

Hewlett, Barry S.
   1986   "Causes of Death Among Aka Pygmies of the Central African Republic." In L. L. Cavalli-Sforza, ed., *African Pygmies*, pp. 45–63. New York: Academic Press.

Janzen, John M.
   1978   *The Quest for Therapy: Medical Pluralism in Lower Zaire.* Los Angeles: University of California Press.

Lewis, I. M.
   1986   *Religion in Context: Cults and Charisma.* Cambridge: Cambridge University Press.

Motte, Elisabeth
   1980   *Les plantes chez les Pygmées Aka et les Monzombode la Lobaye.* Paris: Bibliothèque de la Selaf.

Offiong, Daniel
   1983   "Witchcraft Among the Ibibio of Nigeria." *The African Studies Review*, 26(1): 107–124.

Turnbull, Colin
   1965   *Wayward Servants.* New York: Natural History Press.

Warren, Dennis M.
   1974   "Disease, Medicine, and Religion Among the Techinman-Bono of Ghana; A Study in Culture Change." Doctoral Dissertation: Indiana University.

Yorder, P. Stanley
   1982   "Issues in the Study of Ethnomedical Systems in Africa." In P. Stanley Yorder, ed., *African Health and Healing Systems: Proceedings of a Symposium*, pp. 120. Los Angeles: Crossroads Press, University of California.

The Psychotherapeutic Aspects of Primitive Medicine
Ari Kiev

REFERENCES

Ackerknecht, Erwin H.
   1942a   "Problems of Primitive Medicine," *Bulletin of the History of Medicine*, Vol. 11.
   1942b   "Primitive Medicine and Culture Pattern," *Bulletin of the History of Medicine*, Vol. 12.

Edel, May M.
1957   *The Chiga of Western Uganda.* Oxford: Oxford University Press.

Elkin, Henry
1940   "The Northern Arapaho of Wyoming," in Ralph D. Linton, ed., *Acculturation in Seven American Indian Tribes.* New York: Appleton-Century.

Frank, Jerome D.
1959   "The Dynamics of the Psychotherapeutic Relationship," *Psychiatry,* Vol. 23.

Goldman, Irvin
1940   "The Alkatchoko Carrier of British Columbia," in Ralph D. Linton, ed., *Acculturation in Seven American Indian Tribes.* New York: Appleton-Century.

Harley, George W.
1941   *Native African Medicine.* Cambridge, Mass.: Harvard University Press.

Harris, Jack S.
1940   'The White Knife Shoshoni of Nevada," in Ralph D. Linton, ed., *Acculturation in Seven American Indian Tribes.* New York: Appleton-Century.

Huntingford, G.
1953   *The Nandi of Kenya.* London: Routledge and Kegan Paul.

Joffe, Natalie
1940   "The Fox of Iowa," in Ralph D. Linton, ed., *Acculturation in Seven American Indian Tribes.* New York: Appleton-Century.

Kluckhohn, Clyde, and D. Leighton
1947   *The Navaho.* Cambridge, Mass.: Harvard University Press.

Opler, Marvin K.
1940   "The Southern Ute of Colorado," in Ralph D. Linton, ed., *Acculturation of Seven American Indian Tribes.* New York: Appleton-Century.

Opler, Morris E.
1936   "Some Points of Comparison Between the Treatment of Functional Disorders by Apache Shamans and Modern Psychiatric Practice," *American Journal of Psychiatry,* Vol. 92.

Radcliffe-Brown, A. R.
1984   *The Andaman Islanders.* Glencoe, Ill.: The Free Press.

Radin, Paul
1957   *Primitive Religion: Its Nature and Origin.* New York: Dover Publishing.

Redlich, Frederick, and August Hollingshead
1985   *Social Class and Mental Illness.* New York: John Wiley and Sons.

Smith, Marian W.
1940   "The Puyallup of Washington," in Ralph D. Linton, ed., *Acculturation in Seven American Indian Tribes.* New York: Appleton-Century.

Warner, W. Lloyd
1958   *A Black Civilization.* New York: Harper and Bros.

A School for Medicine Men
Robert Bergman

REFERENCES

Haile, B. O. F. M.
1938   *Origin Legend of the Navaho Enemy Way.* Publications in Anthropology, No. 17. New Haven: Yale University Press.

Kluckhohn, C.
1956   "The Great Chants of the Navaho." In I. T. Sanders *et al.,* eds., *Societies around the World.* New York: Dryden Press.
1967   *Navajo Witchcraft.* Boston: Beacon Press.

Kluckhohn, C., and L. D. Wyman
1940   *An Introduction to Navaho Chant Practice with an Account of the Behaviors Observed in Four Chants.* American Anthropological Association, *Memoirs,* No. 53. Menasha, Wis.: American Anthropological Association.

Kluckhohn, C., and D. Leighton
1962   *The Navajo.* New York: Doubleday & Co.

Leighton, A. H., and D. Leighton
1941   "Elements of Psychotherapy in Navajo Religion." *Psychiatry* 4: 515–23.

Pfister, O.
1932   "Instinctive Psychoanalysis among the

Navajos." *Journal of Nervous and Mental Disease* 76: 234–54.

Reichard, G. A.
1950   *Navajo Religion.* New York: Bollingen Foundation.

Sandner, D.
1970   "Navajo Medicine Men." Paper read at the 123rd Annual Meeting of the American Psychiatric Association, San Francisco, May 11–15.

A Traditional African Psychiatrist
Robert B. Edgerton

REFERENCES

Ackerknecht, Erwin
1943   "Psychopathology, Primitive Medicine and Primitive Culture." *Bulletin of the History of Medicine* 14: 30–67.
1959   *A Short History of Psychiatry.* New York: Hafner.

Alexander, Franz, and Sheldon T. Selesnick
1966   *The History of Psychiatry: An Evaluation of Psychiatric Thought and Practice from Prehistoric Times to the Present.* New York: Harper and Row.

Brown, G. G., and A. McD. Hutt
1935   *Anthropology in Action.* London: Oxford University Press.

Collis, Robert J. M.
1966   "Physical Health and Psychiatric Disorder in Nigeria." *Transactions of the American Philosophical Society* 56: 5–45.

Dawson, John
1964   "Urbanization and Mental Health in a West African Community." In Ari Kiev, ed., *Magic, Faith, and Healing.* New York: Free Press.

Edgerton, Robert B.
1966   "Conceptions on the Psychosis in Four East African Societies." *American Anthropologist* 68: 408–25.
1969   "On the 'Recognition' of Mental Illness." In Stanley C. Plog and Robert B. Edgerton, eds., *Changing Perspectives in Mental Illness.* New York: Holt, Rinehart, and Winston.

Frank, Jerome
1961   *Persuasion and Healing.* Baltimore: Johns Hopkins Press.

Gelfand, Michael
1964   "Psychiatric Disorder as Recognized by the Shona." In Ari Kiev, ed., *Magic, Faith, and Healing.* New York: Free Press.

Honigfeld, Gilbert
1964   "Non-specific Factors in Treatment." *Diseases of the Nervous System* 25: 145–56, 225–39.

Hordern, Anthony
1968   "Psychopharmacology: Some Historical Considerations." In C. R. B. Joyce, ed., *Psychopharmacology: Dimensions and Perspectives.* London: Tavistock.

Kennedy, John G.
MS   "Cultural Psychiatry." In J. J. Honigmann, ed., *Handbook of Social and Cultural Anthropology.* New York: Rand-McNally.

Kiev, Ari, ed.
1964   *Magic, Faith, and Healing.* New York: Free Press.

Koestler, Arthur
1963   *The Sleepwalkers. A History of Man's Changing Vision of the Universe.* New York: Grossett and Dunlap.

Lambo, T. Adeoye
1964   "Patterns of Psychiatric Care in Developing African Countries." In Ari Kiev, ed., *Magic, Faith, and Healing.* New York: Free Press.

Lienhardt, Peter, ed. and trans.
1968   *The Medicine Man. Swifa ya Ngurumali.* Oxford: Clarendon Press.

Loudon, J. B.
1960   "Psychogenic Disorder and Social Conflict Among the Zulu." In Marvin Opler, ed., *Culture and Mental Health.* New York: Macmillan.

Margetts, Edward L.
1965   "Traditional Yoruba Healers in Nigeria." *Man* 65: 115–8.

Mathias, Mildred E.
1965   "Medicinal Plant Hunting in Tanzania."

In David Brokensha, ed., *Ecology and Economic Development in Tropical Africa*. Berkeley: Institute of International Studies, University of California.

Nigmann, E.
1908 *Die Wahehe*. Berlin: Ernst Siegfried Mittler und Sohn.

Prince, Raymond
1964 "Indigenous Yoruba Psychiatry." In Ari Kiev, ed., *Magic, Faith, and Healing*. New York: Free Press.

Turner, Victor
1964 "An Ndembu Doctor in Practice." In Ari Kiev, ed., *Magic, Faith, and Healing*. New York: Free Press.

Whisson, Michael G.
1964 "Some Aspects of Functional Disorders Among the Kenya Luo." In Ari Kiev, ed., *Magic, Faith, and Healing*. New York: Free Press.

Winans, Edgar V.
1965 "The Political Context of Economic Adaptation in the Southern Highlands of Tanzania." *American Anthropologist* 67: 435–41.

Winans, Edgar V., and Robert B. Edgerton
1964 "Hehe Magical Justice." *American Anthropologist* 66: 745–64.

The Sorcerer and His Magic
Claude Lévi-Strauss

REFERENCES

Boas, Franz
1930 *The Religion of the Kwakiutl*. Columbia Contributions to Anthropology, Vol. X. New York.

Cannon, W. B.
1942 "'Voodoo' Death." *American Anthropologist* 44 (New Series).

Lee, D. D.
1941 "Some Indian Texts Dealing with the Supernatural." *Review of Religion* (May).

Lévi-Strauss, C.
1955 *Tristes Tropiques*. Paris.

Mauss, M.
1950 *Sociologie et Anthropologie*. Paris.

Morley, Arthur
1956 *London Sunday Times*, Apr. 22, 1956, p. 11.

Stevenson, M. C.
1905 *The Zuni Indians*. 23rd *Annual Report* of the Bureau of American Ethnology. Washington D.C.: Smithsonian Institution.

Folk Medical Magic and Symbolism in the West
Wayland D. Hand

REFERENCES

Anderson, John Q.
1968 "The Magical Transfer of Disease in Texas Folk Medicine." *Western Folklore* 27: 191–99.

Bakker, Gerard
1960 *Positive Homéopathie*. Ulm.

Black, Pauline Monette
1935 *Nebraska Folk Cures*. University of Nebraska Studies in Language, Literature, and Criticism, No. 15. Lincoln, NE.

Black, William George
1883 *Folk-Medicine: A Chapter in the History of Culture*. Publications of the Folk-Lore Society, Vol. 12. London. p. 61.

Bonser, Wilfrid
1963 "Sympathetic Magic," in *The Medical Background of Anglo-Saxon England: A Study in History, Psychology, and Folklore*.

Brown Frank C.
1952 Frank C. Brown Collection of North
–64 Carolina Folklore. 7 vols. Durham, N.C.

Dictionnaire encyclopedique des sciences medicales. 3eme ser., 6.
1881 9. Paris. pp. 615–618.

Fife, Austin E.
1957 "Pioneer Mormon Remedies." *Western Folklore* 16: 153–62. pp. 153–62.

Folk-lore
1913 Vol. 24, pp. 360–61.

Frazer, James George
1911 *Golden Bough*. 3rd edition. 12 vols.
–15 London. Vol. 1, chap. 3, pp. 52–219.

Hand, Wayland D., ed.
1961 *Popular Beliefs and Superstitions from*
–64 *North Carolina*, Vol. 6, p. 241, no. 1874.

Hand, Wayland D.
1965 "The Magical Transference of Disease." *North Carolina Folklore* 13: 83–109.
1966 "Plugging, Nailing, Wedging, and Kindred Folk Medicine Practices." In Bruce Jackson, ed., *Folklore and Society: Essays in Honor of Benj. A. Botkin*, pp. 63–75. Hatboro, Pa.
1968a "Folk Medical Inhalants in Respiratory Disorders." *Medical History* 12: 153–63.
1968b "'Passin' Through': Folk Medical Magic and Symbolism." *Proceedings of the American Philosophical Society*, Vol. 112, no. 6, pp. 379–402.
1971 "The Common Cold in Utah Folk Medicine." In Thomas E. Cheney, Austin E. Fife, and Juanita Brooks, eds., *Lore of Faith and Folly*, pp. 243–50. Salt Lake City: University of Utah Press.
n.d. *Hangmen, the Gallows, and the Dead Man's Hand in American Folk Medicine.*

Handworterbuch des deutschen Aberglaubens
1927 10 vols. Berlin.
–42

Hendricks, George D.
1966 *Mirrors, Mice & Mustaches: A Sampling of Superstitions and Popular Beliefs in Texas.* Austin: University of Texas. "Paisano Books," No. 1, pp. 32–36, 51.

Journal of American Folklore
1944 Vol. 57, pp. 41 and 46.
1955 Vol. 68, p. 131.

Jungbauer, Gustav
1934 *Deutsche Volksmedizin. Ein Grundriss.* Berlin. pp. 79–85, 89–91.

Lathrop, Amy
1961 "Pioneer Remedies from Western Kansas." *Western Folklore* 20: 1–22.

McKinney, Ida Mae
1952 "Superstitions of the Missouri Ozarks." *Tennessee Folklore Society Bulletin* 18: 107.

Mogk, Eugen
1906 *Germanische Mythologie.* Sammlung Goschen, Bd. 15, Leipzig. p. 98.

Neal, Janice C.
1955 "Grandad—Pioneer Medicine Man." *New York Folklore Quarterly* 11: 289, 291.

Notes and Queries
1903 9th Series, Vol. 12, August 15, 1903, p. 26.

Southern Folklore Quarterly
1946 Vol. 10, p. 166.

Stout, Earl J.
1936 "Folklore from Iowa." *Memoirs of the American Folklore Society*, Vol. 29, no. 761.

Thomas, Daniel Lindsey, and Lucy Blayney Thomas
1920 *Kentucky Superstitions.* Princeton, N.J. No. 1363.

Wuttke, Adolf
1900 *Der deutsche Volksaberglaube der Gegenwart*, ed. Elard Hugo Meyer. pp. 321–22. Section 477.

CHAPTER 6

Witchcraft, Sorcery, and Other Forces of Evil

Witchcraft

Jeffrey Burton Russell

REFERENCES

Baroja, Julio Caro
1964 *The World of the Witches*, trans. O. N. V. Glendinning. Chicago.

Berkout, Carl T., and Jeffrey B. Russell
1981 *Medieval Heresies: A Bibliography, 1960–1979.* Toronto.

Bouisson, Maurice
1960 *Magic: Its History and Principal Rites.* New York.

Boyer, Paul, and Stephen Nissenbaum
1974 *Salem Possessed: The Social Origins of Witchcraft.* Cambridge, Mass.: Harvard University Press.

Briggs, K. M.
1962 *Pale Hecate's Team: An Examination of the Beliefs on Witchcraft and Magic Among Shakespeare's Contemporaries and His Im-*

mediate Successors. London.

Cohn, Norman
    1975   *Europe's Inner Demons: An Enquiry Inspired by the Great Witch-Hunt*. New York.

Demos, John Putnam
    1982   *Entertaining Satan: Witchcraft and the Culture of Early New England*. New York.

Eliade, Mircea
    1976   *Occultism, Witchcraft, and Cultural Fashions: Essays in Comparative Religions*. Chicago.

Evans-Pritchard, E. E.
    1950   *Witchcraft, Oracles and Magic Among the Azande*. 2nd edition. Oxford: Clarendon Press.

Kieckhefer, Richard
    1976   *European Witch Trials: Their Foundations in Popular and Learned Culture, 1300–1500*. London.

Macfarlane, Alan
    1970   *Witchcraft in Tudor and Stuart England: A Regional and Comparative Study*. London.

Mair, Lucy
    1969   *Witchcraft*. London.

Monter, E. William
    1976   *Witchcraft in France and Switzerland: The Borderlands During the Reformation*. Ithaca, N.Y.

Peters, Edward
    1978   *The Magician, the Witch, and the Law*. Philadelphia.

Russell, Jeffrey Burton
    1972   *Witchcraft in the Middle Ages*. Ithaca, N.Y.
    1980   *A History of Witchcraft: Sorcerers, Heretics, and Pagans*. London.

Thomas, Keith
    1971   *Religion and the Decline of Magic*. New York.

Trevor-Roper, Hugh R.
    1969   *The European Witch-Craze of the Sixteenth and Seventeenth Centuries and Other Essays*. New York.

Some Implications of Urban Witchcraft Beliefs
Phillips Stevens, Jr.

REFERENCES

Buffalo Evening News, July 17, 1978.

Cannon, Walter B.
    1942   "The Voodoo Death." *American Anthropologist* 44: 169–81.
    1957   "Voodoo Death." *Psychosomatic Medicine* 19: 182–90.

Cappannari, Stephen C., Bruce Rau, Harry S. Abram, and Denton C. Buchanan
    1975   "Voodoo in the General Hospital: A Case of Hexing and Regional Enteritis." *Journal of the American Medical Association* 232(9): 938–40.

Eastwell, Harry D.
    1982   "Voodoo Death and the Mechanism for Dispatch of the Dying in East Arnhem, Australia." *American Anthropologist* 84(1): 5–18.

Furnham, Adrian, and Bochner, Stephen
    1982   "Social Difficulty in a Foreign Culture: An Empirical Analysis of Culture Shock." In Stephen Bochner, ed., *Cultures in Contact: Studies in Cross-Cultural Interaction*, pp. 161–98. Oxford: Pergamon Press.

Galvin, James A. V., and Ludwig, Arnold M.
    1961   "A Case of Witchcraft." *Journal of Nervous and Mental Disease* 133(2): 161–68.

Gluckman, Max
    1944   "The Logic of African Science and Witchcraft: An Appreciation of Evans-Pritchard's 'Witchcraft, Oracles, and Magic Among the Azande' of the Sudan." *Rhodes-Livingstone Institute Journal* (June).

Golden, Kenneth M.
    1977   "Voodoo in Africa and the United States." *American Journal of Psychiatry* 134(12): 1425–27.

Johns Hopkins Hospital
    1967   "Clinical-pathological Conference."

Johns Hopkins Medical Journal 120: 186–99.

Leininger, Madeleine
1973 "Witchcraft Practices and Psychosocial Therapy with Urban U.S. Families." *Human Organization* 32: 73–83.

Lester, David
1972 "Voodoo Death: Some New Thoughts on an Old Phenomenon." *American Anthropologist* 74(3): 386–90.

Lewis, G. A.
1977 "Fear of Sorcery and the Problem of Death by Suggestion." In J. Blacking, ed., *The Anthropology of the Body*, pp. 111–43. London: Academic Press, ASA Monograph 15.

Lewis, Justin
1958 "The Outlook for a Devil in the Colonies." *Criminal Law Review*, pp. 661–75.

Lex, Barbara
1974 "Voodoo Death: New Thoughts on an Old Explanation." *American Anthropologist* 76(4): 818–23.

Michaelson, Mike
1972 "Can a 'Root Doctor' Actually Put a Hex On, Or Is It All a Great Put-On?" *Today's Health* (March).

New Haven Register
1981 "The Brookfield Demons." Nov. 5.

New York Times
1981 "Florida Hospital Tries to Cope with Refugees." Oct. 4, p. 71.

Oberg, Kalvero
1960 "Cultural Shock: Adjustment to New Cultural Environments." *Practical Anthropology* 7: 177–82.

Pedersen, Paul, ed.
1976 *Counseling Across Cultures*. Honolulu: The University Press of Hawaii.

Prince, Raymond, ed.
1982 "Shamans and Endorphins." *Ethos* 10(4).

Raybin, James B.
1970 "The Curse: A Study in Family Communication." *American Journal of Psychiatry* 127(5): 77–85.

Richter, Curt
1957 "On the Phenomenon of Sudden Death in Animals and Man." *Psychosomatic Medicine* 19: 191–98.

Seelye, Hans
1956 *The Stress of Life*. New York: McGraw-Hill.

Senter, Donovan
1947 "Witches and Psychiatrists." *Psychiatry* 10(1): 49–56.

Snell, John E.
1967 "Hypnosis in the Treatment of the 'Hexed' Patient." *American Journal of Psychiatry* 124(3): 67–72.

Sue, Donald W.
1981 *Counseling the Culturally Different: Theory and Practice*. New York: John Wiley & Sons.

Times-Union, Rochester, N.Y., July 14, 1978.

Tinling, David C.
1967 "Voodoo, Root Work, and Medicine." *Psychosomatic Medicine* 29(5): 483–90.

Tivnan, Edward
1979 "The Voodoo That New Yorkers Do." *New York Times Magazine*. Dec. 2, pp. 181–91.

Warner, Richard
1977 "Witchcraft and Soul Loss: Implications for Community Psychiatry." *Hospital and Community Psychiatry* 28(9): 686–90.

Williams, Glanville
1949 "Homocide and Supernatural." *Law Quarterly Review* 65: 491–503.
1961 *Criminal Law. The General Part*. 2nd edition. London: Stevens & Sons, Ltd. pp. 175–76, 524.

Wintrob, Ronald M.
1973 "The Influence of Others: Witchcraft and Rootwork as Explanations of Behavior Disturbances." *Journal of Nervous and Mental Disease* 156(5): 318–26.

Voodoo Death and the Mechanism for Dispatch of the Dying in East Arnhem, Australia

Harry D. Eastwell

REFERENCES

Barber, Theodore X.
1961 "Death by Suggestion." *Psychosomatic Medicine* 23(2): 153–55.

Cannon, Walter B.
1942 "Voodoo Death." *American Anthropologist* 44: 169–81.

Clune, F. J.
1973 "A Comment on Voodoo Death." *American Anthropologist* 75: 312.

Ellenberger, H. K.
1965 "Ethno-psychiatrie; partie descriptive et clinique." In H. Ey, ed., *Encyclopedie medico-chirugicale: Psychiatrie.* tome 3.

Elkin, A. P.
1977 *Aboriginal Men of High Degree.* 2nd ed. Brisbane: University of Queensland Press.

Engel, G.
1968 "A Life Setting Conducive to Illness, the Giving Up–Given Up Complex." *Annals of Internal Medicine* 69: 293–300.
1971 "Sudden and Rapid Death." *Annals of Internal Medicine* 74: 771–82.

Gelfand, M.
1957 *The Sick African: A Clinical Study.* 3rd ed. Capetown: Juta.

Jones, Ivor H. and David J. Horne
1972 "Diagnosis of Psychiatric Illness Among Tribal Aborigines." *Medical Journal of Australia* 1: 345–49.

Landy, David
1975 "Magical Death Reconsidered: Some Possible Social and Cultural Correlates." Paper presented at American Anthropological Association Meeting, Dec. 3, San Francisco.

Lester, D.
1972 "Voodoo Death: Some New Thoughts on an Old Phenomenon." *American Anthropologist* 74: 386–90.

Lewis, G. A.
1977 "Fear of Sorcery and the Problem of Death by Suggestion." In J. Blacking, ed., *The Anthropology of the Body.* ASA Monograph 15. London: Academic Press.

Lex, Barbara W.
1974 "Voodoo Death: New Thoughts on an Old Explanation." *American Anthropologist* 76: 818–23.

Reid, Janice
1979 "A Time to Live, a Time to Grieve: Patterns and Processes of Mourning among the Yolngu of Australia." *Medicine and Psychiatry* 3(4): 319–46.

Richter, C. P.
1957 "On the Phenomenon of Sudden Death in Animals and Men." *Psychosomatic Medicine* 19: 190–8.

Rubel, A. J.
1964 "The Epidemiology of a Folk Illness: Susto in Hispanic America." *Ethnology* 3: 268–83.

Simon, A., C. C. Herbert and R. Straus
1961 *The Physiology of the Emotions.* Springfield, Ill.: Charles C. Thomas.

Thompson, Donald
1939 *Report on an Expedition to Arnhem Land, 1936–39.* Government Printer. Canberra.

Warner, W. Lloyd
1958 *A Black Civilization. A Social Study of an Australian Tribe.* New York: Harper & Row.

Yap, P. M.
1974 *Comparative Psychiatry: A Theoretical Framework.* Toronto: University of Toronto Press.
1977 "The Culture-Bound Reactive Syndromes." In D. Landy, ed., *Culture, Medicine and Healing: Studies in Medical Anthropology.* New York: McMillan.

The Cannibal's Cauldron
I. M. Lewis

REFERENCES

Alexandre, P.
1974 "On Some Witches and a Predicant." In J. Davis, ed., *Choice and Change: Essays in Honour of Lucy Mair*. London: Athlone Press.

Arens, William
1979 *The Man-Eating Myth: Anthropology and Anthropophagy*. London: Oxford University Press.

Chavunduka, G.
1980 "Witchcraft and the Law." In *Zambezia* 8: 129–47.

Colajanni, A.
1982 "Shamanism and Social Change: The Killing of an Achuar Shaman, Facts and Interpretations." Manuscript Paper, 44th Congress of Americanists, Manchester.

Crawford, J. R.
1967 *Witchcraft and Sorcery in Rhodesia*. London: Oxford University Press.

Devereux, G.
1956 "Normal and Abnormal: The Key Problem of Psychiatric Anthropology." In J. B. Casagrande and T. Gladwin, eds., *Some Uses of Anthropology*. Washington, D.C.: Anthropological Press.

Epstein, A. L.
1958 *Politics in an Urban African Community*. Manchester: Manchester University Press.

Epstein, A.L.
1979 "Unconscious Factors in the Response to Social Crisis: A Case Study from Central Africa." In *The Psychoanalytic Study of Society* 8. New Haven: Yale University Press.

Evans-Pritchard, E. E.
1937 *Witchcraft, Oracles, and Magic Among the Azande*. Oxford: Clarendon Press.

Evans-Pritchard, E. E.
1965 "Zande Cannibalism." In *The Position of Women in Primitive Societies and Other Essays in Social Anthropology*. London: Faber.

Forsyth, D.
1983 "The Beginnings of Brazilian Anthropology." *Journal of Anthropological Research* 2: 147–78.

Foster, G.
1965 "Peasant Society and the Image of Limited Good." *American Anthropologist*, 67: 293–315.

Fraenkel, P. J.
1959 *Wayaleshi*. London: Weidenfield and Nicholson.

Freud, S.
[1913] 1950 *Totem and Taboo*. London: Routledge and Kegan Paul.

Friedland, W. H.
1960 "Some Urban Myths in East Africa." In A. Dubb, ed., *Myth in Modern Africa*. Lusaka: Rhodes Livingston Institute.

Geertz, C.
1984 "Distinguished Lecture: Anti-Lelativism." *American Anthropologist* 86: 263–78.

Harris, M.
1977 *Cannibals and Kings*. New York: Random House.

Hugh-Jones, S.
1980 *The Palm and the Pleiades*. Cambridge: Cambridge University Press.

Jones, E.
1949 *On the Nightmare*. London: Hogarth Press.

Kaberry, P. M.
1969 "Witchcraft of the Sun: Incest in Nso." In M. Douglas and P. Kaberry, eds., *Man in Africa*. London: Tavistock.

Kremser, M.
1981 Das bild der "menschenfressenden Niam-Niam." In *Den Berichten Deutscher Forschengsreisender des 19 Jahrhunderts*. Wiener: Ethnoshhistorische Blatter, 21.

Lévi-Strauss, C.
1966 *Mythologiques II: du miel aux cendres*. Paris: Plon.

Lewis, I. M.
  1976   *Social Anthropology in Perspective*. Harmondsworth: Penguin Books.

MacCormack, C.
  1983   "Human Leopards and Crocodiles." In P. Brown and D. Tuzin, eds., *The Ethnography of Cannibalism*. Washington, D.C.: Society for Psychological Anthropology.

Malinowski, B.
  1922   *Argonauts of the Western Pacific*. London: Routledge and Kegan Paul.

Malinowski, B.
  1929   *The Sexual Life of Savages*. London: Routledge and Kegan Paul.

Reichel-Dolmatoff, G.
  1971   *Amazonian Cosmos*. Chicago: University of Chicago Press.

Richards, A.
  1968   "African Systems of Thought: An Anglo-French Dialogue." *Man*, 2(2): 286–98.

Sahlins, M.
  1983   "Raw Women, Cooked Men and Other 'Great Things' of the Fiji Islands." In P. Brown and D. Tuzin, eds., *The Ethnography of Cannibalism*. Washington, D.C.: Society for Psychological Anthropology.

Seymour-Smith, C.
  1984   "Politics and Ethnicity Among the Peruvian Jivaro of the Rio Communities." Unpublished Ph.D. Thesis, University of London.

Strathern, A.
  1982   "Witchcraft, Greed, Cannibalism and Death: Some Related Themes from the New Guinea Highlands." In M. Bloch and J. Parry, eds., *Death and the Regeneration of Life*. Cambridge: Cambridge University Press.

Watson, W.
  1958   *Tribal Cohesion in a Money Economy*. Manchester: Manchester University Press.

Becoming White: Notes on an Italian-American Explanation of Evil Eye
Michael Buonanno

REFERENCES

Appel, W.
  1976   "The Myth of the Jettatura." In C. Maloney, ed., *The Evil Eye*, pp. 16–27. New York: Columbia University Press.

Chapman, C.
  1971   *Milocca: A Sicilian Village*. Cambridge: Schenkman Publishing Co., Inc. (Written 1935).

DiStasi, L.
  1981   *Malocchio*. San Francisco: North Point Press.

Douglas, M.
  1966   *Purity and Danger: An Analysis of Concepts of Pollution and Taboo*. New York: Frederick A. Praeger.

Garrison, V., and C. Arensberg
  1976   "The Evil Eye: Envy or Risk of Seizure? Paranoia or Patronal Dependency?" In C. Maloney, ed., *The Evil Eye*, pp. 288–328. New York: Columbia University Press.

Goodenough, W.
  1981   *Culture, Language, and Society*. Menlo Park: The Benjamin/Cummings Publishing Co.

Ianni, F.
  1972   *A Family Business*. New York: Russel Sage Foundation.

Pitrè, G.
  [1889] 1981 "The Jettatura and the Evil Eye." In A. Dundes, ed., *The Evil Eye: A Folklore Casebook*, pp. 130–42. New York and London: Garland Publishing, Inc.

Pitt-Rivers, J.
  [1954] 1961 *People of the Sierra*. Chicago: Phoenix Books.

Turner, V.
  1969   *The Ritual Process: Structure and Anti-Structure*. Ithaca: Cornell University Press.

Van Gennep, A.
  [1908] 1960 *The Rites of Passage*, trans. M. Vize-
    dom, and G. Caffee. Chicago: Univer-
    sity of Chicago Press.

Williams, P.
  [1938] 1969 *South Italian Folkways in Europe and
    America.* New York: Russell and Rus-
    sell.

CHAPTER 7
Demons, Exorcism, Divination, and Magic
Psychosocial Interpretations of Exorcism
E. Mansell Pattison

REFERENCES

Ackernecht, E. H.
  1971 *Medicine and Ethnology: Selected Essays.*
    Bern: Verlag Huber.

Bahr, D. M., J. Gregoric, D. I. Lopez and A. Al-
varez
  1974 *Piman Shamanism and Staying Sickness.*
    Tucson: University of Arizona Press.

Bandler, R., and J. Grinder
  1975 *The Structure of Magic.* Palo Alto, Calif.:
    Science and Behavior Books.

Baroja, J. C.
  1964 *The World of the Witches.* Chicago: Uni-
    versity of Chicago Press.

Barrett, W.
  1958 *Irrational Man.* New York: Doubleday.

Becker, E.
  1973 *The Denial of Death.* New York: Free
    Press.
  1975 *Escape from Evil.* New York: Free Press.

Bourguignon, E.
  1968 "World Distribution and Patterns of
    Possession States." In R. Prince, ed.,
    Trance and Possession States. Montreal: R.
    M. Bucke Society.

Bourguignon, E., ed.
  1973 *Religion: Altered States of Consciousness
    and Social Change.* Columbus, Ohio:
    Ohio State University Press.

Carstairs, G. M., and R. L. Kapur
  1976 *The Great Universe of Kota: Stress, Change
    and Mental Disorder in an Indian Village.*
    Berkeley: University of California Press.

Cox, R. H. ed.
  1973 *Religious Systems and Psychotherapy.*
    Springfield, Ill.: C. C. Thomas.

Douglas, M., ed.
  1970 *Witchcraft Confessions and Accusations.*
    London: Tavistock.

Ehrenwald, J., ed.
  1976 *The History of Psychotherapy. From Heal-
    ing Magic to Encounter.* New York: Jason
    Aronson.

Eliade, M.
  1976 *Occultism, Witchcraft, and Cultural Fash-
    ions: Essays in Comparative Religions.* Chi-
    cago: University of Chicago Press.

Ellenberger, H. F.
  1970 *The Discovery of the Unconscious. The His-
    tory and Evolution of Dynamic Psychiatry.*
    New York: Basic Books.

Fairbairn, W. R. D.
  1954 *An Object-Relations Theory of Personality.*
    New York: Basic Books.

Foster, G. M.
  1976 "Disease Etiologies in Non-Western
    Medical Systems." *American Anthropolo-
    gist* 78: 773–82.

Frank, J. D.
  1973 *Persuasion and Healing. A Comparative
    Study of Psychotherapy.* Baltimore: Johns
    Hopkins University Press.

Freud, S.
  1961 "A Seventeenth-Century Demonologi-
    cal Neurosis" (1922). *Collected Works.*
    London: Hogarth.

Galdston, I.
  1963 *Man's Image in Medicine and Anthropol-
    ogy.* New York: International Universi-
    ties Press.

Glock, C. Y., and R. N. Bellah, eds.
  1976 *The New Religious Consciousness.* Berke-
    ley: University of California Press.

Griffith, E. H., and P. Ruiz
  1976 "Cultural Factors in the Training of
    Psychiatric Residents in a Hispanic

Urban Community." *Innovations* 3: 11–16.

Grotjahn, M.
1976 *The Voice of the Symbol.* New York: Mara Books.

Hartmann, H.
1960 *Psychoanalysis and Moral Values.* New York: International Universities Press.

Henderson, D. J.
1976 "Exorcism, Possession, and the Dracula Cult: A Synopsis of Object-Relations Psychology." *Bulletin of the Menninger Clinic* 40: 603–28.

Jilek, W. G.
1974 *Salish Indian Mental Health and Culture Change.* Toronto: Holt, Rinehart & Winston.

Jilek-Aall, L., and W. G. Jilek
1974 "Problems in Transcultural Psychiatry."
–75 *Ethnomedizin* 3: 239–48.

Kiev, A., ed.
1964 *Magic, Faith, and Healing: Studies in Primitive Psychiatry Today.* New York: Free Press.

Kiev, A.
1972 *Transcultural Psychiatry.* New York: Free Press.

Knox, R. A.
1950 *Enthusiasm: A Chapter in the History of Religion.* London: Oxford University Press.

Langer, S. K.
1960 *Philosophy in a New Key: A Study in the Symbolism of Reason, Rite, and Art.* Cambridge, Mass.: Harvard University Press.

Lebra, W. P. ed.
1976 *Cultura-Bound Syndromes, Ethnopsychiatry, and Alternate Therapies.* Honolulu: University of Hawaii Press.

LeVine, R. A.
1973 *Culture, Behavior, and Personality.* Chicago: Aldine.

Lévi-Strauss, C.
1956 "Sorciers et Psychanalyse." *Courrier de l'Unesco* 9: 8–10.

1963 *Structural Anthropology.* New York: Basic Books.

1966 *The Savage Mind.* Chicago: University of Chicago Press.

London, P.
1964 *The Modes and Morals of Psychotherapy.* New York: Holt, Rinehart & Winston.

Loudon, J. B., ed.
1976 *Social Anthropology and Medicine.* New York: Academic Press.

Lubchansky, I., G. Egri, and I. Stokes
1970 "Puerto-Rican Spiritualists View Mental Illness: The Faith Healer as a Para-professional." *American Journal of Psychiatry* 127: 312–21.

Margolis, J.
1966 *Psychotherapy and Morality: A Study of Two Concepts.* New York: Random House.

May, R.
1975 "Value, Myths, and Symbols." *American Journal of Psychiatry* 132: 703–6.

Neaman, J. S.
1975 *Suggestion of the Devil: The Origins of Madness.* New York: Anchor Books.

Pande, S. K.
1968 "The Mystique of Western Psychotherapy: An Eastern Interpretation." *Journal of Nervous and Mental Disease* 146: 425–32.

Parrinder, G.
1958 *Witchcraft: European and African.* London: Faber & Faber.

Pattison, E. M.
1968 "Ego Morality: An Emerging Psychotherapeutic Concept." *Psychoanalytic Review* 55: 187–222.

Pattison, E. M., ed.
1969 *Clinical Psychiatry and Religion.* Boston: Little, Brown.

Pattison E. M., N. A. Lapins, and H. A. Doerr
1973 "Faith Healing: A Study of Personality and Function." *Journal of Nervous and Mental Disease* 157: 397–409.

Pederson, P., W. J. Lonner, and J. G. Draguns
1976 *Counseling Across Cultures.* Honolulu:

University of Hawaii Press.

Prince, R. H.
1976 "Psychotherapy as the Manipulation of Endogenous Healing Mechanisms: A Transcultural Survey." *Transcultural Psychiatric Research Review* 13: 115–33.

Pruyser, P.
1968 *A Dynamic Psychology of Religion.* New York: Harper & Row.

Rivers, W. H. R.
1924 *Medicine, Magic, and Religion.* London: Kegan Paul.

Robbins, R. H.
1959 *The Encyclopedia of Witchcraft and Demonology.* New York: Crown Publishers.

Rosen, G.
1968 *Madness in Society: Chapters in the Historical Sociology of Mental Illness.* Chicago: University of Chicago Press.

Rosenthal, B. G.
1971 *The Images of Man.* New York: Basic Books.

Russell, J. B.
1972 *Witchcraft in the Middle Ages.* Ithaca, N.Y.: Cornell University Press.

Sartre, J. P.
1959 *Existentialism and Human Emotions.* New York: Philosophical Library.

Spiro, M. E.
1965 "Religious Systems as Culturally Constituted Defense Mechanisms." In M. E. Spiro, ed., *Context and Meaning in Cultural Anthropology.* New York: Free Press.
1967 *Burmese Supernaturalism: A Study in the Explanation and Reduction in Suffering.* Englewood Cliffs: Prentice-Hall.

Thomas, K.
1971 *Religion and the Decline of Magic: Studies in Popular Beliefs in Sixteenth and Seventeenth Century England.* London: Weidenfield and Nicholson.

Torrey, E. F.
1972 *The Mind Game/Witchdoctors and Psychiatrists.* New York: Emerson Hall.

Turner, V.
1969 *The Ritual Process.* Chicago: Aldine.

Wardwell, W. I.
1965 "Christian Science Healing." *Journal of the Scientific Study of Religion* 4: 175–81.

Wheelis, A.
1971 *The End of the Modern Age.* New York: Basic Books.

Wijesinghe, C. P., S. A. W. Dissanayake, and N. Mendis
1976 "Possession in a Semi-Urban Community in Sri Lanka." *Aust NZ Journal of Psychiatry* 10: 135–9.

Wilson, M.
1951 "Witch Beliefs and Social Structure." *American Journal of Sociology* 56: 307–13.

Zaretsky, I. I., and M. P. Leone, eds.
1974 *Religious Movements in Contemporary America.* Princeton, N.J.: Princeton University Press.

Characteristics of Sisala Diviners
Eugene Mendonsa

REFERENCES

Bascom, W.
1941 "The Sanctions of Ifa Divination." *Journal of the Royal Anthropological Institute* 81(2): 43–54.

Colson, E.
1970 "The Alien Diviner and Local Politics among the Tonga of Zambia." In W. Simmons, ed., *Man Makes Sense: A Reader in Modern Cultural Anthropology.* Boston: Little, Brown.

Fortes, M.
1959 *Oedipus and Job in West African Religion.* Cambridge, England: Cambridge University Press.
1965 "Some Reflections on Ancestor Worship in Africa." In M. Fortes and G. Dieterlen, *African Systems of Thought.* London: Oxford University Press.
1970 "Pietas and Ancestor Worship." In M. Fortes, *Time and Social Structure and Other Essays.* London: Athlone Press.

Goody, J.
1962 *Death, Property and Ancestors.* London: Tavistock.

Horton, R.
1967   "African Traditional Thought and Western Science" (in two parts). *Africa* 38: 50–71, 155–87.

Kiev, A.
1964   "The Study of Folk Psychiatry." In A. Kiev, ed., *Magic, Faith, and Healing: Studies in Folk Psychiatry Today*. New York: Free Press.

Mendonsa, E.
i.p.   "The Divinatory Process and Temporal-spatial Concepts among the Sisala of Northern Ghana." *Journal of African and Asian Studies*.

Reynolds, B.
1963   *Magic, Divination and Witchcraft among the Barotse of Northern Rhodesia*. London: Chatto and Windus.

Rational Mastery by Man of His Surroundings

Bronislaw Malinowski

REFERENCES

Boas, F.
1910   *The Mind of Primitive Man*.

Brinton, D. G.
1899   *Religions of Primitive Peoples*.

Codrington, R. H.
1891   *The Melanesians*.

Crawley, E.
1902   *The Mystic Rose*.
1905   *The Tree of Life*.

Durkheim, E.
1912   *Les Formes elementaires de la Vie religieuse*.

Ehrenreich, P.
1910   *Die Allgemeine Mythologie*.

Frazer, J. G.
1910   *Totemism and Exogamy*, 4 vols.
1911–14 *The Golden Bough*, 3rd ed., in 12 vols.
1919   *Folklore in the Old Testament*, 3 vols.
1913–24 *The Belief in Immortality and the Worship of the Dead*, 3 vols.

Goldenweiser, A. A.
1923   *Early Civilization*.

Harrison, J.
1910   *Themis*.
–12

Hastings, J.
        Encyclopedia of Religion and Ethics.

Hobhouse, L. T.
1915   *Morals in Evolution*, 2nd ed.

Hubert, H., and M. Mauss
1909   *Melanges d'histoire des religions*.

King, I.
1910   *The Development of Religion*.

Kroeber, A. L.
1923   *Anthropology*.

Lang, A.
1889   *The Making of Religion*.
1901   *Magic and Religion*.

Lévy-Bruhl, M.
1910   *Les Fonctions mentales dans les sociétés inférieures*.

Lowie, R. H.
1920   *Primitive Society*.
1925   *Primitive Religion*.

Malinowski, B.
1915   *The Natives of Mailu*.
1916   "Baloma." *Journal of the Royal Anthropological Institute*.
1922   *Argonauts of the Western Pacific*.
1923–5 *Psyche*. Vols. III(2), IV(4), V(3).

Marett, R. R.
1909   *The Threshold of Religion*.

McLennan, J. F.
1886   *Studies in Ancient History*.

Preuss, K. Th.
1904   *Der Ursprung der Religion und Kunst*.

Schmidt, W.
1912   *Der Ursprung der Gottesidee*.

Seligman, C. G.
1910   *The Melanesians of British New Guinea*.

Smith, W. Robertson
1889   *Lectures on the Religion of the Semites*.

Thurnwald, R.
1912   *Forschungen auf den Solominseln und Bismarckarchipel*.
1921   *Die Gemeinde der Banaro*.
1922   "Psychologie des Primitiven Menschen." In G. Kafka, ed., *Handbuch der Vergl. Psychol.*

Tylor, E. B.
  1903   *Primitive Culture*, 4th ed., 2 vols.

Van Gennep, A.
  1909   *Les Rites de Passage.*

Westermarck, E.
  1905   *The Origin and Development of the Moral Ideas*, 2 vols.

Wundt, Wilh.
  1904   *Volkerpsychologie.*

CHAPTER 8

Ghosts, Souls, and Ancestors: Power of the Dead

Sorcerers, Ghosts, and Polluting Women: An Analysis of Religious Belief and Population Control

Shirley Lindenbaum

REFERENCES

Alland, A.
  1970   *Adaptation in Cultural Evolution: An Approach to Medical Anthropology.* New York.

Berndt, R. M.
  1962   *Excess and Restraint: Social Control among a New Guinea Mountain People.* Chicago.

Brookfield, H. C., and J. White
  1968   "Revolution or Evolution in the Prehistory of the New Guinea Highlands." *Ethnology* 7: 43–52.

Bulmer, R. N. H.
  1965   "The Kyaka of the Western Highlands." In P. Lawrence and M. J. Meggitt, eds., *Gods, Ghosts and Men in Melanesia.* Melbourne.
  1970   "Traditional Forms of Family Limitation in New Guinea." *New Guinea Research Bulletin* 42: 137–62.

Burridge, K. O. L.
  1960   *Mambu: A Melanesian Millennium.* London.
  1965   "Tangu, Northern Madang District." In P. Lawrence and M. J. Meggitt, eds., *Gods, Ghosts and Men in Melanesia.* Melbourne.

Douglas, M.
  1966   *Purity and Danger: An Analysis of Concepts of Pollution and Taboo.* New York.
  1970   *Natural Symbols: Explorations in Cosmology.* New York.

Evans-Pritchard, E. E.
  1937   *Witchcraft, Oracles and Magic Among the Azande.* Oxford.

Forge, A.
  1970a   "Prestige, Influence and Sorcery: A New Guinea Example." In M. Douglas, ed., *Witchcraft Confessions and Accusations.* London.
  1970b   "Learning to See in New Guinea." In P. Mayer, ed., *Socialization: The Approach from Social Anthropology.* London.

Fortune, R. F.
  1963   *Sorcerers of Dobu.* New York.

Gajdusek, D. C., and M. P. Alpers
  1970   *Bibliography of Kuru.* Bethesda, Md.: National Institutes of Health.

Glasse, R. M.
  1969   *Marriage in South Fore.* In R. M. Glasse and M. J. Meggitt, eds., *Pigs, Pearlshells, and Women.* Englewood Cliffs, n.g.

Glasse, R. M., and S. Lindenbaum
  1969   "South Fore Politics." *Anthropological Forum* 2: 308–26.

Goodale, J. C., and A. Chowning
  1971   "The Contaminating Woman." Paper read at 1971 Annual Meeting of the American Anthropological Association.

Hogbin, H. I.
  1958   *Social Change.* London

Kaberry, P. M.
  1940   "The Abelam Tribe, Sepik District, New
  –41   Guinea." *Oceania* 11: 233–58, 345–67.

Langness, L. L.
  1967   "Sexual Antagonism in the New Guinea Highlands: A Bena-Bena Example." *Oceania* 37: 161–77.

Lawrence, P., and M. J. Meggitt
  1965   "Introduction." In P. Lawrence and M. J. Meggitt, eds., *Gods, Ghosts and Men in Melanesia.* Melbourne.

Lea, D. A. M.
   1966   "Yam Growing in the Maprik Area."
          *Papua and New Guinea Agricultural Jour-
          nal* 18: 5–16.

Lindenbaum, S.
   1971   "Sorcery and Structure in Fore Soci-
          ety." *Oceania* 41: 277–87.
   1972   "Kuru Sorcery." In R. W. Hornabrook,
          ed., *Essays on Kuru.*

Lindenbaum, S., and R. M. Glasse
   1969   "Fore Age Mates." *Oceania* 39: 165–73.

Marwick, M. G.
   1967   "The Sociology of Sorcery in a Central
          African Tribe." In J. Middleton, ed.,
          Magic, Witchcraft and Curing. New York.

Meggitt, M. J.
   1964   "Male-Female Relationships in the
          Highlands of Australian New Guinea."
          In J. B. Watson, ed., *New Guinea: The
          Central Highlands.* Special publication of
          American Anthropologist 66 (4), pt. 2.
   1965a *The Lineage System of the Mae-Enga of
          New Guinea.* Edinburgh.
   1965b "The Mae Enga of the Western High-
          lands." In P. Lawrence and M. J. Meg-
          gitt, eds., *Gods, Ghosts, and Men in
          Melanesia.* Melbourne.

Newman, P. L.
   1964   "Religious Belief and Ritual in a New
          Guinea Society." In J. B. Watson, ed.,
          New Guinea: The Central Highlands. Spe-
          cial publication of *American Anthropolo-
          gist* 66 (4), pt. 2.

Rappaport, R. A.
   1967   "Ritual Regulation of Environmental
          Relations in New Guinea." *Ethnology* 6:
          17–30.
   1968   *Pigs for the Ancestors: Ritual in the Ecol-
          ogy of a New Guinea People.* New Haven.

Reay, M.
   1959   *The Kuma.* Melbourne.

Strathern, A. J.
   1968   "Sickness and Frustration: Variations in
          Two New Guinea Highlands Societies."
          Mankind 6: 545–52.

Wagner, R.
   1967   *The Curse of Souw: Principles of Daribi
          Clan Definition and Alliance.* Chicago.

Williams, F. E.
   1930   *Orokaiva Society.* London.

A New Weapon Stirs Up Old Ghosts
William E. Mitchell

SUGGESTED READINGS

Lawrence, P., and M. J. Meggitt, eds.
   1965   *Gods, Ghosts and Men in Melanesia.* New
          York: Oxford University Press.

Lawrence, P.
   1967   *Road Belong Cargo.* Humanities Press.

Voodoo
Karen McCarthy Brown

REFERENCES

Bourguignon, Erika
   1976   *Possession.* San Francisco.

Courlander, Harold
   1960   *The Drum and the Hoe: Life and Lore of the
          Haitian People.* Berkeley: University of
          California Press.

Davis, Wade
   1985   *The Serpent and the Rainbow.* New York.

Deren, Maya
   1953   *Divine Horsemen: The Living Gods of
          Haiti.* New Paltz, N.Y. [Reprint 1983].

Herskovits, Melville J.
   1937   "African Gods and Catholic Saints in
          New World Negro Belief". *American
          Anthropologist* 39: 635–43.
   1937   *Life in a Haitian Village.* New York.

Kiev, Ari
   1964   "The Study of Folk Psychiatry". In Ari
          Kiev, ed., *Magic, Faith, and Healing.*
          New York.

Laguerre, Michel S.
   1981   "Haitian Americans". In Alan Har-
          wood, ed., *Ethnicity and Medical Care.*
          Cambridge, Mass.
   1982   "Voodoo and Urban Life". In *Urban Life
          in the Caribbean: A Study of a Haitian
          Urban Community.* Cambridge, Mass.

Larose, Serge
   1977   "The Meaning of Africa in Haitian
          Vodu". In I. M. Lewis, ed., *Symbols and*

Sentiments: Cross-Cultural Studies in Symbolism. New York.

Leyburn, James G.
  1941 *The Haitian People.* New Haven. [Revised edition 1966.]

Lowenthal, Ira P.
  1978 "Ritual Performance and Religious Experience: A Service for the Gods in Southern Haiti". *Journal of Anthropological Research* 34: 392–415.

Marcelin, Milo
  1949 *Mythologie voodou* (2 volumes).
  –50   Port-au-Prince.

Mars, Louis
  1946 *La crise de possession dans le Vaudou: Essais de psychiatrie comparée.* Port-au-Prince.

Maximilien, Louis
  1945 *Le vodou haïtien: Rite radas-canzo.* Port-au-Prince.

Metraux, Alfred
  1959 *Voodoo in Haiti.* New York.

Simpson, George E.
  1940 "The Vodun Service in Northern Haiti". *American Anthropologist* 42: 236–254.

Thompson, Robert Farris
  1981 *Flash of the Spirit: African and Afro-American Art and Philosophy.* New York.

CHAPTER 9
Old and New Religions: The Search for Salvation
Nativism and Revivalism
Anthony F. C. Wallace

Aberle, David F.
  1962 "A Note on Relative Deprivation Theory as Applied to Millenarian and Other Cult Movements." In Sylvia L. Thrupp, ed., *Millennial Dreams in Action.* Comparative Studies in Society and History, Supplement No. 2. The Hague: Mouton.

Ames, Michael M.
  1957 "Reactions to Stress: A Comparative Study of Nativism." *Davidson Journal of Anthropology* 3: 17–30.

Burridge, Kenelm
  1960 *Mambu: A Melanesian Millennium.* New York: Humanities Press.

Cantril, Hadley
  1941 *The Psychology of Social Movements.* New York: Wiley.

Festinger, Leon, H. W. Riecken, and Stanley Schachter
  1956 *When Prophecy Fails.* Minneapolis: University of Minneapolis Press.

Knox, Ronald A.
  1950 *Enthusiasm: A Chapter in the History of Religion; With Special Reference to the XVII and XVIII Centuries.* New York: Oxford University Press.

Kopytoff, Igor
  1964 *Classifications of Religious Movements: Analytical and Synthetic.* American Ethnological Society, *Proceedings.* New York: The Society.

Lanternari, Vittorio
  1963 *The Religions of the Oppressed: A Study of Modern Messianic Cults.* New York: Knopf.

Linton, Ralph
  [1943] 1965 "Nativistic Movements." In William A. Lessa and Evon Z. Vogt, eds., *Reader in Comparative Religion: An Anthropological Approach.* 2nd ed. New York: Harper.

Mannheim, Karl
  1936 *Ideology and Utopia.* New York: Harcourt.

Mead, Margaret
  1956 *New Lives for Old.* New York: Morrow.

Merton, Robert K.
  [1949] 1957 "Social Structure and Anomie." In Robert K. Merton, *Social Theory and Structure.* Glencoe, Ill.: Free Press.

Metraux, A.
  1941 "Messiahs of South America." *Interamerican Quarterly* 3(2): 53–60.

Mooney, James
  1896 *The Ghost-Dance Religion and the Sioux Outbreak of 1890.* Part 2 of U.S. Bureau

of American Ethnology, *Fourteenth Annual Report*, 1892–1893. Washington, D.C.: Smithsonian Institution.

Morgan, Lewis H.
[1851] 1962 *League of the Iroquois*. Gloucester, Mass.: Peter Smith.

Schwartz, Theodore
1962 *The Paliau Movement in the Admiralty Islands, 1946–1954*. Vol. 49, pt. 2, in American Museum of Natural History, New York, *Anthropological Papers*. New York: The Museum.

Smith, Marian
1959 "Towards a Classification of Cult Movements." *Man: A Record of Anthropological Science* 59: 8–12.

Sundkler, Bengt G. M.
1961 *Bantu Prophets in South Africa*. 2nd ed. Published for the International African Institute. London: Oxford University Press.

Thrupp, Sylvia L., ed.
1962 *Millennial Dreams in Action: Essays in Comparative Study*. Comparative Studies in Society and History, Supplement No. 2. The Hague: Mouton.

Wallace, A. F. C.
1956 "Revitalization Movements." *American Anthropologist* 58 (New Series): 264–81.

Williams, Francis Edgar
1923 "The Vailala Madness and the Destruction of Native Ceremonies in the Gulf Division." *Territory of Papua Anthropology Report*, No. 4. Port Moresby (New Guinea): Baker.

Worsley, Peter
1957 *The Trumpet Shall Sound: A Study of "Cargo" Cults in Melanesia*. London: MacGibbon & Kee.

Cargo Cults
Peter M. Worsley

SUGGESTED READINGS

Worsley, Peter
1957 *The Trumpet Shall Sound: A Study of "Cargo" Cults in Melanesia*. London: MacGibbon & Kee.

Honor Thy Father Moon
Berkeley Rice

SUGGESTED READINGS

Marks, John D.
1974 "From Korea with Love." *Washington Month* (February), pp. 55–61.

Mook, Jane Day
1974 The Unification Church. *A. D.* (May), pp. 32–36.

Sun Myung Moon
n.d. *Divine Principle*. Washington, D.C.: Unification Church Printing Office.
n.d. *The New Future of Christianity*. Washington, D.C.: Unification Church Printing Office.

Rajneeshpuram: The Boom and Bust of a Buddhafield
James E. Myers

REFERENCES

Academy of Rajneeshism, eds.
1983 *Rajneeshism: An Introduction to Bhagwan Shree Rajneesh and His Religion*. Revised 2nd ed. Rajneeshpuram, Or.: Rajneesh Foundation International.

Braun, Kirk
1984 *Rajneeshpuram: the Unwelcome Society*. West Linn, Or.: Scout Creek Press.

Carter, Lewis F.
1987 "The 'New Renunciates' of the Bhagwan Shree Rajneesh." *Journal for the Scientific Study of Religion* 26(2): 148–72.

FitzGerald, Frances
1986 "Rajneeshpuram." *New Yorker*, Sept. 22 and Sept. 29, 1986.

Gordon, James
1987 *The Golden Guru: the Strange Journey of Bhagwan Shree Rajneesh*. Lexington, Mass.: The Stephen Greene Press.

Kanter, Rosabeth Moss
1972 *Commitment and Community*. Cambridge, Mass.: Harvard University Press.

Littman, R. A., R. A. Hagan, C. A. Latkin, and N. D. Sundberg
1984 "Rajneeshpuram: the Development and

Impact of a Utopian Society." Paper presented at a symposium of the Western Psychological Association, April 1984.

Schafer, Walt
1987 "Utopia Gone Awry: Social Dynamics in the Demise of Rajneeshpuram." Paper presented at The Pacific Sociological Association, April 1987.

The Oregonian (June 30, 1985), 25.

CHAPTER 10
The Occult: Paths to the Unknown

Occult Beliefs

Barry Singer and Victor A. Benassi

REFERENCES

Bainbridge, W. S.
1978 "Chariots of the Gullible." *Skeptical Inquirer* 3: 33–48.

Bainbridge, W. S., and R. Stark
1980 "Superstitions: Old and New." *Skeptical Inquirer* 4: 18–32. *Sociological Analysis.*

Beit-Hallahmi, B.
Cults in Our Culture. Unpublished manuscript.

Benassi, V. A., P. D. Sweeney, and G. D. Drevno
1979 "Mind over Matter: Perceived Success at Psychokinesis." *Journal of Personal and Social Psychology* 37: 1377–86.

Benassi, V. A., and B. Singer
1981 "Occult Belief: Seeing Is Believing." *Skeptical Inquirer.*

Benassi, V. A., C. Reynolds, and B. Singer
1981 "Occult Belief: Seeing Is Believing." *Journal for the Scientific Study of Religion.*

Dawes, R. M.
1979 "The Robust Beauty of Improper Lineal Models in Decision-Making." *American Psychologist* 34: 571–82.

Einhorn, H. J., and R. M. Hogarth
1978 "Persistence of the Illusion of Validity." *Psychological Review* 85: 395–416.

Eliade, M.
1976 *Occultism, Witchcraft, and Cultural Fashions.* Chicago: University of Chicago Press.

Evans, C.
"Parapsychology: What the Questionnaire Showed." *New Science* 57: 209.

Freedland, N.
1972 *The Occult Explosion.* Berkeley.

Gallup Opinion Index
1976 132: 25–7.

The Gallup Poll
1978 June 15.

Glock, C. Y., and R. N. Bellah
1976 *The New Religious Consciousness.* Berkeley: University of California Press.

Gmelch, G.
1978 "Baseball Magic." *Human Nature* 1: 32–9.

Godfrey, L. R.
1979 "Science and Evolution in the Public Eye." *Skeptical Inquirer* 4: 21–33.

Godwin, J.
1972 *Occult America.* New York: Doubleday.

Greeley, A. M.
1975 *The Sociology of the Paranormal.* Sage.

Hyman, R., and E. Z. Vogt
1979 *Water Witching, U.S.A.* 2nd ed. Chicago: University of Chicago Press.

Jahoda, G.
1969 *The Psychology of Superstition.* Penguin.

Johnson, H. M., ed.
1979 *Religious Change and Continuity.* Jossey-Bass.

Kahneman, D., and A. Tversky
1973 "On the Psychology of Prediction." *Psychological Review* 80: 237–51.

Keene, M. L.
1976 *The Psychic Mafia.* Dell.

Los Angeles Times
1977 Dec. 25, p. 1.

Mahoney, M.
1976 *Scientist as Subject.* Ballinger.

Malinowski, B.
1954 *Magic, Science, and Religion.* New York: Doubleday.

Marks, D., and R. Kammann
1979   *The Psychology of the Psychic*. Prometheus.

Marshall, E.
1979   "Public Attitudes toward Technological Progress." *Science* 205: 281–85.

Mitroff, I. A.
1974   *The Subjective Side of Science*. Elsevier.

Morison, R. S.
1969   "Science and Social Attitudes." *Science* 165: 150–56.

Myers, D.
1980   *The Inflated Self*. Seabury.

Nisbett, R., and L. Ross
1980   *Human Inference*. Prentice-Hall.

Polzella, D. J., R. J. Popp, and M. C. Hinsman
1975   ESP. American Psychological Association. *JSAS* 5: 1087.

Psychology Today
1978   Nov. 22. "Newsline."

Robbins, T., D. Anthony, and J. Richardson
1978   "Theory and Research on Today's 'New Religions.'" *Sociological Analysis*.

Sagan, E.
1979   "Religion and Magic." In H. M. Johnson, ed., *Religious Change and Continuity*. Jossey-Bass.

Sales, S. M.
1973   "Threat as a Factor in Authoritarianism: An Analysis of Archival Data." *Journal of Personal and Social Psychology* 28: 44–57.

Singer, B.
1977   A Course on Scientific Examinations of Paranormal Phenomena American Psychological Association. JSAS 7: 1404. In G. O. Abell and B. Singer, eds., *Science and the Paranormal*. Scribner's.

Stark, R., and W. S. Bainbridge
1981   *American Journal of Sociology*.

Tversky, A., and D. Kahneman
1974   "Judgement under Uncertainty: Heuristics and Biases." *Science* 185: 1124–31.

Wagner, M. H., and M. Monnet
1979   "Attitudes of College Professors toward Extrasensory Perception." *Zetetic Scholar* 85: 7–16.

Wason, P. C.
1960   "On the Failure to Eliminate Hypotheses in a Conceptual Task." *Quarterly Journal of Experimental Psychology* 12: 129–40.

Wuthnow, R.
1976   *The Consciousness Reformation*. Berkeley: University of California Press.
1978   *Experimentation in American Religion*. Berkeley: University of California Press.

Straight from the Witch's Mouth
John Fritscher

REFERENCES

Burke, Tom
1970   "Princess Leda's Castle in the Air." *Esquire* (March), p. 107.

Carney, William
1968   *The Real Thing*. New York: Putnam.

Coleman, Sy, and C. Leigh
"Witchcraft."

Dunleavy, Steve
1970   "The Incredible Story of Satan and His Fanatic Followers." *National Enquirer*, Jan. 11, 1970.

Henderson, Everett
1969   "What Makes Mick Mighty? Can He Be All Sexes to All People?" *GAY*, Dec. 15, p. 6.

Hyams, Joe
1970   "A Revealing Look into the Mysterious Mind of Charles 'Satan' Manson." *National Enquirer*, Feb. 15.

Johns, June
1969   *Mensa Bulletin*, October, November.

Jone, Heribert, and Urban Adelman
1961   *Moral Theology*. Westminster, MD.: Newman Press.

Klein, Kim
1970   *Washington Post*, "Potomac," May 10.

LaVey, Anton
n.d.   *Notes for the Satanic Mass*. Morgenstrumm Records.

1970   *National Insider*, Jan. 4.

1970   *National Insider*, Feb. 22.

n.d.   Information Brochure for the Church of Satan.

Martello, Dr. Leo Louis

1969   *GAY*, Dec. 31.

1970   *GAY*, Jan. 19.

1970   *GAY*, Apr. 27.

Mercer, Johnny, and Harold Arlen
        "That Old Black Magic."

Robbins, Rossell Hope

1969   *The Encyclopedia of Witchcraft and Demonology*. New York: Crown.

Rodgers, Richard, and Lorenz Hart
        "Bewitched, Bothered, and Bewildered."

Rosenberger, Joseph R.

1969   *The Demon Lovers*. Atlanta: Pendulum Books.

St. Albin-Greene, Daniel

1969   "There May Be a Witch Next Door." *National Observer*, Oct. 13, p. 24.

Trachtenberg, Joshua

1961   *The Devil and the Jews*. New York: Meridian Books of World Publishing Co.

The Occult Revival as Popular Culture: Some Random Observations on the Old and the Nouveau Witch

Marcello Truzzi

REFERENCES

Abramson, M.

1969   "Have You Consulted Your Friendly Astrologer Lately?" *TV Guide*, Oct. 4, pp. 6–8.

Baroja, Julio C.

1964   *The World of the Witches*, trans. O. N. V. Glendinning. Chicago: University of Chicago Press.

Belanger, A. F.

1944   "An Empirical Study of Superstitious and Unfounded Beliefs." *Proceedings of Iowa Academy of Science* 51 (Apr. 15): 355–59.

Berger, B. M.

1963   "On the Youthfulness of Youth Cultures." *Social Research* 30: 319–42.

Berger, Peter

1967   *The Sacred Canopy*. Garden City, N.Y.: Doubleday and Co.

Bloxham, P.

1970   "The Devil and Cecil Williamson." *New York Times*, Apr. 19, p. 5.

Blumberg, P.

1963   "Magic in the Modern World." *Sociology and Social Research* 47: 147–60.

Bok, B., and M. W. Mayall

1941   "Scientists Look at Astrology." *Scientific Monthly* 52: 233–41.

Bone, R.

1964   "We Witches Are Simple People." *Life*. Nov. 13, pp. 55–62.

Bourque, L.

1969   "Social Correlates of Transcendental Experience." *Sociological Analysis* 30: 151–63.

Bourque, L., and K. W. Back

1968   "Values and Transcendental Experiences." *Social Forces* 47: 34–8.

Bracelin, J. L.

1960   *Gerald Gardner: Witch*. London: Octagon Press.

Buckland, Raymond

1970   *Ancient and Modern Witchcraft*. New York: H. C. Publishers, Allograph Books.

Buckley, Tom

1968   "The Signs Are Right for Astrology." *New York Times Magazine*, Dec. 15, p. 30.

Buckner, H. T.

1968   "The Flying Saucerians: An Open Door Cult." In Marcello Truzzi, ed., *Sociology and Everyday Life*. Englewood Cliffs, N.J.: Prentice-Hall.

Burke, T.

1970   "Princess Leda's Castle in the Air." *Esquire* (March) p. 104.

Caldwell, Otis W., and Gerhard E. Lundeen

1937   *Do You Believe It?* Garden City, N.Y.: Garden City Publishing Co.

Carus, Paul
1969   *The History of the Devil and the Idea of Evil.* New York: Land's End Press.

Casey, R. P.
1941   "Transient Cults." *Psychiatry* 4: 525–34.

Conklin, E. S.
1919   "Superstitious Belief and Practice among College Students." *American Journal of Psychology* 30: 83–102.

Consumer Communications Corporation
n.d.   *Dimensions of the Fate Magazine Audience.* Highland Park, Ill.: Fate Magazine.

Coulange, Louis
1930   *The Life of the Devil,* trans. S. H. Guest. New York: Alfred A. Knopf.

Cristiani, Leon
1962   *Evidences of Satan in the Modern World.* New York: Macmillan.

Crow, W. B.
1970   *A History of Witchcraft, Magic and Occultism.* North Hollywood, Calif.: Wilshire Book Co.

Crowley, Aleister
1929   *Magick in Theory and Practice.* Paris: Lecram Press.

Curie, E. P.
1968   "Crimes without Criminals: Witchcraft and Its Control in Renaissance Europe." *Law and Society Review* 3: 7–32.

Darraul, Akron
1966   *Witches and Sorcerers.* New York: Citadel.

De Camp, Lyon S., and Catherine C. De Camp
1966   *Spirits, Stars and Spells: The Profits and Perils of Magic.* New York: Canaveral Press.

Dudycha, G. J.
1933   "The Superstitious Beliefs of College Students." Journal of Abnormal and Social Psychology 27: 457–64.

Durkheim, Emile
1961   *The Elementary Forms of the Religious Life,* trans. Joseph Ward Swain. New York: Collier Books.

Eckman, B.
1969   "Witch Sounds His Trumpet for Satan." *Detroit News,* Oct. 19, p. 18–B.

Erikson, Kai T.
1966   *Wayward Puritans.* New York: John Wiley and Sons.

Eysenck, H. J., D. J. West, J. Beloff, I. Stevenson, C. E. M. Hansel, E. Slater, R. C. B. Aitken, D. H. W. Kelley, C. J. S. Walter, S. M. Cannicott, and R. H. Armin
1968   "Correspondence." *British Journal of Psychiatry* 114: 1471–83.

Feldman, Gene, and Max Gartenberg, eds.
1958   *The Beat Generation and the Angry Young Men.* New York: Citadel Press.

Freedland, N.
1969   "The Witches Are Coming!" *Knight* (October), p. 12.

Fuller, C. G.
1970   Personal communication.

Gallup G., Jr.
1963   "The Gallup Report on Religious Experience." *Fate* (April), pp. 31–7.

Gams, Jan
1970   "From Astrology to Witchcraft: Occult on the Rise on Campus." *Wisconsin State Journal* (Madison), Jan. 18.

Garcon, Maurice, and Jean Vinchon
1929   *The Devil: An Historical Critical and Medical Study,* trans. S. H. Guest. London: Victor Gollancz, Ltd.

Gardner, Gerald
1959   *The Meaning of Witchcraft.* London: Aquarian Press.
1954   *Witchcraft Today.* London: Rider and Co.

Gauquelin, Michel
1969   *The Scientific Basis of Astrology: Myth or Reality.* New York: Stein and Day.

Gilliland, A. R.
1930   "A Study of the Superstitions of the College Student." *Journal of Abnormal and Social Psychology* 24: 472–9.

Glass, Justine
1965   *Witchcraft: The Sixth Sense and Us.* London: Neville Spearman.

Glock, Charles Y., and Rodney Stark
1965   "Is There an American Protestantism?" *Trans-action* (Nov.–Dec.), p. 8.

Graves, R.
1964   "Witches in 1964." *Virginia Quarterly Review* 40: 550–9.

Greeley, A. M.
1969   "There's a New-time Religion on Campus." *New York Times Magazine*, June 1, p. 14.

Hansel, C. E. M.
1966   *ESP: A Scientific Evaluation.* New York: Charles Scribner's Sons.

Hansen, Chadwick
1969   *Witchcraft in Salem.* New York: George Braziller.

Harris, T. G.
1970   "Religion in the Age of Aquarius: A Conversation with Harvey Cox and T. George Harris." *Psychology Today* (April), p. 45.

Hartland, Sidney E.
1921   "Satanism." In James Hastings, ed., *Encyclopedia of Religion and Ethics*, Vol. 11. New York: Charles Scribner's Sons.

Henslin, J. M.
1967   "Craps and Magic." *American Journal of Sociology* 73: 316–30.

Hering, D. W.
1924   *Foibles and Fallacies of Science.* New York: D. Van Nostrand.

Hole, Christina
1957   *A Mirror of Witchcraft.* London: Pedigree.

Holzer, Hans
1969   *The Truth about Witchcraft.* Garden City, N.Y.: Doubleday.

Hudson, Paul
1970   *Mastering Witchcraft: A Practical Guide for Witches, Warlocks and Covens.* New York: G. P. Putnam's Sons.

Huebner, Louise
1969   *Power Through Witchcraft.* Los Angeles: Nash Publishing Co.

Hurston, Z.
1931   "Hoodoo in America." *Journal of American Folk-Lore* 44: 317–418.

Huysmans, Joris-Karl
1958   *Down There*, trans. Keene Wallis. New

Hyde Park, N. Y.: University Books.

Hyman, R., and E. Z. Vogt
1967   *Water Witching: Magical Ritual in Contemporary United States. Psychology Today* (May), pp. 34–42.

Jastrow, Joseph
1962   *Errors and Eccentricity in Human Belief.* New York: Dover.

Jennings, C. R.
1970   "Swinging on the Stars." *Playboy* (March), p. 103.
1969   "Cultsville USA." *Playboy* (March), p. 86.

Johns, June
1970   *King of the Witches. The World of Alex Sanders.* New York: Coward-McCann.

Kittredge, George L.
1956   *Witchcraft in Old and New England.* New York: Russell and Russell.

Klapp, Orrin E.
1969   *Collective Search for Identity.* New York: Holt, Rinehart & Winston.

Klemesrud, J.
1969   "Some People Take This Witch Business Seriously." *New York Times*, Oct. 31, p. 50–C.

Kloman, W.
1970   "Banality of the New Evil." *Esquire* (March), p. 115.

Kobler, J.
1966   "Out for the Night at the Local Caldron." *Saturday Evening Post*, Nov. 5, pp. 76–8.

Kramer, Heinrich, and James Sprenger
1948   *Malleus Maleficarum*, trans. Montague Summers. London: Pushkin Press.

Langston, Edward
1945   *Satan: A Portrait.* London: Skeffington and Sons.

LaVey, Anton Szandor
1970   "Letter from the Devil," Feb. 14, p. 5.
1969   *The Satanic Bible.* New York: Avon Books.
1968   Personal communication.

Lea, Charles Henry
1957   *Materials Toward a History of Witchcraft,*

arr. and ed. A. C. Howard. 3 Vols.
New York: Thomas Yoseloff.

Leek, Sybil
1968   *Diary of a Witch*. Englewood Cliffs, N.J.:
Prentice-Hall.

Lethbridge, T. C.
1968   *Witches*. New York: Citadel Press.

Levin, J.
1968   "The Magic Explosion." *Eye* (Oct.), p.
24.

Levitt, E. E.
1952   "Superstitions: Twenty-five Years Ago
and Today." *American Journal of Psychology* 65 (July): 443–49.

Lewinsohn, Richard
1962   *Science, Prophecy, and Prediction*, trans.
A. J. Pomerons. Greenwich, Conn.:
Fawcett Publications.

Lewis, L. S.
1963   "Knowledge, Danger, Certainty and
the Theory of Magic." *American Journal
of Sociology* 69 (July): 7–12.

Lyons, Arthur
1970   *The Second Coming: Satanism in America*.
New York: Dodd, Mead & Co.

MacFarlane, A. D. J.
1970   *Witchcraft in Tudor and Stuart England*.
London: Routledge and Kegan Paul,
Ltd.

Maple, Eric
1966   *The Domain of Devils*. New York: A. S.
Barnes.
1965   *The Dark World of Witches*. London: Pan.

Martello, Leo L.
1969   *Weird Ways of Witches*. New York: H. C.
Publishers, Allograph Books.

Mather, B.
1969   "Witchcraft and Satanism Are Alive
and Well in Michigan; Meet Bill Who
Believes." *Detroit Free Press Sunday Magazine*, June 15, pp. 8–11.

Mathison, Richard
1960   *Faiths, Cults and Sects of America*. Indianapolis, Ind.: Bobbs-Merrill.

McCall, George J.
1964   "Symbiosis: The Case of Hoodoo and
the Numbers Racket." In Howard S.
Becker, ed., *The Other Side*. New York:
Free Press.

Michelet, Jules
1939   *Satanism and Witchcraft*, trans. A. R. Allinson. New York: Citadel.

Moore, Harry T.
1960   "Enter Beatniks." In Albert Parry, *Garrets and Pretenders: A History of Bohemianism in America*. New York: Dover.

Moore, Martin
1969   *Sex and Modern Witchcraft*. Los Angeles:
Echelon Book Publishers, Impact Library.

Murray, H. A.
1962   "The Personality and Career of Satan."
Journal of Social Issues 18: 36–54.

Murray, Margaret A.
1921   *The Witch Cult in Western Europe*. London: Oxford University Press.

Nash, Ogden
1945   *The Selected Verse of Ogden Nash*. New
York: Modern Library.

Nelson, G. K.
1968   "The Concept of the Occult." *Sociological Review* 16: 351–62.

Newsweek
1970   "The Cult of the Occult." Apr. 13,
pp. 96–97.

Park, R.
1923   "Magic, Mentality, and City Life." *Papers and Proceedings of the American Sociological Society* 18: 102–15.

Parrinder, Geoffrey
1958   *Witchcraft*. Baltimore, Md.: Penguin.

Passin, H., and J. Bennett
1943   "Changing Agricultural Magic in Southern Illinois: A Systematic Analysis of
Folk Urban Transition." *Social Forces* 22:
98–106.

Pileggi, N.
1970   "Occult." *McCalls* (March), p. 62.

Pratt, Antoinette Marie
1915   *The Attitude of the Catholic Church towards Witchcraft and the Allied Practices of
Sorcery and Magic*. Washington, D.C.:

National Capitol Press.

Randolph, Vance
1947   *Ozark Superstitions.* New York: Columbia University Press.

Rascoe, J.
1970   "Church of Satan." *McCalls* (March), p. 74.

Rawcliffe, D. H.
1959   *Illusions and Delusions of the Supernatural and the Occult.* New York: Dover.

Rhodes, H. T. F.
1954   *The Satanic Mass.* London: Rider and Co.

Rigney, Francis T., and L. Douglas Smith
1961   *The Real Bohemia: A Sociological and Psychological Study of the "Beats."* New York: Basic Books.

Robbins, Rossell H.
1959   *The Encyclopedia of Witchcraft and Demonology.* New York: Crown.

Robinson, S.
1970   "Maurice Woodruff: Astrology's Brightest Star." *McCalls* (March), p. 76.

Robson, Peter
1969   *The Devil's Own.* New York: Ace Books.

Rohmer, Sax
1970   *The Romance of Sorcery.* New York: Paperback Library.

Rose, Elliot
1962   *A Razor for a Goat.* Toronto, Ontario: University of Toronto Press.

Roth, J. A.
1957   "Ritual and Magic in the Control of Contagion." *American Sociological Review* 310–14.

Sann, Paul
1967   *Fads, Follies and Delusions of the American People.* New York: Crown.

Sansweet, S. J.
1969   "Strange Doings: Americans Show Burst of Interest in Witches, Other Occult Matters." *Wall Street Journal*, Oct. 23, p. 1.

Sapir, Edward
1937   "Fashion." In *Encyclopedia of the Social Sciences*, Vol. 6. New York: Macmillan.

Seabrook, William
1940   *Witchcraft: Its Power in the World Today.* New York: Harcourt, Brace and Co.

Sechrest, L., and J. M. Bryan
1968   "Astrologers as Useful Marriage Counselors." *Trans-action* (November), pp. 34–6.

Seth, Ronald
1969   *Witches and Their Craft.* New York: Award Books.

Shotwell, J. T.
1910   "The Role of Magic." *American Journal of Sociology* 15: 781–93.

Simpkins, Ozzie
1953   "Magic in Modern Society: A Situational Analysis. University of North Carolina." Unpublished Ph.D. dissertation.

Spence, Lewis
1960   *Encyclopedia of Occultism.* New Hyde Park, N.Y.: University Books.

St. Albin-Greene, D.
1969   "There May Be a Witch Next Door." *National Observer*, Oct. 13, p. 24.

Staude, J. R.
1970   "Alienated Youth and the Cult of the Occult." Paper read at the Annual Meetings of the Midwest Sociological Society, Apr., at St. Louis, Missouri. Mimeographed.

Steiger, Brad
1969   *Sex and Satanism.* New York: Ace Books.

Summers, Montague
1958   *The Geography of Witchcraft.* New Hyde Park, N.Y.: University Books.
1956   *The History of Witchcraft.* New Hyde Park, N.Y.: University Books.
1946   *Witchcraft and Black Magic.* London: Rider and Co.

Thomas, V.
1966   "The Witches of 1966." *Atlantic* (September), pp. 119–25.

Thorndike, L.
1955   "True Place of Astrology in the History of Science." *Isis* 46: 273–78.

Time
1969 "Astrology: Fad and Phenomenon." Mar. 21, pp. 47–56.
1968 "That New Black Magic." Sept. 27, p. 42.

Tindall, Gillian
1967 *The Handbook of Witches.* London: Panther.

Truzzi, Marcello
1972 "Towards a Sociology of the Occult: Notes on Modern Witchcraft." In I. I. Zaretsky and M. P. Leone, eds., *Pragmatic Religions.* Princeton, N.J.: Princeton University Press.
1969 *Caldron Cookery.* New York: Meredith Press.

Valiente, Doreen
1962 *Where Witchcraft Lives.* London: Aquarian Press.

Vogt, E. Z.
1956 "Interview...g Water-dowsers." *American Journal of Sociology* 62: 198.

Vogt, E. Z., and P. Golde
1958 "Some Aspects of the Folklore of Water Witching in the United States." *Journal of American Folklore* 71: 519–31.

Vogt, E. Z., and Ray Hyman
1959 *Water Witching, U.S.A.* Chicago: University of Chicago Press.

Wagner, M. E.
1928 "Superstitions and Their Social and Psychological Correlatives among College Students." *Journal of Educational Sociology* 2: 26–36.

Waite, Arthur E.
1896 *Devil Worship in France.* London: Redward.

Wallace, C. H.
1967 *Witchcraft in the World Today.* New York: Award Books.

Ward, H. H.
1970 "Can Satanists and Christians Talk Together." *Detroit Free Press,* June 27, p. 4–A.

Warren, D. I.
1970 "Status Inconsistency Theory and Flying Saucer Sightings." *Science* 170: 599–603.

Wax, M., and R. Wax
1963 "The Notion of Magic." *Current Anthropology* 4: 495.

Wedeck, Harry
1961 *Treasury of Witchcraft.* New York: Philosophical Library.

Weir, W. W.
1970 "The New Wave of Witches." *Occult* (January), pp. 24–37.

Weiss, H. B.
1944 "Oneirocritica Americana: The Story of American Dream Books." *Bulletin of the New York Public Library,* p. 519.

Wenger, D., and E. L. Quarantelli
1970 "A Voice from the 13th Century: A Study of a Ouija Board Cult." Paper presented at the Annual Meetings of the Ohio Valley Sociological Society, May 1, at Akron, Ohio. Mimeographed.

Whitten, N.
1962 "Contemporary Patterns of Malign Occultism among Negroes in North Carolina." *Journal of American Folklore* 75: 311–25.

Williams, P.
1970 "There's Money in Myths and Magic." *Sunday Telegraph,* April 12.

Wilson, Monique
1968 Interview with Johnny Carson on NBC-TV, the Tonight Show, Oct. 31.

Zapf, R. M.
1945 "Comparison of Responses to Superstitions on a Written Test and in Actual Situations." *Journal of Educational Research* 39: 13–25.
1945 "Relationship between Belief in Superstitions and Other Factors." *Journal of Educational Research* 38: 561–79.

Index